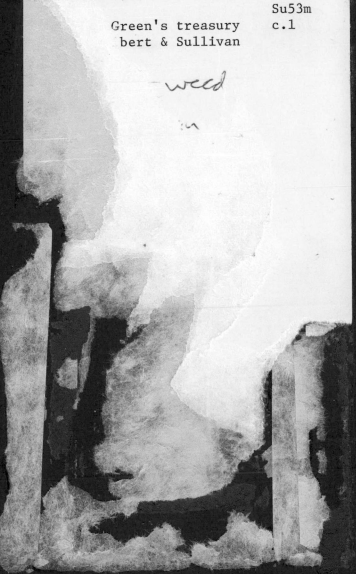

Martyn Green's Treasury of
Gilbert & Sullivan

Trial by Jury   Sorcerer   Pinafore   Pirates   Patience   Iolanthe   Ida   Mikado   Ruddigore   Yeomen   Gondoliers

The Complete Librettos of Eleven Operettas
The Words and the Music of
One Hundred and Two Favorite Songs

Edited and annotated by MARTYN GREEN
Illustrated by LUCILLE CORCOS
Arrangements by DR. ALBERT SIRMAY

SIMON AND SCHUSTER · NEW YORK · 1961

Acknowledgments and grateful thanks to:

The D'Oyly Carte Opera Company and all its members, past and present, for having provided me with much material;

Reginald Allen for a great deal of information and for giving me the opportunity to disagree with him at least once;

Deems Taylor, Leslie Bailey, A. A. Darlington, Hesketh Pearson, Vivian Denison and the Gilbert and Sullivan Society, Barbara Norville, Norman Monath, the Oxford Dictionary and Webster's Dictionary for both witting and unwitting assistance; and to

His Honour the Judge, J. W. Wells, Sir Joseph Porter, Major-General Stanley, Bunthorne, the Lord Chancellor, the Lord High Executioner, R. Oakapple, His Grace the Duke, J. Point.

LIBRARY OF CONGRESS CATALOG CARD NUMBER: 61-12868
MANUFACTURED IN THE UNITED STATES OF AMERICA
BY RAND MC NALLY & CO., BOOK MANUFACTURING DIVISION,
CHICAGO, ILL.

THIS volume is dedicated to the memory of Sir William S. Gilbert, Sir Arthur S. Sullivan, Mr. Richard D'Oyly Carte, and my father, Mr. William Green, and my mother, who turned ninety-two in July 1961. Without any one of these the book would not have been possible.

I would also like to link the names of my manager, Aaron B. Steiner, my editor, Peter Schwed,

and my wife, Yvonne,

who, as my then fiancée, was as much a slave driver as Aaron and Peter were.

CONTENTS

TRIAL BY JURY

THE SORCERER

H.M.S. PINAFORE; or, The Lass That Loved a Sailor

CONTENTS

THE MIKADO; or, The Town of Titipu

RUDDIGORE; or, The Witch's Curse

CONTENTS

Trial by Jury

DRAMATIS PERSONÆ

THE LEARNED JUDGE

THE PLAINTIFF

THE DEFENDANT

COUNSEL FOR THE PLAINTIFF

USHER

FOREMAN OF THE JURY

ASSOCIATE

FIRST BRIDESMAID

First produced at the Royalty Theatre, March 25, 1875

THIS gem of literary and musical wit was originally written by Gilbert for Fun—and, quite probably, for fun itself. Fun was a weekly English magazine, a forerunner of Punch. The whole of Trial by Jury occupied but one page, including the drawings that accompanied it. It was approximately 90 to 100 words long.

Some time later Gilbert hauled it out and elaborated on the theme, having heard that one Carl Rosa, impresario, was looking for something as a vehicle for his wife, Mme. Parepa. Rosa was delighted with it and decided to set it to music himself and to produce it. However, before he could do this, Mme. Parepa died. The libretto was returned and retired to the shelf for a considerable time.

Once again an impresario was looking for a curtain raiser to precede Offenbach's La Périchole, and the name of Gilbert occurred to him. Once again Gilbert hauled out Trial by Jury, now elaborated, and once again, an impresario was delighted with it and decided to produce it. This time the name of Sullivan was suggested as being the perfect composer.

Gilbert was hurried off to see Sullivan and read the script to him. Before he was halfway through the reading Gilbert was in a state of indignation, apparently disgusted with what he had written, and by the end of the reading, he was ready to tear it up. Fortunately for him, for Carte, for Sullivan, and for posterity, he had sold the idea to Sullivan, who was doubled up with laughter.

From such slender threads do the fates of good things depend. Had a curtain raiser not been needed, Trial by Jury would not have been composed by Arthur Sullivan, Richard D'Oyly Carte would not have produced it, and the world might never have seen anything from the joint pens of Gilbert and Sullivan. For it was the curtain raiser's great success that caused it to become the main piece of the evening, and which gave Carte the germ of an idea that was to bring the three of them together for many years.

Only a little over three weeks was to elapse between the moment Sullivan received the libretto and its presentation. Apropos of this a legend has grown up, quite erroneously, that the words, music and all rehearsals were written, composed and completed in the same short space of time. Reginald Allen, in his book, quotes Sullivan as having said: "The words were written and the rehearsals completed within the space of three weeks' time." If these were Sullivan's words then very obviously it was Sullivan who began this legend. Now I wonder if, in the course of time, Sullivan has come to be misquoted. It is more likely that his actual words were: "The music was written and the rehearsals completed within the short space of three weeks' time." The fact remains that the words were written some two years before Sullivan saw them.

Sullivan's brother Fred was the original Judge, and it must have done Gilbert's heart good when he read the reviews, one of which said of Fred Sullivan: "He does not allow the audience to miss a syllable in four or five verses." Words were a fetish with Gilbert; they were "precious concepts, and not to be bandied about!"

Trial by Jury is pure cantata. There is not one word of spoken dialogue. Sullivan, not yet under the "dictionorial" thumb of Gilbert, went to town with his score. Gilbert's later demands, to subdue the music so that every word could be heard, were not yet being made. In subsequent years, however, these demands were to be the seed that eventually grew into their long, bitter and famous quarrel.

Although the shortest of all the Gilbert and Sullivan works, *Trial by Jury* is, nevertheless, one in which I appeared in four separate roles, not counting once having been a member of the Jury. On that occasion I was made up to look as nearly as possible like the late Bernard Shaw. The other roles were: the Associate (a nonspeaking mime role), the Usher, Counsel for the Plaintiff, and the learned Judge.

There is a natural tendency among actors to overplay *Trial by Jury*. This should be avoided at all costs. There is also a tendency in the other direction; directors who are dyed-in-the-wool Gilbertian fanatical purists are likely to order things carried out in so subdued a manner that the whole piece becomes dull and humorless. This, too, should be avoided at any cost. A good rule to follow is that the only people who don't know they are being funny are the actors on the stage. They should be real people—so real they become unreal. *Trial by Jury* is more than a parody, and less than a burlesque—but not by very much!

Trial by Jury

SCENE.—*A Court of Justice. Barristers, Attorneys,* [1] *and Jurymen discovered.*

CHORUS

Hark, the hour of ten is sounding:
Hearts with anxious fears are bounding,
Hall of Justice crowds surrounding,
   Breathing hope and fear—
For to-day in this arena,
Summoned by a stern subpœna,
Edwin, sued by Angelina,
   Shortly will appear.

Enter USHER

SOLO—USHER

Now, Jurymen, hear my advice—
All kinds of vulgar prejudice
   I pray you set aside:
With stern judicial frame of mind
From bias free of every kind,
   This trial must be tried.

CHORUS

From bias free of every kind,
This trial must be tried.

[*During Chorus,* USHER *sings fortissimo, "Silence in Court!"* [2]

USHER.   Oh, listen to the plaintiff's case:
Observe the features of her face—
   The broken-hearted bride.
Condole with her distress of mind:
From bias free of every kind,
   This trial must be tried!

CHORUS.   From bias free, etc.

USHER.   And when amid the plaintiff's shrieks,
The ruffianly defendant speaks—
   Upon the other side;
What *he* may say you needn't mind—
From bias free of every kind,
   This trial must be tried!

CHORUS.   From bias free, etc.

Enter DEFENDANT

RECIT—DEFENDANT

Is this the Court of the Exchequer?
ALL. It is!

[1] Attorney. One who is appointed to act for an-other.
    Barrister. A student of law who has been called to the bar.
    According to the Oxford English Dictionary the title of Attorney was abolished in England in 1873. Either Gilbert forgot this, and failed to make any change in his directions after his li-bretto was returned to him by Carl Rosa, or he deliberately left it this way, which would defi-nitely set the date of the play's action before 1873.
    The libretto gives no direction for the iden-tities of the "strangers" (visitors) in Court who are also discovered.
    Generally speaking there are not enough gen-tlemen of the chorus to permit of more than twelve Jurymen, one or two strangers, and the Associate (Associate Judge). At the most I have seen only two bewigged gentlemen of the law seated under the learned Judge's bench.

[2] "Silence in Court" is sung twice as the Chorus sings the last word, "tried," and the Usher wildly waves his staff in the air in a quieting gesture. This is repeated as the Chorus joins in between each verse and at the end.

From bias free of every kind,
This trial must be tried.

TRIAL BY JURY

[3] A paraphrase of "Keep your pecker up," which, in England, means "Have courage." In the original version the line read: "Be firm, my moral pecker," and in some American editions the line has been changed to: "It is, it is the Exchequer."

[4] Words and music on page 15.

[5] The Defendant strikes a pose here. One knee is slightly bent, the foot turned at an angle and resting on the toe, with the heel touching the ankle of the other foot. He also uses his cane as a banjo. The Chorus assume a similar pose each time they sing "Tink-a-Tank.

The Chorus line is not included in this volume, so for those interested, it is as follows:

DEFENDANT (*aside*). Be firm, be firm, my pecker, [3]
Your evil star's in the ascendant!
ALL. Who are you?
DEFENDANT. I'm the Defendant!

CHORUS OF JURYMEN (*shaking their fists*)

Monster, dread our damages.
We're the jury,
Dread our fury!

DEFENDANT. Hear me, hear me, if you please,
These are very strange proceedings—
For permit me to remark
On the merits of my pleadings,
You're at present in the dark.

[DEFENDANT *beckons to* JURYMEN—*they leave the box and gather round him as they sing the following:*

That's a very true remark—
On the merits of his pleadings
We're at present in the dark!
Ha! ha!—ha! ha!

SONG—DEFENDANT [4]

When first my old, old love I knew,
My bosom welled with joy;
My riches at her feet I threw—
I was a love-sick boy!
No terms seemed too extravagant
Upon her to employ—
I used to mope, and sigh, and pant,
Just like a love-sick boy!
[5] Tink-a-Tank—Tink-a-Tank.

But joy incessant palls the sense;
And love, unchanged, will cloy,
And she became a bore intense
Unto her love-sick boy!
With fitful glimmer burnt my flame,
And I grew cold and coy,
At last, one morning, I became
Another's love-sick boy.
Tink-a-Tank—Tink-a-Tank.

CHORUS OF JURYMEN (*advancing stealthily*)

Oh, I was like that when a lad!
A shocking young scamp of a rover,
I behaved like a regular cad;
But that sort of thing is all over.
I'm now a respectable chap
And shine with a virtue resplendent
And, therefore, I haven't a scrap
Of sympathy with the defendant!
He shall treat us with awe,
If there isn't a flaw,
Singing so merrily—Trial-la-law!
Trial-la-law—Trial-la-law!
Singing so merrily—Trial-la-law!

[*They enter the Jury-box.*

RECIT—USHER (*on Bench*)

Silence in Court, and all attention lend.
Behold your Judge! In due submission bend!

Enter JUDGE *on Bench*

CHORUS

All hail great Judge!
To your bright rays
We never grudge
Ecstatic praise.
All hail!

May each decree
As statute rank
And never be
Reversed in banc.
All hail!

RECIT—JUDGE

For these kind words accept my thanks, I pray.
A Breach of Promise we've to try to-day.
But firstly, if the time you'll not begrudge,
I'll tell you how I came to be a Judge.

ALL. [6] He'll tell us how he came to be a Judge!
JUDGE. I'll tell you how . . .
ALL. He'll tell us how . . .
JUDGE. I'll tell you how . . .
ALL. He'll tell us how . . .
JUDGE. Let me speak . . . !
ALL. Let him speak!
JUDGE. Let me speak!
ALL (*in a whisper*). Let him speak!
        He'll tell us how he came to be a Judge.
USHER. Silence in Court! Silence in Court!

SONG—JUDGE [7]

When I, good friends, was called to the bar,
I'd an appetite fresh and hearty,
But I was, as many young barristers are,
An impecunious party.

I'd a swallow-tail coat of a beautiful blue—
A brief which I bought of a booby—
A couple of shirts and a collar or two,
And a ring that looked like a ruby!

CHORUS.   A couple of shirts, etc.

JUDGE. In Westminster Hall [8] I danced a dance,
Like a semi-despondent fury;
For I thought I should never hit on a chance
Of addressing a British Jury—
But I soon got tired of third-class journeys,
And dinners of bread and water;
So I fell in love with a rich attorney's
Elderly, ugly daughter.

CHORUS.   So he fell in love, etc.

JUDGE. The rich attorney, he jumped with joy,

My riches at her feet I threw—

[6] There is some droll choral singing here, during which the Judge endeavors to make himself heard. Just when he thinks he has them all under control they burst out with a tremendous ffff! and he collapses back into his chair.

[7] Words and music on page 17.

[8] In the city of Westminster, London, and used at this time as a court of justice.

[9] Bailey. *The Old Bailey, the Central Criminal Court.*

[10] *Middlesex, the County of.*

[11] Sessions. *The periodic sittings of justices of the peace. Hence, Middlesex Sessions.*

And a very nice girl you'll find her!

[12] Ancient. *Old Bailey, naturally. Gilbert's way of putting it.*

[13] *The Gurneys were obviously a wealthy family of the day. Sort of 19th-century English Rockefellers.*

[14] Job. *To turn a public office or service or position of trust improperly to a party or private advantage.*

[15] *One of Gilbert's delightful triple entendres. He uses the phrase as a sarcastic acknowledgment of the masterly "job" it was; as a British slang expression implying "it's fortunate"; and finally as a factual synonym for a good performance.*

And replied to my fond professions:
 "You shall reap the reward of your pluck, my boy
  At the Bailey [9] and Middlesex [10] Sessions. [11]
 You'll soon get used to her looks," said he,
  "And a very nice girl you'll find her!
 She may very well pass for forty-three
  In the dusk, with a light behind her!"

CHORUS.   She may very well, etc.

JUDGE. The rich attorney was good as his word;
  The briefs came trooping gaily,
 And every day my voice was heard
  At the Sessions or Ancient [12] Bailey.
 All thieves who could my fees afford
  Relied on my orations,
 And many a burglar I've restored
  To his friends and his relations.

CHORUS.   And many a burglar, etc.

JUDGE. At length I became as rich as the Gurneys— [13]
  An incubus then I thought her,
 So I threw over that rich attorney's
  Elderly, ugly daughter.
 The rich attorney my character high
  Tried vainly to disparage—
 And now, if you please, I'm ready to try
  This Breach of Promise of Marriage!

CHORUS.   And now if you please, etc.

JUDGE. For now I am a Judge!
ALL. And a good Judge too.
JUDGE. Yes, now I am a Judge!
ALL. And a good Judge too!
JUDGE. Though all my law is fudge,
 Yet I'll never, never budge,
 But I'll live and die a Judge!
ALL. And a good Judge too!
JUDGE (*pianissimo*). It was managed by a job— [14]
ALL. And a good job too! [15]
JUDGE. It was managed by a job!
ALL. And a good job too!
JUDGE. It is patent to the mob,
 That my being made a nob
 Was effected by a job.
ALL. And a good job too!

Enter COUNSEL *for* PLAINTIFF. *He takes his place in front row of Counsels' seats*

RECIT—COUNSEL

Swear thou the Jury!

USHER. Kneel, Jurymen, oh, kneel!

[*All the* JURY *kneel in the Jury-box, and so are hidden from audience.*

USHER. Oh, will you swear by yonder skies,
 Whatever question may arise,
 'Twixt rich and poor, 'twixt low and high,
 That you will well and truly try?

JURY (*raising their hands, which alone are visible*)

> To all of this we make reply
> By the dull slate of yonder sky:
> That we will well and truly try.

(*All rise with the last note*) [16]

RECIT—COUNSEL

> Where is the Plaintiff?
> Let her now be brought.

RECIT—USHER

> Oh, Angelina! Come thou into Court!
> Angelina! Angelina!! [17]

Enter the BRIDESMAIDS

CHORUS OF BRIDESMAIDS

> Comes the broken flower—
>   Comes the cheated maid—
> Though the tempest lower,
>   Rain and cloud will fade
> Take, oh take these posies:
>   Though thy beauty rare
> Shame the blushing roses,
>   They are passing fair!
>   Wear the flowers till they fade;
>   Happy be thy life, oh maid!

[*The* JUDGE, *having taken a great fancy to* FIRST BRIDESMAID, *sends her a note by* USHER, *which she reads, kisses rapturously, and places in her bosom.*

Enter PLAINTIFF

SOLO—PLAINTIFF

> O'er the season vernal,
>   Time may cast a shade;
> Sunshine, if eternal,
>   Makes the roses fade!
> Time may do his duty;
>   Let the thief alone—
> Winter hath a beauty,
>   That is all his own.
>   Fairest days are sun and shade:
>   I am no unhappy maid!

[*The* JUDGE *having by this time transferred his admiration to* PLAINTIFF, *directs the* USHER *to take the note from* FIRST BRIDESMAID *and hand it to* PLAINTIFF, *who reads it, kisses it rapturously, and places it in her bosom.*

CHORUS OF BRIDESMAIDS

> Comes the broken flower, etc.

JUDGE. Oh, never, never, never, since I joined the human race,
>   Saw I so exquisitely fair a face.
THE JURY (*shaking their forefingers at him*). Ah, sly dog! Ah, sly dog!
JUDGE (*to* JURY). How say you? Is she not designed for capture?
FOREMAN (*after consulting with the* JURY). We've but one word, my lord, and that is—Rapture.
PLAINTIFF (*curtseying*). Your kindness, gentleman, quite overpowers!

[16] They not only rise but, with the exception of one Juryman, reseat themselves. This calls forth the one spoken line: "Sit down!" from the Usher in a hoarse, loud whisper. Originally he sang the lines:

> This blind devotion is indeed a crusher.
> Pardon the teardrop of a simple Usher!

—whereupon he wept! The cut and the business now used is a vast improvement, I think.

[17] He sings "Angelina!" to one side of the Court, cupping his hand to his mouth while doing so, and Echo—in the shape of the Defendant whose back is to the audience—answers: "Angelina!" He sings it again to the other side of the Court, but this time he finishes an octave lower. Again Echo answers "Angelin . . ." but cannot get down to the ". . . a!" So the Usher, with a sly smile, does it for him.

JURY. We love you fondly and would make you ours!

THE BRIDESMAIDS (*shaking their forefingers at* JURY)

Ah, sly dogs! Ah, sly dogs!

RECIT—COUNSEL *for* PLAINTIFF

May it please you, my lud! [18]
Gentlemen of the jury!

ARIA—COUNSEL [19]

With a sense of deep emotion,
I approach this painful case;
For I never had a notion
That a man could be so base,
Or deceive a girl confiding,
Vows, *etcetera*, deriding.

ALL. He deceived a girl confiding,
Vows, *etcetera*, deriding.

[PLAINTIFF *falls sobbing on* COUNSEL's *breast and remains there.* [20]

COUNSEL. See my interesting client,
Victim of a heartless wile!
See the traitor all defiant
Wear a supercilious smile!
Sweetly smiled my client on him,
Coyly woo'd and gently won him.

ALL. Sweetly smiled, etc.

COUNSEL. Swiftly fled each honeyed hour
Spent with this unmanly male!
Camberwell [21] became a bower,
Peckham [22] an Arcadian Vale,
Breathing concentrated otto! [23]—
An existence *à la* Watteau. [24]

ALL. Bless, us, concentrated otto! etc.

COUNSEL. Picture, then, my client naming,
And insisting on the day:
Picture him excuses framing—
Going from her far away;
Doubly criminal to do so,
For the maid had bought her *trousseau!*

ALL. Doubly criminal, etc.

COUNSEL (*to* PLAINTIFF, *who weeps*)
Cheer up, my pretty—oh, cheer up!

JURY. Cheer up, cheer up, we love you!

[COUNSEL *leads* PLAINTIFF *fondly into Witness-box; he takes a tender leave of her, and resumes his place in Court.* [25]

(PLAINTIFF *reels as if about to faint*)

JUDGE. That she is reeling
Is plain to see!

FOREMAN. If faint you're feeling
Recline on me! [26]

[*She falls sobbing on to the* FOREMAN's *breast.*

---

[18] *My lud. Traditionally, in a British court of law this is pronounced "m'lud" (My Lord). The Judge might not hold a title, not even the law title of Lord Justice—that is to say, he might only be Mr. Justice—but in court he is addressed in the above manner and spoken of as "His Lordship."*

[19] *Words and music on page 21.*

[20] *See Note 26 below.*

[21] *and* [22] *Camberwell and Peckham. Suburbs of London. A part of the East End and South East London, and none too salubrious neighborhoods in those days.*

[23] *Otto. Attar of roses.*

[24] *Antoine Watteau. The French painter who specialized in Arcadian scenes.*

[25] *The D'Oyly Carte set boasted no Witness-box and I cannot say if the original set included one. So Counsel merely leads Plaintiff to the foot of the steps leading up to the Judge's bench.*

[26] *If she had been led to the Witness-box she would not have been able to indulge in what appears to be her favorite pastime.*

PLAINTIFF (*feebly*)
    I shall recover
      If left alone.

ALL (*shaking their fists at* DEFENDANT)
    Oh, perjured lover,
      Atone! atone!

FOREMAN. Just like a father
      I wish to be.   [*Kissing her.*

JUDGE (*approaching her*)
    Or, if you'd rather,
      Recline on me! [27]

[*She jumps on to Bench, sits down by the* JUDGE, *and falls sobbing on his breast.*

COUNSEL. Oh! fetch some water
      From far Cologne! [28]

ALL.   For this sad slaughter
      Atone! atone!

JURY (*shaking fists at* DEFENDANT)
    Monster, monster, dread our fury—
    There's the Judge, and we're the Jury!
    Come! Substantial damages,
    Dam—

USHER.   Silence in Court!

SONG—DEFENDANT [29]

Oh, gentlemen, listen, I pray,
    Though I own that my heart has been ranging,
Of nature the laws I obey,
    For nature is constantly changing.
The moon in her phases is found,
    The time and the wind and the weather,
The months in succession come round,
    And you don't find two Mondays together.
    Consider the moral, I pray,
      Nor bring a young fellow to sorrow,
    Who loves this young lady to-day,
      And loves that young lady to-morrow.

BRIDESMAIDS (*rushing forward, and kneeling to* JURY)

Consider the moral, etc.
You cannot eat breakfast all day,
    Nor is it the act of a sinner,
When breakfast is taken away,
    To turn your attention to dinner;
And it's not in the range of belief,
    To look upon him as a glutton,
Who, when he is tired of beef,
    Determines to tackle the mutton.
    But this I am willing to say,
      If it will appease her sorrow,
    I'll marry this lady to-day,
      And I'll marry the other to-morrow!

BRIDESMAIDS (*rushing forward as before*)

But this he is willing to say, etc.

[27] As it is, she is in a very good position to carry out the directions given here.

[28] Quite obviously the Counsel's call was for the perfumed variety. However, while the Jury and others are demanding atonement the Usher disappears and almost immediately reappears with a glass of plain water which he hands to the Judge. The Judge takes it, drinks it, hands the empty glass back to the Usher, and dabs the Plaintiff's lips with a large red bandanna handkerchief. The Usher meanwhile takes the glass offstage, returning just in time to sing his next line.
    Yes, he has to move very quickly!

[29] Words and music on page 24.

Determines to tackle the mutton.

[30] *Whereas, I suppose, unlawful entry with felonious intent is Bigamee!*

. . . a very serious crime
To marry two wives at one time.

RECIT—JUDGE

That seems a reasonable proposition,
To which, I think, your client may agree.

COUNSEL

But, I submit, my lord, with all submission,
To marry two at once is Burglaree! [30]

[Referring to law book.

In the reign of James the Second,
It was generally reckoned
As a very serious crime
To marry two wives at one time.

[Hands book up to JUDGE, *who reads it.*

ALL.   Oh, man of learning!

QUARTETTE

JUDGE.   A nice dilemma we have here,
            That calls for all our wit:

COUNSEL.   And at this stage, it don't appear
            That we can settle it.

DEFENDANT (*in Witness-box*)
            If I to wed the girl am loth
            A breach 'twill surely be—

PLAINTIFF.   And if he goes and marries both,
            It counts as Burglaree!

ALL.   A nice dilemma, etc.

DUET—PLAINTIFF *and* DEFENDANT

PLAINTIFF (*embracing him rapturously*)

I love him—I love him—with fervour unceasing
    I worship and madly adore;
My blind adoration is always increasing,
    My loss I shall ever deplore.
Oh, see what a blessing, what love and caressing
    I've lost, and remember it, pray,
When you I'm addressing, are busy assessing
    The damages Edwin must pay!

DEFENDANT (*repelling her furiously*)

I smoke like a furnace—I'm always in liquor,
    A ruffian—a bully—a sot;
I'm sure I should thrash her, perhaps I should kick her,
    I am such a very bad lot!
I'm not prepossessing, as you may be guessing,
    She couldn't endure me a day;
Recall my professing, when you are assessing
    The damages Edwin must pay!

*[She clings to him passionately; after a struggle, he throws her off into
    arms of* COUNSEL.

JURY.   We would be fairly acting,
        But this is most distracting!

RECIT—JUDGE

The question, gentlemen—is one of liquor;
You ask for guidance—this is my reply:
He says, when tipsy, he would thrash and kick her,
Let's make him tipsy, gentlemen, and try!

COUNSEL. With all respect
I do object!

PLAINTIFF. I do object!

DEFENDANT. I don't object!

ALL. With all respect
We do object!

JUDGE (*tossing his books and papers about*)

All the legal furies seize you!
No proposal seems to please you,
I can't stop up here all day,
I must shortly go away.
Barristers, and you, attorneys,
Set out on your homeward journeys;
Gentle, simple-minded Usher,
Get you, if you like, to Russ*her*; [31]
Put your briefs upon the shelf,
I will marry her myself!

[*He comes down from Bench to floor of Court. He embraces* ANGELINA.

FINALE

PLAINTIFF. Oh, joy unbounded,
With wealth surrounded,
The knell is sounded
Of grief and woe.

COUNSEL. With love devoted
On you he's doated [32]
To castle moated
Away they go.

DEFENDANT. I wonder whether
They'll live together
In marriage tether
In manner true?

USHER. It seems to me, sir,
Of such as she, sir,
A judge is he, sir,
And a good judge too.

JUDGE. Yes, I am a Judge.

ALL. And a good Judge too!

JUDGE. Yes, I am a Judge.

ALL. And a good Judge too!

JUDGE. Though homeward as you trudge,
You declare my law is fudge.
Yet of beauty I'm a judge.

[31] *These two lines were not in the original script but were added later. Reginald Allen remarks on this in his book, thus:*

"Gentle, simple-minded Usher,
Get you, if you like, to Russia;

(*sometimes spelled Russher*)."

In every edition I have seen it has been spelled "Russher"—including an edition of Chappell & Company, which is obviously a very old one, containing as it does the librettos of both The Sorcerer and Trial by Jury.

Gilbert may have written "Russia" in the first place, but his propensity for misspelling—for the sake of a perfect rhyme and/or double-entendre —inclines me to believe Russher was the original spelling. The italics, too, seem to bear his trademark.

[32] *It is interesting to note that Gilbert deliberately uses an old form of the word—"doated"—to conform with "moated" rather than "devoted."*

[33] Fob. *The small-change (or watch) pocket in the waistband of trousers or breeches. Presumably the learned Judge intends to pay off the Defendant with some small change. For having brought him (the Judge) and the Plaintiff together? Or to ensure the Defendant's keeping his mouth shut over the matter of the Judge's "job"?*

Gilbert's original directions on the finale included a Grand Transformation scene in the form of a quick scenic change to Fairyland! In this many things happened, including "Two Cupids in bar wigs descending from flies. RED FIRE—5 pans each side. One in each entrance— to be lighted when GONG sounds." I wonder why?

ALL.	And a good Judge too!
JUDGE.	Though defendant is a snob,
ALL.	And a great snob, too!
JUDGE.	Though defendant is a snob,
ALL.	And a great snob, too.
JUDGE.	Though defendant is a snob, I'll reward him from my fob. [33] So we've settled with the job,
ALL.	And a good job, too!

Dance

CURTAIN

When First My Old, Old Love I Knew

Animated

mf

p DEFENDANT

1. When first my old, old love I knew, My
2. (But) joy in-ces-sant palls the sense, And

p

bos-om well'd with joy; My rich-es at her feet I threw,
love, un-chang'd, will cloy; And she be-came a bore in-tense

I was a love-sick boy! No terms seem'd too ex-trav-a-gant Up-
Un-to her love-sick boy! With fit-ful glim-mer burnt my flame, And

poco cresc.

on her to — em - ploy, _____ I used to mope and sigh and pant,
I grew cold and coy, _____ At last, one morn - ing, I be - came An-

Just like a love - sick boy! _____ Tink-a - tank, tink-a-tank, tink-a - tank, Tink-a -
oth - er's love - sick boy! _____ Tink-a - tank, tink-a-tank, tink-a - tank, Tink-a -

tank, tink-a-tank, tink-a-tank, I used to mope and sigh and pant,
tank, tink-a-tank, tink-a-tank, At last, one morn - ing, I be - came, An-

Just like a love - sick boy.
oth - er's love - sick boy.

2. But

When I, Good Friends, Was Call'd to the Bar

In spirited tempo

JUDGE

1. When I, good friends, was call'd to the bar, I'd an ap-pe-tite fresh and
2. In West-min-ster Hall I danced a dance, Like a sem-i-de-spond-ent
3. The rich at-tor-ney, he jumped with joy And re-plied to my fond pro-

heart-y, But I was, as man-y young bar-ris-ters are, An
fu-ry; For I thought I nev-er should hit on a chance Of ad-
fes-sions: "You shall reap the re-ward of your pluck, my boy, At the

im-pe-cu-ni-ous par-ty. I'd a swal-low-tail coat of a
dress-ing a Brit-ish Ju-ry. But I soon got tired of third-class
Bai-ley and Mid-dle-sex Ses-sions. You'll soon get used to her

beau-ti-ful blue, A— brief which I bought of a boo-by, A
jour-neys, And— din-ners of bread and— wa-ter, So I
looks," said he, "And a ver-y nice girl— you'll find her! She may

cou-ple of shirts and a col-lar or two, And a ring— that look'd like a
fell in love with a rich at-tor-ney's El-der-ly, ug-ly
ver-y well pass for for-ty-three, In the dusk,— with the light be-

CHORUS

ru—by! He'd a cou-ple of shirts and a col-lar or two, And a
daugh-ter. So he fell in love with a rich at-tor-ney's—
hind her!" She may ver-y well pass for for-ty-three, In the

ring that look'd like a ru—by!
El-der-ly, ug-ly daugh-ter.
dusk, with the light be-hind her!

4. The rich at-tor-ney was good as his word: The briefs came troop-ing gai-ly, And ev-'ry day my voice was heard At the Ses-sions or An-cient Bai-ley. All thieves who could my fees af-ford Re-lied on my o-ra-tions, And man-y a bur-glar I've re-stored To his friends and his re-la-tions, And now, if you please, I'm read-y to try This Breach of Prom-ise of

5. At length I be-came as rich as the Gur-neys, An in-cu-bus then I thought her, So I threw o-ver that rich at-tor-ney's El-der-ly, ug-ly daugh-ter. The rich at-tor-ney my char-ac-ter high Tried vain-ly to dis-par-age. And now, if you please, I'm read-y to try This Breach of Prom-ise of

la - tions. And man-y a bur - glar he's re - stored To his friends and his re -
Mar - riage! And now, if you please, he's read-y to try This Breach of Promise of

la - tions.

Mar - riage. For

now I'm a Judge! And a good Judge too! Yes, now I'm a Judge! And a good Judge too! Though
man-aged by a job, And a good job too! It was man-aged by a job! And a good job too! It is

all my law be fudge, Yet I'll nev-er, nev-er budge, But I'll live and die a Judge! And a
pat - ent to the mob That my be - ing made a nob Was ef-fect-ed by a job. And a

good Judge too! It was good job too!

With a Sense of Deep Emotion

Moderately   COUNSEL

1With a
2(See my)

sense of deep e - mo-tion, I ap - proach this pain-ful case; For I nev - er had a
in - ter-est - ing cli - ent, Vic - tim of a heart-less wile! See the trai-tor, all de-

no - tion That a man could be so base, Or de - ceive a girl con-
fi - ant, Wear a su - per - cil - ious smile! Sweet - ly smil'd my cli - ent

CHORUS

fid - ing, Vows, et - ce - te - ra, de - rid - ing. He de - ceiv'd a girl con-
on him, Coy - ly woo'd and gent - ly won him. Sweet - ly smil'd his cli - ent

fid - ing, Vows, et - ce - te - ra, de - rid - ing.
on him, Coy - ly woo'd and gent - ly

2. See my

2.

won him.

COUNSEL (*with increased energy*)

Swift - ly fled each hon-eyed hour!

Spent with this un - man - ly male! Cam-ber-well be-came a bow'r, Peck-ham an Ar - ca - dian

Vale, Breath - ing con - cen - trat - ed ot - to! An ex - ist - ence à la

CHORUS

Wat - teau. Bless us, con - cen - trat - ed ot - to! An ex - ist - ence à la

Oh, Gentlemen, Listen

Moderately bright

DEFENDANT

1. Oh, gen-tle-men, lis-ten, I pray, Tho' I own that my heart has been rang-ing, Of na-ture the laws I o-bey, For na-ture is con-stant-ly chang-ing. The moon in her phas-es is

2. (You) can-not eat break-fast all day,— Nor is it the act of a sin-ner, When break-fast is tak-en a-way, To turn his at-ten-tion to din-ner; And it's not in the range of be-

The Sorcerer

DRAMATIS PERSONÆ

SIR MARMADUKE POINTDEXTRE, *an Elderly Baronet*

ALEXIS, *of the Grenadier Guards—his Son*

DR. DALY, *Vicar of Ploverleigh*

NOTARY

JOHN WELLINGTON WELLS, *of J. W. Wells & Co., Family Sorcerers*

LADY SANGAZURE, *a Lady of Ancient Lineage*

ALINE, *her Daughter—betrothed to Alexis*

MRS. PARTLET, *a Pew-opener*

CONSTANCE, *her Daughter*

Chorus of Villagers

A C T   I

EXTERIOR OF SIR MARMADUKE'S MANSION. MID-DAY

(Twelve hours are supposed to elapse between Acts I and II)

A C T   I I

EXTERIOR OF SIR MARMADUKE'S MANSION. MIDNIGHT

First produced at the Opéra Comique on November 17, 1877

THE SORCERER is the only opera in which Gilbert used the idea of a magic lozenge. This was an idea to which he was peculiarly addicted. He kept coming up with it over and over again, but neither Carte nor Sullivan felt any great affection for it and rejected it each time it turned up.

Nor was The Sorcerer an outstanding success, as Savoy opera successes were later judged; it ran for only 175 performances.

With the exception of Thespis, Utopia, Limited and The Grand Duke, this particular opera is the one I know least about, having seen it only six or seven times and having appeared in it but twice. Thespis is now in the limbo of the lost, insofar as the music is concerned. But one number has been saved from its ashes, and that is found in The Pirates of Penzance. Utopia, Limited was once considered for revival, but that is as far as it got. The Grand Duke never even got that far.

The Sorcerer, however, did something of great merit. It brought together, on a more or less permanent basis, the great triumvirate—Gilbert, Sullivan and Carte. It was the real beginning of their long and successful partnership. Not that Carte had any such idea in mind when, impressed by the success of Trial by Jury, he decided to form a company that would be devoted to the presentation of works by the best musical and literary talent in England.

French opéra bouffe was still in vogue to some extent, but the success of Trial by Jury had proved that English comic opera could be just as good, if not better. Having obtained the necessary financing, the company was set up under the title of The Comedy Opera Company. Composers Carte had in mind included Burnand, Clay, Cellier, Albery and Sullivan. His search came to an end when he received a letter from Sullivan, who wrote for himself and Gilbert, stating that they would agree to the writing of a two-act operetta— under certain conditions.

Among the conditions were that the company should not consider established West End actors or singers of grand-opera caliber. Rather, unknowns should be engaged, those who could not only sing agreeably and do justice to the music, but who would also be able to present the words clearly and articulately.

(In the beginning was the word. Gilbert's word! It is said that Sullivan, going along with Gilbert on this early idea, privately stated: And in the end it may be the music. Sullivan's music! We all know now that it was neither one nor t'other—it was both.)

Among other things that The Sorcerer did was to introduce in its cast the nucleus of what was to become the more or less permanent company of actors and actresses. First there was George Grossmith, who was an instant success as John Wellington Wells. One must inevitably wonder what would have happened if the advice of one of the directors of the Company had been taken (neither Gilbert nor Sullivan had a financial interest at this time): the director actually went to the extent of sending a telegram to Carte with instructions not to engage Grossmith under any circumstances.

Another stalwart to lay the foundations of a successful career in this medium was Rutland Barrington. No one was more surprised than he when the engagement was offered to him. Up to then he had worked in melodrama, with no thought of singing. As he himself said: "My first big success came with an important role in comic opera for the stupendous salary of £6 a week."*

* About $30 in those days.

The Sorcerer also marked another milestone in the history of the theater. Never before had a librettist and/or composer been given so much authority regarding a production. Even with Thespis, which Gilbert directed and for which Sullivan carried out all musical rehearsals, they did not have the same degree of authority as with The Sorcerer, and with every work that was to follow.

I am inclined to think that, through the years, the original ideas of Sullivan or Gilbert, or of both, have been lost. At one rehearsal, going over one of the duets ("The Family Vault"), Sullivan told his principals that he wished them to imagine themselves at Covent Garden singing grand opera, and not at the Opéra Comique singing comic opera. They were told to imagine themselves a Patti or a Mario, using all the flamboyant gestures that Italian grand opera singers indulged in, and that they needn't consider their own safety while doing so. The latter remark was evoked by an action of Grossmith's who, while carrying out Sullivan's instructions of exaggerated flamboyancy, "nearly fell over the footlights into the orchestra."

This burlesquing seems to be sadly lacking now. I think it's a pity. Can it be that the singing actor of today is unable to indulge in burlesque? Or is it that the Gilbert and Sullivan cult has forgotten such original intentions and now looks upon them as blasphemy?

The Sorcerer was the first opera to be produced under the auspices of Mr. Richard D'Oyly Carte's Comedy Opera Company—and it was also the last but one.

The Sorcerer

ACT I

SCENE.—*Exterior of* SIR MARMADUKE'S *Elizabethan Mansion.*

CHORUS OF VILLAGERS

Ring forth, ye bells,
   With clarion sound—
Forget your knells,
   For joys abound.
Forget your notes
   Of mournful lay,
And from your throats
   Pour joy to-day.

For to-day young Alexis—young Alexis Pointdextre
Is betrothed to Aline—to Aline Sangazure,
And that pride of his sex is—of his sex is to be next her
At the feast on the green—on the green, oh, be sure!

Ring forth, ye bells, etc.

[*Exeunt the men into house.*

Enter MRS. PARTLET [1] *with* CONSTANCE, *her daughter*

RECITATIVE

MRS. P. Constance, my daughter, why this strange depression?
   The village rings with seasonable joy,
   Because the young and amiable Alexis,
   Heir to the great Sir Marmaduke Pointdextre, [2]
   Is plighted to Aline, the only daughter
   Of Annabella, Lady Sangazure. [3]
   You, you alone are sad and out of spirits;
   What is the reason? Speak, my daughter, speak!

CON. Oh, mother, do not ask! If my complexion
   From red to white should change in quick succession,
   And then from white to red, oh, take no notice!
   If my poor limbs should tremble with emotion,
   Pay no attention, mother—it is nothing!
   If long and deep-drawn sighs I chance to utter,
   Oh, heed them not, their cause must ne'er be known!

[MRS. PARTLET *motions to* CHORUS *to leave her with* CONSTANCE. *Exeunt Ladies of* CHORUS.

ARIA—CONSTANCE

When he is here,
   I sigh with pleasure—
When he is gone,
   I sigh with grief.
My hopeless fear
   No soul can measure—

Throughout these operas Gilbert's penchant for the apt naming of his characters is well emphasized, and The Sorcerer is no exception:

[1] Partlet. *The proper name of any hen.*

[2] Pointdextre. *Point: any of nine particular places upon a shield; dextre (or dexter): the right side of a shield as opposed to the left, or sinister. Well, well!*

[3] Sangazure. *This can obviously only be translated as "blue blood."*

His love alone
  Can give my aching heart relief!

When he is cold,
  I weep for sorrow—
When he is kind,
  I weep for joy.
My grief untold
  Knows no to-morrow—
My woe can find
  No hope, no solace, no alloy!

MRS. P. Come, tell me all about it! Do not fear—
  I, too, have loved; but that was long ago!
  Who is the object of your young affections?
CON.   Hush, mother! He is here!

Enter DR. DALY. *He is pensive and does not see them*

MRS. P. (*amazed*).   Our reverend vicar! [4]
CON.   Oh, pity me, my heart is almost broken!
MRS. P. My child, be comforted. To such an union
  I shall not offer any opposition.
  Take him—he's yours! May you and he be happy!
CON.   But, mother dear, he is not yours to give!
MRS. P. That's true, indeed!
CON.   He might object!
MRS. P.   He might.
  But come—take heart—I'll probe him on the subject.
  Be comforted—leave this affair to me.

RECITATIVE—DR. DALY

The air is charged with amatory numbers—
  Soft madrigals, and dreamy lovers' lays.
Peace, peace, old heart! Why waken from its slumbers
  The aching memory of the old, old days?

BALLAD—DR. DALY [5]

Time was when Love and I were well acquainted.
  Time was when we walked ever hand in hand.
A saintly youth, with worldly thought untainted,
  None better-loved than I in all the land!
Time was, when maidens of the noblest station,
  Forsaking even military men,
Would gaze upon me, rapt in adoration—
  Ah me, I was a fair young curate then!

Had I a headache? sighed the maids assembled;
  Had I a cold? welled forth the silent tear;
Did I look pale? then half a parish trembled;
  And when I coughed all thought the end was near!
I had no care—no jealous doubts hung o'er me—
  For I was loved beyond all other men.
Fled gilded dukes and belted earls before me—
  Ah me, I was a pale young curate then!

[*At the conclusion of the ballad,* MRS. PARTLET *comes forward with* CONSTANCE.

MRS. P. Good day, reverend sir.
DR. D. Ah, good Mrs. Partlet, I am glad to see you. And your little

[4] *Mrs. Partlet alludes to Dr. Daly as "Our reverend vicar." He is given the title Vicar of Ploverleigh in the Dramatis Personæ, so Mrs. Partlet's use of it is not surprising—but his costume is! Dr. Daly is still dressed as was the Bishop in the short story, "The Elixir of Love," upon which this opera is based. That is to say, he is attired as a Bishop or a Dean of the Church of England. My knowledge of the niceties of rank in the Church of England does not permit me to say that a Dean may not also be a Vicar—but my experience has not yet brought me in contact with a Dean who was.*

The aching memory of the old, old days . . .

[5] *Words and music on page 55.*

daughter, Constance! Why, she is quite a little woman, I declare!

CON. (*aside*). Oh, mother, I cannot speak to him!

MRS. P. Yes, reverend sir, she is nearly eighteen, and as good as girl as ever stepped. (*Aside to* DR. D.) Ah, sir, I'm afraid I shall soon lose her!

DR. D. (*aside to* MRS. P.). Dear me, you pain me very much. Is she delicate?

MRS. P. Oh no, sir—I don't mean that—but young girls look to get married.

DR. D. Oh, I take you. To be sure. But there's plenty of time for that. Four or five years hence, Mrs. Partlet, four or five years hence. But when the time *does* come, I shall have much pleasure in marrying her myself—

CON. (*aside*). Oh, mother!

DR. D. To some strapping young fellow in her own rank of life.

CON. (*in tears*). He does *not* love me!

MRS. P. I have often wondered, reverend sir (if you'll excuse the liberty), that *you* have never married.

DR. D. (*aside*). Be still, my fluttering heart!

MRS. P. A clergyman's wife does so much good in a village. Besides that, you are not as young as you were, and before very long you will want somebody to nurse you, and look after your little comforts.

DR. D. Mrs. Partlet, there is much truth in what you say. I am indeed getting on in years, and a helpmate would cheer my declining days. Time was when it might have been; but I have left it too long—I am an old fogy, now, am I not, my dear? (*to* CONSTANCE)—a very old fogy, indeed. Ha! ha! No, Mrs. Partlet, my mind is quite made up. I shall live and die a solitary old bachelor.

CON. Oh, mother, mother! (*Sobs on* MRS. PARTLET's *bosom.*)

MRS. P. Come, come, dear one, don't fret. At a more fitting time we will try again—we will try again.

[*Exeunt* MRS. PARTLET *and* CONSTANCE.

DR. D. (*looking after them*). Poor little girl! I'm afraid she has something on her mind. She is rather comely. Time was when this old heart would have throbbed in double-time at the sight of such a fairy form! But tush! I am puling! Here comes the young Alexis with his proud and happy father. Let me dry this tell-tale tear!

A saintly youth . . .

Enter SIR MARMADUKE *and* ALEXIS

RECITATIVE

DR. D. Sir Marmaduke—my dear young friend, Alexis—
On this most happy, most auspicious plighting—
Permit me, as a true old friend, to tender
My best, my very best congratulations!

SIR M. Sir, you are most obleeging! [6]

ALEXIS.   Dr. Daly,
My dear old tutor, and my valued pastor,
I thank you from the bottom of my heart!

(*Spoken through music.*)

DR. D. May fortune bless you! may the middle distance
Of your young life be pleasant as the foreground—
The joyous foreground! and, when you have reached it,
May that which now is the far-off horizon
(But which will then become the middle distance),
In fruitful promise be exceeded only

[6] *The original pronunciation of the word "oblige."
Very olde worlde, obviously.*

By that which will have opened, in the meantime,
Into a new and glorious horizon!

SIR M. Dear Sir, that is an excellent example
Of an old school of stately compliment
To which I have, through life, been much addicted.
Will you obleege me with a copy of it,
In clerkly manuscript, that I myself
May use it on appropriate occasions?

DR. D. Sir, you shall have a fairly-written copy
Ere Sol has sunk into his western slumbers!

[*Exit* DR. DALY.

SIR M. (*to* ALEXIS, *who is in a reverie*). Come, come, my son—your *fiancée* will be here in five minutes. Rouse yourself to receive her.

ALEXIS. Oh rapture!

SIR M. Yes, you are a fortunate young fellow, and I will not disguise from you that this union with the House of Sangazure realizes my fondest wishes. Aline is rich, and she comes of a sufficiently old family, for she is the seven thousand and thirty-seventh in direct descent from Helen of Troy. True, there was a blot [7] on the escutcheon of that lady—that affair with Paris—but where is the family, other than my own, in which there is no flaw? You are a lucky fellow, sir—a very lucky fellow!

ALEXIS. [8] Father, I am welling over with limpid joy! No sicklying taint of sorrow overlies the lucid lake of liquid love, upon which, hand in hand, Aline and I are to float into eternity!

SIR M. Alexis, I desire that of your love for this young lady you do not speak so openly. You are always singing ballads in praise of her beauty, and you expect the very menials who wait behind your chair, to chorus your ecstasies. It is not delicate.

ALEXIS. Father, a man who loves as I love—

SIR M. Pooh pooh, sir! fifty years ago I madly loved your future mother-in-law, the Lady Sangazure, and I have reason to believe that she returned my love. [9] But were we guilty of the indelicacy of publicly rushing into each other's arms, exclaiming—

"Oh, my adored one!"   "Beloved boy!"
"Ecstatic rapture!"   "Unmingled joy!"

which seems to be the modern fashion of love-making? No! it was "Madam, I trust you are in the enjoyment of good health"—"Sir, you are vastly polite, I protest I am mighty well"—and so forth. Much more delicate—much more respectful. But see—Aline approaches—let us retire, that she may compose herself for the interesting ceremony in which she is to play so important a part.

[*Exeunt* SIR MARMADUKE *and* ALEXIS.

Enter ALINE, *on terrace, preceded by Chorus of Girls*

CHORUS OF GIRLS

With heart and with voice
Let us welcome this mating:
To the youth of her choice,
With a heart palpitating,
Comes the lovely Aline!

May their love never cloy!
May their bliss be unbounded!
With a halo of joy

[7] *I think it is quite certain that Gilbert's choice of a family name for Sir Marmaduke was no mere fluke.*

[8] *Doesn't your tongue thoroughly enjoy lapping itself 'round the lovely, laudable alliteration?*

[9] *I have often wondered why, if she returned his love, they never married. Is it possible that the "affair with Paris" still rankled in Sir Marmaduke's mind?*

Notice, a few lines down, Sir Marmaduke's lines which he sings unaccompanied:

Oh, my adored one!   Beloved boy!
Ecstatic rapture!   Unmingled joy!

He is kidding the sentimental hyperbole of Alexis' and Aline's love-making a little later on. His melody is the same as theirs, shown below, except his line should be transposed at least a fourth, maybe a fifth, down. (They're tenor and soprano; he's a bass baritone.)

May their lives be surrounded!
Heaven bless our Aline!

RECITATIVE—ALINE

My kindly friends, I thank you for this greeting,
And as you wish me every earthly joy,
I trust your wishes may have quick fulfilment!

ARIA—ALINE

Oh, happy young heart!
  Comes thy young lord a-wooing
With joy in his eyes,
  And pride in his breast—
Make much of thy prize,
  For he is the best
That ever came a-suing.
  Yet—yet we must part,
            Young heart!
Yet—yet we must part!

Oh, merry young heart,
  Bright are the days of thy wooing!
But happier far
  The days untried—
No sorrow can mar,
  When Love has tied
The knot there's no undoing.
  Then, never to part,
            Young heart!
Then, never to part!

Enter LADY SANGAZURE

RECITATIVE—LADY S.

My child, I join in these congratulations:
Heed not the tear that dims this aged eye!
Old memories crowd upon me. Though I sorrow,
'Tis for myself, Aline, and not for thee!

Enter ALEXIS, *preceded by Chorus of Men*

CHORUS OF MEN AND WOMEN

With heart and with voice
  Let us welcome this mating;
To the maid of his choice,
  With a heart palpitating,
  Comes Alexis the brave!

SIR MARMADUKE *enters.* LADY SANGAZURE *and he exhibit signs of strong emotion at the sight of each other, which they endeavour to repress.* ALEXIS *and* ALINE *rush into each other's arms.*

RECITATIVE

ALEXIS. Oh, my adored one!
ALINE.   Beloved boy!
ALEXIS. Ecstatic rapture!
ALINE.   Unmingled joy!

                    [*They retire up.*

THE SORCERER

[10] *This portion of the duet should be staged with all the stateliness of a minuet.*

[11] *The directions today would be: Emoting in asides all over the stage. An "aside" really means that the line is given to the audience. It is only the thoughts of the actor put into words so the audience may understand.*

[12] *With a return to the stately minuet manner. During Lady Sangazure's verse the same directions are followed, and a minuet is finally danced.*

[13] *In the second act Gilbert's directions are: "Constance leading Notary, who carries an ear-trumpet." No such directions are to be seen here. It may be that Gilbert originally considered two different characters. I say this because in the first-night program there is no such person as the Notary but there is a Counsel. However, in the original script (as printed in Mr. Allen's book, First Night Gilbert and Sullivan), it is the Counsel who draws up the marriage contract—with no ear-trumpet, apparently—in Act I, but it is the Notary who is led on by Constance, and—according to the directions—with no ear-trumpet! At least there are no directions to say that he does carry one, as there are in this later libretto. (See Note 31.)*

SIR M. (*with stately courtesy*) [10]
Welcome joy, adieu to sadness!
　As Aurora gilds the day,
So those eyes, twin orbs of gladness,
　Chase the clouds of care away.
Irresistible incentive
　Bids me humbly kiss your hand;
I'm your servant most attentive—
　Most attentive to command!

(*Aside with frantic vehemence*) [11]
Wild with adoration!
Mad with fascination!
To indulge my lamentation
　No occasion do I miss!
Goaded to distraction
By maddening inaction,
I find some satisfaction
　In apostrophe like this:
"Sangazure immortal,
　"Sangazure divine,
"Welcome to my portal,
　"Angel, oh be mine!"

(*Aloud with much ceremony*) [12]
Irresistible incentive
　Bids me humbly kiss your hand;
I'm your servant most attentive—
　Most attentive to command!

LADY S. Sir, I thank you most politely
　For your graceful courtesee;
Compliment more true and knightly
　Never yet was paid to me!
Chivalry is an ingredient
　Sadly lacking in our land—
Sir, I am your most obedient,
　Most obedient to command!

(*Aside with great vehemence*)
Wild with adoration!
Mad with fascination!
To indulge my lamentation
　No occasion do I miss!
Goaded to distraction
By maddening inaction,
I find some satisfaction
　In apostrophe like this:
"Marmaduke immortal,
　"Marmaduke divine,
"Take me to thy portal,
　"Loved one, oh be mine!"

(*Aloud with much ceremony*)
Chivalry is an ingredient
　Sadly lacking in our land;
Sir, I am your most obedient,
　Most obedient to command!

[*During this the* NOTARY *has entered, with marriage contract.* [13]

RECIT—NOTARY

All is prepared for sealing and for signing,
The contract has been drafted as agreed;
Approach the table, oh, ye lovers pining,
With hand and seal come execute the deed!

[ALEXIS *and* ALINE *advance and sign,* ALEXIS *supported by* SIR MARMA-
DUKE, ALINE *by her Mother.*

CHORUS

See they sign, without a quiver, it—
Then to seal proceed.
They deliver it—they deliver it
As their Act and Deed!

ALEXIS.   I deliver it—I deliver it
As my Act and Deed!

ALINE.   I deliver it—I deliver it
As my Act and Deed!

CHORUS

With heart and with voice,
Let us welcome this mating;
Leave them here to rejoice,
With true love palpitating,
Alexis the brave,
And the lovely Aline!

[*Exeunt all but* ALEXIS *and* ALINE.

ALEXIS. At last we are alone! My darling, you are now irrevocably betrothed to me. Are you not very, very happy?

ALINE. Oh, Alexis, can you doubt it? Do I not love you beyond all on earth, and am I not beloved in return? Is not true love, faithfully given and faithfully returned, the source of every earthly joy?

ALEXIS. Of that there can be no doubt. Oh, that the world could be persuaded of the truth of that maxim! Oh, that the world would break down the artificial barriers of rank, wealth, education, age, beauty, habits, taste, and temper, and recognise the glorious principle, that in marriage alone is to be found the panacea for every ill!

ALINE. Continue to preach that sweet doctrine, and you will succeed, oh, evangel of true happiness!

ALEXIS. [14] I hope so, but as yet the cause progresses but slowly. Still I have made some converts to the principle, that men and women should be coupled in matrimony without distinction of rank. I have lectured on the subject at Mechanics' Institutes, and the mechanics were unanimous in favour of my views. I have preached in workhouses, beershops and Lunatic Asylums, and I have been received with enthusiasm. I have addressed navvies [15] on the advantages that would accrue to them if they married wealthy ladies of rank, and not a navvy dissented!

ALINE. Noble fellows! And yet there are those who hold that the uneducated classes are not open to argument! And what do the countesses say?

ALEXIS. Why, at present, it can't be denied, the aristocracy hold aloof.

ALINE. Ah, the working man is the true Intelligence after all!

ALEXIS. He is a noble creature when he is quite sober. Yes, Aline, true happiness comes of true love, and true love should be independent of external influences. It should live upon itself and by itself—in itself love should live for love alone!

[14] *The humor of the situation is emphasized by the fact that Alexis is clad in the full-dress uniform of the Grenadier Guards.*

[15] *Navvies. Pronounced navv-ies. A "navvy" is a machine for excavating earth, a steam navvy! It is now applied to laborers who are employed on excavation and construction of earthworks, such as canals, railways, drains, roadworks, etc. They are called navvies because they do a navvy's work.*

[16] *It is interesting to note that the word "Alexipharmic" is defined as "having the nature or quality of an antidote against poison."*

[17] *In the short story "The Elixir of Love," the love potion was obtained from Baylis & Culpepper of St. Martin's Lane at a cost of 1s. 0½d. per bottle—one shilling and a halfpenny.*

[18] *Gilbert's love of the pun is put to good use here. One of his funnier puns, I think, unless you don't happen to like that form of humor.*

[19] *Hercules is usually played by the smallest boy who can possibly be obtained.*

BALLAD—ALEXIS [16]

Love feeds on many kinds of food, I know,
    Some love for rank, and some for duty:
Some give their hearts away for empty show,
    And others love for youth and beauty.
To love for money all the world is prone:
    Some love themselves, and live all lonely:
Give me the love that loves for love alone—
    I love that love—I love it only!

What man for any other joy can thirst,
    Whose loving wife adores him duly?
Want, misery, and care may do their worst,
    If loving woman loves you truly.
A lover's thoughts are ever with his own—
    None truly loved is ever lonely:
Give me the love that loves for love alone—
    I love that love—I love it only!

ALINE. Oh, Alexis, those are noble principles!

ALEXIS. Yes, Aline, and I am going to take a desperate step in support of them. Have you ever heard of the firm of J. W. Wells & Co., the old-established Family Sorcerers in St. Mary Axe? [17]

ALINE. I have seen their advertisement.

ALEXIS. They have invented a philtre, which, if report may be believed, is simply infallible. I intend to distribute it through the village, and within half an hour of my doing so there will not be an adult in the place who will not have learnt the secret of pure and lasting happiness. What do you say to that?

ALINE. Well, dear, of course a filter is a very useful thing in a house; but still I don't quite see that it is the sort of thing that places its possessor on the very pinnacle of earthly joy.

ALEXIS. Aline, you misunderstand me. I didn't say a filter—I said a philtre. [18]

ALINE (*alarmed*). You don't mean a love-potion?

ALEXIS. On the contrary—I *do* mean a love-potion.

ALINE. Oh, Alexis! I don't think it would be right. I don't indeed. And then—a real magician! Oh, it would be downright wicked.

ALEXIS. Aline, is it, or is it not, a laudable object to steep the whole village up to its lips in love, and to couple them in matrimony without distinction of age, rank, or fortune?

ALINE. Unquestionably, but—

ALEXIS. Then unpleasant as it must be to have recourse to supernatural aid, I must nevertheless pocket my aversion, in deference to the great and good end I have in view. (*Calling*) Hercules. [19]

Enter a PAGE *from tent*

PAGE. Yes, sir.

ALEXIS. Is Mr. Wells there?

PAGE. He's in the tent, sir—refreshing.

ALEXIS. Ask him to be so good as to step this way.

PAGE. Yes, sir.   [*Exit* PAGE

ALINE. Oh, but, Alexis! A real Sorcerer! Oh, I shall be frightened to death!

ALEXIS. I trust my Aline will not yield to fear while the strong right arm of her Alexis is here to protect her.

ALINE. It's nonsense, dear, to talk of your protecting me with your strong right arm, in face of the fact that this Family Sorcerer could change me into a guinea-pig before you could turn round.

ALEXIS. He *could* change you into a guinea-pig, no doubt, but it is most unlikely that he would take such a liberty. It's a most respectable firm, and I am sure he would never be guilty of so untradesmanlike an act.

Enter MR. WELLS [20] *from tent*

MR. W. Good day, sir. (ALINE *much terrified*)

ALEXIS. Good day—I believe you are a Sorcerer.

MR. W. Yes, sir, we practise Necromancy in all its branches. We've a choice assortment of wishing-caps, divining-rods, amulets, charms, and counter-charms. We can cast you a nativity at a low figure, and we have a horoscope at three-and-six that we can guarantee. Our Abudah chests, each containing a patent Hag who comes out and prophesies disasters, with spring complete, are strongly recommended. Our Aladdin lamps are very chaste, and our Prophetic Tablets, foretelling everything—from a change of Ministry down to a rise in Unified—are much enquired for. Our penny Curse—one of the cheapest things in the trade—is considered infallible. We have some very superior Blessings, too, but they're very little asked for. We've only sold one since Christmas—to a gentleman who bought it to send to his mother-in-law—but it turned out that he was afflicted in the head, and it's been returned on our hands. But our sale of penny Curses, especially on Saturday nights, is tremendous. We can't turn 'em out fast enough.

SONG—MR. WELLS [21]

Oh! my name is John Wellington Wells,
I'm a dealer in magic and spells,
    In blessings and curses
    And ever-filled purses,
In prophecies, witches, and knells.

If you want a proud foe to "make tracks"—
If you'd melt a rich uncle in wax—
    You've but to look in
    On our resident Djinn,
Number seventy, Simmery Axe! [22]

We've a first-class assortment of magic;
    And for raising a posthumous shade
With effects that are comic or tragic,
    There's no cheaper house in the trade.
Love-philtre—we've quantities of it;
    And for knowledge if any one burns,
We keep an extremely small prophet, a prophet
    Who brings us unbounded returns:

    For he can prophesy
    With a wink *of* his eye,
    Peep with security
    Into futurity,
    Sum up your history,
    Clear up a mystery,
    Humour proclivity
    For a nativity—for a nativity;
    With mirrors so magical,
    Tetrapods tragical,
    Bogies spectacular,
    Answers oracular,
    Facts astronomical,
    Solemn or comical,

[20] When *I* was being fitted for my costume for the role of John Wellington Wells for the revival in 1938 at the Scala Theatre, London, I could not get a picture of Sary Gamp (of Dickens fame) out of my mind. Perhaps it was Wells's flaunted "respectability" that gave rise to this image—and, of course, the image of her badge of respectability, her "gamp," or umbrella. I suggested that Wells might carry one for the same purpose—a thing that had not been done before. To my delight, the idea was accepted, and it was to become not only a very useful prop but also the cause of one big laugh (see Note 23).

[21] Words and music on page 57.

[22] Simmery Axe. St. Mary Axe.

. . . effects that are comic or tragic

And, if you want it, he
Makes a reduction on taking a quantity!
Oh!

If any one anything lacks,
He'll find it all ready in stacks,
If he'll only look in
On the resident Djinn,
Number seventy, Simmery Axe!

He can raise you hosts
Of ghosts,
And that without reflectors;
And creepy things
With wings,
And gaunt and grisly spectres.

He can fill you crowds
Of shrouds,
And horrify you vastly;
He can rack your brains
With chains,
And gibberings grim and ghastly!

Then, if you plan it, he
Changes organity,
With an urbanity,
Full of Satanity,
Vexes humanity
With an inanity
Fatal to vanity—
Driving your foes to the verge of insanity!

Barring tautology,
In demonology,
'Lectro-biology,
Mystic nosology,
Spirit philology,
High-class astrology,
Such is his knowledge, he
Isn't the man to require an apology!

Oh!
My name is John Wellington Wells,
I'm a dealer in magic and spells,
In blessings and curses
And ever-filled purses,
In prophecies, witches, and knells.

If any one anything lacks,
He'll find it all ready in stacks,
If he'll only look in
On the resident Djinn,
Number seventy, Simmery Axe! [23]

ALEXIS. I have sent for you to consult you on a very important matter. I believe you advertise a Patent Oxy-Hydrogen Love-at-first-sight Philtre?

MR. W. Sir, it is our leading article. (*Producing a phial.*)

ALEXIS. Now I want to know if you can confidently guarantee it as possessing all the qualities you claim for it in your advertisement?

[23] *The first occasion on which the "brolly" turned out to be useful was at the end of the patter song. John Wellington Wells does a swift walk around the stage as the music winds up the number. No resin had been available at the side of the stage and my new shoes were very slippery— and slip I did. But for my new prop, which I was able to use as a prop (and please excuse the pun), I would have measured my length on the stage floor.*

MR. W. Sir, we are not in the habit of puffing our goods. Ours is an old-established house with a large family connection; and every assurance held out in the advertisement is fully realised. (*Hurt*.)

ALINE (*aside*). Oh, Alexis, don't offend him! He'll change us into something dreadful—I know he will!

ALEXIS. I am anxious from purely philanthropical motives to distribute this philtre, secretly, among the inhabitants of this village. I shall of course require a quantity. How do you sell it?

MR. W. In buying a quantity, sir, we should strongly advise you taking it in the wood, and drawing it off as you happen to want it. We have it in four-and-a-half and nine gallon casks—also in pipes and hogsheads for laying down, and we deduct 10 per cent for prompt cash.

ALEXIS. I should mention that I am a Member of the Army and Navy Stores. [24]

MR. W. In that case we deduct 25 per cent.

ALEXIS. Aline, the villagers will assemble to carouse in a few minutes. Go and fetch the tea-pot.

ALINE. But, Alexis—

ALEXIS. My dear, you must obey me, if you please. Go and fetch the tea-pot.

ALINE (*going*). I'm sure Dr. Daly would disapprove of it.

[*Exit* ALINE.

ALEXIS. And how soon does it take effect?

MR. W. In twelve hours. Whoever drinks of it loses consciousness for that period, and on waking falls in love, as a matter of course, with the first lady he meets who has also tasted it, and his affection is at once returned. One trial will prove the fact.

Enter ALINE *with large tea-pot*

ALEXIS. Good: then, Mr. Wells, I shall feel obliged if you will at once pour as much philtre into this tea-pot as will suffice to affect the whole village.

ALINE. But bless me, Alexis, many of the villagers are married people!

MR. W. Madam, this philtre is compounded on the strictest principles. On married people it has no effect whatever. But are you quite sure that you have nerve enough to carry you through the fearful ordeal?

ALEXIS. In the good cause I fear nothing.

MR. W. Very good, then, we will proceed at once to the Incantation.

(*The stage grows dark*.)

INCANTATION

MR. W.
Sprites of earth and air—
Fiends of flame and fire—
Demon souls,
Come here in shoals,
This dreadful deed inspire!
Appear, appear, appear.

MALE VOICES.
Good master, we are here!

MR. W.
Noisome hags of night—
Imps of deadly shade—
Pallid ghosts,
Arise in hosts,
And lend me all your aid.
Appear, appear, appear!

FEMALE VOICES.
Good master, we are here!

[24] The Army and Navy Stores. *Not, as an American might imagine, an ordnance depot, nor even a department store devoted to the exclusive sale of Army and Navy goods, nor to service personnel only. Just an ordinary store on the lines of Sears, Roebuck.*

ALEXIS (*aside*). Hark, they assemble,
These fiends of the night!
ALINE (*aside*). Oh, Alexis, I tremble,
Seek safety in flight!

ARIA—ALINE

Let us fly to a far-off land,
Where peace and plenty dwell—
Where the sigh of the silver strand
Is echoed in every shell
To the joy that land will give,
On the wings of Love we'll fly;
In innocence there to live—
In innocence there to die!

CHORUS OF SPIRITS

Too late—too late
It may not be!
That happy fate
Is not for thee!

ALEXIS, ALINE, *and* MR. WELLS

Too late—too late,
That may not be!
That happy fate
Is not for { me!
{ thee!

MR. WELLS

Now shrivelled hags, with poison bags,
Discharge your loathsome loads!
Spit flame and fire, unholy choir!
Belch forth your venom, toads!
Ye demons fell, with yelp and yell,
Shed curses far afield—
Ye fiends of night, your filthy blight
In noisome plenty yield!

MR. WELLS (*pouring phial into tea-pot—flash*). [25]
Number One!
CHORUS.   It is done!
MR. W. (*same business*). Number Two! (*flash*).
CHORUS.   One too few!
MR. W. (*same business*). Number Three! (*flash*).
CHORUS.   Set us free!
Set us free—our work is done
Ha! ha! ha!
Set us free—our course is run!
Ha! ha! ha!

ALINE *and* ALEXIS (*aside*)

Let us fly to a far-off land,
Where peace and plenty dwell—
Where the sigh of the silver strand
Is echoed in every shell.

CHORUS OF FIENDS

Ha! ha! ha! ha! ha! ha! ha! ha! ha! ha!

[25] *It was during this scene that my umbrella proved most useful again. Pans of flash powder were placed to each side of the stage and at back stage. As John Wellington Wells sings the words, "Number One! Number Two!" etc., he runs from one side to the other, makes a magic pass, and the flashes go off, being operated by electric impulses. On the opening night, much to my consternation, the third flash failed to co-operate. Without really thinking, though I suppose I must have done so, I put my hand in my pocket, drew out an imaginary piece of billiard chalk, chalked the ferruled tip of my "gamp," once again sang, "Number Three," and again waved my magic wand. To my relief the flash went off, followed by a tremendous laugh from the audience. Naturally I wanted it kept in, and was surprised and delighted that it was, for the remainder of the run. The electrician was warned to hold off the third flash until I had completed my business.*

The run: one more performance!

[*Stage grows light.* MR. WELLS *beckons villagers. Enter villagers and all the* dramatis personæ, *dancing joyously.* MRS. PARTLET *and* MR. WELLS *then distribute tea-cups.*

CHORUS [26]

Now to the banquet we press;
    Now for the eggs, the ham;
Now for the mustard and cress,
    Now for the strawberry jam!

Now for the tea of our host,
    Now for the rollicking bun,
Now for the muffin and toast,
    Now for the gay Sally Lunn!

WOMEN. The eggs and the ham, and the strawberry jam!

MEN.   The rollicking bun, and the gay Sally Lunn!
    The rollicking, rollicking bun!

RECIT—SIR MARMADUKE

Be happy all—the feast is spread before ye;
Fear nothing, but enjoy yourselves, I pray!
Eat, aye, and drink—be merry, I implore ye,
For once let thoughtless Folly rule the day.

TEA-CUP BRINDISI [27]

Eat, drink, and be gay,
    Banish all worry and sorrow,
Laugh gaily to-day,
    Weep, if you're sorry, to-morrow!
Come, pass the cup round—
    I will go bail for the liquor;
It's strong, I'll be bound,
    For it was brewed by the vicar!

CHORUS

None so knowing as he
At brewing a jorum [28] of tea,
    Ha! ha!
A pretty stiff jorum of tea.

TRIO—MR. WELLS, ALINE, *and* ALEXIS (*aside*)

See—see—they drink—
    All thought unheeding,
The tea-cups clink,
    They are exceeding!
Their hearts will melt
    In half-an-hour—
Then will be felt
    The potion's power!

[*During this verse* CONSTANCE *has brought a small tea-pot, kettle, caddy, and cosy to* DR. DALY. *He makes tea scientifically.*

BRINDISI, 2nd Verse—DR. DALY (*with the tea-pot*)

Pain, trouble, and care,
    Misery, heart-ache, and worry,
Quick, out of your lair!
    Get you all gone in a hurry!

[26] Words and music on page 64.

[27] Brindisi. A drinking song.

[28] Jorum. (a.) A large drinking bowl or vessel; also its contents—especially a bowl of punch (1730?). (b.) A large quantity (1872). [Oxford Dictionary]

Toil, sorrow, and plot,
    Fly away quicker and quicker—
Three spoons to the pot—
    That is the brew of your vicar!

CHORUS

None so cunning as he
At brewing a jorum of tea,
    Ha! ha!
A pretty stiff jorum of tea!

ENSEMBLE—ALEXIS *and* ALINE (*aside*)

Oh love, true love—unworldly, abiding!
    Source of all pleasure—true fountain of joy,—
Oh love, true love—divinely confiding,
    Exquisite treasure that knows no alloy,—
O love, true love, rich harvest of gladness,
    Peace-bearing tillage—great garner of bliss,—
Oh love, true love, look down on our sadness—
    Dwell in this village—oh, hear us in this!

[*It becomes evident by the strange conduct of the characters that the charm is working. All rub their eyes, and stagger about the stage as if under the influence of a narcotic.*

TUTTI (*aside*)	ALEXIS, MR. WELLS, *and* ALINE (*aside*)
Oh, marvellous illusion!	A marvellous illusion!
Oh, terrible surprise!	A terrible surprise
What is this strange confusion	Excites a strange confusion
That veils my aching eyes?	Within their aching eyes—
I must regain my senses,	They must regain their senses,
Restoring Reason's law,	Restoring Reason's law,
Or fearful inferences	Or fearful inferences
Society will draw!	Society will draw!

[*Those who have partaken of the philtre struggle in vain against its effects, and, at the end of the chorus, fall insensible on the stage.*

END OF ACT I

ACT II

SCENE.—*Exterior of* SIR MARMADUKE'S *mansion by moonlight. All the peasantry are discovered asleep on the ground, as at the end of Act I.*

Enter MR. WELLS, *on tiptoe, followed by* ALEXIS *and* ALINE. MR. WELLS *carries a dark lantern.*

TRIO—ALEXIS, ALINE, *and* MR. WELLS

'Tis twelve, I think,
    And at this mystic hour
The magic drink
    Should manifest its power.
Oh, slumbering forms,
    How little have ye guessed

               The fire that warms
                  Each apathetic breast!

ALEXIS.   But stay, my father is not here!

ALINE.   And pray where is my mother dear?

MR. WELLS. I did not think it meet to see
              A dame of lengthy pedigree,
              A Baronet and K.C.B.,
              A Doctor of Divinity,
              And that respectable Q.C., [29]
              All fast asleep, al-fresco-ly,
              And so I had them taken home
              And put to bed respectably!
              I trust my conduct meets your approbation.

ALEXIS.   Sir, you have acted with discrimination,
              And shown more delicate appreciation
              Than we expect in persons of your station.

MR. WELLS. But stay—they waken, one by one—
              The spell has worked—the deed is done!
              I would suggest that we retire
              While Love, the Housemaid, lights her kitchen fire!

[*Exeunt* MR. WELLS, ALEXIS, *and* ALINE, *on tiptoe, as the villagers stretch their arms, yawn, rub their eyes, and sit up.*

MEN.   [30] Why, where be oi, and what be oi a doin',
                A sleepin' out, just when the dews du rise?

GIRLS.   Why, that's the very way your health to ruin,
                And don't seem quite respectable likewise!

MEN (*staring at girls*). Eh, that's you!
                Only think o' that now!

GIRLS (*coyly*).   What may you be at, now?
                Tell me, du!

MEN (*admiringly*). Eh, what a nose,
                And eh, what eyes, miss!
              Lips like a rose,
                And cheeks likewise, miss!

GIRLS (*coyly*).   Oi tell you true,
                Which I've never done, sir,
              Oi loike you
                As I never loiked none, sir!

ALL.   Eh, but oi du loike you!

MEN.   If you'll marry me, I'll dig for you and rake
                  for you!

GIRLS.   If you'll marry me, I'll scrub for you and bake
                  for you!

MEN.   If you'll marry me, all others I'll forsake for
                  you!

ALL.   All this will I du, if you'll marry me!

GIRLS.   If you'll marry me, I'll cook for you and brew
                  for you!

MEN.   If you'll marry me, I've guineas not a few for
                  you!

GIRLS.   If you'll marry me, I'll take you in and du
                  for you!

[29] Presumably the Notary. To the best of my knowledge, however, no notary carries the degree or title of Q.C. The use of the initials for Queen's Counsel would seem to suggest one of two things: either Gilbert did intend to call the character in question Counsel, or John Wellington Wells's respectable ignorance leads him astray.

[30] The accent the villagers use is West Country, in all probability Somersetshire; or, as they themselves would say—Zummerzet.

ALL.   All this will I du, if you'll marry me!
Eh, but oi du loike you!

Country dance

[31] *Here's the ear-trumpet! (See Note 13.)*   *At end of dance, enter* CONSTANCE *in tears, leading* NOTARY,
who carries an ear-trumpet [31]

ARIA—CONSTANCE

Dear friends, take pity on my lot,
   My cup is not of nectar!
I long have loved—as who would not?—
   Our kind and reverend rector.
Long years ago my love began
   So sweetly—yet so sadly—
But when I saw this plain old man,
Away my old affection ran—
   I found I loved him madly.
      Oh!

(*To* NOTARY.)   You very, very plain old man,
      I love, I love you madly!

CHORUS.   You very, very plain old man,
      She loves, she loves you madly!

NOTARY.   I am a very deaf old man,
      And hear you very badly!

CONSTANCE.   I know not why I love him so;
      It is enchantment, surely!
He's dry and snuffy, deaf and slow
      Ill-tempered, weak, and poorly!
He's ugly, and absurdly dressed,
      And sixty-seven nearly,
He's everything that I detest,
But if the truth must be confessed,
      I love him very dearly!
         Oh!

(*To* NOTARY.)   You're everything that I detest,
      But still I love you dearly!

CHORUS.   You're everything that girls detest,
      But still she loves you dearly!

NOTARY.   I caught that line, but for the rest,
      I did not hear it clearly!

[*During this verse* ALINE *and* ALEXIS *have entered at back unobserved.*

ALINE *and* ALEXIS

ALEXIS.   Oh joy! oh joy!
     The charm works well,
      And all are now united.

ALINE.   The blind young boy
     Obeys the spell,
      Their troth they all have plighted!

ENSEMBLE

ALINE *and* ALEXIS	CONSTANCE	NOTARY
Oh joy! oh joy!	Oh, bitter joy!	Oh joy! oh joy!
The charm works well,	No words can tell	No words can tell
And all are now united!	How my poor heart is blighted!	My state of mind delighted.
The blind young boy	They'll soon employ	They'll soon employ
Obeys the spell,	A marriage bell,	A marriage bell,
Their troth they all have plighted.	To say that we're united.	To say that we're united.
True happiness	I do confess	True happiness
Reigns everywhere,	A sorrow rare	Reigns everywhere
And dwells with both the sexes,	My humbled spirit vexes,	And dwells with both the sexes,
And all will bless	And none will bless	And all will bless
The thoughtful care	Example rare	Example rare
Of their beloved Alexis.	Of their beloved Alexis!	Of their beloved Alexis!

[*All, except* ALEXIS *and* ALINE, *exeunt lovingly.*

ALINE. How joyful they all seem in their new-found happiness! The whole village has paired off in the happiest manner. And yet not a match has been made that the hollow world would not consider ill-advised!

ALEXIS. But we are wiser—far wiser—than the world. Observe the good that will become of these ill-assorted unions. The miserly wife will check the reckless expenditure of her too frivolous consort, the wealthy husband will shower innumerable bonnets on his penniless bride, and the young and lively spouse will cheer the declining days of her aged partner with comic songs unceasing!

ALINE. What a delightful prospect for him!

ALEXIS. But one thing remains to be done, that my happiness may be complete. We must drink the philtre ourselves, that I may be assured of your love for ever and ever.

ALINE. Oh, Alexis, do you doubt me? Is it necessary that such love as ours should be secured by artificial means? Oh, no, no, no!

ALEXIS. My dear Aline, time works terrible changes, and I want to place our love beyond the chance of change.

ALINE. Alexis, it is already far beyond that chance. Have faith in me, for my love can never, never change!

ALEXIS. Then you absolutely refuse?

ALINE. I do. If you cannot trust me, you have no right to love me— no right to be loved *by* me.

ALEXIS. Enough, Aline, I shall know how to interpret this refusal.

BALLAD—ALEXIS

Thou hast the power thy vaunted love
To sanctify, all doubt above,
    Despite the gathering shade:
To make that love of thine so sure
That, come what may, it must endure
    Till time itself shall fade.
        Thy love is but a flower
        That fades within the hour!
        If such thy love, oh, shame!
        Call it by other name—
            It is not love!

Thine is the power and thine alone,
To place me on so proud a throne

That kings might envy me!
A priceless throne of love untold,
More rare than orient pearl and gold.
But no! Thou wouldst be free!
Such love is like the ray
That dies within the day:
If such thy love, oh, shame!
Call it by other name—
It is not love!

Enter DR. DALY

DR. D. (*musing*). It is singular—it is very singular. It has overthrown all my calculations. It is distinctly opposed to the doctrine of averages. I cannot understand it.

ALINE. Dear Dr. Daly, what has puzzled you?

DR. D. My dear, this village has not hitherto been addicted to marrying and giving in marriage. Hitherto the youths of this village have not been enterprising, and the maidens have been distinctly coy. Judge then of my surprise when I tell you that the whole village came to me in a body just now, and implored me to join them in matrimony with as little delay as possible. Even your excellent father has hinted to me that before very long it is not unlikely that he also may change his condition.

ALINE. Oh, Alexis—do you hear that? Are you not delighted?

ALEXIS. Yes. I confess that a union between your mother and my father would be a happy circumstance indeed. (*Crossing to* DR. DALY.) My dear sir—the news that you bring us is very gratifying.

DR. D. Yes—still, in my eyes, it has its melancholy side. This universal marrying recalls the happy days—now, alas, gone for ever—when I myself might have—but tush! I am puling. I am too old to marry—and yet, within the last half-hour, I have greatly yearned for companionship. I never remarked it before, but the young maidens of this village are very comely. So likewise are the middle-aged. Also the elderly. All are comely—and (*with a deep sigh*) all are engaged!

ALINE. Here comes your father.

Enter SIR MARMADUKE *with* MRS. PARTLET, *arm-in-arm*

ALINE *and* ALEXIS (*aside*). Mrs. Partlet!

SIR M. Dr. Daly, give me joy. Alexis, my dear boy, you will, I am sure, be pleased to hear that my declining days are not unlikely to be solaced by the companionship of this good, virtuous, and amiable woman.

ALEXIS (*rather taken aback*). My dear father, this is not altogether what I expected. I am certainly taken somewhat by surprise. Still it can hardly be necessary to assure you that any wife of yours is a mother of mine. (*Aside to* ALINE.) It is not quite what I could have wished.

MRS. P. (*crossing to* ALEXIS). Oh, sir, I entreat your forgiveness. I am aware that socially I am not everything that could be desired, nor am I blessed with an abundance of worldly goods, but I can at least confer on your estimable father the great and priceless dowry of a true, tender, and lovin' 'art! [32]

ALEXIS (*coldly*). I do not question it. After all, a faithful love is the true source of every earthly joy.

SIR M. I knew that my boy would not blame his poor father for acting on the impulse of a heart that has never yet misled him. Zorah is not perhaps what the world calls beautiful—

DR. D. Still she is comely—distinctly comely. (*Sighs.*)

[32] *The original edition uses the correct spelling with no attempt to convey Mrs. Partlet's habit of dropping her aitches.*

ALINE. Zorah is very good, and very clean, and honest, and quite, quite sober in her habits: and that is worth far more than beauty, dear Sir Marmaduke.

DR. D. Yes; beauty will fade and perish, but personal cleanliness is practically undying, for it can be renewed whenever it discovers symptoms of decay. My dear Sir Marmaduke, I heartily congratulate you. (*Sighs.*)

QUINTETTE

ALEXIS, ALINE, SIR MARMADUKE, ZORAH, *and* DR. DALY

ALEXIS. I rejoice that it's decided,
   Happy now will be his life,
  For my father is provided
   With a true and tender wife.

ENSEMBLE

 She will tend him, nurse him, mend him,
  Air his linen, dry his tears;
 Bless the thoughtful fates that send him
  Such a wife to soothe his years!

ALINE. No young giddy thoughtless maiden,
   Full of graces, airs, and jeers—
  But a sober widow, laden
   With the weight of fifty years!

SIR M. No high-born exacting beauty,
   Blazing like a jewelled sun—
  But a wife who'll do her duty,
   As that duty should be done!

MRS. P. I'm no saucy minx and giddy—
   Hussies such as them abound—
  But a clean and tidy widdy
   Well be-known for miles around!

DR. D. All the village now have mated,
   All are happy as can be—
  I to live alone am fated:
   No one's left to marry me!

ENSEMBLE.   She will tend him etc.

 [*Exeunt* SIR MARMADUKE, MRS. PARTLET, *and* ALINE,
   with ALEXIS. DR. DALY *looks after them sentimentally, then exits with a sigh.*

Enter MR. WELLS

RECITATIVE—MR. WELLS

Oh, I have wrought much evil with my spells!
 And ill I can't undo!
This is too bad of you, J. W. Wells—
 What wrong have they done you?
And see—another love-lorn lady comes—
 Alas, poor stricken dame!
A gentle pensiveness her life benumbs—
 And mine, alone, the blame!

LADY SANGAZURE *enters. She is very melancholy*

LADY S.　　Alas, ah me! and well-a-day!
　　　　　　I sigh for love, and well I may,
　　　　　　For I am very old and grey.
　　　　　　But stay!

(Sees MR. WELLS, *and becomes fascinated by him.)*

RECITATIVE

LADY S.　What is this fairy form I see before me?
MR. W.　Oh, horrible!—she's going to adore me!
　　　　This last catastrophe is overpowering!
LADY S.　Why do you glare at one with visage lowering?
　　　　For pity's sake recoil not thus from me!
MR. W.　My lady, leave me—this may never be!

DUET—LADY SANGAZURE *and* MR. WELLS

MR. W.　Hate me! I drop my H's—have through life!
LADY S.　　Love me! I'll drop them too!
MR. W.　Hate me! I always eat peas with a knife!
LADY S.　　Love me! I'll eat like you!
MR. W.　Hate me! I spend the day at Rosherville! [33]
LADY S.　　Love me! that joy I'll share!
MR. W.　Hate me! I often roll down One Tree Hill! [34]
LADY S.　　Love me! I'll join you there!

LADY S.　Love me! my prejudices I will drop! [35]
MR. W.　　Hate me! that's not enough!
LADY S.　Love me! I'll come and help you in the shop!
MR. W.　　Hate me! the life is rough!
LADY S.　Love me! my grammar I will all forswear!
MR. W.　　Hate me! abjure my lot!
LADY S.　Love me! I'll stick sunflowers in my hair!
MR. W.　　Hate me! they'll suit you not!

RECITATIVE—MR. WELLS

　　　　At what I am going to say be not enraged—
　　　　I may not love you—for I am engaged!
LADY S. *(horrified)*.　　　　Engaged!
MR. W.　　　　　　　　　　　　　Engaged!
　　　　　　To a maiden fair,
　　　　　　With bright brown hair,
　　　　　　　And a sweet and simple smile,
　　　　　　Who waits for me
　　　　　　By the sounding sea,
　　　　　　　On a South Pacific isle.
MR. W. *(aside)*.　A lie! No maiden waits me there!
LADY S. *(mournfully)*.　She has bright brown hair.
MR. W. *(aside)*.　A lie! No maiden smiles on me!
LADY S. *(mournfully)*.　By the sounding sea!

ENSEMBLE

LADY SANGAZURE	MR. WELLS
Oh, agony, rage, despair!	Oh, agony, rage, despair!
The maiden has bright brown hair,	Oh, where will this end—oh, where?
And mine is as white as snow!	I should like very much to know!
False man, it will be your fault,	It will certainly be my fault,
If I go to my family vault,	If she goes to her family vault,
And bury my life-long woe!	To bury her life-long woe!

[33] Rosherville. *Obviously an invented name. A sort of Coney Island, Hampstead Heath, or Southend on Sea.*

[34] One Tree Hill. *About four miles from London, where a fair is held.*

[35] *The question has often been put to me: What are her prejudices? I can only presume they are against tradespeople and bad grammar.*

BOTH.   The family vault—the family vault.

It will certainly be $\begin{Bmatrix} \text{your} \\ \text{my} \end{Bmatrix}$ fault.

If $\begin{Bmatrix} \text{I go} \\ \text{she goes} \end{Bmatrix}$ to $\begin{Bmatrix} \text{my} \\ \text{her} \end{Bmatrix}$ family vault,

To bury $\begin{Bmatrix} \text{my} \\ \text{her} \end{Bmatrix}$ life-long woe!

[*Exit* LADY SANGAZURE, *in great anguish, accompanied by* MR. WELLS. [36]

Enter ALINE, RECITATIVE

Alexis! Doubt me not, my loved one! See,
Thine uttered will is sovereign law to me!
All fear—all thought of ill I cast away!
It is my darling's will, and I obey!

(*She drinks the philtre.*)

The fearful deed is done,
    My love is near!
I go to meet my own
    In trembling fear!
If o'er us aught of ill
    Should cast a shade,
It was my darling's will,
    And I obeyed!

[*As* ALINE *is going off, she meets* DR. DALY, *entering pensively. He is playing on a flageolet. Under the influence of the spell she at once becomes strangely fascinated by him, and exhibits every symptom of being hopelessly in love with him.*

SONG—DR. DALY

Oh, my voice is sad and low
And with timid step I go—
For with load of love o'erladen
I enquire of every maiden,
"Will you wed me, little lady?
Will you share my cottage shady?"
    Little lady answers "No!
    Thank you for your kindly proffer—
    Good your heart, and full your coffer;
    Yet I must decline your offer—
    I'm engaged to So-and-so!"
    So-and-so!
    So-and-so! (*flageolet solo*) [37]
She's engaged to So-and-so!
What a rogue young hearts to pillage;
What a worker on Love's tillage!
Every maiden in the village
    Is engaged to So-and-so!
    So-and-so!
    So-and-so! (*flageolet solo*)
All engaged to So-and-so!

[*At the end of the song* DR. DALY *sees* ALINE, *and, under the influence of the potion, falls in love with her.*

[36] In actual production, Lady Sangazure, as far as I remember, does not exit in great anguish, accompanied by John Wellington Wells. My recollection of the end of this number is that Wells backs away from Lady Sangazure as they sing the final bars, she ending up with a most threatening gesture, whereupon Wells turns tail and flees, hotly pursued by Lady Sangazure.

The music itself would seem to debar any show of great anguish on her part, though Mr. Wells's lyric does give an indication of a knowledge of his guilt, if not of absolute repentance.

[37] This solo should be, and is, actually played by Dr. Daly, and during rehearsals for any budding principal, the "air is charged," but not, I'm afraid, "with amatory numbers." Rather it is charged with the frenzied efforts of a tyro Dr. Daly frantically trying to produce a reasonable facsimile of Sullivan's intentions musically, and of Mr. Gilbert's, lyrically.

Actually, the flageolet part is not so very difficult. The difficulty seems to be in co-ordinating vocal cords and fingers.

FLAGEOLET

ENSEMBLE—ALINE *and* DR. DALY

Oh, joyous boon! oh, mad delight;
Oh, sun and moon! oh, day and night!
   Rejoice, rejoice with me!
Proclaim our joy, ye birds above—
Yet brooklets, murmur forth our love,
   In choral ecstasy:

ALINE. Oh, joyous boon!
DR. D.   Oh, mad delight!
ALINE. Oh, sun and moon!
DR. D.   Oh, day and night!
BOTH. Ye birds, and brooks, and fruitful trees,
    With choral joy delight the breeze—
      Rejoice, rejoice with me!

Enter ALEXIS

ALEXIS (*with rapture*). Aline my only love, my happiness!
The philtre—you have tasted it?
ALINE (*with confusion*). Yes! Yes!
ALEXIS. Oh, joy, mine, mine for ever, and for aye!

(*Embraces her.*)

ALINE. Alexis, don't do that—you must not!

(DR. DALY *interposes between them.*)

ALEXIS (*amazed*). Why?

DUET—ALINE *and* DR. DALY

ALINE. Alas! that lovers thus should meet:
    Oh, pity, pity me!
  Oh, charge me not with cold deceit;
    Oh, pity, pity me!
  You bade me drink—with trembling awe
  I drank, and, by the potion's law,
  I loved the very first I saw!
    Oh, pity, pity me!

DR. D. My dear young friend, consolèd be—
    We pity, pity you.
  In this I'm not an agent free—
    We pity, pity you.
  Some most extraordinary spell
  O'er us has cast its magic fell—
  The consequence I need not tell.
    We pity, pity you.

ENSEMBLE

Some most extraordinary spell

Oe'r { us / them } has cast its magic fell—

The consequence { we / they } need not tell.

We / They } pity, pity { thee! / me.

ALEXIS (*furiously*).   False one, begone—I spurn thee,
      To thy new lover turn thee!
      Thy perfidy all men shall know.
ALINE (*wildly*).   I could not help it!
ALEXIS (*calling off*).   Come one, come all!

DR. D.   We could not help it!
ALEXIS (*calling off*).   Obey my call!
ALINE (*wildly*).   I could not help it!
ALEXIS (*calling off*).   Come hither, run!
DR. D.   We could not help it!
ALEXIS (*calling off*).   Come, every one!

Enter all the characters except LADY SANGAZURE *and* MR. WELLS

CHORUS

Oh, what is the matter, and what is the clatter?
He's glowering at her, and threatens a blow!
Oh, why does he batter the girl he did flatter?
And why does the latter recoil from him so?

RECITATIVE—ALEXIS

Prepare for sad surprises—
My love Aline despises!
No thought of sorrow shames her—
Another lover claims her!
Be his, false girl, for better or for worse—
But, ere you leave me, may a lover's curse—

DR. D. (*coming forward*). Hold! Be just. This poor child drank the philtre at your instance. She hurried off to meet you—but, most unhappily, she met me instead. As you had administered the potion to both of us, the result was inevitable. But fear nothing from me—I will be no man's rival. I shall quit the country at once—and bury my sorrow in the congenial gloom of a Colonial Bishopric.

ALEXIS. My excellent old friend! (*Taking his hand—then turning to* MR. WELLS, *who has entered with* LADY SANGAZURE.) Oh, Mr. Wells, what, what is to be done?

MR. W. I do not know—and yet—there is one means by which this spell may be removed.

ALEXIS. Name it—oh, name it!

MR. W. Or you or I must yield up his life to Ahrimanes. [38] I would rather it were you. I should have no hesitation in sacrificing my own life to spare yours, but we take stock next week, and it would not be fair on the Co.

ALEXIS. True. Well, I am ready!

ALINE. No, no—Alexis—it must not be! Mr. Wells, if he must die that all may be restored to their old loves, what is to become of me? I should be left out in the cold, with no love to be restored to!

MR. W. True—I did not think of that. (*To the others.*) My friends, I appeal to you, and I will leave the decision in your hands.

[38] Ahrimanes. Zoroastrianism. *The supreme spirit of evil in opposition to Ormazd.*

FINALE

MR. W.   Or I or he
            Must die!
        Which shall it be?
            Reply!
SIR M.   Die thou!
        Thou art the cause of all offending!
DR. D.   Die thou!
        Yield thou to this decree unbending!
ALL.   Die thou!
MR. W. So be it! I submit! My fate is sealed.
      To public execration thus I yield!

[39] One reason why The Sorcerer is not presented as frequently as it might be is the trap. Few theaters today are built with traps, and when they are, they are invariably in the wrong places. This means that a special trap must be installed in the right place, which, apart from the owner's natural disinclination to cut his stage, is expensive.

[40] During this chorus John Wellington Wells takes out his handkerchief and wipes his brow and the inside of his hatband. He takes out his watch and holds it to his ear, then winds it and puts it back in his pocket. He takes his shoes off and places them neatly beside him. By this time the trap should be ready to descend amidst "red fire." As soon as the curtain goes up for the first bow, after its fall, Wells's hat, shoes, gloves and umbrella are thrown back onto the stage from below.

On Sir Henry's last appearance in the role he also pushed a sign up through the trap, thus calling down on his head the wrath of the powers that be. Mae West was at her peak at this time, and the sign read: "Come down and see me sometime!"

(Falls on trap.) [39]

Be happy all—leave me to my despair—
I go—it matters not with whom—or where!

(Gong.)

[*All quit their present partners, and rejoin their old lovers.* SIR MARMADUKE *leaves* MRS. PARTLET, *and goes to* LADY SANGAZURE. ALINE *leaves* DR. DALY, *and goes to* ALEXIS. DR. DALY *leaves* ALINE, *and goes to* CONSTANCE. NOTARY *leaves* CONSTANCE, *and goes to* MRS. PARTLET. *All the* CHORUS *make a corresponding change.*

ALL

GENTLEMEN.	Oh, my adored one!
LADIES.	Unmingled joy!
GENTLEMEN.	Ecstatic rapture!
LADIES.	Beloved boy!

(They embrace.)

SIR M. Come to my mansion, all of you! At least
We'll crown our rapture with another feast!

ENSEMBLE
SIR MARMADUKE, LADY SANGAZURE, ALEXIS, *and* ALINE

Now to the banquet we press—
Now for the eggs and the ham—
Now for the mustard and cress—
Now for the strawberry jam!

CHORUS. Now to the banquet, etc. [40]

DR. DALY, CONSTANCE, NOTARY, *and* MRS. PARTLET

Now for the tea of our host—
Now for the rollicking bun—
Now for the muffin and toast—
Now for the gay Sally Lunn!

CHORUS. Now for the tea, etc.

(General Dance.)

[*During the symphony* MR. WELLS *sinks through trap, amid red fire.*

CURTAIN

Time Was, When Love and I

DR. DALY

With tranquillity

mf legato

p sempre legato

1. Time
2. Had I a

was, when Love and I were well ac - quaint - ed. Time was, when we walk'd ev - er hand in
head-ache? sigh'd the maids as - sem - bled; Had I a cold? well'd forth the si - lent

hand. A saint - ly youth, with world-ly thought un-taint - ed,
tear; Did I look pale? then half a par - ish trem - bled;

None bet - ter lov'd than I in all the land! Time
And when I cough'd all thought the end was near! I had no

was, when maid-ens of the no-blest sta-tion, For-sak-ing ev-en mil-i-ta-ry

care, no jeal-ous doubts hung o'er me, For I was lov'd be-yond all oth-er

cresc. *mf*

men, Would gaze up-on me, rapt in ad-o-ra-tion, Ah

men. Fled gild-ed dukes and belt-ed earls be-fore me, Ah

p *rit.* **1.**

me, Ah me, I was a fair young cu-rate then!

me, Ah me, I was a pale young cu-rate

mf a tempo

2.

then! A pale young cu-rate, a pale young cu-rate, Ah

cresc. *mf*

mf *cresc.* *mf*

me, I was a pale young cu-rate then!

rit.

p a tempo *mf*

My Name Is John Wellington Wells

Very lively

MR. WELLS

My name is John Well-ing-ton Wells,____ I'm a

deal-er in mag-ic and spells,____ In bless-ings and curs-es And ev-er-fill'd purs-es, In

proph-e-cies, witch-es, and knells.____ If you want a proud foe to "make tracks"____ If you'd

melt a rich un-cle in wax___ You've but to look in On the res - i - dent Djinn, Num-ber

sev - en - ty, Sim-mer - y Axe.___We've a first-rate as-sort-ment of mag - ic; And for

rais-ing a post-hu-mous shade, With ef - fects that are com-ic or trag-ic, There's

no cheap-er house in the trade.___ Love-phil-tre, we've quan-ti-ties of it! And for

knowl-edge if an-y-one burns,___ We're keep-ing a ver - y small proph-et, a proph-et Who

brings us un-bound-ed re - turns___ For he can proph-e-sy

With a wink of his eye, Peep with se-cu-ri-ty In-to fu-tu-ri-ty,

Sum up your his-to-ry, Clear up a mys-ter-y, Hu-mour pro-cliv-i-ty

For a na-tiv-i-ty, for a na-tiv-i-ty; He has

an-swers o-rac-u-lar, Bo-gies spec-tac-u-lar, Tet-ra-pods trag-i-cal,

Mir-rors so mag-i-cal, Facts as-tro-nom-i-cal, Sol-emn or com-i-cal,

And, if you want it, he Makes a re-duc-tion on tak-ing a quan-ti-ty!

cresc.

Oh! If an-y-one an-y-thing lacks, He'll

find it all read-y in stacks, If he'll on-ly look in On the

res-i-dent Djinn, Num-ber sev-en-ty, Sim-mer-y Axe.

He can raise you hosts Of ghosts,. And

that, with-out re-flec - tors; And creep - y things With wings, And

gaunt and gris - ly spec - tres; He can fill you crowds Of shrouds, And

hor - ri - fy you vast - ly; He can rack your brains With chains,___ And

quire an a-pol-o-gy! Oh! _____ My name is John Well-ing-ton Wells, ___ I'm a
deal-er in mag-ic and spells, ___ In bless-ings and curs-es, And ev-er fill'd purs-es, In
proph-e-cies, witch-es, and knells. ___ And if an-y-one an-y-thing lacks, ___ He'll
find it all read-y in stacks, ___ If he'll on-ly look in On the res-i-dent Djinn, Num-ber
sev-en-ty, Sim-mer-y Axe!

Now to the Banquet We Press

Light and cheerful

CHORUS

Now to the ban-quet we press, Now for the eggs and the ham!___

Now for the mus-tard and cress, Now for the straw-ber-ry jam!___

Now for the tea of our host!___ Now for the rol-lick-ing

gay Sal - ly Lunn! The eggs and the ham And the straw - ber - ry jam, And the

rol - lick - ing bun! The rol - lick - ing bun And the gay Sal - ly Lunn And the

straw - ber - ry jam, jam, bun, jam, bun, Oh! the

straw - ber - ry, straw - ber - ry jam, bun, jam, bun, jam, Oh! ___

___ the rol - lick - ing, rol - lick - ing bun! ___

H.M.S. Pinafore

OR, THE LASS THAT LOVED A SAILOR

DRAMATIS PERSONÆ

THE RT. HON. SIR JOSEPH PORTER, K.C.B. (*First Lord of the Admiralty*).

CAPTAIN CORCORAN (*Commanding H.M.S. Pinafore*).

TOM TUCKER (*Midshipmite*).

RALPH RACKSTRAW (*Able Seaman*).

DICK DEADEYE (*Able Seaman*).

BILL BOBSTAY (*Boatswain's Mate*).

BOB BECKET (*Carpenter's Mate*).

JOSEPHINE (*the Captain's Daughter*).

HEBE (*Sir Joseph's First Cousin*).

MRS. CRIPPS (LITTLE BUTTERCUP) (*a Portsmouth Bumboat Woman*).

First Lord's Sisters, his Cousins, his Aunts, Sailors, Marines, etc.

Scene: QUARTER-DECK OF H.M.S. *Pinafore*, OFF PORTSMOUTH.

ACT I.—*Noon.*   ACT II.—*Night.*

First produced at the Opéra Comique on May 25, 1878

imitated or not, there was a certain resemblance to the portraits of Nelson in Mr. Grossmith's make-up." The make-up could very well have been one of Gilbert's tricks to avoid any suggestion that Sir Joseph was little more than a caricature of W. H. Smith, the then First Lord in Disraeli's cabinet. It wasn't carried to extremes, however. Grossmith did not wear a black patch over one eye, nor did anyone amputate his arm.

At one time the very minor roles of the Midshipmite and the Sergeant of Marines were mentioned in the program. The former was dignified (?) with the name of Tommy Tucker. Today they are frequently missing from the printed program, though "Tom Tucker, a Midshipmite" does occasionally appear in some of the published editions of the opera. Conversely, Little Buttercup had no name in the original first-night program, but somewhere along the line she acquired one—Mrs. Cripps.

One character who has in past years been presented as a frightening, glary-eyed, cronelike creature is Dick Deadeye. I have never agreed with this conception of the role, and, from contemporary sketches, neither did Gilbert. Deadeye is shown simply as wearing a black patch over one eye, and as being slightly humpbacked. Any distortion or hideousness in his make-up is conspicuous by its absence. Deadeye is at a physical disadvantage, certainly, but his ugliness is of the mind. This is due, possibly, to the fact that he considers his "a beast of a name," and therefore they, the crew, all "hate him for it." But he's not frightening. He should be booed and hissed, yes, but should not look so frightful that children are likely to run screaming out of the theater.

H.M.S. Pinafore is unique in that it was the cause of a split between Richard Carte and the other directors of the Opéra Comique. When, because of the heat wave and other factors, business was at a low ebb they (the other directors) wished to close the show and cut their losses. Carte, however, was adamant in keeping it on, with the result that relations became strained. But when Sullivan played one of Pinafore's selections at the prom, the show became a gold mine, their attitude changed, and with the change came a most extraordinary decision. They would split with Carte and open their own

(W. S. GILBERT'S LETTER ON THE FACING PAGE READS:)

8th Feb. 1908

Dear Miss Woodward,

The "Northumberland" will do perfectly well as far as regards *masts, yards & rigging*—but she has a flush deck (that is, a deck that is on the same level throughout) whereas a ship of the "Pinafore" class would have what is called a "raised poop"—that is to say, the after part of the deck is raised some 10 ft above the general run, with two ladders giving access to it; & entrance to cabins, & also the steering wheel, under the overhanging part of the poop-deck. You will find exactly what you want in the model of the "Albion" which stands on the left of the Northumberland as you enter from Imperial Institute Road. I give you a rough idea of it on the other side. Faithfully,

W. S. Gilbert

(The words on the illustration, from left to right, are):
Mizzen Rigging   Mizzen Mast   Mizzen Rigging
Fire buckets
(not shown in model of Albion)
Gun   Door   Wheel   Door   Windows   Gun
Hatchway

"A FROTHY production destined soon to subside into nothingness."

This excerpt is taken from the review from the London Daily Telegraph, May 27, 1878. It refers to the opening-night performance of Pinafore. I imagine the writer would feel pretty silly if he were still around these days. Or does over seventy years of continued popularity constitute "nothingness"?

There was, however, a time when it looked as if the critic had hit the nail on the head, for, in spite of the fact that other papers were, if not lavish with their praise, at least kindly disposed toward the piece, Pinafore gave no indication of being an immediate smash hit. A variety of causes was responsible, among which was a heat wave in May followed by a flaming June; a theater in a not-too-good neighborhood; and a public to whom the theater was still not quite the place for "nice" people to be seen in.

Luckily, Sullivan, who had just been appointed conductor of the justly famous Queen's Hall Promenade Concerts, decided to include a selection from Pinafore in one of these proms. The result was staggering, to say the least. The following morning the theater box office was besieged, and a near failure became a smash hit overnight. It ran for 700 performances.

On Sunday, May 26, 1878, Gilbert and Sullivan, having read the reviews, decided to cut out a hornpipe in Act I, as well as Rutland Barrington's serenade in Act II. I imagine the hornpipe is the dance music sung and danced by the crew at the end of "A British tar is a soaring soul," or perhaps it was extra music not now used, but I cannot say for certain. Barrington's serenade undoubtedly refers to "Fair moon, to thee I sing." Fortunately, the advice of others prevailed, and I strongly suspect that Mr. Barrington himself was among those presenting his case. The serenade was allowed to remain.

The scene of this nautical comic opera is set on board the H.M.S. Pinafore riding at anchor in Portsmouth Harbor, with H.M.S. Victory visible in the background. The general outline of the scene is as nearly authentic as can be. Gilbert spent a whole day on board the Victory, lunched with Lord Charles Beresford on the Thunderer, and made copious sketches the while. Such was Gilbert's passion for correctness and detail that the uniforms were made by a Portsmouth naval tailor. Sir Joseph's costume was probably the only exception. In the first place, it is not a uniform. It is the court dress of a high-ranking cabinet minister, and as such would not come under the head of naval tailoring. In all probability it was obtained from one of the court tailors in London. The slight resemblance to Lord Nelson may have been the original cause of the thought, particularly in the United States, that Sir Joseph is an admiral. It has carried over even to the charming illustration of this volume.

Quite frequently Sir Joseph is alluded to as "the admiral." Sir Joseph is in no way at all a Navy man. He is a civilian, and the post he holds is a political one insofar as he is a member of the Cabinet. As First Lord of the Admiralty he should not be confused with the First Sea Lord, who is not a member of the Cabinet but who is regular Royal Navy and an admiral.

The Order of the Bath, the insignia of which Sir Joseph wears on his left breast and at his throat, was, in those days, as authentic and correct as his court dress, and as authentic as the dress, sword and K.C.B. which I wore.

The Era, a theatrical weekly, said in its review of Pinafore that ". . . Grossmith's 'Sir Joseph' was a very effective study of a British admiral. [This may partly account for the confusion regarding his real status.] Whether purposely

TELEPHONE: 1426 VICTORIA.

90. EATON SQUARE,
S.W.

8th Feb. 1908.

Dear Miss Woodward.

The "Northumberland" will do perfectly well as far as regards masts, yards & rigging – but she has a flush deck (that is, a deck that is on the same level throughout) whereas a ship of the "Pinafore" class would have what is called a "raised poop" – that is to say, the after part of the deck is raised some 10 ft above the general run, with two ladders giving access to it, & entrance to cabins, & also the steering wheel, under the overhanging part of the poop-deck. You will find exactly what you want in the model of the "Albion" which stands on the left of the Northumberland as you enter from Imperial Institute Road. I give you a rough idea of it on the other side.

Yours truly

W. S. Gilbert.

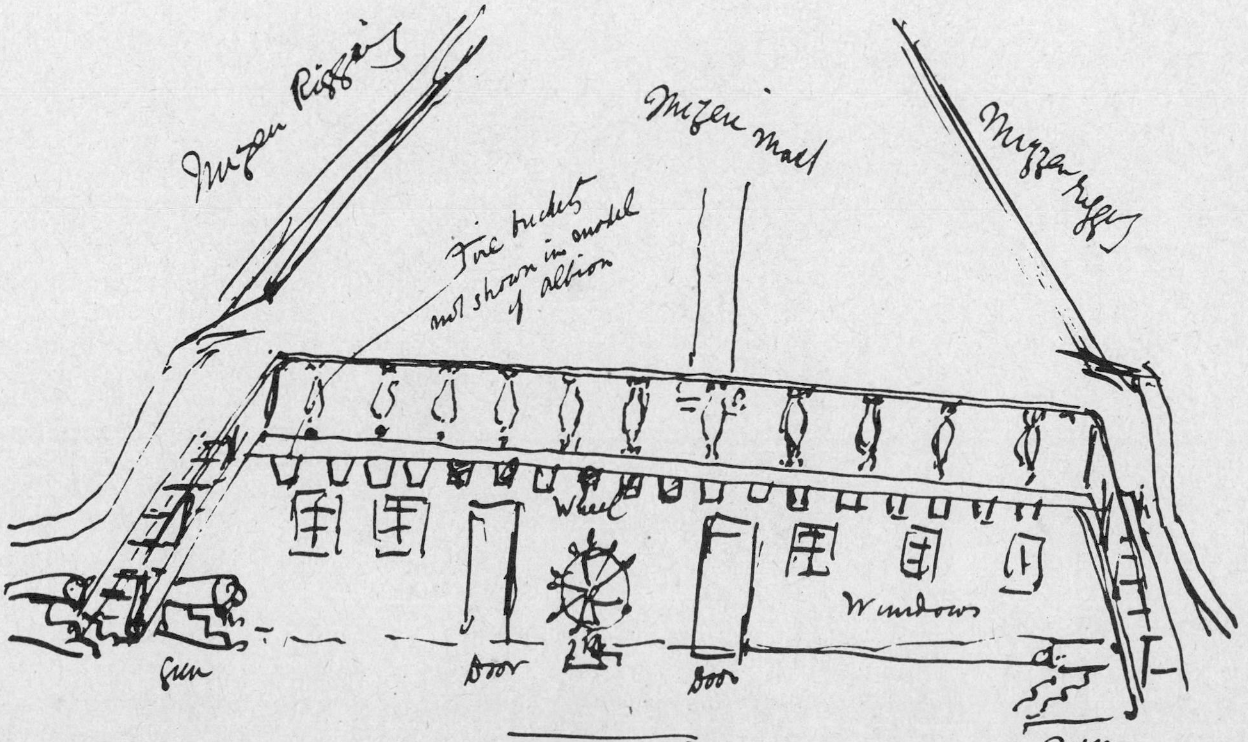
Mizen Rigging
Mizen Mast
Mizzen Rigging
Fire buckets not shown in model of Albion
Wheel
Windows
Gun
Door
Door
Gun
Hatches

production at another theater. Equipped with vans and men they arrived at the Opéra Comique, intending to remove the scenery. The show was in actual performance, but that did not deter them.

Shouts of "Come on!" and "Now's the time!" were heard and the actors saw crowds of "roughs" (in American parlance, "toughs") rushing toward the stage. Roughs are somewhat worse than a rat (see Note 45 of Patience) and, not unnaturally, the ladies became panicky. This led to a belief in the audience that a fire had broken out, and there were shouts to that effect. Alfred Cellier, the conductor, stopped the performance; Grossmith, as Sir Joseph, came forward and tried to reassure the audience, while Miss Everard, the Little Buttercup, gallantly attempted to proceed with her role. The Opéra Comique's stagehands were hurriedly called and a free-for-all lasting a full hour took place before the intruders were driven from the theater, leaving Richard Carte the victor.

The rival company carried on with their version, however, and later had the audacity to move almost next door. Lack of public support soon put an end to their efforts, and the lawsuits that went on only served to advertise Carte's "official" version—to the intense chagrin of his rivals.

H.M.S. Pinafore

ACT I

SCENE.—*Quarter-deck of H.M.S. Pinafore. Sailors, led by* BOATSWAIN, *discovered cleaning brasswork, splicing rope, etc.* [1]

CHORUS—MEN [2]

We sail the ocean blue,
And our saucy ship's a beauty;
We're sober men and true,
And attentive to our duty.
When the balls whistle free
O'er the bright blue sea,
We stand to our guns all day;
When at anchor we ride
On the Portsmouth tide,
We've plenty of time for play.

Enter LITTLE BUTTERCUP, *with large basket on her arm*

RECIT

Hail, men-o'-war's men—safeguards of your nation,
Here is an end, at last, of all privation;
You've got your pay—spare all you can afford
To welcome Little Buttercup on board.

ARIA—BUTTERCUP [3]

For I'm called Little Buttercup—dear Little Buttercup,
  Though I could never tell why,
But still I'm called Buttercup—poor little Buttercup,
  Sweet Little Buttercup I!

I've snuff and tobaccy, and excellent jacky, [4]
  I've scissors, and watches, and knives;
I've ribbons and laces to set off the faces
  Of pretty young sweethearts and wives.

I've treacle and toffee, I've tea and I've coffee,
  Soft tommy [5] and succulent chops;
I've chickens and conies, [6] and pretty polonies, [7]
  And excellent peppermint drops.

Then buy of your Buttercup—dear Little Buttercup;
  Sailors should never be shy;
So, buy of your Buttercup—poor Little Buttercup;
  Come, of your Buttercup buy! [8]

BOAT. Aye, Little Buttercup—and well called—for you're the rosiest, the roundest, and the reddest [9] beauty in all Spithead.

BUT. Red, am I? and round—and rosy! Maybe, for I have dissembled well! But hark ye, my merry friend—hast ever thought that beneath a

[1] Tommy Tucker, the Midshipmite, is also discovered. He is the officer in charge, or, in naval parlance, the officer of the watch, and he is always the very smallest boy who can be obtained. He carries a telescope under his arm in approved fashion, and occasionally calls a man to task for slovenly work. At one moment he is saluted smartly by the Boatswain, Bill Bobstay.

[2] Words and music on page 97.

[3] Words and music on page 100.

[4] Jacky. Tobacco in twists, soaked in rum; for chewing.

[5] Tommy. Also known as soft tommy. A soft bread or bun. This would be a delicacy after the ship's hardtack.

[6] European term for rabbit.

[7] A kind of sausage. Like the American baloney, polony derives its name from Bologna..

[8] As she finishes her song the sailors crowd around her and buy all she has, with the exception of one stick of peppermint rock of a beautiful pink and about nine inches long. This she hands to Tommy Tucker, saying: "And that's for you, little man." Tommy exits, happily sucking the rock.

[9] Buttercups are yellow! By what process of reasoning does the Boatswain consider her "well called"?

gay and frivolous exterior there may lurk a canker-worm which is slowly but surely eating its way into one's very heart?

BOAT. No, my lass, I can't say I've ever thought that.

Enter DICK DEADEYE. *He pushes through sailors, and comes down*

DICK. I have thought it often. (*All recoil from him.*)

BUT. Yes, you look like it! What's the matter with the man? Isn't he well?

BOAT. Don't take no heed of *him;* that's only poor Dick Deadeye.

DICK. I say—it's a beast of a name, ain't it—Dick Deadeye?

BUT. It's not a nice name.

DICK. I'm ugly too, ain't I?

BUT. You are certainly plain.

DICK. And I'm three-cornered too, ain't I?

BUT. You are rather triangular.

DICK. Ha! ha! That's it. I'm ugly, and they hate me for it; for you all hate me, don't you?

ALL. We do!

DICK. There!

BOAT. Well, Dick, we wouldn't go for to hurt any fellow-creature's feelings, but you can't expect a chap with such a name as Dick Deadeye to be a popular character—now can you? [10]

DICK. No.

BOAT. It's asking too much, ain't it?

DICK. It is. From such a face and form as mine the noblest sentiments sound like the black utterances of a depraved imagination. It is human nature—I am resigned.

RECIT

BUT. (*looking down hatchway*).
    But, tell me—who's the youth whose faltering feet
      With difficulty bear him on his course?

BOAT. That is the smartest lad in all the fleet—
    Ralph [11] Rackstraw!

BUT.   Ha! That name! Remorse! remorse!

Enter RALPH *from hatchway*

MADRIGAL—RALPH

RALPH.   The Nightingale
            Sighed for the moon's bright ray,
              And told his tale
            In his own melodious way!
            He sang "Ah, well-a-day!"

ALL.   He sang "Ah, well-a-day!"

RALPH.   The lowly vale
            For the mountain vainly sighed,
              To his humble wail
            The echoing hills replied.
            They sang "Ah, well-a-day!"

ALL.   They sang "Ah, well-a-day!"

RECIT—RALPH

I know the value of a kindly chorus,
    But choruses yield little consolation
When we have pain and sorrow too before us!
    I love—and love, alas, above my station!

[10] *Deadeye is really quite a philosopher. Gilbert emphasizes this and at the same time points up the instinctive cruelty of man when he gives the Boatswain the line: ". . . you can't expect a chap with such a name as Dick Deadeye to be a popular character—now can you?" No matter how sympathetically this is said, the inherent cruelty is there. And here comes Dick, the philosopher: "No. . . . It is human nature—I am resigned." Deadeye is more to be pitied than blamed.*

Going back to the Boatswain's speech—for some reason or another the word "character" has (during my time, at any rate) always been pronounced ker-rack-ter. So far as I know, the county-of-origin of the Boatswain has never been established, nor do I know if this special pronunciation was at Gilbert's instigation. Quite possibly it was, and quite possibly that is the way any cockney or even coster would have pronounced it in Gilbert's day. As far as I'm concerned either of these personalities would pronounce it kar-ick-ter. As ker-rack-ter, though, it does have a quaint, Dickensian quality.

[11] *Ralph is pronounced Raife.*

BUT. (*aside*). He loves—and loves a lass above his station! [12]
ALL (*aside*). Yes, yes, the lass is much above his station!

[*Exit* LITTLE BUTTERCUP.

[12] A very obscure pun that reads well but, I'm afraid, is lost to the ear—until it is explained by the sailors!

BALLAD—RALPH [13]

[13] Words and music on page 103.

A maiden fair to see,
The pearl of minstrelsy,
  A bud of blushing beauty;
For whom proud nobles sigh,
And with each other vie
  To do her menial's duty.
ALL.   To do her menial's duty.

RALPH. A suitor, lowly born,
With hopeless passion torn,
  And poor beyond denying,
Has dared for her to pine
At whose exalted shrine
  A world of wealth is sighing.
ALL.   A world of wealth is sighing.

RALPH. Unlearned he in aught
Save that which love has taught
  (For love had been his tutor);
Oh, pity, pity me—
Our captain's daughter she,
  And I that lowly suitor!
ALL.   And he that lowly suitor!

BOAT. Ah, my poor lad, you've climbed too high: our worthy captain's child won't have nothin' to say to a poor chap like you. Will she, lads?
ALL. No, no.
DICK. No, no, captains' daughters don't marry fore-mast hands.
ALL (*recoiling from him*). Shame! shame!
BOAT. Dick Deadeye, them sentiments o' yourn are a disgrace to our common natur'.
RALPH. But it's a strange anomaly, that the daughter of a man who hails from the quarter-deck may not love another who lays out on the fore-yard arm. For a man is but a man, whether he hoists his flag at the main-truck or his slacks on the main-deck.
DICK. Ah, it's a queer world!
RALPH. Dick Deadeye, I have no desire to press hardly on you, but such a revolutionary sentiment is enough to make an honest sailor shudder.
BOAT. My lads, our gallant captain has come on deck; let us greet him as so brave an officer and so gallant a seaman deserves.

Enter CAPTAIN CORCORAN [14]

RECIT—CAPT. *and* CREW

CAPT. My gallant crew, good morning.
ALL (*saluting*). Sir, good morning!
CAPT. I hope you're all quite well.
ALL (*as before*). Quite well; and you, sir?
CAPT. I am in reasonable health, and happy
    To meet you all once more.
ALL (*as before*). You do us proud, sir!

[14] Captain Corcoran is a typical Royal Navy type: good-looking, forty-five to fifty years old, proud of his uniform (in this case, full ceremonial dress, sword, cocked hat and aiglet, and complete decorations, viz., battle medals, etc.). Proud, too, of his abilities as an officer, sailor and gentleman. Well liked by his crew, even if they are at times likely to question some of his statements.

SONG—CAPT. [15]

CAPT.   I am the Captain of the *Pinafore*;

[15] Words and music on page 106.

[16] *Just you wait, Captain Corcoran, just you wait!*

[17] *Selvagee. A hank or skein of ropeyarn marled together and used as a strap to fasten around a shroud or stay, or as slings, etc. We may presume that Captain Corcoran is alluding to his ability to be able actually to fasten one.*

[18] *It is a well-established fact that Gilbert drew on his Bab Ballads for many of his plots and characters. There is a close resemblance to Captain Reece, R.N., of the good ship Mantelpiece, in Captain Corcoran, and a little more than a touch of the Bishop of Rum-ti-Foo:*

> *Some sailors whom he did not know*
> *Had landed there not long ago,*
> *And taught them "Bother," also "Blow"*
>   *(Of wickedness the germs).*
> *No need to use a casuist's pen*
> *To prove that they were merchantmen;*
> *No sailor of the Royal N.*
>   *Would use such awful terms.*

Also, Ralph Rackstraw can be traced to Jo Golightly, and the First Lord's Daughter, and The Bumboat Woman's Story will reveal a distinct likeness to Little Buttercup.

ALL.   And a right good captain, too!

CAPT.   You're very, very good,
     And be it understood,
   I command a right good crew,

ALL.   We're very, very good,
     And be it understood,
   He commands a right good crew.

CAPT.   Though related to a peer, [16]
   I can hand, reef, and steer,
     And ship a selvagee; [17]
   I am never known to quail
   At the fury of a gale,
     And I'm never, never sick at sea!

ALL.   What, never?

CAPT.   No, never!

ALL.   What, *never*?

CAPT.   Hardly ever!

ALL.   He's hardly ever sick at sea!
Then give three cheers, and one cheer more,
For the hardy Captain of the *Pinafore*!

CAPT.   I do my best to satisfy you all—

ALL.   And with you we're quite content.

CAPT.   You're exceedingly polite,
     And I think it only right
   To return the compliment.

ALL.   We're exceedingly polite,
     And he thinks it's only right
   To return the compliment.

CAPT.   Bad language or abuse, [18]
   I never, never use,
   Whatever the emergency;
     Though "Bother it" I may
     Occasionally say,
   I never use a big, big D—

ALL.   What, never?

CAPT.   No, never!

ALL.   What, *never*?

CAPT.   Hardly ever!

ALL.   Hardly ever swears a big, big D—
Then give three cheers, and one cheer more,
For the well-bred Captain of the *Pinafore*!

       [*After song exeunt all but* CAPTAIN

Enter LITTLE BUTTERCUP

RECIT—BUTTERCUP *and* CAPT.

BUT. Sir, you are sad! The silent eloquence
Of yonder tear that trembles on your eyelash
Proclaims a sorrow far more deep than common;
Confide in me—fear not—I am a mother!

CAPT. Yes, Little Buttercup, I'm sad and sorry—
My daughter, Josephine, the fairest flower
That ever blossomed on ancestral timber,
Is sought in marriage by Sir Joseph Porter,
Our Admiralty's First Lord, but for some reason
She does not seem to tackle kindly to it.

BUT. (*with emotion*). Ah, poor Sir Joseph! Ah, I know too well

The anguish of a heart that loves but vainly!
But see, here comes your most attractive daughter.
I go—Farewell!   [*Exit.*
CAPT. (*looking after her*). A plump and pleasing person!   [*Exit.*

Enter JOSEPHINE, [19] *twining some flowers which she carries
in a small basket*

[19] Josephine is a very presentable young lady of marriageable age. Ralph, as it turns out later, is the "humble sailor" with whom she is in love. Ralph, it is well to remember, is generally depicted as a young man about her own age.

BALLAD—JOSEPHINE [20]

Sorry her lot who loves too well,
    Heavy the heart that hopes but vainly,
Sad are the sighs that own the spell,
    Uttered by eyes that speak too plainly;
        Heavy the sorrow that bows the head
        When love is alive and hope is dead!

Sad is the hour when sets the sun—
    Dark is the night to earth's poor daughters,
When to the ark the wearied one
    Flies from the empty waste of waters!
        Heavy the sorrow that bows the head
        When love is alive and hope is dead!

[20] Words and music on page 109.

Enter CAPTAIN

CAPT. My child, I grieve to see that you are a prey to melancholy. You should look your best to-day, for Sir Joseph Porter, K.C.B., [21] will be here this afternoon to claim your promised hand.

JOS. Ah, father, your words cut me to the quick. I can esteem—reverence—venerate Sir Joseph, for he is a great and good man; but oh, I cannot love him! My heart is already given.

CAPT. (*aside*). It is then as I feared. (*Aloud.*) Given? And to whom? Not to some gilded lordling?

JOS. No, father—the object of my love is no lordling. Oh, pity me, for he is but a humble sailor on board your own ship!

CAPT. Impossible!

JOS. Yes, it is true—too true.

CAPT. A common sailor? Oh fie!

JOS. I blush for the weakness that allows me to cherish such a passion. I hate myself when I think of the depth to which I have stooped in permitting myself to think tenderly of one so ignobly born, but I love him! I love him! I love him! (*Weeps.*)

CAPT. Come, my child, let us talk this over. In a matter of the heart I would not coerce my daughter—I attach but little value to rank or wealth, but the line must be drawn somewhere. A man in that station may be brave and worthy, but at every step he would commit solecisms that society would never pardon.

JOS. Oh, I have thought of this night and day. But fear not, father, I have a heart, and therefore I love; but I am your daughter, and therefore I am proud. Though I carry my love with me to the tomb, he shall never, never know it.

CAPT. You *are* [22] my daughter after all. But see, Sir Joseph's barge approaches, manned by twelve trusty oarsmen and accompanied by the admiring crowd of sisters, cousins, and aunts that attend him wherever he goes. Retire, my daughter, to your cabin—take this, his photograph, with you—it may help to bring you to a more reasonable frame of mind.

JOS. My own thoughtful father!

[*Exit* JOSEPHINE. CAPTAIN *remains and ascends the poop-deck.*

[21] Captain Corcoran is the complete snob and very conscious of rank. He raises his cocked hat every time he mentions Sir Joseph's name and rank. A most un-Royal Navy proceeding. Normally he would salute, but apparently he feels that to raise his hat shows a deeper respect.

K.C.B. Knight Companion of the Most Noble Order of the Bath is one of the two highest honors awarded in Britain. The other is the Garter. It may be of interest to know that the Order of the Bath is so called from the bath which preceded installation, and was instituted in 1603.

[22] This line has frequently given rise to the question of whether the Captain had up to this point had some real doubts. (The italics in the libretto are Gilbert's, not mine.)

[23] *It is, of course, impossible to present a comic opera without a full chorus and one must admire the insouciant way in which Gilbert arranges for a complete ladies' chorus quite logically to find itself present on board one of Her Majesty's warships.*

During the Barcarolle, the crew, who have changed into their dress whites, pea jackets and straw sailor hats, have tiptoed onto the deck and crowd along the ship's side in an effort to catch a glimpse of the barge-load of beauty that is approaching. One of the crew notices that the Midshipmite cannot see over the heads of the crowd and lifts him up, whereupon the Midshipmite adjusts his telescope, takes a good look and waves wildly.

[24] *". . . devoid of fe-ar." In the libretto the word is printed like this and must be sung as fee-arr to rhyme with the next line but one: ". . . we are."*

[25] *A moment before Sir Joseph and Hebe appear one of the ship's officers should give the command "Attention!" When directing this myself in 1952, I gave the command line to Tommy Tucker. This is followed by the Sergeant of Marines' order: "Pree-sen-n-'tumps!" Interpreted, this means "Present arms!"*

[26] *Hebe. Vide the Oxford Dictionary: "Youthful, prime." And she usually is.*

Traditionally Sir Joseph wears a monocle. I've often wondered whether this prop could possibly be the reason why practically every principal comedian in the D'Oyly Carte Opera Company has since affected a monocle. I am no exception to this rule, but at least mine is real; in fact, it is a bifocal. It was not only the principal comedians who affected this form of visual correction when I first knew them, and the fact that I sported a monocle placed me in a very embarrassing situation. The first three people I met were the stage manager, Fred Hobbs, the business manager, Charles Poole, and Henry Lytton. All three were present at the same time, and all three were wearing monocles. So was I, but not for long. The three monocles were too much for me, and as surreptitiously as I could I slipped mine out of my eye and for several months never wore it if there was any chance of one or more of the others being present.

[27] *Words and music on page 111.*

BARCAROLLE (*invisible*) [23]
SIR JOSEPH'S FEMALE RELATIVES

Over the bright blue sea
Comes Sir Joseph Porter, K.C.B.,
Wherever he may go
Bang-bang the loud nine-pounders go!
Shout o'er the bright blue sea
For Sir Joseph Porter, K.C.B.

[*During this the Crew have entered on tiptoe, listening attentively to the song.*

CHORUS OF SAILORS

Sir Joseph's barge is seen,
And its crowd of blushing beauties,
We hope he'll find us clean,
And attentive to our duties.
We sail, we sail the ocean blue,
And our saucy ship's a beauty.
We're sober, sober men and true
And attentive to our duty.
We're smart and sober men,
And quite devoid of fe-ar, [24]
In all the Royal N.
None are so smart as we are.

Enter SIR JOSEPH'S FEMALE RELATIVES

(*They dance round stage*)

REL. Gaily tripping,
   Lightly skipping,
Flock the maidens to the shipping.
SAILORS. Flags and guns and pennants dipping!
All the ladies love the shipping.
REL. Sailors sprightly
   Always rightly
Welcome ladies so politely.
SAILORS. Ladies who can smile so brightly,
Sailors welcome most politely.
CAPT. (*from poop*). Now give three cheers, I'll lead the way
ALL. Hurrah! hurrah! hurrah! hurray!

[25] *Enter* SIR JOSEPH *with* COUSIN HEBE [26]

SONG—SIR JOSEPH [27]

I am the monarch of the sea,
  The ruler of the Queen's Navee,
Whose praise Great Britain loudly chants.
COUSIN HEBE. And we are his sisters, and his cousins, and his aunts!
REL. And we are his sisters, and his cousins, and his aunts!
SIR JOSEPH. When at anchor here I ride,
  My bosom swells with pride,
And I snap my fingers at a foeman's taunts;
COUSIN HEBE. And so do his sisters, and his cousins, and his aunts!
ALL. And so do his sisters, and his cousins, and his aunts!
SIR JOSEPH. But when the breezes blow,
  I generally go below,
And seek the seclusion that a cabin grants;

COUSIN HEBE.   And so do his sisters, and his cousins, and his aunts!
ALL.   And so do his sisters, and his cousins, and his aunts!
                His sisters and his cousins,
                Whom he reckons up by dozens,
                And his aunts!

SONG—SIR JOSEPH [28]

When I was a lad I served a term
As office boy to an Attorney's firm.
I cleaned the windows and I swept the floor,
And I polished up the handle of the big front door.
    I polished up that handle so carefullee
    That now I am the Ruler of the Queen's Navee! [29]

    CHORUS.—He polished, etc.

As office boy I made such a mark
That they gave me the post of a junior clerk. [30]
I served the writs with a smile so bland,
And I copied all the letters in a big round hand—
    I copied all the letters in a hand so free,
    That now I am the Ruler of the Queen's Navee!

    CHORUS.—He copied, etc.

In serving writs I made such a name
That an articled clerk I soon became;
I wore clean collars and a brand-new suit
For the pass examination at the Institute,
    And that pass examination did so well for me,
    That now I am the Ruler of the Queen's Navee!

    CHORUS.—And that pass examination, etc.

Of legal knowledge I acquired such a grip
That they took me into the partnership.
And that junior partnership, I ween,
Was the only ship that I ever had seen.
    But that kind of ship so suited me,
    That now I am the Ruler of the Queen's Navee!

    CHORUS.—But that kind, etc.

I grew so rich that I was sent
By a pocket borough into Parliament.
I always voted at my party's call,
And I never thought of thinking for myself at all.
    I thought so little, they rewarded me
    By making me the Ruler of the Queen's Navee!

    CHORUS.—He thought so little, etc.

Now landsmen all, whoever you may be,
If you want to rise to the top of the tree,
If your soul isn't fettered to an office stool,
Be careful to be guided by this golden rule—
    Stick close to your desks and never go to sea,
    And you all may be Rulers of the Queen's Navee!

    CHORUS.—Stick close, etc.

SIR JOSEPH. You've a remarkably fine crew, Captain Corcoran.
CAPT. It *is* a fine crew, Sir Joseph.

[28] Words and music on page 114.

[29] ". . . Queen's Nay-vee" not "Nah-vee."

[30] ". . . gave me the post of a junior clerk." Pronounced clark in the British fashion.

. . . an articled clerk I soon became

[31] *Even Sir Joseph's poise is shaken when he sees Deadeye, but he very quickly recovers himself and in dismissing Dick is consideration itself.*

[32] *The original text read: "Ralph Rackstraw, come here!"—a most un-naval command. When it was decided to change it to its present form, I know not.*

[33] *A lesson Sir Joseph teaches that is not forgotten by either the Boatswain or, in due time, by the Captain.*

[34] *There is some quite amusing business between Sir Joseph and Ralph. As soon as he has stepped forward, he gives Sir Joseph a smart salute and at the same time stamps his right foot. Sir Joseph is a little surprised at this, but continues with his inspection of this "splendid seaman" by tapping him on the shoulder and indicating that he wishes him to turn around. Ralph does so and again salutes with the stamp of the foot. Sir Joseph returns his salute while displaying interest in the stamp of the foot. Finally he addresses Ralph: "You're a remarkably fine fellow." As Ralph replies, "Yes, your honour," he salutes once more, again stamping his foot. Not to be outdone, Sir Joseph returns the salute and this time stamps his foot, only to bring it down on his own toe. One of the lowest forms of visual humor but nevertheless always good for a laugh.*

[35] *Right at this point the rest of the crew breaks into a hornpipe step. Sir Joseph stops them with an imperious wave of his hand.*

[36] *Traditionally, Ralph drops the aitch in "hum." This gives rise to Sir Joseph's also dropping the aitch—then quickly covering it with a cough that also becomes the aitch. (This is the only time he does commit such a crime.)*

SIR JOSEPH (*examining a very small midshipman*). A British sailor is a splendid fellow, Captain Corcoran.

CAPT. A splendid fellow indeed, Sir Joseph.

SIR JOSEPH. I hope you treat your crew kindly, Captain Corcoran.

CAPT. Indeed I hope so, Sir Joseph.

SIR JOSEPH. Never forget that they are the bulwarks of England's greatness, Captain Corcoran.

CAPT. So I have always considered them, Sir Joseph.

SIR JOSEPH. No bullying, I trust—no strong language of any kind, eh?

CAPT. Oh, never, Sir Joseph.

SIR JOSEPH. What, *never*?

CAPT. Hardly ever, Sir Joseph. They are an excellent crew, and do their work thoroughly without it.

SIR JOSEPH. Don't patronise them, sir—pray, don't patronise them.

CAPT. Certainly not, Sir Joseph.

SIR JOSEPH. That you are their captain is an accident of birth. I cannot permit these noble fellows to be patronised because an accident of birth has placed you above them and them below you.

CAPT. I am the last person to insult a British sailor, Sir Joseph.

SIR JOSEPH. You are the last person who did, Captain Corcoran. Desire that splendid seaman to step forward.

(DICK *comes forward.*)

SIR JOSEPH. No, no, the other splendid seaman. [31]

CAPT. Ralph Rackstraw, three paces to the front—march! [32]

SIR JOSEPH (*sternly*). If what?

CAPT. I beg your pardon—I don't think I understand you.

SIR JOSEPH. If you *please*. [33]

CAPT. Oh, yes, of course. If you please. (RALPH *steps forward.*)

SIR JOSEPH. You're a remarkably fine fellow. [34]

RALPH. Yes, your honour.

SIR JOSEPH. And a first-rate seaman, I'll be bound.

RALPH. There's not a smarter topman in the Navy, your honour, though I say it who shouldn't.

SIR JOSEPH. Not at all. Proper self-respect, nothing more. Can you dance a hornpipe?

RALPH. No, your honour.

SIR JOSEPH. That's a pity: all sailors should dance hornpipes. [35] I will teach you one this evening, after dinner. Now tell me—don't be afraid—how does your captain treat you, eh?

RALPH. A better captain don't walk the deck, your honour.

ALL. Aye; Aye!

SIR JOSEPH. Good. I like to hear you speak well of your commanding officer; I daresay he don't deserve it, but still it does you credit. Can you sing?

RALPH. I can hum a little, your honour. [36]

SIR JOSEPH. Then hum this at your leisure. (*Giving him MS. music.*) It is a song that I have composed for the use of the Royal Navy. It is designed to encourage independence of thought and action in the lower branches of the service, and to teach the principle that a British sailor is any man's equal, excepting mine. Now, Captain Corcoran, a word with you in your cabin, on a tender and sentimental subject.

CAPT. Aye, aye, Sir Joseph. (*Crossing.*) Boatswain, in commemoration of this joyous occasion, see that extra grog is served out to the ship's company at seven bells.

BOAT. Beg pardon. If what, your honour?

CAPT. If what? I don't think I understand you.

BOAT. If you *please*, your honour.

CAPT. What!

SIR JOSEPH. The gentleman is quite right. If you *please*.

CAPT. (*stamping his foot impatiently*). If you *please*!

[*Exit.*

SIR JOSEPH.   For I hold that on the seas
        The expression, "if you please,"
        A particularly gentlemanly tone implants.

COUSIN HEBE. And so do his sisters, and his cousins, and his aunts!

ALL.   And so do his sisters, and his cousins, and his aunts!

[*Exeunt* SIR JOSEPH *and* RELATIVES.

BOAT. Ah! Sir Joseph's true gentleman; courteous and considerate to the very humblest. [37]

RALPH. True, Boatswain, but we are not the very humblest. Sir Joseph has explained our true position to us. As he says, a British seaman is any man's equal excepting his, and if Sir Joseph says that, is it not our duty to believe him?

ALL. Well spoke! well spoke!

DICK. You're on a wrong tack, and so is he. He means well, but he don't know. When people have to obey other people's orders, equality's out of the question.

ALL (*recoiling*). Horrible! horrible!

BOAT. Dick Deadeye, if you go for to infuriate this here ship's company too far, I won't answer for being able to hold 'em in. I'm shocked! That's what I am—shocked! [38]

RALPH. Messmates, my mind's made up. I'll speak to the captain's daughter, and tell her, like an honest man, of the honest love I have for her.

ALL. Aye, aye!

RALPH. Is not my love as good as another's? Is not my heart as true as another's? Have I not hands and eyes and ears and limbs like another?

ALL. Aye, aye!

RALPH. True, I lack birth—

BOAT. You've a berth on board this very ship.

RALPH. Well said—I had forgotten that. Messmates—what do you say? Do you approve my determination?

ALL. We do.

DICK. *I* don't.

BOAT. What is to be done with this here hopeless chap? Let us sing him the song that Sir Joseph has kindly composed for us. Perhaps it will bring this here miserable creetur to a proper state of mind.

GLEE—RALPH, BOATSWAIN, BOATSWAIN'S MATE, *and* CHORUS

A British tar is a soaring soul,
    As free as a mountain bird,
His energetic fist should be ready to resist
    A dictatorial word.
His nose should pant and his lip should curl,
His cheeks should flame and his brow should furl,
His bosom should heave and his heart should glow,
And his fist be ever ready for a knock-down blow.

CHORUS.—His nose should pant, etc.

His eyes should flash with an inborn fire,
    His brow with scorn be wrung;
He never should bow down to a domineering frown,
    Or the tang of a tyrant tongue.

[37] *The Boatswain employs throughout the play a very Dickensian Sam Wellerish manner of speech: ". . . cortchuss and cunsiderate ter the werry 'umblest."*

[38] *The Boatswain not only drops his aitches, he inserts a few: ". . . hif you go for ter hinfuriate this 'ere ship's comp'ny too far, I won't hanswer fer bein' hable ter 'old 'em hin. I'm shocked! That's wot I ham—shocked!"*

. . . his customary attitude—

His foot should stamp and his throat should growl,
His hair should twirl and his face should scowl;
His eyes should flash and his breast protrude,
And this should be his customary attitude—(*pose*).

CHORUS.—His foot should stamp, etc.

[*All dance off excepting* RALPH, *who remains, leaning pensively against bulwark.*]

Enter JOSEPHINE *from cabin*

JOS. It is useless—Sir Joseph's attentions nauseate me. I know that he is a truly great and good man, for he told me so himself, but to me he seems tedious, fretful, and dictatorial. Yet his must be a mind of no common order, or he would not dare to teach my dear father to dance a hornpipe on the cabin table. (*Sees* RALPH.) Ralph Rackstraw! (*Overcome by emotion.*)

RALPH. Aye, lady—no other than poor Ralph Rackstraw!

JOS. (*aside*). How my heart beats! (*Aloud.*) And why poor, Ralph?

RALPH. [39] I am poor in the essence of happiness, lady—rich only in never-ending unrest. In me there meet a combination of antithetical elements which are at eternal war with one another. Driven hither by objective influences—thither by subjective emotions—wafted one moment into blazing day, by mocking hope—plunged the next into the Cimmerian darkness of tangible despair, I am but a living ganglion of irreconcilable antagonisms. I hope I make myself clear, lady?

JOS. Perfectly. (*Aside.*) His simple eloquence goes to my heart. Oh, if I dared—but no, the thought is madness! (*Aloud.*) Dismiss these foolish fancies, they torture you but needlessly. Come, make one effort.

RALPH (*aside*). I will—one. (*Aloud.*) Josephine!

JOS. (*indignantly*). Sir!

RALPH. Aye, even though Jove's armoury were launched at the head of the audacious mortal whose lips, unhallowed by relationship, dared to breathe that precious word, yet would I breathe it once, and then perchance be silent evermore. Josephine, in one brief breath I will concentrate the hopes, the doubts, the anxious fears of six weary months. Josephine, I am a British sailor, and I love you!

JOS. Sir, this audacity! (*Aside.*) Oh, my heart, my beating heart! (*Aloud.*) This unwarrantable presumption on the part of a common sailor! (*Aside.*) Common! oh, the irony of the word! (*Crossing, aloud.*) Oh, sir, you forget the disparity in our ranks.

RALPH. I forget nothing, haughty lady. I love you desperately, my life is in your hand—I lay it at your feet! Give me hope, and what I lack in education and polite accomplishments, that I will endeavour to acquire. Drive me to despair, and in death alone I shall look for consolation. I am proud and cannot stoop to implore. I have spoken and I wait your word.

JOS. You shall not wait long. Your proffered love I haughtily reject. Go, sir, and learn to cast your eyes on some village maiden in your own poor rank—they should be lowered before your captain's daughter.

DUET—JOSEPHINE *and* RALPH [40]

JOS.   Refrain, audacious tar,
            Your suit from pressing,
        Remember what you are,
            And whom addressing!
(*Aside.*)   I'd laugh my rank to scorn
            In union holy,

[39] *To obtain the full humor of this scene, Ralph must be absolutely sincere. At the same time he must deliver his lines with all the vigor of an old Shakespearean ham declaiming one of the more florid speeches from Henry IV. Wide gestures must be used. But never for one instant must Ralph be aware that he is hamming it up. One line, and one line only, is given in a purely conversational voice: "I hope I make myself clear, lady?"*

Similarly, in the duet with Josephine (who, like Ralph, must be completely unaware that anything she says is even remotely funny), they both must employ wide gestures and a vocal delivery similar to the Italian operatic style in vogue in the days of Verdi.

Gilbert's own definition of the character of Ralph is very interesting. He (Ralph) is extremely good-looking and very well spoken for a man with so little education. A fine fellow, but not so fine as he himself thinks. He has heard, in song and story, that a British tar possesses every good quality, whereas the truth is that there is room for a lot more good qualities than are usually found inside a sailor. (Précis of a quote from The Pinafore Picture Book, G. Bell & Sons.)

[40] *Words and music on page 118.*

                      Were he more highly born
                          Or I more lowly!
RALPH.   Proud lady, have your way,
                          Unfeeling beauty!
                      You speak and I obey,
                          It is my duty!
                      I am the lowliest tar
                          That sails the water,
                      And you, proud maiden, are
                          My captain's daughter!
(*Aside.*)   My heart with anguish torn
                          Bows down before her,
                      She laughs my love to scorn,
                          Yet I adore her!

> [*Repeat refrain, ensemble, then exit* JOSEPHINE *into cabin.*]

RALPH (*Recit*). Can I survive this overbearing
                      Or live a life of mad despairing,
                      My proffered love despised, rejected?
                      No, no, it's not to be expected!
                                (*Calling off.*)
           Messmates, ahoy!
                      Come here! Come here!

> *Enter* SAILORS, HEBE, *and* RELATIVES

ALL.   Aye, aye, my boy,
                      What cheer, what cheer?
                          Now tell us, pray,
                          Without delay,
                          What does she say—[41]
                      What cheer, what cheer?

RALPH (*to* COUSIN HEBE).
           The maiden treats my suit with scorn,
               Rejects my humble gift, my lady;
           She says I am ignobly born,
               And cuts my hopes adrift, my lady.

ALL.   Oh, cruel one.

DICK.   She spurns your suit? Oho! Oho!
           I told you so, I told you so.

SAILORS *and* RELATIVES.

           Shall $\begin{Bmatrix} \text{we} \\ \text{they} \end{Bmatrix}$ submit? Are $\begin{Bmatrix} \text{we} \\ \text{they} \end{Bmatrix}$ but slaves?
               Love comes alike to high and low—
           Britannia's sailors rule the waves,
               And shall they stoop to insult? No!

DICK.   You must submit, you are but slaves;
               A lady she! Oho! Oho!
           You lowly toilers of the waves,
               She spurns you all—I told you so!

RALPH. My friends, my leave of life I'm taking,
           For oh, my heart, my heart is breaking.
           When I am gone, oh, prithee tell
           The maid that, as I died, I loved her well!

ALL (*turning away, weeping*).

[41] *Apparently Sir Joseph and Captain Corcoran are the only persons on the ship who were not, and are not, aware of Ralph's intention to speak to Josephine.*

[42] *The Boatswain's sympathetic concern for Ralph is one of the most amusingly touching scenes. But Dick Deadeye is the only person present who finds any delight in the situation. Nevertheless, he too stops up his ears, though his face is wreathed in a puckish grin.*

Of life, alas! his leave he's taking,
For ah! his faithful heart is breaking;
When he is gone we'll surely tell
The maid that, as he died, he loved her well.

[*During Chorus* BOATSWAIN *has loaded pistol, which he hands to* RALPH. [42]

RALPH. Be warned, my messmates all
      Who love in rank above you—
  For Josephine I fall!

[*Puts pistol to his head. All the sailors stop their ears.*

Enter JOSEPHINE *on deck*

JOS. Ah! stay your hand! I love you!
ALL. Ah! stay your hand—she loves you!
RALPH (*incredulously*). Loves me?
JOS.   Loves you!
ALL. Yes, yes—ah, yes, she loves you!

ENSEMBLE
SAILORS *and* **RELATIVES,** **JOSEPHINE,** *and* **RALPH**

Oh joy, oh rapture unforeseen,
For now the sky is all serene;
The god of day—the orb of love—
Has hung his ensign high above,
  The sky is all ablaze.

With wooing words and loving song,
We'll chase the lagging hours along,
And if $\begin{Bmatrix} \text{I find} \\ \text{we find} \end{Bmatrix}$ the maiden coy,
$\begin{matrix} \text{I'll} \\ \text{We'll} \end{matrix}\Big\}$ murmur forth decorous joy
  In dreamy roundelays!

DICK DEADEYE [43]

He thinks he's won his Josephine,
But though the sky is now serene,
A frowning thunderbolt above
May end their ill-assorted love
  Which now is all ablaze.

Our captain, ere the day is gone,
Will be extremely down upon
The wicked men who art employ
To make his Josephine less coy
  In many various ways.

[*Exit* DICK.

[43] *After Ralph's near demise has been halted by Josephine's admission of her love, Dick Deadeye's glee gives us an indication of his intention to spill the beans to the Captain. I do not know why Gilbert should have given the direction for Dick to exit at this point, i.e., after his solo, for Dick is back onstage within a very few moments. One can only assume that he has gone off to seek the Captain and has found him busy with Sir Joseph. It is extremely difficult to suggest this possibility to an audience, so whenever I have directed Pinafore I have kept him onstage, though withdrawn from the general company. It is plain then that he hears the making of the plan for Josephine and Ralph to elope that very night. What is more, in this way, his next lines do not come out of left field, and his final exit is all the stronger —and funnier. This is the point where, Dick having been forced off by the unanimous anger of everyone, Bill Bobstay hurls the revolver, which is no longer needed, at him. This is followed by a tremendous crash offstage and the audience is supposed to imagine that Dick has tripped while dodging the weapon and has fallen through the skylight—a source of great amusement to the crew and ladies present.*

JOS.	This very night,
HEBE.	With bated breath
RALPH.	And muffled oar—
JOS.	Without a light,
HEBE.	As still as death,
RALPH.	We'll steal ashore
JOS.	A clergyman
RALPH.	Shall make us one
BOAT.	At half-past ten,

JOS.	And then we can
RALPH.	Return, for none
BOAT.	Can part them then!
ALL.	This very night, etc.

(DICK *appears at hatchway.*)

DICK. Forbear, nor carry out the scheme you've planned;
  She is a lady—you a foremast hand!
  Remember, she's your gallant captain's daughter,
  And you the meanest slave that crawls the water!

ALL.   Back, vermin, back,
         Nor mock us!
         Back, vermin, back,
         You shock us!

[*Exit* DICK.

Let's give three cheers for the sailor's bride
Who casts all thought of rank aside—
Who gives up home and fortune too
For the honest love of a sailor true!
     For a British tar is a soaring soul
       As free as a mountain bird!
     His energetic fist should be ready to resist
       A dictatorial word!
His foot should stamp and his throat should growl,
His hair should twirl and his face should scowl,
His eyes should flash and his breast protrude,
And this should be his customary attitude—(*pose*).

GENERAL DANCE

END OF ACT I

ACT II

Same Scene. Night. Awning removed. Moonlight. CAPTAIN *discovered singing on poop-deck, and accompanying himself on a mandolin.* LITTLE BUTTERCUP *seated on quarter-deck, gazing sentimentally at him.* [44]

SONG—CAPTAIN

Fair moon, to thee I sing,
  Bright regent of the heavens,
Say, why is everything
  Either at sixes or at sevens?
I have lived hitherto
  Free from breath of slander,
Beloved by all my crew—
  A really popular commander.
But now my kindly crew rebel,
  My daughter to a tar is partial,
Sir Joseph storms, and, sad to tell,
  He threatens a court martial!
    Fair moon, to thee I sing,
      Bright regent of the heavens,
      Say, why is everything
        Either at sixes or at sevens?

[44] Captain Corcoran is now dressed in full naval mess dress: tails (naval cut, of course), black tie, white waistcoat, gold-striped trousers, epaulets, insignia of rank on the sleeves, and full decorations, but—no aiglet.

  Little Buttercup has no change of costume. She is, naturally, visible to the audience but is not seen by Captain Corcoran who remains in blissful ignorance of her presence until the appropriate moment. For this reason she is usually placed to the side or rear, in one of the less well lighted positions on the stage.

[45] *There is a temptation in this scene to play it for low comedy. Falling for this temptation spells disaster for the scene. It is a burlesque of every melodrama that went before it, and the secret of burlesque is absolute seriousness.*

[46] *Words and music on page 121.*

[47] *The first, but not the last, time that Gilbert utilized good old proverbs for the purpose of a lyric.*

[45] BUT. How sweetly he carols forth his melody to the unconscious moon! Of whom is he thinking? Of some high-born beauty? It may be! Who is poor Little Buttercup that she should expect his glance to fall on one so lowly! And yet if he knew—if he only knew!

CAPT. (*coming down*). Ah! Little Buttercup, still on board? That is not quite right, little one. It would have been more respectable to have gone on shore at dusk.

BUT. True, dear Captain—but the recollection of your sad pale face seemed to chain me to the ship. I would fain see you smile before I go.

CAPT. Ah! Little Buttercup, I fear it will be long before I recover my accustomed cheerfulness, for misfortunes crowd upon me, and all my old friends seem to have turned against me!

BUT. Oh no—do not say "all," dear Captain. That were unjust to one, at least.

CAPT. True, for you are staunch to me. (*Aside.*) If ever I gave my heart again, methinks it would be to such a one as this! (*Aloud.*) I am touched to the heart by your innocent regard for me, and were we differently situated, I think I could have returned it. But as it is, I fear I can never be more to you than a friend.

BUT. I understand! You hold aloof from me because you are rich and lofty—and I poor and lowly. But take care! The poor bumboat woman has gipsy blood in her veins, and she can read destinies.

CAPT. Destinies?

BUT. There is a change in store for you!

CAPT. A change?

BUT. Aye—be prepared!

DUET—LITTLE BUTTERCUP *and* CAPTAIN [46]

BUT.	Things are seldom what they seem, [47] Skim milk masquerades as cream; Highlows pass as patent leathers; Jackdaws strut in peacock's feathers.
CAPT. (*puzzled*).	Very true, So they do.
BUT.	Black sheep dwell in every fold; All that glitters is not gold; Storks turn out to be but logs; Bulls are but inflated frogs.
CAPT. (*puzzled*).	So they be, Frequentlee.
BUT.	Drops the wind and stops the mill; Turbot is ambitious brill; Gild the farthing if you will, Yet it is a farthing still.
CAPT. (*puzzled*).	Yes, I know. That is so. Though to catch your drift I'm striving, It is shady—it is shady; I don't see at what you're driving, Mystic lady—mystic lady.
(*Aside.*)	Stern conviction's o'er me stealing, That the mystic lady's dealing In oracular revealing.
BUT. (*aside*).	Stern conviction's o'er him stealing, That the mystic lady's dealing In oracular revealing.
BOTH.	Yes, I know— That is so!
CAPT.	Though I'm anything but clever,

I could talk like that for ever:
Once a cat was killed by care;
Only brave deserve the fair.

BUT. Very true,
So they do.

CAPT. Wink is often good as nod;
Spoils the child who spares the rod;
Thirsty lambs run foxy dangers;
Dogs are found in many mangers.

BUT. Frequentlee,
I agree.

CAPT. Paw of cat the chestnut snatches;
Worn-out garments show new patches;
Only count the chick that hatches;
Men are grown-up catchy-catchies.

BUT. Yes, I know,
That is so.

(*Aside.*) Though to catch my drift he's striving,
I'll dissemble—I'll dissemble;
When he sees at what I'm driving,
Let him tremble—let him tremble!

ENSEMBLE

Though a mystic tone $\begin{Bmatrix} I \\ you \end{Bmatrix}$ borrow,

$\left. \begin{matrix} You\ will \\ I\ shall \end{matrix} \right\}$ learn the truth with sorrow,

Here to-day and gone to-morrow;
Yes, I know—
That is so!

[*At the end exit* LITTLE BUTTERCUP *melodramatically.*

CAPT. Incomprehensible as her utterances are, I nevertheless feel that they are dictated by a sincere regard for me. But to what new misery is she referring? Time alone can tell!

Enter SIR JOSEPH

SIR JOSEPH. Captain Corcoran, I am much disappointed with your daughter. In fact, I don't think she will do.

CAPT. She won't do, Sir Joseph!

SIR JOSEPH. I'm afraid not. The fact is, that although I have urged my suit with as much eloquence as is consistent with an official utterance, I have done so hitherto without success. How do you account for this?

CAPT. Really, Sir Joseph, I hardly know. Josephine is of course sensible of your condescension.

SIR JOSEPH. She naturally would be.

CAPT. But perhaps your exalted rank dazzles her.

SIR JOSEPH. You think it does?

CAPT. I can hardly say; but she is a modest girl, and her social position is far below your own. It may be that she feels she is not worthy of you.

SIR JOSEPH. That is really a very sensible suggestion, and displays more knowledge of human nature than I had given you credit for.

CAPT. See, she comes. If your lordship would kindly reason with her and assure her officially that it is a standing rule at the Admiralty that love levels all ranks, her respect for an official utterance might induce her to look upon your offer in its proper light.

SIR JOSEPH. It is not unlikely. I will adopt your suggestion. But soft, she is here. Let us withdraw, and watch our opportunity. [48]

[48] At the end of the scene between Sir Joseph and the Captain there is a nice bit of business not included in the printed libretto. The Captain, pleased with Sir Joseph's acceptance of his suggestion, and agreeing that it would be wise to withdraw, forgets himself so far as to precede Sir Joseph. However, the First Lord, conscious of his rank and precedence, halts the Captain with an imperious: "Captain Corcoran!" Then, with a flick of his silk handkerchief, he motions him to step back and aside. The Captain is for a moment at a loss, and again the First Lord motions him back. This time the Captain gets the idea and he steps back while Sir Joseph stalks past him very haughtily, hands behind his back, swishing his handkerchief up and down in an irritated manner. This is just a shade too much for a British sailor. Throwing his dignity to the winds, the Captain behaves like any small boy and gives a highly exaggerated imitation of our haughty Cabinet minister. This is always good for a laugh. In fact, when Leslie Rands was playing the role it became almost a tradition for me to turn in the wings and greet him as he came off with: "Hey! Who's the blooming comic in this 'ere comic opry company—you or me?"

Enter JOSEPHINE *from cabin.* FIRST LORD *and* CAPTAIN *retire*

SCENA—JOSEPHINE

The hours creep on apace,
 My guilty heart is quaking!
Oh, that I might retrace
 The step that I am taking!
Its folly it were easy to be showing,
What I am giving up and whither going.
On the one hand, papa's luxurious home,
 Hung with ancestral armour and old brasses,
Carved oak and tapestry from distant Rome,
 Rare "blue and white" Venetian finger-glasses,
Rich oriental rugs, luxurious sofa pillows,
And everything that isn't old, from Gillow's. [49]
And on the other, a dark and dingy room,
 In some back street with stuffy children crying,
Where organs yell, and clacking housewives fume,
 And clothes are hanging out all day a-drying.
With one cracked looking-glass to see your face in,
And dinner served up in a pudding basin!

A simple sailor, lowly born,
 Unlettered and unknown,
Who toils for bread from early morn
 Till half the night has flown!
No golden rank can he impart—
 No wealth of house or land—
No fortune save his trusty heart
 And honest brown right hand!
And yet he is so wondrous fair
That love for one so passing rare,
So peerless in his manly beauty,
Were little else than solemn duty!
Oh, god of love, and god of reason, say,
Which of you twain shall my poor heart obey!

SIR JOSEPH *and* CAPTAIN *enter*

SIR JOSEPH. Madam, it has been represented to me that you are appalled by my exalted rank. I desire to convey to you officially my assurance, that if your hesitation is attributable to that circumstance, it is uncalled for.

JOS. Oh! then your lordship is of opinion that married happiness is *not* inconsistent with discrepancy in rank?

SIR JOSEPH. I am officially of that opinion.

JOS. That the high and the lowly may be truly happy together, provided that they truly love one another?

SIR JOSEPH. Madam, I desire to convey to you officially my opinion that love is a platform upon which all ranks meet.

JOS. I thank you, Sir Joseph. I *did* hesitate, but I will hesitate no longer. (*Aside.*) He little thinks how eloquently he has pleaded his rival's cause!

TRIO [50]
FIRST LORD, [51] CAPTAIN, *and* JOSEPHINE

CAPT.
 Never mind the why and wherefore,
 Love can level ranks, and therefore,
 Though his lordship's station's mighty,
  Though stupendous be his brain,

[49] *A well-known firm of home furnishers. In a recent production in New York—not under the auspices of D'Oyly Carte—I am told that "Gillow's" was changed to "Saks Fifth Avenue"! I may be a renegade, but I am not such a renegade as all that. Granted, when in New York, I would stand on the side of the stage and murmur sotto voce when this line was reached, ". . . everything that isn't old from Gimbels." But never on the stage would I have dreamed of permitting it, even though Gimbels is not far removed from Gillow's, sound-wise. And, too, I might have found a rhyme in the preceding line (gold thimbles?), whereas even Gilbert would have been hard pressed to come up with one for Saks Fifth Avenue.*

[50] *Words and music on page 124.*

[51] *During the trio Sir Joseph is allowed to go—and as far as I was concerned, did go—completely haywire, starting with a wild dance—well, moderately wild—and with a suggestion of ringing a hand bell. With each succeeding encore (I think seven is my record) a wilder series of dances*

Though your tastes are mean and flighty
And your fortune poor and plain,

CAPT. *and*   Ring the merry bells on board-ship,
SIR JOSEPH.   Rend the air with warbling wild,

For the union of $\begin{Bmatrix} his \\ my \end{Bmatrix}$ lordship

With a humble captain's child!

CAPT.   For a humble captain's daughter—
JOS.   For a gallant captain's daughter—
SIR JOSEPH.   And a lord who rules the water—
JOS. (*aside*).   And a *tar* who ploughs the water!
ALL.   Let the air with joy be laden,
Rend with songs the air above,
For the union of a maiden
With the man who owns her love!

SIR JOSEPH.   Never mind the why and wherefore,
Love can level ranks, and therefore,
Though your nautical relation (*alluding to* CAPT.)
In my set could scarcely pass—
Though you occupy a station
In the lower middle class—

CAPT. *and*   Ring the merry bells on board-ship,
SIR JOSEPH.   Rend the air with warbling wild,

For the union of $\begin{Bmatrix} my \\ his \end{Bmatrix}$ lordship

With a humble captain's child!

CAPT.   For a humble captain's daughter—
JOS.   For a gallant captain's daughter—
SIR JOSEPH.   And a lord who rules the water—
JOS. (*aside*).   And a *tar* who ploughs the water!
ALL.   Let the air with joy be laden,
Rend with songs the air above,
For the union of a maiden
With the man who owns her love!

JOS.   Never mind the why and wherefore,
Love can level ranks, and therefore
I admit the jurisdiction;
Ably have you played your part;
You have carried firm conviction
To my hesitating heart.

CAPT. *and*   Ring the merry bells on board-ship,
SIR JOSEPH.   Rend the air with warbling wild,

For the union of $\begin{Bmatrix} my \\ his \end{Bmatrix}$ lordship

With a humble captain's child!

CAPT.   For a humble captain's daughter—
JOS.   For a gallant captain's daughter—
SIR JOSEPH.   And a lord who rules the water—
JOS. (*aside*).   And a *tar* who ploughs the water!
(*Aloud.*)   Let the air with joy be laden.
CAPT. *and* SIR JOSEPH. Ring the merry bells on board-ship—
JOS.   For the union of a maiden—
CAPT. *and* SIR JOSEPH. For her union with his lordship.
ALL.   Rend with songs the air above
For the man who owns her love!

[*Exit* JOS.

CAPT. Sir Joseph, I cannot express to you my delight at the happy result of your eloquence. Your argument was unanswerable.

ensue. At one time I endeavored to perform a toe dance; at another, a hornpipe, dropping my handkerchief and trying to pick it up (a difficult feat in those tight white breeches). The bells became more and more exaggerated and included a carillon, a piano, a hurdy-gurdy, a triangle (to coincide with the actual instrument in the orchestra), a try-your-strength machine like those found in carnivals (one of those things where you hit a knob with a heavy sledge hammer and if you are strong enough a bell at the top rings), a telephone, and an electric front-doorbell. One purist questioned my use of the telephone and the doorbell; electric bells and telephones were not invented at this time, said he. I presume he was speaking of the days of sail.. However, as Gilbert actually makes an allusion to the telephone later on in this opera I felt I was justified in using one. And if the telephone, why not an electric doorbell? One sure-fire road to a further encore was for me to appear in a state of collapse, just after having escorted Josephine to the cabin door, and then lean on the wheel for support. The wheel, of course, immediately spun 'round and 'round and neatly sent me spinning too.

I well remember the first time I essayed the role of Sir Joseph Porter. I was at the time second understudy to Frank Steward, the principal comedian of the small Company ("small" because it carried only four operas as opposed to the repertory Company's ten and two curtain raisers). Both Frank and the first understudy were ill so it fell to me to try to keep the curtain up. I made my big entrance to one of the most deafening silences it has ever been my misfortune to experience. The scene over, I made my exit to an even deathlier silence. In fear and trepidation I embarked upon the second act. The most notable thing about that was the continued stony silence. This got my dander up. I determined that, come what might, they were going to like me, or (with Ralph) "in death alone would I seek consolation." Something had to be done, and I did it. Discretion was thrown to the four winds of heaven. I danced; I pranced; I cavorted. I rang bells. I was as funny as all what-have-you. The air was pregnant with disapproval. There was no encore. I was the only one who had any idea I was being funny. And therein lay my mistake. I was forcing myself on people who, if I had only known it, did not dislike me, even if they didn't actually like me. I should have wooed them; let them do the forcing. And so the various "bells" were invented, and, as I invented, the more I enjoyed myself. Of course, there was the problem of inducing the powers that be to accept my inventions. That they did is now an obvious fact, if not history, as my invented bells and many other pieces of business were never cut out. I do wonder, at times, if Gilbert, who was a stickler for his business, would also have accepted mine?

[52] *This is probably one of the greatest exit lines ever written by any playwright.*

[53] *Words and music on page 128.*

[54] *Words and music on page 130.*

[55] *One very funny incident occurred during a performance given by the small Company. I was not performing Sir Joseph that night; I was one of the sailors. We had just reached the point where the directions in the printed text read: "(Captain stamps.)—Chord." In actual fact, he not only stamps his foot, he brings the cat-o'-nine-tails down hard on Dick Deadeye's back. "Goodness me," asks the Chorus, "what was that?" and Dick assures them "It was the cat." This night a cat—a real cat, not yet fully grown and still rather kittenish in its ways—chased something, probably its own shadow, onto the stage just as the Captain stamped his foot and brought the cat-o'-nine-tails down and the chord in the music crashed out. The cat gave one wild leap, came down on all fours, and stood there with arched back, spitting and glaring at everyone. The effect on the audience was terrific. The Company gallantly tried to carry on, but Dick's assurance that it was only the cat was too much. The Company broke up; the audience broke up; gales of laughter swept the house; and the cat fled into the ship's rigging. I'm afraid the rest of the scene was lost.*

SIR JOSEPH. Captain Corcoran, it is one of the happiest characteristics of this glorious country that official utterances are invariably regarded as unanswerable. [52]

[*Exit* SIR JOSEPH.

CAPT. At last my fond hopes are to be crowned. My only daughter is to be the bride of a Cabinet Minister. The prospect is Elysian. (*During this speech* DICK DEADEYE *has entered.*)

DICK. Captain.

CAPT. Deadeye! You here? Don't! (*Recoiling from him.*)

DICK. Ah, don't shrink from me, Captain. I'm unpleasant to look at, and my name's agin me, but I ain't as bad as I seem.

CAPT. What would you with me?

DICK (*mysteriously*). I'm come to give you warning.

CAPT. Indeed! do you propose to leave the Navy then?

DICK. No, no, you misunderstand me; listen!

DUET [53]
CAPTAIN *and* DICK DEADEYE

DICK. Kind Captain, I've important information,
　　　　Sing hey, the kind commander that you are,
　　　About a certain intimate relation,
　　　　Sing hey, the merry maiden and the tar.
BOTH.　　　　The merry maiden and the tar.

CAPT. Good fellow, in conundrums you are speaking,
　　　　Sing hey, the mystic sailor that you are;
　　　The answer to them vainly I am seeking;
　　　　Sing hey, the merry maiden and the tar.
BOTH.　　　　The merry maiden and the tar.

DICK. Kind Captain, your young lady is a-sighing,
　　　　Sing hey, the simple captain that you are,
　　　This very night with Rackstraw to be flying;
　　　　Sing hey, the merry maiden and the tar.
BOTH.　　　　The merry maiden and the tar.

CAPT. Good fellow, you have given timely warning,
　　　　Sing hey, the thoughtful sailor that you are,
　　　I'll talk to Master Rackstraw in the morning:
　　　　Sing hey, the cat-o'-nine-tails and the tar.
　　　　　　　　(*Producing a "cat."*)
BOTH.　　　The merry cat-o'-nine-tails and the tar!

CAPT. Dick Deadeye—I thank you for your warning—I will at once take means to arrest their flight. This boat cloak will afford me ample disguise—So! (*Envelops himself in a mysterious cloak, holding it before his face.*)

DICK. Ha, ha! They are foiled—foiled—foiled!

Enter Crew on tiptoe, with RALPH *and* BOATSWAIN *meeting* JOSEPHINE, *who enters from cabin on tiptoe, with bundle of necessaries, and accompanied by* LITTLE BUTTERCUP.

ENSEMBLE—MEN [54]

Carefully on tiptoe stealing,
　Breathing gently as we may,
Every step with caution feeling,
　We will softly steal away.

(CAPTAIN *stamps.*)—*Chord.* [55]

ALL (*much alarmed*). Goodness me—
                Why, what was that?
DICK.   Silent be,
                It was the cat!
ALL (*reassured*). It was—it was the cat!
CAPT. (*producing cat-o'-nine-tails*). They're right, it was the cat!

ALL.   Pull ashore, in fashion steady,
                Hymen will defray the fare,
              For a clergyman is ready
                To unite the happy pair!

          (*Stamp as before, and Chord.*)

ALL.   Goodness me,
                Why, what was that?
DICK.   Silent be,
                Again the cat!
ALL.   It was again that cat!
CAPT. (*aside*).   They're right, it was the cat!
CAPT. (*throwing off cloak*). Hold! (*All start.*)
              Pretty daughter of mine,
                I insist upon knowing
                Where you may be going
              With these sons of the brine,
                For my excellent crew,
              Though foes they could thump any,
                Are scarcely fit company,
                My daughter, for you.
CREW.   Now, hark at that, do!
              Though foes we could thump any,
              We are scarcely fit company
              For a lady like you!

RALPH.   Proud officer, that haughty lip uncurl!
         Vain man, suppress that supercilious sneer,
      For I have dared to love your matchless girl,
        A fact well known to all my messmates here!

CAPT.   Oh, horror!

RALPH *and* JOS. { I, / He, } humble, poor, and lowly born,
         The meanest in the port division—
          The butt of epauletted scorn—
          The mark of quarter-deck derision—
         Have / Has } dared to raise { my / his } wormy eyes
        Above the dust to which you'd mould { me / him
        In manhood's glorious pride to rise,
        I am / He is } an Englishman—behold { me! / him!

ALL.   He is an Englishman!

BOAT.   He is an Englishman! [56]
        For he himself has said it,
         And it's greatly to his credit,
       That he is an Englishman!

ALL.   That he is an Englishman!

[56] *Words and music on page 132.*

... in spite of all temptations

[57] *Sir Joseph makes his entrance on the bridge here. Given directions are for Sir Joseph, Hebe and the female relatives to enter the scene during the Captain's solo: "In uttering a reprobation, etc." I found it much more in keeping with the turn the plot is now taking to have them come on gradually as if the singing "He is an Englishman" has roused their pride. Sir Joseph, listening from the bridge, is obviously very pleased to think they are all aware of this most important fact. The shock, when Captain Corcoran in his anger so far forgets himself as to use a "big, big D," is all the greater, and the impact stronger. Sir Joseph, having started to descend the companion ladder from the bridge to the deck, and being a little distressed by Corcoran's show of temper, is so horrified when the big, big D bursts on his ears that he loses his footing on the ladder and slithers down the remaining steps, into the arms of one of the sailors who happens to be conveniently nearby.*

[58] *A traditional joke in the D'Oyly Carte Company is to ask at each performance, "Who's playing Celerity tonight?"*

BOAT.   For he might have been a Roosian,
        A French, or Turk, or Proosian,
        Or perhaps Itali-an!

ALL.   Or perhaps Itali-an!
BOAT.   But in spite of all temptations
        To belong to other nations,
           He remains an Englishman!

ALL.   For in spite of all temptations, etc. [57]

CAPT. (*trying to repress his anger*).
        In uttering a reprobation
           To any British tar,
        I try to speak with moderation,
           But you have gone too far.
        I'm very sorry to disparage
           A humble foremast lad,
        But to seek your captain's child in marriage,
           Why damme, it's too bad!

[*During this,* COUSIN HEBE *and* FEMALE RELATIVES *have entered.*

ALL (*shocked*). Oh!
CAPT.   Yes, damme, it's too bad!
ALL.   Oh!
CAPT. *and* DICK DEADEYE. Yes, damme, it's too bad.

[*During this,* SIR JOSEPH *has appeared on poop-deck. He is horrified at the bad language.*

HEBE.   Did you hear him—did you hear him?
        Oh, the monster overbearing!
        Don't go near him—don't go near him—
        He is swearing—he is swearing!
SIR JOSEPH.   My pain and my distress,
        I find it is not easy to express;
        My amazement—my surprise—
        You may learn from the expression of my eyes!
CAPT.   My lord—one word—the facts are not before you
        The word was injudicious, I allow—
        But hear my explanation, I implore you,
        And you will be indignant too, I vow!
SIR JOSEPH.   I will hear of no defence,
        Attempt none if you're sensible.
        That word of evil sense
        Is wholly indefensible.
        Go, ribald, get you hence
        To your cabin with celerity. [58]
        This is the consequence
        Of ill-advised asperity!

[*Exit* CAPTAIN, *disgraced, followed by* JOSEPHINE

ALL.   This is the consequence,
        Of ill-advised asperity!
SIR JOSEPH.   For I'll teach you all, ere long,
        To refrain from language strong
        For I haven't any sympathy for ill-bred taunts!
HEBE.   No more have his sisters, nor his cousins, nor his aunts.
ALL.   For he is an Englishman, etc.

SIR JOSEPH. Now, tell me, my fine fellow—for you *are* a fine fellow——

RALPH. Yes, your honour.

SIR JOSEPH. How came your captain so far to forget himself? I am quite sure you had given him no cause for annoyance.

RALPH. Please your honour, it was thus-wise. You see I'm only a topman—a mere foremast hand——

SIR JOSEPH. Don't be ashamed of that. Your position as a topman is a very exalted one.

RALPH. Well, your honour, love burns as brightly in the fo'c'sle as it does on the quarter-deck, and Josephine is the fairest bud that ever blossomed upon the tree of a poor fellow's wildest hopes.

Enter JOSEPHINE; *she rushes to* RALPH's *arms*

JOS. Darling! (SIR JOSEPH *horrified*.) [59]

RALPH. She is the figurehead of my ship of life—the bright beacon that guides me into my port of happiness—the rarest, the purest gem that ever sparkled on a poor but worthy fellow's trusting brow!

ALL. Very pretty, very pretty!

SIR JOSEPH. Insolent sailor, you shall repent this outrage. Seize him!
(*Two Marines seize him and handcuff him*.)

JOS. Oh, Sir Joseph, spare him, for I love him tenderly.

SIR JOSEPH. Pray, don't. I will teach this presumptuous mariner to discipline his affections. Have you such a thing as a dungeon on board?

ALL. We have!

DICK. They have!

SIR JOSEPH. Then load him with chains and take him there at once!

OCTETTE [60]

RALPH.
    Farewell, my own,
        Light of my life, farewell!
    For crime unknown
        I go to a dungeon cell.

JOS.
    I will atone.
        In the meantime farewell!
    And all alone
        Rejoice in your dungeon cell!

SIR JOSEPH.
    A bone, a bone
        I'll pick with this sailor fell;
    Let him be shown
        At once to his dungeon cell.

BOATSWAIN, DICK DEADEYE, *and* COUSIN HEBE

    He'll hear no tone
        Of the maiden he loves so well!
    No telephone
        Communicates with his cell!

BUT. (*mysteriously*).
    But when is known
        The secret I have to tell,
    Wide will be thrown
        The door of his dungeon cell.

ALL.
    For crime unknown
        He goes to a dungeon cell!
                [RALPH *is led off in custody*.

SIR JOSEPH.
    My pain and my distress [61]
    Again it is not easy to express.

[59] Upon Josephine's rushing into Ralph's arms as she cries, "Darling!" Sir Joseph's horror is such that he collapses completely and is prevented from falling only because Buttercup is nearby and saves him. Then, supporting him with one hand, she fans him with a red bandanna handkerchief. Ralph should not carry on with his speech ("She is the figurehead . . .") until the comedy business and the laughs are over. When he does begin to speak, Sir Joseph's horror should mount and mount to such a pitch that by the time he (Ralph) reaches the end of his speech (". . . but worthy fellow's trusting brow") Sir Joseph's anger overcomes normal control of his dignity and he attempts to draw his sword. As it is a ceremonial sword and not intended to be drawn in anger—in fact, not intended to be drawn at all, other than for cleaning—it is not surprising that it has become stuck. Not to be foiled by this he turns to Hebe and asks her, in mime, to pull on the hilt while he hangs on to the scabbard. Woman-like, she cannot abide the sight of cold steel, and she refuses. This added frustration sends Sir Joseph's blood pressure soaring and he promptly orders the arrest and placing in irons of poor Ralph.

[60] Words and music on page 134.

[61] In the place of Sir Joseph's solo, the original script contains the following lines for him: "Josephine, I cannot tell you the distress I feel at this most painful revelation. I desire to express to you, officially, that I am hurt. You whom I honoured by seeking in marriage—you, the Daughter of a Captain in the Royal Navy!" and Buttercup's present lines as sung were spoken: "Hold! I have something to say to that!" Could Sullivan have had something to do with the change?

My amazement, my surprise,
Again you may discover from my eyes.
ALL.   How terrible the aspect of his eyes!
BUT.   Hold! Ere upon your loss
You lay much stress,
A long-concealèd crime
I would confess.

SONG—BUTTERCUP

A many years ago,
When I was young and charming,
As some of you may know,
I practised baby-farming.

ALL.   Now this is most alarming!
When she was young and charming,
She practised baby-farming,
A many years ago.

BUT.   Two tender babes I nussed:
One was of low condition,
The other, upper crust,
A regular patrician.

ALL (*explaining to each other*).
Now, this is the position:
One was of low condition,
The other a patrician,
A many years ago.

BUT.   Oh, bitter is my cup!
However could I do it?
I mixed those children up,
And not a creature knew it!

ALL.   However could you do it?
Some day, no doubt, you'll rue it,
Although no creature knew it,
So many years ago.

BUT.   In time each little waif
Forsook his foster-mother,
The well-born babe was Ralph—
Your captain was the other!!!

ALL.   They left their foster-mother,
The one was Ralph, our brother,
Our captain was the other,
A many years ago. [62]

[62] *One must admit that Ralph certainly managed to keep at least the appearance of youth.*

SIR JOSEPH. Then I am to understand that Captain Corcoran and Ralph were exchanged in childhood's happy hour—that Ralph is really the Captain, and the Captain is Ralph?
BUT. That is the idea I intended to convey, officially!
SIR JOSEPH. And very well you have conveyed it.
BUT. Aye! aye! yer 'onour.
SIR JOSEPH. Dear me! Let them appear before me, at once!

RALPH *enters as* CAPTAIN; CAPTAIN *as a common sailor.*
JOSEPHINE *rushes to his arms*

JOS. My father—a common sailor!
CAPT. It is hard, is it not, my dear?

SIR JOSEPH. This is a very singular occurrence; I congratulate you both. (*To* RALPH.) Desire that remarkably fine seaman to step forward.

RALPH. Corcoran. Three paces to the front—march!

CAPT. If what?

RALPH. If what? I don't think I understand you.

CAPT. If you please.

SIR JOSEPH. The gentleman is quite right. If you *please*.

RALPH. Oh! If you *please*. (CAPTAIN *steps forward*.)

SIR JOSEPH (*to* CAPTAIN). You are an extremely fine fellow.

CAPT. Yes, your honour.

SIR JOSEPH. So it seems that you were Ralph, and Ralph was you.

CAPT. So it seems, your honour.

SIR JOSEPH. Well, I need not tell you that after this change in your condition, a marriage with your daughter will be out of the question.

CAPT. Don't say that, your honour—love levels all ranks. [63]

SIR JOSEPH. It does to a considerable extent, but it does not level them as much as that. (*Handing* JOSEPHINE *to* RALPH.) Here—take her, sir, and mind you treat her kindly.

RALPH *and* JOS. Oh bliss, oh rapture!

CAPT. *and* BUT. Oh rapture, oh bliss!

SIR JOSEPH.   Sad my lot and sorry,
      What shall I do? I cannot live alone!

HEBE. Fear nothing—while I live I'll not desert you.
      I'll soothe and comfort your declining days.

SIR JOSEPH. No, don't do that.

HEBE.   Yes, but indeed I'd rather—

SIR JOSEPH (*resigned*). [64] To-morrow morn our vows shall all be plighted,
      Three loving pairs on the same day united!

QUARTETTE

JOSEPHINE, HEBE, RALPH, *and* DEADEYE

Oh joy, oh rapture unforeseen,
The clouded sky is now serene,
The god of day—the orb of love,
Has hung his ensign high above,
    The sky is all ablaze.

With wooing words and loving song,
We'll chase the lagging hours along,
And if $\begin{Bmatrix} \text{he finds} \\ \text{I find} \end{Bmatrix}$ the maiden coy,
We'll murmur forth decorous joy,
    In dreamy roundelay.

CAPT.   For he's the Captain of the *Pinafore*.
ALL.   And a right good captain too!
CAPT.   And though before my fall
        I was captain of you all,
      I'm a member of the crew.

ALL.   Although before his fall, etc.
CAPT.   I shall marry with a wife,
      In my humble rank of life! (*turning to* BUT.)
        And you, my own, are she—
      I must wander to and fro;
      But wherever I may go,
        I shall never be untrue to thee!

[63] *It helps the scene considerably if Corcoran adds the words "y'know!" and if Sir Joseph puts in an "M'yes," before proceeding with "It does, etc." After all, he's just been hoist with his own petard and it gives him time to think.*

[64] *A line is interpolated here by Sir Joseph: "Oh, very well, then!" And incidentally, before he says it, he takes a good look at all the rest of his sisters, cousins and aunts—well, at his cousins and aunts—finally coming face to face with Dick Deadeye!*

[65] *In spite of Sir Joseph's statement, "I'll be true to
the devotion that my love implants," he nevertheless goes visiting with all his female relations,
chucking them under their chins and generally
behaving like a man who is going to miss the
sisters, cousins and aunts who accompany him
where he—in the past had "gone!" Hebe, finding
him missing from her side, goes in quest of him
and brings him to heel in quick fashion, proving,
as ever, that the woman is the real master in the
house. Not that I think that it was Gilbert's intention to prove this; it just happened. In fact,
Sir Joseph's and Hebe's business here is just a
repetition of that of Captain (now A.B.) Corcoran and Buttercup when he is chased by her
after having stated that he will "never be untrue
to thee!" "What, never?" "No, never!" "What,
never?" "Hardly ever!" This is a line, incidentally,
that Leslie Rands once managed to either ruin
or improve, depending on which way you look at
it, by singing:*

*". . . I shall always be untrue to thee!" "What,
always?" "Yes, always!" "What, always?" "Well
—nearly never!"*

ALL.   What, never?
CAPT.   No, never!
ALL.   What, *never*?
CAPT.   Hardly ever!
ALL.   Hardly ever be untrue to thee.
Then give three cheers, and one cheer more
For the former Captain of the *Pinafore*.

BUT.   For he loves Little Buttercup, dear Little Buttercup,
    Though I could never tell why;
But still he loves Buttercup, poor Little Buttercup,
    Sweet Little Buttercup, aye!
ALL.   For he loves, etc.

SIR JOSEPH.   I am the monarch of the sea,
And when I've married thee (*to* HEBE),
I'll be true to the devotion that my love implants,
    [65]
HEBE.   Then good-bye to his sisters, and his cousins, and
        his aunts,
Especially his cousins,
Whom he reckons up by dozens,
His sisters, and his cousins, and his aunts!

ALL.   For he is an Englishman,
    And he himself hath said it,
    And it's greatly to his credit
That he is an Englishman!

CURTAIN

We Sail the Ocean Blue

With vigor and ponderously CHORUS of MEN

We sail the o - cean blue, And our sau - cy ship's a beau - ty; We're so - ber men and true, And at - ten - tive to our du - ty. When the balls whis - tle free o'er the bright blue sea, We stand to our guns all day. When at

an - chor we ride On the Ports - mouth tide, We've plen - ty of time for play. A - hoy! A - hoy! The balls whis - tle free. A - hoy! A - hoy! O'er the bright blue sea, We stand to our guns, to our guns all day. We sail the o - cean blue, And our sau - cy ship's a beau - ty; We're so - ber men and true, And at -

ten - tive to our du - ty; Our sau - cy ship's a beau - ty, We're at -

ten - tive to our du - ty; We're so - ber men and true, We sail the

o - - - - cean blue!

I'm Called Little Buttercup

Moderate Waltz tempo

LITTLE BUTTERCUP

I'm called lit-tle But-ter-cup, Dear lit-tle

But-ter-cup, Though I could nev-er tell why; But still I'm called

But-ter-cup, Poor lit-tle But-ter-cup, Sweet lit-tle But-ter-cup

I. I've snuff and to-bac-cy, and ex-cel-lent jack-y; I've scis-sors and watch-es and knives; I've rib-bons and lac-es to set off the fac-es Of pret-ty young sweet-hearts and wives. I've trea-cle and tof-fee, I've tea and I've cof-fee, Soft tom-my and suc-cu-lent chops; I've chick-ens and co-nies, And

pret - ty po - lo - nies, And ex - cel - lent pep - per - mint drops. Then

buy of your But - ter - cup, Dear lit - tle But - ter - cup; Sail - ors should

nev - er be shy; So buy of your But - ter - cup,

Poor lit - tle But - ter - cup; Come, of your But - ter - cup buy.

A Maiden Fair to See

With restraint, as a ballad

mf

RALPH

p

A maid-en fair to see, The pearl of min-strel-sy, A bud of blush-ing beau-ty; For whom proud no-bles sigh, And with each oth-er vie To do her me-nial's du-ty. To do her me-nial's

CHORUS
mp

RALPH

du - ty. A suit - or, low - ly born, With hope - less pas - sion torn, And

poor be - yond de - ny - ing, Has dared for her to pine, At

whose ex - alt - ed shrine A world of wealth is sigh - ing. **CHORUS** A world of wealth is

RALPH

sigh - ing. Un - learn - ed he in aught Save that which love has taught (For

love had been his tu-tor); Oh, pit-y, pit-y me, Our

cap-tain's daugh-ter, she, And I that low-ly suit-or. Oh,

pit-y, pit-y me, Our cap-tain's daugh-ter, she, And I that low-ly

suit - or.

I Am the Captain of the Pinafore

Sprightly

CAPTAIN CORCORAN

1. I am the Cap-tain of the
(2. I) do my best to sat-is-

MEN

CAPTAIN CORCORAN

Pin-a-fore! And a right-good-cap-tain, too! You're ver-y, ver-y good, And,
fy you all! And with you we're quite con-tent. You're ex-ceed-ing-ly po-lite, And I

MEN

be it un-der-stood, I com-mand a right good crew. We're
think it on-ly right To re-turn the com-pli-ment. We're ex-

ver-y, ver-y good, And, be it un-der-stood, He com-mands a____ right good
ceed-ing-ly po-lite, And he thinks it on-ly right To re-turn the____ com-pli-

CAPTAIN

crew. Though re-lat-ed to a peer, I can hand, reef and steer, Or
ment. Bad lan-guage or a-buse, I nev-er, nev-er use, What-

ship a sel-va-gee; I am nev-er known to quail At the
ev-er the e-mer-gen-cy; Though "both-er it" I may Oc-

MEN

fu-ry of a gale, And I'm nev-er, nev-er sick at sea! What,
ca-sion-al-ly say, I nev-er use a big, big D! What,

Sorry Her Lot

Slowly, with expression

JOSEPHINE

1. Sor-ry her lot____ who loves_ too well, Heav-y the
2. Sad is the hour____ when sets_ the sun, Dark is the

heart____ that hopes but vain - ly, Sad____ are the sighs_ that
night____ to earth's poor daugh - ters, When ____ to the ark_ the

own the spell Ut-tered by eyes____ that speak too plain - ly; Sor-ry her lot ____ who
wea-ried one Flies from the emp - ty waste of wa - ters. Sad is the hour_ when

loves too well,
Heav-y the heart that hopes but vain-ly.

sets the sun,
Dark is the night to earth's poor daugh-ters.

Somewhat livelier

Heav-y the sor-row that bows the head When love is a-

live and hope is dead! When love is a-live and

follow the voice

hope is dead!

love is a-live And hope is dead!

follow the voice

I Am the Monarch of the Sea

Very lively

SIR JOSEPH

I am the mon-arch of the sea, The rul-er of the Queen's Na - vee, Whose praise Great Brit-ain

COUSIN HEBE

loud-ly chants. And we are his sis-ters and his cous-ins and his aunts, And

COUSIN HEBE and CHORUS

we are his sis-ters and his cous-ins and his aunts, His sis-ters and his cous-ins and his

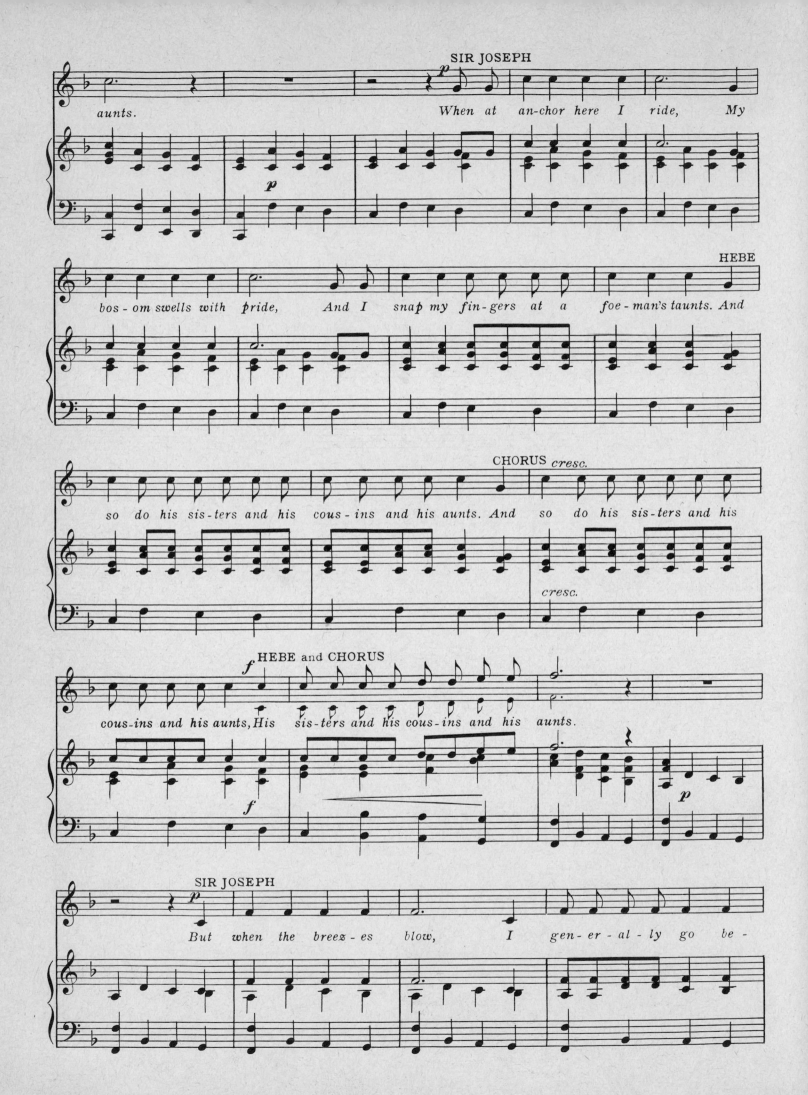

When I Was a Lad

Brightly, but not too fast

SIR JOSEPH

1. When I was a lad I served a term As
(2. As) of-fice boy I made such a mark That they
(3. In) serv-ing writs I made such a name That an

of - fice boy to an at - tor - ney's firm. I cleaned the win - dows and I
gave me the post of a jun - ior clerk. I served the writs with a
ar - ti-cled clerk I soon be - came; I wore clean col - lars and a

staccato

swept the floor, And I pol-ished up the han-dle of the big front door. He
smile so bland, And I cop-ied all the let-ters in a big round hand. He
brand-new suit For the pass ex-am-i-na-tion at the In-sti-tute. For the

pol-ished up the han-dle of the big front door. I pol-ished up that han-dle so
cop-ied all the let-ters in a big round hand. I cop-ied all the let-ters in a
pass ex-am-i-na-tion at the In-sti-tute. That pass ex-am-i-na-tion did so

care-ful-lee That now I am the rul-er of the Queen's Na-vee! He
hand so free That now I am the rul-er of the Queen's Na-vee! He
well for me That now I am the rul-er of the Queen's Na-vee! That

pol-ished up that han-dle so care-ful-lee That now he is the rul-er of the
cop-ied all the let-ters in a hand so free That now he is the rul-er of the
pass ex-am-i-na-tion did so well for him That now he is the rul-er of the

SIR JOSEPH

ev - er had   seen. But   that   kind of   ship   so   suit - ed   me That
self   at   all. I   thought   so   lit - tle, they re - ward - ed   me By
gold - en   rule. Stick   close   to your desks   and   nev - er go to sea, And you

CHORUS

now I   am   the rul - er   of   the Queen's Na - vee! But   that   kind of   ship   so
mak - ing me   the rul - er   of   the Queen's Na - vee! He   thought   so   lit - tle, they re -
all   may be rul - ers   of   the Queen's Na - vee! Stick   close   to   your desks   and

4.-5.   SIR JOSEPH

suit - ed   him That   now he is   the rul - er of the Queen's Na - vee!   5. I
ward - ed   him By   mak - ing him the rul - er   of   the Queen's Na - vee!   6. Now
nev - er go to sea, And you all ── may be rul - ers of the

6.

Queen's Na - vee!

117

Refrain, Audacious Tar

Things Are Seldom What They Seem

Moderately fast

Little Buttercup 1. Things are sel-dom what they seem,
Captain Corcoran 2. Tho' I'm an-y-thing but clev-er,

Skim milk mas-quer-ades as cream;
I could talk like that for-ev-er:

High-lows pass as pat-ent leath-ers;
Once a cat was killed by care;

Jack-daws strut in pea-cock's feath-ers. Capt. Corcoran Ver-y true, so they do.
On-ly brave de-serve the fair. Little Buttercup Ver-y true, so they do.

Little Buttercup Black sheep dwell in ev-'ry fold; All that glit-ters is not gold;
Captain Corcoran Wink is oft-en good as nod; Spoils the child who spares the rod;

Storks turn out to be but logs; Bulls are but in-flat-ed frogs. Capt. C. So they be,
Thirst-y lambs run fox-y dan-gers; Dogs are found in man-y man-gers. Buttercup Fre-quent-lee,

fre-quent-lee. Buttercup Drops the wind and stops the mill; Tur-bot is am-
I a-gree. Capt. Cor. Paw of cat the chest-nut snatch-es; Worn-out gar-ments

bi-tious brill; Gild the farth-ing if you will, Yet it is a farth-ing still.
show new patch-es; On-ly count the chick that hatch-es; Men are grown-up catch-y-catch-ies.

Capt. C. Yes, I know, That is so. Tho' to catch your drift I'm striv-ing, It is shad-y, it is
Buttercup Yes, I know, That is so. Tho' to catch my drift he's striv-ing, I'll dis-sem-ble, I'll dis-

shad-y; I don't see at what you're driv-ing, Mys-tic la-dy, mys-tic la-dy.
sem-ble! When he sees at what I'm driv-ing, Let him trem-ble, let him trem-ble!

Never Mind the Why and Wherefore

Joyful and full of life

Captain Corcoran 1. Nev-er mind the why and
Sir Joseph 2. Nev-er mind the why and
Josephine 3. Nev-er mind the why and

where-fore, Love can lev-el ranks, and there-fore, Though his Lord-ship's sta-tion's
where-fore, Love can lev-el ranks, and there-fore, Though your nau-ti-cal re-
where-fore, Love can lev-el ranks, and there-fore, I ad-mit the ju-ris-

might-y, Though stu-pen-dous be his brain, Though her tastes are mean and
la-tion In my set could scarce-ly pass, Though you oc-cu-py a
dic-tion; A-bly have you play'd your part, You have car-ried firm con-

flight - y And her for - tune poor____ and plain.
sta - tion In the low - er mid - dle class.
vic - tion To my hes - i - tat - ing heart.

mf CAPT. CORCORAN and SIR JOSEPH (each verse)

Ring the mer - ry bells on board-ship, Rend the air with

war - bling wild, For the un - ion of {his/my} Lord-ship With a hum - ble

CAPT. CORCORAN (each verse)   JOSEPHINE

cap - tain's child. For a hum - ble cap - tain's daugh - ter, For a

(each verse)   SIR JOSEPH (each verse)   JOSEPHINE

gal - lant cap - tain's daugh - ter. And a Lord who rules the wa - ter. And a

125

tar who ploughs the wa-ter. Let the air with

joy be lad-en, Rend with songs the air a-bove, For the un-ion

of a maid-en With the man who owns her love.

3. JOSEPHINE

Let the air with joy be lad-en. Ring the mer-ry bells on board-ship,

JOSEPHINE

For the un-ion of a maid-en, For her un-ion with his Lord-ship.

126

f ALL THREE

Rend with songs the air a-bove, For the man who owns her love,

Rend with songs the air a-bove, For the man who owns her

love.

f a tempo

Kind Captain, I've Important Information

Moderately lively

Dick Deadeye   *1. Kind*
(Capt. Corcoran   *2. Good*)
(Dick Deadeye   *3. Kind*)
(Capt. Corcoran   *4. Good*)

Cap - tain, I've im - por - tant in - for - ma - tion, Sing
fel - low, in co - nun - drums you are speak - ing, Sing
Cap - tain, your young la - dy is a - sigh - ing, Sing
fel - low, you have giv - en time - ly warn - ing, Sing

hey, the kind com - man - der that you are, A -
hey, the mys - tic sail - or that you are; The
hey, the sim - ple Cap - tain that you are, This
hey, the thought - ful sail - or that you are; I'll

bout a cer - tain in - ti - mate re - la - tion, Sing
an - swer to them vain - ly I am seek - ing, Sing
ver - y night with Rack - straw to be fly - ing, Sing
talk to Mas - ter Rack - straw in the morn - ing, Sing

hey, the mer - ry maid - en and the tar.   Capt. Corcoran *The*
hey, the mer - ry maid - en and the tar.   Capt. Corcoran *The*
hey, the mer - ry maid - en and the tar.   Capt. Corcoran *The*
hey, the cat - o' - nine - tails and the tar.   Capt. Corcoran *The*

mer - ry, mer - ry maid - en, The mer - ry, mer - ry maid - en, Sing
mer - ry, mer - ry maid - en, The mer - ry, mer - ry maid - en, Sing
mer - ry, mer - ry maid - en, The mer - ry, mer - ry maid - en, Sing
mer - ry cat - o' - nine - tails, The mer - ry cat - o' - nine - tails, The

hey, the mer - ry maid - en __ and the tar.
hey, the mer - ry maid - en __ and the tar.
much too mer - ry maid - en __ and the tar.
mer - ry cat - o' - nine - tails __ and the tar.

1.   2.

Capt. Corcoran *2. Good*
Dick Deadeye *3. Kind*
Capt. Corcoran *4. Good*

Carefully on Tiptoe Stealing

Moderately

MEN

1. Care-ful - ly on tip - toe
2. (Pull a -) shore in fash - ion

steal - ing, Breath - ing gent - ly as we may, Ev - 'ry
stead - y, Hy - men will de - fray the fare, For a

step with cau - tion feel - ing, We__ will__ soft - ly steal a -
cler - gy - man is read - y To__ u - nite the hap - py

DEADEYE

way. Good - ness me! Why, what was that? Si - lent
pair. Good - ness me! Why, what was that? Si - lent

He Is an Englishman

BOATSWAIN (*freely*)   Moderately (*almost solemnly*)

He is an Eng-lish-man! For— he him-self has said— it, And it's great-ly to his cred-it, That he is an Eng-lish-

MEN

man! That he is an Eng-lish-man! For he might have been a Roo-sian, A

BOATSWAIN

French or Turk or Proo-sian, Or per-haps I-tal-i-an! Or per-

MEN

Farewell, My Own

With warmth and animation

RALPH

Fare-well, my own, Light of my life, fare-well! For crime un-known I go to a dun-geon cell.

JOSEPHINE

I will a-tone; In the mean-time, fare-well! And all a-

lone Re-joice in your dun-geon cell! ___ A bone, ___ a

bone, ___ I'll pick with this sail-or fell; Let him be

shown At once to his dun-geon cell. He'll hear no

tone ___ Of the maid-en he loves so well! No tel-e-

phone Com-mu-ni-cates with his cell! But when is known The

se - cret I have to tell, Wide will be thrown The door of his dun - geon

cell. Fare - well, my own, Light of my life, fare - well!

And all a - lone Re - joice in your dun - geon, your dun -

geon cell!

The Pirates of Penzance

OR, THE SLAVE OF DUTY

DRAMATIS PERSONÆ

MAJOR-GENERAL STANLEY

THE PIRATE KING

SAMUEL (*his Lieutenant*)

FREDERIC (*the Pirate Apprentice*)

SERGEANT OF POLICE

MABEL

EDITH

KATE   } (*General Stanley's Daughters*)

ISABEL

RUTH (*a Pirate Maid of all Work*)

Chorus of Pirates, Police, and General Stanley's
Daughters

ACT I

A ROCKY SEA-SHORE ON THE COAST OF CORNWALL

ACT II

A RUINED CHAPEL BY MOONLIGHT

First produced at the Opéra Comique on April 3, 1880

THIS was the only opera of the series that had its world première outside of England. The program of that historic opening has, in a note immediately above the title of the opera, the words "First production of the New Melo-Dramatic Opera, in Two Acts . . . written and composed expressly for production in the United States."

In this it is unique among the Gilbert and Sullivan operas. But although it was the true world première, it was not its first actual performance. That took place at the Bijou Theatre in Paignton, Devonshire.

H.M.S. Pinafore had been pirated in many versions in the United States, and Mr. Carte, Gilbert and Sullivan determined to put a stop to this sort of thing in the future. Litigation had already been resorted to in the case of Pinafore, and Gilbert, Sullivan and Carte were the losers. The court's ruling had been that versions of the libretto and score (vocal score only) placed the work in the public domain.

The result of this was that the three partners—as they were by now—decided that they would produce their next opera in New York, that no printed versions would be published, and that no one other than those directly connected with their company would be permitted in the theater at any time during rehearsals. While they were rehearsing, it came to their notice that if they were to produce in America before doing so in England, the English copyright would become null and void. To overcome this it was decided to give one performance in England, but one that would in no way upset the American première. A touring company playing Pinafore in the provinces was rapidly rehearsed—very rapidly, indeed—as the music arrived from America only just in time for the members of the company to take a quick glance at it before going on to perform it. This was the performance rushed on at the Bijou Theatre. Dressed in their Pinafore costumes, the pirates, wearing nothing but colored handkerchiefs around their heads to distinguish them from able seamen of the Royal Navy, their parts in their hands, performed The Pirates of Penzance in England only a few hours before the world première opened at the Fifth Avenue Theater in New York City— and the British copyright was safe.

But the trials and tribulations of the three partners were not over so far as the United States was concerned. Following the American opening, it was not long before pirated versions of The Pirates began to appear. Once again litigation was resorted to—and once again the three partners were the losers. It must be remembered that the United States was not a signatory to the then existing International Copyright Agreement. In spite of the rule not permitting anyone to enter the theater unless duly authorized, piratical producers managed to get spies into the opening—people versed in the art of taking musical dictation rapidly (aided, one cannot help thinking, by unscrupulous members of the orchestra)—and obtained sufficient material to produce their own versions of this successful opera. The ruling of the courts on this occasion was: Public performance constituted publication, and as publication rendered anything open to public domain, the verdict in this case would be for the defendants. But the British copyright was safe, and with that the authors and producer had to rest content, nor did they try to open any one of their future operas first in the United States. Iolanthe had simultaneous—or nearly simultaneous—openings and some of the subsequent operas were performed in New York and on the road, notably Patience.

The London première of The Pirates did not take place until some three months later at the Opéra Comique. The Pirates of Penzance was, one might say, the last of the Gilbert and Sullivan operas to be played at the Opéra Comique and so is not one of the true Savoy operas. It is true that Patience opened there, but only while waiting for the Savoy Theatre to be completed.

Of the New York cast only one member returned to appear in the London production. This was Jessie Bond, a young lady destined to remain with the company for many years. Another member of the New York cast who was to become quite a favorite in subsequent English operettas was Rosina Brandram.

One of the strangest things about this world première was that in spite of very bad notices for a certain member of the company, the whole was hailed as a brilliant success for author, composer and everyone else concerned. That Carte, Gilbert and, especially, Sullivan should have kept the offending artist on after such devastating reviews would seem very surprising, but, as the one surviving member of the D'Oyly Carte Company has put it: It's really quite obvious. No other tenor was available! In the entire history of these operas no other single artist ever received such a panning as did Mr. Hugh Talbot in the role of Frederic: ". . . a make-up that gave an appearance of advanced age"; ". . . he [Mr. Talbot] did not know his lines"; ". . . his singing was weak"; ". . . making nonsense of his role"; and so on.

The Paignton program reveals one name that was to become a byword in the D'Oyly Carte Company, the very first Sergeant of Police, Fred Billington (Mr. Billington, in the program). Although practically unknown in London, he was a great favorite in the provinces for many years. In 1916, a heart attack felled him as he was waiting for a train to Cambridge, where the company was playing, after a lunch at the Savoy Hotel with Mr. Rupert D'Oyly Carte, the son of Richard. Carte had called Billington to town to inform him that, much as he regretted it, he felt that Billington was getting a little too old and he had decided to retire him. "Billy" apparently took his congé with particularly good grace, but only a few hours later he was dead, dying as he always said he would wish to—after a good meal, some good wine, coffee, and a good cigar.

The patterns of both H.M.S. Pinafore and The Pirates of Penzance are similar, though the plot of The Pirates is, on the whole, more complicated. There is, however, one main departure. Sir Joseph's first song in Pinafore makes a number of different points (a point number) whereas Major-General Stanley's is pure patter. And, apropos of that, I have often—er—orfen—been asked not only, "How do you remember the words?" but, as well, "And how do you manage to get them out at such a speed?" Well, the memorizing of words is each person's problem. No two people use quite the same method. My own best advice is that once one has got the words into one's head, never think of the lines that are to come. Concentrate on the immediate words. To think ahead spells catastrophe to the line you are singing. As for the speed of delivery, the secret there is not to set the pace too fast, and once the speed is set—stick to it! The even tempo gives an illusion of greater speed. There is one moment when you may increase the beat slightly, and very gradually, and that is right at the end of the number. This is the speed the members of your audience will retain in their minds. Try it and see!

The Pirates of Penzance

ACT I

SCENE.—*A rocky sea-shore on the coast of Cornwall. In the distance is a calm sea, on which a schooner is lying at anchor. As the curtain rises groups of pirates are discovered—some drinking, some playing cards.* SAMUEL, [1] *the Pirate Lieutenant, is going from one group to another, filling the cups from a flask.* FREDERIC *is seated in a despondent attitude at the back of the scene.*

OPENING CHORUS

> Pour, oh, pour the pirate sherry; [2]
>   Fill, oh, fill the pirate glass;
> And, to make us more than merry,
>   Let the pirate bumper pass.

SAM.
> For to-day our pirate 'prentice
>   Rises from indenture freed;
> Strong his arm and keen his scent is,
>   He's a pirate now indeed!

ALL.
> Here's good luck to Frederic's ventures!
> Frederic's out of his indentures.

SAM.
> Two-and-twenty now he's rising,
>   And alone he's fit to fly,
> Which we're bent on signalizing
>   With unusual revelry.

ALL.
> Here's good luck to Frederic's ventures!
> Frederic's out of his indentures.
> Pour, oh, pour the pirate sherry, etc.

FREDERIC *rises and comes forward with* PIRATE KING, [3] *who enters*

KING. [4] Yes, Frederic, from to-day you rank as a full-blown member of our band.

ALL. Hurrah.

FRED. My friends, I thank you all, from my heart, for your kindly wishes. Would that I could repay them as they deserve!

KING. What do you mean?

FRED. To-day I am out of my indentures, and to-day I leave you for ever.

KING. But this is quite unaccountable; a keener hand at scuttling a Cunarder or cutting out a P. & O. [5] never shipped a handspike.

FRED. Yes, I have done my best for you. And why? It was my duty under my indentures, and I am the slave of duty. As a child I was regularly apprenticed to your band. It was through an error—no matter, the mistake was ours, not yours, and I was in honour bound by it.

SAM. An error? What error?

RUTH *enters* [6]

[1] In the Paignton program Samuel is coupled with another Pirate character, James. That was his one and only appearance.

[2] I have always had a sneaking feeling that these Pirates' main criminal activities were confined to rum- and sherry-running, in spite of the Pirate King's later allusions to Frederic's keenness.

[3] Many portrayers of the Pirate King are inclined to go overboard in the matter of make-up. Beyond the black, full-bottomed wig and black mustache, he should not attempt to give any impression of fierceness. The reverse is more in order—geniality, almost a touch of gay righteousness.

[4] In the New York world première program the King is dignified with a name, "Richard," and called "a Pirate Chief."

[5] P. & O.—Peninsula & Orient Line. In the original American version this line was changed to ". . . or cutting out a White Star," Gilbert having decided that the American public would recognize that reference more easily than P. & O. D'Oyly Carte visits to the United States in more recent years, however, retain P. & O.

[6] While the name "Ruth" is always retained, a study of the three opening programs finds her variously described as: "A piratical maid-of-all-work" (New York); "A Pirate maid of all-work" (London); and "Frederic's nurse" (Paignton).

FRED. I may not tell you; it would reflect upon my well-loved Ruth.

RUTH. Nay, dear master, my mind has long been gnawed by the cankering tooth of mystery. Better have it out at once.

SONG—RUTH [7]

[7] *Words and music on page 168.*

When Frederic was a little lad he proved so brave and daring,
His father thought he'd 'prentice him to some career seafaring.
I was, alas! his nurserymaid, and so it fell to *my* lot
To take and bind the promising boy apprentice to a *pilot*—
A life not bad for a hardy lad, though surely not a high lot,
Though I'm a nurse, you might do worse than make your boy a pilot.
I was a stupid nurserymaid, on breakers always steering,
And I did not catch the word aright, through being hard of hearing; [8]
Mistaking my instructions, which within my brain did gyrate,
I took and bound this promising boy apprentice to a *pirate*.
A sad mistake it was to make and doom him to a vile lot,
I bound him to a pirate—you—instead of to a pilot.

[8] *For the sake of the plot she had to be, but except for one reference immediately after this song, to the two words being so much alike, there is no further evidence of her deafness. Gilbert conveniently forgets the fact.*

I soon found out, beyond all doubt, the scope of this disaster,
But I hadn't the face to return to my place, and break it to my master.
A nurserymaid is not afraid of what you people *call* work,
So I made up my mind to go as a kind of piratical maid-of-all-work. [9]
And that is how you find me now, a member of your shy lot,
Which you wouldn't have found, had he been bound apprentice to a
     pilot.

[9] *See Note 6.*

RUTH. Oh, pardon! Frederic, pardon! (*Kneels.*)

FRED. Rise, sweet one, I have long pardoned you.

RUTH (*rises*). The two words were so much alike!

FRED. They were. They still are, though years have rolled over their heads. But this afternoon my obligation ceases. Individually, I love you all with affection unspeakable, but, collectively, I look upon you with a disgust that amounts to absolute detestation. Oh! pity me, my beloved friends, for such is my sense of duty that, once out of my indentures, I shall feel myself bound to devote myself heart and soul to your extermination!

ALL. Poor lad—poor lad! (*All weep.*)

KING. Well, Frederic, if you conscientiously feel that it is your duty to destroy us, we cannot blame you for acting on that conviction. Always act in accordance with the dictates of your conscience, my boy, and chance the consequences.

SAM. Besides, we can offer you but little temptation to remain with us. We don't seem to make piracy pay. I'm sure I don't know why, but we don't.

FRED. *I* know why, but, alas! I mustn't tell you; it wouldn't be right.

KING. Why not, my boy? It's only half-past eleven, and you are one of us until the clock strikes twelve. [10]

[10] *The Pirate King does a most delightful piece of stage business at this point. Says he: ". . . it's only . . . er . . ." and here he turns upstage, shades his eyes and scans the sun above the sea's horizon. He then goes on: ". . . half-past eleven . . ." but follows with the most paradoxical remark: ". . . and you are one of us until the clock strikes twelve"!*

SAM. True, and until then you are bound to protect our interests.

ALL. Hear, hear!

FRED. Well, then, it is my duty, as a pirate, to tell you that you are too tender-hearted. For instance, you make a point of never attacking a weaker party than yourselves, and when you attack a stronger party you invariably get thrashed.

KING. There is some truth in that.

FRED. Then, again, you make a point of never molesting an orphan!

SAM. Of course: we are orphans ourselves, and know what it is.

FRED. Yes, but it has got about, and what is the consequence? Every one we capture says he's an orphan. The last three ships we took proved to be manned entirely by orphans, and so we had to let them go. One would think that Great Britain's mercantile navy was recruited solely from her orphan asylums—which we know is not the case.

SAM. But, hang it all! you wouldn't have us absolutely merciless?

FRED. There's my difficulty; until twelve o'clock I would, after twelve I wouldn't. Was ever a man placed in so delicate a situation.

RUTH. And Ruth, your own Ruth, whom you love so well, and who has won her middle-aged way into your boyish heart, what is to become of *her*? [11]

KING. Oh, he will take you with him.

FRED. Well, Ruth, I feel some little difficulty about you. It is true that I admire you very much, but I have been constantly at sea since I was eight years old, and yours is the only woman's face that I have seen during that time. I think it is a sweet face.

RUTH. It is—oh, it is!

FRED. I say I *think* it is; that is my impression. But as I have never had an opportunity of comparing you with other women, it is just possible I may be mistaken.

KING. True.

FRED. What a terrible thing it would be if I were to marry this innocent person, and then find out that she is, on the whole, plain!

KING. Oh, Ruth is very well, very well indeed.

SAM. Yes, there are the remains of a fine woman about Ruth. [12]

FRED. Do you really think so?

SAM. I do.

FRED. Then I will not be so selfish as to take her from you. In justice to her, and in consideration for you, I will leave her behind. (*Hands* RUTH *to* KING.)

KING. No, Frederic, this must not be. We are rough men who lead a rough life, but we are not so utterly heartless as to deprive thee of thy love. I think I am right in saying that there is not one here who would rob thee of this inestimable treasure for all the world holds dear. [13]

ALL (*loudly*). Not one!

KING. No, I thought there wasn't. Keep thy love, Frederic, keep thy love. (*Hands her back to* FREDERIC.) [14]

FRED. You're very good, I'm sure. [*Exit* RUTH.

KING. Well, it's the top of the tide, and we must be off. Farewell, Frederic. [15] When your process of extermination begins, let our deaths be as swift and painless as you can conveniently make them.

FRED. I will! By the love I have for you, I swear it! Would that you could render this extermination unnecessary by accompanying me back to civilization!

KING. No, Frederic, it cannot be. I don't think much of our profession, but, contrasted with respectability, it is comparatively honest. No, Frederic, I shall live and die a Pirate King.

SONG—PIRATE KING [16]

Oh better far to live and die
Under the brave black flag I fly,
Than play a sanctimonious part,
With a pirate head and a pirate heart.
Away to the cheating world go you,
Where pirates all are well-to-do;
But I'll be true to the song I sing,
And live and die a Pirate King.
For I am a Pirate King.

[11] *This is the first time that Gilbert's later tendency to think an elderly spinster one of the best jokes imaginable really begins to show itself. The joking with respect to Buttercup in Pinafore is placed more on social differences than on her being elderly or a spinster.*

[12] *See what I mean? See Note 11.*

[13] *If more evidence is needed!*

[14] ! !

[15] *Can it be that the King is just making sure?*

[16] *Words and music on page 170.*

ALL.   You are!
              Hurrah for our Pirate King!
KING.   And it is, it is a glorious thing
              To be a Pirate King.
ALL.   Hurrah!
              Hurrah for our Pirate King!

KING.   When I sally forth to seek my prey
              I help myself in a royal way:
              I sink a few more ships, it's true,
              Than a well-bred monarch ought to do;
              But many a king on a first-class throne,
              If he wants to call his crown his own,
              Must manage somehow to get through
              More dirty work than ever I do,
                  Though I am a Pirate King.
ALL.   You are!
              Hurrah for our Pirate King!
KING.   And it is, it is a glorious thing
              To be a Pirate King!
ALL.   It is!
              Hurrah for our Pirate King!

[*Exeunt all except* FREDERIC.

Enter RUTH

RUTH. Oh, take me with you! I cannot live if I am left behind.

FRED. Ruth, I will be quite candid with you. You are very dear to me, as you know, but I must be circumspect. You see, you are considerably older than I. A lad of twenty-one usually looks for a wife of seventeen.

RUTH. A wife of seventeen! You will find me a wife of a thousand!

FRED. No, but I shall find you a wife of forty-seven, and that is quite enough. Ruth, tell me candidly, and without reserve: compared with other women—how are *you*?

RUTH. I will answer you truthfully, master—I have a slight cold, but otherwise I am quite well. [17]

FRED. I am sorry for your cold, but I was referring rather to your personal appearance. Compared with other women, are you beautiful?

RUTH (*bashfully*). I have been told so, dear master.

FRED. Ah, but lately?

RUTH. Oh, no, years and years ago.

FRED. What do you think of yourself?

RUTH. It is a delicate question to answer, but I think I am a fine woman.

FRED. That is your candid opinion?

RUTH. Yes, I should be deceiving you if I told you otherwise.

FRED. Thank you, Ruth, I believe you, for I am sure you would not practise on my inexperience; I wish to do the right thing, and if— I say *if*—you are really a fine woman, your age shall be no obstacle to our union! (*Chorus of Girls heard in the distance.*) Hark! Surely I hear voices! Who has ventured to approach our all but inaccessible lair? Can it be Custom House? No, it does not sound like Custom House. [18]

RUTH (*aside*). Confusion! it is the voices of young girls! If he should see them I am lost.

FRED. (*looking off*). By all that's marvellous, a bevy of beautiful maidens!

[17] *No, I'm afraid this isn't an example of Ruth's being hard of hearing, but a deliberate misconstruction of a straightforward question.*

[18] *This more than ever convinces me that the Pirates' main (and no pun intended) activity was rum-running. No pirate would be afraid of Custom House; but a rum-runner would.*

RUTH (*aside*). Lost! lost! lost!

FRED. How lovely! how surpassingly lovely is the plainest of them! What grace—what delicacy—what refinement! And Ruth—Ruth told me she was beautiful!

RECIT

FRED.   Oh, false one, you have deceived me!

RUTH.   I have deceived you?

FRED.   Yes, deceived me!

(*Denouncing her.*)

DUET—FRED. *and* RUTH

FRED.   You told me you were fair as gold!

RUTH (*wildly*). And, master, am I not so?

FRED.   And now I see you're plain and old.

RUTH.   I am sure I am not a jot so. [19]

FRED.   Upon my innocence you play.

RUTH.   I'm not the one to plot so.

FRED.   Your face is lined, your hair is grey.

RUTH.   It's gradually got so.

FRED.   Faithless woman, to deceive me,
                    I who trusted so!

RUTH.   Master, master, do not leave me!
                    Hear me, ere you go!
                My love without reflecting,
                Oh, do not be rejecting.
Take a maiden tender—her affection raw and green,
                At very highest rating,
                Has been accumulating
Summers seventeen—summers seventeen.
                Don't, beloved master,
                Crush me with disaster.
What is such a dower to the dower I have here?
                My love unabating
                Has been accumulating
Forty-seven year—forty-seven year!

ENSEMBLE

RUTH	FRED.
Don't, beloved master,	Yes, your former master
Crush me with disaster.	Saves you from disaster.
What is such a dower to the dower	Your love would be uncomfortably
I have here?	fervid, it is clear,
My love unabating	If, as you are stating,
Has been accumulating	It's been accumulating
Forty-seven year—forty-seven year!	Forty-seven year—forty-seven year!

[*At the end he renounces her, and she goes off in despair.*

RECIT—FRED.

What shall I do? Before these gentle maidens
I dare not show in this alarming costume.
No, no, I must remain in close concealment
Until I can appear in decent clothing!

(*Hides in cave as they enter climbing over the rocks.*)

GIRLS.   Climbing over rocky mountain, [20]
            Skipping rivulet and fountain,
            Passing where the willows quiver

[19] How small children can take notice and listen! Many years ago our then Sergeant of Police had his five-year-old boy at a matinee. On his return home for a between-shows meal his small boy asked him:

"What is a Jottso, Daddy?"

"Well," said he, "I don't think there is any such thing, son."

"Oh, yes, there is, Daddy. It was in the play!"

"In the play?" Daddy's eyes opened wide. "Where?"

"The lady says she is sure she isn't a Jottso. What is a Jottso, Daddy?"

[20] Words and music on page 173.

[21] Near-tragedy was experienced when it was discovered that Sullivan had forgotten to bring his notes on the music with him to New York, where he was to complete scoring it. His prodigious memory, however, enabled him to remember practically every note he had written. There was but one exception. He could not recall the entrance of General Stanley's daughters. Opening night was looming. Gilbert came to his rescue and suggested that they transfer the entrance of the "Thespians" (from Thespis, their first collaboration) lock, stock and barrel. The two entrances were so much alike anyway. The girls' entrance was originally quite different from that now extant, but Gilbert's brain wave saved the show and the first-night curtain went up on schedule. One or two minor changes had to be made in the original Thespis wording, of course —for instance, "Till the mountain top they gain!" became "Till the bright sea-shore they gain!" Had it not been for this bright thought, nothing would today remain of the music of Thespis.

By the ever-rolling river,
    Swollen with the summer rain;
Threading long and leafy mazes
Dotted with unnumbered daisies;
Scaling rough and rugged passes,
Climb the hardy little lasses,
    Till the bright sea-shore they gain! [21]

EDITH. Let us gaily tread the measure,
Make the most of fleeting leisure;
Hail it as a true ally,
Though it perish by and by.

ALL.   Hail it as a true ally,
    Though it perish by and by.

EDITH. Every moment brings a treasure
Of its own especial pleasure,
Though the moments quickly die,
Greet them gaily as they fly.

KATE. Far away from toil and care,
Revelling in fresh sea air,
Here we live and reign alone
In a world that's all our own.
Here in this our rocky den,
Far away from mortal men,
We'll be queens, and make decrees—
They may honour them who please.

ALL. Let us gaily tread the measure, etc.

KATE. What a picturesque spot! I wonder where we are!

EDITH. And I wonder where papa is. We have left him ever so far behind.

ISABEL. Oh, he will be here presently! Remember poor papa is not as young as we are, and we have come over a rather difficult country.

KATE. But how thoroughly delightful it is to be so entirely alone! Why, in all probability we are the first human beings who ever set foot on this enchanting spot.

ISABEL. Except the mermaids—it's the very place for mermaids.

KATE. Who are only human beings down to the waist!

EDITH. And who can't be said strictly to set *foot* anywhere. Tails they may, but feet they *cannot*.

KATE. But what shall we do until papa and the servants arrive with the luncheon?

EDITH. We are quite alone, and the sea is as smooth as glass. Suppose we take off our shoes and stockings and paddle?

ALL. Yes, yes! The very thing! (*They prepare to carry out the suggestion. They have all taken off one shoe, when* FREDERIC *comes forward from cave.*)

FRED. (*recitative*). Stop, ladies, pray!

ALL (*hopping on one foot*).   A man!

FRED.   I had intended
Not to intrude myself upon your notice
In this effective but alarming costume,
But under these peculiar circumstances
It is my bounden duty to inform you
That your proceedings will not be unwitnessed!

EDITH. But who are you, sir? Speak! (*All hopping.*)

FRED.   I am a pirate!

ALL (*recoiling, hopping*).   A pirate! Horror!

FRED.   Ladies, do not shun me!
This evening I renounce my wild profession;
And to that end, oh, pure and peerless maidens!
Oh, blushing buds of ever-blooming beauty!
I, sore at heart, implore your kind assistance.

EDITH. How pitiful his tale!

KATE.   How rare his beauty!

ALL.   How pitiful his tale!   How rare his beauty!

SONG—FRED. [22]

Oh, is there not one maiden breast
    Which does not feel the moral beauty
Of making worldly interest
    Subordinate to sense of duty?

Who would not give up willingly
    All matrimonial ambition,
To rescue such a one as I
    From his unfortunate position?

ALL.   Alas! there's not one maiden breast
    Which seems to feel the moral beauty
Of making worldly interest
    Subordinate to sense of duty!

FRED.   Oh, is there not one maiden here
    Whose homely face and bad complexion
Have caused all hopes to disappear
    Of ever winning man's affection?
To such a one, if such there be,
    I swear by Heaven's arch above you,
If you will cast your eyes on me—
    However plain you be—I'll love you!

ALL.   Alas! there's not one maiden here
    Whose homely face and bad complexion
Have caused all hope to disappear
    Of ever winning man's affection!

FRED. (*in despair*). Not one?

ALL.   No, no—not one!

FRED.   Not one?

ALL.   No, no!

MABEL *enters*

MABEL.   Yes, one! [23]

ALL.   'Tis Mabel!

MABEL.   Yes, 'tis Mabel! [24]

RECIT—MABEL

Oh, sisters, deaf to pity's name,
       For shame!
It's true that he has gone astray,
       But pray
Is that a reason good and true
       Why you
Should all be deaf to pity's name?

[22] Words and music on page 176.

[23] *Like all Gilbert and Sullivan heroines, from Yum-Yum down the line, Mabel is consciously naïve. She will pipe up with "Yes, one!" to the query about whether there isn't one maiden whose homely face and bad complexion, etc., etc. However, like her sister Savoy heroines, she knows very well she's the prettiest of the lot.*

[24] *Almost immediately on her entrance Mabel goes into a cadenza admitting she is Mabel—which takes her about ten or more seconds to sing!*

ALL (*aside*). The question is, had he not been
        A thing of beauty,
    Would she be swayed by quite as keen
        A sense of duty?

MABEL.   For shame, for shame, for shame!

SONG—MABEL [25]

Poor wandering one!
Though thou hast surely strayed,
    Take heart of grace,
    Thy steps retrace,
Poor wandering one!
Poor wandering one!
If such poor love as mine
    Can help thee find
    True peace of mind—
Why, take it, it is thine!
    Take heart, fair days will shine;
    Take any heart—take mine! [26]

ALL.   Take heart; no danger lowers;
    Take any heart—but ours!

[*Exeunt* MABEL *and* FREDERIC.

(EDITH *beckons her sisters, who form in a semicircle around her.*)

EDITH

What ought we to do,
    Gentle sisters, say?
Propriety, we know,
    Says we ought to stay;
While sympathy exclaims,
    "Free them from your tether—
Play at other games—
    Leave them here together."

KATE

Her case may, any day,
    Be yours, my dear, or mine.
Let her make her hay
    While the sun doth shine.
Let us compromise,
    (Our hearts are not of leather).
Let us shut our eyes,
    And talk about the weather.

GIRLS.   Yes, yes, let's talk about the weather.
        Chattering chorus
How beautifully blue the sky,
The glass is rising very high, [27]
Continue fine I hope it may,
And yet it rained but yesterday.
To-morrow it may pour again
(I hear the country wants some rain),
Yet people say, I know not why,
That we shall have a warm July.

[25] Words and music on page 180.

[26] *This is the point where Sullivan really gives a coloratura a chance to show off.*

[27] *In the beginning was the word . . . Clarity of diction was a thing about which Gilbert was adamant, but while talking this volume over with me, my editor informed me that up to the age of ten he was convinced the line read: "The grass is rising very high."*
Poor Mr. Gilbert!

Enter MABEL *and* FREDERIC

[*During* MABEL'*s solo the* GIRLS *continue chatter pianissimo,
but listening eagerly all the time.*

SOLO—MABEL

Did ever maiden wake
    From dream of homely duty,
To find her daylight break
    With such exceeding beauty?
Did ever maiden close
    Her eyes on waking sadness,
To dream of such exceeding gladness?

FRED.   Oh, yes! ah, yes! this is exceeding gladness.
GIRLS.   How beautifully blue the sky, etc.

SOLO—FRED.

[*During this,* GIRLS *continue their chatter pianissimo as before,
but listening intently all the time.*

Did ever pirate roll
    His soul in guilty dreaming,
And wake to find that soul
    With peace and virtue beaming?

ENSEMBLE [28]

MABEL	FRED.	GIRLS
Did ever maiden wake, etc.	Did ever pirate roll, etc.	How beautifully blue the sky, etc.

RECIT—FRED.

Stay, we must not lose our senses;
    Men who stick at no offences
        Will anon be here.
Piracy their dreadful trade is
    Pray you, get you hence, young ladies,
        While the coast is clear.

[FREDERIC *and* MABEL *retire.*

GIRLS. No, we must not lose our senses,
    If they stick at no offences
        We should not be here.
Piracy their dreadful trade is—
    Nice companions for young ladies!
        Let us disappear. [29]

[*During this chorus the* PIRATES *have entered stealthily, and formed in
a semicircle behind the* GIRLS. *As the* GIRLS *move to go off each*
PIRATE *seizes a girl.* KING *seizes* EDITH *and* ISABEL, SAMUEL *seizes*
KATE.

ALL.   Too late!
PIRATES.   Ha! Ha!
ALL.   Too late!
PIRATES.   Ha! Ha!
    Ha! ha! ha! ha!   Ha! ha! ha! ha!

[28] Sullivan was not only a master of melody but a master of counterpoint as well, and the close of Frederic's and Mabel's duet with contrapuntal chorus is one of the best examples:

[29] This line is never actually completed in performance. As they (the girls) are about to sing the last note the Pirates, having crept up behind them, seize them by their wrists and the note resolves itself into a shriek: Let us dis - a - oh!

THE PIRATES OF PENZANCE

[30] *Legal wards of the Lord Chancellor (the senior legal dignitary of Great Britain). And how come? The program maintains—and so do the girls— that they are the daughters of General Stanley. It could be presumed that General Stanley and the girls are incapable of attending to their own affairs.*

[31] *Words and music on page 185.*

[32] *By the end of the introductory music the Major-General is downstage center. He brushes his mustaches to each side, takes a deep breath and launches into the number. Near the end of each stanza he is momentarily stumped for a rhyme, and has to repeat the next-to-last line a couple of times before he finally bursts out triumphantly with the last line, thus:*

> *About binomial theorem I'm teeming with a lot o' news—*
> *(Oh! lot o' news . . . lot o' news . . . Ah!)*
> *With many cheerful facts about the square of the hypotenuse.*

When he finishes the last stanza with "sat a gee" he straddles his sword as a child would a hobbyhorse and prances about the stage. There is always at least one encore to this patter song, taken from the beginning of the last stanza. This time our model Major-General is utterly confident:

> *In short, when I've a smattering of elemental strategy,*
> *(He continues without a pause)*
> *You'll say a better Major-General has never rode a horse!*

This evokes a tremendous guffaw from all the Pirates and consternation from his daughters. Edith at once jumps forward and whispers in his ear; he is nonplused and she repeats her whisper. Then, with a bright smile, he says:

> *Of course it is!*
> *You'll say a better Major-General has never sat a gee!*

Not infrequently a second encore would be called for, and in this case I picked up at the coda: "For my military knowledge . . ." and raced through the whole thing just as fast as I could possibly take it. There came a time when a third encore was being demanded, and the set business left no further changes to ring, so I decided that the only thing to do was to make the second encore longer, picking it up at top speed at the beginning of the stanza. As I neared the line where I had "goofed" earlier, I arranged that the Pirates should be waiting for still another blooper, while my daughters should hold their breath in concern. This time I would sing absolutely correctly and without pause, at which the Pirates would be very disappointed and my daughters would heave a sigh of relief. Should a third encore still be demanded, I was then able to use just the coda. However, it had to be taken at such speed that the chorus invariably found they couldn't mouth the words, so it was arranged that they should merely accompany me in this manner:

> *But still in matters vegetable-lubalubaluba-lubalubalubalubalubalubaluba Gineral!*

ENSEMBLE

(Pirates pass in front of Girls.)   *(Girls pass in front of Pirates.)*

PIRATES	GIRLS
Here's a first-rate opportunity	We have missed our opportunity
To get married with impunity,	Of escaping with impunity;
And indulge in the felicity	So farewell to the felicity
Of unbounded domesticity.	Of our maiden domesticity!
You shall quickly be parsonified,	We shall quickly be parsonified,
Conjugally matrimonified,	Conjugally matrimonified,
By a doctor of divinity,	By a doctor of divinity,
Who resides in this vicinity.	Who resides in this vicinity.

MABEL *(coming forward)*.

RECIT

Hold, monsters! Ere your pirate caravanserai
   Proceed, against our will, to wed us all,
Just bear in mind that we are Wards in Chancery, [30]
   And father is a Major-General!

SAM. *(cowed)*. We'd better pause, or danger may befall,
   Their father is a Major-General.

GIRLS. Yes, yes; he is a Major-General!

The MAJOR-GENERAL *has entered unnoticed, on rock*

GEN.   Yes, I am a Major-General!
SAM.   For he is a Major-General!
ALL.   He is! Hurrah for the Major-General!
GEN.   And it is—it is a glorious thing
     To be a Major-General!
ALL.   It is! Hurrah for the Major-General!

SONG—MAJOR-GENERAL [31]

I am the very model of a modern Major-General, [32]
I've information vegetable, animal, and mineral,
I know the kings of England, and I quote the fights historical,

I am the very model
of a modern Major-General

From Marathon [33] to Waterloo, in order categorical;
I'm very well acquainted too with matters mathematical,
I understand equations, both the simple and quadratical,
About binomial theorem I'm teeming with a lot o' news—
With many cheerful facts about the square of the hypotenuse.

ALL. With many cheerful facts, etc.

GEN. I'm very good at integral and differential calculus,
I know the scientific names of beings animalculous; [34]
In short, in matters vegetable, animal, and mineral,
I am the very model of a modern Major-General.

ALL. In short, in matters vegetable, animal, and mineral,
He is the very model of a modern Major-General.

GEN. I know our mythic history, King Arthur's and Sir Caradoc's, [35]
I answer hard acrostics, I've a pretty taste for paradox,
I quote in elegiacs all the crimes of Heliogabalus, [36]
In conics I can floor peculiarities parabolous.
I can tell undoubted Raphaels from Gerard Dows [37] and
Zoffanies, [38]
I know the croaking chorus from the *Frogs* of Aristophanes,
Then I can hum a fugue of which I've heard the music's din afore,
And whistle all the airs from that infernal nonsense *Pinafore*.

ALL. And whistle all the airs, etc.

GEN. Then I can write a washing bill in Babylonic cuneiform,
And tell you every detail of Caractacus's [39] uniform;
In short, in matters vegetable, animal, and mineral,
I am the very model of a modern Major-General.

ALL. In short, in matters vegetable, animal, and mineral,
He is the very model of a modern Major-General.

GEN. In fact, when I know what is meant by "mamelon" and
"ravelin," [40]
When I can tell at sight a chassepôt [41] rifle from a javelin,
When such affairs as sorties and surprises I'm more wary at,
And when I know precisely what is meant by "commissariat,"
When I have learnt what progress has been made in modern
gunnery,
When I know more of tactics than a novice in a nunnery:
In short, when I've a smattering of elemental strategy,
You'll say a better Major-Gene*ral* has never *sat* a gee—

ALL. You'll say a better, etc.

GEN. For my military knowledge, though I'm plucky and adventury,
Has only been brought down to the beginning of the century; [42]
But still in matters vegetable, animal, and mineral,
I am the very model of a modern Major-General.

ALL. But still in matters vegetable, animal, and mineral,
He is the very model of a modern Major-General.

GEN. And now that I've introduced myself I should like to have some
idea of what's going on.
KATE. Oh, papa—we——
SAM. Permit me, I'll explain in two words: we propose to marry your
daughters.
GEN. Dear me!
GIRLS. Against our wills, papa—against our wills!

[33] Marathon. *A Greek city. Scene of a victory by the Athenians over the Persians, 490* B.C.

[34] Animalculous. *Of the family of animalcules; small or microscopic animals; mice, etc.*

[35] Sir Caradoc. *A knight of King Arthur's Round Table.*

[36] Heliogabalus. *Proclaimed emperor of Rome in 218* A.D. *and assassinated four years later. Famed for his licentiousness, he left the running of government to his wife and in-laws.*

[37] Gerard Dow. *Anglicization of Dou, Dutch painter (1613–75), student of Rembrandt.*

[38] Zoffany. *Pseudonym for Johann Zauffely (1733–1810). Bohemian painter, who came to England in 1758. He was a member of the British Royal Academy and known for his portraits of actors in character.*

[39] Caractacus. *British king under Roman rule, c. 50* A.D.

[40] Mamelon. *A rounded eminence or hummock.* Ravelin. *Earthworks connected with a fort.*

[41] Chassepôt. *Although still printed in libretti the word "Mauser" is now used, and has been for many years. Both are rifles, but the chassepôt became outdated, and anyway was not as familiar to people as the (then) newfangled Mauser.*

It is interesting to note that when performed at Paignton this number had a notation preceding it in the script to the effect that it was to be recited. This was probably because it was doubted whether the music would reach England from America in time. Not for a moment can it be thought that it was Sullivan's original intention, since it was most certainly sung to his music on the first night at the Fifth Avenue Theater.
Major-General Stanley is probably the most nerve-racking of all roles to play, inasmuch as the actor has only two introductory lines and then goes into what is probably the most difficult patter song in the series. It is the role I played on the opening night of the Savoy Theatre season, after having been announced as Sir Henry Lytton's successor. Never have I been so grateful for a sword. It gave me a third leg that couldn't buckle at the knees.

[42] *Of the last century!*

[43] *For reasons that will become obvious, the word "often" must be pronounced to sound like "orphan." The correct Queen's English (vide the Oxford English Dictionary) is "offen," though in the south of England "off-ten" is becoming more frequent. "Orfen" is—and was—an extreme and exaggerated pronunciation prevalent among adherents of Oxford English, as opposed to the Queen's. Major-General Stanley is obviously of the former class. If he were not, he would have no misunderstanding with the Pirate King.*

[44] *The section from the beginning of this speech of General Stanley's down to the Pirate King's line "But not often" has in recent years been cut by the D'Oyly Carte Company. Mr. Rupert D'Oyly Carte—quite rightly, I feel—decided that the pun was becoming labored. This cut speeded up the fun, and the pun—to the distinct advantage of both.*

[45A] *It is a matter of opinion whether the General should emphasize the "off-ten" here, or let it remain "orf-en" and leave it to the explanatory "frequently" to clear things up. I, personally, prefer, and did use, the latter.*

[45B] *This was in view of the General's using the word "orf-en" again within the space of two lines.*

GEN. Oh, but you mustn't do that! May I ask—this is a picturesque uniform, but I'm not familiar with it. What are you?

KING. We are all single gentlemen.

GEN. Yes, I gathered that—anything else?

KING. No, nothing else.

EDITH. Papa, don't believe them; they are pirates—the famous Pirates of Penzance!

GEN. The Pirates of Penzance! I have often [43] heard of them.

MABEL. All except this gentleman—(*indicating* FREDERIC)—who was a pirate once, but who is out of his indentures to-day, and who means to lead a blameless life evermore.

GEN. But wait a bit. I object to pirates as sons-in-law.

KING. We object to Major-Generals as fathers-in-law. But we waive that point. We do not press it. We look over it.

GEN. (*aside*). Hah! an idea! (*Aloud*). And do you mean to say that you would deliberately rob me of these, the sole remaining props of my old age, and leave me to go through the remainder of my life unfriended, unprotected, and alone?

KING. Well, yes, that's the idea.

GEN. Tell me, have you ever known what it is to be an orphan?

PIRATES (*disgusted*). Oh, dash it all!

KING. Here we are again!

GEN. I ask you, have you ever known what it is to be an orphan?

KING. Often!

GEN. Yes, orphan. Have you ever known what it is to be one?

KING. I say, often.

ALL (*disgusted*). Often, often, often. (*Turning away*).

GEN. [44] I don't think we quite understand one another. I ask you, have you ever known what it is to be an orphan, and you say "orphan." As I understand you, you are merely repeating the word "orphan" to show that you understand me.

KING. I didn't repeat the word often.

GEN. Pardon me, you did indeed.

KING. I only repeated it once.

GEN. True, but you repeated it.

KING. But not often.

GEN. Stop: I think I see where we are getting confused. When you said "orphan," did you mean "orphan"—a person who has lost his parents, or "often" [45A]—frequently?

KING. Ah! I beg pardon—I see what you mean—frequently.

GEN. Ah! you said often [45B]—frequently.

KING. No, only once.

GEN. (*irritated*). Exactly—you said often, frequently, only once.

RECIT—GENERAL

Oh, men of dark and dismal fate,
Forgo your cruel employ,
Have pity on my lonely state,
I am an orphan boy!

KING *and* SAM. An orphan boy?

GEN. An orphan boy!

PIRATES. How sad—an orphan boy.

SOLO—GENERAL

These children whom you see
Are all that I can call my own!

PIRATES. Poor fellow!

GEN. Take them away from me
   And I shall be indeed alone.
PIRATES.   Poor fellow!
GEN. If pity you can feel,
   Leave me my sole remaining joy—
   See, at your feet they kneel;
   Your hearts you cannot steel
  Against the sad, sad tale of the lonely orphan boy! [46]
PIRATES (*sobbing*).   Poor fellow!
   See at our feet they kneel;
   Our hearts we cannot steel
  Against the sad, sad tale of the lonely orphan boy! [47]
KING. The orphan boy!
SAM.   The orphan boy!
ALL. The lonely orphan boy! Poor fellow! [48]

ENSEMBLE

GENERAL (*aside*)	GIRLS (*aside*)	PIRATES (*aside*)
I'm telling a terrible story,	He's telling a terrible story,	If he's telling a terrible story,
But it doesn't diminish my glory;	Which will tend to diminish his glory;	He shall die by a death that is gory,
For they would have taken my daughters	Though they would have taken his daughters	One of the cruellest slaughters
Over the billowy waters,	Over the billowy waters.	That ever were known in these waters;
If I hadn't, in elegant diction,	It's easy, in elegant diction,	And we'll finish his moral affliction
Indulged in an innocent fiction;	To call it an innocent fiction,	By a very complete malediction,
Which is not in the same category	But it comes in the same category	As a compliment valedictory,
As a regular terrible story.	As a regular terrible story.	If he's telling a terrible story.

KING. Although our dark career
   Sometimes involves the crime of stealing,
  We rather think that we're
   Not altogether void of feeling.
  Although we live by strife,
   We're always sorry to begin it,
  For what, we ask, is life
   Without a touch of Poetry in it? [49]

ALL (*kneeling*). [50]
   Hail, Poetry, thou heaven-born maid!
   Thou gildest e'en the pirate's trade:
   Hail, flowing fount of sentiment!
   All hail, Divine Emollient! (*All rise.*)

KING. You may go, for you're at liberty, our pirate rules protect you,
  And honorary members of our band we do elect you!

SAM.   For he is an orphan boy.
CHORUS. He is! Hurrah for the orphan boy.
GEN.   And it sometimes is a useful thing
    To be an orphan boy.
CHORUS. It is! Hurrah for the orphan boy!

   Oh, happy day, with joyous glee
   They will away and married be;
   Should it befall auspiciously,
   Our sisters all will bridesmaids be!

[46] *I rather imagine that as a general rule the vast majority of people of the General's age would be orphans. In this, however, General Stanley and I are more or less unique, neither, as I write, being an orphan. My mother turned ninety-one in 1960.*

The vocalizing of this passage is considerably exaggerated:

MAJOR-GENERAL

Lone - ly — e - e - e - e or—phan boy!

[47] *So, too, is the duet passage for the King and Samuel:*

SAMUEL and KING

lone - ly — or - or- or- or - or- or or — phan

PIRATES

boy. Poor fel - low!

*Singers take deep breath

[48] *They fall sobbing on each other's shoulders, big, red handkerchiefs in their hands with which they dab at their eyes. All the other Pirates do likewise.*

[49] *In this solo, phrasing is even more important than diction—and diction, as we know, is of paramount importance. For quite a long time— that is, until I read the book and noticed the comma after "what"—I was under the impression that the last few lines meant something entirely different from their actual sense:*

  For what we ask, is life
  Without a touch of Poetry in it.

Poor phrasing gave me a wrong meaning, and I never could understand why pirates, who were "not altogether void of feeling," should ask for life without a touch of poetry in it.

[50] *Sullivan's propensity for using organ music is well illustrated in his scoring of "Hail, Poetry." That he should have this propensity is not really strange; his early training set him off in this direction. What is strange is the variety of reactions to this ensemble number. Some say, "Why a hymn in the middle of a comic opera, especially this opera?"; others, "I think this is one of the loveliest things in the series."*

RUTH *enters and comes down to* FREDERIC

RUTH.   Oh, master, hear one word, I do implore you!
          Remember Ruth, your Ruth, who kneels before you!
CHORUS.   Yes, yes, remember Ruth, who kneels before you!
FRED.   (PIRATES *threaten* RUTH.) Away, you did deceive me!
CHORUS.   Away, you did deceive him!

RUTH.   Oh, do not leave me!
CHORUS.   Oh, do not leave her! [51]

FRED.   Away, you grieve me!
CHORUS.   Away, you grieve him!
FRED.   I wish you'd leave me!

(FREDERIC *casts* RUTH *from him.*)

CHORUS.   We wish you'd leave him!

ENSEMBLE

Pray observe the magnanimity
We ⎫
They ⎭ display to lace and dimity!
Never was such opportunity
To get married with impunity,
But ⎧ we ⎫ give up the felicity
    ⎩ they ⎭
Of unbounded domesticity,
Though a doctor of divinity
Resides in this vicinity.

[GIRLS *and* GENERAL *go up rocks, while* PIRATES *indulge in a wild dance of delight on stage. The* GENERAL *produces a British flag, and the* PIRATE KING *produces a black flag with skull and cross-bones. Enter* RUTH, *who makes a final appeal to* FREDERIC, *who casts her from him.*

END OF ACT I

[51] *What a delightful set of ruffians the Pirates are! Sort of sitting on the fence: one moment with Ruth, the next with Frederic; ready to go with the cat whichever way it jumps—and delighted at the final outcome!*

ACT II

SCENE.—*A Ruined Chapel by Moonlight. Ruined Gothic windows at* back. GENERAL STANLEY *discovered seated pensively, surrounded by his daughters.* [52]

CHORUS

Oh, dry the glistening tear
    That dews that martial cheek;
Thy loving children hear,
    In them thy comfort seek.
With sympathetic care
    Their arms around thee creep,
For oh, they cannot bear
    To see their father weep!

Enter MABEL

[52] *Most of the second act openings are beautiful or poignant, and that of The Pirates is perhaps the most beautiful of the whole series, both musically and visually.*

154

SOLO—MABEL

Dear father, why leave your bed
At this untimely hour,
When happy daylight is dead,
And darksome dangers lower?
See heaven has lit her lamp,
The midnight hour is past,
The chilly night air is damp,
And the dews are falling fast!
Dear father, why leave your bed
When happy daylight is dead?

FREDERIC *enters* [53]

MABEL. Oh, Frederic, cannot you, in the calm excellence of your wisdom, reconcile it with your conscience to say something that will relieve my father's sorrow?

FRED. I will try, dear Mabel. But why does he sit, night after night, in this draughty old ruin?

GEN. Why do I sit here? To escape from the pirates' clutches, I described myself as an orphan, and, heaven help me, I am no orphan! I come here to humble myself before the tombs of my ancestors, and to implore their pardon for having brought dishonour on the family escutcheon.

FRED. But you forget, sir, you only bought the property a year ago, and the stucco in your baronial hall is scarcely dry.

GEN. Frederic, in this chapel are ancestors: you cannot deny that. With the estate, I bought the chapel and its contents. I don't know whose ancestors they *were*, but I know whose ancestors they *are*, and I shudder to think that their descendant by purchase (if I may so describe myself) should have brought disgrace upon what, I have no doubt, was an unstained escutcheon.

FRED. Be comforted. Had you not acted as you did, these reckless men would assuredly have called in the nearest clergyman, and have married your large family on the spot.

GEN. I thank you for your proffered solace, but it is unavailing. I assure you, Frederic, that such is the anguish and remorse I feel at the abominable falsehood by which I escaped these easily deluded pirates, that I would go to their simple-minded [54] chief this very night and confess all, did I not fear that the consequences would be most disastrous to myself. [55] At what time does your expedition march against these scoundrels?

FRED. At eleven, and before midnight I hope to have atoned for my involuntary association with the pestilent scourges by sweeping them from the face of the earth—and then, dear Mabel, you will be mine!

GEN. Are your devoted followers at hand?

FRED. They are, they only wait my orders.

RECIT—GENERAL

Then, Frederic, let your escort lion-hearted
Be summoned to receive a General's blessing,
Ere they depart upon their dread adventure.

FRED. Dear, sir, they come.

Enter POLICE, *marching in single file. They form in line, facing audience*

[53] *If one can judge by contemporary drawings, Frederic wore a full beard and mustache. In one drawing in particular, in his second-act uniform, he also appears to be many years older than his twenty-one years. He is also depicted wearing a pillbox hat and a sword.*

Generally speaking, this costume impresses me more as being that of a Hussar than that of a Lieutenant of Police, which I have always presumed him to have become. Nor does it impress me as being the sort of dress in which to sally forth to do battle with a gang of desperate pirates. But in the same connection, no Major-General in his right mind would sally forth to a beach picnic in full ceremonial dress, cocked hat and sword, not to mention spurs!

[54] *Perhaps there should be a touch of the simple-minded in the Pirate King's make-up, too. (See Note 3.)*

[55] *The perfect armchair strategist.*

[56] Words and music on page 193.

[57] Sergeant. *In the New York opening night program he is given a name: Edward. In neither the Paignton or Opéra Comique program is he so dignified, nor has he ever been again in any subsequent program, so far as I know.*

[58] Emeutes. *A popular rising or disturbance. How Gilbert intended this to be pronounced is difficult to determine. According to the Oxford Dictionary the "eut" is pronounced as in the French word "peu," and would very nearly rhyme with "boots." However, for as far back as my memory takes me, it has always been pronounced "e-mutes" and "boots" made to rhyme with it: "b-yutes." Well, it cannot be gainsaid that there is a degree more humor in the latter, so it is within the bounds of possibility that it was Gilbert's intention.*

[59] More often than not two encores are demanded for this number. When this happens the vocal is picked up at this point, though the introductory music is played to enable the Police to make their re-entrance. And here's where the Sergeant's "trip up" on his first entrance pays off. For the first encore he very carefully jumps over the spot, and the General, intrigued by this, searches for the offending unevenness—and, of course, finds nothing. Also, in his rising irritability at the Police for "not going" he loses his patience to such a degree he actually swears ("But, damme! You don't go!"), shocking everyone present.

For the second encore the Sergeant most carefully and ostentatiously walks around the offending spot, and again General Stanley searches in vain for the danger spot. (See Note 61.)

[56] SONG—SERGEANT [57]

When the foeman bares his steel,
   Tarantara! tarantara!
We uncomfortable feel,
   Tarantara!
And we find the wisest thing,
   Tarantara! tarantara!
Is to slap our chests and sing
   Tarantara!
For when threatened with emeutes, [58]
   Tarantara! tarantara!
And your heart is in your boots,
   Tarantara!
There is nothing brings it round,
   Tarantara! tarantara!
Like the trumpet's martial sound,
   Tarantara! tarantara!
Tarantara-ra-ra-ra-ra!

ALL. Tarantara-ra-ra-ra-ra!

MABEL. Go, ye heroes, go to glory,
Though you die in combat gory,
Ye shall live in song and story.
  Go to immortality!
Go to death, and go to slaughter;
Die, and every Cornish daughter
With her tears your grave shall water.
  Go, ye heroes, go and die!

ALL.   Go, ye heroes, go and die!

POLICE. [59] Though to us it's evident,
   Tarantara! tarantara!
These intentions are well meant,
   Tarantara!
Such expressions don't appear,
   Tarantara! tarantara!
Calculated men to cheer,
   Tarantara!
Who are going to meet their fate
In a highly nervous state,
   Tarantara!
Still to us it's evident
These intentions are well meant.
   Tarantara!

EDITH. Go and do your best endeavour,
And before all links we sever,
We will say farewell for ever.
  Go to glory and the grave!

GIRLS. For your foes are fierce and ruthless,
False, unmerciful, and truthless.
Young and tender, old and toothless,
  All in vain their mercy crave.

SERG. We observe too great a stress,
On the risks that on us press,
And of reference a lack
To our chance of coming back.

Still, perhaps it would be wise
Not to carp or criticise,
For it's very evident
These attentions are well meant.

ALL.   Yes, to them it's evident
Our attentions are well meant.
                  Tarantara-ra-ra-ra-ra!

Go, ye heroes, go to glory, etc.

ENSEMBLE [60]

Chorus of all but Police	*Chorus of Police*
Go and do your best endeavour,	Such expressions don't appear,
And before all links we sever	Tarantara, tarantara!
We will say farewell for ever.	Calculated men to cheer,
Go to glory and the grave!	Tarantara!
For your foes are fierce and ruthless,	Who are going to their fate,
False, unmerciful, and truthless.	Tarantara, tarantara!
Young and tender, old and toothless,	In a highly nervous state—
All in vain their mercy crave.	Tarantara!
	We observe too great a stress,
	Tarantara, tarantara!
	On the risks that on us press,
	Tarantara!
	And of reference a lack,
	Tarantara, tarantara!
	To our chance of coming back,
	Tarantara!

GEN.   Away, away!
POLICE (*without moving*). Yes, yes, we go.
GEN.   These pirates slay.
POLICE.   Tarantara!
GEN.   Then do not stay.
POLICE.   Tarantara!
GEN.   Then why this delay?
POLICE.   All right—we go.
Yes, forward on the foe!
GEN.   Yes, but you *don't* go!
POLICE.   We go, we go!
Yes, forward on the foe!
GEN.   Yes, but you *don't* go! [61]
ALL.   At last they really go.

[MABEL *tears herself from* FREDERIC *and exits, followed by her sisters, consoling her. The* GENERAL *and others follow.* FREDERIC *remains.*]

RECIT—FRED.

Now for the pirates' lair! Oh, joy unbounded!
Oh, sweet relief! Oh, rapture unexampled!
At last I may atone, in some slight measure,
For the repeated acts of theft and pillage
Which, at a sense of duty's stern dictation,
I, circumstance's victim, have been guilty.

(KING *and* RUTH *appear at the window, armed.*)

KING.   Young Frederic! (*Covering him with pistol.*)
FRED.   Who calls?
KING.   Your late commander!

[60] The Ensemble here provides another example of Sullivan's genius for counterpoint, with the girls and the Police each singing a reprise of their own very different original melodies. If you want to do it yourself, let the gentlemen sing from "Though to us it's evident" (see page 196 of the score) while the ladies sing Mabel and Edith's passage, "Go, ye heroes, go to glory" (page 199), and continue for sixteen bars.

[61] General Stanley, reaching the same place where his indignation had risen before, remembers just in time to refrain from strong language: "Yes, but . . . bother . . . you don't go!" The trouble is that on each occasion one of his daughters starts to flirt with the Sergeant and he has had to admonish her severely (in pantomime, of course). But on this, the third time, as he goes forward to remove her from the embraces of the Sergeant, he trips over the nonexistent hump, lump or mamelon, thus presenting her with the opportunity of sneaking off to her place in the chorus behind his back.

RUTH.   And I, your little Ruth! (*Covering him with pistol.*)

FRED.   Oh, mad intruders,
How dare ye face me? Know ye not, oh rash ones,
That I have doomed you to extermination?

(KING *and* RUTH *hold a pistol to each ear.*)

KING.   Have mercy on us, hear us, ere you slaughter.

FRED.   I do not think I ought to listen to you.
Yet, mercy should alloy our stern resentment,
And so I will be merciful—say on!

TRIO—RUTH, KING, *and* FRED.

RUTH.   When you had left our pirate fold
                We tried to raise our spirits faint,
According to our customs old,
                With quips and quibbles quaint.
But all in vain the quips we heard,
                We lay and sobbed upon the rocks,
Until to somebody occurred
                A startling paradox.

FRED.   A paradox?

KING (*laughing*).   A paradox!

RUTH.   A most ingenious paradox!
                We've quips and quibbles heard in flocks,
But none to beat this paradox!
                Ha! ha! ha! ha! Ho! ho! ho! ho!

KING.   We knew your taste for curious quips,
                For cranks and contradictions queer,
And with the laughter on our lips,
                We wished you there to hear.
We said, "If we could tell it him,
                How Frederic would the joke enjoy!"
And so we've risked both life and limb
                To tell it to our boy.

FRED. (*interested*). That paradox? That paradox?

KING
and   } (*laughing*). That most ingenious paradox!
RUTH

                We've quips and quibbles heard in flocks,
                But none to beat that paradox!
                Ha! ha! ha! ha! Ho! ho! ho! ho!

CHANT—KING [62]

For some ridiculous reason, to which, however, I've no desire to be
        disloyal,
Some person in authority, I don't know who, very likely the Astronomer
        Royal,
Has decided that, although for such a beastly month as February,
        twenty-eight days as a rule are plenty,
One year in every four his days shall be reckoned as nine-and-twenty.
Through some singular coincidence—I shouldn't be surprised if it were
        owing to the agency of an ill-natured fairy—
You are the victim of this clumsy arrangement, having been born in
        leap-year, on the twenty-ninth of February, [63]
And so, by a simple arithmetical process, you'll easily discover,
That though you've lived twenty-one years, yet, if we go by birthdays,
        you're only five and a little bit over!

[62] *The King's chant is definitely sung in a monotone. It is a vocalized recitative.*

[63] *Frederic was born in the year 1856, in case you
don't wish to be bothered working it out for
yourself, and because of the copyright situation
he was born three times: once in America and
twice in England. How quaint the ways of paradox!*

RUTH
and } Ha! ha! ha! ha! Ho! ho! ho! ho!
KING
FRED. Dear me!
Let's see! (*counting on fingers*).
Yes, yes; with yours my figures do agree!

RUTH
and } Ha! ha! ha! Ho! ho! ho! ho! (FREDERIC *more amused than*
KING *any*.)

FRED. How quaint the ways of Paradox!
At common sense she gaily mocks!
Though counting in the usual way,
Years twenty-one I've been alive,
Yet, reckoning by my natal day, [64]
I am a little boy of five!

RUTH
and } He is a little boy of five! Ha! ha!
KING

A paradox, a paradox,
A most ingenious paradox!

RUTH
KING } Ha! ha! ha! ha! Ho! ho! ho! ho! (RUTH *and* KING *throw them-*
FRED. *selves back on seats, exhausted with laughter.*)

FRED. Upon my word, this is most curious—most absurdly whimsical! Five-and-a-quarter! No one would think it to look at me!

RUTH. You are glad now, I'll be bound, that you spared us. You would never have forgiven yourself when you discovered that you had killed *two of your comrades*.

FRED. My comrades?

KING (*rises*). I'm afraid you don't appreciate the delicacy of your position. You were apprenticed to us——

FRED. Until I reached my twenty-first year.

KING. No, until you reached your twenty-first *birthday* (*producing document*), and, going by birthdays, you are as yet only five-and-a-quarter.

FRED. You don't mean to say you are going to hold me to that?

KING. No, we merely remind you of the fact, and leave the rest to your sense of duty.

RUTH. Your sense of duty!

FRED. (*wildly*). Don't put it on that footing! As I was merciful to you just now, be merciful to me! I implore you not to insist on the letter of your bond just as the cup of happiness is at my lips!

RUTH. We insist on nothing; we content ourselves with pointing out to you *your duty*.

KING. Your duty!

FRED. (*after a pause*). Well, you have appealed to my sense of duty, and my duty is only too clear. I abhor your infamous calling; I shudder at the thought that I have ever been mixed up with it; but duty is before all—at any price I will do my duty.

KING. Bravely spoken! Come, you are one of us once more.

FRED. Lead on, I follow. (*Suddenly.*) Oh, horror!

KING. } What is the matter?
RUTH.

FRED. Ought I to tell you? No, no, I cannot do it; and yet, as one of your band——

KING. Speak out, I charge you by that sense of conscientiousness to which we have never yet appealed in vain.

FRED. General Stanley, the father of my Mabel——

KING. } Yes, yes!
RUTH.

[64] *There is a definite pause while he reckons on his fingers his actual age. Quite a number of Gilbert's characters are not particularly adept at arithmetic.*

FRED. He escaped from you on the plea that he was an orphan!

KING. He did!

FRED. It breaks my heart to betray the honoured father of the girl I adore, but as your apprentice I have no alternative. It is my duty to tell you that General Stanley is no orphan!

KING. } What!
RUTH. }

FRED. More than that, he never was one!

KING. Am I to understand that, to save his contemptible life, he dared to practise on our credulous simplicity? (FREDERIC *nods as he weeps*.) Our revenge shall be swift and terrible. We will go and collect our band and attack Tremorden Castle this very night.

FRED. But—stay——

KING. Not a word! He is doomed!

TRIO

KING *and* RUTH	FRED.
Away, away! my heart's on fire,	Away, away! ere I expire—
I burn this base deception to repay,	I find my duty hard to do to-day!
This very night my vengeance dire	My heart is filled with anguish dire,
Shall glut itself in gore. Away, away!	It strikes me to the core. Away, away!

KING.
With falsehood foul
He tricked us of our brides.
Let vengeance howl;
The Pirate so decides.
Our nature stern
He softened with his lies,
And, in return,
To-night the traitor dies.

ALL. Yes, yes! to-night the traitor dies.

RUTH. To-night he dies!

KING. Yes, or early to-morrow.

FRED. His girls likewise?

RUTH. They will welter in sorrow.

KING. The one soft spot

FRED. In their natures they cherish—

RUTH. And all who plot

KING. To abuse it shall perish! [65]

ALL. Yes, all who plot
To abuse it shall perish!
Away, away! etc.

[*Exeunt* KING *and* RUTH.

Enter MABEL

RECIT—MABEL

All is prepared, your gallant crew await you.
My Frederic in tears? It cannot be
That lion-heart quails at the coming conflict?

FRED. No, Mabel, no. A terrible disclosure
Has just been made! Mabel, my dearly-loved one,
I bound myself to serve the pirate captain [66]
Until I reached my one-and-twentieth birthday—

MABEL. But you *are* twenty-one?

FRED. I've just discovered
That I was born in leap-year, and that birthday
Will not be reached by me till 1940. [67]

[65] Open letter to the ghost of Gilbert:

Sir:

I have been questioned quite often regarding the interpretation of this lyric, especially from the point:

The one soft spot
In their natures they cherish—
And all who plot
To abuse it shall perish!

Please, Mr. Gilbert, to what, and to whom are they alluding? Whose "soft spot"? The Pirates'? The girls'?

It would clearly seem to be the Pirates' soft spot, since the King says: "Our nature stern he softened with his lies." Yet, if Frederic sings the line he should say: "In our natures we cherish," since, after all, Frederic is still a pirate, isn't he?

[66] *I wonder, does Frederic deliberately demote the Pirate King?*

[67] *An odd thought: If the opera were to be brought up to date the year of his birth would be 1936 and his coming of age—if we go by birthdays—would be 2020! In which case, how would that be sung:*

. . . and that birthday
Will not be reached by me till . . .
(Twenty twenty? or
Two thousand and twenty?)

MABEL. Oh, horrible! catastrophe appalling!
FRED. And so, farewell!
MABEL. No, no! Ah, Frederic, hear me.

DUET—MABEL *and* FRED.

MABEL. Stay, Frederic, stay!
  They have no legal claim,
  No shadow of a shame
  Will fall upon thy name.
 Stay, Frederic, stay!

FRED. Nay, Mabel, nay!
  To-night I quit these walls,
  The thought my soul appalls,
  But when stern Duty calls,
 I must obey.

MABEL. Stay, Frederic, stay!
FRED. Nay, Mabel, nay!
MABEL. They have no claim—
FRED. But Duty's name!
  The thought my soul appalls,
  But when stern Duty calls,
 I must obey.

BALLAD—MABEL [68]   [68] Words and music on page 201.

Ah, leave me not to pine
 Alone and desolate;
No fate seemed fair as mine,
 No happiness so great!
And nature, day by day,
 Has sung, in accents clear,
This joyous roundelay,
 "He loves thee—he is here.
  Fa-la, fa-la, fa-la."

FRED. Ah, must I leave thee here
 In endless night to dream,
Where joy is dark and drear,
 And sorrow all supreme!
Where nature, day by day,
 Will sing, in altered tone,
This weary roundelay,
 "He loves thee—he is gone.
  Fa-la, fa-la, fa-la."

FRED. In 1940 I of age shall be,
I'll then return, and claim you—I declare it!
MABEL.   It seems so long!
FRED. Swear that, till then, you will be true to me.
MABEL.   Yes, I'll be strong!
By all the Stanleys dead and gone, I swear it!

ENSEMBLE

Oh, here is love, and here is truth,
 And here is food for joyous laughter.
He⎱ will be faithful to ⎰his⎱ sooth
She⎰   ⎱her⎰
Till we are wed, and even after.

[FREDERIC *rushes to window and leaps out*

THE PIRATES OF PENZANCE

[69] *In the original libretto the line read: "Yes, I am brave!" Today, however, as for many years now, the accepted version is "No! I'll be brave!" (as sung in the D'Oyly Carte Company).*

[70] *Whereas Mabel speaks her lines, as does the Sergeant up to a point, the responses by the chorus are intoned on one note. This goes on until the Sergeant reaches ". . . to capture these pirates alone." From that point through ". . . so dear to us all" is intoned on the same note that the Policemen have been using, almost to the very end. He then picks up in an almost matter-of-fact speaking voice. The "It is!" of the chorus is an octave lower than before.*

Sullivan is at his musically whimsical best here. Not that it takes a great deal of talent to compose a monotone, but it does require a first-rate appreciation of humorous musical possibilities to think of presenting spoken dialogue in such an absurd and beguiling manner.

[71] *Words and music on page 203.*

MABEL (*almost fainting*). No, I am brave! [69] Oh, family descent,
How great thy charm, thy sway how excellent!
Come, one and all, undaunted men in blue,
A crisis, now, affairs are coming to!

Enter Police, marching in single file

SERG.   Though in body and in mind,
                        Tarantara, tarantara!
              We are timidly inclined,
                        Tarantara!
              And anything but blind,
                        Tarantara, tarantara!
              To the danger that's behind,
                        Tarantara!
              Yet, when the danger's near,
                        Tarantara, tarantara!
              We manage to appear,
                        Tarantara!
              As insensible to fear
              As anybody here.
                        Tarantara, tarantara-ra-ra-ra-ra!

MABEL. Sergeant, approach! Young Frederic was to have led you to death and glory. [70]

ALL. That is not a pleasant way of putting it.

MABEL. No matter; he will not so lead you, for he has allied himself once more with his old associates.

ALL. He has acted shamefully!

MABEL. You speak falsely. You know nothing about it. He has acted nobly.

ALL. He has acted nobly!

MABEL. Dearly as I loved him before, his heroic sacrifice to his sense of duty has endeared him to me tenfold. He has done his duty. I will do mine. Go ye and do yours.   [*Exit* MABEL.

ALL. Right oh!

SERG. This is perplexing.

ALL. We cannot understand it at all.

SERG. Still, as he is actuated by a sense of duty——

ALL. That makes a difference, of course. At the same time we repeat, we cannot understand it at all.

SERG. No matter; our course is clear. We must do our best to capture these pirates alone. It is most distressing to us to be the agents whereby our erring fellow-creatures are deprived of that liberty which is so dear to all—but we should have thought of that before we joined the Force.

ALL. We should!

SERG. It is too late now!

ALL. It is!

SONG—SERGEANT [71]

SERG.   When a felon's not engaged in his employment—
ALL.   His employment,
SERG.   Or maturing his felonious little plans—
ALL.   Little plans,
SERG.   His capacity for innocent enjoyment—
ALL.   'Cent enjoyment
SERG.   Is just as great as any honest man's—
ALL.   Honest man's.
SERG.   Our feelings we with difficulty smother—

ALL.	'Culty smother
SERG.	When constabulary duty's to be done—
ALL.	To be done.
SERG.	Ah, take one consideration with another—
ALL.	With another,
SERG.	A policeman's lot is not a happy one.
ALL.	When constabulary duty's to be done— To be done, The policeman's lot is not a happy one.

SERG.	When the enterprising burglar's not a-burgling—
ALL.	Not a-burgling,
SERG.	When the cut-throat isn't occupied in crime—
ALL.	'Pied in crime,
SERG.	He loves to hear the little brook a-gurgling—
ALL.	Brook a-gurgling,
SERG.	And listen to the merry village chime—
ALL.	Village chime.
SERG.	When the coster's [72] finished jumping on his mother—
ALL.	On his mother,
SERG.	He loves to lie a-basking in the sun—
ALL.	In the sun.
SERG.	Ah, take one consideration with another—
ALL.	With another,
SERG.	The policeman's lot is not a happy one.
ALL. [73]	When constabulary duty's to be done— To be done, The policeman's lot is not a happy one— Happy one.

(*Chorus of Pirates without, in the distance.*)

A rollicking band of pirates we,
Who, tired of tossing on the sea,
Are trying their hand at a burglaree,
With weapons grim and gory.

SERG. Hush, hush! I hear them on the manor poaching,
With stealthy step the pirates are approaching.

(*Chorus of Pirates, resumed nearer.*)

We are not coming for plate or gold—
A story General Stanley's told—
We seek a penalty fifty-fold,
For General Stanley's story.

POLICE.	They seek a penalty—
PIRATES (*without*).	Fifty-fold,
	We seek a penalty—
POLICE.	Fifty-fold,
ALL.	We } They } seek a penalty fifty-fold, For General Stanley's story.
SERG.	They come in force, with stealthy stride, Our obvious course is now—to hide.

[*Police conceal themselves. As they do so, the Pirates are seen appearing at ruined window. They enter cautiously, [74] and come down stage. SAMUEL is laden with burglarious tools and pistols, etc.*

A policeman's lot is not a happy one.

[72] Coster. *In this case, short for "costermonger." I really take issue with Gilbert over this. A "coster" is a small French apple. A costermonger is a man who peddles them for sale, though in the last forty years, at least, the term costermonger has come to cover a general vender of all fruits and greenstuffs. But as a rule, he is a well-behaved and generous man, even though he be of rude speech.*

[73] *So great was the popularity of this song that it invariably received two encores, and it is said of Rutland Barrington, the original Sergeant of Police, that he actually approached Gilbert and suggested that he write a special encore verse. Gilbert's reply was: "Mr. Barrington, 'encore' means 'sing it again'!"*

[74] *They enter cautiously and on tiptoe—but see Note 76.*

THE PIRATES OF PENZANCE

[75] Words and music on page 205.

[76] *As soon as the Pirates begin to sing double-forte they promptly begin to stamp their feet:*

    With cat-like tread, (stamp!)
      Upon our prey we steal, (stamp!)
    In silence dread (stamp!)
      Our cautious way we feel. (stamp!)
        etc.

[77] *In case some readers are still in doubt, Sullivan was the original composer of this tune, and not some college youths, as my dresser in Seattle in 1929 so fondly believed. The words "Hail, hail, the gang's all here" were in all probability adapted to the tune sometime during the run in New York. But the tune is Sullivan's, believe me.*

[78] *In a sketch contemporary with the period in which this opera was written, General Stanley is depicted wearing not only a dressing gown and carrying a lighted candle but also wearing gold-striped trousers (and, presumably, spurs) and his cocked hat! The accepted headwear today is a nightcap, sleeping or bed socks, and felt carpet slippers. I must say that I like the idea of the cocked hat. I get an immediate picture of the General in bed—apart from his terrible story, no wonder he lay upon a sleepless bed and tossed and turned and moaned.*

CHORUS—PIRATES [75] (*very loud*) [76]

    With cat-like tread,
      Upon our prey we steal,
    In silence dread
      Our cautious way we feel.
    No sound at all,
      We never speak a word,
    A fly's foot-fall
      Would be distinctly heard—

POLICE (*pianissimo*).   Tarantara, tarantara!

PIRATES. So stealthily the pirate creeps,
    While all the household soundly sleeps.
    Come, friends, who plough the sea, [77]
      Truce to navigation,
      Take another station;
    Let's vary piracee
    With a little burglaree!

POLICE (*pianissimo*).   Tarantara, tarantara!

SAM. (*distributing implements to various members of the gang*).
    Here's your crowbar and your centrebit,
    Your life-preserver—you may want to hit;
    Your silent matches, your dark lantern seize,
    Take your file and your skeletonic keys.

Enter KING, FREDERIC, *and* RUTH

ALL (*fortissimo*). With cat-like tread, etc.

RECIT

FRED.   Hush, hush, not a word! I see a light inside!
    The Major-General comes, so quickly hide!

PIRATES.   Yes, yes, the Major-General comes!

[*Exeunt* KING, FREDERIC, SAMUEL, *and* RUTH.

POLICE.   Yes, yes, the Major-General comes!

GEN. (*entering in dressing-gown, carrying a light*). [78]
    Yes, yes, the Major-General comes!

SOLO—GENERAL

Tormented with the anguish dread
    Of falsehood unatoned,
I lay upon my sleepless bed,
    And tossed and turned and groaned.
The man who finds his conscience ache
    No peace at all enjoys,
And as I lay in bed awake
    I thought I heard a noise.

PIRATES. } He thought he heard a noise—ha! ha!
POLICE. } He thought he heard a noise—ha! ha! (*Very loud.*)

GEN.   No, all is still
       In dale, on hill;
       My mind is set at ease.
       So still the scene—
       It must have been
       The sighing of the breeze.

BALLAD—GENERAL [79]

Sighing softly to the river
　Comes the loving breeze,
Setting nature all a-quiver,
　Rustling through the trees—

ALL. 　　　　　　　　　　Through the trees.
GEN. 　And the brook, in rippling measure,
　Laughs for very love,
While the poplars, in their pleasure,
　Wave their arms above.

POLICE. ⎫ Yes, the trees, for very love,
and ⎬ Wave their leafy arms above,
PIRATES. ⎭ 　River, river, little river,
　May thy loving prosper ever.
Heaven speed thee, poplar tree,
　May thy wooing happy be.

GEN. 　Yet, the breeze is but a rover;
　When he wings away,
Brook and poplar mourn a lover!
　Sighing well-a-day!
ALL. 　　　　　　　　　　Well-a-day!
GEN. 　Ah! the doing and undoing,
　That the rogue could tell!
When the breeze is out a-wooing,
　Who can woo so well?

POLICE. ⎫ Shocking tales the rogue could tell
and ⎬ Nobody can woo so well.
PIRATES. ⎭ 　Pretty brook, thy dream is over,
　For thy love is but a rover!
Sad the lot of poplar trees,
　Courted by the fickle breeze!

[Enter the GENERAL's *daughters, all in white peignoirs and
night-caps, and carrying lighted candles*

GIRLS. 　Now what is this, and what is that, and why does father leave
　　his rest
At such a time of night as this, so very incompletely dressed?
Dear father is, and always was, the most methodical of men!
It's his invariable rule to go to bed at half-past ten.
What strange occurrence can it be that calls dear father from
　his rest
At such a time of night as this, so very incompletely
　dressed? [80]

Enter KING, SAMUEL, *and* FREDERIC

KING. 　Forward, my men, and seize that General there!
　　　　　(*They seize the* GENERAL.)
GIRLS. 　The pirates! the pirates! Oh, despair!
PIRATES. Yes, we're the pirates, so despair!
GEN. 　Frederic here! Oh, joy! Oh, rapture!
　Summon your men and effect their capture!
MABEL. 　Frederic, save us!
FRED. 　　　　　　Beautiful Mabel,
　I would if I could, but I am not able. [81]

[79] Among the reasons that the role of General
Stanley is a difficult one is the fact that Sullivan
never seemed quite to make up his mind whether
the General was a baritone, bass or tenor. His
patter song is baritone, the line given him in
"Hail, Poetry" is with the bass, and in "Sighing
Softly" he is a tenor. Most confusing.

When the breeze is out a-wooing

[80] *In trousers, boots (and spurs) and cocked hat?*

[81] *Two of the Pirates have seized Frederic and are
by this time holding pistols to his head.*

PIRATES. He's telling the truth, he is not able.
KING.   With base deceit
        You worked upon our feelings!
    Revenge is sweet,
        And flavours all our dealings!
    With courage rare
        And resolution manly,
    For death prepare,
        Unhappy General Stanley.

MABEL (*wildly*). Is he to die, unshriven—unannealed?
GIRLS.   Oh, spare him!
MABEL. Will no one in his cause a weapon wield?
GIRLS.   Oh, spare him!
POLICE (*springing up*). Yes, we are here, though hitherto concealed! [82]
GIRLS.   Oh, rapture!
POLICE. So to the Constabulary, pirates, yield!
GIRLS.   Oh, rapture!

[*A struggle ensues between Pirates and Police. Eventually the Police are overcome, and fall prostrate, the Pirates standing over them with drawn swords.*

CHORUS OF POLICE AND PIRATES

    You ⎫
    We ⎭ triumph now, for well we trow
    Our mortal career's cut short,
  No pirate band will take its stand
    At the Central Criminal Court.
SERG. To gain a brief advantage you've contrived.
    But your proud triumph will not be long-lived.
KING. Don't say you are orphans, for we know that game.
SERG. On your allegiance we've a stronger claim—
    We charge you yield, in Queen Victoria's name!
KING (*baffled*). You do!
POLICE.   We do!
    We charge you yield, in Queen Victoria's name!

      [*Pirates kneel, Police stand over them triumphantly.*

KING. We yield at once, with humbled mien, [83]
    Because, with all our faults, we love our Queen.
POLICE. Yes, yes, with all their faults, they love their Queen.
GIRLS. Yes, yes, with all, etc.

    [*Police, holding Pirates by the collar, take out handkerchiefs and weep.*

GEN. Away with them, and place them at the bar!

Enter RUTH

RUTH. One moment! let me tell you who they are.
    They are no members of the common throng;
    They are all noblemen who have gone wrong!
GEN. No Englishman unmoved that statement hears,
    Because, with all our faults, we love our House of Peers.

RECIT—GENERAL

    I pray you, pardon me, ex-Pirate King,
    Peers will be peers, and youth will have its fling.

[82] *For some reason or other, the Sergeant of Police is twirling a ratchet type of noisemaker around and around. Perhaps it's on the theory that sudden and unexpected noise will divert the enemy and make their overthrow so much the easier? Alas, the plans of mice and men and police sergeants gang aft agley. The truncheon is no match for the sword.*

[83] *It is said that Gilbert, in view of the fact that he had been taken to task over his lampooning of a high-ranking Cabinet Minister and of Her Majesty's Royal Navy in Pinafore, wrote these words deliberately in the hope that they would put an end to any suggestion of his slighting Her Majesty in any possible way.*

An interesting thought. Should anyone in the future decide to bring the opera up to date, in whose name would the pirates be charged to yield? And suppose it were a king on the throne? "King" does not rhyme with "mien."

Perhaps the line could be changed to something like this:

With all our faults, we can but humbly sing,
We yield at once because we love our King.

Resume your ranks and legislative duties,
And take my daughters, all of whom are beauties.

FINALE—MABEL, EDITH AND ENSEMBLE [84]

Poor wandering ones! [85]
    Though ye have surely strayed,
    Take heart of grace.
    Your steps retrace,
Poor wandering ones!

Poor wandering ones!
    If such poor love as ours
    Can help you find
    True peace of mind,
Why, take it, it is yours!
    Poor wandering ones! etc.

CURTAIN

[84] *Part of the scoring of the finale is given to a duet between Mabel and Edith. The printed script does not indicate this*

[85] *During the singing of the finale General Stanley makes his way around the stage, conferring his blessing on the pirates and his daughters. He reaches the spot where the Sergeant is making eyes at Ruth, attempts to congratulate him for a job well done, but "Edward" promptly half turns his back and sticks his hand out for a tip. The General finds a few loose pennies in his dressing-gown pocket, hands them over, and is blessing Frederic and Mabel as the*

Curtain Falls

When Frederic Was a Little Lad

With speed, but ponderously

RUTH

1. When
2. I
3. I

Fred-'ric was a — lit-tle lad He — proved so brave and dar-ing, His
was a stu-pid nur'-s'ry maid, On — break-ers al-ways steer-ing, And I
soon found out, be-yond all doubt, The — scope of this dis-as-ter, But I

fa-ther thought he'd — 'pren-tice him To — some ca-reer sea-far-ing. I —
did not catch the — word a-right, Through be-ing hard of hear-ing; Mis-
had-n't the face to re-turn to my place, And — break it to my mas-ter. A —

was, a-las! his — nur-s'ry maid, And — so it fell to my lot To
tak-ing my in-struc-tions, which With-in my brain did gy-rate, To I
nur-s'ry maid is — not a-fraid Of — what you peo-ple call work, So I

take and   bind the_   prom-is-ing   boy   Ap - pren-tice to a   pi-lot!   A
took and   bound this_   prom-is-ing   boy   Ap - pren-tice to a   pi-rate!   A
made up my mind to_   go   as a   kind   Of pi - rat-i-cal maid-of-_ all-work. And

life   not   bad   for   a   har - dy   lad,   Though_   sure - ly   not   a
sad   mis - take   it___   was   to   make,   And_   doom   him   to   a
that   is   how   you___   find   me   now,   A ___   mem - ber   of   your

high   lot,   Though   I'm   a   nurse, you   might do worse Than make your boy a
vile   lot.   I   bound   him   to   a   pi - rate, you!   In - stead   of   to   a
shy   lot,   Which you   would-n't   have found, had   he been bound Ap - pren-tice to a

1.-2.   3.

pi - lot!
pi - lot!
         pi - lot!

Oh Better Far to Live and Die

Moderately fast

_f_ marcato

_mp_ PIRATE KING

_p_

1. Oh   bet - ter far   to   live_ and die
2. When I   sal - ly forth to   seek_ my prey   I

Un - der the brave black flag I fly, Than play a sanc - ti - mo - nious part, With a
help my - self in a roy - al way; I sink a few more ships, it's true, Than a

Chorus *You are! Hur- rah for our Pi - rate*

be a Pi - rate King!_ For I am a Pi - rate King!_

King! ——— PIRATE KING

And it is, it is a glo - rious thing_ To be a Pi - rate

CHORUS   PIRATE KING and CHORUS

King! It is! Hur - rah for our Pi - rate King! Hur - rah for {the / our} Pi - rate

*King!*_

Climbing Over Rocky Mountain

Gracefully and not too fast

CHORUS of GIRLS

Climb-ing o - ver— rock-y moun-tain, Skip-ping riv-u - let and foun-tain,

Pass-ing where the— wil - lows— quiv - er,

bright sea - shore they gain; Scal-ing rough and_ rug-ged pass-es,

Climb the har - dy_ lit - tle lass-es Till_ the _ bright sea -

shore they gain!

Oh, Is There Not One Maiden Breast

Slowly and tenderly

FREDERIC

Oh,

is there not one maid - en breast Which does not feel the mor - al

beau - ty Of mak - ing world - ly in - ter - est Sub - or - di - nate to sense of

duty? Who would not give up will-ing-ly All mat-ri-mo-nial am-

bi - tion, To res - cue such an one as I From his un-for-tu-nate po-

si - tion? From his __ po - si - tion, To res - cue such an one as I From

his __ un-for-tu - nate po - si - tion? A - las! there's not one

maid-en breast Which seems to feel the mor-al beau-ty Of mak-ing world-ly

in - ter - est Sub - or - di - nate to sense of du - ty!

FREDERIC

Oh, is there not one maid - en here Whose home - ly face and bad com - plex - ion Have caused all hope to dis - ap - pear Of ev - er win - ning man's af - fec - tion? To such an one, if such there be, I swear by Heav - en's arch a - bove you, If you will cast your eyes on me, How-

ev-er plain you be, I'll love you! How-ev-er plain you be, If
you will cast your eyes on me, How-ev-er plain you be, I'll love you, I'll
love you, I'll love, I'll love you.

CHORUS of GIRLS

A-las! there's not one
maid-en here Whose home-ly face and bad com-plex-ion Have caused all hope to
dis-ap-pear Of ev-er win-ning man's af-fec-tion!

follow the voice

Poor Wandering One

Moderate Waltz tempo

MABEL

Poor wan - d'ring one!

Tho' thou hast sure - ly strayed, Take heart of grace, Thy steps re-

trace, Poor wan - d'ring one! Poor

wan - d'ring one! If such poor love as mine

Can help thee find True peace of mind, Why, take it,

it ___ is thine! **f**CHORUS of GIRLS Take heart, no dan-ger

lowers; Take an - y heart ___ but ours! **p**MABEL Take

heart, fair days will shine;___ Take an - y heart, take mine!

fCHORUS Take heart, no dan-ger lowers; Take ___

181

Model of a Modern Major-General

Cheerfully

ff

MAJOR-GENERAL

pp   *p*

1. I am the ver-y mod-el of a mod-ern Ma-jor-Gin-er-al; I've
2. I know our myth-ic his-to-ry, King Ar-thur's and Sir Car-a-doc's; I

in-for-ma-tion veg-e-ta-ble, an-i-mal and min-er-al; I
an-swer hard a-cros-tics, I've a pret-ty taste for par-a-dox; I

With man-y cheer-ful facts a-bout the square of the hy-pot-e-nuse.
And whis-tle all the airs from that in-fer-nal non-sense, Pin-a-fore!

CHORUS

With man-y cheer-ful facts a-bout the square of the hy-pot-e-nuse, With
And whis-tle all the airs from that in-fer-nal non-sense, Pin-a-fore, And

man-y cheer-ful facts a-bout the square of the hy-pot-e-nuse, With
whis-tle all the airs from that in-fer-nal non-sense, Pin-a-fore, And

man-y cheer-ful facts a-bout the square of the hy-pot-e-pot-e-
whis-tle all the airs from that in-fer-nal non-sense, Pin-a-pin-a-

MAJOR-GENERAL

nuse.
fore.
I'm ver-y good at in-te-gral and
Then I can write a wash-ing bill in

differ - en - tial cal - cu - lus; I know the sci - en - tif - ic names of
Bab - y - lon - ic cu - nei - form, And tell you ev - 'ry de - tail of Ca -

be - ings an - i - mal - cu - lous.⎫
rac - ta - cus - 's u - ni - form.⎭ In short, in mat - ters veg - e - ta - ble,

an - i - mal and min - er - al, I am the ver - y mod - el of a mod - ern Ma - jor - Gin - er - al!

CHORUS

In short, in mat - ters veg - e - ta - ble, an - i - mal and min - er - al, He

is the ver - y mod - el of a mod - ern Ma - jor - Gin - er - al!

188

Slower

3. In fact, when I know what is meant by "mam-e-lon" and "rave-lin"; When I can tell at sight a Mau-ser ri-fle from a jave-lin; When such af-fairs as sor-ties and sur-pris-es I'm more war-y at, And when I know pre-cise-ly what is meant by "com-mis-sar-i-at"; When I have learnt what pro-gress has been

made in mod-ern gun-ner-y; When I know more of tac-tics than a

nov-ice in a nun-ner-y; In short, when I've a smat-ter-ing of

el-e-men-tal strat-e-gy,

Fast again

You'll

say a bet-ter Ma-jor-Gen-er-al has nev-er sat a gee;

CHORUS

You'll say a bet-ter Ma-jor-Gen-er-al has nev-er sat a gee, You'll

say a bet - ter Ma - jor - Gen - er - al has nev - er sat a gee, You'll

poco a poco cresc.

say a bet - ter Ma - jor - Gen - er - al has nev - er sat a, sat a

gee!

MAJOR-GENERAL

4. For my

mil - i - tar - y knowl - edge, tho' I'm pluck - y and ad - ven - tur - y, Has

on - ly been brought down to the be - gin - ning of the cen - tu - ry, But

still, in mat-ters veg-e-ta-ble, an-i-mal and min-er-al, I

am the ver-y mod-el of a mod-ern Ma-jor-Gen-er-al.

CHORUS

But still, in mat-ters veg-e-ta-ble, an-i-mal and min-er-al He

is the ver-y mod-el of a mod-ern Ma-jor-Gen-er-al.

When the Foeman Bares His Steel

Spirited march tempo

SERGEANT

When the foe-man bares his steel, Ta-ran-ta-ra, ta-ran-ta-ra! We un-com-fort-a-ble feel! Ta-ran-ta-ra! And we find the wis-est thing, Ta-ran-ta-ra, ta-ran-ta-ra! Is to slap our chests and sing Ta-ran-ta-ra! For when threat-en'd with e-meutes, Ta-ran-ta-

SERG.   Police   SERG.

ra, ta-ran-ta-ra! And your heart is in your boots, Ta-ran-ta-ra! There is

noth-ing brings it round, Like the trum-pet's mar-tial sound, Like the trum-pet's mar-tial

sound, Ta-ran-ta-ra, ta-ran-ta-ra, ta-ran-ta-ra, ta-ran-ta-ra, ta-ran-ta-ra, ta-ran-ta-

ra, ta-ran-ta-ra, ta-ran-ta-ra, ta-ran-ta-ra, ta-ran-ta-ra, ta-ran-ta-ra, ta-ran-ta-

ra, ta-ran-ta-ra, ta-ran-ta-ra, ra, ra, ta-ran-ta-ra!

194

die! Go, ye he-roes, go__ and die! Go, ye he-roes, go__ and die! Tho' to

us it's ev-i-dent, Ta-ran-ta-ra, ta-ran-ta-ra! These at-ten-tions are well meant, Ta-ran-ta-

ra! Such ex-pres-sions don't ap-pear, Ta-ran-ta-ra, ta-ran-ta-ra! Cal-cu-

lat-ed men to cheer, Ta-ran-ta-ra! Who are going to meet their fate In a

high-ly nerv-ous state, Ta-ran-ta-ra, ta-ran-ta-ra, ta-ran-ta-ra! Still to

us it's ev-i-dent These at-ten-tions are well meant. Ta-ran-ta-ra, ta-ran-ta-ra, ta-ran-ta-

ra! Go___ and do your best___ en-deav - our,

And___ be-fore all links we sev - er, We___ will say fare-

well___ for-ev - er. Go to glo - ry and the grave!

Go to glo - ry and the grave! For your foes are fierce and ruth-less, False, un-

mer-ci-ful, and truth-less. Young and ten-der, old and tooth-less, All in vain their mer-cy crave!

SERG.

We ob-serve too great a stress On the

risks that on us press, And of ref-er-ence a-lack To our chance of com-ing back; Still, per-

haps it would be wise Not to carp or crit-i-cise, For it's ver-y ev-i-dent These at-

POLICE

ten-tions are well meant. Yes, it's ver-y ev-i-dent These at-ten-tions are well meant, Ev-i-

198

SERG. and POLICE

dent, yes, well meant, ev - i - dent, Ah, yes, well meant!

MABEL and EDITH

Go,_____ ye he - roes, go _____ to glo - ry! Though _____ ye die_ in com_ bat

gor - - y, Ye _____ shall live in song_____ and sto - ry.

Go _____ to im - mor - tal - i - ty! Go to death,___ and go to

slaugh - ter; Die,___ and ev - 'ry Cor - nish daugh - ter With her

tears your grave shall wa - ter. Go,— ye he-roes, go and die! Go, ye he - roes, go to im - mor - tal - i - ty! Go ye he - roes, go to im - mor - tal - i - ty! Tho' ye die in com-bat gor-y, Ye shall live in song and sto - ry; Go to im - mor - tal - i - ty!

Ah, Leave Me Not to Pine

A Policeman's Lot Is Not a Happy One

Moderately fast

SERGEANT

CHORUS of POLICE   SERG.

1. When a fel-on's not en-gaged in his em-ploy-ment (his em-ploy-ment), Or ma-
2. When the en-ter-pris-ing burg-lar's not a-burg-ling (not a-burg-ling), When the

CHORUS   SERG.

tur-ing his fe-lo-nious lit-tle plans (lit-tle plans), His ca-pac-i-ty for in-no-cent en-
cut-throat is-n't oc-cu-pied in crime ('pied in crime), He loves to hear the lit-tle brook a-

CHORUS   SERG.   CHORUS   SERG.

joy-ment ('cent en-joy-ment) Is just as great as an-y hon-est man's (hon-est man's). Our
gur-gling (brook a-gur-gling) And lis-ten to the mer-ry vil-lage chime (vil-lage chime). When the

feel-ings we with dif-fi-cul-ty smoth-er ('cul-ty smoth-er) When con - stab-u-lar-y du-ty's to be
cos-ter's fin-ished jump-ing on his moth-er (on his moth-er), He loves to lie a-bask-ing in the

done (to be done). Ah, take one con-sid-er-a-tion with an-oth-er (with an-oth-er), A po-
sun (in the sun).

lice-man's lot is not a hap-py one. Ah, When con - stab-u-lar-y du-ty's to be

done, to be done, A po-lice-man's lot is not a hap-py one, hap-py one.

one, hap-py one!

With Catlike Tread

Strong march tempo

mf CHORUS of PIRATES

With cat - like tread Up - on our prey we steal, In si - lence dread Our

cau - tious way we feel! No sound at all, We nev - er speak a word;

fly's foot - fall Would be dis - tinct - ly heard! Ta - ran - ta - ra,

Chorus of Police

ta - ran - ta -

pi - ra - cee, ___ With a lit - tle bur - gla - ree!

SAMUEL

Here's your ___ crow-bar and ___ your ___ cen - tre-bit, Your

life ___ pre - serv - er, you may want to hit.

Your si - lent match-es, your dark lan-tern seize! ___

Take your file ___ and your skel-e - ton-ic keys! Ta-ran-ta-ra! With cat-like

Police   PIRATES

Police PIRATES

tread, Ta-ran-ta-ra! In si-lence dread.
With

cat-like tread Up-on our prey we steal, In si-lence dread Our

cau-tious way we feel! No sound at all, We nev-er speak a word; A

fly's foot-fall Would be dis-tinct-ly heard! Come, friends, who

plough the sea, Truce to nav-i-ga-tion, Take an-oth-er sta-tion;

Let's var - y pi - ra - cee— With a lit - tle bur - gla -

ree! With cat - like tread Up - on our prey we

steal, In si - lence dread Our cau - tious way we

feel!

209

ACCORDING to what has been described as "an hitherto unpublished letter (November 7, 1880) to his friend, the critic, Clement Scott," Gilbert said that he had to rewrite The Sorcerer for early performance, and had to get it finished quickly and that he was upset over this as he had already written two thirds of it and now had to start all over again. Reginald Allen, in his foreword to Patience in The First Night Gilbert and Sullivan, states that there was no question that The Sorcerer was inspired by the Bab Ballad "The Rival Curates."

Isaac Goldberg, in his biography, The Story of Gilbert and Sullivan, writes: "Gilbert and Carte were fanatical in the lengths they would go to foil American pirates. . . . It may well be that Gilbert's reference to rewriting The Sorcerer was a deliberate red herring for Clement Scott to spread among the press. There is no evidence of any kind that the three partners had any concern with the reviving of The Sorcerer at this time, let alone rewriting it."

I myself can see no resemblance between "The Rival Curates" and The Sorcerer other than the fact that Dr. Daly, like the Curate in the Ballad, plays on a wind instrument. Dr. Daly plays a flageolet, the Curate an airy flute. The rest of The Sorcerer deals with the efforts of an amorous-minded young gent to influence everyone so that all may be "coupled in matrimony without distinction of rank." To this end he employs a magician and a love potion. I find no reference to magician or love potion in "The Rival Curates."

I do, however, see a strong resemblance between the Ballad and Patience. Another possibility would seem to be that, when writing to Scott, Gilbert inadvertently penned the words The Sorcerer when he really meant Patience, or whatever title he had in mind for his new work (if he had a title in mind at that time). Scott apparently never thought of this, nor did Mr. Goldberg nor anyone else, and a misconception has grown out of it.

In a letter to Arthur Sullivan, dated just six days prior to the one addressed to Scott, Gilbert says that he would very much like to see him about a "new piece" which is two-thirds finished but about which he is having some qualms. His qualms concerned the possible public reaction to the portrayal of the clergy in a comic opera in which two rival curates compete for the hand of a "dairy-maid." In all probability these qualms arose from criticism leveled at him for his handling of Dr. Daly in The Sorcerer. It seems likely that these qualms and the probable cause were so much in his mind that he penned the words to Scott unthinkingly and failed to catch his error.

Later on in his letter to Sullivan he alludes to his "original idea" in which the two rivals were to be long-haired poets—aesthetics—with a chorus of devoted followers of the aesthetic cult. It has, I believe, been generally considered that the "poet" idea was his second thought, but this letter would seem to belie that.

Further evidence as to which opera was based on the Ballad appears in an introduction which Gilbert wrote for a new American edition of Patience in which he expressly states that the idea for the theme of Patience lay in his Bab Ballad, "The Rival Curates." He then goes on to say (and this appears to give the lie to his reference to his "original idea of two long-haired poets" in his letter to Sullivan) that his first idea had been for the two rivals to be curates from adjoining parishes, but the necessity for "protecting [himself] from a charge of irreverence . . . becomes a stumbling block."

Still further evidence: There is a scene in Patience wherein Bunthorne threatens Grosvenor with a formidable curse ("a nephew's curse") if he does not alter his mode and manner immediately. In alarm, Grosvenor agrees, having long wished for an excuse to do this very thing. Now the excuse has come—but he does it "on compulsion."

For "Bunthorne" read "Clayton Hooper"; for "Grosvenor" read "Hopley Porter"; and then read the Bab Ballad, "The Rival Curates," the twenty-first verse of which is:

> For years I've longed for some
> Excuse for this revulsion:
> Now that excuse has come
> I do it on compulsion.

Well, if I've convinced no one else, I've convinced myself that The Sorcerer was not connected with "The Rival Curates," but that Patience was.

But enough of babble—come!

Patience is a lot of fun, and as Bunthorne I never failed to enjoy myself when appearing in the role. I even enjoyed rehearsing it.

At one rehearsal our stage director pointed out to me that I was going somewhat overboard in my portrayal of this poseur-charlatan.

"Remember," he said, "remember that Bunthorne is a gentleman."

From then on, at all rehearsals, I went through the part in as gentlemanly a manner as possible, never emphasizing the poseur or the charlatan aspects of Bunthorne, not even in that delightfully satirical song, "If you're anxious for to shine, etc."

Later there came a rehearsal at which this same director pulled me up short with: "Mr. Green, I am not seeing anything of Bunthorne. There must be more flamboyancy, more of the poseur, of the fraud!"

That I had been playing the role on stage in this manner for some time seemed to have escaped his notice. I said, "But you've already told me that Bunthorne is a gentleman! Surely no gentleman would behave that way . . . ?"

I thought for a moment he would explode. Then: "Of course he's a gentleman," he said. "Of course he's a gentleman, but—er—only financially!"

And between you and me, I don't think Gilbert could have come up with a better answer.

There is a general belief that Reginald Bunthorne is a caricature of Oscar Wilde. Actually he is not a caricature of any single person but of a type. If he approaches anyone physically it is Whistler: gray streak, small imperial, and monocle. (As for Grosvenor, if he is to be likened to anyone it is Swinburne.)

Oscar Wilde was, however, used by Mr. Carte. Patience was running at the Standard Theater on Broadway and, according to a letter from Helen Lenoir (later Mrs. Richard Carte) who was managing his business in New York, "receipts have gone down." It seems that Colonel F. W. Morse, manager for the New York Patience, suggested that a cable be sent to Oscar Wilde, asking if he would consider an offer for fifty readings. Wilde accepted. It is quite certain that he did not go to the United States with any motive of advertising Patience—he did not—but it is also quite evident that Carte knew what he was doing when he approved the idea. Papers in England were saying that he was sending Wilde over as a sandwichman for his new piece Patience. Others later said that Carte had canceled the engagement because "he could get sandwichmen in America with longer hair for half the money."

Perhaps Carte did not send Wilde out with any hidden motive, but he certainly took advantage of his going—he even suggested that Wilde attend a performance of Patience, letting it be known that he was there, as it would be a boon for him!

It is also on record (in a letter from Helen Lenoir to Carte) that ". . . absurd as it may appear, it seems that Oscar Wilde's visit here, which has caused a regular 'craze,' has given the business a fillip up."

Patience opened originally at the Opéra Comique on April 23, 1881, and enjoyed a second opening when it moved on October 10 of the same year to the brand-new Savoy Theatre in the Strand. Here, for the first time, there was electric lighting for both auditorium and stage. Both openings were gala performances and both received reviews. However, the two collaborators, to their chagrin, found that Richard D'Oyly Carte, the builder of the theater, had completely stolen their thunder by virtue of the newfangled "electricity"!

Some interesting facts emerge from the programs for these two openings. The one for the Opéra Comique, dated April 23, lists a curtain raiser—In the Sulks—but states it will not be performed that evening; that on subsequent evenings the doors will open at 7:30 P.M. and In the Sulks will go on at 8 P.M. At the Savoy Theatre no curtain raiser is listed. Presumably it was dropped because of the length of the performance; the two shows plus two intermissions must have run at least three if not three and a quarter hours.

The Opéra Comique program also gives no indication of the identity of the conductor. Sullivan was unquestionably in the chair as usual, since there is no evidence that this was any exception (as in the case of Princess Ida in a future instance).

There is one very interesting note in the program for April 23, the first-night program:

> NOTE: The Management considers it advisable to state that the Libretto of this Opera was completed in November last.

Sullivan had been on the Riviera and had found it very difficult to settle down to work. Although the libretto was finished, both Carte and Gilbert found it an impossible task to get Sullivan to come through with the music. Apparently the show was to have been produced in the autumn of 1880 but had to be put off until the following spring because of Sullivan's indolence. Meanwhile, however, F. C. Burnand had produced The Colonel late in 1880, a piece with a very similar theme—aestheticism. Thus the notice in the Opéra Comique's program was clearly intended as a refutation of any charge of imitation or plagiarism on Gilbert's part. The same notice, however, was not deemed necessary for the Savoy opening; The Colonel, by that time, had run its course.

Patience

ACT I

SCENE.—*Exterior of Castle Bunthorne. Entrance to Castle by drawbridge over moat. Young ladies dressed in æsthetic draperies are grouped about the stage. They play on lutes, mandolins, etc., as they sing, and all are in the last stage of despair.* ANGELA, ELLA, *and* SAPHIR *lead them.*

CHORUS—MAIDENS [1]

Twenty [2] love-sick maidens we,
　Love-sick all against our will.
Twenty years hence we shall be
　Twenty love-sick maidens still.
Twenty love-sick maidens we,
And we die for love of thee.

SOLO—ANGELA

Love feeds on hope, they say, or love will die—

ALL. 　　　　　Ah, miserie!

Yet my love lives, although no hope have I!

ALL. 　　　　　Ah, miserie!

Alas, poor heart, go hide thyself away—
To weeping concords tune thy roundelay!
　　　　　Ah, miserie!

CHORUS

All our love is all for one,
　Yet that love he heedeth not.
He is coy and cares for none,
　Sad and sorry is our lot!
　　　　Ah, miserie!

SOLO—ELLA

Go, breaking heart,
　Go, dream of love requited;
Go, foolish heart,
　Go, dream of lovers plighted;
Go, madcap heart,
　Go, dream of never waking;
And in thy dream
　Forget that thou art breaking!

CHORUS. 　　　　Ah, miserie!

ELLA. 　　Forget that thou art breaking!

CHORUS. 　　Twenty love-sick maidens, etc.

ANG. There is a strange magic in this love of ours! Rivals as we all

[1] Words and music on page 247.

[2] *Gilbert landed succeeding generations of the D'Oyly Carte Company in quite a pickle: "Twenty love-sick maidens we." In Gondoliers it was "We, alas, are four-and-twenty." In a long run of one piece it was possible to conform to the figures Gilbert set in regard to the number of ladies required. But in a touring repertory company this became not only difficult but expensive. So many more ladies meant so many more men —or less, as the case might be. Throughout my experience, Rupert D'Oyly Carte compromised with a more or less fixed number—sixteen to eighteen women and the same number of men— and Devil take the two or six who just weren't there!*

I thank thee, Love, thou comest not to me!

[3] "... *a sealed book!*" *Traditionally, "sealed" is pronounced with two distinct syllables.*

[4] *Can Gilbert have taken these stage directions from Shakespeare's "Patience on a monument"?*

[5] Words and music on page 249.

are in the affections of our Reginald, the very hopelessness of our love is a bond that binds us to one another!

SAPH. Jealousy is merged in misery. While he, the very cynosure of our eyes and hearts, remains icy insensible—what have we to strive for?

ELLA. The love of maidens is, to him, as interesting as the taxes!

SAPH. Would that it were! He pays his taxes.

ANG. And cherishes the receipts!

Enter LADY JANE

SAPH. Happy receipts!

JANE (*suddenly*). Fools!

ANG. I beg your pardon?

JANE. Fools and blind! The man loves—wildly loves!

ANG. But whom? None of us!

JANE. No, none of us. His weird fancy has lighted, for the nonce, on Patience, the village milkmaid!

SAPH. On Patience? Oh, it cannot be!

JANE. Bah! But yesterday I caught him in her dairy, eating fresh butter with a tablespoon. To-day he is not well!

SAPH. But Patience boasts that she has never loved—that love is, to her, a sealed book! [3] Oh, he cannot be serious!

JANE. 'Tis but a fleeting fancy—'twill quickly pass away. (*Aside.*) Oh, Reginald, if you but knew what a wealth of golden love is waiting for you, stored up in this rugged old bosom of mine, the milkmaid's triumph would be short indeed!

PATIENCE *appears on an eminence.* [4] *She looks down with pity on the despondent Ladies*

RECIT—PATIENCE

Still brooding on their mad infatuation!
    I thank thee, Love, thou comest not to me!
Far happier I, free from thy ministration,
    Than dukes or duchesses who love can be!

SAPH. (*looking up*). 'Tis Patience—happy girl! Loved by a Poet!

PA.   Your pardon, ladies. I intrude upon you. (*Going.*)

ANG.   Nay, pretty child, come hither. Is it true
            That you have never loved?

PA.   Most true indeed.

SOPRANOS.   Most marvellous!

CONTRALTOS.   And most deplorable!

SONG—PATIENCE [5]

I cannot tell what this love may be
That cometh to all, but not to me.
It cannot be kind as they'd imply,
Or why do these ladies sigh?

It cannot be joy and rapture deep,
Or why do these gentle ladies weep?
It cannot be blissful as 'tis said,
Or why are their eyes so wondrous red?

    Though everywhere true love I see
    A-coming to all, but not to me
    I cannot tell what this love may be!
        For I am blithe and I am gay,
        While they sit sighing night and day

Think of the gulf 'twixt them and me,
"Fal la la la!"—and "Miserie!"

CHORUS.   Yes, she is blithe, etc.

PA. [6]   If love is a thorn, they show no wit
Who foolishly hug and foster it.
If love is a weed, how simple they
Who gather it, day by day!

If love is a nettle that makes you smart,
Then why do you wear it next your heart?
And if it be none of these, say I,
Ah, why do you sit and sob and sigh?
Though everywhere, etc.

CHORUS.   For she is blithe, etc.

ANG. Ah, Patience, if you have never loved, you have never known true happiness! (*All sigh.*)

PA. But the truly happy always seem to have so much on their minds. The truly happy never seem quite well.

JANE. There is a transcendentality of delirium—an acute accentuation of a supremest ecstasy—which the earthy might easily mistake for indigestion. But it is *not* indigestion—it is æsthetic transfiguration! (*To the others.*) Enough of babble. Come!

PA. But stay, I have some news for you. The 35th Dragoon Guards have halted in the village, and are even now on their way to this very spot.

ANG. The 35th Dragoon Guards!

SAPH. They are fleshly men, of full habit!

ELLA. We care nothing for Dragoon Guards!

PA. But, bless me, you were all engaged to them a year ago!

SAPH. A year ago!

ANG. My poor child, you don't understand these things. A year ago they were very well in our eyes, but since then our tastes have been etherealized, our perceptions exalted. (*To others.*) Come, it is time to lift up our voices in morning carol to our Reginald. Let us to his door.

[*The Ladies go off, two and two, into the Castle, singing refrain of "Twenty love-sick maidens we," and accompanying themselves on harps and mandolins.* [7] PATIENCE *watches them in surprise, as she climbs the rock by which she entered.*

March. Enter Officers of Dragoon Guards, led by MAJOR [8]

CHORUS OF DRAGOONS

The soldiers of our Queen
Are linked in friendly tether;
Upon the battle scene
They fight the foe together.
There every mother's son
Prepared to fight and fall is;
The enemy of one
The enemy of all is!

Enter COLONEL

SONG—COLONEL [9]

If you want a receipt for that popular mystery,
Known to the world as a Heavy Dragoon,

[6] *Gilbert uses a very similar theme for Fairfax in* The Yeomen of the Guard. *A comparison of the two songs, particularly their second verses (see page 562, Note 20), shows how very easily Gilbert might have given Fairfax Patience's lines:*

If [life] is a thorn, they show no wit
Who foolishly hug and foster it

or Patience Fairfax's:

Is [love] a thorn?
Then count it not a whit!
Man is well done with it.

Patience would have sung "Woman's well done with it," of course.

[7] *During my time the love-sick maidens went off accompanying themselves on lutes and lyres only. I could have wished—and did wish often—that they had also used mandolins as directed. It is such a delightfully satirical Gilbertian touch!*

[8] *In actual performance the Major delayed his entrance until the Dragoons were on stage and singing. Then he came in with a flourish, dusted his boots, dusted his nose, and awaited the arrival of Colonel Calverley.*

[9] *Words and music on page 252.*

PATIENCE

Many people have told me that they would enjoy this song much more if they understood the more obscure allusions, so—herewith a glossary of the lesser-known names:

  a) Sir James Paget (1814–1899). British surgeon and pathologist.

  b) Louis Antoine Jullien (1812–1860). French composer and music director.

  c) Dion Boucicault (1820–1890). Born in Ireland of Irish and French parentage. Became famous, however, as an American dramatist, manager and actor.

  d) Sodor and Man. Medieval diocese comprising the Hebrides and the Isle of Man. (The diocese now consists of only the latter.)

  e) Alfred, Count d'Orsay (1801–1852). A French dandy who lived in London.

  f) Peveril of the Peak. An historical novel by Sir Walter Scott.

  g) Henry Sacheverell (1674–1724). English clergyman and politician.

  h) Martin Farquhar Tupper (1810–1889). English poet whose chief work was Proverbial Philosophy, a collection of moral statements in blank verse.

  i) François Pierre Guillaume Guizot (1787–1874). French historian and statesman with a prodigious output of literary criticism, history and biography. Was Ambassador to England in 1840 (for a few months).

  j) Lord Waterford. An Irish Peer, famous for his reckless sporting activities, especially when following hounds!

  k) Roderick Dhu. Highland chieftain, one of the principal characters in Scott's The Lady of the Lake.

  l) Paddington Pollaky. Ignatius Paul, who was a detective in the CID, Scotland Yard. He was attached to the Paddington District of London and was the scourge of criminals in that quarter.

  m) Sir Garnet. Better known as Field Marshal Lord Wolseley.

  n) Manfred. Onetime King of Sicily.

  o) Beadle of Burlington. Probably the uniformed attendant in the Burlington Arcade. And, if one may believe the gesture made by the Colonel, of portly dimensions.

  p) Richardson's show. A traveling show, similar to Barnum and Bailey's, but before them.

  q) Tussaud. Pronounced Too-so, with accent on the last syllable, to rhyme with "show."

[11] An unearned income of £1,000 a day.

Take all the remarkable people in history, [10]
  Rattle them off to a popular tune.
The pluck of Lord Nelson on board of the Victory—
  Genius of Bismarck devising a plan—
The humour of Fielding (which sounds contradictory)—
  Coolness of Paget [a] about to trepan—
The science of Jullien, [b] the eminent musico—
  Wit of Macaulay, who wrote of Queen Anne—
The pathos of Paddy, as rendered by Boucicault—[c]
  Style of the Bishop of Sodor and Man—[d]
The dash of a D'Orsay, [e] divested of quackery—
Narrative powers of Dickens and Thackeray—
Victor Emmanuel—peak-haunting Peveril—[f]
Thomas Aquinas, and Doctor Sacheverell—[g]
  Tupper [h] and Tennyson—Daniel Defoe—
  Anthony Trollope and Mr. Guizot! [i]
    Take of these elements all that is fusible,
    Melt them all down in a pipkin or crucible,
    Set them to simmer and take off the scum,
    And a Heavy Dragoon is the residuum!

CHORUS.   Yes! yes! yes! yes!
        A Heavy Dragoon is the residuum!

COL.   If you want a receipt for this soldier-like paragon,
    Get at the wealth of the Czar (if you can)—
The family pride of a Spaniard from Aragon—
    Force of Mephisto pronouncing a ban—
A smack of Lord Waterford, [j] reckless and rollicky—
    Swagger of Roderick, [k] heading his clan—
The keen penetration of Paddington Pollaky—[l]
    Grace of an Odalisque on a divan—
The genius strategic of Cæsar or Hannibal—
Skill of Sir Garnet [m] in thrashing a cannibal—
Flavour of Hamlet—the Stranger, a touch of him—
Little of Manfred [n] (but not very much of him)—
    Beadle of Burlington [o]—Richardson's show—[p]
    Mr. Micawber and Madame Tussaud! [q]
      Take of these elements all that is fusible,
      Melt them all down in a pipkin or crucible,
      Set them to simmer and take off the scum,
      And a Heavy Dragoon is the residuum!

ALL.   Yes! yes! yes! yes!
       A Heavy Dragoon is the residuum!

COL. Well, here we are once more on the scene of our former triumphs. But where's the Duke?

Enter DUKE, *listlessly, and in low spirits*

DUKE. Here I am! (*Sighs.*)
COL. Come, cheer up, don't give way!
DUKE. Oh, for that, I'm as cheerful as a poor devil can be expected to be who has the misfortune to be a duke, with a thousand a day! [11]
MAJ. Humph! Most men would envy you!
DUKE. Envy *me?* Tell me, Major, are you fond of toffee?
MAJ. Very!
COL. We are all fond of toffee.
ALL. We are!
DUKE. Yes, and toffee in moderation is a capital thing. But to *live* on

toffee—toffee for breakfast, toffee for dinner, toffee for tea—to have it supposed that you care for nothing *but* toffee, and that you would consider yourself insulted if anything but toffee were offered to you—how would you like *that?*

COL. I can quite believe that, under those circumstances, even toffee would become monotonous.

DUKE. For "toffee" read flattery, adulation, and abject deference, carried to such a pitch that I began, at last, to think that man was born bent at an angle of forty-five degrees! [12] Great Heavens, what is there to adulate in me! [a] Am I particularly intelligent, [b] or remarkably studious, [c] or excruciatingly witty, [d] or unusually accomplished, [e] or exceptionally virtuous? [f]

COL. You're about as commonplace a young man as ever I saw.

ALL. You are!

DUKE. Exactly! That's it exactly! That describes me to a T! Thank you all very much! Well, I couldn't stand it any longer, so I joined this second-class cavalry regiment. [13] In the Army, thought I, I shall be occasionally snubbed, perhaps even bullied, who knows? The thought was rapture, and here I am.

COL. (*looking off*). Yes, and here are the ladies!

DUKE. But who is the gentleman with the long hair?

COL. I don't know.

DUKE. He seems popular!

COL. He *does* seem popular!

BUNTHORNE *enters, followed by Ladies, two and two, singing and playing on harps as before. He is composing a poem, and quite absorbed.* [14] *He sees no one, but walks across the stage, followed by Ladies. They take no notice of Dragoons—to the surprise and indignation of those Officers.*

CHORUS OF LADIES

In a doleful train
　Two and two we walk all day—
For we love in vain!
　None so sorrowful as they
　　Who can only sigh and say,
　　Woe is me, alackaday!

CHORUS OF DRAGOONS

Now is not this ridiculous—and is not this preposterous?
　A thorough-paced absurdity—explain it if you can.
Instead of rushing eagerly to cherish us and foster us,
　They all prefer this melancholy literary man.
　　Instead of slyly peering at us,
　　Casting looks endearing at us,
Blushing at us, flushing at us—flirting with a fan;
They're actually sneering at us, fleering at us, jeering at us!
　　Pretty sort of treatment for a military man!
　　Pretty sort of treatment for a military man!

ANG.　　　Mystic poet, hear our prayer,
　　　Twenty love-sick maidens we—
　　Young and wealthy, dark and fair—
　　　All of county family.
　　And we die for love of thee—
　　Twenty love-sick maidens we!

CHORUS OF LADIES.　　Yes, we die for love of thee—
　　　Twenty love-sick maidens we!

[12] An allusion to the constant bowing to which he had been subjected. During the remainder of this speech his remarks are punctuated by responses from the Colonel, the Major and the Chorus:
　(a) Good Lord, nothing!
　(b) No!
　(c) I should say not!
　(d) Heavens, no!
　(e) Definitely not!
　(f) Virtuous! Ha! Ha! Ha!

[13] At the Duke's allusion to a "second-class cavalry regiment" there is a most indignant shout of "What!" from all the others, and at the same time they half draw their sabers.

[14] Bunthorne carries a small, gold bound notebook and gold pencil. Although the directions say he is "quite absorbed," he is, in fact, only apparently so. He sees the Dragoons all right. And while appearing to be engrossed in his poem he takes an occasional sly look at the girls to make sure that he still has their full attention. His very first lines reveal this fact.

A Heavy Dragoon is the residuum!

[15] *Here again strict attention to the directions must be ignored. That is to say, an "aside" usually means that the audience alone is supposed to hear the words, but in this case Bunthorne's "aside" is not quite as private as he thinks. The Dragoons hear what he says . . . and repeat it to each other.*

BUN. (*aside—slyly*). [15] Though my book I seem to scan
    In a rapt ecstatic way,
    Like a literary man
    Who despises female clay,
    I hear plainly all they say,
    Twenty love-sick maidens they!

OFFICERS (*to each other*).   He hears plainly, etc.

SAPH.   Though so excellently wise,
    For a moment mortal be,
    Deign to raise thy purple eyes
    From thy heart-drawn poesy.
    Twenty love-sick maidens see—
    Each is kneeling on her knee! (*All kneel.*)

CHORUS OF LADIES.   Twenty love-sick, etc.

BUN. (*aside*).   Though, as I remarked before,
    Any one convinced would be
    That some transcendental lore
    Is monopolizing me,
    Round the corner I can see
    Each is kneeling on her knee!

OFFICERS (*to each other*).   Round the corner, etc.

ENSEMBLE

OFFICERS   LADIES
Now is not this ridiculous, etc.   Mystic poet, hear our prayer, etc.

COL. Angela! what is the meaning of this?

ANG. Oh, sir, leave us; our minds are but ill-tuned to light love-talk.

MAJ. But what in the world has come over you all?

JANE. Bunthorne! *He* has come over us. He has come among us, and he has idealized us.

DUKE. Has he succeeded in idealizing *you*? [16]

JANE. He has!

DUKE. Good old Bunthorne!

JANE. My eyes are open; I droop despairingly; I am soulfully intense; I am limp and I cling! [17]

[*During this* BUNTHORNE *is seen in all the agonies of composition. The Ladies are watching him intently as he writhes. At last he hits on the word he wants and writes it down. A general sense of relief.*

BUN. Finished! At last! Finished!

[*He staggers, overcome with the mental strain, into arms of* COLONEL

COL. Are you better now?

BUN. Yes—oh, it's you—I am better now. The poem is finished, and my soul had gone out into it. That was all. It was nothing worth mentioning, it occurs three times a day. (*Sees* PATIENCE, *who has entered during this scene.*) Ah, Patience! Dear Patience! (*Holds her hand; she seems frightened.*)

ANG. Will it please you to read it to us, sir?

SAPH. This we supplicate. (*All kneel.*)

BUN. Shall I?

ALL THE DRAGOONS. No! [18]

BUN. (*annoyed—to* PATIENCE). I will read it if *you* bid me!

PA. (*much frightened*). You can if you like! [19]

BUN. It is a wild, weird, fleshly thing; yet very tender, very yearning, very precious. It is called, "Oh, Hollow! Hollow! Hollow!"

[16] *The Duke's line should emphasize Lady Jane's "ample and rugged bosom."*

[17] *I have always wanted to see Lady Jane fall limply on her knees at Bunthorne's feet and literally cling to him. It would help Bunthorne to find the word he wanted with great rapidity and motivate his cross to a place near where the Colonel is standing (by virtue of a keen desire to escape). As it stands now, his cross is completely unmotivated—but perhaps I am treading on dangerous ground.*

[18] *This is a tremendous shout and should really frighten Bunthorne.*

[19] *Reactions from the Dragoons are interpolated: "Oh, no! Anything but that!"*

PA. Is it a hunting song? [20]

BUN. A hunting song? No, it is *not* a hunting song. It is the wail of the poet's heart on discovering that everything is commonplace. To understand it, cling passionately to one another and think of faint lilies. (*They do so as he recites*)—[21]

"OH, HOLLOW! HOLLOW! HOLLOW!"

What time the poet hath hymned
The writhing maid, lithe-limbed,
    Quivering on amaranthine asphodel,
How can he paint her woes,
Knowing, as well he knows,
    That all can be set right with calomel?

When from the poet's plinth
The amorous colocynth
    Yearns for the aloe, faint with rapturous thrills,
How can he hymn their throes
Knowing, as well he knows,
    That they are only uncompounded pills?

Is it, and can it be,
Nature hath this decree,
    Nothing poetic in the world shall dwell?
Or that in all her works
Something poetic lurks,
    Even in colocynth and calomel?
                    I cannot tell.

                    [*Exit* BUNTHORNE.

ANG. How purely fragrant!

SAPH. How earnestly precious!

PA. Well, it seems to me to be nonsense.

SAPH. Nonsense, yes, perhaps—but oh, what precious nonsense!

COL. This is all very well, but you seem to forget that you are engaged to us.

SAPH. It can never be. You are not Empyrean. You are not Della Cruscan. [22] You are not even Early English. Oh, be Early English ere it is too late! (*Officers look at each other in astonishment.*)

JANE (*looking at uniform*). Red and yellow! [23] Primary colours! Oh, South Kensington!

DUKE. We didn't design our uniforms, but we don't see how they could be improved.

JANE. No, you wouldn't. Still, there *is* a cobwebby grey velvet, with a tender bloom like cold gravy, which, made Florentine fourteenth-century, trimmed with Venetian leather and Spanish altar lace, and surmounted with something Japanese—it matters not what—would at least be Early English! Come, maidens.

        [*Exeunt Maidens, two and two, singing refrain of
        "Twenty love-sick maidens we". The Officers
        watch them off in astonishment.*

DUKE. Gentlemen, this is an insult to the British uniform——

COL. A uniform that has been as successful in the courts of Venus as on the field of Mars!

SONG—COLONEL [24]

When I first put this uniform on,
    I said, as I looked in the glass,
        "It's one to a million

[20] *A not-as-good-as-usual pun on the Huntsman's "View Hollo!"*

[21] *We-e-ll—they try to look as if they are!*

[22] Della Cruscan. (*Academy of the bran or chaff.*) *Of or pertaining to the Accademia Della Crusca, established in Florence in 1582 to sift and purify the Italian language (hence its name; and hence its emblem: a sieve).*

[23] *The allusion "red and yellow" in regard to their uniform refers to the "yellow" cloth stripe on the breeches. Which is as it should be—in undress uniform, but in this instance it is Parade Dress, and the stripes are gold!*

[24] *Words and music on page 257. The Hessians the Colonel alludes to in this song are high tasseled boots—riding boots—and a part of a Dragoon's dress uniform. They were also very fashionable in England in the early 19th century.*

I said, as I looked in the glass

That any civilian
My figure and form will surpass.
Gold lace has a charm for the fair,
And I've plenty of that, and to spare,
While a lover's professions,
When uttered in Hessians,
Are eloquent everywhere!"
A fact that I counted upon,
When I first put this uniform on!

CHORUS OF DRAGOONS

By a simple coincidence, few
Could ever have counted upon,
The same thing occurred to me, too,
When I first put this uniform on!

. . . the peripatetics
Of long-haired aesthetics

COL.   I said, when I first put it on,
"It is plain to the veriest dunce
That every beauty
Will feel it her duty
To yield to its glamour at once.
They will see that I'm freely gold-laced
In a uniform handsome and chaste"—
But the peripatetics
Of long-haired æsthetics
Are very much more to their taste—
Which I never counted upon,
When I first put this uniform on!

CHORUS.   By a simple coincidence, few
Could ever have reckoned upon,
I didn't anticipate that,
When I first put this uniform on!

[*The Dragoons go off angrily.*

Enter BUNTHORNE, *who changes his manner and
becomes intensely melodramatic*

RECIT AND SONG—BUNTHORNE

Am I alone,
And unobserved? I am!
Then let me own
I'm an æsthetic sham!

This air severe
Is but a mere
Veneer!

This cynic smile
Is but a wile
Of guile!

A languid love for lilies . . .

This costume chaste
Is but good taste
Misplaced!

Let me confess!
A languid love for lilies does *not* blight me!
Lank limbs and haggard cheeks do *not* delight me!
I do *not* care for dirty greens [25]

[25] A pun *that Gilbert did not intend—not even if
he had known that I would one day play the
role.*

224

By any means.
    I do *not* long for all one sees
        That's Japanese.
    I am *not* fond of uttering platitudes
        In stained-glass attitudes.
    In short, my mediævalism's affectation,
    Born of a morbid love of admiration!

SONG—BUNTHORNE [26]

[27] If you're anxious for to shine in the high æsthetic line as a man of culture rare,

You must get up all the germs of the transcendental terms, and plant them everywhere.

You must lie upon the daisies and discourse in novel phrases of your complicated state of mind,

The meaning doesn't matter if it's only idle chatter of a transcendental kind.

      And every one will say,
      As you walk your mystic way,

"If this young man expresses himself in terms too deep for *me*,

Why, what a very singularly deep young man this deep young man must be!"

Be eloquent in praise of the very dull old days which have long since passed away,

And convince 'em, if you can, that the reign of good Queen Anne was Culture's palmiest day.

Of course you will pooh-pooh whatever's fresh and new, and declare it's crude and mean,

For Art stopped short in the cultivated court of the Empress Josephine.

      And every one will say,
      As you walk your mystic way,

"If that's not good enough for him which is good enough for *me*,

Why, what a very cultivated kind of youth this kind of youth must be!"

Then a sentimental passion of a vegetable fashion must excite your languid spleen,

An attachment *à la* Plato for a bashful young potato, or a not-too-French French bean!

Though the Philistines may jostle, you will rank as an apostle in the high æsthetic band,

If you walk down Piccadilly with a poppy or a lily in your mediæval hand.

      And every one will say,
      As you walk your flowery way,

"If he's content with a vegetable love which would certainly not suit *me*,

Why, what a most particularly pure young man this pure young man must be!"

At the end of his song PATIENCE *enters. He sees her*

BUN. Ah! Patience, come hither. [28] I am pleased with thee. The bitter-hearted one, who finds all else hollow, is pleased with thee. For you are not hollow. *Are you?*

PA. No, thanks, I have dined; but—I beg your pardon—I interrupt you.

[26] *Words and music on page 259.*

[27] *The treatment for this song should be similar to that for Sir Joseph Porter's "When I was a lad." While being a form of patter song, it should not be treated as a tour de force or in any way similarly to the Major General's song, the Nightmare Song from Iolanthe or "Oh my name is John Wellington Wells" from The Sorcerer. These are pure patter, the points made being secondary to the rapid delivery. Here, however, as with Sir Joseph's song, the points made are of greater importance than the patter. The tempo, therefore, should be held back rather than speeded up. But don't lose the suggestion of patter in doing so!*

[28] *A warning to all would-be performers of Gilbert and Sullivan—remember which opera you are playing. I once said, as Patience entered: "Ah, Phyllis, come hither . . ." (Consternation on the face of Patience) "Oh! Sorry! That's Iolanthe—uh—Patience, come hither . . ."*

BUN. Life is made up of interruptions. The tortured soul, yearning for solitude, writhes under them. Oh, but my heart is a-weary! Oh, I am a cursed thing! Don't go.

PA. Really, I'm very sorry——

BUN. Tell me, girl, do you ever yearn?

PA. (*misunderstanding him*). I earn my living. [29]

BUN. (*impatiently*). No, no! Do you know what it is to be heart-hungry? Do you know what it is to yearn for the Indefinable, and yet to be brought face to face, daily, with the Multiplication Table? Do you know what it is to seek oceans and to find puddles?—to long for whirlwinds and yet to have to do the best you can with the bellows? That's my case. Oh, I am a cursed thing! Don't go.

PA. If you please, I don't understand you—you frighten me!

BUN. Don't be frightened—it's only poetry.

PA. Well, if that's poetry, I don't like poetry.

BUN. (*eagerly*). Don't you? (*Aside.*) Can I trust her? (*Aloud.*) Patience, you don't like poetry—well, between you and me, I don't like poetry. It's hollow, unsubstantial—unsatisfactory. What's the use of yearning for Elysian Fields when you know you can't get 'em, and would only let 'em out on building leases if you had 'em?

PA. Sir, I——

BUN. Patience, I have long loved you. Let me tell you a secret. I am not as bilious as I look. If you like, I will cut my hair. There is more innocent fun within me than a casual spectator would imagine. You have never seen me frolicsome. Be a good girl—a very good girl—and one day you shall. If you are fond of touch-and-go jocularity—this is the shop for it.

PA. Sir, I will speak plainly. In the matter of love I am untaught. I have never loved but my great-aunt. But I am quite certain, under any circumstances, I couldn't possibly love *you*.

BUN. Oh, you think not?

PA. I'm quite sure of it. Quite sure. Quite.

BUN. Very good. Life is henceforth a blank. I don't care what becomes of me. I have only to ask that you will not abuse my confidence; though *you* despise me, I am extremely popular with the other young ladies.

PA. I only ask that you will leave me and never renew the subject.

BUN. Certainly. Broken-hearted and desolate, I go. (*Recites.*) [30]

> "Oh, to be wafted away
> From this black Aceldama [31] of sorrow,
> Where the dust of an earthy to-day
> Is the earth of a dusty to-morrow!"

It is a little thing of my own. I call it "Heart Foam." I shall not publish it. Farewell! Patience, Patience, farewell!

[*Exit* BUNTHORNE

PA. What on earth does it all mean? Why does he love me? Why does he expect me to love him? He's not a relation! It frightens me!

Enter ANGELA

ANG. Why, Patience, what is the matter?

PA. Lady Angela, tell me two things. Firstly, what on earth is this love that upsets everybody; and, secondly, how is it to be distinguished from insanity?

ANG. Poor blind child! Oh, forgive her, Eros! Why, love is of all passions the most essential! It is the embodiment of purity, the abstraction of refinement! It is the one unselfish emotion in this whirlpool of grasping greed!

PA. Oh, dear, oh! (*Beginning to cry.*)

ANG. Why are you crying?

PA. To think that I have lived all these years without having experienced this ennobling and unselfish passion! Why, what a wicked girl I must be! For it *is* unselfish, isn't it?

ANG. Absolutely! Love that is tainted with selfishness is no love. [32] Oh, try, try, try to love! It really isn't difficult if you give your whole mind to it.

PA. I'll set about it at once. I won't go to bed until I'm head over ears in love with somebody.

ANG. Noble girl! But is it possible that you have never loved anybody?

PA. Yes, one.

ANG. Ah! Whom?

PA. My great-aunt——

ANG. Great-aunts don't count.

PA. Then there's nobody. At least—no, nobody. Not since I was a baby. But *that* doesn't count, I suppose.

ANG. I don't know. Tell me all about it.

[32] *An example of Gilbert's love of uttering a profound truth, only to knock it down a second later by making fun of it.*

DUET—PATIENCE *and* ANGELA

Long years ago—fourteen, maybe—
    When but a tiny babe of four,
Another baby played with me,
    My elder by a year or more;
A little child of beauty rare,
With marvellous eyes and wondrous hair,
Who, in my child-eyes, seemed to me
All that a little child should be!
        Ah, how we loved, that child and I!
            How pure our baby joy!
        How true our love—and, by the by,
            He was a little boy!

ANG.   Ah, old, old tale of Cupid's touch!
                       I thought as much—I thought as much!
                           He *was* a little boy!

PA. (*shocked*).   Pray don't misconstrue what I say—
                       Remember, pray—remember, pray,
                           He was a *little* boy!

ANG.   No doubt! Yet, spite of all your pains,
                       The interesting fact remains—
                           He was a little *boy*!

ENSEMBLE. $\left\{ \begin{matrix} \text{Ah, yes, in} \\ \text{No doubt! Yet} \end{matrix} \right\}$ spite of all $\left\{ \begin{matrix} \text{my} \\ \text{your} \end{matrix} \right\}$ pains, etc.

[*Exit* ANGELA.

PA. It's perfectly dreadful to think of the appalling state I must be in! I had no idea that love was a duty. No wonder they all look so unhappy! Upon my word, I hardly like to associate with myself. I don't think I'm respectable. I'll go at once and fall in love with—— (*Enter* GROSVENOR.) A stranger!

Prithee, pretty maiden—

DUET—PATIENCE *and* GROSVENOR [33]

[33] *Words and music on page 262.*

GROS.   Prithee, pretty maiden—prithee, tell me true,
              (Hey, but I'm doleful, willow willow waly)
          Have you e'er a lover a-dangling after you?
              Hey willow waly O!
              I would fain discover

<blockquote>
If you have a lover?
Hey willow waly O!
</blockquote>

PA. Gentle sir, my heart is frolicsome and free—
    (Hey, but he's doleful, willow willow waly!)
  Nobody I care for comes a-courting me—
    Hey willow waly O!
      Nobody I care for
      Comes a-courting—therefore,
    Hey willow waly O!

GROS. Prithee, pretty maiden, will you marry me?
    (Hey, but I'm hopeful, willow willow waly!)
  I may say, at once, I'm a man of propertee—
    Hey willow waly O!
      Money, I despise it;
      Many people prize it,
    Hey willow waly O!

PA. Gentle sir, although to marry I design—
    (Hey, but he's hopeful, willow willow waly!)
  As yet I do not know you, and so I must decline.
    Hey willow waly O!
      To other maidens go you—
      As yet I do not know you,
    Hey willow waly O!

GROS. Patience! Can it be that you don't recognise me?

PA. Recognise you? No, indeed I don't!

GROS. Have fifteen years so greatly changed me?

PA. Fifteen years? What do you mean?

GROS. Have you forgotten the friend of your youth, your Archibald? —your little playfellow? Oh, Chronos, Chronos, this is too bad of you!

PA. Archibald! Is it possible? Why, let me look! It is! It is! It must be! Oh, how happy I am! I thought we should never meet again! And how you've grown!

GROS. Yes, Patience, I am much taller and much [34] stouter than I was.

PA. And how you've improved!

GROS. Yes, Patience, I am very beautiful! (*Sighs.*)

PA. But surely *that* doesn't make you unhappy.

GROS. Yes, Patience. Gifted as I am with a beauty which probably has not its rival on earth, I am, nevertheless, utterly and completely miserable.

PA. Oh—but why?

GROS. My child-love for you has never faded. Conceive, then, the horror of my situation when I tell you that it is my hideous destiny to be madly loved at first sight by every woman I come across!

PA. But why do you make yourself so picturesque? Why not disguise yourself, disfigure yourself, anything to escape this persecution?

GROS. No, Patience, that may not be. These gifts—irksome as they are—were given to me for the enjoyment and delectation of my fellow-creatures. I am a trustee for Beauty, and it is my duty to see that the conditions of my trust are faithfully discharged.

PA. And you, too, are a Poet?

GROS. Yes, I am the Apostle of Simplicity. I am called "Archibald the All-Right"—for I am infallible!

PA. And is it possible that you condescend to love such a girl as I?

GROS. Yes, Patience, is it not strange? I have loved you with a

[34] *The word "much" has, for many years now, been changed to "little." This is because, since the days when the late Leo Sheffield played the role (the last of the portly Grosvenors), the actors in the role have been on the slim side.*

Florentine fourteenth-century frenzy for full fifteen years!

PA. Oh, marvellous! I have hitherto been deaf to the voice of love. I seem now to know what love is! It has been revealed to me—it is Archibald Grosvenor!

GROS. Yes, Patience, it is!

PA. (*as in a trance*). We will never, never part!

GROS. We will live and die together!

PA. I swear it!

GROS. We both swear it!

PA. (*recoiling from him*). But—oh, horror!

GROS. What's the matter?

PA. Why, you are perfection! A source of endless ecstasy to all who know you!

GROS. I know I am. Well?

PA. Then, bless my heart, there can be nothing unselfish in loving *you*!

GROS. Merciful powers! I never thought of that!

PA. To monopolize those features on which all women love to linger! It would be unpardonable!

GROS. Why, so it would! Oh, fatal perfection, again you interpose between me and my happiness!

PA. Oh, if you were but a thought less beautiful than you are!

GROS. Would that I were; but candour compels me to admit that I'm not!

PA. Our duty is clear; we must part, and for ever!

GROS. Oh, misery! And yet I cannot question the propriety of your decision. Farewell, Patience!

PA. Farewell, Archibald! But stay!

GROS. Yes, Patience?

PA. Although I may not love *you*—for you are perfection—there is nothing to prevent your loving *me*. I am plain, homely, unattractive!

GROS. Why, that's true!

PA. The love of such a man as you for such a girl as I must be unselfish!

GROS. Unselfishness itself!

DUET—PATIENCE *and* GROSVENOR

PA.	Though to marry you would very selfish be—
GROS.	Hey, but I'm doleful—willow willow waly!
PA.	You may, all the same, continue loving me—
GROS.	Hey willow waly O!
BOTH.	All the world ignoring,
	You'll⎫
	I'll ⎬ go on adoring—
	Hey willow waly O!

[*At the end, exeunt despairingly, in opposite directions.*

FINALE—ACT I

Enter BUNTHORNE, *crowned with roses and hung about with garlands, and looking very miserable. He is led by* ANGELA *and* SAPHIR (*each of whom holds an end of the rose-garland by which he is bound*), *and accompanied by procession of Maidens. They are dancing classically, and playing on cymbals, double pipes, and other archaic instruments.*

[35] *Pandaean. Pertaining to the cloven-hoofed Pan.*

[36] *To my intense regret I never saw any one of the love-sick maidens take a Daphnephoric bound! I have always wanted to know what one looked like. I presume it was the sort of leap Daphne took in order to avoid Apollo.*

CHORUS

Let the merry cymbals sound,
　　Gaily pipe Pandæan [35] pleasure,
With a Daphnephoric [36] bound
　　Tread a gay but classic measure.
Every heart with hope is beating,
For at this exciting meeting
　　Fickle Fortune will decide
　　Who shall be our Bunthorne's bride!

Enter Dragoons, led by COLONEL, MAJOR, *and* DUKE.
They are surprised at proceedings

CHORUS OF DRAGOONS

Now tell us, we pray you,
Why thus they array you—
Oh, poet, how say you—
　　What is it you've done?

DUKE.　　　　　Of rite sacrificial,
By sentence judicial,
This seems the initial,
　　Then why don't you run?

COL.　　　　　They cannot have led you
To hang or behead you,
Nor may they *all* wed you,
　　Unfortunate one!

CHORUS OF DRAGOONS

Then tell us, we pray you,
Why thus they array you—
Oh, poet, how say you—
　　What is it you've done?

RECIT—BUNTHORNE

Heart-broken at my Patience's barbarity,
　By the advice of my solicitor
　　　　　　(*introducing his* SOLICITOR),
In aid—in aid of a deserving charity,
　I've put myself up to be raffled for!

MAIDENS.　　　By the advice of his solicitor
　　He's put himself up to be raffled for!

DRAGOONS.　　Oh, horror! urged by his solicitor,
　　He's put himself up to be raffled for!

MAIDENS.　　　Oh, heaven's blessing on his solicitor!

DRAGOONS.　　A hideous curse on his solicitor!

[*The* SOLICITOR, *horrified at the Dragoons' curse,
　　rushes off.*

COL.　　　　　Stay, we implore you,
　　Before our hopes are blighted;
You see before you
　　The men to whom you're plighted!

CHORUS OF DRAGOONS

Stay, we implore you,
For we adore you;
To us you're plighted
To be united—
    Stay, we implore you!

SOLO—DUKE

Your maiden hearts, ah, do not steel
To pity's eloquent appeal,
Such conduct British soldiers feel.
(*Aside to Dragoons.*) Sigh, sigh, all sigh!
                (*They all sigh.*)

To foeman's steel we rarely see
A British soldier bend the knee,
Yet, one and all, they kneel to ye—
(*Aside to Dragoons.*) Kneel, kneel, all kneel!
                (*They all kneel.*)

Our soldiers very seldom cry,
And yet—I need not tell you why—
A tear-drop dews each martial eye!
(*Aside to Dragoons.*) Weep, weep, all weep!
                (*They all weep.*)

ENSEMBLE

Our soldiers very seldom cry,
And yet—I need not tell you why—
A tear-drop dews each manly eye!
Weep, weep, all weep!

BUNTHORNE (*who has been impatient during this appeal*). [37]

Come, walk up, and purchase with avidity,
Overcome your diffidence and natural timidity,
Tickets for the raffle should be purchased with avidity,
    Put in half a guinea and a husband you may gain—
Such a judge of blue-and-white and other kinds of pottery—
From early Oriental down to modern terra-cotta-ry—
Put in half a guinea—you may draw him in a lottery—
    Such an opportunity may not occur again.

CHORUS. Such a judge of blue-and-white, etc.

[MAIDENS *crowd up to purchase tickets; during this* DRAGOONS *dance in single file round stage, to express their indifference.* [38]

DRAGOONS. We've been thrown over, we're aware,
    But we don't care—but we don't care!
    There's fish in the sea, no doubt of it,
    As good as ever came out of it,
    And some day we shall get our share,
    So we don't care—so we don't care!

[*During this the* MAIDENS *have been buying tickets. At last* JANE *presents herself.* [39] BUNTHORNE *looks at her with aversion.*

RECIT

BUN.   And are *you* going a ticket for to buy?
JANE (*surprised*). Most certainly I am; why shouldn't I?

[37] Bunthorne's raffling himself off probably stems from Gilbert's original (or second) conception (see Foreword) of "The Rival Curates," where the idea of a curate offering himself as a prize in a raffle would strike one as being particularly amusing. The raffle has always been a prime means of raising money for a church. A sweepstake, no. A sweepstake would be gambling, and that is frowned upon. But a raffle is just fun, and the prize, of course, is never money! Nevertheless, it is chance.

    Bunthorne's raffle is by no means the only instance in which a character of Gilbert's uses chance as a means of winning a wife. (Bunthorne actually doesn't get his wife, but he uses the element of chance with the apparent intention of doing so.) Marco and Giuseppe in The Gondoliers gain their wives through a game of blindman's buff; Fairfax, in The Yeomen of the Guard, obtains his bride through a form of chance: "So, my good lieutenant . . . find me the first that comes . . ."

[38] As they dance around the stage they all pull out cigarettes which they wave nonchalantly but never light.

[39] Our Lady Jane on one occasion had a most embarrassing experience. She had been seated in her dressing-room chair over the back of which she had draped her corsets. When she rose to come onto the stage they got caught in her gown, unknown to her. Suppressed giggles greeted her entrance, which made her furious. Some of the girls tried to tell her of her plight, and that only made her more furious. Turning her back to the audience she demanded in an angry stage whisper, "What is so damn funny?" A huge burst of laughter came from out front. Her blush, when at last she realized the situation, showed even through her make-up.

BUN. (*aside*). Oh, Fortune, this is hard! (*Aloud.*) Blindfold your
            eyes;
        Two minutes will decide who wins the prize! (MAIDENS
        blindfold themselves.)

CHORUS OF MAIDENS

Oh, Fortune, to my aching heart be kind!
Like us, thou art blindfolded, but not blind; (*Each uncovers one eye.*)
Just raise your bandage, thus, that you may see,
And give the prize, and give the prize to me! (*They cover their eyes
    again.*)

BUN. Come, Lady Jane, I pray you draw the first!
JANE (*joyfully*). He loves me best!
BUN. (*aside*).   I want to know the worst!

[JANE *puts hand in bag to draw ticket.* PATIENCE *enters
    and prevents her doing so.*

PA. Hold! Stay your hand!
ALL (*uncovering their eyes*). What means this interference?
    Of this bold girl I pray you make a clearance!
JANE. Away with you, and to your milk-pails go!
BUN. (*suddenly*). She wants a ticket! Take a dozen!
PA.   No!

SOLO—PATIENCE (*kneeling to* BUNTHORNE)

If there be pardon in your breast
    For this poor penitent,
Who, with remorseful thought opprest,
    Sincerely doth repent;
If you, with one so lowly, still
    Desire to be allied,
Then you may take me, if you will,
    For I will be your bride!

ALL.   Oh, shameless one!
          Oh, bold-faced thing!
        Away you run,
          Go, take you wing,
        You shameless one!
        You bold-faced thing!

BUN.   How strong is love! For many and many a week
        She's loved me fondly and has feared to speak
        But Nature, for restraint too mighty far,
        Has burst the bonds of Art—and here we are!

PA.   No, Mr. Bunthorne, no—you're wrong again;
         Permit me—I'll endeavour to explain!

SONG—PATIENCE

PA.   True love must single-hearted be—
BUN.   Exactly so!
PA.   From every selfish fancy free—
BUN.   Exactly so!
PA.   No idle thought of gain or joy
        A maiden's fancy should employ—
        True love must be without alloy.
ALL.   Exactly so!

PA.	Imposture to contempt must lead—
COL.	Exactly so!
PA.	Blind vanity's dissension's seed—
MAJ.	Exactly so!
PA.	It follows, then, a maiden who
	Devotes herself to loving you (*indicating*
	BUNTHORNE)
	Is prompted by no selfish view—
ALL.	Exactly so!
SAPH.	Are you resolved to wed this shameless one?
ANG.	Is there no chance for any other?
BUN.	(*decisively*). None! (*Embraces* PATIENCE.) [40]

[*Exeunt* PATIENCE *and* BUNTHORNE.

[ANGELA, SAPHIR, *and* ELLA *take* COLONEL, DUKE, *and* MAJOR *down, while*
GIRLS *gaze fondly at other* OFFICERS.

SEXTETTE [41]

I hear the soft note of the echoing voice
Of an old, old love, long dead—
It whispers my sorrowing heart "rejoice"—
For the last sad tear is shed—
The pain that is all but a pleasure will change
For the pleasure that's all but pain,
And never, oh never, this heart will range
From that old, old love again!
(GIRLS *embrace* OFFICERS.)

CHORUS. Yes, the pain that is all, etc. (*Embrace.*)

Enter PATIENCE *and* BUNTHORNE

[As *the* DRAGOONS *and* GIRLS *are embracing, enter* GROSVENOR, *reading.
He takes no notice of them, but comes slowly down, still reading.
The* GIRLS *are all strangely fascinated by him, and gradually with-
draw from* DRAGOONS.

ANG.	But who is this, whose god-like grace
	Proclaims he comes of noble race?
	And who is this, whose manly face
	Bears sorrow's interesting trace?

ENSEMBLE—TUTTI

Yes, who is this, etc.

GROS.	I am a broken-hearted troubadour,
	Whose mind's æsthetic and whose tastes are pure!
ANG.	Æsthetic! He is æsthetic!
GROS.	Yes, yes—I am æsthetic
	And poetic!
ALL THE LADIES.	Then, we love you!

[*The* GIRLS *leave* DRAGOONS *and group, kneeling, around* GROSVENOR. *Fury
of* BUNTHORNE, *who recognizes a rival.*

DRAGOONS. They love him! Horror!
BUN. *and* PA. They love him! Horror! [42]
GROS. They love me! Horror! Horror! Horror!

[40] Stage directions notwithstanding, so far as I ever knew, Bunthorne did not embrace Patience—to the intense disappointment of more than one Bunthorne I've known, including myself. No, he just takes her hand and leads her off.

[41] Another example of Gilbert's love of the bizarre. Here he has a beautiful lyric expressing a beautiful sentiment, with a perfect musical setting . . .
. . . only to turn it to ridicule a few seconds later.

[42] Bunthorne's fury is so intense that it is only with great difficulty—or apparently so—that Patience prevents him from laying hands on Grosvenor. Held back by her he expresses his final intense disapproval by taking a small daisy out of his breast pocket and throwing it in Grosvenor's face. That done, he turns back to Patience to find that she is about to attack the girls in a frenzy of jealousy. He now restrains her, at the same time turning to make a moue at his hated rival.

ENSEMBLE—TUTTI

GIRLS

Oh, list while we a love confess
That words imperfectly express.
Those shell-like ears, ah, do not close
To blighted love's distracting woes!

GROSVENOR

Again my cursed comeliness
Spreads hopeless anguish and distress!
Thine ears, oh Fortune, do not close
To my intolerable woes.

PATIENCE

List, Reginald, while I confess
A love that's all unselfishness;
That it's unselfish, goodness knows,
You won't dispute it, I suppose?

BUNTHORNE

My jealousy I can't express,
Their love they openly confess;
His shell-like ears he does not close
To their recital of their woes.

DRAGOONS. Now is not this ridiculous, etc.

END OF ACT I

ACT II

SCENE.—*A glade.* JANE *is discovered leaning on a violon-cello, upon which she presently accompanies herself. Chorus of* MAIDENS *are heard singing in the distance.*

JANE. The fickle crew have deserted Reginald and sworn allegiance to his rival, and all, forsooth, because he has glanced with passing favour on a puling milkmaid! Fools! of that fancy he will soon weary—and then I, who alone am faithful to him, shall reap my reward. But do not dally too long, Reginald, for my charms are ripe, Reginald, and already they are decaying. Better secure me ere I have gone too far!

RECIT—JANE [43]

Sad is that woman's lot who, year by year,
Sees, one by one, her beauties disappear,
When Time, grown weary of her heart-drawn sighs,
Impatiently begins to "dim her eyes"!
Compelled, at last, in life's uncertain gloamings,
To wreathe her wrinkled brow with well-saved "combings,"
Reduced, with rouge, lip-salve, and pearly grey,
To "make up" for lost time as best she may!

SONG—JANE [44]

Silvered is the raven hair,
     Spreading is the parting straight,
Mottled the complexion fair,
     Halting is the youthful gait,
Hollow is the laughter free,
     Spectacled the limpid eye—
Little will be left of me
     In the coming by and by!

Fading is the taper waist,
     Shapeless grows the shapely limb,
And although severely laced,
     Spreading is the figure trim!
Stouter than I used to be,
     Still more corpulent grow I—
There will be too much of me
     In the coming by and by!

[*Exit* JANE.

To wreathe her wrinkled brow . . .

[43] *This is not the first, and certainly not the last time that Gilbert strongly ridicules the elderly spinster. Other instances are to be found in The Mikado, The Pirates, Iolanthe and The Yeomen of the Guard. And yet, strangely enough, Jane has always been one of the favorite roles among all "heavy" contraltos.*

[44] *Chappell & Company, the publishers of the libretto and vocal scores, were very struck with Lady Jane's song and were convinced that it would make an excellent drawing-room ballad if given different words. It was eventually published by them as a separate song with new lyrics by Hugh Conway. Retaining its sad and mournful mood the song began:*

     In the twilight of our love,
     In the darkness falling fast
     Broken by no gleam above . . .

and ended with

     Would we two had never met.

There's a sentiment calculated to bring tears to the eyes of the most hardened listener to the drawing-room ballad!

Words and music, as they appear in Patience, are on page 264.

[*Enter* GROSVENOR, *followed by* MAIDENS, *two and two, each playing on an archaic instrument, as in Act I. He is reading abstractedly, as* BUNTHORNE *did in Act I, and pays no attention to them.*

CHORUS OF MAIDENS

Turn, oh, turn in this direction,
Shed, oh, shed a gentle smile,
With a glance of sad perfection
Our poor fainting hearts beguile!
On such eyes as maidens cherish
Let thy fond adorers gaze,
Or incontinently perish
In their all-consuming rays!

[*He sits—they group around him.* [45]

GROS. (*aside*). The old, old tale. How rapturously these maidens love me, and how hopelessly! Oh, Patience, Patience, with the love of thee in my heart, what have I for these poor mad maidens but an unvalued pity? Alas, they will die of hopeless love for me, as I shall die of hopeless love for thee!

ANG. Sir, will it please you read to us?

GROS. (*sighing*). Yes, child, if you will. What shall I read?

ANG. One of your own poems.

GROS. One of my own poems? Better not, my child. *They* will not cure thee of thy love.

ELLA. Mr. Bunthorne used to read us a poem of his own every day.

SAPH. And, to do him justice, he read them extremely well.

GROS. Oh, did he so? Well, who am I that I should take upon myself to withhold my gifts from you? What am I but a trustee? Here is a decalet—a pure and simple thing, a very daisy [46]—a babe might understand it. To appreciate it, it is not necessary to think of anything at all.

ANG. Let us think of nothing at all!

GROSVENOR *recites*

Gentle Jane was good as gold,
She always did as she was told;
She never spoke when her mouth was full,
Or caught bluebottles [47] their legs to pull,
Or spilt plum jam on her nice new frock,
Or put white mice in the eight-day clock,
Or vivisected her last new doll,
Or fostered a passion for alcohol.
And when she grew up she was given in marriage
To a first-class earl who keeps his carriage!

GROS. I believe I am right in saying that there is not one word in that decalet which is calculated to bring the blush of shame to the cheek of modesty.

ANG. Not one; it is purity itself.

GROS. Here's another.

Teasing Tom was a very bad boy,
A great big squirt was his favourite toy;
He put live shrimps in his father's boots,
And sewed up the sleeves of his Sunday suits;
He punched his poor little sisters' heads,
And cayenne-peppered their four-post beds,

[45] The fortitude of the ladies was twice put to the test in this scene. Intense cold in 1946–47 plus a coal strike rendered the theater so cold it was difficult to know, among those girls who were wearing any shade of blue, where they started and their dresses ended. Yet they carried on without so much as one visible shiver. On another occasion, when all were lying on the stage, looking up adoringly at Grosvenor, a rat made its way onto the stage and actually ran over a couple of the girls. Not one moved. Not one lost her rapt expression. But, I'm told, there was many a silent sigh of relief when the rat made its way off on the far side of the stage.

[46] A . . . daisy. In England this is a colloquialism meaning "the tops," of high quality.

[47] Bluebottle. Known in the United States as a horsefly. According to Webster's Dictionary, it is "any of the several large metallic blue and green flies of the dipterous family calliphoridae." So now we know.

[48] Halfpennies. *Pronounced hayp-nees.*

[49] Totally. *Pronounced toe-tally to rhyme with* de bally.

[50] Damning. *Pronounced dam-ning.*

[51] Ungallant. *Pronounced unga-lant.*

[52] *Words and music on page 266.*

He plastered their hair with cobbler's wax,
And dropped hot halfpennies [48] down their backs.
The consequence was he was lost tot*a*lly, [49]
And married a girl in the *corps de bally*!

ANG. Marked you how grandly—how relentlessly—the damning [50] catalogue of crime strode on, till Retribution, like a poisèd hawk, came swooping down upon the Wrong-Doer? Oh, it was terrible!

ELLA. Oh, sir, you are indeed a true poet, for you touch our hearts, and they go out to you!

GROS. (*aside*). This is simply cloying. (*Aloud.*) Ladies, I am sorry to appear ungallant, [51] but this is Saturday, and you have been following me about ever since Monday. I should like the usual half-holiday. I shall take it as a personal favour if you will kindly allow me to close early to-day.

SAPH. Oh, sir, do not send us from you!

GROS. Poor, poor girls! It is best to speak plainly. I know that I am loved by you, but I never can love you in return, for my heart is fixed elsewhere! Remember the fable of the Magnet and the Churn.

ANG. (*wildly*). But we don't know the fable of the Magnet and the Churn!

GROS. Don't you? Then I will sing it to you.

SONG—GROSVENOR [52]

A magnet hung in a hardware shop,
And all around was a loving crop
Of scissors and needles, nails and knives,
Offering love for all their lives;
But for iron the magnet felt no whim,
Though he charmed iron, it charmed not him;
From needles and nails and knives he'd turn,
For he'd set his love on a Silver Churn!

ALL. A Silver Churn?

GROS. A Silver Churn!

His most æsthetic,
Very magnetic
Fancy took this turn—
"If I can wheedle
A knife or a needle,
Why not a Silver Churn?"

CHORUS.   His most æsthetic, etc.

GROS.   And Iron and Steel expressed surprise,
The needles opened their well-drilled eyes,
The penknives felt "shut up," no doubt,
The scissors declared themselves "cut out,"
The kettles they boiled with rage, 'tis said,
While every nail went off its head,
And hither and thither began to roam,
Till a hammer came up—and drove them home.

ALL. It drove them home?
GROS. It drove them home!

While this magnetic,
Peripatetic
Lover he lived to learn,

For he'd set his love on a Silver Churn!

> By no endeavour
> Can magnet ever
> Attract a Silver Churn!

ALL.   While this magnetic, etc.

[They go off in low spirits, gazing back at him from time to time.

GROS. At last they are gone! What is this mysterious fascination that I seem to exercise over all I come across? A curse on my fatal beauty, for I am sick of conquests! [53]

PATIENCE *appears*

PA. Archibald!

GROS. (*turns and sees her*). Patience!

PA. I have escaped with difficulty from my Reginald. I wanted to see you so much that I might ask you if you still love me as fondly as ever?

GROS. Love you? If the devotion of a lifetime—— (*Seizes her hand.*)

PA. (*indignantly*). Hold! Unhand me, or I scream! (*He releases her.*) If you are a gentleman, pray remember that I am another's! (*Very tenderly.*) But you *do* love me, don't you?

GROS. Madly, hopelessly, despairingly!

PA. That's right! I never can be yours; but that's right!

GROS. And you love this Bunthorne?

PA. With a heart-whole ecstasy that withers, and scorches, and burns, and stings! (*Sadly.*) It is my duty.

GROS. Admirable girl! But you are not happy with him?

PA. Happy? I am miserable beyond description!

GROS. That's right! I never can be yours; but that's right!

PA. But go now. I see dear Reginald approaching. Farewell, dear Archibald; I cannot tell you how happy it has made me to know that you still love me.

GROS. Ah, if I only dared—— (*Advances towards her.*)

PA. Sir! this language to one who is promised to another! (*Tenderly.*) Oh, Archibald, think of me sometimes, for my heart is breaking! He is so unkind to me, and you would be so loving!

GROS. Loving! (*Advances towards her.*)

PA. Advance one step, and as I am a good and pure woman, I scream! (*Tenderly.*) Farewell, Archibald! (*Sternly.*) Stop there! (*Tenderly.*) Think of me sometimes! (*Angrily.*) Advance at your peril! Once more, adieu!

*[*GROSVENOR *sighs, gazes sorrowfully at her, sighs deeply, and exit. She bursts into tears*

Enter BUNTHORNE, *followed by* JANE. *He is moody and preoccupied*

JANE *sings*

> In a doleful train,
>   One and one I walk all day;
> For I love in vain—
>   None so sorrowful as they
>   Who can only sigh and say,
>   Woe is me, alackaday!

BUN. (*seeing* PATIENCE). Crying, eh? What are you crying about?

PA. I've only been thinking how dearly I love you!

BUN. Love me! Bah!

JANE. Love him! Bah!

Till a hammer came up—and drove them home.

[53] Patience was the cause of embarrassment to another performer on the stage. The usual Grosvenor had been rushed off to hospital for an appendectomy and an ex-member of the Company was hurriedly recalled to play the role. The only costume available was the one belonging to the hospitalized gentleman—and he was considerably slimmer than the newcomer. The latter did get into it, however, and for the first act everything went well. But the effort of sitting on the stump to sing "The Magnet and the Churn" was too much for the tightly stretched velvet breeches. The back seam gave way. As the girls made their exit, he, obeying directions as given, followed them upstage, giving the audience an unimpeded view of the damage. If you will go back and read Grosvenor's dialogue immediately following the ladies' exit, you will get some idea of the effect this speech had on the audience.

[54] *It might be well to describe a certain bit of business that takes place here. As he speaks the line Bunthorne whips around on Lady Jane. (He is seated on a stump with Lady Jane standing by his side.)*

[55] *Again he whips around toward her.*

[56] *He makes to turn on her but this time she refuses to be crushed.*

[57] *As he speaks this line he looks first at Patience, then to the front, and finally to Lady Jane. But this is too much for her, and she turns on him. Result—Bunthorne's delight suffers a serious setback!*

[58] *He has crossed to Patience and is standing close by her, and as she finishes speaking he snaps his fingers in her face, and then moves upstage. Lady Jane does likewise—snaps fingers, etc. He tries to dodge Jane and finally rushes offstage, hotly pursued by her.*

[59] Words and music on page 269.

BUN. (*to* JANE). Don't you interfere. [54]

JANE. He always crushes me!

PA. (*going to him*). What is the matter, dear Reginald? If you have any sorrow, tell it to me, that I may share it with you. (*Sighing.*) It is my duty!

BUN. (*snappishly*). Whom were you talking with just now?

PA. With dear Archibald.

BUN. (*furiously*). With dear Archibald! Upon my honour, this is too much!

JANE. A great deal too much!

BUN. (*angrily to* JANE). Do be quiet! [55]

JANE. Crushed again!

PA. I think he is the noblest, purest, and most perfect being I have ever met. But I don't love him. It is true that he is devotedly attached to me, but indeed I don't love *him*. Whenever he grows affectionate, I scream. It is my duty! (*Sighing.*)

BUN. I dare say!

JANE. So do I! I dare say! [56]

PA. Why, how could I love him and love you too? You can't love two people at once!

BUN. Oh, can't you, though! [57]

PA. No, you can't; I only wish you could.

BUN. I don't believe you know what love is!

PA. (*sighing*). Yes, I do. There was a happy time when I didn't, but a bitter experience has taught me.

[*Exeunt* BUNTHORNE *and* JANE. [58]

BALLAD—PATIENCE [59]

Love is a plaintive song,
    Sung by a suffering maid,
Telling a tale of wrong,
    Telling of hope betrayed;
Tuned to each changing note,
    Sorry when *he* is sad,
Blind to his every mote,
    Merry when he is glad!
        Love that no wrong can cure,
            Love that is always new,
        That is the love that's pure,
            That is the love that's true!

Rendering good for ill,
    Smiling at every frown,
Yielding your own self-will,
    Laughing your tear-drops down;
Never a selfish whim,
    Trouble, or pain to stir;
Everything for him,
    Nothing at all for her!
        Love that will aye endure,
            Though the rewards be few,
        That is the love that's pure,
            That is the love that's true!

[*At the end of ballad exit* PATIENCE, *weeping.*

Enter BUNTHORNE *and* JANE

BUN. Everything has gone wrong with me since that smug-faced idiot came here. Before that I was admired—I may say, loved.

JANE. Too mild—adored!

BUN. Do let a poet soliloquize! The damozels used to follow me wherever I went; now they all follow him!

JANE. Not all! *I* am still faithful to you.

BUN. Yes, and a pretty damozel *you* are!

JANE. No, not pretty. Massive. Cheer up! I will never leave you, I swear it!

BUN. Oh, thank you! I know what it is; it's his confounded mildness. They find me too highly spiced, if you please! And no doubt I *am* highly spiced.

JANE. Not for my taste!

BUN. (*savagely*). No, but I am for theirs. But I will show the world I can be as mild as he. If they want insipidity, they shall have it. I'll meet this fellow on his own ground and beat him on it.

JANE. You shall. And I will help you.

BUN. You will? Jane, there's a good deal of good in you, after all!

DUET—BUNTHORNE *and* JANE [60]

JANE. So go to him and say to him, with compliment ironical—
BUN.   Sing "Hey to you—
                         Good day to you"—
                   And that's what I shall say!

JANE. "Your style is much too sanctified—your cut is too canonical"—
BUN.   Sing "Bah to you—
                         Ha! ha! to you"—
                   And that's what I shall say!

JANE. "I was the beau ideal of the morbid young æsthetical—
       To doubt my inspiration was regarded as heretical—
       Until you cut me out with your placidity emetical."—
BUN.   Sing "Booh to you—
                         Pooh, pooh to you"—
                   And that's what I shall say!

BOTH.   Sing "Hey to you—good day to you"—
         Sing "Bah to you—ha! ha! to you"—
         Sing "Booh to you—pooh, pooh to you"—
         And that's what ${you \atop I}$ shall say!

BUN. I'll tell him that unless he will consent to be more jocular—
JANE.   Sing "Booh to you—
                         Pooh, pooh to you"—
                   And that's what you should say!

BUN. To cut his curly hair, and stick an eyeglass in his ocular—
JANE.   Sing "Bah to you—
                         Ha! ha! to you"—
                   And that's what you should say!

BUN. To stuff his conversation full of quibble and of quiddity—
      To dine on chops and roly-poly pudding with avidity—
      He'd better clear away with all convenient rapidity.
JANE.   Sing "Hey to you—
                         Good day to you"—
                   And that's what you should say!

BOTH.   Sing "Booh to you—pooh, pooh to you"—
         Sing "Bah to you—ha! ha! to you"—
         Sing "Hey to you—good day to you"—
         And that's what ${I \atop you}$ shall say!

[60] *This duet is a great deal of fun to do and invariably receives two encores, the final business being varied each time, with more exaggeration by Bunthorne. At the end of the original number, Bunthorne skips off, followed by Jane in hot pursuit. At the end of the first encore she nearly catches him; and the entrance for the second encore carries on with that theme, as she has apparently caught him offstage. She comes on with Bunthorne's head under her arm (Bunthorne is still attached to it). At the end of this encore Bunthorne has come near enough to Jane for her to pick him up bodily, head hanging down, and carry him off in triumph. This always calls for at least a call. He brings her on and suddenly turns as if to pick her up. Jane retires with a scream. At the next call, he again leads her on and then, after taking a bow, dashes off the far side of the stage, Jane chasing him. He comes on again through another entrance with Jane still in hot pursuit and exits by the way he came in. Should there be a still further call (not unlikely), he leads her on as before and while she is busy acknowledging the applause he sneaks behind her and off. Jane reacts accordingly and goes off.*

All this is very well, providing the Jane is strong enough. One Jane, unfortunately, dropped me—to the intense delight of the audience as well as of everyone backstage.

[61] The "other outward signs" are a sunflower, an orchid, and a poppy, carried respectively by the Colonel, the Duke and the Major.

[Exeunt JANE and BUNTHORNE together.

Enter DUKE, COLONEL, and MAJOR. They have abandoned their uniforms, and are dressed and made up in imitation of Æsthetics. They have long hair, and other outward signs [61] of attachment to the brotherhood. As they sing they walk in stiff, constrained, and angular attitudes—a grotesque exaggeration of the attitudes adopted by BUNTHORNE and the young Ladies in Act I.

TRIO—DUKE, COLONEL, and MAJOR

It's clear that mediæval art alone retains its zest,
To charm and please its devotees we've done our little best.
We're not quite sure if all we do has the Early English ring;
But, as far as we can judge, it's something like this sort of thing:
   You hold yourself like this (attitude),
   You hold yourself like that (attitude),
By hook and crook you try to look both angular and flat (attitude).
   We venture to expect
   That what we recollect,
Though but a part of true High Art, will have its due effect.

If this is not exactly right, we hope you won't upbraid;
You can't get high Æsthetic tastes, like trousers, ready made.
True views on Mediævalism Time alone will bring,
But, as far as we can judge, it's something like this sort of thing:
   You hold yourself like this (attitude),
   You hold yourself like that (attitude),
By hook and crook you try to look both angular and flat (attitude).
   To cultivate the trim
   Rigidity of limb,
You ought to get a Marionette, and form your style on him (attitude).

COL. (attitude). Yes, it's quite clear that our only chance of making a lasting impression on these young ladies is to become as æsthetic as they are.

MAJ. (attitude). No doubt. The only question is how far we've succeeded in doing so. I don't know why, but I've an idea that this is not quite right.

DUKE (attitude). I don't like it. I never did. I don't see what it means. I do it, but I don't like it.

COL. My good friend, the question is not whether we like it, but whether they do. They understand these things—we don't. Now I shouldn't be surprised if this is effective enough—at a distance.

MAJ. I can't help thinking, we're a little stiff at it. It would be extremely awkward if we were to be "struck" so!

COL. I don't think we shall be struck so. Perhaps we're a little awkward at first—but everything must have a beginning. Oh, here they come! 'Tention! [62]

They strike fresh attitudes, as ANGELA and SAPHIR enter

ANG. (seeing them). Oh, Saphir—see—see! The immortal fire has descended on them, and they are of the Inner Brotherhood—perceptively intense and consummately utter. (The OFFICERS have some difficulty in maintaining their constrained attitudes.)

SAPH. (in admiration). How Botticellian! How Fra Angelican! Oh, Art, we thank thee for this boon!

COL. (apologetically). I'm afraid we're not quite right.

ANG. Not supremely, perhaps, but oh, so, all-but! (To SAPHIR.) Oh, Saphir, are they not quite too all-but?

[62] This is spoken as if giving a military command: "Ten-SHUN!" The three of them carry out a change of posture (still exaggerated aestheticism) with true British Army parade-ground precision.

240

SAPHIR. They are indeed jolly utter!

MAJ. (*in agony*). I wonder what the Inner Brotherhood usually recommend for cramp? [63]

COL. Ladies, we will not deceive you. We are doing this at some personal inconvenience with a view of expressing the extremity of our devotion to you. We trust that it is not without its effect.

ANG. We will not deny that we are much moved by this proof of your attachment.

SAPH. Yes, your conversion to the principles of Æsthetic Art in its highest development has touched us deeply.

ANG. And if Mr. Grosvenor should remain obdurate—

SAPH. Which we have every reason to believe he will—

MAJ. (*aside, in agony*). I wish they'd make haste.

ANG. We are not prepared to say that our yearning hearts will not go out to you.

COL. (*as giving a word of command*). By sections of threes—Rapture! (*All strike a fresh attitude, expressive of æsthetic rapture.*) [64]

SAPH. Oh, it's extremely good—for beginners it's admirable. [65]

MAJ. The only question is, who will take who?

COL. Oh, the Duke chooses first, as a matter of course.

DUKE. Oh, I couldn't think of it—you are really too good!

COL. Nothing of the kind. You are a great matrimonial fish, and it's only fair that each of these ladies should have a chance of hooking you. It's perfectly simple. Observe, suppose you choose Angela, I take Saphir, Major takes nobody. Suppose you choose Saphir, Major takes Angela, I take nobody. Suppose you choose neither, I take Angela, Major takes Saphir. Clear as day!

QUINTET

DUKE, COLONEL, MAJOR, ANGELA, *and* SAPHIR

DUKE (*taking* SAPHIR)

If Saphir I choose to marry,
  I shall be fixed up for life;
Then the Colonel need not tarry,
  Angela can be his wife.

[DUKE *dances with* SAPHIR, COLONEL *with* ANGELA, MAJOR *dances alone.*

MAJOR (*dancing alone*)

In that case unprecedented,
  Single I shall live and die—
I shall have to be contented
  With their heartfelt sympathy! [66]

ALL (*dancing as before*)

He will have to be contented
  With our heartfelt sympathy!

DUKE (*taking* ANGELA)

If on Angy I determine,
  At my wedding she'll appear
Decked in diamonds and in ermine,
  Major then can take Saphir!

[DUKE *dances with* ANGELA, MAJOR *with* SAPHIR, COLONEL *dances alone.*

[63] *The position has become too much for the Major whose leg shoots out straight, causing him to hop madly on the other to regain his balance.*

[64] *Again, this is given as if it were a military drill command, and all strike a fresh attitude, carrying the movement out in three distinct and precise moves.*

[65] *Saphir's approval is a signal for the officers to break their attitudes and the Major wastes no time in putting his leg up on a stump and slapping it vigorously to restore the circulation.*

[66] *At one time "sympathy" was always pronounced to rhyme with die. Some time around the 1930s this was changed and is now pronounced in the usual way. Quite rightly so. Had Gilbert desired the offbeat pronunciation, I think he would have spelled it that way, or accented the syllable, as he invariably did in such cases.*

COLONEL (*dancing*)

In that case unprecedented,
Single I shall live and die—
I shall have to be contented
With their heartfelt sympathy!

ALL (*dancing as before*)

He will have to be contented
With our heartfelt sympathy!

DUKE (*taking both* ANGELA *and* SAPHIR)

After some debate internal,
If on neither I decide,
Saphir then can take the Colonel,

(*Handing* SAPHIR *to* COLONEL.)

Angy be the Major's bride!

(*Handing* ANGELA *to* MAJOR.)

[COLONEL *dances with* SAPHIR, MAJOR *with* ANGELA, DUKE *dances alone.*

DUKE (*dancing*)

In that case unprecedented,
Single I must live and die—
I shall have to be contented
With their heartfelt sympathy!

ALL (*dancing as before*)

He will have to be contented
With our heartfelt sympathy.

[*At the end,* DUKE, COLONEL, *and* MAJOR, *and two girls
dance off arm-in-arm.*

Enter GROSVENOR

GROS. It is very pleasant to be alone. It is pleasant to be able to gaze at leisure upon those features which all others may gaze upon at their good will! (*Looking at his reflection in hand-mirror.*) [67] Ah, I am a very Narcissus!

Enter BUNTHORNE, *moodily*

BUN. It's no use; I can't live without admiration. Since Grosvenor came here, insipidity has been at a premium. Ah, he is there!
GROS. Ah, Bunthorne! come here—look! Very graceful, isn't it! [68]
BUN. (*taking hand-mirror*). Allow me; I haven't seen it. Yes, it is graceful.
GROS. (*re-taking hand-mirror*). Oh, good gracious! not that—this——
BUN. You don't mean that! Bah! I am in no mood for trifling.
GROS. And what is amiss?
BUN. Ever since you came here, you have entirely monopolized the attentions of the young ladies. I don't like it, sir!
GROS. My dear sir, how can I help it? They are the plague of my life. My dear Mr. Bunthorne, with your personal disadvantages, you can have no idea of the inconvenience of being madly loved, at first sight, by every woman you meet.
BUN. Sir, until you came here I was adored!
GROS. Exactly—until I came here. That's my grievance. I cut everybody out! I assure you, if you could only suggest some means whereby,

[67] *Gilbert's original stage directions call for Grosvenor to recline "on bank of lake, and look at his reflection in the water." In view of his speech this would seem to be most appropriate. When the directions were changed, I cannot say, nor why. I can only assume that scenic difficulties had something to do with it.*

[68] *The original script for this and the next few lines read:*

GROS. *Ah, Bunthorne, come here. Is it not beautiful?*
BUN. *Which?*
GROS. *Mine!*
BUN. *Bah! I am in no mood for trifling!*

consistently with my duty to society, I could escape these inconvenient attentions, you would earn my everlasting gratitude.

BUN. I will do so at once. However popular it may be with the world at large, your personal appearance is highly objectionable to *me*.

GROS. It is? (*Shaking his hand.*) Oh, thank you! thank you! How can I express my gratitude?

BUN. By making a complete change at once. Your conversation must henceforth be perfectly matter-of-fact. You must cut your hair, and have a back parting. [69] In appearance and costume you must be absolutely commonplace.

GROS. (*decidedly*). No. Pardon me, that's impossible.

BUN. Take care! When I am thwarted I am very terrible.

GROS. I can't help that. I am a man with a mission. And that mission must be fulfilled.

BUN. I don't think you quite appreciate the consequences of thwarting me.

GROS. I don't care what they are.

BUN. Suppose—I won't go so far as to say that I will do it—but suppose for one moment I were to curse you? (GROSVENOR *quails.*) Ah! Very well. Take care.

GROS. But surely you would never do that? (*In great alarm.*)

BUN. I don't know. It would be an extreme measure, no doubt. Still——

GROS. (*wildly*). But you would not do it—I am sure you would not. (*Throwing himself at* BUNTHORNE's *knees, and clinging to him.*) Oh, reflect, reflect! You had a mother once.

BUN. Never!

GROS. Then you had an aunt! (BUNTHORNE *affected.*) Ah! I see you had! By the memory of that aunt, I implore you to pause ere you resort to this last fearful expedient. Oh, Mr. Bunthorne, reflect, reflect! (*Weeping.*)

BUN. (*aside, after a struggle with himself*). I must not allow myself to be unmanned! (*Aloud.*) It is useless. Consent at once, or may a nephew's curse——

GROS. Hold! Are you absolutely resolved?

BUN. Absolutely.

GROS. Will nothing shake you?

BUN. Nothing. I am adamant.

GROS. Very good. (*Rising.*) Then I yield.

BUN. Ha! You swear it?

GROS. I do, cheerfully. I have long wished for a reasonable pretext for such a change as you suggest. It has come at last. I do it on compulsion! [70]

BUN. Victory! I triumph!

DUET [71]—BUNTHORNE *and* GROSVENOR [72]

BUN.
      When I go out of door,
      Of damozels a score
        (All sighing and burning,
        And clinging and yearning)
      Will follow me as before.
      I shall, with cultured taste,
      Distinguish gems from paste,
        And "High diddle diddle"
        Will rank as an idyll,
      If I pronounce it chaste!

BOTH.
      A most intense young man,
      A soulful-eyed young man,

[69] ". . . and have a back parting." *Several lines in the original script were cut, but this was a line added at a later date.*

[70] *Compare these lines with Verse 21 in "The Rival Curates" (Bab Ballads).*

[71] *It was just at this point, when we were appearing at the Shakespeare Memorial Theatre, Stratford-upon-Avon, that the aftermath of a fire that broke out under the stage that same evening caught up with us. The auditorium had become filled with smoke, and though nobody left his seat, there had been some alarm. However, in the intermission, the manager calmed the audience by saying that the sliding roof would be opened to clear the air. It was a nice night and not raining. As we began our duet they started to close the roof. It had never been opened before, and so never closed. The large pulley wheel that was part of the mechanism had a flaw in it and the strain was too much. It broke, and large pieces of cast iron rained down on the stage. I sang the first verse with one eye up and one eye looking for Grosvenor who had adopted the wisdom of discretion and had disappeared. All I could think of was that I hoped I would see the next piece in time to dodge it, and be able to remember Grosvenor's lines of the duet well enough to adapt them to myself. Fortunately, there was no other piece and I was saved from the ultimate by the timely reappearance of Grosvenor.*

[72] *Words and music on page 271.*

An ultra-poetical, super-æsthetical,
Out-of-the-way young man!

GROS.
Conceive me, if you can,
An every-day young man:
A commonplace type,
With a stick and a pipe,
And a half-bred black-and-tan;
Who thinks suburban "hops" [73]
More fun than "Monday Pops," [74]
Who's fond of his dinner,
And doesn't get thinner
On bottled beer and chops.

BOTH.
A commonplace young man,
A matter-of-fact young man,
A steady and stolid-y, jolly Bank-holiday [75]
Every-day young man!

BUN.
A Japanese young man,
A blue-and-white young man,
Francesca da Rimini, miminy, piminy, [76]
Je-ne-sais-quoi young man!

GROS.
A Chancery Lane [77] young man,
A Somerset House [78] young man,
A very delectable, highly respectable,
Threepenny-bus young man! [79]

BUN.
A pallid and thin young man,
A haggard and lank young man,
A greenery-yallery, Grosvenor Gallery, [80]
Foot-in-the-grave young man!

GROS.
A Sewell & Cross [81] young man,
A Howell & James [82] young man,
A pushing young particle—"What's the next
  article?"
Waterloo House [83] young man!

ENSEMBLE

BUN.	GROS.
Conceive me, if you can,	Conceive me, if you can,
A crotchety, cracked young man,	A matter-of-fact young man,
An ultra-poetical, super-æsthetical,	An alphabetical, arithmetical,
Out-of-the-way young man!	Every-day young man!

[*At the end,* GROSVENOR *dances off.* BUNTHORNE *remains.*

BUN. It is all right! I have committed my last act of ill-nature, and henceforth I'm a changed character. (*Dances about stage, humming refrain of last air.*)

Enter PATIENCE. *She gazes in astonishment at him*

PA. Reginald! Dancing! And—what in the world is the matter with you?

BUN. Patience, I'm a changed man. Hitherto I've been gloomy, moody, fitful—uncertain in temper and selfish in disposition—

PA. You have, indeed! (*Sighing.*)

BUN. All that is changed. I have reformed. I have modelled myself upon Mr. Grosvenor. Henceforth I am mildly cheerful. My conversation will blend amusement with instruction. I shall still be æsthetic; but my æstheticism will be of the most pastoral kind.

[73] Suburban hops. *Weekly dances held in the suburbs, usually on a Saturday night.*

[74] Monday Pops. *Popular concerts (probably held in Queen's Hall).*

[75] Jolly Bank-holiday. *The reference here is to the type of person who frequents the Hampstead Heath August Bank Holiday Fair.*

[76] Miminy, piminy. *Ridiculously affected, finicking.*

[77] Chancery Lane. *The law center of London. Obviously the allusion is to a lawyer's clerk.*

[78] Somerset House. *The office of the Registrar General, where all records—births, deaths, wills, testaments, etc.—are kept.*

[79] Threepenny-bus young man. *As opposed to one who hails a taxi.*
I think that it's interesting that the line "Threepenny-bus young man" became for a time "Twopenny-tube young man." This was when the "Tuppenny Tube," as it became known, was opened. Later, the rise in tube fares brought the original line back—and so it has remained ever since. (Incidentally, it is pronounced Thrippenny bus.)

[80] Grosvenor Gallery. *A picture gallery (from whence Gilbert chose Grosvenor's name). Whistler exhibited some of his "Nocturnes" paintings here.*

[81] Sewell & Cross.
[82] Howell & James. } *Department stores.*
[83] Waterloo-House.

PA. Oh, Reginald! Is all this true?

BUN. Quite true. Observe how amiable I am. (*Assuming a fixed smile.*)

PA. But, Reginald, how long will this last?

BUN. With occasional intervals for rest and refreshment, as long as I do.

PA. Oh, Reginald, I'm so happy! (*In his arms.*) Oh, dear, dear Reginald, I cannot express the joy I feel at this change. It will no longer be a duty to love you, but a pleasure—a rapture—an ecstasy!

BUN. My darling!

PA. But—oh, horror! (*Recoiling from him.*)

BUN. What's the matter?

PA. Is it quite certain that you have absolutely reformed—that you are henceforth a perfect being—utterly free from defect of any kind?

BUN. It is quite certain. I have sworn it.

PA. Then I never can be yours!

BUN. Why not?

PA. Love, to be pure, must be absolutely unselfish, and there can be nothing unselfish in loving so perfect a being as you have now become!

BUN. But, stop a bit! I don't want to change—I'll relapse—I'll be as I was—interrupted!

Enter GROSVENOR, *followed by all the young Ladies, who are followed by Chorus of Dragoons. He has had his hair cut, and is dressed in an ordinary suit of dittoes* [84] *and a pot hat.* [85] *They all dance cheerfully round the stage in marked contrast to their former languor.*

CHORUS—GROSVENOR *and* GIRLS

GROS.	GIRLS
I'm a Waterloo House young man,	We're Swears & Wells [86] young girls,
A Sewell & Cross young man,	We're Madame Louise [87] young girls,
A steady and stolid-y, jolly Bank-holiday,	We're prettily pattering, cheerily chattering,
Every-day young man!	Every-day young girls!

BUN. Angela—Ella—Saphir—what—what does this mean?

ANG. It means that Archibald the All-Right cannot be all-wrong; and if the All-Right chooses to discard æstheticism, it proves that æstheticism ought to be discarded.

PA. Oh, Archibald! Archibald! I'm shocked—surprised—horrified!

GROS. I can't help it. I'm not a free agent. I do it on compulsion.

PA. This is terrible. Go! I shall never set eyes on you again. But—oh, joy!

GROS. What is the matter?

PA. Is it quite, quite certain that you will always be a commonplace young man?

GROS. Always—I've sworn it.

PA. Why, then, there's nothing to prevent my loving you with all the fervour at my command!

GROS. Why, that's true.

PA. My Archibald!

GROS. My Patience! (*They embrace.*)

BUN. Crushed again!

Enter JANE

JANE (*who is still æsthetic*). Cheer up! I am still here. I have never left you, and I never will!

BUN. Thank you, Jane. After all, there is no denying it, you're a fine figure of a woman!

[84] Dittoes. *A suit made of the same material throughout.*

[85] Pot hat. *A hard felt or bowler. A "derby." (The ladies' dresses included such attire as tennis frocks, riding habits, and even Scottish Highland dress—kilts, sporran, spats and all!)*

[86] Swears & Wells. *An exclusive department store still in existence.*

[87] Madame Louise. *A Bond Street establishment that catered to the ladies.*

JANE. My Reginald!

BUN. My Jane!

Flourish. Enter COLONEL, DUKE, *and* MAJOR

COL. Ladies, the Duke has at length determined to select a bride! (*General excitement.*)

DUKE. I have a great gift to bestow. Approach such of you as are truly lovely. (*All come forward, bashfully, except* JANE *and* PATIENCE.) In personal appearance you have all that is necessary to make a woman happy. In common fairness, I think I ought to choose the only one among you who has the misfortune to be distinctly plain. (*Girls retire disappointed.*) Jane!

JANE (*leaving* BUNTHORNE'S *arms*). Duke! (JANE *and* DUKE *embrace.* BUNTHORNE *is utterly disgusted.*)

BUN. Crushed again!

FINALE

DUKE.
> After much debate internal,
> I on Lady Jane decide,
> Saphir now may take the Colonel,
> Angy be the Major's bride!

[SAPHIR *pairs off with* COLONEL, ANGELA *with* MAJOR, ELLA *with* SOLICITOR

BUN.
> In that case unprecedented,
> Single I must live and die—
> I shall have to be contented
> With a tulip or li*ly!* [88]

[*Takes a lily from button-hole and gazes affectionately at it.* [89]

ALL.
> He will have to be contented
> With a tulip or li*ly!*
>
> Greatly pleased with one another,
> To get married we decide.
> Each of us will wed the other,
> Nobody be Bunthorne's Bride!

DANCE

CURTAIN

[88] *Here the accent is definitely on the last syllable, and the pronunciation is li-lie.*

[89] *. . . and sinks down onto the stage to contemplate it.*

Twenty Love-Sick Maidens We

I Cannot Tell What This Love May Be

Lightly and gracefully

PATIENCE

I can-not tell what this love may
If love is a thorn, they show no

be That com-eth to all, but not to me; It can-not be kind as they'd im-
wit Who fool-ish-ly hug and fost-er it. If love is a weed, how sim-ple

ply, Or why do these la - dies sigh? It can-not be joy and rap - ture
they Who gath-er it day by day! If love is a net-tle that makes you

deep, Or why do these gen - tle la - dies weep? It can-not be bliss - ful as 'tis
smart, Then why do you wear it next your heart? And if it be none of these, say

said,— Or why are their eyes so _____ won-drous red?
I, — Ah, why do you sit and _____ sob and sigh?

rit.
follow the voice
mf *a tempo*

Though ev - 'ry - where_ true love I see

A - com-ing to all_ but not to me, I can-not tell what_ this love_ may

mf *a tempo*

be!_____ For I_ am blithe and I_ am gay, While they_ sit

sigh - ing night_ and day; For I_ am blithe and I_ am gay, Think of the

250

gulf_ 'twixt them_ and me. Think of the gulf_ 'twixt them_ and

me, Fal- la- la- la- la, la- la- la- la- la- la- la- la- la, la- la- la- la- la- la- la- la- la-

1.

la, and mi - se - rie!

2.

la, and mi - se - rie!

If You Want a Receipt

yes, yes, yes, yes, yes! Take

all the re-mark-a-ble peo-ple in his-to-ry, Rat-tle them off to a

pop-u-lar Chorus: Yes, yes, yes, yes,

yes, yes, yes! 1. The
(2. If you)

pluck of Lord Nel-son on board of the Vic-to-ry, Ge-nius of Bis-marck de-
want a re-ceipt for this sol-dier-like par-a-gon, Get at the wealth of the

staccato

vis - ing a plan, The hu - mour of Field - ing (which sounds con - tra - dic - to - ry),
Czar (if you can), The fam - i - ly pride of a Span - iard from Ar - a - gon,

Cool - ness of Pa - get a - bout to tre - pan, The sci - ence of Jul - lien, the
Force of Me - phis - to pro - nounc - ing a ban, A smack of Lord Wa - ter - ford,

em - i - nent mu - si - co, Wit of Mac - au - ley, who wrote of Queen Anne, The
reck - less and rol - lick - y, Swag - ger of Ro - der - ick, head - ing his clan, The

pa - thos of Pad - dy, as ren - dered by Bou - ci - cault, Style of the Bish - op of
keen pen - e - tra - tion of Pad - ding - ton Pol - la - ky, Grace of an O - da - lisque

So - dor and Man, The dash of a D'Or - say, di - vest - ed of quack - er - y
on a di - van, The ge - nius stra - te - gic of Cae - sar or Han - ni - bal,

Nar - ra - tive pow - ers of Dick - ens and Thac - ke - ray, Vic - tor Em - man - u - el
Skill of Sir Gar - net in thrash - ing a can - ni - bal, Fla - vour of Ham - let, the

poco a

peak-haunt-ing Po - ve - ril, Thom - as A - qui - nas, And Doc - tor Sa - che - ve - rell,
Strang-er, a touch of him, Lit - tle of Man - fred (but not ver - y much of him),

poco cresc.

Tup - per and Ten - ny - son, Dan - iel De - foe, An - tho - ny Trol - lope and
Bea - dle of Bur - ling - ton, Ri - chard - son's show, Mis - ter Mi - caw - ber and

più cresc.

Mis - ter Gui - zot! Ah!
Ma - dame Tus - saud!

Chorus Yes, yes, yes, yes, yes, yes,

f deciso

yes, yes! Take of these el - e - ments all that is fu - si - ble,

Melt them all down in a pip-kin or cru - ci - ble, Set them to sim - mer and

take off the scum, ___ And a Heav - y Dra - goon is the re - si -

du - um!

2. If you

When I First Put This Uniform On

In a spirited march tempo

COLONEL

1. When I   first put this u - ni - form
(2. I)   said, when I first put it

on, I   said, as I looked in the glass,   "It's one to a mil - lion That
on, "It is plain to the ver - i - est dunce,   That ev - er - y beau - ty Will

an - y ci - vil - ian My fig - ure and form will sur - pass.   Gold   lace has a charm for the
feel it her du - ty To yield to its glam - our at once.   They will see that I'm free - ly gold-

fair, And I've plen- ty of that, and to spare," While a lov- er's pro-fes-sions, When
laced In a u- ni-form hand-some and chaste." But the per- i -pa- tet- ics Of

ut- tered in Hes-sians, Are el - o-quent ev-'ry - where!" A__ fact that I count- ed up-
long-haired aes-thet- ics Are ver-y much more to their taste, Which I nev-er count- ed up-

CHORUS

on, When I first put this u - ni -form on! By a sim- ple co-
on, When I first put this u - ni -form on! By a sim- ple co-

in - ci- dence, few Could ev- er have count- ed up- on, The same thing oc- curred to
in - ci- dence, few Could ev- er have count- ed up- on, I did-n't an - tic- i- pate

1.   COLONEL 2.

me, When I first put this u - ni - form on! 2. I
that, When I first put this u - ni - form on!

If You're Anxious For to Shine

Gracefully

mf

BUNTHORNE

p

1. If you're anx-ious for to shine— in the high aes-thet-ic line— as a
(2. Be —) el - o-quent in praise of the ver-y dull old days— which have
(3. Then a) sen-ti-men-tal pas-sion of a ve-ge-ta-ble fash-ion must ex-

man of cul-ture rare, You must get up all the germs— of the
long since passed a-way, And con-vince 'em, if you can,— that the
cite your lan-guid spleen, An at-tach-ment à la Pla-to for a

sempre staccato

tran-scen-den-tal terms— and— plant them ev-'ry-where. You must
reign of good Queen Anne— was— Cul-ture's palm-iest day. Of—
bash-ful young po-ta-to, or a not-too-French French bean! Though the

lie up-on the dais-ies and dis-course in nov-el phras-es of your
course you will pooh-pooh what-ev-er's fresh and new,___ and de-
Phi-lis-tines may jos-tle, you will rank as an a-pos-tle in the

com-pli-cat-ed state of mind, The mean-ing does-n't mat-ter if it's
clare it's crude and mean. For Art stopped short in the
high aes-thet-ic band, If you walk down Pic-ca-dil-ly with a

on-ly i-dle chat-ter of a tran-scen-den-tal kind.
cul-ti-vat-ed court of the Em-press Jo-se-phine.
pop-py or a lil-y in your me-di-ae-val hand.

And ev-'ry one will say, As you walk your mys-tic
And ev-'ry one will say, As you walk your mys-tic
And ev-'ry one will say, As you walk your flow-ery

way,   "If— this— young man ex - press-es him - self in
way,   "If— that's not good e - nough— for him which is
way,   "If— he's— con - tent with a ve - ge - ta - ble love which would

terms too deep for me,   Why, what a ver - y sin - gu - lar - ly
good e - nough · for me,   Why, what a ver - y cul - ti - vat - ed
cer - tain - ly not suit me,   Why, what a most par - tic - u - lar - ly

deep young man this deep young man must be!"
kind of youth this kind of youth must be!"
pure young man this pure young man must be!"

rit.

f   a tempo

rit.

1.-2.   p   3.

2. Be—
3. Then a

p

sf

Prithee, Pretty Maiden

Very tenderly and rather slow   *p* GROSVENOR

1. Pri-thee, pret-ty maid-en,
2. Pri-thee, pret-ty maid-en,

pri-thee, tell me true.   (Hey, but I'm dole-ful, wil-low, wil-low wa-ly!)
will you mar-ry me?   (Hey, but I'm hope-ful, wil-low, wil-low wa-ly!)

Have you e'er a lov-er a-dang-ling af-ter you?   Hey, wil-low wa-ly O!
I may say at once, I'm a man of pro-per-tee,   Hey, wil-low wa-ly O!

I would fain dis-cov-er If you have a lov-er!   Hey,_ wil-low wa-ly_ O!
Mon-ey, I des-pise it; Man-y peo-ple prize it,   Hey,_ wil-low wa-ly_ O!

Silvered Is the Raven Hair

Moderately slow tempo

JANE

Sil - vered is the ra - ven hair, Spread - ing is the part - ing straight,
Fad - ing is the ta - per waist, Shape - less grows the shape - ly limb,

Mot - tled the com - plex - ion fair, Halt - ing is the youth - ful gait,
And al - though se - vere - ly laced, Spread - ing is the fi - gure trim!

Hol - low is the laugh - ter free, Spec - ta - cled the lim - pid eye,
Stout - er than I used to be, Still more cor - pu - lent grow I,

rall.

The Magnet and the Churn

Gaily

GROSVENOR

1. A mag-net hung in a hard-ware shop, And all a-round was a
(2. And) i-ron and steel ex-pressed sur-prise, The nee-dles o-pened their

lov-ing crop Of scis-sors and nee-dles, nails and knives, Of-fer-ing love for
well-drilled eyes, The pen-knives felt "shut up," no doubt, The scis-sors de-clared them-

all_ their_ lives;   But for
selves_ "cut_ out";   The

Fan - cy took this— turn: "If I can whee-dle A knife or a nee-dle,
Lov - er he lived to— learn, By no en-deav-our Can mag-net ev-er At-

_mf_ CHORUS of MAIDENS

Why not a Sil - ver Churn?" His— most aes-thet-ic— Ver-y mag-net-ic—
tract a Sil - ver Churn! While this mag-net-ic— Per-i-pa-tet-ic—

_mf_

(2nd time) CHORUS and GROSVENOR

Fan - cy took this— turn. "If I can whee-dle A knife or a nee-dle,
Lov - er he lived to— learn, By no en-deav-our Can mag-net ev-er At-

1.

Why not a Sil - ver Churn?"

_f_

GROSVENOR **2.**

_p_

2. And tract a Sil - ver Churn!—

_p_

_fz_

Love Is a Plaintive Song

Moderately fast

p PATIENCE

1. Love is a plain-tive song,   Sung by a suf-f'ring
2. Ren-der-ing good for ill,   Smil-ing at ev - 'ry

maid,   Tell-ing a tale of wrong,   Tell-ing of hope be - trayed;
frown,   Yield-ing your own self - will,   Laugh-ing your tear-drops down;

Tuned to each chang-ing note,   Sor - ry when he is sad,___   Blind to his ev - 'ry
Nev - er a self-ish whim,   Trou-ble or pain to stir;___   Ev - er - y-thing for

rall.

mote, Mer - ry when he_ is glad! Mer - ry when he_ is glad!_
him, Noth - ing at all_ for her! Noth - ing at all_ for her!_

rall. follow the voice

When I Go Out of Door

man, Fran - ces - ca da Ri - mi - ni, mim - i - ny, pim - i - ny,
man, A ver - y de - lec - ta - ble, high - ly re - spect - a - ble,
man, A green - er - y yal - ler - y, Gros - ve - nor Gal - ler - y,
man, A push - ing young par - ti - cle, "What's the next ar - ti - cle?"

1.-2.-3.   4. Grosvenor Con - ceive me, if you

Je ne sais quoi young man! Grosvenor 4. A
Three - pen - ny - bus young man! Bunthorne 5. A   Bunthorne Con - ceive me, if you
Foot - in - the - grave young man! Grosvenor 6. A
Wa - ter - loo House young   man!

can, A mat - ter - of - fact young man, An al - pha - bet - i - cal,
can, A crotch - et - y, cracked young man, An ul - tra - po - et - i - cal,

ar - ith - met - i - cal, ev - er - y - day young man!

su - per - aes - thet - i - cal, out - of - the - way young man!

Iolanthe

OR, THE PEER AND THE PERI

DRAMATIS PERSONÆ

THE LORD CHANCELLOR

EARL OF MOUNTARARAT

EARL TOLLOLLER

PRIVATE WILLIS (*of the Grenadier Guards*)

STREPHON (*an Arcadian Shepherd*)

QUEEN OF THE FAIRIES

IOLANTHE (*a Fairy, Strephon's Mother*)

CELIA ⎫
LEILA ⎬ *Fairies*
FLETA ⎭

PHYLLIS (*an Arcadian Shepherdess and Ward in Chancery*)

Chorus of Dukes, Marquises, Earls, Viscounts, Barons, and Fairies

ACT I

AN ARCADIAN LANDSCAPE

ACT II

PALACE YARD, WESTMINSTER

First produced at the Savoy Theatre, November 25, 1882

IOLANTHE; or, The Peer and the Peri* *was written under most tragic circumstances so far as Sullivan was concerned—his mother, whom he adored, died in May of 1881. Yet Iolanthe remains one of the gayest of scores. Tragedy seemed to inspire him to write: his father died and "In Memoriam" followed; his brother Fred died and Sullivan wrote "The Lost Chord."*

But that wasn't all. On the day of the opening night his bankers, Cooper, Hall & Company, went bankrupt. Every penny Sullivan had was wrapped up in that company, and when he entered the pit to conduct the first performance he was a financially ruined man. A few pounds in a current account represented his sole assets.

But once again Gilbert and Sullivan "did it." Although Iolanthe was not unanimously hailed the next morning by the critics as a smash hit (one weekly said it didn't come "within a mile of Pinafore"), it ran for fourteen months, and Sullivan's fortunes were once again in the ascendant.

Iolanthe is notable because it is the only one of the series for which the overture was composed by Sullivan. Usually it was Alfred Cellier, the regular conductor, who made the arrangements. In fact, he was making an arrangement for the American company of Iolanthe in New York, but this time Sullivan was composing one in England as well. Time was short—a not unusual circumstance where Sullivan was concerned in the matter of a score— and he could not get his overture ready in time for it to reach New York for the opening there, so he wrote to Cellier, telling him to "write one himself." The official overture used today, however, is Sullivan's. There is a famous story concerning this overture. Sullivan had gone into the theater one evening and was leaning on the rail at the back of the circle, listening to the orchestra playing his music. Quite soon he began to hum along with them. A patron of the theater, also leaning over the rail and only a few yards away (obviously a full house with standing room only), tapped Sullivan on the shoulder and said: "Excuse me, sir, but I came to hear Sullivan's music—not yours."

It was also during the writing and the run of Iolanthe that two other events of some significance occurred. Patience was still running at the Savoy while Iolanthe was being evolved from the pen of Gilbert and music manuscript of Sullivan. But Gilbert's pen was busy in another direction too. He wrote a letter to Sullivan in which he alluded to the outrageously high nightly expenses that Patience was incurring at the Savoy. The letter contained a mild threat, it seems. Gilbert closed it with a statement that if he (Sullivan) and Carte agreed on any one point (as opposed to his own ideas of economizing) he would consider the matter decided and would act accordingly. A forerunner of the later and famous "carpet" quarrel? In May of 1883, during the run of Iolanthe, Sullivan was knighted. Gilbert was not. It cannot be said that Gilbert was so jealous of this honor that the seeds of their final breakup were sown then, but there is no doubt the snub accorded him rankled. On top of which, in any difference of opinion, Sullivan usually sided with Carte, a thing Gilbert was aware of, as witness the mild threat in his letter. Actually,

* See note 80.

Sullivan's knighthood was not conferred on him for his work in collaboration with Gilbert. Queen Victoria had little sympathy with those "frivolities" and didn't even consider them. The accolade was given "in recognition of your distinguished talents as a composer and of the services which you have rendered to the promotion of the art of music generally in this country." It was his "Te Deum," "In Memoriam," religious music, the Prom Concerts, etc., that were the factors in her decision to honor him.*

* Gilbert was knighted twenty-four years later, in 1902, by Edward VII.

Iolanthe

ACT I

SCENE.—*An Arcadian Landscape. A river runs around the back of the stage. A rustic bridge crosses the river.*

Enter Fairies, led by LEILA, CELIA, *and* FLETA. *They trip around the stage, singing as they dance*

CHORUS [1]

Tripping hither, tripping thither,
Nobody knows why or whither;
We must dance and we must sing
Round about our fairy ring!

SOLO—CELIA [2]

We are dainty little fairies,
   Ever singing, ever dancing;
We indulge in our vagaries
   In a fashion most entrancing.
If you ask the special function
   Of our never-ceasing motion,
We reply, without compunction,
   That we haven't any notion!

CHORUS

No, we haven't any notion!
Tripping hither, etc.

SOLO—LEILA

If you ask us how we live,
Lovers all essentials give—
   We can ride on lovers' sighs,
   Warm ourselves in lovers' eyes,
   Bathe ourselves in lovers' tears,
   Clothe ourselves with lovers' fears,
   Arm ourselves with lovers' darts,
   Hide ourselves in lovers' hearts.
When you know us, you'll discover
That we almost live on lover!

CHORUS

Tripping hither, etc.
(*At the end of Chorus, all sigh wearily.*)

CELIA. Ah, it's all very well, but since our Queen banished Iolanthe, [3] fairy revels have not been what they were!
LEILA. Iolanthe was the life and soul of Fairyland. Why, she wrote all our songs and arranged all our dances! We sing her songs and we trip her measures, but we don't enjoy ourselves!

[1] As long as I have known this opera the entrance of the Fairies has always been taken with all the delicacy possible. The tendency has been toward the delicious, delightful and (de) lovely! Beautiful girls, delightful and fairylike music, and equally delightful and airy dances.

Arthur Sullivan's marking in the vocal score (and, I presume, in his original orchestral score) is "f" (forte!), and, I think, a "lazy V." If the music is played and sung as marked, the whole conception of the presentation changes.

The question arises, how did Gilbert conceive these ladies? As fairies? Or as a delightful parody of Grimm or Hans Andersen? Sullivan's scoring would appear to me to lean toward the latter. And in that case, who was the real wit of the team? More frequently than not it turns out to be Sullivan. That is to say, from a musical point of view! (Although he was once sentences ahead of Gilbert when he was heard to say, apropos of the pirating of these operas by American producers and certain remarks in respect to the results of litigation regarding same: "It would appear to me to be most undemocratic to deprive these people of their right to rob us of our rights!")

As a matter of interest, the vocal score as published in the official and authorized versions is marked forte staccato.

The inference I draw from such marking is one of heavy-footedness rather than the light and dainty. And do not overlook Gilbert's directions at the end of the opening chorus. They are all weary and all very distressed—a state of mind not conducive to lightsomeness, as Leila's first speech points out.

[2] Words and music on page 310.

[3] Iolanthe. Up to the night of the opening the name had been Perola. At the last rehearsal Sullivan told the Company that "on the night" they were to use the name "Iolanthe." ("Iolanthe" had been the selected name and title all along, but "officially" they were rehearsing "Perola" in an effort to throw American pirates off the scent.) One young lady was afraid she would not remember the name. Sullivan told her not to mind about that; so long as the music was sung she could use any name she liked. Only Gilbert would notice the mistake—and he wouldn't be there! Nor was he. He prowled about the Thames Embankment, arriving at the theater just in time to answer the calls for author and composer at the end of the show.

[4] *One young lady, not very long with the D'Oyly Carte Company, was suddenly entrusted with the role of Fleta. Very young and very nervous, she got her first lines out in a trembling voice. Then came her next line—and a word that suddenly became a monster! Said she: "Oh! Ith it injudithash to marry a mortal?" Her blush could be seen through her make-up. But poor Leila. Not sure if she had heard aright, she stared at Fleta, wide-eyed, and then said: "Injudiciouth? It thtriketh at the root of the whole fairy thythtem!"*

Such is the force of thuggethtion—oops! sorry—suggestion.

[5] *The Queen, please remember, is, one might say, the counterpart of Lady Jane in Patience, only in the Queen's case she does not allude directly to her portliness. It is brought to the attention of the eye by the ludicrousness of her ability to "dive into a dewdrop." As Leila says, Iolanthe certainly did surprising things.*

In the very early days, before the final draft of Iolanthe was reached, the Fairy Queen bore a name—Varine. This she lost, along with a number of other characters Gilbert had had in mind but discarded—such as an Admiral of the Fleet, Attorney-General and Commander-in-Chief. She has also suffered many a costume change. The original costume bore a definite similarity to that of Brünnhilde in Die Walküre. From thence through a variety of changes to the heavy satin crinoline and red hair of today (designed in 1932 by George Sheringham).

[6] *It is a great pity that modern stages do not contain the number of traps that practically all the old ones did. Iolanthe actually rose through a shallow trough of water and crossed it by means of steppingstones painted as lily leaves. Today she sits behind a small bush and just stands up when called. A beautiful effect once, now lost. The cost of cutting and fitting a trap is too great for one short effect.*

FLETA. To think that five-and-twenty years have elapsed since she was banished! What could she have done to have deserved so terrible a punishment?

LEILA. Something awful! She married a mortal!

FLETA. Oh! Is it injudicious to marry a mortal? [4]

LEILA. Injudicious? It strikes at the root of the whole fairy system! By our laws, the fairy who marries a mortal dies!

CELIA. But Iolanthe didn't die!

Enter FAIRY QUEEN

QUEEN. No, because your Queen, who loved her with a surpassing love, commuted her sentence to penal servitude for life, on condition that she left her husband and never communicated with him again!

LEILA. That sentence of penal servitude she is now working out, on her head, at the bottom of that stream!

QUEEN. Yes, but when I banished her, I gave her all the pleasant places of the earth to dwell in. I'm sure I never intended that she should go and live at the bottom of a stream! It makes me perfectly wretched to think of the discomfort she must have undergone!

LEILA. Think of the damp! And her chest was always delicate.

QUEEN. And the frogs! Ugh! I never shall enjoy any peace of mind until I know why Iolanthe went to live among the frogs!

FLETA. Then why not summon her and ask her?

QUEEN. Why? Because if I set eyes on her I should forgive her at once!

CELIA. Then why not forgive her? Twenty-five years—it's a long time!

LEILA. Think how we loved her!

QUEEN. Loved her? What was your love to mine? Why, she was invaluable to me! Who taught me to curl myself inside a buttercup? Iolanthe! Who taught me to swing upon a cobweb? Iolanthe! Who taught me to dive into a dewdrop [5]—to nestle in a nutshell—to gambol upon gossamer? Iolanthe!

LEILA. She certainly did surprising things!

FLETA. Oh, give her back to us, great Queen, for your sake if not for ours! (*All kneel in supplication.*)

QUEEN (*irresolute*). Oh, I should be strong, but I am weak! I should be marble, but I am clay! Her punishment has been heavier than I intended. I did not mean that she should live among the frogs—and—well, well, it shall be as you wish—it shall be as you wish!

INVOCATION—QUEEN

Iolanthe!
From thy dark exile thou art summoned!
Come to our call—
Come, Iolanthe!

CELIA.	Iolanthe!
LEILA.	Iolanthe!
ALL.	Come to our call,
	Come, Iolanthe!

[IOLANTHE *rises from the water.* [6] *She is clad in waterweeds. She approaches the* QUEEN *with head bent and arms crossed.*

IOLANTHE. With humbled breast
And every hope laid low,
To thy behest,
Offended Queen, I bow!

QUEEN. For a dark sin against our fairy laws
      We sent thee into life-long banishment;
      But mercy holds her sway within our hearts—
      Rise—thou art pardoned!
IOL.   Pardoned!
ALL.   Pardoned!

[*Her weeds fall from her, and she appears clothed as a fairy. The* QUEEN *places a diamond coronet on her head, and embraces her. The others also embrace her.*

CHORUS

Welcome to our hearts again,
    Iolanthe! Iolanthe!
We have shared thy bitter pain,
    Iolanthe! Iolanthe!

Every heart, and every hand
In our loving little band
Welcomes thee to Fairyland,
    Iolanthe!

QUEEN. And now, tell me, with all the world to choose from, why on earth did you decide to live at the bottom of that stream?

IOL. To be near my son, Strephon.

QUEEN. Bless my heart, I didn't know you had a son.

IOL. He was born soon after I left my husband by your royal command—but he does not even know of his father's existence.

FLETA. How old is he?

IOL. Twenty-four.

LEILA. Twenty-four! No one, to look at you, would think you had a son of twenty-four! But that's one of the advantages of being immortal. We never grow old! Is he pretty?

IOL. He's extremely pretty, but he's inclined to be stout.

ALL (*disappointed*). Oh!

QUEEN. I see no objection to stoutness, in moderation.

CELIA. And what is he?

IOL. He's an Arcadian shepherd—and he loves Phyllis, a Ward in Chancery.

CELIA. A mere shepherd! and he half a fairy!

IOL. He's a fairy down to the waist—but his legs are mortal.

ALL. Dear me!

QUEEN. I have no reason to suppose that I am more curious than other people, but I confess I should like to see a person who is fairy down to the waist, but whose legs are mortal.

IOL. Nothing easier, for here he comes!

Enter STREPHON, [7] *singing and dancing and playing on a flageolet. He does not see the Fairies, who retire upstage as he enters.*

SONG—STREPHON

Good morrow, good mother!
    Good mother, good morrow!
By some means or other,
    Pray banish your sorrow!
      With joy beyond telling
      My bosom is swelling,
      So join in a measure
      Expressive of pleasure,
For I'm to be married to-day—to-day—
    Yes, I'm to be married to-day!

[7] *In the first concept Strephon was given the name of Corydon, and he was in the employ of Phyllis, a shepherdess à la Watteau.*

Both Phyllis and Strephon, when I first saw them, were models of a Dresden china shepherd and shepherdess. At the same time that the Queen got her crinoline the two lovers cast off the Dresden and took on Chelsea china.

CHORUS (*aside*). Yes, he's to be married to-day—to-day—
Yes, he's to be married to-day!

IOL. Then the Lord Chancellor [8] has at last given his consent to your marriage with his beautiful ward, Phyllis?

STREPH. Not he, indeed. To all my tearful prayers he answers me, "A shepherd lad is no fit helpmate for a Ward of Chancery." I stood in court, and there I sang him songs of Arcadee, with flageolet accompaniment—in vain. At first he seemed amused, so did the Bar; but quickly wearying of my song and pipe, bade me get out. A servile usher then, in crumpled bands and rusty bombazine, led me, still singing, into Chancery Lane! [9] I'll go no more; I'll marry her to-day, and brave the upshot, be it what it may! (*Sees Fairies.*) But who are these?

IOL. Oh, Strephon! rejoice with me, my Queen has pardoned me!

STREPH. Pardoned you, mother? This is good news indeed.

IOL. And these ladies are my beloved sisters.

STREPH. Your sisters! Then they are—my aunts!

QUEEN. A pleasant piece of news for your bride on her wedding day!

STREPH. Hush! My bride knows nothing of my fairyhood. I dare not tell her, lest it frighten her. She thinks me mortal, and prefers me so.

LEILA. Your fairyhood doesn't seem to have done you much good.

STREPH. Much good! My dear aunt! it's the curse of my existence! What's the use of being half a fairy? My body can creep through a keyhole, but what's the good of that when my legs are left kicking behind? I can make myself invisible down to the waist, but that's of no use when my legs remain exposed to view. My brain is a fairy brain, but from the waist downwards I'm a gibbering idiot. My upper half is immortal, but my lower half grows older every day, and some day or other must die of old age. What's to become of my upper half when I've buried my lower half I really don't know!

FAIRIES. Poor fellow!

QUEEN. I see your difficulty, but with a fairy brain you should seek an intellectual sphere of action. Let me see. I've a borough or two at my disposal. Would you like to go into Parliament?

IOL. A fairy Member! That would be delightful!

STREPH. I'm afraid I should do no good there—you see, down to the waist, I'm a Tory of the most determined description, but my legs are a couple of confounded Radicals, and, on a division, they'd be sure to take me into the wrong lobby. You see, they're two to one, which is a strong working majority.

QUEEN. Don't let that distress you; you shall be returned as a Liberal-Unionist, [10] and your legs shall be our peculiar care.

STREPH. (*bowing*). I see your Majesty does not do things by halves.

QUEEN. No, we are fairies down to the feet.

ENSEMBLE

QUEEN.	Fare thee well, attractive stranger.
FAIRIES.	Fare thee well, attractive stranger.
QUEEN.	Shouldst thou be in doubt or danger,
	Peril or perplexitee,
	Call us, and we'll come to thee!
FAIRIES.	Call us, and we'll come to thee!
	Tripping hither, tripping thither,
	Nobody knows why or whither;
	We must now be taking wing
	To another fairy ring!

[*Fairies and* QUEEN *trip off,* IOLANTHE, *who takes an affectionate farewell of her son, going off last.*

[8] Lord Chancellor. *Originally the official secretary of the King. In modern usage he is the highest judicial functionary in England, ranking immediately after the princes of the blood and the Archbishop of Canterbury. Styled "the keeper of the King's conscience," he is the general guardian of infants, lunatics and idiots, etc. And Phyllis is his ward! (She must be among the etceteras.)*

[9] Chancery Lane. *Named for the Court of Chancery (a division of the Supreme Court).*

[10] Unionist. *The Unionist Party. Tories. One might say the right-wing Conservatives. The name has been dropped from politics for some years now, and the word Conservative has replaced Unionist in the D'Oyly Carte Company since about the middle of the twenties.*

Enter PHYLLIS, *singing and dancing, and accompanying herself on a flageolet*

SONG—PHYLLIS [11]

Good morrow, good lover!
Good lover, good morrow!
I prithee discover,
Steal, purchase, or borrow
Some means of concealing
The care you are feeling,
And join in a measure
Expressive of pleasure,
For we're to be married to-day—to-day!
For we're to be married to-day!

BOTH.　　　　　Yes, we're to be married, etc.

STREPH. (*embracing her*). My Phyllis! And to-day we are to be made happy for ever.

PHYL. Well, we're to be married. [12]

STREPH. It's the same thing.

PHYL. I suppose it is. But oh, Strephon, I tremble at the step I'm taking! I believe it's penal servitude for life to marry a Ward of Court without the Lord Chancellor's consent! I shall be of age in two years. Don't you think you could wait two years?

STREPH. Two years. Have you ever looked in the glass?

PHYL. No, never.

STREPH. Here, look at that (*showing her a pocket mirror*), and tell me if you think it rational to expect me to wait two years?

PHYL. (*looking at herself*). No. You're quite right—it's asking too much. One must be reasonable.

STREPH. Besides, who knows what will happen in two years? Why, you might fall in love with the Lord Chancellor himself by that time!

PHYL. Yes. He's a clean old gentleman.

STREPH. As it is, half the House of Lords are sighing at your feet.

PHYL. The House of Lords are certainly extremely attentive.

STREPH. Attentive? I should think they were! Why did five-and-twenty Liberal Peers come down to shoot over your grass-plot last autumn? It couldn't have been the sparrows. Why did five-and-twenty Conservative Peers come down to fish your pond? Don't tell me it was the gold-fish! No, no—delays are dangerous, and if we are to marry, the sooner the better.

DUET—STREPHON *and* PHYLLIS [13]

PHYLLIS.　　None shall part us from each other,
　　　　　　　One in life and death are we:
　　　　　　All in all to one another—
　　　　　　　I to thee and thou to me!

BOTH.　　　Thou the tree and I the flower—
　　　　　　　Thou the idol; I the throng—
　　　　　　Thou the day and I the hour—
　　　　　　　Thou the singer; I the song!

STREPH.　　All in all since that fond meeting
　　　　　　　When in joy, I woke to find
　　　　　　Mine the heart within thee beating,
　　　　　　　Mine the love that heart enshrined!

[11] Words and music on page 314.

[12] *Mr. Gilbert's cynicism is somewhat belied by the fact that he was a married man, and remained that way for forty-odd years. It has been said that Gilbert was helped quite a bit by Mrs. Gilbert, and that many of his bon mots were adapted from some remark of hers. I did once hear her say, in reply to a statement that she certainly seemed to enjoy life, "Oh, yes, life has been much more enjoyable as Sir William Gilbert's widow than ever it was as Mr. Gilbert's wife!" And yet they lived together for forty years or more. He couldn't have been too bad! And there was a twinkle in her eye when she said it!*

[13] Words and music on page 316.

IOLANTHE

[14] *Changes may come and changes may go but, to misquote Lord Mountararat slightly, "If there is an institution that is susceptible of no change whatsoever it is the House of Lords." Through the years the bright scarlets, royal blues, emerald greens and pale blues of the Peers, together with the black and gold of the Lord Chancellor, have suffered no change. The "unique procession passes" as colorfully as always. These robes, by the way, are the robes of the various high orders of knighthood: the Garter,* the Bath, St. Patrick, the Thistle, etc. They do not denote their ranks. This is denoted by the coronet they wear, the number of gold balls, leaves, and how they are placed. (Costumes for the first-night opening were made by the court robe makers to Her Majesty, Messrs. Ede & Son.)*

Originally the Peers were preceded by the band of the Grenadier Guards in full scarlet, busbys and all. But they have been conspicuous by their absence for many years in the D'Oyly Carte Company, though the Winthrop Ames production, in the late twenties, utilized them, I believe.

* The Most Noble Order of the Garter derives its name from the action of King Henry VIII who picked up and placed around his own leg, just below the knee, a garter dropped by one of the ladies of the Court. The falling of the garter had brought a titter from the assembled courtiers. King Henry said sternly, as he placed it on his own leg, "Honi soit qui mal y pense," which has remained the motto of the Order ever since.

[15] Words and music on page 319.

A rather susceptible Chancellor!

[16] *At one performance of this opera at the Sadler's Wells Theatre I was surprised during the intermission by a visit from the then Lord Chancellor. After I had been presented to him he remarked that he was very surprised that Mr. Carte should permit a Lord Chancellor to appear on the stage in a robe that was too short and a wig that was too small! I promptly reported these words to our general manager, Richard Collet, who in turn reported them to Mr. Carte, and three days later I was in a court and legal tailor's in Chancery Lane being properly fitted.*

[17] Words and music on page 324.

[18] *As the highest legal functionary in the land.*

BOTH.

Thou the stream and I the willow—
Thou the sculptor; I the clay—
Thou the ocean; I the billow—
Thou the sunrise; I the day!

[*Exeunt* STREPHON *and* PHYLLIS *together.*

March. Enter Procession of Peers [14]

CHORUS [15]

Loudly let the trumpet bray!
Tantantara!
Proudly bang the sounding brasses!
Tzing! Boom!
As upon its lordly way
This unique procession passes,
Tantantara! Tzing! Boom!
Bow, bow, ye lower middle classes!
Bow, bow, ye tradesmen, bow, ye masses!
Blow the trumpets, bang the brasses!
Tantantara! Tzing! Boom!
We are peers of highest station,
Paragons of legislation,
Pillars of the British nation!
Tantantara! Tzing! Boom!

Enter the LORD CHANCELLOR, [16] *followed by his train-bearer*

SONG—LORD CHANCELLOR [17]

The Law is the true embodiment
Of everything that's excellent.
It has no kind of fault or flaw,
And I, my Lords, embody the Law. [18]
The constitutional guardian I
Of pretty young Wards in Chancery,
All very agreeable girls—and none
Are over the age of twenty-one.
A pleasant occupation for
A rather susceptible Chancellor!

ALL.

A pleasant, etc.

LORD CH.

But though the compliment implied
Inflates me with legitimate pride,
It nevertheless can't be denied
That it has its inconvenient side.
For I'm not so old, and not so plain,
And I'm quite prepared to marry again,
But there'd be the deuce to pay in the Lords
If I fell in love with one of my Wards!
Which rather tries my temper, for
I'm *such* a susceptible Chancellor!

ALL.

Which rather, etc.

And every one who'd marry a Ward
Must come to me for my accord,
And in my court I sit all day,
Giving agreeable girls away,
With one for him—and one for he—
And one for you—and one for ye—

And one for thou—and one for thee—
But never, oh, never a one for me!
Which is exasperating for
A highly susceptible Chancellor!

ALL. Which is, etc.

But never, oh, never a one for me!

Enter LORD TOLLOLLER

LORD TOLL. And now, my Lords, to the business of the day.

LORD CH. By all means. Phyllis, who is a Ward of Court, has so powerfully affected your Lordships, that you have appealed to me in a body to give her to whichever one of you she may think proper to select, and a noble Lord has just gone to her cottage to request her immediate attendance. It would be idle to deny that I, myself, have the misfortune to be singularly attracted by this young person. My regard for her is rapidly undermining my constitution. Three months ago I was a stout man. I need say no more. If I could reconcile it with my duty, I should unhesitatingly award her to myself, for I can conscientiously say that I know no man who is so well fitted to render her exceptionally happy. (*Peers:* Hear, hear!) But such an award would be open to misconstruction, and therefore, at whatever personal inconvenience, I waive my claim.

LORD TOLL. My Lord, I desire, on the part of this House, to express its sincere sympathy with your Lordship's most painful position.

LORD CH. I thank your Lordships. The feelings of a Lord Chancellor who is in love with a Ward of Court are not to be envied. What is his position? Can he give his own consent to his own marriage with his own Ward? Can he marry his own Ward without his own consent? And if he marries his own Ward without his own consent, can he commit himself for contempt of his own Court? And if he commit himself for contempt of his own Court, can he appear by counsel before himself, to move for arrest of his own judgment? Ah, my Lords, it is indeed painful to have to sit upon a woolsack [19] which is stuffed with such thorns as these!

Enter LORD MOUNTARARAT

LORD MOUNT. My Lords, I have much pleasure in announcing that I have succeeded in inducing the young person to present herself at the Bar of this House.

Enter PHYLLIS

RECIT—PHYLLIS

My well-loved Lord and Guardian dear,
You summoned me, and I am here!

CHORUS OF PEERS

Oh, rapture, how beautiful!
How gentle—how dutiful!

SOLO—LORD TOLLOLLER [20]

Of all the young ladies I know
    This pretty young lady's the fairest;
Her lips have the rosiest show,
    Her eyes are the richest and rarest.
Her origin's lowly, it's true,
    But of birth and position I've plenty;
I've grammar and spelling for two,

[19] Woolsack. *A large package or bale of wool. The usual seat of the Lord Chancellor in the House of Lords is made out of a large square bag of wool and covered with cloth (maroon, if my memory serves me right) and without back or arms. When being shown around the House of Lords by an M.P. friend I had the temerity to seat myself upon the woolsack, while my friend kept a good lookout to make sure I was not observed by one of the custodians of the Chamber. I gather I was committing sacrilege!*

[20] *Words and music on page 327.*

And blood and behaviour for twenty!
Her origin's lowly, it's true,
I've grammar and spelling for two;

CHORUS.   Of birth and position he's plenty,
With blood and behaviour for twenty!

SOLO—LORD MOUNTARARAT

Though the views of the House have diverged
On every conceivable motion,
All questions of Party [21] are merged
In a frenzy of love and devotion;
If you ask us distinctly to say
What Party we claim to belong to,
We reply, without doubt or delay,
The Party [22] I'm singing this song to!

SOLO—PHYLLIS

I'm very much pained to refuse,
But I'll stick to my pipes and my tabors; [23]
I can spell all the words that I use,
And my grammar's as good as my neighbours'.
As for birth—I was born like the rest,
My behaviour is rustic but hearty,
And I know where to turn for the best,
When I want a particular Party!

CHORUS.   Though her station is none of the best,
I suppose she was born like the rest;
And she knows where to look for her hearty,
When she wants a particular Party!

RECIT—PHYLLIS

Nay, tempt me not.
To rank I'll not be bound;
In lowly cot
Alone is virtue found!

CHORUS.   No, no; indeed high rank will never hurt you,
The Peerage is not destitute of virtue.

BALLAD—LORD TOLLOLLER [24]

Spurn not the nobly born
With love affected,
Nor treat with virtuous scorn
The well-connected.
High rank involves no shame—
We boast an equal claim
With him of humble name
To be respected!
Blue blood! blue blood!
When virtuous love is sought
Thy power is naught,
Though dating from the Flood,
Blue blood!

CHORUS.   Blue blood! blue blood! etc.

Spare us the bitter pain
Of stern denials,

[21] Party. *Used here in its political sense . . .*

[22] *. . . and here to denote a particular person. One of Gilbert's best efforts, to my mind, of a play on a word.*

[23] *Phyllis' pipes are clearly the pipes of Pan which she carries onstage at her entrance. But to the best of my knowledge, no one has ever seen her with her tabors (little drums). Perhaps she confines her musical efforts on percussion instruments to the privacy of her own home.*

[24] *Words and music on page 329.*

Spurn not the nobly born

Nor with low-born disdain
　　Augment our trials.
Hearts just as pure and fair
May beat in Belgrave Square [25]
As in the lowly air
　　Of Seven Dials! [26]
Blue blood! Blue blood!
　　Of what avail art thou
　　To serve us now?
Though dating from the Flood,
　　Blue blood!

CHORUS.　　Blue blood! blue blood! etc.

RECIT—PHYLLIS

My Lords, it may not be.
　　With grief my heart is riven!
You waste your time on me,
　　For ah! my heart is given!

ALL.　　Given!
PHYL.　　Yes, given!
ALL.　　Oh, horror!!!

RECIT—LORD CHANCELLOR

And who has dared to brave our high displeasure,
And thus defy our definite command?

Enter STREPHON

STREPH. 'Tis I—young Strephon—mine this priceless treasure!
Against the world I claim my darling's hand!

[PHYLLIS *rushes to his arms.*

A shepherd I—
ALL.　　　　A shepherd he!
STREPH. Of Arcady—[27]
ALL.　　　　Of Arcadee!
STREPH. Betrothed are we!
ALL.　　　　Betrothed are they—
STREPH. And mean to be—
ALL.　　　　Espoused to-day!

ENSEMBLE

STREPH.	THE OTHERS
A shepherd I	A shepherd he
Of Arcady,	Of Arcadee,
Betrothed are we,	Betrothed is he,
And mean to be	And means to be
Espoused to-day!	Espoused to-day!

DUET—LORD MOUNTARARAT *and* LORD TOLLOLLER
(*aside to each other*)

'Neath this blow,
　　Worse than stab of dagger—
Though we mo-
　　Mentarily stagger,
In each heart
　　Proud are we innately—
Let's depart
　　Dignified and stately!

[25] Belgrave Square. *The site of homes of many of the noble families of England.*

[26] Seven Dials. *A district in the East End of London. In the days of Gilbert, almost on a par with the Bowery.*

[27] *Pronounced to rhyme with I.*

ALL.   Let's depart,
                  Dignified and stately!

CHORUS OF PEERS

Though our hearts she's badly bruising,
In another suitor choosing,
Let's pretend it's most amusing.
    Ha! ha! ha! Tan-ta-ra!

[*Exeunt all the Peers, marching round stage with much dignity.* LORD CHANCELLOR *separates* PHYLLIS *from* STREPHON *and orders her off. She follows Peers. Manent* LORD CHANCELLOR *and* STREPHON.

LORD CH. Now, sir, what excuse have you to offer for having disobeyed an order of the Court of Chancery?

STREPH. My Lord, I know no Courts of Chancery; I go by Nature's Acts of Parliament. The bees—the breeze—the seas—the rooks—the brooks—the gales—the vales—the fountains and the mountains cry, "You love this maiden—take her, we command you!" 'Tis writ in heaven by the bright barbèd dart that leaps forth into lurid light from each grim thundercloud. [28] The very rain pours forth her sad and sodden sympathy! When chorused Nature bids me take my love, shall I reply, "Nay, but a certain Chancellor forbids it"? Sir, you are England's Lord High Chancellor, but are you Chancellor of birds and trees, King of the winds and Prince of thunderclouds?

LORD CH. No. It's a nice point. I don't know that I ever met it before. But my difficulty is that at present there's no evidence before the Court that chorused Nature has interested herself in the matter.

STREPH. No evidence! You have my word for it. I tell you that she bade me take my love.

LORD CH. Ah! but, my good sir, you mustn't tell us what she told you —it's not evidence. Now an affidavit from a thunderstorm, or a few words on oath from a heavy shower, would meet with all the attention they deserve.

STREPH. And have you the heart to apply the prosaic rules of evidence to a case which bubbles over with poetical emotion?

LORD CH. Distinctly. I have always kept my duty strictly before my eyes, and it is to that fact that I owe my advancement to my present distinguished position.

SONG—LORD CHANCELLOR [29]

When I went to the Bar as a very young man,
    (Said I to myself—said I),.
I'll work on a new and original plan
    (Said I to myself—said I),
I'll never assume that a rogue or a thief
Is a gentleman worthy implicit belief,
Because his attorney has sent me a brief
    (Said I to myself—said I!).

Ere I go into court I will read my brief through
    (Said I to myself—said I).
And I'll never take work I'm unable to do
    (Said I to myself—said I),
My learned profession I'll never disgrace
By taking a fee with a grin on my face,
When I haven't been there to attend to the case
    (Said I to myself—said I!).

[28] Theaters are not soundproof, especially not against loud noises. During one performance Leslie Rands had just completed the line ". . . from each grim thundercloud," when a terrific clap of thunder broke the momentary silence. The timing was perfect. For a moment I feel sure the audience thought it was an arranged effect. Then came the rain—right on cue! It was so heavy the noise of it on the roof almost drowned out the last of Strephon's speech. But—and this sounds exaggerated, I know, but it is not—the most perfect piece of timing was a second peal of thunder just as I said, ". . . there's no evidence before the Court that chorused Nature has interested herself in the matter." Fortunately for the sake of our own gravity, there was no further thunder that might have been interpreted as an "affidavit."

[29] Words and music on page 330.

I'll never throw dust in a juryman's eyes
    (Said I to myself—said I),
Or hoodwink a judge who is not over-wise
    (Said I to myself—said I),
Or assume that the witnesses summoned in force
In Exchequer, Queen's Bench, Common Pleas, or
    Divorce, [30]
Have perjured themselves as a matter of course
    (Said I to myself—said I!).

In other professions in which men engage
    (Said I to myself—said I),
The Army, the Navy, the Church, and the Stage
    (Said I to myself—said I),
Professional license, if carried too far,
Your chance of promotion will certainly mar—
And I fancy the rule might apply to the Bar
    (Said I to myself—said I!).

[*Exit* LORD CHANCELLOR. [31]

Enter IOLANTHE

STREPH. Oh, Phyllis, Phyllis! To be taken from you just as I was on the point of making you my own! Oh, it's too much—it's too much!

IOL. (*to* STREPHON, *who is in tears*). My son in tears—and on his wedding day!

STREPH. My wedding day! Oh, mother, weep with me, for the Law has interposed between us, and the Lord Chancellor has separated us for ever!

IOL. The Lord Chancellor! (*Aside.*) Oh, if he did but know!

STREPH. (*overhearing her*). If he did but know what?

IOL. No matter! The Lord Chancellor has no power over you. Remember you are half a fairy. [32] You can defy him—down to the waist.

STREPH. Yes, but from the waist downwards he can commit me to prison for years! Of what avail is it that my body is free, if my legs are working out seven years' penal servitude?

IOL. True. But take heart—our Queen has promised you her special protection. I'll go to her and lay your peculiar case before her.

STREPH. My beloved mother! how can I repay the debt I owe you?

FINALE—QUARTET [33]

As it commences, the Peers appear at the back, advancing unseen and on tiptoe. LORD MOUNTARARAT *and* LORD TOLLOLLER *lead* PHYLLIS *between them, who listens in horror to what she hears.*

STREPH. (*to* IOLANTHE). When darkly looms the day,
    And all is dull and grey,
    To chase the gloom away,
        On thee I'll call!

PHYL. (*speaking aside to* LORD MOUNTARARAT). What was that? [34]

LORD MOUNT. (*aside to* PHYLLIS).
    I think I heard him say,
    That on a rainy day,
    To while the time away,
        On her he'd call!

CHORUS. We think we heard him say, etc.

[PHYLLIS *much agitated at her lover's supposed faithlessness.*

I'll never throw dust in a juryman's eyes

[30] Various divisions of the High Court of Justice.

[31] A very narrow shave was mine on one occasion during this number. I had just reached the end of the last verse when one of the scenery flats worked loose from its supporting brace and fell forward. I felt the swish as it fell past my ear, and heard the audience gasp. I finished the verse with "And I fancy the rule might apply to the scenery's Bar, Said I to myself—said I!"

[32] The first inkling of an idea for Iolanthe came to Gilbert from his Bab Ballad "The Fairy Curate."

[33] Sullivan is quoted as saying that this, he thought, was the longest finale he ever wrote—"Goodness knows how many pages of score it covered!" Actually, it runs to thirty-five pages of the vocal score, with The Grand Duke running it a close second with thirty-four.

[34] This line she speaks in a moderately high squeak, as if bordering on tears, and yet unable to believe her ears.

[35] *Again the squeak, but even more agitated.*

[36] *For the benefit of those readers who do not know London, St. James's Park was originally the private grounds of St. James's Palace, at one time the official residence of the King (the Court of St. James's). It is now a public park and adjacent to Green Park.*

IOL. (*to* STREPHON). When tempests wreck thy bark,
   And all is drear and dark,
   If thou shouldst need an Ark,
    I'll give thee one!

PHYL. (*speaking aside to* LORD TOLLOLLER). What was that? [35]

LORD TOLL. (*aside to* PHYLLIS).
   I heard the minx remark,
   She'd meet him after dark,
   Inside St. James's Park, [36]
    And give him one!

PHYL.   The prospect's very bad,
   My heart so sore and sad
   Will never more be glad
    As summer's sun.

IOL., LORD TOLL., STREPH., LORD MOUNT.
   The prospect's not so bad,
   $\left.\begin{array}{l}\text{My}\\\text{Thy}\end{array}\right\}$ heart so sore and sad
   May very soon be glad
    As summer's sun;

PHYL., IOL., LORD TOLL., STREPH., LORD MOUNT.
   For when the sky is dark
   And tempests wreck $\left\{\begin{array}{l}\text{my}\\\text{thy}\\\text{his}\end{array}\right\}$ bark,
   If $\left\{\begin{array}{l}\text{he should}\\\text{I should}\\\text{thou shouldst}\end{array}\right\}$ need an Ark,
   $\left.\begin{array}{l}\text{She'll}\\\text{I'll}\end{array}\right\}$ give $\left\{\begin{array}{l}\text{him}\\\text{me}\\\text{thee}\end{array}\right\}$ one!

PHYL. (*revealing herself*). Ah!
   [IOLANTHE *and* STREPHON *much confused.*

PHYL.   Oh, shameless one, tremble!
    Nay, do not endeavour
   Thy fault to dissemble,
    We part—and for ever!
   I worshipped him blindly,
   He worships another—

STREPH.   Attend to me kindly,
    This lady's my mother!

TOLL.   This lady's his *what*?
STREPH.   This lady's my mother!
TENORS.   This lady's his *what*?
BASSES.   He says she's his mother!

[*They point derisively to* IOLANTHE, *laughing heartily at her. She goes for protection to* STREPHON.

   Enter LORD CHANCELLOR. IOLANTHE *veils herself*

LORD CH. What means this mirth unseemly,
   That shakes the listening earth?

LORD TOLL. The joke is good extremely,
   And justifies our mirth.

LORD MOUNT. This gentleman is seen,
    With a maid of seventeen;
   A-taking of his *dolce far niente*; [37]
    And wonders he'd achieve,
    For he asks us to believe
   She's his mother—and he's nearly five-and-twenty.

LORD CH. (*sternly*). Recollect yourself, I pray,
    And be careful what you say—
   As the ancient Romans said, *festina lente* [38]
    For I really do not see
    How so young a girl could be
   The mother of a man of five-and-twenty. [39]

ALL.   Ha! ha! ha! ha! ha!

STREPH. My Lord, of evidence I have no dearth—
   She is—has been—my mother from my birth!

BALLAD

   In babyhood
   Upon her lap I lay,
    With infant food
   She moistenèd my clay;
    Had she withheld
   The succour she supplied,
    By hunger quelled,
   Your Strephon might have died!

LORD CH. (*much moved*).
    Had that refreshment been denied,
    Indeed our Strephon might have died!

ALL (*much affected*).
    Had that refreshment been denied,
    Indeed our Strephon might have died!

LORD MOUNT. But as she's not
   His mother, it appears,
    Why weep these hot
   Unnecessary tears?
    And by what laws
   Should we so joyously
    Rejoice, because
   Our Strephon did not die?
   Oh, rather let us pipe our eye [40]
   Because our Strephon did not die!

ALL.   That's very true—let's pipe our eye
   Because our Strephon did not die!

[*All weep.* IOLANTHE, *who has succeeded in hiding her face from* LORD CHANCELLOR, *escapes unnoticed.*

PHYL. Go, traitorous one—for ever we must part:
   To one of you, my Lords, I give my heart!

ALL.   Oh, rapture!

STREPH. Hear me, Phyllis, ere you leave me.

PHYL. Not a word—you did deceive me.

ALL.   Not a word—you did deceive her.

       [*Exit* STREPHON.

[37] Dolce far niente. *Literally translated: "sweet doing nothing." Here, I rather imagine, Gilbert means "whispering sweet nothings."*

[38] Festina lente. *Make haste slowly. (Don't make rash and foolish statements. Think before you speak. Look before you leap.)*

[39] *Compare Strephon's lines, and those of Lord Mountararat and the Lord Chancellor with this verse from "The Fairy Curate":*
   "Who is this, sir,
    Ballet miss, sir?"
  Said the Bishop, coldly.
   " 'Tis my mother
    And no other,"
  Georgie answered boldly.
   "Go along, sir!
    You are wrong, sir,
  You have years in plenty;
   While this hussy
    (Gracious mussy!)
  Isn't two and twenty!"

[40] Pipe our eye. *A colloquialism: to shed tears.*

BALLAD—PHYLLIS

For riches and rank I do not long—
    Their pleasures are false and vain;
I gave up the love of a lordly throng
    For the love of a simple swain.
But now that simple swain's untrue,
With sorrowful heart I turn to you—
    A heart that's aching,
    Quaking, breaking,
As sorrowful hearts are wont to do!

The riches and rank that you befall
    Are the only baits you use,
So the richest and rankiest of you all
    My sorrowful heart shall choose.
As none are so noble—none so rich
As this couple of lords, I'll find a niche
    In my heart that's aching,
    Quaking, breaking,
For one of you two—and I don't care which!

ENSEMBLE

PHYL. (*to* LORD MOUNTARARAT *and* LORD TOLLOLLER).
    To you I give my heart so rich!
ALL (*puzzled*).   To which?
PHYL.   I do not care!
    To you I yield—it is my doom!
ALL.   To whom?
PHYL.   I'm not aware!
    I'm yours for life if you but choose.
ALL.   She's whose?
PHYL.   That's your affair!
    I'll be a countess, shall I not?
ALL.   Of what?
PHYL.   I do not care! [41]
ALL.   Lucky little lady!
    Strephon's lot is shady;
    Rank, it seems, is vital,
    "Countess" [42] is the title,
    But of what I'm not aware;

Enter STREPHON

STREPH.   Can I inactive see my fortunes fade?
    No, no!
    Mighty protectress, hasten to my aid!

Enter Fairies, tripping, headed by CELIA, LEILA, *and*
FLETA, and followed by QUEEN

CHORUS   Tripping hither, tripping thither,
OF   Nobody knows why or whither;
FAIRIES   Why you want us we don't know,
    But you've summoned us, and so
    Enter all the little fairies
    To their usual tripping measure!
    To oblige you all our care is—
    Tell us, pray, what is your pleasure!

[41] *The Lord Chancellor has been seated on a stump upstage, on a sort of Arcadian woolsack. However, at this point he hurries down to Tolloller and Mountararat to let them know that before any choice is made he must first grant permission.*

[42] *Countess. The wife of an Earl.*

STREPH. The lady of my love has caught me talking to another—
PEERS.   Oh, fie! our Strephon is a rogue!
STREPH. I tell her very plainly that the lady is my mother—
PEERS.   Taradiddle, taradiddle, tol lol lay!
STREPH. She won't believe my statement, and declares we must be
        parted,
Because on a career of double-dealing I have started,
Then gives her hand to one of these, and leaves me broken-
        hearted—

PEERS.   Taradiddle, taradiddle, tol lol lay!
QUEEN. Ah, cruel ones, to separate two lovers from each other!
FAIRIES.   Oh, fie! our Strephon's not a rogue!
QUEEN. You've done him an injustice, for the lady *is* his mother!
FAIRIES.   Taradiddle, taradiddle, tol lol lay!
LORD CH. That fable p'r'aps may serve his turn as well as any other.
(*Aside.*) I didn't see her face, but if they fondled one another,
And she's but seventeen—I don't believe it was his mother!
      Taradiddle, taradiddle.
ALL.   Tol lol lay!

LORD TOLL.   I have often had a use
    For a thorough-bred excuse
Of a sudden (which is English for "*repente*"),
    But of all I ever heard
    This is much the most absurd,
For she's seventeen, and he is five-and-twenty!

ALL.   Though she is seventeen, and he's four or five-and-twenty!
      Oh, fie! our Strephon is a rogue!

LORD MOUNT.   Now, listen, pray to me, [43]
    For this paradox will be
Carried, nobody at all *contradicente.*
    Her age, upon the date
    Of his birth, was *minus* eight,
If she's seventeen, and he is five-and-twenty!
ALL. To say she is his mother is an utter bit of folly!
      Oh, fie! our Strephon is a rogue!
Perhaps his brain is addled, and it's very melancholy!
      Taradiddle, taradiddle, tol lol lay!
I wouldn't say a word that could be reckoned as injurious,
But to find a mother younger than her son is very curious,
And that's a kind of mother that is usually spurious.
      Taradiddle, taradiddle, tol lol lay!

LORD CH.   Go away, madam;
      I should say, madam,
      You display, madam,
        Shocking taste.

      It is rude, madam,
      To intrude, madam,
      With your brood, madam,
        Brazen-faced!

      You come here, madam,
      Interfere, madam,
      With a peer, madam.
        (I am one.)

[43] Mountararat has been working this out in a small notebook he carries (in fact, all the Peers carry notebooks and pencils). While singing this solo he is showing the result of his mathematics to the Chancellor, who then works it out on his fingers, apparently achieving the same result!

You're aware, madam,
What you dare, madam,
So take care, madam,
And begone!

ENSEMBLE

FAIRIES (*to* QUEEN)	PEERS
Let us stay, madam;	Go away, madam;
I should say, madam,	I should say, madam,
They display, madam,	You display, madam,
Shocking taste.	Shocking taste.
It is rude, madam,	It is rude, madam,
To allude, madam,	To intrude, madam,
To your brood, madam,	With your brood, madam,
Brazen-faced!	Brazen-faced!
We don't fear, madam,	You come here, madam,
Any peer, madam,	Interfere, madam,
Though, my dear madam,	With a peer, madam,
This is one.	(I am one.)
They will stare, madam,	You're aware, madam,
When aware, madam,	What you dare, madam,
What they dare, madam—	So take care, madam,
What they've done!	And begone!

QUEEN.   Bearded by these puny mortals!
(*furious*). I will launch from fairy portals
    All the most terrific thunders
    In my armory of wonders!

PHYL. (*aside*). Should they launch terrific wonders,
    All would then repent their blunders.
    Surely these must be immortals.

[*Exit* PHYLLIS.

QUEEN.   Oh! Chancellor unwary
    It's highly necessary
      Your tongue to teach
      Respectful speech—
    Your attitude to vary!

    Your badinage so airy,
    Your manner arbitrary,
      Are out of place
      When face to face
    With an influential Fairy.

ALL THE PEERS We never knew
(*aside*).   We were talking to
    An influential Fairy!

LORD CH.   A plague on this vagary,
    I'm in a nice quandary!
      Of hasty tone
      With dames unknown
    I ought to be more chary;
    It seems that she's a fairy
    From Andersen's library,
      And I took her for
      The proprietor
    Of a Ladies' Seminary!

PEERS.   We took her for
    The proprietor
    Of a Ladies' Seminary!

QUEEN. When next your Houses do assemble,
You may tremble!

CELIA. Our wrath, when gentlemen offend us, [44]
Is tremendous!

LEILA. They meet, who underrate our calling,
Doom appalling!

QUEEN. Take down our sentence as we speak it,
And *he* shall wreak it!

[*Indicating* STREPHON.

PEERS. Oh, spare us!

QUEEN. Henceforth, Strephon, cast away [45]
Crooks and pipes and ribbons so gay—
Flocks and herds that bleat and low;
Into Parliament you shall go!

ALL. Into Parliament he shall go!
Backed by our supreme authority,
He'll command a large majority!
Into Parliament he shall go!

QUEEN. In the Parliamentary hive,
Liberal or Conservative—
Whig or Tory—I don't know—
But into Parliament you shall go!

FAIRIES. Into Parliament, etc.

QUEEN (*speaking through music*)

Every bill and every measure
That may gratify his pleasure,
Though your fury it arouses,
Shall be passed by both your Houses!
PEERS. Oh!
You shall sit, if he sees reason,
Through the grouse and salmon season; [46]
PEERS. No!
He shall end the cherished rights
You enjoy on Friday nights: [47]
PEERS. No!
He shall prick that annual blister,
Marriage with deceased wife's sister: [48]
PEERS. Mercy!
Titles shall ennoble, then,
All the Common Councilmen:
PEERS. Spare us!
Peers shall teem in Christendom,
And a Duke's exalted station
Be attainable by Com-
Petitive Examination! [49]

PEERS
Oh, horror!

FAIRIES *and* PHYLLIS
Their horror
They can't dissemble
Nor hide the fear that makes them
tremble!

[44] *Each of the Fairies (other than the Queen) levels her fairy wand at the Lord Chancellor whose nervousness mounts with each action. (And do, please, pronounce "wrath" in the British fashion: "wrawth"—unless you have very strong feelings about it! I do really believe the broader "a" has a more pleasing sound.)*

As Leila sings her line she makes a motion as if to impale the Lord Chancellor, who backs hurriedly away and into Mountararat, rebounding almost onto the point of the wand.

[45] *The Peers take out their notebooks and proceed to "take down the sentence." The Lord Chancellor uses Mountararat's back as a rest. At the end of the Queen's first verse he turns to her, but she promptly begins to sing again. So back he whips to Mountararat's back. Once more he turns to the Queen (possibly to ask her how to spell a word). She frowns on him and again he returns to Mountararat's back, but continues to look over his shoulder at the Queen. In the meantime, Mountararat has gone down on his knees, the better to rest his book, with the obvious result to the Chancellor.*

[46] *The "grouse and salmon season" most happily coincides with the Parliamentary summer recess!*

[47] *Friday nights were reserved for the consideration and possible discussion of "private members'" bills, as opposed to the Government's bills. Actually, all who sit in the House of Commons are Members of Parliament. They are, however, divided into "front bench" or members with Cabinet rank and "back bench" or "Private" members. Why these Friday nights should be so cherished by the House of Lords I am unable to say—not being a Peer of the Realm myself—and the Lord Chancellor never told me!*

[48] *This was for many, many years a big bone of Parliamentary contention!*

[49] *This is too much for the Lord Chancellor who promptly faints into the arms of Mountararat. Lord Tolloller tucks his robe under one arm, picks up the Chancellor's legs by the ankles, and he is borne off the stage. (See Note 58.)*

[50] Words and music on page 332.

PEERS	FAIRIES, PHYLLIS *and* STREPHON
Young Strephon is the kind of lout	With Strephon for your foe, no doubt,
We do not care a fig about!	A fearful prospect opens out,
We cannot say	And who shall say
What evils may	What evils may
Result in consequence.	Result in consequence?
But lordly vengeance will pursue	A hideous vengeance will pursue
All kinds of common people who	All noblemen who venture to
Oppose our views,	Oppose his views,
Or boldly choose	Or boldly choose
To offer us offence.	To offer him offence.
He'd better fly at humbler game,	'Twill plunge them into grief and shame;
Or our forbearance he must claim,	His kind forbearance they must claim,
If he'd escape	If they'd escape
In any shape	In any shape
A very painful wrench!	A very painful wrench.
Your powers we dauntlessly pooh-pooh:	Although our threats you now pooh-pooh,
A dire revenge will fall on you,	A dire revenge will fall on you,
If you besiege	Should he besiege
Our high *prestige*—	Your high *prestige*—
(The word "*prestige*" is French).	(The word "*prestige*" is French).

[51] Canaille. Pack of dogs. (The vile populace; the mob; the rabble.)

[52] *I was interested to discover that a "plebe" is a member of the lowest class at the United States Military Academy, though I don't think Gilbert used it with that definition in mind!*

[53] όι πολλοι. Hoi polloi: the common people.

PEERS. Our lordly style
    You shall not quench
  With base *canaille*! [51]
FAIRIES.   (That word is French.)
PEERS. Distinction ebbs
    Before a herd
  Of vulgar *plebs*! [52]
FAIRIES.   (A Latin word.)
PEERS. 'Twould fill with joy,
    And madness stark
  The όι πολλοι! [53]
FAIRIES.   (A Greek remark.)

PEERS. One Latin word, one Greek remark,
And one that's French.

FAIRIES. Your lordly style
    We'll quickly quench
  With base *canaille*!
PEERS.   (That word is French.)
FAIRIES. Distinction ebbs
    Before a herd
  Of vulgar *plebs*!
PEERS.   (A Latin word.)
FAIRIES. 'Twill fill with joy
    And madness stark
  The όι πολλοι!
PEERS.   (A Greek remark.)

FAIRIES. One Latin word, one Greek remark,
And one that's French.

PEERS	FAIRIES
You needn't wait:	We will not wait:
Away you fly!	We go sky-high!
Your threatened hate	Our threatened hate
We won't defy!	You won't defy!

[FAIRIES *threaten* PEERS *with their wands.* PEERS *kneel as begging for mercy.* PHYLLIS *implores* STREPHON *to relent. He casts her from him, and she falls fainting into the arms of* LORD MOUNTARARAT *and* LORD TOLLOLLER. [54]

END OF ACT I

ACT II

SCENE.—*Palace Yard, Westminster. Westminster Hall,* L. *Clock tower up,* R.C. PRIVATE WILLIS [55] *discovered on sentry,* R. *Moonlight.*

SONG—PRIVATE WILLIS [56]

When all night long a chap remains
 On sentry-go, to chase monotony
He exercises of his brains,
 That is, assuming that he's got any.
Though never nurtured in the lap
 Of luxury, yet I admonish you,
I am an intellectual chap,
 And think of things that would astonish you.
  I often think it's comical—Fal, lal, la!
  Now Nature always does contrive—Fal, lal, la!
   That every boy and every gal
    That's born into the world alive
   Is either a little Liberal
    Or else a little Conservative!
     Fal, lal, la!
When in that House M.P.'s divide,
 If they've a brain and cerebellum, too,
They've got to leave that brain outside,
 And vote just as their leaders tell 'em to.
But then the prospect of a lot
 Of dull M.P.'s in close proximity,
All thinking for themselves, is what
 No man can face with equanimity.
  Then let's rejoice with loud Fal la—Fal lal la!
  That Nature always does contrive—Fal lal la!
   That every boy and every gal
    That's born into the world alive
   Is either a little Liberal
    Or else a little Conservative!
     Fal lal la!

Enter FAIRIES, *with* CELIA, LEILA, *and* FLETA. *They trip round stage*

CHORUS OF FAIRIES

Strephon's a Member of Parliament!
Carries every Bill he chooses.
To his measures all assent—
 Showing that fairies have their uses.
  Whigs and Tories
  Dim their glories,

[54] *Phyllis, the Lord Chancellor, Lords Mountararat and Tolloller rush onto the stage. Strephon takes Phyllis by her wrists and throws her off and across the Lord Chancellor into the arms of Mountararat and Tolloller. The Lord Chancellor turns and chides Strephon (or threatens him) while the Queen protects him with her fairy wand. (In spite of anything the printed directions may say!)*

[55] *The original Private Willis was later to become quite well known in England as the founder of the Moody-Manners Opera Company, a company which specialized in presenting operas such as The Bohemian Girl and The Emerald Isle.*

 He scored a distinct success with his first song which was, in fact, the show stopper of the evening. In a letter to Sullivan, Gilbert stated that he intended to cast Barrington for the part. Why he changed his mind I do not know, but it may have been partly due to the fact that, according to J. M. Gordon, stage director for many years for the D'Oyly Carte, he wanted to get the "smallest man, with the biggest and deepest voice possible." This would have been very funny, since the average Grenadier is about six feet and some inches tall. However, the combination he sought was not to be found, so he settled for the tallest, with the biggest and deepest voice.

[56] *Words and music on page 335.*

Giving an ear to all his stories—
Lords and Commons are both in the blues!
Strephon makes them shake in their shoes!
Shake in their shoes!
Shake in their shoes!
Strephon makes them shake in their shoes!

Enter PEERS *from Westminster Hall*

CHORUS OF PEERS

Strephon's a Member of Parliament!
Running a-muck of all abuses.
His unqualified assent
Somehow nobody now refuses.
Whigs and Tories
Dim their glories,
Giving an ear to all his stories
Carrying every Bill he may wish:
Here's a pretty kettle of fish!
Kettle of fish!
Kettle of fish!
Here's a pretty kettle of fish!

Enter LORD MOUNTARARAT *and* LORD TOLLOLLER *from Westminster Hall*

CELIA. You seem annoyed.

LORD MOUNT. Annoyed! I should think so! Why, this ridiculous *protégé* of yours is playing the deuce with everything! To-night is the second reading of his Bill to throw the Peerage open to Competitive Examination!

LORD TOLL. And he'll carry it, too!

LORD MOUNT. Carry it? Of course he will! He's a Parliamentary Pickford—he carries everything! [57]

LEILA. Yes. If you please, that's our fault!

LORD MOUNT. The deuce it is!

CELIA. Yes; we influence the members, and compel them to vote just as he wishes them to.

LEILA. It's our system. It shortens the debates.

LORD TOLL. Well, but think what it all means. I don't so much mind for myself, but with a House of Peers with no grandfathers worth mentioning, the country must go to the dogs!

LEILA. I suppose it must!

LORD MOUNT. I don't want to say a word against brains—I've a great respect for brains—I often wish I had some myself—but with a House of Peers composed exclusively of people of intellect, what's to become of the House of Commons? [58]

LEILA. I never thought of that!

LORD MOUNT. This comes of women interfering in politics. It so happens that if there is an institution in Great Britain which is not susceptible of any improvement at all, it is the House of Peers!

SONG—LORD MOUNTARARAT [59]

When Britain really ruled the waves—
(In good Queen Bess's time)
The House of Peers made no pretence [60]
To intellectual eminence,
Or scholarship sublime;

[57] Parliamentary Pickford. *Pickford's Ltd. were, and still are, a well-known firm of carriers whose slogan was "We carry everything." Gilbert here plays on the word "carries," his allusion being to the carrying of a Parliamentary bill.*

[58] *An allusion to the Fairy Queen's threat to throw the Peerage open to competitive examination. (See note 49.)*

[59] *Words and music on page 338.*

[60] *It is interesting to note that while Lord Mountararat gibes at the Upper House, Private Willis's gibes are directed toward the Lower, or House of Commons. Can it be that Gilbert wanted to make it quite clear that he was in no way taking sides, especially with the Commons, against the House of Lords? 'S possible!*

Yet Britain won her proudest bays
In good Queen Bess's glorious days!

CHORUS.   Yes, Britain won, etc.

When Wellington thrashed Bonaparte,
   As every child can tell,
The House of Peers, throughout the war,
Did nothing in particular,
   And did it very well:
Yet Britain set the world ablaze
In good King George's glorious days!

CHORUS.   Yes, Britain set, etc.

And while the House of Peers withholds
   Its legislative hand,
And noble statesmen do not itch
To interfere with matters which
   They do not understand,
As bright will shine Great Britain's rays
As in King George's glorious days!

CHORUS.   As bright will shine, etc.

LEILA (*who has been much attracted by the* PEERS *during this song*). Charming persons, are they not?

CELIA. Distinctly. For self-contained dignity, combined with airy condescension, give me a British Representative Peer!

LORD TOLL. Then pray stop this *protégé* of yours before it's too late. Think of the mischief you're doing!

LEILA (*crying*). But we *can't* stop him now. (*Aside to* CELIA.) Aren't they lovely! (*Aloud.*) Oh, why did you go and defy us, you great geese!

When Wellington thrashed Bonaparte
(I quite often get the feeling, in England especially, that this is looked on as a most patriotic song!)

And while the House of Peers withholds
Its legislative hand . . .

DUET—LEILA *and* CELIA

LEILA.   In vain to us you plead—
                        Don't go!
            Your prayers we do not heed—
                        Don't go!
                  It's true we sigh,
                        But don't suppose
                  A tearful eye
                        Forgiveness shows:
                              Oh, no!
            We're very cross indeed—
                        Don't go!

FAIRIES.   It's true we sigh, etc.

CELIA.   Your disrespectful sneers—
                        Don't go!
            Call forth indignant tears—
                        Don't go!
            You break our laws—
                  You are our foe:
            We cry because
                  We hate you so!
                        You know!
            You very wicked Peers!
                        Don't go!

FAIRIES	LORDS MOUNT. *and* TOLL.
You break our laws—	Our disrespectful sneers,
You are our foe:	Ha, ha!
We cry because	Call forth indignant tears,
We hate you so!	Ha, ha!
You know!	If that's the case, my dears—
You very wicked peers!	FAIRIES. Don't go!
Don't go!	PEERS. We'll go!

[*Exeunt* LORD MOUNTARARAT, LORD TOLLOLLER, *and* PEERS. FAIRIES *gaze wistfully after them.*

Enter FAIRY QUEEN

QUEEN. Oh, shame—shame upon you! Is this your fidelity to the laws you are bound to obey? Know ye not that it is death to marry a mortal?

LEILA. Yes, but it's not death to *wish* to marry a mortal!

FLETA. If it were, you'd have to execute us all!

QUEEN. Oh, this is weakness! Subdue it!

CELIA. We know it's weakness, but the weakness is so strong!

LEILA. We are not all as tough as you are!

QUEEN. Tough! Do you suppose that I am insensible to the effect of manly beauty? Look at that man! [61] (*Referring to* SENTRY.) A perfect picture! (*To* SENTRY.) Who are you, sir?

WILLIS (*coming to "attention"*). Private Willis, B Company, 1st Grenadier Guards.

QUEEN. You're a very fine fellow, sir.

WILLIS. I am generally admired.

QUEEN. I can quite understand it. (*To* FAIRIES.) Now here is a man whose physical attributes are simply godlike. That man has a most extraordinary effect upon me. If I yielded to a natural impulse, I should fall down and worship that man. But I mortify this inclination; I wrestle with it, and it lies beneath my feet! That is how I treat my regard for that man!

[61] *How delightfully ludicrous, how laughably absurd this would have been had Gilbert been able to find the combination of voice and stature he is quoted as having wanted!*

If I yielded to a natural impulse . . .

[62] Words and music on page 340.

[63] *The allusion, of course, is to the poet's dissertations in The Art of Love.*

SONG—FAIRY QUEEN [62]

Oh, foolish fay,
    Think you, because
His brave array
    My bosom thaws,
I'd disobey
    Our fairy laws?
Because I fly
    In realms above,
In tendency
    To fall in love,
Resemble I
    The amorous dove?

(*Aside.*) Oh, amorous dove!
    Type of Ovidius Naso! [63]
      This heart of mine
      Is soft as thine,
    Although I dare not say so!

CHORUS. Oh, amorous dove, etc.
On fire that glows
    With heat intense
I turn the hose
    Of common sense,
And out it goes
    At small expense!

We must maintain
   Our fairy law;
That is the main
   On which to draw—
In that we gain
   A Captain Shaw! [64]
     Oh, Captain Shaw!
       Type of true love kept under!
       Could thy Brigade
       With cold cascade
      Quench my great love, I wonder!

(*Aside.*)

CHORUS.   Oh, Captain Shaw! etc.

[*Exeunt* FAIRIES *and* FAIRY QUEEN, *sorrowfully.*

Enter PHYLLIS

PHYL. (*half crying*). I can't think why I'm not in better spirits. I'm engaged to two noblemen at once. That ought to be enough to make any girl happy. But I'm miserable! Don't suppose it's because I care for Strephon, for I hate him! No girl *could* care for a man who goes about with a mother considerably younger than himself!

Enter LORD MOUNTARARAT *and* LORD TOLLOLLER

LORD MOUNT. Phyllis! My darling!

LORD TOLL. Phyllis! My own!

PHYL. Don't! How dare you? Oh, but perhaps you're the two noblemen I'm engaged to?

LORD MOUNT. I am one of them.

LORD TOLL. I am the other.

PHYL. Oh, then, my darling! (*to* LORD MOUNTARARAT). My own! (*to* LORD TOLLOLLER). Well, have you settled which it's to be?

LORD TOLL. Not altogether. It's a difficult position. It would be hardly delicate to toss up. On the whole we would rather leave it to you.

PHYL. How can it possibly concern me? You are both Earls, and you are both rich, and you are both plain.

LORD MOUNT. So we are. At least I am.

LORD TOLL. So am I.

LORD MOUNT. No, no!

LORD TOLL. I am indeed. Very plain.

LORD MOUNT. Well, well—perhaps you are.

PHYL. There's really nothing to choose between you. If one of you would forgo his title, and distribute his estates among his Irish tenantry, why, then, I should then see a reason for accepting the other.

LORD MOUNT. Tolloller, are you prepared to make this sacrifice?

LORD TOLL. No!

LORD MOUNT. Not even to oblige a lady?

LORD TOLL. No! not even to oblige a lady.

LORD MOUNT. Then, the only question is, which of us shall give way to the other? Perhaps, on the whole, she would be happier with me. I don't know. I may be wrong.

LORD TOLL. No. I don't know that you are. I really believe she would. But the awkward part of the thing is that if you rob me of the girl of my heart, we must fight, and one of us must die. It's a family tradition that I have sworn to respect. It's a painful position, for I have a very strong regard for you, George.

LORD MOUNT. (*much affected*). My dear Thomas!

[64] Captain Shaw. *The Chief of the London Fire Brigade at the time (Captain Eyre Massey Shaw). He was an inveterate first-nighter and was at the opening of Iolanthe. Whether it was by accident or design, I wouldn't venture to say, but his seat was right in the center of the front row of the orchestra stalls, where the Fairy Queen could not fail to see him, and this gave her the opportunity of stretching her arms out toward the gallant captain when she reached the appropriate words.*

**Could thy Brigade
With cold cascade**
(The fireman with the hose is dressed correctly, including the ax, in the uniform of the London Fire Brigade.)

LORD TOLL. You are very dear to me, George. We were boys together—at least *I* was. If I were to survive you, my existence would be hopelessly embittered.

LORD MOUNT. Then, my dear Thomas, you must not do it. I say it again and again—if it will have this effect upon you, you must not do it. No, no. If one of us is to destroy the other, let it be me!

LORD TOLL. No, no!

LORD MOUNT. Ah, yes!—by our boyish friendship I implore you!

LORD TOLL. (*much moved*). Well, well, be it so. But, no—no!—I cannot consent to an act which would crush you with unavailing remorse.

LORD MOUNT. But it would not do so. I should be very sad at first—oh, who would not be?—but it would wear off. I like you *very much*—but not, perhaps, as much as you like me.

LORD TOLL. George, you're a noble fellow, but that telltale tear betrays you. No, George; you are very fond of me, and I cannot consent to give you a week's uneasiness on my account.

LORD MOUNT. But, dear Thomas, it would not last a week! Remember, you lead the House of Lords! on your demise I shall take your place! Oh, Thomas, it would not last a day!

PHYL. (*coming down*). Now, I do hope you're not going to fight about me, because it's really not worth while.

LORD TOLL. (*looking at her*). Well, I don't believe it is!

LORD MOUNT. Nor I. The sacred ties of Friendship are paramount.

QUARTETTE—LORD MOUNTARARAT,
LORD TOLLOLLER, PHYLLIS, *and* PRIVATE WILLIS

LORD TOLL.   Though p'r'aps I may incur your blame,
               The things are few
               I would not do
            In Friendship's name!

LORD MOUNT.   And I may say I think the same;
               Not even love
               Should rank above
            True Friendship's name!

PHYL.   Then free me, pray; be mine the blame;
               Forget your craze
               And go your ways
            In Friendship's name!

ALL.   Oh, many a man, in Friendship's name,
            Has yielded fortune, rank, and fame!
            But no one yet, in the world so wide,
            Has yielded up a promised bride!

WILLIS.   Accept, O Friendship, all the same,

ALL.   This sacrifice to thy dear name!

[*Exeunt* LORD MOUNTARARAT *and* LORD TOLLOLLER, *lovingly, in one direction, and* PHYLLIS *in another. Exit* SENTRY. [65]

Enter LORD CHANCELLOR, *very miserable*

RECIT—LORD CHANCELLOR

Love, unrequited, robs me of my rest:
    Love, hopeless love, my ardent soul encumbers:
Love, nightmare-like, lies heavy on my chest,
    And weaves itself into my midnight slumbers!

[65] The Sentry's exit is carried out in true sentinel fashion: smartly to attention, then sloping arms. A smart turn to the left and a march across the stage. Halt, turn about, and march back across the stage and off—giving the audience a knowing wink and nod of the head!

SONG—LORD CHANCELLOR [66]

When you're lying awake with a dismal headache, and repose is taboo'd by anxiety, [67]

I conceive you may use any language you choose to indulge in, without impropriety;

For your brain is on fire—the bedclothes conspire of usual slumber to plunder you:

First your counterpane goes, and uncovers your toes, and your sheet slips demurely from under you;

Then the blanketing tickles—you feel like mixed pickles—so terribly sharp is the pricking,

And you're hot, and you're cross, and you tumble and toss till there's nothing 'twixt you and the ticking.

Then the bedclothes all creep to the ground in a heap, and you pick 'em all up in a tangle;

Next your pillow resigns and politely declines to remain at its usual angle!

Well, you get some repose in the form of a doze, with hot eye-balls and head ever aching,

But your slumbering teems with such horrible dreams that you'd very much better be waking;

For you dream you are crossing the Channel, and tossing about in a steamer from Harwich—[68]

Which is something between a large bathing machine and a very small second-class carriage—

And you're giving a treat (penny ice and cold meat) to a party of friends and relations—

They're a ravenous horde—and they all came on board at Sloane Square and South Kensington Stations. [69]

And bound on that journey you find your attorney (who started that morning from Devon);

He's a bit undersized, and you don't feel surprised when he tells you he's only eleven.

Well, you're driving like mad with this singular lad (by the by, the ship's now a four-wheeler),

And you're playing round games, and he calls you bad names when you tell him that "ties pay the dealer";

But this you can't stand, so you throw up your hand, and you find you're as cold as an icicle,

In your shirt and your socks (the black silk with gold clocks), crossing Salisbury Plain on a bicycle:

And he and the crew are on bicycles too—which they've somehow or other invested in—

And he's telling the tars all the particu*lars* of a company he's interested in—

It's a scheme of devices, to get at low prices all goods from cough mixtures to cables

(Which tickled the sailors), by treating retailers as though they were all vege*ta*bles—

You get a good spadesman to plant a small tradesman (first take off his boots with a boot-tree),

And his legs will take root, and his fingers will shoot, and they'll blossom and bud like a fruit-tree—

From the greengrocer tree you get grapes and green pea, cauliflower, pineapple, and cranberries,

While the pastrycook plant cherry brandy will grant, apple puffs, and three-corners, and Banburys—[70]

[66] Words and music on page 343.

[67] *Probably the perfect prototype of a patter song. I say this because it is the only one of its length that I know that keeps going without pause, almost to the end. And well I know it! There is hardly time to take a breath. And if you miss one word, or stumble—so easy to do, especially if you begin to think ahead—the whole thing goes. It's fun singing it, though—after you've sung it!*

[68] *Harwich. A smallish seaport in England. Pronounced "Harrich."*

[69] *Two stations on the London Metropolitan Line, the equivalent of New York's subway. (Not the Tube, however, which I doubt was in operation at the time anyway.)*

You get a good spadesman to plant a small tradesman . . .

[70] *Banbury. A particularly pleasant form of cake, invented at Banbury, a small County town not far from Oxford. At one time noted for its Puritan zeal, now for its cakes!*

The shares are a penny, and ever so many are taken by Rothschild and Baring,

And just as a few are allotted to you, you awake with a shudder despairing—

You're a regular wreck, with a crick in your neck, and no wonder you snore, for your head's on the floor, and you've needles and pins from your soles to your shins, and your flesh is a-creep, for your left leg's asleep, and you've cramp in your toes, and a fly on your nose, and some fluff in your lung, and a feverish tongue, and a thirst that's intense, and a general sense that you haven't been sleeping in clover;

But the darkness has passed, and it's daylight at last, and the night has been long—ditto ditto my song—and thank goodness they're both of them over!

[LORD CHANCELLOR *falls exhausted on a seat.*

LORDS MOUNTARARAT *and* TOLLOLLER *come forward*

LORD MOUNT. I am much distressed to see your Lordship in this condition.

LORD CH. Ah, my Lords, it is seldom that a Lord Chancellor has reason to envy the position of another, but I am free to confess that I would rather be two Earls engaged to Phyllis than any other half-dozen noblemen upon the face of the globe.

LORD TOLL. (*without enthusiasm*). Yes. It's an enviable position when you're the only one.

LORD MOUNT. Oh yes, no doubt—most enviable. At the same time, seeing you thus, we naturally say to ourselves, "This is very sad. His Lordship is constitutionally as blithe as a bird—he trills upon the bench like a thing of song and gladness. His series of judgments in F sharp minor, given *andante* in six-eight time, are among the most remarkable effects ever produced in a Court of Chancery. He is, perhaps, the only living instance of a judge whose decrees have received the honour of a double *encore*. How can we bring ourselves to do that which will deprive the Court of Chancery of one of its most attractive features?"

LORD CH. I feel the force of your remarks, but I am here in two capacities, and they clash, my Lords, they clash! I deeply grieve to say that in declining to entertain my last application to myself, I presumed to address myself in terms which render it impossible for me ever to apply to myself again. It was a most painful scene, my Lord—most painful!

LORD TOLL. This is what it is to have two capacities! Let us be thankful that we are persons of no capacity whatever.

LORD MOUNT. Come, come. Remember you are a very just and kindly old gentleman, and you need have no hesitation in approaching yourself, so that you do so respectfully and with a proper show of deference.

LORD CH. Do you really think so?

LORD MOUNT. I do.

LORD CH. Well, I will nerve myself to another effort, and, if that fails, I resign myself to my fate!

TRIO—LORD CHANCELLOR, [71] LORDS MOUNTARARAT *and* TOLLOLLER [72]

LORD MOUNT. If you go in
You're sure to win—
Yours will be the charming maidie:
Be your law
The ancient saw,
"Faint heart never won fair lady!"

[71] *One of the D'Oyly Carte tenors was the cause of my getting one of my biggest laughs in the opera. At the beginning of the introductory music to the trio the three men would go into a dance, and I would make a pirouette at the end that would bring me face to face with Mountararat; similarly between the first and second verses. But as I pirouetted I did an exaggerated version of it as I came vis-à-vis with Tolloller. This had been the usual business for as many years as I could remember. However, this particular tenor complained that the ensuing small laugh that followed prevented him from picking up his musical cue and would I please refrain from any antics? For one moment I was amazed. But I quickly said that, yes, of course, I would refrain from antics (!) at that point, if it interfered with him. The next time we played Iolanthe I didn't move, either at the introductory music or between first and second verses, but as soon as the inter-verse music began—between second and third verses—I did! Picking up my long and heavy robe, so that my legs could be seen, I broke into a wild version of the "scissors," a step so called because the legs carry out a scissorslike action. The sudden change from dignity to wild abandon was too much for the audience and they collapsed in the aisles. This again brought forth angry comment from our tenor, but this time I was not so easygoing; I refused to cut these antics, and I was solidly backed up by Mr. Carte. Tenors! Ha!*

[72] Words and music on page 349.

ALL.   Faint heart never won fair lady!
              Every journey has an end—
              When at the worst affairs will mend—
              Dark the dawn when day is nigh—
              Hustle your horse and don't say die!

LORD TOLL.   He who shies
              At such a prize
      Is not worth a maravedi,
            Be so kind
            To bear in mind—
      Faint heart never won fair lady!

ALL.   Faint heart never won fair lady!
              While the sun shines make your hay—
              Where a will is, there's a way—
              Beard the lion in his lair—
              None but the brave deserve the fair!

LORD CH.   I'll take heart
              And make a start—
      Though I fear the prospect's shady—
            Much I'd spend
            To gain my end—
      Faint heart never won fair lady!

ALL.   Faint heart never won fair lady!
              Nothing venture, nothing win—
              Blood is thick, but water's thin—
              In for a penny, in for a pound—
              It's Love that makes the world go round!

[*Dance, and exeunt arm-in-arm together.*

Enter STREPHON, *in very low spirits*

STREPH. I suppose one ought to enjoy oneself in Parliament, when one leads both Parties, as I do! But I'm miserable, poor, broken-hearted fool that I am! Oh, Phyllis, Phyllis!——

Enter PHYLLIS

PHYL. Yes.

STREPH. (*surprised*). Phyllis! But I suppose I should say "My Lady." I have not yet been informed which title your ladyship has pleased to select.

PHYL. I—I haven't quite decided. You see *I* have no *mother* to advise *me*!

STREPH. No. I have.

PHYL. Yes; a *young* mother.

STREPH. Not very—a couple of centuries or so.

PHYL. Oh! She wears well.

STREPH. She does. She's a fairy.

PHYL. I beg your pardon—a what?

STREPH. Oh, I've no longer any reason to conceal the fact—she's a fairy.

PHYL. A fairy! Well, but—that would account for a good many things! Then—I suppose *you're* a fairy?

STREPH. I'm half a fairy.

PHYL. Which half?

STREPH. The upper half—down to the waistcoat.

PHYL. Dear me! (*Prodding him with her fingers.*) There is nothing to show it!

STREPH. Don't do that.

PHYL. But why didn't you tell me this before?

STREPH. I thought you would take a dislike to me. But as it's all off, you may as well know the truth—I'm only half a mortal!

PHYL. (*crying*). But I'd rather have half a mortal I do love, than half a dozen I don't! [73]

STREPH. (*crying*). But I think not—go to your half-dozen.

PHYL. (*crying*). It's only two! and I hate 'em! Please forgive me!

STREPH. I don't think I ought to. Besides, all sorts of difficulties will arise. You know, my grandmother looks quite as young as my mother. So do all my aunts.

PHYL. I quite understand. Whenever I see you kissing a very young lady, I shall know it's an elderly relative.

STREPH. You will? Then, Phyllis, I think we shall be very happy! (*Embracing her.*)

PHYL. We won't wait long.

STREPH. No. We might change our minds. We'll get married first.

PHYL. And change our minds afterwards?

STREPH. That's the usual course.

DUET—STREPHON *and* PHYLLIS [74]

STREPH.
> If we're weak enough to tarry
> Ere we marry,
> You and I,
> Of the feeling I inspire
> You may tire
> By and by,
> For peers with flowing coffers
> Press their offers—
> That is why
> I am sure we should not tarry
> Ere we marry,
> You and I!

PHYL.
> If we're weak enough to tarry
> Ere we marry,
> You and I,
> With a more attractive maiden,
> Jewel-laden,
> You may fly.
> If by chance we should be parted,
> Broken-hearted
> I should die—
> So I think we will not tarry
> Ere we marry,
> You and I.

PHYL. But does your mother know you're—[75] I mean, is she aware of our engagement?

Enter IOLANTHE

IOL. She is; and thus she welcomes her daughter-in-law! (*Kisses her.*)

PHYL. She kisses just like other people! But the Lord Chancellor?

STREPH. I forgot him! Mother, none can resist your fairy eloquence; you will go to him and plead for us?

IOL. (*much agitated*). No, no; impossible!

STREPH. But our happiness—our very lives—depend upon our obtaining his consent!

PHYL. Oh, madam, you cannot refuse to do this!

[73] *In one of the American editions this line reads:* "I'd rather have half a mortal I do love, than have a dozen I don't!" *The correct line is* ". . . half a dozen . . ." *but it is not beyond the bounds of possibility that the American version was inspired by the way the word is pronounced in the United States. It is a delightful play on words, and I can easily believe that had Gilbert been writing for Americans he would have written it so himself.*

[74] Words and music on page 353.

[75] *One of Gilbert's enigmatic lines. I once asked J. M. Gordon if he knew exactly what it was Phyllis intended saying. His reply was,* "Of course. Phyllis was going to say, 'Does your mother know you're out?'" *Mr. Gordon, what is more, directed the line to be spoken as if she were saying that, and remembering herself just in time. I cannot argue with him. He knew Gilbert. I only (once) sat on his knee!*

IOL. You know not what you ask! The Lord Chancellor is—my husband!

STREPH. *and* PHYL. Your husband!

IOL. My husband and your father! (*Addressing* STREPHON, *who is much moved.*)

PHYL. Then our course is plain; on his learning that Strephon is his son, all objection to our marriage will be at once removed!

IOL. No; he must never know! He believes me to have died childless, and, dearly as I love him, I am bound, under penalty of death, not to undeceive him. But see—he comes! Quick—my veil!

[IOLANTHE *veils herself.* STREPHON *and* PHYLLIS *go off on tiptoe.*

Enter LORD CHANCELLOR

LORD CH. Victory! Victory! Success has crowned my efforts, and I may consider myself engaged to Phyllis! At first I wouldn't hear of it—it was out of the question. But I took heart. I pointed out to myself that I was no stranger to myself; that, in point of fact, I had been personally acquainted with myself for some years. This had its effect. I admitted that I had watched my professional advancement with considerable interest, and I handsomely added that I yielded to no one in admiration for my private and professional virtues. This was a great point gained. I then endeavoured to work upon my feelings. Conceive my joy when I distinctly perceived a tear glistening in my own eye! Eventually, after a severe struggle with myself, I reluctantly—most reluctantly—consented.

[IOLANTHE *comes down veiled.*

RECIT—IOLANTHE

My lord, a suppliant at your feet I kneel,
Oh, listen to a mother's fond appeal!
Hear me to-night! I come in urgent need—
'Tis for my son, young Strephon, that I plead!

BALLAD—IOLANTHE [76]

He loves! If in the bygone years
  Thine eyes have ever shed
Tears—bitter, unavailing tears,
  For one untimely dead—
If, in the eventide of life,
  Sad thoughts of her arise,
Then let the memory of thy wife
  Plead for my boy—he dies!

He dies! If fondly laid aside
  In some old cabinet,
Memorials of thy long-dead bride
  Lie, dearly treasured yet,
Then let her hallowed bridal dress—
  Her little dainty gloves—
Her withered flowers—her faded tress—
  Plead for my boy—he loves!

[*The* LORD CHANCELLOR *is moved by this appeal. After a pause.*

LORD CH. It may not be—for so the fates decide!
    Learn thou that Phyllis is my promised bride.
IOL. (*in horror*).   Thy bride! No! no!
LORD CH.   It shall be so!
    Those who would separate us woe betide!

[76] *Without any doubt, I think this is the most beautiful lyric Gilbert ever wrote. And Sullivan was with him every inch of the way in providing exquisite music.*

There have been Chancellors who have carried out varying degrees of comedy during the singing of this ballad. Even without the directions of Gordon, who was adamant in his belief that the Lord Chancellor should remain still, I could never have brought myself to do anything which would upset the mood of the scene, let alone indulge in comedy business. This mood should carry right through—it's a serious mood—to . . .

IOL. My doom thy lips have spoken—
      I plead in vain!

CHORUS OF FAIRIES (*without*). Forbear! forbear!

IOL. A vow already broken
      I break again!

CHORUS OF FAIRIES (*without*). Forbear! forbear!

IOL. For him—for her—for thee
      I yield my life.
    Behold—it may not be!
      I am thy wife.

CHORUS OF FAIRIES (*without*). Aiaiah! Aiaiah! Willaloo!

LORD CH. (*recognizing her*). Iolanthe! thou livest?

IOL.   Aye!
    I live! Now let me die!

Enter FAIRY QUEEN *and* FAIRIES. IOLANTHE *kneels to her*

QUEEN. Once again thy vows are broken:
    Thou thyself thy doom hast spoken!

CHORUS OF FAIRIES.   Aiaiah! Aiaiah!
      Willahalah! Willaloo!
      Willahalah! Willaloo!

QUEEN. Bow thy head to Destiny:
    Death thy doom, and thou shalt die!

CHORUS OF FAIRIES.   Aiaiah! Aiaiah! etc.

PEERS and SENTRY *enter. The* QUEEN *raises her spear*

LEILA. Hold! If Iolanthe must die, so must we all; for, as she has sinned, so have we!

QUEEN. What?

CELIA. We are all fairy duchesses, marchionesses, countesses, viscountesses, and baronesses.

LORD MOUNT. It's our fault. They couldn't help themselves.

QUEEN. It seems they *have* helped themselves, and pretty freely, too! (*After a pause.*) You have all incurred death; but I can't slaughter the whole company! And yet (*unfolding a scroll*) the law is clear—every fairy must die who marries a mortal!

[77] LORD CH. Allow me, as an old Equity draftsman, [78] to make a suggestion. The subtleties of the legal mind are equal to the emergency. The thing is really quite simple—the insertion of a single word will do it. Let it stand that every fairy shall die who doesn't marry a mortal, and there you are, out of your difficulty at once!

QUEEN. We like your humour. Very well! (*Altering the MS. in pencil.*) Private Willis!

SENTRY (*coming forward*). Ma'am!

QUEEN. To save my life, it is necessary that I marry at once. How should you like to be a fairy guardsman?

SENTRY. Well, ma'am, I don't think much of the British soldier who wouldn't ill-convenience [79] himself to save a female in distress.

QUEEN. You are a brave fellow. You're a fairy from this moment. (*Wings spring from* SENTRY's *shoulders.*) And you, my Lords, how say you, will you join our ranks?

[FAIRIES *kneel to* PEERS *and implore them to do so*

[77] . . . here.

[78] Equity draftsman. In jurisprudence, "The recourse to general principles of justice to correct or supplement the ordinary law."

[79] "Ill-convenience." Generally given the Dickensian Sam Wellerish pronunciation: "ill-conwenience."

PHYLLIS *and* STREPHON *enter*

LORD MOUNT. (*to* LORD TOLLOLLER). Well, now that the Peers are to be recruited entirely from persons of intelligence, I really don't see what use *we* are, down here, do you, Tolloller?

LORD TOLL. None whatever.

QUEEN. Good (*Wings spring from shoulders of* PEERS). Then away we go to Fairyland.

FINALE

PHYL.	Soon as we may, Off and away! We'll commence our journey airy— Happy are we— As you can see, Every one is now a fairy!
ALL.	Every one is now a fairy!
IOL., QUEEN, *and* PHYL.	Though as a general rule we know Two strings go to every bow, Make up your minds that grief 'twill bring, If you've two beaux to every string.
ALL.	Though as a general rule, etc.
LORD CH.	Up in the sky, Ever so high, Pleasures come in endless series; We will arrange Happy exchange— House of Peers for House of Peris! [80]
ALL.	House of Peers for House of Peris!
LORDS CH., MOUNT., *and* TOLL.	Up in the air, sky-high, sky-high, Free from Wards in Chancery, I } He } will be surely happier, for I'm } He's } such a susceptible Chancellor.
ALL.	Up in the air, etc.

CURTAIN

[80] Peris. Members of a race of beautiful fairylike beings of Persian mythology, represented as descended from fallen angels and excluded from Paradise until their penance is accomplished.

We Are Dainty Little Fairies

In a light, playful manner, but not fast

CELIA

We are dain - ty lit - tle fair - ies, Ev - er sing - ing, ev - er danc - ing; We in - dulge in our va - gar - ies In a fash - ion most en - tranc - ing. If you ask the spec - ial func - tion Of our nev - er ceas - ing

mo - tion, We re - ply with - out com - punc - tion That we

mf CHORUS

have - n't an - y no - tion. No, we have - n't an - y no - tion! An - y

mp

no - tion! Trip-ping hith-er, trip-ping thith-er, No-bod-y knows why or whith-er; We must

f　　　　　　　　　　　*dim.*

dance and we must sing, Round a - bout our fair - y

p LEILA

ring. If you ask us how we live, Lov-ers all es - sen - tials give;

p calmato

311

dance and we must sing, Round a - bout our fair - y

ring. We are dain-ty lit - tle fair-ies, Ev - er sing-ing ev - er danc -ing;

We in - dulge in our va - ga -ries In a fash-ion most en - tranc - ing,

most en - tranc - ing, most en - tranc - ing.

Trip-ping hith-er, trip-ping thith-er, No-bod-y knows why or whith-er.

Good Morrow, Good Lover

Gracefully

PHYLLIS

Good mor - row, good lov - er!

Good lov - er, good mor - row! I

pri - thee dis - cov - er,

Steal, pur - chase, or bor - row

Some means of con-ceal-ing The care you are feel-ing, And join in a meas-ure Ex-pres-sive of pleas-ure, For we're to be mar-ried to-day, to-day; Yes, we're to be mar-ried to-day!— Yes, we're to be mar-ried to-day, to-day; Yes, we're to be mar-ried to-day!—

mf PHYLLIS and STREPHON

315

None Shall Part Us

Slowly with much sentiment

f

p

Phyllis 1. None shall part us from each oth - er, One in
Strephon 2. All in all since that fond meet - ing When, in

p

mf

life and death are we: All in all to one an - oth - er, I to
joy, I woke to find Mine the heart, with - in thee beat - ing, Mine the

mf

thee and thou to me! All in all to one an - oth - er, I to
love that heart en - shrined! Mine the heart, with - in thee beat - ing, Mine the

Loudly Let the Trumpet Bray

Pompous march tempo

CHORUS

Loud - ly let the trum - pet bray, Tan - tan - ta - ra, tan - ta - ta - ra!

Proud - ly bang the sound - ing— brass - es,—

As up - on its lord - ly— way This u - nique pro - ces - sion— pass - es.

320

trades-men, bow, ye mass - es! Blow the trum-pets, bang the brass-es! Tan-tan-ta-ra, tan-ta-

cresc.　　　　　　　　　　　　　　　　　　　ff

ra, tan - ta - ra, tan - ta - ra, tan - ta - ra! Tzing, boom, tzing, boom!

p

We are Peers of high - est sta - tion,

Par - a - gons of leg - is - la - tion,

cresc.

Pil - lars of the Brit - ish na - tion.

masses, Bow, ye low-er mid-dle class-es, Bow, ye trades-men, bow, ye

masses. Tan-tan-ta-ra, Tan-tan-ta-ra, Tan-tan-ta-ra, tan-ta-ra, tan-ta-

ra, tan-ta-ra, tan-ta-ra, ra, ra, ra, ra! Tan-ta-

ra! Tan-ta-ra!

The Law Is the True Embodiment

Vivaciously

LORD CHANCELLOR

1. The Law is the true em-
2. But though the com - pli -
3. And ev - 'ry - one who'd

bod - i - ment Of ev - 'ry - thing that's ex - cel - lent. It
ment im - plied In - flates me with le - gi - ti - mate pride, It
mar - ry a Ward Must come to me for my ac - cord, And

has no kind of fault or flaw, And I, my lords, em -
nev - er - the - less can't be de - nied That it has its in - con -
in my court I sit all day, Giv - ing a - gree - a - ble

pleas- ant oc- cu- pa- tion for A rath- er sus- cep- ti- ble
rath- er tries my tem- per, for I'm such a sus- cep- ti- ble
is ex- as- per- at- ing for A high- ly sus- cep- ti- ble

f CHORUS of PEERS

Chan - cel - lor! A pleas - ant oc - cu - pa - tion for A
Chan - cel - lor! Which rath - er tries his tem - per, for He's
Chan - cel - lor! Which is ex - as - per - at - ing for A

1.-2.

rath - er sus - cep - ti - ble Chan - cel - lor!
such a sus - cep - ti - ble Chan - cel - lor!
high - ly sus - cep - ti - ble

3.

Chan - cel - lor!

Of All the Young Ladies I Know

Smoothly, like a Barcarole

Lord Tolloller 1. Of all the young la-dies I know,___ This pret-ty young la-dy's the fair-est: Her lips have the ros-i-est show,___ Her eyes are the rich-est and rar-est. Her or-i-gin's low-ly, it's true,___ But of birth and po-si-tion I've plen-ty; I've gram-mar and spell-ing for

Phyllis 2. I'm ver-y much pain'd to re-fuse,___ But I'll stick to my pipes and my ta-bors; I can spell all the words that I use,___ And my gram-mar's as good as my neigh-bor's. As for birth, I was born like the rest.___ My be-hav-iour is rus-tic but heart-y, And I know where to turn for the

two,   And blood and be - hav - iour for twen - ty!   Ah! _____
best, When I want a par - tic - u - lar par - ty!   Ah! _____

mp espressivo

Her   or - i - gin's low - ly, it's true, I've   gram - mar and
Though my sta - tion is none of the best, I sup - pose ___ I was

poco cresc.

spell - ing for two; Of birth and po - si - tion I've plen - ty, With blood and be - hav - iour for
born like the rest. I know where to look for my heart - y, When I want a par - tic - u - lar

mf   *f*

twen - ty! Of birth and po - si - tion I've plen - ty, With blood and be - hav - iour for twen -
par - ty! I know where to look for my heart - y, When - ev - er I want ___ a par -

mf   *f follow the voice*

ty!
ty!
dolce
p a tempo

1.   **2.**

8va   *8va*

Spurn Not the Nobly Born

Sustained and with expression

p LORD TOLLOLER

1. Spurn not the no-bly born With love af-fect-ed! Nor treat with vir-tuous scorn The
2. Spare us the bit-ter pain Of stern de-ni-als, Nor with low-born dis-dain Aug-

mf *p legato*

well_ con-nect-ed! High rank in-volves no shame, We boast an e-qual claim
ment_ our_ tri-als. Hearts just as pure and fair May beat in Bel-grave Square

cresc. *mp*

With him of hum-ble name To be re-spect-ed! Blue blood! Blue blood! When
As in the low-ly air Of Sev-en Di-als! Blue blood! Blue blood! Of

cresc. *mp*

cresc. *allargando* *f*

vir-tuous love is sought, Thy pow'r_ is_ naught, Though dat-ing from the Flood, Blue blood, ah, blue blood!
what a-vail art thou To serve_ us_ now? Though dat-ing from the Flood, Blue blood, ah, blue blood!

cresc. *allargando* *f*

When I Went to the Bar

Fast but easily

LORD CHANCELLOR

1. When I went to the Bar as a ver-y young man (Said
2. Ere I go in-to court I will read my brief through (Said
3. I'll nev-er throw dust in a ju-ry-man's eyes (Said
4. In oth-er pro-fes-sions in which men en-gage (Said

I to my-self, said I),   I'll work on a new and o-
I to my-self, said I),   And I'll nev-er take work I'm un-
I to my-self, said I),   Or hood-wink a judge who is
I to my-self, said I),   The Ar-my, the Na-vy, the

rig-i-nal plan (Said I to my-self, said I),   I'll nev-er as-sume that a
a-ble to do (Said I to my-self, said I),   My learn-ed pro-fes-sion I'll
not o-ver-wise (Said I to my-self, said I),   Or as-sume that the wit-ness-es
Church and the Stage (Said I to my-self, said I),   Pro-fes-sion-al li-cense, if

rogue or a thief is a gen - tle-man worth - y im - plic - it be - lief, Be -
nev - er dis-grace By tak - ing a fee with a grin on my face, When I
sum-moned in force In Ex - che - quer, Queen's Bench, Com - mon Pleas, or Di - vorce, Have
car - ried too far, Your chance of pro - mo - tion will cer - tain - ly mar, And I

cause his at - tor - ney has sent me a brief (Said I to my-self, said
have - n't been there to at - tend to the case (Said I to my-self, said
per - jur'd them-selves as a mat - ter of course (Said I to my-self, said
fan - cy the rule might ap - ply to the Bar (Said I to my-self, said

I!).

1. - 2. - 3.   4.

Young Strephon Is the Kind of Lout

Gay march tempo

mf CHORUS

Girls: With Strephon for your foe, no doubt, A fearful prospect opens out! And who shall say What evils may Result in consequence? A hideous vengeance will pursue All noblemen who venture to Oppose his views, Or

Men: Young Strephon is the kind of lout We do not care a fig about! We cannot say What evils may Result in consequence. But lordly vengeance will pursue All kinds of common people who Oppose our views, Or

bold - ly choose To of - fer us of - fence. 'Twill plunge them in - to

bold - ly choose To of - fer us of - fence.

grief and shame; His kind for - bear - ance they must claim, If they'd es - cape, In

an - y shape A ver - y pain - ful wrench. Your pow'rs we daunt - less -

ly pooh-pooh: A dire re - venge will fall on you If you be - siege Our

GIRLS

high pres-tige. (The word "pres-tige" is French, The word "pres-tige" is

French.) Girls: Al - though our threats you now pooh-pooh, A dire re - venge will
Men: Your pow'rs we daunt - less - ly pooh-pooh: A dire re - venge will

cresc.

fall on you. With Stre - phon for your foe, no doubt, A fear - ful pros - pect
fall on you. Young Stre - phon is the kind of lout We do not care a

o - pens out! And who shall say What e - vils may Re - sult in con - se - quence?
fig a - bout! We can - not say What e - vils may Re - sult in con - se - quence.

When All Night Long

Moderately

PRIVATE WILLIS

1. When
(2. When)

all night long a chap re - mains On sen - try - go, to chase mo -
in that House M. P.'s di - vide, If they've a brain and cer - e -

not - o - ny He ex - er - cis - es of his brains, That
bel - lum, too, They've got to leave that brain out - side, And

is, as - sum - ing that he's got an - y. Tho' nev - er nur - tur'd
vote just as their lead - ers tell 'em to. But then the pros - pect

in the lap Of lux-u-ry, Yet I ad-mon-ish you, I am an in-tel-
of a lot Of dull M. P.'s in close prox-im-i-ty, All think-ing for them-

lec-tual chap, And think of things that would as-ton-ish you. I
selves, is what No man can face with e-qua-nim-i-ty. Then

A little more animated

oft-en think it's com-i-cal Fal, lal,— la! Fal, lal,— la! How
let's re-joice with loud Fal, lal, Fal, lal,— la! Fal, lal,— la! That

Na-ture al-ways does con-trive, Fal, lal,— la, la! That—

ev-'ry boy and— ev-'ry gal That's born in-to the—

When Britain Really Ruled the Waves

With majesty and grandeur

ff *marcato*

LORD MOUNTARARAT

mf

1. When Brit-ain real-ly ruled the waves (In
(2.When) Wel-ling-ton thrash'd Bo-na-parte, As
(3. And) while the House of Peers with-holds Its

good Queen Bess-'s __ time), The House of Peers made no pre-tence To
ev-'ry child can __ tell, The House of Peers, through-out the war, Did
leg-is-la-tive __ hand, And no-ble states-men do not itch To

in-tel-lec-tual em-i-nence, Or scho-lar-ship su-blime; Yet
noth-ing in par-tic-u-lar, And did it ver-y well: Yet
in-ter-fere with mat-ters which They do not un-der-stand, As

Brit - ain won her proud-est bays In good Queen Bess - 's
Brit - ain set the world a - blaze In good King George - 's
bright will shine Great Brit - ain's rays As in King George - 's

glo - rious days! Yet Brit - ain won her proud-est bays In good Queen
glo - rious days! Yet Brit - ain set the world a - blaze In good King
glo - rious days! As bright will shine Great Brit - ain's rays As in King

CHORUS

Bess - 's glo - rious days. Yes, Brit - ain won her proud-est bays In good Queen
George - 's glo - rious days. Yes, Brit - ain set the world a - blaze In good King
George - 's glo - rious days. As bright will shine Great Brit - ain's rays As in King

Bess - 's glo - rious days. 2. When
George - 's glo - rious days. 3. And

George - 's glo - rious days.

339

Oh, Foolish Fay

Quietly, in a singing style

f *poco rit*

p QUEEN
p a tempo

1. Oh, fool - ish fay, Think you, be - cause His brave ar -
2. On fire that glows With heat in - tense I turn the

ray My bo - som thaws, I'd dis - o - bey Our fair - y
hose Of com - mon sense, And out it goes At small ex -

laws? Be - cause I fly In realms a - bove, In ten - den -
pense! We must main - tain Our fair - y law; That is the

cy To fall in love, Re - sem - ble I The am - 'rous
main On which to draw, In that we gain A Cap - tain

dove? Re - sem - ble I the am - 'rous dove? (Aside) Oh, am - 'rous
Shaw! In that we gain A Cap - tain Shaw! (Aside) Oh, Cap - tain

dove! Type of O - vi - dius Na - so!
Shaw! Type of true love kept un - der!

This heart of mine Is soft as thine, Al - though I dare not
Could thy Bri - gade With cold cas - cade Quench my great love, I

When You're Lying Awake

Quick but not too fast

LORD CHANCELLOR

1. When you're
(2. For you)
(3. And)

ly - ing a - wake with a dis-mal head-ache and re - pose is ta-boo'd by anx-
dream you are cross - ing the Chan-nel, and toss-ing a - bout in a steam - er from
he and the crew are on bi - cy - cles too, which they've some-how or oth - er in -

i - e - ty, I con - ceive you may use an - y lan-guage you choose to in -
Har - wich, Which is some - thing be - tween a large bath - ing ma - chine and a
vest - ed in, And he's tell - ing the tars all the par - tic - u - lars of a

dulge in, with - out im - pro - pri - e - ty; For your brain is on fire,— the
ver - y small sec - ond-class car - riage, And you're giv - ing a treat (pen - ny
com - pa - ny he's in - ter - est - ed in; It's a scheme of de - vic - es, to

bed - clothes con - spire ____ of u - su - al slum - ber to plun-der you: First your
ice and cold meat) to a par - ty of friends and re - la - tions; They're a
get at low pric - es, all goods from cough mix - tures to ca - bles (Which

coun - ter - pane goes, and un - cov-ers your toes, and your sheet slips de - mure - ly from
rav - en - ous horde, and they all came on board at Sloane Square and South Ken - sing - ton
tick - led the sail - ors), by treat - ing re - tail - ers as though they were all veg - e -

poco   a   poco   cresc.

un - der you; Then the blank - et - ing tick - les, you feel like mixed pick - les, so
Sta - tions.   And bound on that jour - ney you find your at - tor - ney (who
ta - bles;   You get a good spades-man to plant a small trades-man (first

poco   a   poco   cresc.

ter - ri - bly sharp is the prick - ing,   And you're hot, and you're cross, and you
start - ed that morn - ing from Dev - on);   He's a bit un - der - siz'd, and you
take off his boots with a boot - tree),   And his legs will take root, and his

tum - ble and toss till there's noth - ing 'twixt you and the tick - ing. Then the
don't feel sur-pris'd when he tells you he's on - ly e - lev - en. Well, you're
fin - gers will shoot, and they'll blos - som and bud like a fruit tree; From the

bed - clothes all creep to the ground in a heap and you pick 'em all up in a
driv - ing like mad with this sing - u - lar lad (by the bye the ship's now a four-
green-gro - cer tree you get grapes and green pea, cau - li - flow - er, pine - ap - ple and

tan - gle; Next your pil - low re - signs and po - lite - ly de - clines to re-
wheel - er), And you're play-ing round games, and he calls you bad names when you
cran - ber-ries, While the pas - try-cook plant cher-ry bran-dy will grant, ap - ple

main at its u - su - al an - gle! Well, you get some re - pose in the
tell him that "ties pay the deal - er"; But this you can't stand, so you
puffs, and three - cor - ners, and ban - bur-ys; The shares are a pen - ny, and

form of a doze, with hot eye-balls and head ev-er ach-ing, But your
throw up your hand, and you find you're as cold as an i-ci-cle; In your
ev-er so ma-ny are tak-en by Roth-schild and Bar-ing, And

slum-ber-ing teems with such hor-ri-ble dreams that you'd ver-y much bet-ter be
shirt and your socks (the black silk with gold clocks), cross-ing Sal's-bu-ry Plain on a
just as a few are al-lot-ted to you, you a-

wak-ing; 2. For you
bi-cy-cle: 3. And wake with a shud-der des-pair-ing; You're a

reg-u-lar wreck, with a crick in your neck, and no won-der you snore, for your

dark - ness has pass'd, and it's day - light at last, and the

cresc.

night has been long, dit - to, dit - to my song,

f freely   *Very fast*

And thank good-ness they're both of them o - ver!

f follow the voice   *ff*

sff

Faint Heart Never Won Fair Lady

Waltz tempo

Lord Mountararat 1. *If you go*
Lord Tolloller 2. *He — who*

in You're sure to win, Yours— will be the charm - ing
shies At such a prize Is — not worth a mar - a -

maid - ie: Be — your law The an - cient saw, } "Faint — heart
ve - di, Be — so kind To bear in mind:

nev - er won fair la - dy!" Nev - er, nev - er, nev - er.

"Faint heart nev - er won fair la - dy!"

1. Ev - 'ry jour - ney has _ an end, When at the
2. While _ the sun shines make _ your hay, Where _ a

worst af - fairs _ will mend, Dark _ the dawn when day is
will is, there's _ a way, Beard _ the li - on in his

nigh, Hus - tle your horse and don't say die!
lair, None but the brave de - serve the fair!

LORD CHANCELLOR

I'll_ take heart And make a start, Though_ I fear the pros - pect's shad - y, Much_ I'd spend To gain_ my end:

mf **ALL THREE**

"Faint heart nev - er won fair la - dy!" Nev - er, nev - er

nev - er. "Faint heart nev - er won fair la - dy!"

Noth - ing ven - ture, noth - ing win;

Blood is thick, but wa - ter's thin; In for a pen - ny,

in for a pound; It's Love that makes the world go round!

If We're Weak Enough to Tarry

Joyously

STREPHON

If we're weak e-nough to tar-ry

Ere we mar-ry, You_ and I, Of the feel-ing I in-spire

You may tire___ By_ and bye; For peers with flow-ing cof-fers

Press their of - fers, That is why I am sure we should not tar - ry

mp PHYLLIS

Ere we mar - ry, You and I. If we're weak e - nough to tar - ry

mp

Ere we mar - ry, You and I, With a more at - trac - tive maid - en,

Jew - el lad - en, You may fly; If by chance we should be part - ed,

Bro - ken-heart - ed I should die. So I think we will not tar - ry

Princess Ida

OR, CASTLE ADAMANT

DRAMATIS PERSONÆ

KING HILDEBRAND

HILARION (*his Son*)

CYRIL
FLORIAN } (*Hilarion's Friends*)

KING GAMA

ARAC
GURON } (*his Sons*)
SCYNTHIUS

PRINCESS IDA (*Gama's Daughter*)

LADY BLANCHE (*Professor of Abstract Science*)

LADY PSYCHE (*Professor of Humanities*)

MELISSA (*Lady Blanche's Daughter*)

SACHARISSA
CHLOE } (*Girl Graduates*)
ADA

Soldiers, Courtiers, "Girl Graduates," "Daughters of the Plough," etc.

ACT I

PAVILION IN KING HILDEBRAND'S PALACE

ACT II

GARDENS OF CASTLE ADAMANT

ACT III

COURTYARD OF CASTLE ADAMANT

First produced at the Savoy Theatre on January 5, 1884

I AM often asked, "Which is your favorite part?" My reply to that question is either "I do not have one," or "The part I am going to play next." I found that it was inadvisable to have a favorite. If I did, then every other one of my roles would be likely to suffer. Now if the question were, "Which is your favorite opera?" I could answer quite freely, "I think it is Princess Ida." I am not alone in this, but I realize I am one among a tiny minority.

Princess Ida, in my opinion, contains the very best of both Gilbert's and Sullivan's work. For consistency of literary and musical charm throughout, it seems to me to have no peer. Not even Yeomen of the Guard or Iolanthe, both extremely beautiful, can measure up to it. For some reason, though, it is not among the more popular of the Gilbert and Sullivan series. It is performed less often and is less well known. The songs, therefore, are not so familiar, which is why so few of them are represented in the music section of this book.

Then why do I rank it so high? Well, I doubt if Die Walküre commands as great a popularity as La Bohème or Carmen, or—to select one of Wagner's own compositions—Die Meistersinger, but does that preclude it from being great, if not greater music?

I will admit that some first reviews of Princess Ida contained such adjectives as "dull," "clumsy," "tedious," etc., and that its original run at the Savoy was not considered by the three partners a success by their standards. Sullivan came off by far the better of the two collaborators. The music critic of the Sunday Times said: ". . . it is the best in every way that Sir Arthur Sullivan has produced . . . I cannot detect a single piece that does not bear obvious traces of artistic thought and care. . . . Besides its exquisite orchestration, Princess Ida is rich in vocal concerted music. Humor is almost as strong a point with Sir Arthur as with his clever collaborator, and when attained by such legitimate means, it is simply irresistible!"

Gilbert described Princess Ida as a "respectful operatic perversion of Tennyson's Princess." He had already written a "respectful perversion" in his The Princess and it was from this that he adapted the operatic version, in both cases retaining blank verse dialogue. The program announced the piece as being in "A Prologue and Two Acts," but somehow the critics ignored the program and alluded to it as "In three acts," and in three acts it has been ever since.

Quarrels, or at least incidents, were beginning to occur at more frequent intervals about now. Richard D'Oyly Carte, quite unwittingly, set off the spark to one. In March 1884, a little less than two months after Princess Ida had been produced, he wrote to both Gilbert and Sullivan, saying ". . . business, as they must have observed, was dropping, and it seemed possible that a new piece would be needed for the autumn." Carte was required to give Gilbert and Sullivan six months' notice if a new opera was deemed necessary, and this letter was intended to fulfill this contractual clause.

Sullivan was in Brussels when he received his copy of the letter. He astonished both Carte and Gilbert with his reply, in which he stated that it was impossible for him to compose another piece of the character of those already written by Gilbert and himself. Gilbert exercised considerable restraint in his reply to Sullivan. He pointed out that, according to the terms of their contract, they would be liable for any losses that Carte might incur *if they defaulted in providing a new piece. By this time Sullivan was in Paris, from where he wrote again in the same vein. He maintained that in Princess Ida he had come to the end of his tether for that kind of piece; that his tunes were becoming repetitions of his former pieces, and that his concerted movements were beginning to bear a strong family resemblance!*

All this was not entirely Sir Arthur Sullivan's own thinking. He had only recently received the accolade of knighthood, and his friends (?) were telling him that such light nonsense as the comic operas to which he had affixed his name hitherto as Arthur Sullivan were beneath Sir Arthur Sullivan. He should turn his talents to more serious work—grand opera, for instance. Queen Victoria herself had urged him in this direction, saying, ". . . you would do it so well!" Undoubtedly this had its effect on him, leading him to reply to Gilbert as he did.

Eventually, a more realistic factor resolved the impasse. Serious music was not as lucrative as comic opera, and Sullivan was fond of the good things of life, being a great gambler and a frequent visitor to Monte Carlo and the Casino—all to the detriment of his pocketbook! So Sullivan rediscovered his head that he had so nearly lost.

Two lots of programs were printed for the first night of Princess Ida. Sullivan was a very sick man, unable to move from his bed. Mr. Carte, realizing the situation, withdrew the programs bearing Sir Arthur's name as the conductor for this occasion and printed fresh ones announcing the musical conductor as Mr. Frank Cellier. At noon on January 5, 1884, the day of the opening, Sullivan dragged himself out of his bed, collapsed, but then crawled to his chair. He had made up his mind. He would conduct that night. His diary records that after having a strong injection to ease his pain, and a big cup of black coffee to keep him awake, he managed to dress, get to the theater, and into the pit. It was too late to replace the new programs with the originals that bore Sullivan's name, and so, according to "official" records, Sullivan did not conduct the opening night of Princess Ida.

Princess Ida

ACT I

SCENE.—*Pavilion attached to* KING HILDEBRAND's *palace. Soldiers and Courtiers discovered looking out through opera-glasses, telescopes, etc.,* FLORIAN *leading.* [1]

CHORUS.　　　Search throughout the panorama
　　　　　　For a sign of royal Gama,
　　　　　　　　Who to-day should cross the water
　　　　　　　　With his fascinating daughter—
　　　　　　　　Ida is her name.

　　　　　　Some misfortune evidently
　　　　　　Has detained them—consequently
　　　　　　　　Search throughout the panorama
　　　　　　　　For the daughter of King Gama,
　　　　　　　　Prince Hilarion's flame!

SOLO

FLOR.　Will Prince Hilarion's hopes be sadly blighted?
ALL.　　　　　　　　　Who can tell?
FLOR.　Will Ida break the vows that she has plighted?
ALL.　　　　　　　　　Who can tell?
FLOR.　Will she back out, and say she did not mean them?
ALL.　　　　　　　　　Who can tell?
FLOR.　If so, there'll be the deuce to pay between them!

ALL.　　　　　No, no—we'll not despair,
　　　　　　For Gama would not dare
　　　　　　To make a deadly foe
　　　　　　Of Hildebrand, and so,
　　　　　　　　Search throughout, etc.

Enter KING HILDEBRAND, *with* CYRIL

HILD.　See you no sign of Gama?
FLOR.　　　　　　　　None, my liege!
HILD.　It's very odd indeed. If Gama fail
　　　To put in an appearance at our Court
　　　Before the sun has set in yonder west,
　　　And fail to bring the Princess Ida here
　　　To whom our son Hilarion was betrothed [2]
　　　At the extremely early age of one,
　　　There's war between King Gama and ourselves!
　　　　(*Aside to* CYRIL.) Oh, Cyril, how I dread this interview.
　　　It's twenty years since he and I have met.
　　　He was a twisted monster—all awry—
　　　As though Dame Nature, angry with her work,
　　　Had crumpled it in fitful petulance!
CYR.　But, sir, a twisted and ungainly trunk
　　　Often bears goodly fruit. Perhaps he was
　　　A kind, well-spoken gentleman?

[1] How many people, I wonder, have stopped to realize that Princess Ida *is the only opera of the series that does not specify, either by direct statement or by definite implication, either the period or the country in which the plot is set? The original costuming would suggest the period as being medieval, and probably European, but no more than that. The name Hildebrand could suggest Rome as the locale. Pope Gregory VII (1073–85) was no more unbending in his assertions of his own power and the celibacy of the clergy than King Hildebrand is of his power and the early marriage vows of his son and Gama's daughter.*

But one moment. Opera glasses? Telescopes? No matter what the country is, the period must be 19th century, and fairly late 19th century at that, despite what the costumes may suggest.

[2] *King Hildebrand refers to Hilarion's "betrothal" to Princess Ida. It will later be observed that Hilarion refers to his marriage with her when he was a year old.*

361

[3] *It has always struck me as strange that Gilbert could permit himself to make such a grossly inaccurate statement regarding the venomous organ of the snake for the sake of a vague and not overly humorous pun. A snake's venom is ejected through its fangs.*

[4] *Cigars. Another indication that this opera is meant not to be set in medieval times. "Mustachios," of course, would still suggest the Latin locale.*

HILD.   Oh, no!
For, adder-like, his sting lay in his tongue. [3]
(His "sting" is present, though his "stung" is past.)

FLOR.   (*looking through glass*). But stay, my liege; o'er yonder mountain's brow
Comes a small body, bearing Gama's arms;
And now I look more closely at it, sir,
I see attached to it King Gama's legs;
From which I gather this corollary
That that small body must be Gama's own!

HILD.   Ha! Is the Princess with him?

FLOR.   Well, my liege,
Unless her highness is full six feet high,
And wears mustachios too—and smokes cigars—[4]
And rides *en cavalier* in coat of steel—
I do not think she is.

HILD.   One never knows.
She's a strange girl, I've heard, and does odd things!
Come, bustle there!
For Gama place the richest robes we own—
For Gama place the coarsest prison dress—
For Gama let our best spare bed be aired—
For Gama let our deepest dungeon yawn—
For Gama lay the costliest banquet out—
For Gama place cold water and dry bread!
For as King Gama brings the Princess here,
Or brings her not, so shall King Gama have
Much more than everything—much less than nothing!

SONG AND CHORUS

HILD.   Now hearken to my strict command
On every hand, on every hand—

CHORUS.   To your command,
On every hand,
We dutifully bow!

HILD.   If Gama bring the Princess here,
Give him good cheer, give him good cheer.

CHORUS.   If she come here
We'll give him a cheer,
And we will show you how.
Hip, hip, hurrah! hip, hip, hurrah!
Hip, hip, hurrah! hurrah! hurrah!
We'll shout and sing
Long live the King,
And his daughter, too, I trow!
Then shout ha! ha! hip, hip, hurrah!
Hip, hip, hip, hip, hurrah!
For the fair Princess and her good papa,
Hurrah! hurrah!

HILD.   But if he fail to keep his troth,
Upon our oath, we'll trounce them both!

CHORUS.   He'll trounce them both,
Upon his oath,
As sure as quarter-day!

HILD.   We'll shut him up in a dungeon cell,
         And toll his knell on a funeral bell.

CHORUS.   From his dungeon cell,
                     His funeral knell
                 Shall strike him with dismay!
         Hip, hip, hurrah! hip, hip, hurrah!
         Hip, hip, hurrah! hurrah! hurrah!
                  As up we string
                  The faithless King,
              In the old familiar way!
         We'll shout ha! ha! hip, hip, hurrah!
         Hip, hip, hip, hip, hurrah!
         As we make an end of her false papa,
                  Hurrah! hurrah!

                                    [*Exeunt all.*

                Enter HILARION

            RECIT.—HILARION [5]

         To-day we meet, my baby bride and I—
           But ah, my hopes are balanced by my fears!
         What transmutations have been conjured by
           The silent alchemy of twenty years!

            [6] BALLAD—HILARION [7]

              Ida was a twelvemonth old,
                Twenty years ago!
              I was twice her age, I'm told,
                Twenty years ago!
              Husband twice as old as wife
              Argues ill for married life
              Baleful prophecies were rife,
                Twenty years ago!

              Still, I was a tiny prince
                Twenty years ago.
              She has gained upon me, since
                Twenty years ago.
              Though she's twenty-one, it's true,
              I am barely twenty-two—
              False and foolish prophets you,
                Twenty years ago!

                Enter HILDEBRAND

HIL.   Well, father, is there news for me at last?
HILD.   King Gama is in sight, but much I fear
         With no Princess!
HIL.   Alas, my liege, I've heard
         That Princess Ida has forsworn the world,
         And, with a band of women, shut herself
         Within a lonely country house; and there
         Devotes herself to stern philosophies!
HILD.   Then I should say the loss of such a wife
         Is one to which a reasonable man
         Would easily be reconciled.
HIL.   Oh, no!
         Or I am not a reasonable man.
         She *is* my wife—has been for twenty years!
         (*Holding glass.*) [8] I think I see her now.

[5] *One of Sullivan's most tuneful recitatives, and particularly effective following, as it does, the vigorous solo and chorus.*

[6] *Although the theme of this ballad is different, one can find a distinct similarity in its form to that of Fairfax's song, "Is Life a Boon?" (see The Yeomen of the Guard, Note 20). Gilbert takes a hypothesis or a statement of fact in the first verse, enlarges upon it, and comes to a conclusion. In the second verse, he takes another hypothesis or statement of fact, enlarges upon it, and comes to an opposite conclusion.*

In my opinion, this is one of the most delightful of all Sullivan's tenor songs.

[7] *Words and music on page 395.*

[8] *Hilarion picks up a telescope when he comes to the end of his previous song, and is actually looking through it in the direction from which Gama is approaching while the dialogue is going on. Hildebrand's "Ha! let me look!" is a reaction of pleased surprise at the thought that Princess Ida is with her father, in spite of Florian's statement that he thought she wasn't.*

HILD.   Ha! let me look!

HIL.   In my mind's eye, I mean—a blushing bride,
All bib and tucker, frill and furbelow!
How exquisite she looked as she was borne,
Recumbent, in her foster-mother's arms!
How the bride wept—nor would be comforted
Until the hireling mother-for-the-nonce
Administered refreshment in the vestry.
And I remember feeling much annoyed
That she should weep at marrying with me.
But then I thought, "These brides are all alike.
You cry at marrying me? How much more cause
You'd have to cry if it were broken off!"
These were my thoughts; I kept them to myself,
For at that age I had not learned to speak.

                                          [Exeunt.

Enter Courtiers

CHORUS.   From the distant panorama
Come the sons of royal Gama.
They are heralds evidently,
And are sacred consequently,
Sons of Gama, hail! oh, hail!

Enter ARAC, GURON, *and* SCYNTHIUS [9]

SONG—ARAC

We are warriors three,
Sons of Gama, Rex.
Like most sons are we,
Masculine in sex.

ALL THREE.   Yes, yes, yes,
Masculine in sex.

ARAC.   Politics we bar,
They are not our bent;
On the whole we are
Not intelligent.

ALL THREE.   No, no, no,
Not intelligent.

ARAC.   But with doughty heart,
And with trusty blade [10]
We can play our part—
Fighting is our trade.

ALL THREE.   Yes, yes, yes,
Fighting is our trade.

Bold, and fierce, and strong, ha! ha! [11]
For a war we burn,
With its right or wrong, ha! ha!
We have no concern.
Order comes to fight, ha! ha!
Order is obeyed,
We are men of might, ha! ha!
Fighting is our trade.
Yes, yes, yes,
Fighting is our trade, ha! ha!

[9] *The entrance of Gama's sons is, I think, one of the funniest in the series. Clad in heavy armor from head to foot, which makes it extremely difficult for them to move, they stomp onto the stage in time to a slow and truly Handelian piece of writing.*

[10] *Each one's "trusty blade" is a two-handed sword practically as tall as its owner.*

[11] *In appearance they are truly "bold, and fierce, and strong." All have fearsome beards, one bright ginger, one a true blond, and the other jet black. We do not see their close-cropped heads at the moment, covered as they are with steel helmets.*

CHORUS.   They are men of might, ha! ha!
              Fighting is their trade.
              Order comes to fight, ha! ha!
              Order is obeyed, ha! ha!
                  Fighting is their trade!

Enter KING GAMA

SONG—GAMA [12]

If you give me your attention, I will tell you what I am: [13]
I'm a genuine philanthropist—all other kinds are sham.
Each little fault of temper and each social defect
In my erring fellow-creatures I endeavour to correct.
To all their little weaknesses I open people's eyes;
And little plans to snub the self-sufficient I devise;
I love my fellow-creatures—I do all the good I can—
Yet everybody says I'm such a disagreeable man!
        And I can't think why!

To compliments inflated I've a withering reply;
And vanity I always do my best to mortify;
A charitable action I can skilfully dissect;
And interested motives I'm delighted to detect;
I know everybody's income and what everybody earns;
And I carefully compare it with the income tax returns;
But to benefit humanity however much I plan,
Yet everybody says I'm such a disagreeable man!
        And I can't think why!

I'm sure I'm no ascetic; I'm as pleasant as can be;
You'll always find me ready with a crushing repartee,
I've an irritating chuckle, I've a celebrated sneer,
I've an entertaining snigger, I've a fascinating leer.
To everybody's prejudice I know a thing or two;
I can tell a woman's age in half a minute—and I do.
But although I try to make myself as pleasant as I can,
Yet everybody says I am a disagreeable man!
        And I can't think why!

CHORUS.   He can't think why!

Enter HILDEBRAND, HILARION, CYRIL, *and* FLORIAN

GAMA.   So this is Castle Hildebrand? Well, well!
            Dame Rumour whispered that the place was grand;
            She told me that your taste was exquisite,
            Superb, unparalleled!
HILD. (*gratified*).   Oh, really, King!
GAMA.   But she's a liar! Why, how old you've grown!
            Is this Hilarion? Why, you've changed too—
            You were a singularly handsome child!
(*To* FLOR.) Are you a courtier? Come, then, ply your trade,
            Tell me some lies. How do you like your King?
            Vile rumour says he's all but imbecile.
            Now, that's not true?
FLOR.   My lord, we love our King.
            His wise remarks are valued by his court
            As precious stones.
GAMA.   And for the self-same cause,
            Like precious stones, his sensible remarks
            Derive their value from their scarcity!

[12] Words and music on page 397.

[13] *"If you give me your attention, etc." is Gilbert's jocular self-description. As he told George Grossmith, the original King Gama, during one rehearsal, "I meant it for myself: I thought it my duty to live up to my reputation."*

[14] Princess Ida was re-dressed by the D'Oyly Carte Opera Company in 1955 and I was shocked to see that King Gama's appearance had been changed so radically that he was practically not deformed, and his make-up, with the exception of a gray pointed beard, was "straight"! Meeting the stage director after a performance at the Shubert Theater during the company's visit in 1956, I remarked on this, and to my astonishment was told that this

"... twisted monster—all awry—
As though Dame Nature, angry with her work,
Had crumpled it in fitful petulance!"

was twisted and ungainly only in the mind! Pardon me, Mr. Stage Director, but . . .

"This leg is crooked—this foot is ill-designed—
This shoulder wears a hump! Come, out with it!
Look, here's my face! Now, am I not the worst
Of Nature's blunders?"

and as Florian says:

"Nature never errs.
To those who know the workings of your mind,
Your face and figure, sir, suggest a book
Appropriately bound."

[15] Oh, no, King Gama is no snob—so he says!

[16] Here, of course, "match" means "prove equal to or better than." In the next reference . . .

[17] . . . Florian deliberately misconstrues Gama's use of the word, and in doing so would appear to set the period of Princess Ida no earlier than 1831 when matches were invented.

Come now, be honest, tell the truth for once!
Tell it of me. [14] Come, come, I'll harm you not.
This leg is crooked—this foot is ill-designed—
This shoulder wears a hump! Come, out with it!
Look, here's my face! Now, am I not the worst
Of Nature's blunders?

CYR.   Nature never errs.
To those who know the workings of your mind,
Your face and figure, sir, suggest a book
Appropriately bound.

GAMA (enraged).   Why, harkye, sir,
How dare you bandy words with me?

CYR.   No need
To bandy aught that appertains to you.

GAMA (furiously). Do you permit this, King?

HILD.   We are in doubt
Whether to treat you as an honoured guest
Or as a traitor knave who plights his word
And breaks it.

GAMA (quickly).   If the casting vote's with me,
I give it for the former!

HILD.   We shall see.
By the terms of our contract, signed and sealed,
You're bound to bring the Princess here to-day:
Why is she not with you?

GAMA.   Answer me this:
What think you of a wealthy purse-proud man,
Who, when he calls upon a starving friend,
Pulls out his gold and flourishes his notes,
And flashes diamonds in the pauper's eyes?
What name have you for such an one?

HILD.   A snob.

GAMA. Just so. The girl has beauty, virtue, wit,
Grace, humour, wisdom, charity, and pluck.
Would it be kindly, think you, to parade
These brilliant qualities, before your eyes?
Oh no, King Hildebrand, I am no snob!

HILD. (furiously). Stop that tongue,
Or you shall lose the monkey head that holds it!

GAMA.   Bravo! your King deprives me of my head,
That he and I may meet on equal terms!

HILD.   Where is she now?

GAMA.   In Castle Adamant,
One of my many country houses. [15] There
She rules a woman's University,
With full a hundred girls, who learn of her.

CYR.   A hundred girls! A hundred ecstasies!

GAMA.   But no mere girls, my good young gentleman;
With all the college learning that you boast,
The youngest there will prove a match [16] for you.

CYR.   With all my heart, if she's the prettiest!
(To FLOR.) Fancy, a hundred matches [17]—all alight!—
That's if I strike them as I hope to do!

GAMA.   Despair your hope; their hearts are dead to men.
He who desires to gain their favour must
Be qualified to strike their teeming brains,
And not their hearts. They're safety matches, sir,

And they light only on the knowledge box—
So *you've* no chance!

FLOR.   And there are no males whatever in those walls?

GAMA.   None, gentlemen, excepting letter mails— [18]
And they are driven (as males often are
In other large communities) by women.
Why, bless my heart, she's so particular
She'll scarcely suffer Dr. Watts's [19] hymns—
And all the animals she owns are "hers"!
The ladies rise at cockcrow every morn—

CYR.   Ah, then they have male poultry?

GAMA.   Not at all,
(*Confidentially.*) The crowing's done by an accomplished hen!

DUET—GAMA *and* HILDEBRAND

GAMA.   Perhaps if you address the lady
      Most politely, most politely—
    Flatter and impress the lady,
      Most politely, most politely—
    Humbly beg and humbly sue—
    She may deign to look on you,
    But your doing you must do
      Most politely, most politely! [20]

ALL.   Humbly beg and humbly sue, etc.

HILD.   Go you, and inform the lady,
      Most politely, most politely,
    If she don't, we'll storm the lady
      Most politely, most politely!

(*To* GAMA.)   You'll remain as hostage here;
    Should Hilarion disappear,
    We will hang you, never fear,
      Most politely, most politely!

ALL.   He'll ⎫
    I'll ⎬ remain as hostage here, etc.
    You'll ⎭

[GAMA, ARAC, GURON, *and* SCYNTHIUS *are marched off in custody,*
    HILDEBRAND *following.*

RECIT.—HILARION

Come, Cyril, Florian, our course is plain,
    To-morrow morn fair Ida we'll engage;
But we will use no force her love to gain,
    Nature has armed us for the war we wage!

TRIO—HILARION, CYRIL, *and* FLORIAN [21]

HIL.   Expressive glances
    Shall be our lances,
      And pops of Sillery [22]
      Our light artillery.
    We'll storm their bowers
    With scented showers
    Of fairest flowers
    That we can buy!

[18] *Gilbert's fondness for that lowest form of humor is amply illustrated here, as is his fondness for the punless play on words.*

[19] *Dr. Isaac Watts (1674–1748). A nonconformist theologian and a prolific writer of hymns.*
The word "hymns" should be spoken with enough stress to imply "hims," and in the next line the suggestion is, of course, that every animal she owns, quite naturally, is hers, and each is a "her."

[20] *The business here calls for the ladies to make a curtsy to Hilarion. Gilbert, wanting them all to carry out this movement at exactly the same moment, fixed on the word "politely" when it was sung for the last time in each verse, as the cue. Even so, the ladies were not quite together, and at last in desperation, Gilbert roared: "No, ladies—you go down on the 'po' and come up 'lightly.'" Gilbert's love of the pun was here again very evident, though perhaps not quite of the "drawing-room order"! It is based on the French pot de chambre, a bedroom article referred to in England as the "po."*

[21] Words and music on page 400.

[22] *Pops of Sillery. The popping of corks from bottles of Sillery, a high-class wine produced in and around the village of Sillery in the Champagne district of France.*

CHORUS.   Oh, dainty triolet!
              Oh fragrant violet!
              Oh, gentle heigho-let
                 (Or little sigh).
On sweet urbanity, [23]
Though mere inanity,
To touch their vanity
      We will rely!

[23] *Gilbert's rhyming genius combines with Sullivan's brilliant gift of melody in a particularly mellifluous fashion to make this trio outstanding. To obtain its full beauty, it must be sung with consistent smoothness and at a steady rhythm. Sullivan gives the directions "Moderately slow, and with tenderness." A suggested metronomic time would be: ♩ = 100.*

It is one of the few numbers in the series that may be sung without further action after the singers form a picture on the stage. In fact, action here tends very strongly to distract from the beauty of the harmony.

CYR.   When day is fading,
With serenading
      And such frivolity
      We'll prove our quality.
A sweet profusion
Of soft allusion
This bold intrusion
      Shall justify.

CHORUS.   Oh, dainty triolet, etc.

FLOR.   We'll charm their senses
With verbal fences,
      With ballads amatory
      And declamatory.
Little heeding
Their pretty pleading,
Our love exceeding
      We'll justify!

CHORUS.   Oh, dainty triolet, etc.

Re-enter GAMA, ARAC, GURON, *and* SCYNTHIUS
heavily ironed [24]

[24] *If the above manner of staging is carried out, the re-entrance of Gama, and what follows, takes on added impact by reason of contrast.*

RECIT.

GAMA. Must we, till then, in prison cell be thrust?
HILD.   You must!
GAMA. This seems unnecessarily severe!
ARAC, GURON, *and* SCYNTHIUS. Hear, hear!

TRIO—ARAC, GURON, *and* SCYNTHIUS [25]

[25] *Similarly, the trio, with its vastly different tempo, becomes stronger and far more effective.*

For a month to dwell
In a dungeon cell;
      Growing thin and wizen
      In a solitary prison,
Is a poor look-out
For a soldier stout,
      Who is longing for the rattle
      Of a complicated battle—
For the rum-tum-tum
Of the military drum
      And the guns that go boom! boom!

ALL.   The rum-tum-tum
Of the military drum, etc.

HILD.   When Hilarion's bride
Has at length complied
      With the just conditions
      Of our requisitions,
You may go in haste

And indulge your taste
    For the fascinating rattle
    Of a complicated battle—
For the rum-tum-tum,
Of the military drum,
    And the guns that go boom! boom!

ALL.   For the rum-tum-tum
Of the military drum, etc.

ALL.   But till that time { we'll / you'll } here remain,

And bail { they / we } will not entertain,

Should she { his / our } mandate disobey,

Our / Your } lives the penalty will pay!

[GAMA, ARAC, GURON, *and* SCYNTHIUS *are marched off.*

END OF ACT I

ACT II

Gardens in Castle Adamant. A river runs across the back of the stage, crossed by a rustic bridge. Castle Adamant in the distance.

Girl graduates discovered seated at the feet of LADY PSYCHE

CHORUS.   Towards the empyrean heights
    Of every kind of lore,
We've taken several easy flights,
    And mean to take some more.
In trying to achieve success
    No envy racks our heart,
And all the knowledge we possess,
    We mutually impart.

SOLO—MELISSA

Pray, what authors should she read
Who in Classics would succeed?

PSYCHE   If you'd climb the Helicon, [26]
You should read Anacreon, [27]
Ovid's *Metamorphoses*,
Likewise Aristophanes,
And the works of Juvenal: [28]
These are worth attention, all;
But, if you will be advised,
You will get them Bowdlerized! [29]

CHORUS.   Ah! we will get them Bowdlerized!

SOLO—SACHARISSA

Pray you, tell us, if you can,
What's the thing that's known as Man?

[26] Helicon. *A mountain in Boeotia, sacred to the Muses.*

[27] Anacreon. *A Greek poet known for his songs of love and drinking.*

[28] Juvenal. *The Roman poet of satire. Lived circa 60–140* A.D.

[29] Bowdlerized. *Expurgated. After Thomas Bowdler, who published an expurgated version of Shakespeare in 1818.*

PSYCHE
Man will swear and Man will storm—
Man is not at all good form—
Man is of no kind of use—
Man's a donkey—Man's a goose—
Man is coarse and Man is plain—
Man is more or less insane—
Man's a ribald—Man's a rake,
Man is Nature's sole mistake!

CHORUS.
We'll a memorandum make—
Man is Nature's sole mistake!

And thus to empyrean height
　Of every kind of lore,
In search of wisdom's pure delight,
　Ambitiously we soar.
In trying to achieve success
　No envy racks our heart,
For all we know and all we guess,
　We mutually impart!

Enter LADY BLANCHE. *All stand up demurely*

BLA.
Attention, ladies, while I read to you
The Princess Ida's list of punishments.
The first is Sacharissa. She's expelled!

ALL.
Expelled!

BLA.
　　　　Expelled, because although she knew
No man of any kind may pass our walls,
She dared to bring a set of chessmen here!

SACH. (*crying*). I meant no harm; they're only men of wood!

BLA.
They're men with whom you give each other mate,
And that's enough! The next is Chloe.

CHLOE.
　　　　　　　　　　　　　　　　　Ah!

BLA.
Chloe will lose three terms, for yesterday,
When looking through her drawing-book, I found
A sketch of a perambulator!

ALL (*horrified*).　　　　　　　　Oh!

BLA.
Double perambulator, shameless girl!
That's all at present. Now, attention, pray;
Your Principal the Princess comes to give
Her usual inaugural address [30]
To those young ladies who joined yesterday.

Enter the PRINCESS

CHORUS.
Mighty maiden with a mission,
　Paragon of common sense,
Running fount of erudition,
　Miracle of eloquence,
We are blind, and we would see;
We are bound, and would be free;
We are dumb, and we would talk;
We are lame, and we would walk.
Mighty maiden with a mission—
　Paragon of common sense;
Running fount of erudition—
　Miracle of eloquence!

PRIN. (*recit.*).　　　Minerva, [31] oh, hear me!

[30] *Since Castle Adamant is a college, one presumes there will be vacations. As the Princess is about to give her inaugural address, this must be the beginning of a new semester. I'm curious to know where the young ladies went during vacation. Or did they remain confined within the walls of the castle?*

[31] *Minerva. Goddess of wisdom.*

370

ARIA [32]

Oh, goddess wise
　　That lovest light
　　Endow with sight
Their unillumined eyes.

At this my call,
　　A fervent few
　　Have come to woo
The rays that from thee fall.

Let fervent words and fervent thoughts be mine,
That I may lead them to thy sacred shrine!

Women of Adamant, fair Neophytes—
Who thirst for such instruction as we give,
Attend, while I unfold a parable.
The elephant is mightier than Man,
Yet Man subdues him. Why? The elephant
Is elephantine everywhere but here (*tapping her forehead*),
And Man, whose brain is to the elephant's
As Woman's brain to Man's—(that's rule of three),—
Conquers the foolish giant of the woods,
As Woman, in her turn, shall conquer Man.
In Mathematics, Woman leads the way:
The narrow-minded pedant still believes
That two and two make four! Why, we can prove,
We women—household drudges as we are—
That two and two make five—or three—or seven;
Or five-and-twenty, if the case demands!
Diplomacy? The wiliest diplomat
Is absolutely helpless in our hands,
He wheedles monarchs—woman wheedles him!
Logic? Why, tyrant Man himself admits
It's waste of time to argue with a woman!
Then we excel in social qualities:
Though Man professes that he holds our sex
In utter scorn, I venture to believe
He'd rather pass the day with one of you,
Than with five hundred of his fellow-men!
In all things we excel. Believing this,
A hundred maidens here have sworn to place
Their feet upon his neck. If we succeed,
We'll treat him better than he treated us:
But if we fail, why, then let hope fail too!
Let no one care a penny how she looks—
Let red be worn with yellow—blue with green—
Crimson with scarlet—violet with blue!
Let all your things misfit, and you yourselves
At inconvenient moments come undone!
Let hair-pins lose their virtue: let the hook
Disdain the fascination of the eye—
The bashful button modestly evade
The soft embraces of the button-hole!
Let old associations all dissolve,
Let Swan secede from Edgar—Gask from Gask,
Sewell from Cross—Lewis from Allenby! [33]
In other words—let Chaos come again!
(*Coming down.*) Who lectures in the Hall of Arts to-day?

[32] *In the Princess's aria, "Oh, goddess wise," Sullivan's music begins to achieve grand operatic proportions. According to Reginald Allen's First Night Gilbert and Sullivan, the original libretto had these two quatrains in reverse order. Apparently Sullivan, for purposes of musical scansion, placed them in the order now shown.*

[33] *These are all department stores. Perhaps the country in which Princess Ida is set is England, after all.*

BLA. I, madam, on Abstract Philosophy.
There I propose considering, at length,
Three points—The Is, the Might Be, and the Must.
Whether the Is, from being actual fact,
Is more important than the vague Might Be,
Or the Might Be, from taking wider scope,
Is for that reason greater than the Is:
And lastly, how the Is and Might Be stand
Compared with the inevitable Must!
PRIN. The subject's deep—how do you treat it, pray?
BLA. Madam, I take three possibilities,
And strike a balance, then, between the three:
As thus: The Princess Ida Is our head,
The Lady Psyche Might Be,—Lady Blanche,
Neglected Blanche, inevitably Must.
Given these three hypotheses—to find
The actual betting against each of them!
PRIN. Your theme's ambitious: pray you, bear in mind
Who highest soar fall farthest. Fare you well,
You and your pupils! Maidens, follow me.

[*Exeunt* PRINCESS *and Maidens singing refrain of chorus, "And
thus to empyrean heights," etc. Manet* LADY BLANCHE.

BLA. I should command here—I was born to rule,
But do I rule? I don't. Why? I don't know.

I shall some day. Not yet. I bide my time.
I once was Some One—and the Was Will Be.
The Present as we speak becomes the Past, [34]
The Past repeats itself, and so is Future!
This sounds involved. It's not. It's right enough.

SONG—LADY BLANCHE [35]

Come, mighty Must!
    Inevitable Shall!
In thee I trust.
    Time weaves my coronal!
Go, mocking Is!
    Go, disappointing Was!
That I am this
    Ye are the cursed cause!
Yet humble second shall be first,
        I ween;
And dead and buried be the curst
        Has Been!

Oh, weak Might Be!
    Oh, May, Might, Could, Would, Should!
How powerless ye
    For evil or for good!
In every sense
    Your moods I cheerless call,
Whate'er your tense
    Ye are Imperfect, all!
Ye have deceived the trust I've shown
        In ye!
Away! The Mighty Must alone
        Shall be!

[*Exit* LADY BLANCHE.

[34] *Dr. Daly uses a similar theme in his speech to
Alexis in* The Sorcerer *(see page 33).*

[35] *This song has been cut from the performance for
many years, though not deleted from printed
editions of the libretto. Reginald Allen says, in
his* First Night Gilbert and Sullivan, *"In the
1955 revival the only casualty among the lyrics
in the official cuts was Lady Blanche's song,
'Come, Mighty Must!'" To my certain knowledge, the cut took effect years before that. I
would not say for certain that it goes back as far
as the 1922 revival, but I do not recall its being
included in 1925.*

Enter HILARION, CYRIL, *and* FLORIAN, *climbing over wall, and creeping cautiously among the trees and rocks at the back of the stage.*

TRIO—HILARION, CYRIL, FLORIAN

Gently, gently,
Evidently
　　We are safe so far,
After scaling
Fence and paling,
　　Here, at last, we are!
In this college
Useful knowledge
　　Everywhere one finds,
And already,
Growing steady,
　　We've enlarged our minds.

CYR.　We've learnt that prickly cactus
Has the power to attract us
　　　　When we fall.

ALL.　　　　　　　When we fall!

HIL.　That nothing man unsettles
Like a bed of stinging nettles,
　　　　Short or tall.

ALL.　　　　　　　Short or tall!

FLOR.　That bull-dogs feed on throttles—
That we don't like broken bottles
　　　　On a wall.

ALL.　　　　　　　On a wall!

HIL.　That spring-guns breathe defiance!
And that burglary's a science
　　　　After all!

ALL.　　　　　　　After all!

RECIT.—FLORIAN [36]

A Woman's college! maddest folly going!
What can girls learn within its walls worth knowing?
I'll lay a crown (the Princess shall decide it)
I'll teach them twice as much in half-an-hour outside it.

HILARION

Hush, scoffer; ere you sound your puny thunder,
List to their aims, and bow your head in wonder!

They intend to send a wire
　　To the moon—to the moon;
And they'll set the Thames on fire
　　Very soon—very soon;
Then they learn to make silk purses
　　With their rigs—with their rigs,
From the ears of Lady Circe's
　　Piggy-wigs—piggy-wigs.
And weasels at their slumbers
　　They trepan—they trepan;
To get sunbeams from cucumbers,

[36] One writer,* on the subject of Gilbert and Sullivan and Princess Ida, accuses Gilbert of prejudice and bad temper with respect to the strides that were being made in the higher education of women. He asserts that Gilbert's attitude was crystallized in Florian's recitative, "A Woman's college! maddest folly going!" and the ensuing solos of Hilarion and Cyril.

I disagree. Gilbert was satirical, invariably, and cynical, often, but bad-tempered in his writings, never. He was merely voicing the thoughts of all young men of that period about the pseudo-intellectual woman who had no use for men. What can they learn in a world without men? The argument is not so much against learning as it is against male-less society. Give Florian half an hour with one of the girls outside the college and there is, as Lady Blanche says later, ". . . an unbounded field of speculation on which I could discourse for hours!" Does not the accuser of Gilbert display prejudice and bad temper himself toward Gilbert?

* W. A. Darlington: The World of Gilbert and Sullivan.

[37] Sullivan transposed these words and the vocal parts now read:

hop-ing at her U- ni- ver-si-

tee we shall see!

[38] The word "nigger" is used here by Gilbert to mean a Negro, and not, as in The Mikado, to indicate a minstrel made up with burnt cork. I have no doubt that, if and when Princess Ida is performed in the United States again, the word will be changed, as it has been in The Mikado. (See The Mikado, page 435, Note 79.)

For they do not care about him

[39] To overcome the glaring coincidence of these opportunely placed academic robes, three of the young ladies are discovered stitching away at them as the curtain rises. When they make their exit, the gowns and three academic caps are conveniently forgotten. The caps, incidentally, must be made in such a way that they will hide the fact that the three men have male haircuts.

They've a plan—they've a plan.
They've a firmly rooted notion
They can cross the Polar Ocean,
And they'll find Perpetual Motion,
    If they can—if they can.

ALL.   These are the phenomena
That every pretty domina
    Is hoping we shall see
    At her Universitee! [37]

CYR.   As for fashion, they forswear it,
    So they say—so they say;
And the circle—they will square it
    Some fine day—some fine day;
Then the little pigs they're teaching
    For to fly—for to fly;
And the niggers [38] they'll be bleaching,
    By and by—by and by!
Each newly-joined aspirant
    To the clan—to the clan—
Must repudiate the tyrant
    Known as Man—known as Man.
They mock at him and flout him,
For they do not care about him,
And they're "going to do without him"
    If they can—if they can!

ALL.   These are the phenomena, etc.

    In this college
    Useful knowledge
    Ev'rywhere one finds,
    And already growing steady
    We've enlarg'd our minds.

HIL.   So that's the Princess Ida's castle! Well,
They must be lovely girls, indeed, if it requires
Such walls as those to keep intruders off!

CYR.   To keep men off is only half their charge,
And that the easier half. I much suspect
The object of these walls is not so much
To keep men off as keep the maidens in!

FLOR.   But what are these? (Examining some Collegiate robes.) [39]

HIL. (looking at them). Why, Academic robes,
Worn by the lady undergraduates
When they matriculate. Let's try them on.
    (They do so.)
Why, see—we're covered to the very toes.
Three lovely lady undergraduates
Who, weary of the world and all its wooing—

FLOR.   And penitent for deeds there's no undoing—

CYR.   Looked at askance by well-conducted maids—

ALL.   Seek sanctuary in these classic shades!

TRIO—HILARION, CYRIL, FLORIAN

HIL.   I am a maiden, cold and stately,
    Heartless I, with a face divine.
    What do I want with a heart, innately?
    Every heart I meet is mine!

ALL.
　　Haughty, humble, coy, or free,
　　　　Little care I what maid may be.
　　So that a maid is fair to see,
　　　　Every maid is the maid for me!

(*Dance.*)

CYR.
　　I am a maiden frank and simple,
　　　　Brimming with joyous roguery;
　　Merriment lurks in every dimple,
　　　　Nobody breaks more hearts than I!

ALL.
　　Haughty, humble, coy, or free,
　　　　Little care I what maid may be.
　　So that a maid is fair to see,
　　　　Every maid is the maid for me!

(*Dance.*)

FLOR.
　　I am a maiden coyly blushing,
　　　　Timid am I as a startled hind;
　　Every suitor sets me flushing:
　　　　I am the maid that wins mankind!

ALL.
　　Haughty, humble, coy, or free,
　　　　Little care I what maid may be.
　　So that a maid is fair to see,
　　　　Every maid is the maid for me!

Enter the PRINCESS *reading. She does not see them*

FLOR. But who comes here? The Princess, as I live! What shall we do?
HIL. (*aside*).　　　　　　　　　　Why, we must brave it out!
(*Aloud.*) Madam, accept our humblest reverence.

[*They bow, then, suddenly recollecting themselves, curtsey.*

PRIN. (*surprised*). We greet you, ladies. What would you with us?
HIL. (*aside*). What shall I say? (*Aloud.*) We are three students, ma'am,
　　Three well-born maids of liberal estate,
　　Who wish to join this University.

[HILARION *and* FLORIAN *curtsey again.* CYRIL *bows extravagantly, then, being recalled to himself by* FLORIAN, *curtseys.*

PRIN.　If, as you say, you wish to join our ranks,
　　And will subscribe to all our rules, 'tis well. [40]
FLOR.　To all your rules we cheerfully subscribe.
PRIN.　You say you're noblewomen. Well, you'll find
　　No sham degrees for noblewomen here.
　　You'll find no sizars [41] here, or servitors,
　　Or other cruel distinctions, meant to draw
　　A line 'twixt rich and poor: you'll find no tufts
　　To mark nobility, except such tufts
　　As indicate nobility of brain.
　　As for your fellow-students, mark me well:
　　There are a hundred maids within these walls,
　　All good, all learned, and all beautiful:
　　They are prepared to love you: will you swear
　　To give the fullness of your love to them?
HIL.　Upon our words and honours, ma'am, we will!
PRIN.　But we go further: will you undertake
　　That you will never marry any man?
FLOR.　Indeed we never will!

[40] *Is it not extraordinary that the Princess Ida should be in no way curious or perturbed at finding three "aspirants to the cause" already wearing the approved academic uniform of the college?*

[41] *At Cambridge and at Trinity College, Dublin, a "sizar" was an undergraduate who received an allowance from the college to enable him to study. He performed certain duties and, in effect, partially worked his way through college.*

[42] *Gilbert uses the word "homely" in its original and correct sense, i.e., "belonging to the home, unpretentious." He possibly also means "plain," but he does not mean "ugly," which is the accepted interpretation of the word in the United States.*

[43] *Cyril, of course, is the one who is constantly putting his foot in it.*

PRIN.   Consider well,
You must prefer our maids to all mankind!

HIL.   To all mankind we much prefer your maids!

CYR.   We should be dolts indeed, if we did not,
Seeing how fair——

HIL. (*aside to* CYRIL). Take care—that's rather strong!

PRIN.   But have you left no lovers at your home
Who may pursue you here?

HIL.   No, madam, none.
We're homely [42] ladies, as no doubt you see,
And we have never fished for lover's love.
We smile at girls who deck themselves with gems,
False hair, and meretricious ornament,
To chain the fleeting fancy of a man,
But do not imitate them. What we have
Of hair, is all our own. Our colour, too,
Unladylike, but not unwomanly,
Is Nature's handiwork, and man has learnt
To reckon Nature an impertinence.

PRIN.   Well, beauty counts for naught within these walls;
If all you say is true, you'll pass with us
A happy, happy time!

CYR.   If, as you say,
A hundred lovely maidens wait within, [43]
To welcome us with smiles and open arms,
I think there's very little doubt we shall!

QUARTETTE—PRINCESS, HILARION, CYRIL, FLORIAN

PRIN.   The world is but a broken toy,
Its pleasure hollow—false its joy,
Unreal its loveliest hue,
Alas!
Its pains alone are true,
Alas!
Its pains alone are true.

HIL.   The world is everything you say,
The world we think has had its day.
Its merriment is slow,
Alas!
We've tried it, and we know.
Alas!
We've tried it and we know.

TUTTI

PRINCESS	HILARION, CYRIL, FLORIAN
The world is but a broken toy,	The world is but a broken toy,
Its pleasure hollow—false its joy,	We freely give it up with joy,
Unreal its loveliest hue,	Unreal its loveliest hue,
Alas!	Alas!
Its pains alone are true,	Its pains alone are true,
Alas!	Alas!
Its pains alone are true!	Its pains alone are true!

[*Exit* PRINCESS. *The three gentlemen watch her off.* LADY PSYCHE *enters, and regards them with amazement.*

HIL.   I'faith, the plunge is taken, gentlemen!
For, willy-nilly, we are maidens now,
And maids against our will we must remain!

(*All laugh heartily.*)

PSY. (*aside*). These ladies are unseemly in their mirth.

> [*The gentlemen see her, and, in confusion, resume their modest demeanour.*

FLOR. (*aside*). Here's a catastrophe, Hilarion!
This is my sister! She'll remember me,
Though years have passed since she and I have met!

HIL. (*aside to* FLORIAN). Then make a virtue of necessity,
And trust our secret to her gentle care.

FLOR. (*to* PSYCHE, *who has watched* CYRIL *in amazement*). Psyche!
Why, don't you know me? Florian!

PSY. (*amazed*). Why, Florian!

FLOR. My sister (*embraces her*).

PSY. Oh, my dear!
What are you doing here—and who are these?

HIL. I am that Prince Hilarion to whom
Your Princess is betrothed. I come to claim
Her plighted love. Your brother Florian
And Cyril came to see me safely through.

PSY. The Prince Hilarion? Cyril too? How strange!
My earliest playfellows!

HIL. Why, let me look!
Are you that learned little Psyche who
At school alarmed her mates because she called
A buttercup "ranunculus bulbosus"?

CYR. Are you indeed that Lady Psyche, who
At children's parties drove the conjuror wild,
Explaining all his tricks before he did them?

HIL. Are you that learned little Psyche, who
At dinner parties, brought in to dessert,
Would tackle visitors with "You don't know
Who first determined longitude—I do—
Hipparchus 'twas—B.C. one sixty-three!"
Are you indeed that small phenomenon?

PSY. That small phenomenon indeed am I!
But, gentlemen, 'tis death to enter here:
We have all promised to renounce mankind!

FLOR. Renounce mankind? On what ground do you base
This senseless resolution?

PSY. Senseless? No.
We are all taught, and, being taught, believe
That Man, sprung from an Ape, is Ape at heart.

CYR. That's rather strong.

PSY. The truth is always strong!

SONG—LADY PSYCHE [44]

> A Lady fair, of lineage high,
> Was loved by an Ape, in the days gone by.
> The Maid was radiant as the sun,
> The Ape was a most unsightly one—
> So it would not do—
> His scheme fell through,
> For the Maid, when his love took formal shape,
> Expressed such terror
> At his monstrous error,
> That he stammered an apology and made his 'scape,
> The picture of a disconcerted Ape.

[44] *The inspiration for this lyric obviously came from Charles Darwin's theory of the evolution of man, written in 1871. It was the cause of much discussion and controversy at the time. The wonder is that Gilbert waited so long before lampooning it.*

I suspect that, by this time, we can all agree that the period in which Princess Ida is intended to be placed is late 19th century, no matter what the costumes.

He bought white ties, and he bought dress suits

With a view to rise in the social scale,
He shaved his bristles, and he docked his tail,
He grew mustachios, and he took his tub,
And he paid a guinea to a toilet club—
    But it would not do,
    The scheme fell through—
For the Maid was Beauty's fairest Queen,
    With golden tresses,
    Like a real princess's,
While the Ape, despite his razor keen,
Was the apiest Ape that ever was seen!

He bought white ties, and he bought dress suits,
He crammed his feet into bright tight boots—
And to start in life on a brand-new plan,
He christened himself Darwinian Man!
    But it would not do,
    The scheme fell through—
For the Maiden fair, whom the monkey craved,
    Was a radiant Being,
    With a brain far-seeing—
While a Darwinian Man, though well-behaved,
At best is only a monkey shaved!

ALL.   While Darwinian Man, etc.

During this MELISSA *has entered unobserved; she
looks on in amazement*

MEL. (*coming down*). Oh, Lady Psyche!
PSY. (*terrified*).   What! you heard us then?
    Oh, all is lost!
MEL.   Not so! I'll breathe no word!
    (*Advancing in astonishment to* FLORIAN.)
    How marvellously strange! and are you then
    Indeed young men?
FLOR.   Well, yes, just now we are—
    But hope by dint of study to become,
    In course of time, young women.
MEL. (*eagerly*).   No, no, no—
    Oh, don't do that! Is this indeed a man?
    I've often heard of them, but, till to-day,
    Never set eyes on one. They told me men
    Were hideous, idiotic, and deformed!
    They're quite as beautiful as women are!
    As beautiful, they're infinitely more so!
    Their cheeks have not that pulpy softness which
    One gets so weary of in womankind:
    Their features are more marked—and—oh, their chins!
    How curious! (*Feeling his chin.*)
FLOR.   I fear it's rather rough.
MEL. (*eagerly*). Oh, don't apologize—I like it so!

QUINTETTE—PSYCHE, MELISSA, HILARION, CYRIL, FLORIAN [45]

PSY.   The woman of the wisest wit
        May sometimes be mistaken, O!
      In Ida's views, I must admit,
        My faith is somewhat shaken, O!

[45] *Sullivan here uses a musical gimmick very similar
to the one he employed in the Sergeant's song
in* The Pirates of Penzance:
    His capacity for innocent enjoyment
          —cent enjoyment
Compare that with Hilarion's:
    Your powers of observation, O!
        —servation, O!

CYR. On every other point than this
    Her learning is untainted, O!
  But Man's a theme with which she is
    Entirely unacquainted, O!
      —acquainted, O!
      —acquainted, O!
  Entirely unacquainted, O!

ALL. Then jump for joy and gaily bound,
  The truth is found—the truth is found!
  Set bells a-ringing through the air—
  Ring here and there and everywhere—
  And echo forth the joyous sound,
  The truth is found—the truth is found!

           (*Dance.*)

MEL. My natural instinct teaches me
    (And instinct is important, O!)
  You're everything you ought to be,
    And nothing that you oughtn't, O!

HIL. That fact was seen at once by you
    In casual conversation, O!
  Which is most creditable to
    Your powers of observation, O!
      —servation, O!
      —servation, O!
  Your powers of observation, O!

ALL. Then jump for joy, etc.

[*Exeunt* PSYCHE, HILARION, CYRIL, *and* FLORIAN. MELISSA *going.*

Enter LADY BLANCHE

BLA. Melissa!
MEL. (*returning*). Mother!
BLA.   Here—a word with you.
  Those are the three new students?
MEL. (*confused*).   Yes, they are.
  They're charming girls.
BLA.   Particularly so.
  So graceful, and so very womanly!
  So skilled in all a girl's accomplishments!
MEL. (*confused*). Yes—very skilled.
BLA.   They sing so nicely too!
MEL. They *do* sing nicely!
BLA.   Humph! It's very odd.
  Two are tenors, one is a baritone!
MEL. (*much agitated*). They've all got colds!
BLA.   Colds! Bah! D'ye think I'm blind?
  These "girls" are men disguised!
MEL.   Oh no—indeed!
  You wrong these gentlemen—I mean—why, see,
  Here is an *étui* dropped by one of them (*picking up an étui*).
  Containing scissors, needles, and——
BLA. (*opening it*).   Cigars!
  Why, these *are* men! And you knew this, you minx!
MEL. Oh, spare them—they are gentlemen indeed.
  The Prince Hilarion (married years ago
  To Princess Ida) with two trusted friends!

Consider, mother, he's her husband now,
And has been, twenty years! Consider, too,
You're only second here—you should be first.
Assist the Prince's plan, and when he gains
The Princess Ida, why, you *will* be first.
You will design the fashions—think of that—
And always serve out all the punishments!
The scheme is harmless, mother—wink at it!

BLA. (*aside*). The prospect's tempting! Well, well, well, I'll try—
Though I've not winked at anything for years!
'Tis but one step towards my destiny—
The mighty Must! the inevitable Shall!

[46] Rule the roast. *This is not a misprint. The modern accepted version, "rule the roost," is a corruption of the original expression. To "rule the roast" is to be in supreme charge of an ox roasting on a spit.*

DUET—MELISSA *and* LADY BLANCHE

MEL.
Now wouldn't you like to rule the roast, [46]
And guide this University?

BLA.
I must agree
'Twould pleasant be.
(Sing hey, a Proper Pride!)

MEL.
And wouldn't you like to clear the coast
Of malice and perversity?

BLA.
Without a doubt
I'll bundle 'em out,
Sing hey, when I preside!

BOTH.
Sing, hoity, toity! Sorry for some!

Marry, come up and {my / her} day will come!

Sing, Proper Pride
Is the horse to ride,
And Happy-go-lucky, my Lady, O!

BLA.
For years I've writhed beneath her sneers,
Although a born Plantagenet!

MEL.
You're much too meek,
Or you would speak.
(Sing hey, I'll say no more!)

BLA.
Her elder I, by several years,
Although you'd ne'er imagine it.

MEL.
Sing, so I've heard
But never a word
Have I e'er believed before!

BOTH.
Sing, hoity, toity! Sorry for some!

Marry, come up and {my / her} day will come!

Sing, she shall learn
That a worm will turn.
Sing Happy-go-lucky, my Lady, O!

[*Exit* LADY BLANCHE.

MEL.
Saved for a time, at least!

Enter FLORIAN, *on tiptoe*

FLOR. (*whispering*).
Melissa—come!

MEL.   Oh, sir! you must away from this at once—
     My mother guessed your sex! It was my fault—
     I blushed and stammered so that she exclaimed,
     "Can these be men?" Then, seeing this, "Why these——"
     "*Are men*," she would have added, but "*are men*" [47]
     Stuck in her throat! She keeps your secret, sir,
     For reasons of her own—but fly from this
     And take me with you—that is—no—not that!
FLOR.   I'll go, but not without you! (*Bell.*) Why, what's that?
MEL.   The luncheon bell.
FLOR.   I'll wait for luncheon then!

Enter HILARION *with* PRINCESS, CYRIL *with* PSYCHE, LADY BLANCHE *and* LADIES. *Also "Daughters of the Plough" bearing luncheon.* [48]

CHORUS.   Merrily ring the luncheon bell!
     Here in meadow of asphodel,
     Feast we body and mind as well,
     So merrily ring the luncheon bell!

SOLO—BLANCHE

     Hunger, I beg to state,
     Is highly indelicate,
     This is a fact profoundly true,
     So learn your appetites to subdue. [49]

ALL.   Yes, yes,
     We'll learn our appetites to subdue!

SOLO—CYRIL (*eating*)

     Madame, your words so wise,
     Nobody should despise,
     Cursed with appetite keen I am
     And I'll subdue it—
     And I'll subdue it—
     And I'll subdue it with cold roast lamb! [50]

ALL.   Yes—yes—
     We'll subdue it with cold roast lamb!

CHORUS.   Merrily ring, etc.

PRIN.   You say you know the court of Hildebrand?
     There is a Prince there—I forget his name—
HIL.   Hilarion?
PRIN.   Exactly—is he well?
HIL.   If it be well to droop and pine and mope,
     To sigh "Oh, Ida! Ida!" all day long,
     "Ida! my love! my life! Oh, come to me!"
     If it be well, I say, to do all this,
     Then Prince Hilarion is very well.
PRIN.   He breathes *our* name? Well, it's a common one!
     And is the booby comely? [51]
HIL.   Pretty well.
     I've heard it said that if I dressed myself
     In Prince Hilarion's clothes (supposing this
     Consisted with my maiden modesty),
     I might be taken for Hilarion's self.
     But what is this to you or me, who think
     Of all mankind with undisguised contempt?

[47] A punning paraphrase of Shakespeare. Compare this line with the words of Macbeth (Act II, Scene 2): "But wherefore could I not pronounce 'Amen'? I had most need of blessing then, and 'Amen' stuck in my throat!"
    If you look back, however, you will see that Lady Blanche, in spite of Melissa's statement, has said, "these are men!" and there is no earthly reason for Melissa to tell this lie now other than to bring in a punning paraphrase.

[48] *Princess Ida was wrong; the college does have servitors, and they serve luncheon. Generally the Daughters of the Plough are men, extras or supers, engaged locally and rigged out in long, tow-colored wigs, rough tweed blouses, shawls, and skirts. They are really homely—in the American sense of the word.*

[49] *Blanche herself would not appear, from her proportions, to carry out her dietary counsel. It was ever thus with some dieters.*

[50] *To Cyril, however, a healthy appetite, wine, women and song, are all things to be enjoyed to the fullest extent. It was, again, ever thus.*

[51] *This is too much for Cyril, who promptly splutters over his wine, of which he is drinking his full share. It may be a college for young ladies where man is eschewed, but wine certainly is not.*

PRIN.   Contempt? Why, damsel, when I think of man,
      Contempt is not the word.

CYR. (*getting tipsy*).   I'm sure of that,
      Or if it is, it surely should not be!

HIL. (*aside to* CYRIL). Be quiet, idiot, or they'll find us out.

CYR.   The Prince Hilarion's a goodly lad!

PRIN.   *You* know him then?

CYR. (*tipsily*).   I rather think I do!
      We are inseparables!

PRIN.   Why, what's this?
      You love him then?

CYR.   We do indeed—all three!

HIL.   Madam, she jests! (*Aside to* CYRIL.) Remember where you
      are!

CYR.   Jests? Not at all! Why, bless my heart alive,
      You and Hilarion, when at the Court,
      Rode the same horse!

PRIN. (*horrified*).   Astride?

CYR.   Of course! Why not?
      Wore the same clothes—and once or twice, I think,
      Got tipsy in the same good company!

PRIN.   Well, these are nice young ladies, on my word!

CYR. (*tipsy*). Don't you remember that old kissing-song
      He'd sing to blushing Mistress Lalage,
      The hostess of the Pigeons? Thus it ran:

SONG—CYRIL [52]

[*During symphony* HILARION *and* FLORIAN *try to stop*
CYRIL. *He shakes them off angrily* [53]

Would you know the kind of maid
  Sets my heart aflame-a?
Eyes must be downcast and staid,
  Cheeks must flush for shame-a!
    She may neither dance nor sing,
    But, demure in everything,
    Hang her head in modest way,
    With pouting lips that seem to say,
  "Oh, kiss me, kiss me, kiss me, kiss me,
   Though I die of shame-a!"
Please you, that's the kind of maid
  Sets my heart aflame-a!

When a maid is bold and gay
  With a tongue goes clang-a,
Flaunting it in brave array,
  Maiden may go hang-a
    Sunflower gay and hollyhock
    Never shall my garden stock;
    Mine the blushing rose of May,
    With pouting lips that seem to say,
  "Oh, kiss me, kiss me, kiss me, kiss me,
   Though I die for shame-a!"
Please you, that's the kind of maid
  Sets my heart aflame-a!

PRIN.   Infamous creature, get you hence away!

Eyes must be downcast and staid

[52] Words and music on page 404.

[53] Cyril begins singing to the whole stage, still grasping his mug of wine. At the end of the first verse, he takes a long pull, and then sees Lady Blanche standing rigid, arms akimbo, to one side. He addresses the next verse directly to her, gradually drawing closer to her as he proceeds with the song. As he reaches the repeat phrase of "Oh, kiss me, kiss me," he stops singing (though the music carries on), seizes her around the waist and plants a big kiss on her cheek. As he carries on with the song, Lady Blanche screams in horror, and that really puts the cat among the pigeons.

[HILARION, *who has been with difficulty restrained by* FLORIAN *during this song, breaks from him and strikes* CYRIL *furiously on the breast.*

HIL.   Dog! there is something more to sing about!

CYR. (*sobered*). Hilarion, are you mad?

PRIN. (*horrified*).   Hilarion? Help!
Why, these are men! Lost! lost! betrayed, undone!
                         (*Running on to bridge.*)
Girls, get you hence! Man-monsters, if you dare
Approach one step, I—— Ah!

             (*Loses her balance, and falls into the stream.*) [54]

PSY.   Oh! save her, sir!

BLA.   It's useless, sir—you'll only catch your death!

                         (HILARION *springs in.*)

SACH.   He catches her!

MEL.   And now he lets her go!
Again she's in his grasp—

PSY.   And now she's not.
He seizes her back hair!

BLA. (*not looking*).   And it comes off!

PSY.   No, no! She's saved!—she's saved!—she's saved!—she's saved!

FINALE

CHORUS OF LADIES

Oh! joy, our chief is saved,
And by Hilarion's hand;
The torrent fierce he braved,
And brought her safe to land!
For his intrusion we must own
This doughty deed may well atone!

PRIN.   Stand forth ye three,
Whoe'er ye be,
And hearken to our stern decree!

HIL., CYR., *and* FLOR. Have mercy, lady,—disregard your oaths!

PRIN.   I know not mercy, men in women's clothes!
The man whose sacrilegious eyes
Invade our strict seclusion, dies.
Arrest these coarse intruding spies!

[*They are arrested by the "Daughters of the Plough."*

FLOR., CYR., *and* LADIES. Have mercy, lady—disregard your oaths!

PRIN.   I know not mercy, men in women's clothes!

[CYRIL *and* FLORIAN *are bound.*

SONG—HILARION [55]

Whom thou hast chained must wear his chain,
Thou canst not set him free,
He wrestles with his bonds in vain
Who lives by loving thee!
If heart of stone for heart of fire,
Be all thou hast to give,
If dead to me my heart's desire,
Why should I wish to live?

[54] Reviews of the opening performance varied from unqualified praise to downright blasting. But the big joke of the day was the two separate notices in the same newspaper. One, by the dramatic critic, said: ". . . Desperately dull . . . not three jokes worth remembering . . . the tumble of the Princess and rescue from drowning is so ludicrously mismanaged as to evoke hisses and laughter." The other, by the music critic, said: "Mr. Gilbert has rendered this piece as amusing as his immense talent so many times has proved was safe to do . . . the performance going as smoothly as in the whole world, first evenings go only at this theatre . . . there is never a hitch [emphasis mine] in the performance!"

[55] Hilarion's song is a typical example of Gilbert's use of a further hypothesis and an opposite conclusion, and here the two conclusions are very similar to the philosophy of Fairfax in "Is Life a Boon?" in The Yeomen of the Guard.

FLOR., CYR., *and* LADIES. Have mercy, O lady!

No word of thine—no stern command
    Can teach my heart to rove,
Then rather perish by thy hand,
    Than live without thy love!
A loveless life apart from thee
    Were hopeless slavery,
If kindly death will set me free,
    Why should I fear to die?

[*He is bound by two of the attendants, and the three gentlemen are marched off.*

Enter MELISSA.

MEL.   Madam, without the castle walls
            An armed band
        Demand admittance to our halls
            For Hildebrand!

ALL.   Oh, horror!

PRIN.   Deny them!
        We will defy them!

ALL.   Too late—too late!
        The castle gate
        Is battered by them!

[*The gate yields.* SOLDIERS *rush in.* ARAC, GURON, *and* SCYNTHIUS *are with them, but with their hands handcuffed.*

ENSEMBLE [56]

GIRLS	MEN
Rend the air with wailing,	Walls and fences scaling,
Shed the shameful tear!	Promptly we appear;
Walls are unavailing,	Walls are unavailing,
Man has entered here!	We have entered here.
Shame and desecration	Female execration
Are his staunch allies,	Stifle if you're wise,
Let your lamentation	Stop your lamentation,
Echo to the skies!	Dry your pretty eyes!

Enter HILDEBRAND

RECIT.

PRIN.   Audacious tyrant, do you dare
        To beard a maiden in her lair?

HILD.   Since you inquire,
            We've no desire
        To beard a maiden here, or anywhere!

SOL.   No, no—we've no desire
        To beard a maiden here, or anywhere!

SOLO—HILDEBRAND

Some years ago
No doubt you know
(And if you don't I'll tell you so)
You gave your troth
Upon your oath
To Hilarion my son.

[56] The finale to Princess Ida, Act II, is among the busiest and musically best that Sullivan wrote. There is constant movement, and very careful rehearsing is essential. Musically, it progresses to a tremendously defiant ending. To my mind, it can compare favorably with many grand operas.

A vow you make
You must not break,
(If you think you may, it's a great mistake),
For a bride's a bride
Though the knot were tied
At the early age of one!
And I'm a peppery kind of King,
Who's indisposed for parleying
To fit the wit of a bit of a chit,
And that's the long and the short of it!

SOL. For he's a peppery kind of King, etc.

HILD.
If you decide
To pocket your pride
And let Hilarion claim his bride,
Why, well and good,
It's understood
We'll let bygones go by—
But if you choose
To sulk in the blues
I'll make the whole of you shake in your shoes.
I'll storm your walls,
And level your halls,
In the twinkling of an eye!
For I'm a peppery Potentate,
Who's little inclined his claim to bate,
To fit the wit of a bit of a chit,
And that's the long and the short of it!

SOL. For he's a peppery kind of King, etc.

TRIO—ARAC, GURON, *and* SCYNTHIUS

We may remark, though nothing can [57]
Dismay us,
That if you thwart this gentleman,
He'll slay us.
We don't fear death, of course—we're taught
To shame it;
But still upon the whole we thought
We'd name it.

(*To each other*.) Yes, yes, yes, better perhaps to name it.

Our interests we would not press
With chatter,
Three hulking brothers more or less
Don't matter;
If you'd pooh-pooh this monarch's plan,
Pooh-pooh it,
But when he says he'll hang a man,
He'll do it.

(*To each other*.) Yes, yes, yes, devil doubt he'll do it.

PRIN. (*Recit*.) Be reassured, nor fear his anger blind,
His menaces are idle as the wind.
He dares not kill you—vengeance lurks behind!

AR., GUR., SCYN. We rather think he dares, but never mind!
No, no,—never, never mind!

[57] *At one time the role of King Hildebrand boosted the sale of dental-plate adhesive by at least a tin a month. As his solo comes to an end, Princess Ida openly flouts Hildebrand and snaps her fingers in his face. His reactions are those of extreme indignation, and he is supposed to puff and blow to indicate this. Some years ago, Joseph Griffin puffed and blew with such a will that he blew his upper plate right out. With admirable dexterity, he managed to catch the denture before it fell to the stage and quickly pop it back in. It was too late. The audience had seen and had realized what had happened. So had Arac, Guron and Scynthius. They were fascinated, and still staring at Joe Griffin, they sang: "We may remark, though nothing can dismay us . . ."*

Thereafter, that particular King Hildebrand took precautions against any repetition.

HILD.
I rather think I dare, but never, never mind!
Enough of parley—as a special boon,
We give you till to-morrow afternoon;
Release Hilarion, then, and be his bride,
Or you'll incur the guilt of fratricide!

ENSEMBLE

PRINCESS	THE OTHERS
To yield at once to such a foe	Oh! yield at once, 'twere better so
With shame were rife;	Than risk a strife!
So quick! away with him, although	And let the Prince Hilarion go—
He saved my life!	He saved thy life!
That he is fair, and strong, and tall,	Hilarion's fair, and strong, and tall—
Is very evident to all,	A worse misfortune might befall—
Yet I will die before I call	It's not so dreadful, after all,
Myself his wife!	To be his wife!

SOLO—PRINCESS

Though I am but a girl,
Defiance thus I hurl,
Our banners all
On outer wall
We fearlessly unfurl.

ALL.
Though she is but a girl, etc.

PRINCESS	THE OTHERS
That he is fair, etc.	Hilarion's fair, etc.

[*The* PRINCESS *stands, surrounded by girls kneeling.* HILDEBRAND *and soldiers stand on built rocks at back and sides of stage. Picture.*

CURTAIN

END OF ACT II

ACT III

SCENE.—*Outer Walls and Courtyard of Castle Adamant.* MELISSA, SACHARISSA, *and ladies discovered, armed with battleaxes.*

CHORUS.
Death to the invader!
Strike a deadly blow,
As an old Crusader
Struck his Paynim foe! [58]
Let our martial thunder
Fill his soul with wonder,
Tear his ranks asunder,
Lay the tyrant low!

SOLO—MELISSA

Thus our courage, all untarnished,
We're instructed to display:
But to tell the truth unvarnished,
We are more inclined to say,
"Please you, do not hurt us."

ALL.   "Do not hurt us, if it please you!"
MEL.   "Please you let us be."
ALL.   "Let us be—let us be!"
MEL.   "Soldiers disconcert us."

[58] Paynim foe. *The Crusaders' Mohammedan enemy.* "Paynim" *is Middle English for* "pagan."

ALL.   "Disconcert us, if it please you!"
MEL.   "Frightened maids are we!"
ALL.   "Maids are we—maids are we!"

MELISSA

But 'twould be an error
To confess our terror,
So, in Ida's name,
Boldly we exclaim:

CHORUS.   Death to the invader!
Strike a deadly blow,
As an old Crusader
Struck his Paynim foe!

Flourish. Enter PRINCESS, *armed, attended by* BLANCHE *and* PSYCHE

PRIN.   I like your spirit, girls! [59] We have to meet
Stern bearded warriors in fight to-day:
Wear naught but what is necessary to
Preserve your dignity before their eyes,
And give your limbs full play.
BLA.   One moment, ma'am,
Here is a paradox we should not pass
Without inquiry. We are prone to say,
"This thing is Needful—that, Superfluous"—
Yet they invariably co-exist!
We find the Needful comprehended in
The circle of the grand Superfluous,
Yet the Superfluous cannot be bought
Unless you're amply furnished with the Needful.
These singular considerations are—
PRIN.   Superfluous, yet not Needful—so you see
The terms may independently exist.
(*To Ladies.*) Women of Adamant, we have to show
That women, educated to the task,
Can meet Man, face to face, on his own ground,
And beat him there. Now let us set to work:
Where is our lady surgeon?
SAC.   Madam, here!
PRIN.   We shall require your skill to heal the wounds
Of those that fall.
SAC. (*alarmed*).   What, heal the wounded?
PRIN.   Yes!
SAC.   And cut off real live legs and arms?
PRIN.   Of course!
SAC.   I wouldn't do it for a thousand pounds!
PRIN.   Why, how is this? Are you faint-hearted, girl?
You've often cut them off in theory!
SAC.   In theory I'll cut them off again
With pleasure, and as often as you like,
But not in practice.
PRIN.   Coward! get you hence,
I've craft enough for that, and courage too,
I'll do your work! My fusiliers, advance!
Why, you are armed with axes! Gilded toys!
Where are your rifles, pray?
CHLOE.   Why, please you, ma'am,
We left them in the armoury, for fear

[59] *The same writer who accused Gilbert of prejudice and bad temper also goes so far as to say: "Time and two World Wars have conspired to make utter nonsense of the last act." He then goes on to draw attention to the girls, ". . . outwardly brave, but inwardly shaking with fear . . . theater audiences today know how bravely the women can stand up to bombardment." He cites the various women's corps.*

Granted! Florence Nightingale wasn't squeamish either, but she and her few followers were the exception in Gilbert's day, when the women were more generally noted for climbing onto a table if they saw a mouse than they were for bearing arms.

"The way in which Princess Ida's girls desert her is a very poor joke indeed," says Mr. Darlington. Now really, sir. It would be a poor joke if Princess Ida and all her girls had been WACS *or* WAVES, *or their English counterparts, the* ATS, WRENS *or* WAAFS, *but they weren't; they hadn't been thought of when Gilbert wrote this play. Women definitely preferred to be the weaker sex—most still do—and Gilbert's gibe is directed exclusively at the pseudo-Amazon. He wasn't poking fun at women generally here—he just preferred in his women the inherent and traditional softness of women.*

That in the heat and turmoil of the fight,
They might go off!

PRIN.   "They might!" Oh, craven souls!
Go off yourselves! Thank heaven, I have a heart
That quails not at the thought of meeting men;
I will discharge your rifles! Off with you!
Where's my bandmistress?

ADA.   Please you, ma'am, the band
Do not feel well, and can't come out to-day!

PRIN.   Why, this is flat rebellion! I've no time
To talk to them just now. But, happily,
I can play several instruments at once,
And I will drown the shrieks of those that fall
With trumpet music, such as soldiers love!
How stand we with respect to gunpowder?
My Lady Psyche—you who superintend
Our lab'ratory [60]—are you well prepared
To blow these bearded rascals into shreds?

PSY.   Why, madam—

PRIN.   Well?

PSY.   Let us try gentler means.
We can dispense with fulminating grains
While we have eyes with which to flash our rage!
We can dispense with villainous saltpetre
While we have tongues with which to blow them up!
We can dispense, in short, with all the arts
That brutalize the practical polemist! [61]

PRIN. (*contemptuously*). I never knew a more dispensing chemist!
                Away, away—I'll meet these men alone
                Since all my women have deserted me!

[*Exeunt all but* PRINCESS, *singing refrain of "Please you, do not hurt us,"*
    pianissimo.

PRIN.   So fail my cherished plans—so fails my faith—
           And with it hope, and all that comes of hope!

SONG—PRINCESS

I built upon a rock,
    But ere Destruction's hand
        Dealt equal lot
        To Court and cot,
    My rock had turned to sand!
I leant upon an oak,
    But in the hour of need,
        Alack-a-day,
        My trusted stay
    Was but a bruisèd reed!
        Ah, faithless rock,
        My simple faith to mock!
        Ah, trait'rous oak,
        Thy worthlessness to cloak.
        Thy worthlessness to cloak.

I drew a sword of steel,
    But when to home and hearth
        The battle's breath
        Bore fire and death,
    My sword was but a lath!
I lit a beacon fire,

[60] *To maintain the correct meter of these two lines, the word "superintend" should be pronounced as if it had three syllables only: su-prin-tend. The word "laboratory" is written to indicate that it should be pronounced in the American fashion.*

[61] *Psyche's speech, I think, sums up Gilbert's thinking about what women should be.*

But on a stormy day
    Of frost and rime,
    In wintertime,
My fire had died away, had died away!
    Ah, coward steel,
    That fear can unanneal!
    False fire indeed,
    To fail me in my need!
    To fail me in my need!

She sinks on a seat. Enter CHLOE *and all the ladies*

CHLOE.   Madam, your father and your brothers claim
    An audience!

PRIN.   What do they do here?

CHLOE.   They come
To fight for you!

PRIN.   Admit them!

BLA.   Infamous!
One's brothers, ma'am, are men!

PRIN.   So I've heard.
But all my women seem to fail me when
I need them most. In this emergency,
Even one's brothers may be turned to use.

Enter GAMA, *quite pale and unnerved*

GAMA.   My daughter!

PRIN.   Father! thou art free!

GAMA.   Aye, free!
Free as a tethered ass! I come to thee
With words from Hildebrand. Those duly given
I must return to blank captivity.
I'm free so far.

PRIN.   Your message.

GAMA.   Hildebrand
Is loth to war with women. Pit my sons,
My three brave sons, against these popinjays,
These tufted jack-a-dandy featherheads,
And on the issue let thy hand depend!

PRIN.   Insult on insult's head! Are we a stake
For fighting men? What fiend possesses thee,
That thou hast come with offers such as these
From such as he to such an one as I?

GAMA.   I am possessed
By the pale devil of a shaking heart!
My stubborn will is bent. I dare not face
That devilish monarch's black malignity!
He tortures me with torments worse than death,
I haven't anything to grumble at!
He finds out what particular meats I love,
And gives me them. The very choicest wines,
The costliest robes—the richest rooms are mine:
He suffers none to thwart my simplest plan,
And gives strict orders none should contradict me!
He's made my life a curse! (*weeps*).

PRIN.   My tortured father!

SONG—GAMA [62]

Whene'er I poke
Sarcastic joke

[62] As in Gama's first song, "If you give me your attention" (Note 13), Gilbert is living up to his own reputation.

For some reason encores have been arranged in an unusual way for this song. Usually it is the last verse that is repeated, or the encore picks up at some point in the last verse, although there are some variations, as in The Yeomen of the Guard, where two verses of Jack Point's song, "If you wish to succeed," are held back. However, in this song of Gama's, the second verse is repeated for the first encore, the first verse for the second and the last verse for the third.

Replete with malice spiteful,
This people mild
Politely smiled,
    And voted me delightful!
Now when a wight
Sits up all night
    Ill-natured jokes devising,
And all his wiles
Are met with smiles
    It's hard, there's no disguising!

O, don't the days seem lank and long
When all goes right and nothing goes wrong,
And isn't your life extremely flat
With nothing whatever to grumble at!

When German bands [63]
    From music stands
Played Wagner imperfectly—
    I bade them go—
    They didn't say no,
But off they went directly!
    The organ boys
    They stopped their noise
With readiness surprising,
    And grinning herds
    Of hurdy-gurds [64]
Retired apologising!

Oh, don't the days seem lank and long, etc.

I offered gold
In sums untold
To all who'd contradict me—
    I said I'd pay
    A pound a day
To any one who kicked me—
    I bribed with toys
    Great vulgar boys
To utter something spiteful,
    But, bless you, no!
    They *would* be so
Confoundedly politeful!

In short, these aggravating lads,
They tickle my tastes, they feed my fads,
They give me this and they give me that,
And I've nothing whatever to grumble at!

[*He bursts into tears, and falls sobbing on a seat.*

PRIN.   My poor old father! How he must have suffered!
    Well, well, I yield!
GAMA (*hysterically*). She yields! I'm saved, I'm saved!   [*Exit.*
PRIN.   Open the gates—admit these warriors,
    Then get you all within the castle walls.   [*Exit.*

[*The gates are opened, and the girls mount the battlements as soldiers
    enter. Also* ARAC, GURON, *and* SCYNTHIUS.

[63] German bands. At the time Gilbert was writing *Princess Ida* London was being invaded by a number of itinerant German brass and wind instrumentalists, who had formed themselves into small bands and were roaming the streets. That they should play Wagner—pronounced Varg-ner, please—imperfectly was not unexpected. They would not have been street musicians otherwise.

[64] Hurdy-gurds. Hurdy-gurdies. Gilbert is alluding to another form of itinerant street musician, in this case the Italian hurdy-gurdy man. The hurdy-gurdy is a lutelike instrument, the sound of which is produced by the turning of a rosined wheel against the strings. This is enclosed in a box with a crank handle on the outside, and the whole is supported by a single central leg. Generally a monkey, seated on the top, holds a bag for money to be dropped into. The word is now popularly applied to the barrel organ which creates its music quite differently and produces an entirely different musical sound.

To all who'd contradict me—

CHORUS OF SOLDIERS

When anger spreads his wing,
 And all seems dark as night for it,
 There's nothing but to fight for it,
But ere you pitch your ring,
 Select a pretty site for it,
 (This spot is suited quite for it),
And then you gaily sing,

"Oh, I love the jolly rattle
Of an ordeal [65] by battle,
There's an end of tittle-tattle
 When your enemy is dead.
It's an arrant molly-coddle
Fears a crack upon his noddle
And he's only fit to swaddle
 In a downy feather-bed!"—

ALL.   For a fight's a kind of thing
That I love to look upon,
 So let us sing,
 Long live the King,
And his son Hilarion!

[*During this,* HILARION, FLORIAN, *and* CYRIL *are brought out by the "Daughters of the Plough." They are still bound and wear the robes. Enter* GAMA.

GAMA. Hilarion! Cyril! Florian! dressed as women!
    Is this indeed Hilarion?
HIL.   Yes, it is!
GAMA. Why, you look handsome in your women's clothes!
    Stick to 'em! men's attire becomes you not!
(*To* CYRIL *and* FLORIAN). And you, young ladies, will you please to pray
    King Hildebrand to set me free again?
    Hang on his neck and gaze into his eyes,
    He never could resist a pretty face!
HIL. You dog, you'll find, though I wear woman's garb,
    My sword is long and sharp!
GAMA.   Hush, pretty one!
    Here's a virago! Here's a termagant!
    If length and sharpness go for anything,
    You'll want no sword while you can wag your tongue!
CYR. What need to waste your words on such as he?
    He's old and crippled.
GAMA.   Aye, but I've three sons,
    Fine fellows, young, and muscular, and brave,
    They're well worth talking to! Come, what d'ye say?
ARAC. Aye, pretty ones, engage yourselves with us,
    If three rude warriors affright you not!
HIL. Old as you are, I'd wring your shrivelled neck
    If you were not the Princess Ida's father,
GAMA. If I were not the Princess Ida's father,
    And so had not her brothers for my sons,
    No doubt you'd wring my neck—in safety too!
    Come, come, Hilarion, begin, begin!
    Give them no quarter—they will give you none.

[65] To maintain the meter it is necessary that the word "ordeal" be pronounced with three syllables: or-dee-al, with the accent coming on the first. Sullivan writes it this way:

rat - tle Of an or - de - al by bat - tle

You've this advantage over warriors
Who kill their country's enemies for pay—
You know what you are fighting for—look there!

(*Pointing to Ladies on the battlements.*)

[*Exit* GAMA. HILARION, FLORIAN, *and* CYRIL *are led off.*

SONG—ARAC

This helmet, I suppose,
Was meant to ward off blows,
It's very hot,
And weighs a lot,
As many a guardsman knows,
So off that helmet goes.

ALL.   Yes, yes, yes,
So off that helmet goes!

(*Giving their helmets to attendants.*)

[66] Cuirass. Body armor, reaching to the waist, with back and front piece. There is a very good reason for Gilbert pointing out that it was made of steel. Originally, it was made of leather.

ARAC.   This tight-fitting cuirass [66]
Is but a useless mass,
It's made of steel,
And weighs a deal,
A man is but an ass
Who fights in a cuirass,
So off goes that cuirass.

ALL.   Yes, yes, yes,
So off goes that cuirass!

(*Removing cuirasses.*)

[67] Brassets. (*Brassart; brassard.*) Armor for the upper arm. The brassets worn here, though, reach down to the wrists.

ARAC.   These brassets, [67] truth to tell,
May look uncommon well,
But in a fight
They're much too tight,
They're like a lobster shell!

[68] It's quite possible that Gilbert actually had forgotten the name for the leg piece, could not be bothered to look it up, and turned out a deliciously amusing verse in consequence. (*By the way, it's "jamb."*)

Sullivan's setting for this song is a charming musical parody with a strong hint of a Handelian oratorio.

ALL.   Yes, yes, yes,
They're like a lobster shell.

(*Removing their brassets.*)

ARAC.   These things I treat the same (*indicating leg pieces*).
(I quite forget their name) [68]
They turn one's legs
To cribbage pegs—
Their aid I thus disclaim,
Though I forget their name!

[69] The "desperate fight" must be thoroughly planned and rehearsed, and under no circumstances must it look real. Sullivan has written a perfect accompaniment for it, and the "fight" must be planned to go along with it. The music is precise and well marked, and in some ways reminds one a little of the "Anvil Chorus," with the clashing of the swords adding to the musical effect. At a given moment, without having been struck by so much as the flat of a sword, Arac, Guron and Scynthius collapse to the ground.

The swords they use are not the big, two-handed weapons they originally carry. The Daughters of the Plough bring on six more easily wielded swords as soon as Arac and his brothers have divested themselves of their armor.

The costumes which the three sons of Gama Rex wear under their armor invariably made me wonder if King Gama was the father of three sons masquerading as Superman.

ALL.   Yes, yes, yes,
Their aid $\begin{Bmatrix} \text{we} \\ \text{they} \end{Bmatrix}$ thus disclaim!

[*They remove their leg pieces and wear close-fitting shape suits.*

Enter HILARION, FLORIAN, *and* CYRIL

[*Desperate fight* [69] *between the three Princes and the three Knights, during which the Ladies on the battlements and the Soldiers on the stage sing the following chorus.*

This is our duty plain towards
 Our Princess all immaculate,
We ought to bless her brothers' swords
 And piously ejaculate:
  Oh, Hungary! [70]
  Oh, Hungary!
 Oh, doughty sons of Hungary!
 May all success
 Attend and bless
Your warlike ironmongery!

Hilarion! Hilarion! Hilarion!

[*By this time,* ARAC, GURON, *and* SCYNTHIUS *are on the ground, wounded* —HILARION, CYRIL, *and* FLORIAN *stand over them.*

PRIN. (*entering through gate and followed by Ladies,* HILDEBRAND, *and* GAMA). Hold! stay your hands—we yield ourselves to you!
 Ladies, my brothers all lie bleeding there!
 Bind up their wounds—but look the other way.
(*Coming down*). Is this the end? (*bitterly to* LADY BLANCHE). How say you, Lady Blanche—
 Can I with dignity my post resign?
 And if I do, will you then take my place?

BLA. To answer this, it's meet that we consult
 The great Potential Mysteries; I mean
 The five Subjunctive Possibilities—
 The May, the Might, the Would, the Could, the Should.
 Can you resign? The prince May claim you; if
 He Might, you Could—and if you Should, I Would!

PRIN. I thought as much! Then, to my fate I yield—
 So ends my cherished scheme! Oh, I had hoped
 To band all women with my maiden throng,
 And make them all abjure tyrannic Man!

HILD. A noble aim!

PRIN.   You ridicule it now!
 But if I carried out this glorious scheme,
 At my exalted name Posterity
 Would bow in gratitude!

HILD.   But pray reflect—
 If you enlist all women in your cause,
 And make them all abjure tyrannic Man,
 The obvious question then arises, "How
 Is this Posterity to be provided?"

PRIN. I never thought of that! My Lady Blanche,
 How do you solve the riddle?

BLA.   Don't ask me—
 Abstract Philosophy won't answer it.
 Take him—he is your Shall. Give in to Fate!

PRIN. And you desert me. I alone am staunch!

HIL. Madam, you placed your trust in Woman—well,
 Woman has failed you utterly—try Man,
 Give him one chance, it's only fair—besides,
 Women are far too precious, too divine, [71]
 To try unproven theories upon.
 Experiments, the proverb says, are made
 On humble subjects—try our grosser clay,
 And mould it as you will!

[70] *Well, regardless of the setting of the opera, it's clear that Gama and Sons are Hungarian.*

[71] *Any suggestion of sourness about women on Gilbert's part must surely be dispelled by Hilarion's words. W. S. Gilbert and his wife had been married forty years when he died, and as one writer put it, "A man whose wife can put up with him for that length of time cannot be such a curmudgeon as reputation would have it!"*

393

CYR.   Remember, too,
Dear Madam, if at any time you feel
A-weary of the Prince, you can return
To Castle Adamant, and rule your girls
As heretofore, you know.

PRIN.   And shall I find
The Lady Psyche here?

PSY.   If Cyril, ma'am,
Does not behave himself, I think you will.

PRIN.   And you, Melissa, shall I find *you* here?

MEL.   Madam, however Florian turns out,
Unhesitatingly I answer, No!

GAMA.   Consider this, my love, if your mamma
Had looked on matters from your point of view
(I wish she had), why where would you have been?

BLA.   There's an unbounded field of speculation,
On which I could discourse for hours!

PRIN.   No doubt!
We will not trouble you. Hilarion,
I have been wrong—I see my error now.
Take me, Hilarion—"We will walk the world
Yoked in all exercise of noble end!
And so through those dark gates across the wild
That no man knows! Indeed, I love thee—Come!" [72]

FINALE

PRIN.   With joy abiding,
       Together gliding
            Through life's variety,
            In sweet society,
       And thus enthroning
       The love I'm owning,
       On this atoning
            I will rely!

CHORUS.   It were profanity
       For poor humanity
       To treat as vanity
            The sway of Love.
       In no locality
       Or principality
       Is our mortality
            Its sway above!

HILARION.   When day is fading,
       With serenading
            And such frivolity
            Of tender quality—
       With scented showers
       Of fairest flowers,
       The happy hours
            Will gaily fly!

CHORUS.   It were profanity, etc. [73]

CURTAIN

[72] *Gilbert is quoting directly from Tennyson's poem
The Princess (Part VII), of which Princess Ida
is "a respectful operatic perversion . . ."*

[73] *While the chorus is bringing the opera to its
close, Gama makes a couple of passes at Lady
Blanche, who remains completely aloof until he
gets down on his knees and taps her arm to attract her attention. His ardor is quelled by the
look she gives him, so he rises to his feet and
turns to watch Ida and Hilarion as they go into
an embrace. He is finally using Lady Blanche as
a leaning post as*
                the
                     curtain
                          falls.

Ida Was a Twelvemonth Old

HILARION

1. I - da was a twelve - month old, Twen - ty years a - go!
2. Still, I was a ti - ny Prince Twen - ty years a -

go! I was twice her age, I'm told, Twen - ty years a - go!
go. She has gain'd up - on me, since Twen - ty years a - go!

Hus - band— twice— as—
Though she's— twen - ty -

If You Give Me Your Attention

Quick but not too fast

f marcato

legato

GAMA

1. If you give me your at-ten-tion, I will tell you what I am: I'm a
(2. To) com-pli-ments in-flat-ed I've a with-er-ing re-ply; And
(3. I'm) sure I'm not as-cet-ic; I'm as pleas-ant as can be; You'll

gen-u-ine phi-lan-thro-pist, all oth-er kinds are sham. Each
van-i-ty I al-ways do my best to mor-ti-fy; A
al-ways find me read-y with a crush-ing re-par-tee. I've an

cresc.

lit-tle fault of tem-per and each so-ci-al de-fect In my
char-i-ta-ble ac-tion I can skil-ful-ly dis-sect; And
ir-ri-tat-ing chuck-le, I've a cel-e-brat-ed sneer, I've an

cresc.

erring fel-low crea-tures, I en-deav-our to cor-rect. To
in-ter-est-ed mo-tives I'm de-light-ed to de-tect; I know
en-ter-tain-ing snig-ger, I've a fas-ci-nat-ing leer. To

all their lit-tle weak-ness-es I o-pen peo-ple's eyes; And
ev-'ry-bod-y's in-come and what ev-'ry-bod-y earns; And I
ev-'ry-bod-y's prej-u-dice I know a thing or two; I can

lit-tle plans to snub the self-suf-fi-cient I de-vise; I
care-ful-ly com-pare it with the in-come-tax re-turns; But to
tell a wom-an's age in half a min-ute, and I do. But al-

love my fel-low crea-tures, I do all the good I can; Yet
ben-e-fit hu-man-i-ty how-ev-er much I plan,
though I try to make my-self as pleas-ant as I can,

ev - 'ry - bod - y says I'm such a dis - a - gree - able man! And I

1.-2.
can't think why!
2. To
3. I'm

legato

3. CHORUS GAMA
can't think why! He can't think why! I can't think

why!

a tempo

Expressive Glances

Would You Know the Kind of Maid

Gracefully

CYRIL

1. Would you know the kind of maid Sets my heart a flame-a?
2. When a maid is bold and gay, With a tongue goes clang-a,

Eyes must be down-cast and staid, Cheeks must flush for shame-a!
Flaunt-ing it in brave ar-ray, Maid-en may go hang-a!

She may neith-er dance nor sing, But, de mure in ev-'ry-thing,
Sun-flow'r gay and hol-ly-hock, Nev-er shall my gar-den stock;

Hang her head in mod-est way,
Mine the blush-ing rose of May,
With pout-ing lips,— with pout-ing

lips_ that seem_____ to say, "Oh, kiss me, kiss me, kiss me, kiss me,

Though I_ die of shame-a!" Please you, that's the kind of maid Sets_ my heart a-

flame-a! "Kiss me, kiss me, kiss me, kiss me, Though I_ die of

shame-a!" Please you, that's the kind of maid Sets_ my heart a-flame-a!

The Mikado

OR, THE TOWN OF TITIPU

DRAMATIS PERSONÆ

THE MIKADO OF JAPAN

NANKI-POO (*his Son, disguised as a wandering minstrel, and in love with* YUM-YUM)

KO-KO (*Lord High Executioner of Titipu*)

POOH-BAH (*Lord High Everything Else*)

PISH-TUSH (*a Noble Lord*)

YUM-YUM
PITTI-SING ⎱ *Three Sisters—Wards of* KO-KO
PEEP-BO

KATISHA (*an elderly Lady, in love with* NANKI-POO)

Chorus of School-girls, Nobles, Guards, and Coolies

ACT I

COURTYARD OF KO-KO'S OFFICIAL RESIDENCE.

ACT II

KO-KO'S GARDEN.

First produced at the Savoy Theatre on March 14, 1885

MARCH of 1884 saw the beginnings of an impasse. Both Sullivan and Carte had once again categorically rejected Gilbert's new "magic lozenge" plot. Gilbert countered with the suggestion that perhaps Sullivan had better try another dramatist, saying that the length of their association had perhaps turned him stale. Sullivan saw no reason why they should come to a standstill just because he did not like a story line that failed to afford him sufficient musical scope. Could they not try something new? A story that had some human interest with a degree of probability in it? Sullivan's latest thoughts reached Gilbert when he was in the throes of revising his "lozenge" plot again, which was rather unfortunate. He promptly replied, saying that ". . . anxious though he was to give due consideration to any suggestions . . ." he felt the time had come when, with great reluctance, he must state that he ". . . could not consent to concoct another plot for a further opera!" Regretful though Gilbert seemed to be, this letter convinced Sullivan that the decision was final.

Well—here was a pretty kettle of fish! Here was a state of things! In fact—here was a how-de-do! Gilbert was unhappy too, and fuming at the impasse. One day he was pacing up and down his study, on the wall of which there hung a Japanese ceremonial sword. His heavy tread was too much for the Oriental serenity of the weapon; the sword finally gave up the unequal battle and fell to the floor with a clang. Whatever thoughts Gilbert had in mind at that moment—and they may well have been another "magic lozenge" idea—were rudely shattered, and his ire rose at this unlooked-for interruption. Picking it up (and thanks be to whatever gods there are whose labor in life is looking after lozenge-loving librettists), he was struck with a new idea. It was but a germ of an idea at first. His mind had at once turned toward a Japanese exhibition that had recently opened in London. The exotic robes worn by these Far Eastern visitors to the shores of England began to form pictures in his mind's eye. By the time dawn broke he had written a sheaf of notes and the vague outlines of a plot. He immediately sent these over to Sullivan, whose reaction was instantaneous, full of relief, and bubbling with excitement.

But there was little enough time left. In fact, Princess Ida finished its run at the Savoy Theatre long before "the new piece" was ready, and it was decided to revive Trial by Jury and The Sorcerer. In the case of The Sorcerer it was a happy revival. It had not been a really big success during its original run, but now it achieved that distinction.

Like all the other operas The Mikado has had its changes over the years with respect to scenery, costumes, etc. The most sweeping change was made in 1926 when Rupert D'Oyly Carte engaged the services of Charles Ricketts, A.R.A. At the time there was no intention on the part of Carte to redesign The Mikado. His mind was actually set on a revival of Utopia, Ltd., and it was to this end that he had approached Ricketts, actually sending him photos of the original production. Ricketts turned this offer down, the subject being "quite outside his line." But he did suggest that perhaps The Gondoliers in Louis XIV costumes; or maybe a Mikado in ". . . exquisite 18th-century Japanese dresses . . ."

Carte abandoned the idea of Utopia, Ltd. in favor of Ricketts' intriguing notion, giving the artist the go-ahead sign without further ado.

Some license was taken, but there was nothing that was unacceptable, though Ricketts was severely criticized in some quarters for not adhering to the traditional Japanese form of dress. He was quick to reply, saying that up to date ". . . The Geisha Girl, Madam Butterfly and The Mikado had created nothing but a dreary dressing-gown style unlike anything Japanese . . ."; that his costumes were as authentic as could be, being based on 18th-century Japanese prints. Care and thought had gone into the designs, two qualities that were sadly lacking in the original Mikado costumes. Staged, as it was, in a great hurry, a costumer had been told to "do the best he could," and he, in common with most people at that time, knew little or nothing about the Japanese and so dressed everyone in kimonos. A kimono is not a dress so much as an indoor robe for women.

One big departure from tradition was Ko-Ko's sword—the one that fell from the study wall, this being replaced by a huge ax. A delightfully humorous twist was given to Ko-Ko by including a hat that suggested "the big black block," and the insignia of his rank and position, in the shape of crossed axes on his sleeves. The Mikado's costume, out of deference to the feelings of the Japanese Emperor himself, was more the costume of a Shogun than of the ruler. (The actual date of Ricketts' chosen period is approximately 1720.) Ricketts kept the scenery itself simple and almost severe. There was more suggestion of the "screen and fan" than there had hitherto been. The first act was carried out in dark-green and scarlet against which the pastel blues, pinks and greens of the ladies stood out. More color was given to the second act by the simple removal of the pagoda arch and rostrum and replacing them with large silver screens.

Of the Company which opened the 1926 D'Oyly Carte season at the Prince's Theatre, the tenor was the only person to make any complaint regarding the costume. He found it extremely difficult to sing his first song from under the large coolie-type hat that he had been given to wear. The next evening saw the hat hanging down his back, and promptly he had trouble with his Japanese guitar. So—he got used to wearing the hat.

The original Mikado ran continuously at the Savoy Theatre for 672 performances. Since then it has been performed in many foreign languages, including Japanese, and, I believe, Chinese and Hindustani. I myself have performed the role of Ko-Ko well over 1,500 times, and that is in addition to performances in which I was one of the noblemen or Pish-Tush. The late Fred Billington, who was the original Pooh-Bah in New York, played the role over 5,000 times during his career. Yes, I think one might say that The Mikado is Number One in popularity!

The Mikado

ACT I

SCENE.—*Courtyard of* KO-KO's *Palace in Titipu. Japanese nobles discovered standing and sitting in attitudes suggested by native drawings.* [1]

CHORUS OF NOBLES [2]

If you want to know who we are,
    We are gentlemen of Japan;
On many a vase and jar—
    On many a screen and fan,
      We figure in lively paint:
      Our attitude's queer and quaint—
      You're wrong if you think it ain't, oh!

If you think we are worked by strings,
    Like a Japanese marionette,
You don't understand these things:
    It is simply Court etiquette.
      Perhaps you suppose this throng
      Can't keep it up all day long?
      If that's your idea, you're wrong, oh!

Enter NANKI-POO [3] *in great excitement. He carries a native guitar on his back and a bundle of ballads in his hand.*

RECIT—NANKI-POO

Gentlemen, I pray you tell me
Where a gentle maiden dwelleth,
Named Yum-Yum, the ward of Ko-Ko?
In pity speak—oh, speak, I pray you!

A NOBLE.   Why, who are you who ask this question?
NANK.   Come gather round me, and I'll tell you.

SONG AND CHORUS—NANKI-POO [4]

A wandering minstrel I—
    A thing of shreds and patches,
    Of ballads, songs and snatches,
And dreamy lullaby!

My catalogue is long,
    Through every passion ranging,
    And to your humours changing
I tune my supple song!

    Are you in sentimental mood?
      I'll sigh with you,
        Oh, sorrow, sorrow!
    On maiden's coldness do you brood?
      I'll do so, too—
        Oh, sorrow, sorrow! [5]

[1] *In spite of his directions (native drawings), quite obviously Gilbert's mind was still influenced by the "arty" type he lambasted in* Patience, *to whom ". . . something Japanese" went hand in hand with Spanish altar lace and lilies. "You're wrong if you think it ain't"—and furthermore, "You don't understand these things!" Et cetera.*

[2] Words and music on page 445.

[3] *Gilbert was a great man for finding the right name for the right character. What Nanki-Poo's real name is no one knows. According to his father, the Emperor, this is only the name he goes by. But somehow, Nanki-Poo is the perfect name for the disguised son of the Mikado.*

[4] Words and music on page 450.

[5] *Gilbert's original script for this lyric ran:*
    I'll do so, too—
      Oh, willow, willow!
He obviously thought better of it later and decided to reserve this word of lament for "Tit-willow" in Act II.

I'll charm your willing ears
With songs of lovers' fears,
While sympathetic tears
My cheeks bedew—
Oh, sorrow, sorrow!

But if patriotic sentiment is wanted,
I've patriotic ballads cut and dried;
For where'er our country's banner may be planted,
All other local banners are defied!
Our warriors, in serried ranks assembled,
Never quail—or they conceal it if they do—
And I shouldn't be surprised if nations trembled
Before the mighty troops of Titipu!

CHORUS.   We shouldn't be surprised, etc.

NANK.   And if you call for a song of the sea,
We'll heave the capstan round,
With a yeo heave ho, for the wind is free,
Her anchor's a-trip and her helm's a-lee,
Hurrah for the homeward bound!

CHORUS.   Yeo-ho—heave ho—
Hurrah for the homeward bound!

To lay aloft in a howling breeze
May tickle a landsman's taste,
But the happiest hour a sailor sees
Is when he's down
At an inland town,
With his Nancy on his knees, yeo ho!
And his arm around her waist!

CHORUS.   Then man the capstan—off we go,
As the fiddler swings us round,
With a yeo heave ho,
And a rum below,
Hurrah for the homeward bound!

A wandering minstrel I, etc.

Enter PISH-TUSH [6]

PISH. And what may be your business with Yum-Yum?

NANK. I'll tell you. A year ago I was a member of the Titipu town band. It was my duty to take the cap round for contributions. While discharging this delicate office, I saw Yum-Yum. We loved each other at once, but she was betrothed to her guardian Ko-Ko, a cheap tailor, and I saw that my suit was hopeless. Overwhelmed with despair, I quitted the town. Judge of my delight when I heard, a month ago, that Ko-Ko had been condemned to death for flirting! I hurried back at once, in the hope of finding Yum-Yum at liberty to listen to my protestations.

PISH. It is true that Ko-Ko was condemned to death for flirting, but he was reprieved at the last moment, and raised to the exalted rank of Lord High Executioner under the following remarkable circumstances:

SONG—PISH-TUSH *and* CHORUS [7]

Our great Mikado, virtuous man,
When he to rule our land began,

[6] Pish-Tush. *This marvelous, double-barreled name conveys immediately the "compleat Noble Lord."*

[7] *This is by way of being a patter song but, unlike most of Gilbert's patter songs, it is of the utmost importance from a plot point of view, as opposed to the mere tour de force. Not one word must be lost in the singing. One of the main plot lines is contained in this song. Nanki-Poo mentioned Ko-Ko's being condemned to death for flirting in an earlier speech, but he did not explain why flirting was a capital offense. It is left to Pish-Tush to explain in this song—as well as the reason for Ko-Ko's sudden elevation to his present high post.*

In a TV cut version of The Mikado, which I both cut and staged in 1960, the role of Pish-Tush was eliminated, and so was the song. Much as I regretted this, it had to go. TV's top tyrant, the stop watch, had to be placated. My main worry was to retain the plot line, which I did by giving some of Pish-Tush's lines to Pooh-Bah.

Resolved to try
A plan whereby
Young men might best be steadied.

So he decreed, in words succinct,
That all who flirted, leered or winked
(Unless connubially linked),
Should forthwith be beheaded.

And I expect you'll all agree
That he was right to so decree.
And I am right,
And you are right,
And all is right as right can be!

CHORUS.
And you are right,
And we are right, etc.

This stern decree, you'll understand,
Caused great dismay throughout the land!
For young and old
And shy and bold
Were equally affected.
The youth who winked a roving eye,
Or breathed a non-connubial sigh,
Was thereupon condemned to die—
He usually objected.

And you'll allow, as I expect,
That he was right to so object.
And I am right,
And you are right,
And everything is quite correct!

CHORUS.
And you are right,
And we are right, etc.

And so we straight let out on bail,
A convict from the county jail,
Whose head was next
On some pretext
Condemned to be mown off,
And made *him* Headsman, for we said,
"Who's next to be decapited
Cannot cut off another's head
Until he's cut his own off."

And we are right, I think you'll say,
To argue in this kind of way;
And I am right,
And you are right,
And all is right—too-looral-lay!

CHORUS.
And you are right,
And we are right, etc.

[*Exeunt* CHORUS.

Enter POOH-BAH [8]

NANK. Ko-Ko, the cheap tailor, Lord High Executioner of Titipu!
Why, that's the highest rank a citizen can attain!

POOH. It is. Our logical Mikado, seeing no moral difference between
the dignified judge who condemns a criminal to die, and the industrious

[8] Pooh-Bah. *In Gilbert's own words: ". . . may be
described without hesitation as the most remarkable man in ancient or modern history." This
was written for Gilbert's book The Story of The
Mikado for Children. In the same book he pictures Pooh-Bah as being constantly followed by
a small boy carrying an enormous volume into
which he enters any scrap of evidence that will
help Pooh-Bah prove that he can trace his ancestry back to, and perhaps beyond, a "protoplasmal primordial atomic globule."*

*Going back to the subject of good Gilbertian
nomenclature, Pooh-Bah has become a name in
our language symbolizing the sort of character
he was.*

mechanic who carries out the sentence, has rolled the two offices into one, and every judge is now his own executioner.

NANK. But how good of you (for I see that you are a nobleman of the highest rank) to condescend to tell all this to me, a mere strolling minstrel!

POOH. Don't mention it. I am, in point of fact, a particularly haughty and exclusive person, of pre-Adamite ancestral descent. You will understand this when I tell you that I can trace my ancestry back to a protoplasmal primordial atomic globule. Consequently, my family pride is something inconceivable. I can't help it. I was born sneering. But I struggle hard to overcome this defect. I mortify my pride continually. When all the great officers of State resigned in a body, because they were too proud to serve under an ex-tailor, did I not unhesitatingly accept all their posts at once?

PISH. And the salaries attached to them? You did.

POOH. It is consequently my degrading duty to serve this upstart as First Lord of the Treasury, Lord Chief Justice, Commander-in-Chief, Lord High Admiral, Master of the Buckhounds, Groom of the Back Stairs, Archbishop of Titipu, and Lord Mayor, both acting and elect, all rolled into one. And at a salary! A Pooh-Bah paid for his services! I a salaried minion! But I do it! It revolts me, but I do it!

NANK. And it does you credit.

POOH. But I don't stop at that. [9] I go and dine with middle-class people on reasonable terms. I dance at cheap suburban parties for a moderate fee. I accept refreshment at any hands, however lowly. I also retail State secrets at a very low figure. [10] For instance, any further information about Yum-Yum would come under the head of a State secret. (NANKI-POO *takes the hint, and gives him money.*) (*Aside.*) Another insult, and, I think, a light one!

SONG—POOH-BAH *with* NANKI-POO *and* PISH-TUSH

> Young man, despair,
>   Likewise go to,
> Yum-Yum the fair
>   You must not woo.
>   It will not do:
>   I'm sorry for you,
> You very imperfect ablutioner!
>   This very day
>   From school Yum-Yum
> Will wend her way,
>   And homeward come,
>   With beat of drum
>   And a rum-tum-tum,
> To wed the Lord High Executioner!
>   And the brass will crash,
>   And the trumpets bray,
>   And they'll cut a dash
>   On their wedding day.
> She'll toddle away, as all aver,
> With the Lord High Executioner!

NANK. *and* POOH. And the brass will crash, etc.

> It's a hopeless case,
>   As you may see,
> And in your place
>   Away I'd flee;
>   But don't blame me—

[9] *A similar idea is carried out in The Gondoliers in the form of the duet between the Duke and Duchess of Plaza-Toro (see pages 664-665) where this noble couple sell their services without being too particular about their clients.*

[10] *Some years ago a certain cabinet minister was accused and found guilty of revealing some budget details before they were officially given out by the Chancellor of the Exchequer in Parliament on Budget Day. The news of the verdict came out in the late editions of the evening papers. That same evening the D'Oyly Carte Company was playing The Mikado, and when Sydney Granville, as Pooh-Bah, spoke this line, the house nearly fell in!*

I'm sorry to be
Of your pleasure a diminutioner.
They'll vow their pact
Extremely soon,
In point of fact
This afternoon.
Her honeymoon
With that buffoon
At seven commences, so *you* shun her!

ALL.   And the brass will crash, etc.

            [*Exit* PISH-TUSH.

   RECIT NANKI-POO *and* POOH-BAH

NANK. And I have journeyed for a month, or nearly,
    To learn that Yum-Yum, whom I love so dearly,
    This day to Ko-Ko is to be united!

POOH. The fact appears to be as you've recited:
    But here he comes, equipped as suits his station;
    He'll give you any further information.

      [*Exeunt* POOH-BAH *and* NANKI-POO.

   Enter CHORUS OF NOBLES [11]

Behold the Lord High Executioner
  A personage of noble rank and title—
A dignified and potent officer,
  Whose functions are particularly vital!
   Defer, defer,
To the Lord High Executioner!

   Enter KO-KO *attended* [12]

    SOLO—KO-KO [13]

Taken from the county jail
  By a set of curious chances;
Liberated then on bail,
  On my own recognizances;
Wafted by a favouring gale
  As one sometimes is in trances,
To a height that few can scale,
  Save by long and weary dances;
Surely, never had a male
  Under such like circumstances
So adventurous a tale
  Which may rank with most romances.

CHORUS.   Defer, defer,
   To the Lord High Executioner, etc.

KO. [14] Gentlemen, I'm much touched by this reception. I can only trust that by strict attention to duty I shall ensure a continuance of those favours which it will ever be my study to deserve. [15] If I should ever be called upon to act professionally, I am happy to think that there will be no difficulty in finding plenty of people whose loss will be a distinct gain to society at large.

   SONG—KO-KO *with* CHORUS OF MEN [16]

As some day it may happen that a victim must be found,
  I've got a little list—I've got a little list
Of society offenders who might well be underground,

[11] Words and music on page 456.

[12] Ko-Ko's attendant is a small boy—the smallest that can be found. He is there for the purpose of carrying Ko-Ko's badge of office—that is, the "snickersnee." In the original production this weapon was the actual sword that once fell from the wall of Gilbert's study and thus gave birth to an idea that has gone on for seventy-five years.

  With the exception of the Mikado himself, Ko-Ko is the only character who has a truly Japanese name. Translated, the word means "pickles."

[13] For words and music for Ko-Ko's solo, see Note 11 above.

[14] In performance, this speech is split up by interpolations from the Nobles:

  KO. Gentlemen, I'm much touched by this reception.
  NOB. M-a-a-a-a! (Like the bleating of sheep. They do this as they bow.)
  KO. (Returning the compliment) M-a-a-a-a! (Continues his speech) I can only trust . . . study to deserve.
  NOB. M-a-a-a-a!
  KO. M-a-a-a-a! If I should ever be called . . . gain to society at large.
  NOB. M-a-a-a-a!
  KO. M-a-a-a-a!
  NOB. M-a-a-a-a!
  KO. M-a-a-a-a!

The last four bleats continue through the introductory music to the following song.

[15] Ko-Ko's "Little List" song was not in this position in the original production. Following the words ". . . ever be my study to deserve" Ko-Ko continued with dialogue as follows: "Gentlemen, I expect my three beautiful wards, Yum-Yum, Peep-Bo, and Pitti-Sing, in a few minutes. If you will kindly receive them with a show of abject deference, I shall feel obliged to you. I know how painful it must be to noblemen of your rank to have to humiliate yourselves before a person of my antecedents, but discipline must be observed." Nobles bow and exeunt and he goes right on with: "Pooh-Bah, it seems that the festivities, etc."

[16] Words and music on page 460.

[17] *It was not until 1947 that any form of criticism was leveled at the use of this word, yet the D'Oyly Carte had played in the United States many times from 1934 on. However, serious objections were expressed in 1947. Rupert D'Oyly Carte approached Sir Alan P. Herbert, a contemporary lyricist, to provide alternatives to the word, both in this song and in the Mikado's song. There was no difficulty over this one—the word was simply changed to "banjo player," basing the change on Gilbert's meaning of the word when he wrote it, viz., the itinerant street singer who, in imitation of the Negro minstrel, a craze that had come over from the United States, was using burnt cork and twanging away on a banjo at virtually every street corner. It was impossible to miss him.*

[18] *The lady novelist. At the time Gilbert wrote The Mikado, she was regarded as a most singular anomaly, but as time went on and she became accepted, the point got lost, so Gilbert authorized the topicalization of the line. For many years the anomaly was the "prohibitionist." When that became obsolete another "ist" was chosen. Among those used were the scorching motorist, jazz-time pianist, and—one I found to be more successful than all the others combined—the girl who's not been kissed!*

The present chorus at the end of each verse was written in after the original chorus was deleted. It went:

> *As a victim must be found*
> *If you'll only look around,*
> *There are criminals at large*
> *(And enough to fill a barge),*
> *Whose swift decapitation*
> *Would be hailed with acclamation,*
> *If accomplished by the nation*
> *At a reasonable charge.*

Quite obviously Gilbert realized that this was not one of his better efforts, especially the contrived line just for the sake of a rhyme, "And enough to fill a barge." The surprising thing is that he let the chorus remain in for the first night.

[19] *As a general rule, certain mimed business was used to point up certain statesmen. In spite of Gilbert's stopping short of mentioning actual names, there is little doubt that he directed this mimed business. I can still remember the time when Joseph Chamberlain was indicated by inserting a monocle in the eye, and in later years I suggested Neville Chamberlain by opening, in mime, an umbrella. Lloyd George was suggested by making a golf stroke, which would have done very well for Dwight D. Eisenhower in recent years. Occasionally I was taken to task by people who wrote deploring this "insult" to great men. My experience has been that those who were so "insulted" never took it in any other way than that in which it was intended—a spirit of good fun. The London season of 1951 (Festival of Britain Year) opened at the Savoy Theatre with The Mikado. Winston Churchill was one of the brilliant opening-night audience, seated in the Royal Box on the right of the auditorium. Churchill was not, at the time, Prime Minister. He was Leader of the Opposition, and a General*

And who never would be missed—who never would be missed!
There's the pestilential nuisances who write for autographs—
All people who have flabby hands and irritating laughs—
All children who are up in dates, and floor you with 'em flat—
All persons who in shaking hands, shake hands with you like *that*—
And all third persons who on spoiling *tête-à-têtes* insist—
    They'd none of 'em be missed—they'd none of 'em be missed!

CHORUS. He's got 'em on the list—he's got 'em on the list;
        And they'll none of 'em be missed—they'll none of 'em
        be missed.

There's the nigger [17] serenader, and the others of his race,
    And the piano-organist—I've got him on the list!
And the people who eat peppermint and puff it in your face,
    They never would be missed—they never would be missed!
Then the idiot who praises, with enthusiastic tone,
All centuries but this, and every country but his own;
And the lady from the provinces, who dresses like a guy,
And who "doesn't think she waltzes, but would rather like to try";
And that singular anomaly, the lady novelist—[18]
    I don't think she'd be missed—I'm *sure* she'd not be missed!

CHORUS. He's got her on the list—he's got her on the list;
        And I don't think she'll be missed—I'm *sure* she'll not be
        missed!

And that *Nisi Prius* nuisance, who just now is rather rife,
    The Judicial humorist—I've got *him* on the list!
All funny fellows, comic men, and clowns of private life—
    They'd none of 'em be missed—they'd none of 'em be missed.
And apologetic statesmen of a compromising kind,
Such as—What d'ye call him—Thing'em-bob, and likewise—Never-mind,
And 'St—'st—'st—and What's-his-name, and also You-know-who—[19]
The task of filling up the blanks I'd rather leave to *you*.
But it really doesn't matter whom you put upon the list,
    For they'd none of 'em be missed—they'd none of 'em be missed!

CHORUS. You may put 'em on the list—you may put 'em on the list;
        And they'll none of 'em be missed—they'll none of 'em be
        missed!

Enter POOH-BAH

KO. Pooh-Bah, it seems that the festivities in connection with my approaching marriage must last a week. I should like to do it handsomely, and I want to consult you as to the amount I ought to spend upon them.

POOH. Certainly. In which of my capacities? [20] As First Lord of the Treasury, Lord Chamberlain, Attorney-General, Chancellor of the Exchequer, Privy Purse, or Private Secretary?

KO. Suppose we say as Private Secretary.

POOH. Speaking as your Private Secretary, I should say that, as the city will have to pay for it, don't stint yourself, do it well.

KO. Exactly—as the city will have to pay for it. That is your advice.

POOH. As Private Secretary. Of course you will understand that, as Chancellor of the Exchequer, I am bound to see that due economy is observed.

KO. Oh! But you said just now "Don't stint yourself, do it well."

POOH. As Private Secretary.

KO. And now you say that due economy must be observed.

POOH. As Chancellor of the Exchequer.

KO. I see. Come over here, where the Chancellor can't hear us. (*They cross the stage.*) Now, as my Solicitor, how do you advise me to deal with this difficulty?

POOH. Oh, as your Solicitor, I should have no hesitation in saying "Chance it——"

KO. Thank you. (*Shaking his hand.*) I will.

POOH. If it were not that, as Lord Chief Justice, I am bound to see that the law isn't violated.

KO. I see. Come over here where the Chief Justice can't hear us. (*They cross the stage.*) Now, then, as First Lord of the Treasury?

POOH. Of course, as First Lord of the Treasury, I could propose a special vote that would cover all expenses, if it were not that, as Leader of the Opposition, it would be my duty to resist it, tooth and nail. Or, as Paymaster-General, I could so cook the accounts that, as Lord High Auditor, I should never discover the fraud. But then, as Archbishop of Titipu, it would be my duty to denounce my dishonesty and give myself into my own custody as First Commissioner of Police.

KO. That's extremely awkward.

POOH. I don't say that all these distinguished people couldn't be squared; but it is right to tell you that they wouldn't be sufficiently degraded in their own estimation unless they were insulted with a very considerable bribe. [21]

KO. The matter shall have my careful consideration. But my bride and her sisters approach, and any little compliment on your part, such as an abject grovel in a characteristic Japanese attitude, would be esteemed a favour. [22]

[*Exeunt together.*

Enter procession of YUM-YUM's *schoolfellows, heralding* YUM-YUM, PEEP-BO, *and* PITTI-SING [23]

CHORUS OF GIRLS

Comes a train of little ladies
　　From scholastic trammels free,
Each a little bit afraid is,
　　Wondering what the world can be!

Is it but a world of trouble—
　　Sadness set to song?
Is its beauty but a bubble
　　Bound to break ere long?

Are its palaces and pleasures
　　Fantasies that fade?
And the glory of its treasures
　　Shadow of a shade?

Schoolgirls we, eighteen and under,
　　From scholastic trammels free,
And we wonder—how we wonder!—
　　What on earth the world can be!

TRIO [24]

YUM-YUM, PEEP-BO, *and* PITTI-SING, *with* CHORUS OF GIRLS

THE THREE. 　Three little maids from school are we,
　　　　　　Pert as a school-girl well can be,
　　　　　　Filled to the brim with girlish glee,
　　　　　　　Three little maids from school!
YUM-YUM. 　Everything is a source of fun. (*Chuckle.*)

Election was looming. As I made my entrance as Ko-Ko I knew that I had some very pointed words to sing. I also knew that on no account should I look in his direction, unless I could find the right moment. Up to the point of halfway through the last verse I had not found that moment in my mind. I reached the line:

And apologetic statesmen of a compromising
　kind (gusts of laughter)
Such as—What d'ye call him—Thing'em-bob,
　and likewise—Never-mind (shrieks of laugh-
　ter)
And 'St—'st—'st—and What's-his-name (in a
　blinding flash the right moment came to
　me) and also (I deliberately, and pointedly,
　looked at Mr. Churchill) You-know-who—

[20] There is little doubt that Gilbert was, at times, something of a plagiarist. The ensuing scene, or at least the idea thereof, could hardly have come from any other place than The Sleeping Beauty (Planché, 1840) in which the Lord Factotum (Lord High Everything Else?) says:

As Lord High Chamberlain, I slumber never;
As Lord High Steward, in a stew for ever;
As Lord High Treasurer, I've the deuce to pay;
Etc.

and ending with

In other States, the honors are divided,
But here, they're one and all to me confided.

[21] Referring back to the retailing of state secrets and the guilty cabinet minister, Gilbert expands his joke. He now brings in the cause of a possible fall from grace and high officialdom—bribery. In the case of the British cabinet minister's fall, another well-known though not political name was involved, who by virtue of a pre-knowledge of Budget intentions was able to carry out a deal that netted him and his informer a considerable sum of money.
　　How I adore that word "insulted."

[22] For many years, certainly from the first moment that I knew The Mikado, it was traditional for Pooh-Bah to add one further line: "No money, no grovel!" before the exeunt. There came a time when this was cut, and the result, in my opinion, was to leave Ko-Ko and Pooh-Bah with a most tame exit. So I have always kept the words in whenever I have directed a performance.

[23] Yum-Yum! And how very Yum-Yummy she is—like all Gilbert's heroines—and oh, how consciously naïve!
　　Pitti-Sing! So suitably pert, and pertly suitable.
　　Peep-Bo! Did the writer of "Little Bo-Peep" originally reverse the name, or was it left to Gilbert? Who really cares? It fits the young lady like a glove.

[24] Words and music on page 463.

417

[25] *Gilbert, that facile rhymester, contents himself with but two rhymes for "seminary" here. But just take another glance at the Finale, page 294 of Iolanthe, beginning "Oh, Chancellor unwary."*

[26] *To the intense dismay of all lovers of Gilbert and Sullivan in general, and of The Mikado in particular, the following scene was one which I cut in its entirety from the TV version. No one was more dismayed than I; I was cutting one of my favorite gags. But as it does little or nothing for the furtherance of the plot, and is only good for a couple of laughs, and as our TV tyrant, the Time Teller, still insisted on sacrifice, out it had to go.*

[27] *One of the gags was some visual business just at this point. As Ko-Ko said: "One at a time, if you please," he would flick open his fan very sharply. Yum-Yum, Pitti-Sing, Peep-Bo, Nanki-Poo, and Pish-Tush flick theirs in rapid succession, followed by the slow Bronx-cheerish-sounding opening of Pooh-Bah's very large fan. (The larger, the better—and funnier.)*

[28] *An instance of Gilbert's occasional heavy-handedness with a joke. Rupert D'Oyly Carte cut this line several years ago—and "it never has been missed!"*

[29] *This is where my favorite gag—insofar as this scene is concerned—came in. Nanki would go down on one knee and lower his head as near the ground as possible. I, who had been looking to the front and so not seeing him go down, would turn to him—and address nothing. Then, realizing he was on the floor, I would get down on my back and wriggle my face under his so that we were nose to nose—I looking up, he looking down. The whole of my next speech was delivered in this position—once the audience had got over its convulsions!*

Boasting? No; it was funny, and I knew it. And so, apparently, did Mr. Carte for he never cut it out.

PEEP-BO.   Nobody's safe, for we care for none! (*Chuckle.*)
PITTI-SING.   Life is a joke that's just begun! (*Chuckle.*)
THE THREE.   Three little maids from school!
ALL (*dancing*). Three little maids who, all unwary,
                Come from a ladies' seminary, [25]
                Freed from its genius tutelary—
THE THREE (*suddenly demure*). Three little maids from school!

YUM-YUM.   One little maid is a bride, Yum-Yum—
PEEP-BO.   Two little maids in attendance come—
PITTI-SING.   Three little maids is the total sum.
THE THREE.   Three little maids from school!
YUM-YUM.   From three little maids take one away.
PEEP-BO.   Two little maids remain, and they—
PITTI-SING.   Won't have to wait very long, they say—
THE THREE.   Three little maids from school!
ALL (*dancing*). Three little maids who, all unwary,
                Come from a ladies' seminary,
                Freed from its genius tutelary—
THE THREE (*suddenly demure*). Three little maids from school!

Enter KO-KO *and* POOH-BAH [26]

KO. At last, my bride that is to be! (*About to embrace her.*)

YUM. You're not going to kiss me before all these people?

KO. Well, that was the idea.

YUM. (*aside to* PEEP-BO). It seems odd, doesn't it?

PEEP. It's rather peculiar.

PITTI. Oh, I expect it's all right. Must have a beginning, you know.

YUM. Well, of course I know nothing about these things; but I've no objection if it's usual.

KO. Oh, it's quite usual, I think. Eh, Lord Chamberlain? (*Appealing to* POOH-BAH.)

POOH. I have known it done. (KO-KO *embraces her.*)

YUM. Thank goodness that's over! (*Sees* NANKI-POO, *and rushes to him.*) Why, that's never you? (*The Three Girls rush to him and shake his hands, all speaking at once.*)

YUM. Oh, I'm so glad! I haven't seen you for ever so long, and I'm right at the top of the school, and I've got three prizes, and I've come home for good, and I'm not going back any more!

PEEP. And have you got an engagement?—Yum-Yum's got one, but she doesn't like it, and she'd ever so much rather it was you! I've come home for good, and I'm not going back any more!

PITTI. Now tell us all the news, because you go about everywhere, and we've been at school, but, thank goodness, that's all over now, and we've come home for good, and we're not going back any more!

(*These three speeches are spoken together in one breath.*)

KO. I beg your pardon. Will you present me?

YUM. Oh, this is the musician who used—
PEEP. Oh, this is the gentleman who used—
PITTI. Oh, it is only Nanki-Poo who used—

KO. One at a time, if you please. [27]

YUM. Oh, if you please, he's the gentleman who used to play so beautifully on the—on the——

PITTI. On the Marine Parade.

YUM. Yes, I think that was the name of the instrument. [28]

NANK. Sir, I have the misfortune to love your ward, Yum-Yum—oh, I know I deserve your anger! [29]

KO. Anger! not a bit, my boy. Why, I love her myself. Charming little girl, isn't she? Pretty eyes, nice hair. Taking little thing, altogether. Very glad to hear my opinion backed by a competent authority. Thank you very much. Good-bye. (*To* PISH-TUSH.) Take him away. (PISH-TUSH *removes him.*)

PITTI. (*who has been examining* POOH-BAH). I beg your pardon, but what is this? Customer come to try on?

KO. That is a Tremendous Swell.

PITTI. Oh, it's alive. (*She starts back in alarm.*)

POOH. Go away, little girls. Can't talk to little girls like you. Go away, there's dears.

KO. Allow me to present you, Pooh-Bah. These are my three wards. The one in the middle is my bride elect.

POOH. What do you want me to do to them? Mind, I *will not* kiss them.

KO. No, no, you shan't kiss them; a little bow—a mere nothing—you needn't mean it, you know.

POOH. It goes against the grain. They are not young ladies, they are young persons.

KO. Come, come, make an effort, there's a good nobleman.

POOH. (*aside to* KO-KO). Well, I shan't mean it. (*With a great effort.*) How de do, little girls, how de do? (*Aside.*) Oh, my protoplasmal ancestor!

KO. That's very good. (*Girls indulge in suppressed laughter.*)

POOH. I see nothing to laugh at. It is very painful to me to have to say "How de do, little girls, how de do?" to young persons. I'm not in the habit of saying "How de do, little girls, how de do?" to anybody under the rank of a Stockbroker.

KO. (*aside to girls*). Don't laugh at him, he can't help it—he's under treatment for it. (*Aside to* POOH-BAH.) Never mind them, they don't understand the delicacy of your position. [30]

POOH. We know how delicate it is, don't we?

KO. I should think we did! How a nobleman of your importance can do it at all is a thing I never can, never shall understand.

[KO-KO *retires up and goes off.*

QUARTET AND CHORUS OF GIRLS
YUM-YUM, PEEP-BO, PITTI-SING, *and* POOH-BAH

YUM., PEEP. *and* PITTI.	So please you, Sir, we much regret If we have failed in etiquette Towards a man of rank so high— We shall know better by and by.
YUM.	But youth, of course, must have its fling, So pardon us, So pardon us,
PITTI.	And don't, in girlhood's happy spring, Be hard on us, Be hard on us, If we're inclined to dance and sing. Tra la la, etc. (*Dancing.*)
CHORUS OF GIRLS.	But youth, of course, etc.
POOH.	I think you ought to recollect You cannot show too much respect Towards the highly titled few; But nobody does, and why should you? That youth at us should have its fling,

[30] One line I was never fond of and longed to cut but there, like Ko-Ko a little later on, Mr. Carte was adamant, and the line remained.

Is hard on us,
Is hard on us;
To our prerogative we cling—
So pardon us,
So pardon us,
If we decline to dance and sing.
Tra la la, etc. (*Dancing.*)

CHORUS OF GIRLS. But youth, of course, must have its fling, etc.

[*Exeunt all but* YUM-YUM.

Enter NANKI-POO

NANK. Yum-Yum, at last we are alone! I have sought you night and day for three weeks, in the belief that your guardian was beheaded, and I find that you are about to be married to him this afternoon!

YUM. Alas, yes!

NANK. But you do not love him?

YUM. Alas, no!

NANK. Modified rapture! [31] But why do you not refuse him?

YUM. What good would that do? He's my guardian, and he wouldn't let me marry you!

NANK. But I would wait until you were of age!

YUM. You forget that in Japan girls do not arrive at years of discretion until they are fifty.

NANK. True; from seventeen to forty-nine are considered years of indiscretion.

YUM. Besides—a wandering minstrel, who plays a wind instrument outside tea-houses, is hardly a fitting husband for the ward of a Lord High Executioner.

NANK. But—— (*Aside.*) Shall I tell her? Yes! She will not betray me! (*Aloud.*) What if it should prove that, after all, I am no musician?

YUM. There! I was certain of it, directly I heard you play!

NANK. What if it should prove that I am no other than the son of his Majesty the Mikado?

YUM. The son of the Mikado! But why is your Highness disguised? And what has your Highness done? And will your Highness promise never to do it again?

NANK. Some years ago I had the misfortune to captivate Katisha, an elderly lady of my father's Court. She misconstrued my customary affability into expressions of affection, and claimed me in marriage, under my father's law. My father, the Lucius Junius Brutus of his race, ordered me to marry her within a week, or perish ignominiously on the scaffold. That night I fled his Court, and, assuming the disguise of a Second Trombone, I joined the band in which you found me when I had the happiness of seeing you! (*Approaching her.*)

YUM. (*retreating*). If you please, I think your Highness had better not come too near. The laws against flirting are excessively severe.

NANK. But we are quite alone, and nobody can see us.

YUM. Still, that don't [32] make it right. To flirt is capital.

NANK. It *is* capital!

YUM. And we must obey the law.

NANK. Deuce take the law!

YUM. I wish it would, but it won't!

NANK. If it were not for that, how happy we might be! [33]

YUM. Happy indeed!

NANK. If it were not for the law, we should now be sitting side by side, like that. (*Sits by her.*)

YUM. Instead of being obliged to sit half a mile off, like that. (*Crosses and sits at other side of stage.*)

[31] *Gilbert's original line was just "Oh, rapture!" However, during rehearsals, Mr. Durward Lely, the Nanki-Poo, was inclined to be a little too rapturous for Gilbert's taste, and Gilbert had him go over the line time and again. The tempers of both were wearing thin. Gilbert eventually exploded: " 'Rapture'—yes, Mr. Lely, definitely 'rapture'—but modified rapture, please!"*

Lely was also seething by this time. The scene was begun again:

"But you do not love him?" speaks Lely.

"Alas, no!" replies Miss Leonora Braham, his Yum-Yum.

Lely flung discretion to the four winds. "Oh, modified rapture!" he declaimed.

Gilbert gasped with astonishment and then collapsed in his seat. Lely was equally astonished at this, and even more so when Gilbert, having recovered himself, said: "Modified rapture, indeed! Oh, very good. But don't speak the 'Oh,' Mr. Lely. Just leave it 'modified rapture.' "

And some people will insist that Gilbert was so adamant about his words that he would brook no suggestions!

[32] *Many modern editions of The Mikado have altered this to "doesn't." By doing this they completely spoil the apparent unworldliness of Yum-Yum; besides which, "don't" was quite acceptable in those days for "does not," in the same way that "ain't" was acceptable for "is not." Incidentally, Gilbert's original line was: "That don't make it right. To flirt is illegal, and we must obey the law."*

The next two lines were not there, Nanki-Poo coming in with: "Deuce take the law!"

[33] *An almost identical situation is found in The Gondoliers. (See page 642, Note 24.)*

NANK. We should be gazing into each other's eyes, like that. (*Gazing at her sentimentally.*)

YUM. Breathing sighs of unutterable love—like that. (*Sighing and gazing lovingly at him.*)

NANK. With our arms round each other's waists, like that. (*Embracing her.*)

YUM. Yes, if it wasn't for the law.

NANK. If it wasn't for the law.

YUM. As it is, of course we couldn't do anything of the kind.

NANK. Not for worlds!

YUM. Being engaged to Ko-Ko, you know!

NANK. Being engaged to Ko-Ko!

[34] DUET—YUM-YUM *and* NANKI-POO [35]

NANK.
Were you not to Ko-Ko plighted,
I would say in tender tone,
"Loved one, let us be united—
Let us be each other's own!"
I would merge all rank and station,
Worldly sneers are nought to us,
And, to mark my admiration,
I would kiss you fondly thus—
(*Kisses her.*)

BOTH.
{I / He} would kiss {you / me} fondly thus—(*Kiss.*)

YUM.
But as I'm engaged to Ko-Ko,
To embrace you thus, *con fuoco*,
Would be distinctly no *giuoco*,
And for yam I should get toko—

BOTH.
Toko, toko, toko, toko!

NANK.
So, in spite of all temptation,
Such a theme I'll not discuss,
And on no consideration
Will I kiss you fondly thus—
(*Kissing her.*)
Let me make it clear to you,
This is what I'll never do!
This, oh, this, oh, this, oh, this—
(*Kissing her.*)

TOGETHER.
This, oh, this, etc.

[*Exeunt in opposite directions.*

Enter KO-KO

KO. (*looking after* YUM-YUM). There she goes! To think how entirely my future happiness is wrapped up in that little parcel! Really, it hardly seems worth while! [36] Oh, matrimony!— (*Enter* POOH-BAH *and* PISH-TUSH.) Now then, what is it? Can't you see I'm soliloquizing? You have interrupted an apostrophe, sir!

PISH. I am the bearer of a letter from his Majesty the Mikado. [37]

KO. (*taking it from him reverentially*). A letter from the Mikado! What in the world can he have to say to me? (*Reads letter.*) Ah, here it is at last! I thought it would come sooner or later! The Mikado is struck by the fact that no executions have taken place in Titipu for a year and decrees that unless somebody is beheaded within one month the post of Lord High Executioner shall be abolished, and the city reduced to the rank of a village!

[34] *This duet originally consisted of four verses. It is doubtful if it was sung as first written more than two or three times. My guess is that it was probably among the cuts and transpositions that were made the morning after the opening. As a matter of interest, the duet went as follows:*

YUM.
Were I not to Ko-Ko plighted,
I would say in tender tone,
"Loved one, let us be united—
Let us be each other's own!"
I would say, "Oh, gentle stranger,
Press me closely to thy heart,
Sharing every joy and danger
We will never part

BOTH.
We will never part
We will never part.

YUM.
But as I'm to marry Ko-Ko,
To express my love con fuoco
Would distinctly be no giuocco
And for yam, I should get toco!

BOTH.
Toco, toco, toco, toco!

YUM.
So I will not say, "Oh, stranger,
Press me closely to thy heart,
Sharing every joy and danger,
We will never, never part!"
Clearly understand, I pray,
This is what I'll never say—
This, oh, this, oh, this, oh, this—
This is what I'll never say.

NANK.
Were you not to Ko-Ko plighted,
I should thrill at words like those.
Joy of joys is love requited,
Love despised is woe of woes.
I would merge all rank and station—
Worldly sneers are nought to us—
And to mark my admiration,
I would kiss you fondly thus—
(Kisses her.)

The duet then concluded from the point where both sing

{I / He} would kiss {you / me} fondly thus—

substantially as it does in the present version.

[35] Words and music on page 467.

[36] *"Really, it hardly seems worth while!" The number of times I have spoken that line and wondered to myself what hardly seemed worth while? Ko-Ko's future happiness? Marrying the girl? Giving up his freedom? And what was Gilbert going to say about matrimony?*

He leaves us in exactly the same state of suspense in The Yeomen of the Guard *with an unanswered conundrum. (See page 568, Note 35.)*

[37] *For the first few performances only, Ko-Ko's "Little List" song came during this scene. Pish-Tush entered alone. The dialogue was the same up to:—*PISH. *"But that will involve us all in irretrievable ruin." Ko-Ko replied with: "Yes—somebody will have to suffer. Send the Recorder to me."* (Exit PISH-TUSH.) *"I expected something of this sort! I knew it couldn't go on! Well, they've brought it on themselves, and the only question is, Who shall it be? Fortunately, there will be no difficulty in pitching upon somebody*

whose death will be a distinct gain to society."
Then came the "Little List."

There were but two minor changes. The first line used to be: "As it seems to be essential . . . etc." and the fourth line: "Of social offenders . . . etc."

At the end of the number, Pooh-Bah and Pish-Tush entered, with Pooh-Bah saying: "This is very uncomfortable news." Beyond some very minor word changes and eliminations, the rest of the scene remained as is.

[38] *See The Gondoliers, page 654, Note 51.*

[39] *Pooh-Bah, Ko-Ko and Pish-Tush have been seated tailor fashion on the floor. In rising, Pooh-Bah's bulk causes him to assume a ridiculously awkward position, with both hands and feet on the ground. Ko-Ko's following line is not really needed, and is generally lost, anyway, in the laugh that follows Pooh-Bah's line and business.*

[40] *This trio contains what is probably one of the most perfect examples of Sullivan's genius with counterpoint, in this case, triple counterpoint.*

The reader should note that the printed libretto does not give complete instructions for the order in which the verses are sung. The order is as follows:

POOH-BAH.   *"I am so proud . . ." to "And mortified."*
KO-KO.   *"My brain it teems . . ." to "As best he can."*
PISH-TUSH.   *"I heard one day . . ." to "To bid us adieu."*
ALL TOGETHER.   *Repeat their respective verses.*
KO-KO.   *"And so, Although . . ." to "So I object—"*
POOH-BAH.   *"And so, Although . . ." to "I must decline—"*
PISH-TUSH.   *"And go And show . . ." to "I don't much care—"*

PISH. But that will involve us all in irretrievable ruin!

KO. Yes. There is no help for it, I shall have to execute somebody at once. The only question is, who shall it be?

POOH. Well, it seems unkind to say so, but as you're already under sentence of death for flirting, everything seems to point to *you.*

KO. To me? What are you talking about? I can't execute myself.

POOH. Why not?

KO. Why not? Because, in the first place, self-decapitation is an extremely difficult, not to say dangerous, thing to attempt; and, in the second, it's suicide, and suicide is a capital offence.

POOH. That is so, no doubt.

PISH. We might reserve that point. [38]

POOH. True, it could be argued six months hence, before the full Court.

KO. Besides, I don't see how a man *can* cut off his own head.

POOH. A man might try.

PISH. Even if you only succeeded in cutting it half off, that would be something.

POOH. It would be taken as an earnest of your desire to comply with the Imperial will.

KO. No. Pardon me, but there I am adamant. As official Headsman, my reputation is at stake, and I can't consent to embark on a professional operation unless I see my way to a successful result.

POOH. This professional conscientiousness is highly creditable to *you,* but it places us in a very awkward position. [39]

KO. My good sir, the awkwardness of your position is grace itself compared with that of a man engaged in the act of cutting off his own head.

PISH. I am afraid that, unless you can obtain a substitute——

KO. A substitute? Oh, certainly—nothing easier. (*To* POOH-BAH.) I appoint you Lord High Substitute.

POOH. I should be delighted. Such an appointment would realize my fondest dreams. But no, at any sacrifice, I must set bounds to my insatiable ambition!

TRIO [40]

KO-KO	POOH-BAH	PISH-TUSH
My brain it teems	I am so proud,	I heard one day
With endless schemes	If I allowed	A gentleman say
Both good and new	My family pride	That criminals who
For Titipu;	To be my guide,	Are cut in two
But if I flit,	I'd volunteer	Can hardly feel
The benefit	To quit this sphere	The fatal steel,
That I'd diffuse	Instead of you,	And so are slain
The town would lose!	In a minute or two.	Without much pain.
Now every man	But family pride	If this is true,
To aid his clan	Must be denied,	It's jolly for you;
Should plot and plan	And set aside,	Your courage screw
As best he can,	And mortified.	To bid us adieu,
And so,	And so,	And go
Although	Although	And show
I'm ready to go,	I wish to go,	Both friend and foe
Yet recollect	And greatly pine	How much you dare.
'Twere disrespect	To brightly shine,	I'm quite aware
Did I neglect	And take the line	It's your affair,
To thus effect	Of a hero fine,	Yet I declare
This aim direct.	With grief condign	I'd take your share,
So I object—	I must decline—	But I don't much care—
So I object—	I must decline—	I don't much care—
So I object—	I must decline—	I don't much care—

ALL.   To sit in solemn silence in a dull, dark dock,
      In a pestilential prison, with a life-long lock,
      Awaiting the sensation of a short, sharp shock,
      From a cheap and chippy chopper on a big black block!

[*Exeunt* POOH. *and* PISH.

KO. This is simply appalling! I, who allowed myself to be respited at the last moment, simply in order to benefit my native town, am now required to die within a month, and that by a man whom I have loaded with honours! Is this public gratitude? Is this—— (*Enter* NANKI-POO, *with a rope in his hands.*) [41] Go away, sir! How dare you? Am I never to be permitted to soliloquize?

NANK. Oh, go on—don't mind me.

KO. What are you going to do with that rope?

NANK. I am about to terminate an unendurable existence.

KO. Terminate your existence? Oh, nonsense! What for?

NANK. Because you are going to marry the girl I adore.

KO. Nonsense, sir. I won't permit it. I am a humane man, and if you attempt anything of the kind I shall order your instant arrest. Come, sir, desist at once or I summon my guard.

NANK. That's absurd. If you attempt to raise an alarm, I instantly perform the Happy Despatch with this dagger.

KO. No, no, don't do that. This is horrible! (*Suddenly.*) Why, you cold-blooded scoundrel, are you aware that, in taking your life, you are committing a crime which—which—which is—— Oh! (*Struck by an idea.*) Substitute!

NANK. What's the matter?

KO. Is it *absolutely certain* that you are resolved to die?

NANK. Absolutely!

KO. Will *nothing* shake your resolution?

NANK. Nothing.

KO. Threats, entreaties, prayers—all useless?

NANK. All! My mind is made up.

KO. Then, if you really mean what you say, and if you are absolutely resolved to die, and if nothing whatever will shake your determination—don't spoil yourself by committing suicide, but be beheaded handsomely at the hands of the Public Executioner!

NANK. I don't see how that would benefit me.

KO. You don't? Observe: you'll have a month to live, and you'll live like a fighting-cock at my expense. When the day comes there'll be a grand public ceremonial—you'll be the central figure—no one will attempt to deprive you of that distinction. There'll be a procession—bands [42]—dead march—bells tolling—all the girls in tears—Yum-Yum distracted—then, when it's all over, general rejoicings, and a display of fireworks in the evening. *You* won't see them, but they'll be there all the same.

NANK. Do you think Yum-Yum would really be distracted at my death?

KO. I am convinced of it. Bless you, she's the most tender-hearted little creature alive.

NANK. I should be sorry to cause her pain. Perhaps, after all, if I were to withdraw from Japan, and travel in Europe for a couple of years, I might contrive to forget her.

KO. Oh, I don't think you could forget Yum-Yum so easily; and, after all, what is more miserable than a love-blighted life?

NANK. True.

KO. Life without Yum-Yum—why, it seems absurd!

[41] *Nanki-Poo's rope has a running noose, with a hangman's knot and it is around his neck. A question often asked is: Is Nanki-Poo serious in this attempt to commit suicide, or, since he is aware of Ko-Ko's aversion to killing things, is he pulling a fast one? I don't think there is any doubt that Gilbert intends Nanki to be quite serious about this at first. There is also no doubt that Nanki gets an inkling of an idea as soon as Ko-Ko mentions Yum-Yum and her distraction.*

The whole of this scene, in my opinion, may be numbered among Gilbert's funniest, in spite of the fact that the main theme is one of violent death.

When Ko-Ko realizes that in Nanki-Poo he has a possible substitute, he traditionally breaks into a little jig of pleasure. This was always good for a slight laugh, but one day I placed my fan on the floor and put the knife, which Ko-Ko has by this time wrested from Nanki's hand, on top, making a cross, and broke into a wild suggestion of a Scottish sword dance. This was so successful I kept it in from then on.

[42] *Sir Henry Lytton used to break this speech here, hold his nose, hum "The Campbells Are Coming" while he struck his throat with his free hand. This produced a noise similar to the bagpipes. I personally never used this because I felt it held the speech up and killed the spoken gag immediately following.*

[43] *Nanki-Poo prepares the rope by coiling it, still with the noose around his neck, and goes to throw it over the branch of a tree. The loose end falls back over his shoulder and Ko-Ko grabs at and catches it, immediately marching away from the tree, dragging Nanki by the neck. And this is about the only time that he is in any sort of danger from the rope.*

[44] *The Mikado of Japan was looked upon by his people as someone of divine origin, and the Japanese Ambassador made a protest, and called for the banning of the operetta The Mikado on the grounds that it subjected his monarch to ridicule. Strangely enough, Queen Victoria took no steps, in spite of her feelings regarding some of Gilbert's previous operas, and the protest was not upheld. It was, of course, obvious to all Englishmen that Gilbert was lampooning British institutions with no thought in his head of Japan or the Japanese Emperor other than scenery and costumes. Again, in 1907, another protest of a similar nature was made, and this time The Mikado was banned, and remained under the ban for some time.*

In 1939, when the D'Oyly Carte Company was in Boston, The Mikado was again the subject of a protest and a request that it be banned. This time the susceptibilities of the Japanese were not the reason. "Indecency" was cited in a letter to one of the local papers from a resident of Boston, who declared that he could not take his wife and child to a performance wherein one of the characters was willing to sell the body of his fiancée to another man simply in order to save his own life. It was nothing but a form of white slavery—or words to that effect. This letter was answered by another Bostonian, in which the writer agreed wholeheartedly, and furthermore suggested that perhaps the children's tale of Little Red Ridinghood be banned from the bookstores, because that told the story of a little girl lured by a "wolf" into his bedroom!

NANK. And yet there are a good many people in the world who have to endure it.

KO. Poor devils, yes! You are quite right not to be of their number.

NANK. (*suddenly*). I *won't* be of their number!

KO. Noble fellow!

NANK. I'll tell you how we'll manage it. Let me marry Yum-Yum to-morrow, and in a month you may behead me.

KO. No, no. I draw the line at Yum-Yum.

NANK. Very good. If you can draw the line, so can I. (*Preparing rope.*) [43]

KO. Stop, stop—listen one moment—be reasonable. How can I consent to your marrying Yum-Yum if I'm going to marry her myself?

NANK. My good friend, she'll be a widow in a month, and you can marry her then.

KO. That's true, of course. I quite see that. But, dear me! my position during the next month will be most unpleasant—most unpleasant.

NANK. Not half so unpleasant as my position at the end of it.

KO. But—dear me!—well—I agree—after all, it's only putting off my wedding for a month. But you won't prejudice her against me, will you? You see, I've educated her to be my wife; she's been taught to regard me as a wise and good man. Now I shouldn't like her views on that point disturbed.

NANK. Trust me, she shall never learn the truth from me.

FINALE

Enter CHORUS, POOH-BAH, *and* PISH-TUSH

CHORUS

With aspect stern
   And gloomy stride,
We come to learn
   How you decide.

Don't hesitate
   Your choice to name,
A dreadful fate
   You'll suffer all the same.

POOH.   To ask you what you mean to do we punctually appear.

KO.   Congratulate me, gentlemen, I've found a Volunteer!

ALL.   The Japanese equivalent for Hear, Hear, Hear!

KO. (*presenting him*).   'Tis Nanki-Poo!

ALL.   Hail, Nanki-Poo!

KO.   I think he'll do?

ALL.   Yes, yes, he'll do!

KO. [44] He yields his life if I'll Yum-Yum surrender.
   Now I adore that girl with passion tender,
   And could not yield her with a ready will,
      Or her allot
      If I did not
   Adore myself with passion tenderer still!

Enter YUM-YUM, PEEP-BO, *and* PITTI-SING

ALL.   Ah, yes!
   He loves himself with passion tenderer still!

KO. (*to* NANKI-POO). Take her—she's yours!

[*Exit* KO-KO.

ENSEMBLE

NANKI-POO. The threatened cloud has passed away, [45]
YUM-YUM. And brightly shines the dawning day;
NANKI-POO. What though the night may come too soon, [46]
YUM-YUM. There's yet a month of afternoon!

NANKI-POO, POOH-BAH, YUM-YUM, PITTI-SING, *and* PEEP-BO

Then let the throng
Our joy advance,
With laughing song
And merry dance,

CHORUS. With joyous shout and ringing cheer,
Inaugurate our brief career!

PITTI-SING. A day, a week, a month, a year—[47]
YUM. Or far or near, or far or near,
POOH. Life's eventime comes much too soon,
PITTI-SING. You'll live at least a honeymoon! [48]

ALL. Then let the throng, etc.

CHORUS. With joyous shout, etc.

SOLO—POOH-BAH [49]

As in a month you've got to die,
If Ko-Ko tells us true,
'Twere empty compliment to cry
"Long life to Nanki-Poo!"
But as one month you have to live
As fellow citizen,
This toast with three times three we'll give—
"Long life to you—till then!"

[*Exit* POOH-BAH.

CHORUS. May all good fortune prosper you,
May you have health and riches too,
May you succeed in all you do!
Long life to you—till then!

(*Dance.*)

Enter KATISHA *melodramatically*

KAT. Your revels cease! Assist me, all of you!
CHORUS. Why, who is this whose evil eyes
Rain blight on our festivities?
KAT. I claim my perjured lover, Nanki-Poo!
Oh, fool! to shun delights that never cloy! [50]
CHORUS. Go, leave thy deadly work undone!
KAT. Come back, oh, shallow fool! come back to joy! [51]
CHORUS. Away, away! ill-favoured one!

NANK. (*aside to* YUM-YUM). Ah!
'Tis Katisha!
The maid of whom I told you. (*About to go.*)

KAT. (*detaining him*). No!
You shall not go,
These arms shall thus enfold you!

[45] and [46] *Two delightfully typical Gilbertian couplets, the one full of promise for the future, the other equally full of foreboding!*

[47] and [48] *Pitti-Sing's pert philosophy, with which she is plentifully endowed, is delightfully empha-sized. The average honeymoon of the well-to-do, which, of course, in Gilbert's book included Royalty, was of four weeks' duration!*

[49] *As in all vocal passages, recitative or aria, breath-ing is of the utmost importance. A wrongly taken breath can alter the meaning of a sung phrase quicker than a cat can wink his eye. This par-ticular solo is one of the glaring examples, so much so that for many years I was foxed as to the meaning. Practically all the Pooh-Bahs I have known always took a breath, or at least made a break, between the two lines: "But as one month you have to live" and "As fellow citizen" and invariably cut the comma that follows. The result was that it sounded as if Pooh-Bah was saying, or singing, that it was as a fellow citizen that he was giving this toast, and not that Nanki-Poo as a fellow citizen had a month to live. Neither the lyric nor the score indicates comma, pause or breath after "live."*

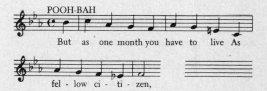

[50] and [51] *I have a sneaking suspicion that Gilbert was quite familiar with at least one of Benjamin Franklin's letters.*

SONG—KATISHA

KAT. (*addressing* NANKI-POO).

Oh fool, that fleest
My hallowed joys!
Oh blind, that seest
No equipoise!
Oh rash, that judgest
From half, the whole!
Oh base, that grudgest
Love's lightest dole!
Thy heart unbind,
Oh fool, oh blind!
Give me my place,
Oh rash, oh base!

CHORUS.

If she's thy bride, restore her place,
Oh fool, oh blind, oh rash, oh base!

KAT. (*addressing* YUM-YUM).

Pink cheek, that rulest
Where wisdom serves! [52]
Bright eye, that foolest
Heroic nerves!
Rose lip, that scornest
Lore-laden years!
Smooth tongue, that warnest
Who rightly hears!
Thy doom is nigh,
Pink cheek, bright eye!
Thy knell is rung,
Rose lip, smooth tongue!

CHORUS.

If true her tale, thy knell is rung,
Pink cheek, bright eye, rose lip, smooth tongue!

PITTI-SING.

Away, nor prosecute your quest—
From our intention, well expressed,
You cannot turn us!
The state of your connubial views
Towards the person you accuse
Does not concern us!
For he's going to marry Yum-Yum—

ALL. Yum-Yum! [53]

PITTI. Your anger pray bury,
For all will be merry,
I think you had better succumb—

ALL. Cumb—cumb!

PITTI. And join our expressions of glee.
On this subject I pray you be dumb—

ALL. Dumb—dumb.

PITTI. You'll find there are many
Who'll wed for a penny—
The word for your guidance is "Mum"—

ALL. Mum—mum!

PITTI. There's lots of good fish in the sea!

ALL. On this subject we pray you be dumb, etc.

SOLO—KATISHA [54]

The hour of gladness
Is dead and gone;

[52] *Benjamin Franklin? Of this there is no shadow of doubt, no possible, probable shadow of doubt whatever!*

[53] *Words and music on page 471.*

[54] *Was Gilbert always as harsh toward elderly women as has been maintained? He pokes a certain amount of fun at them, but was he invariably poking fun? Or did he sometimes emphasize the cruel fun other people poke at plain or homely people? In other words, did he try to show up human cruelty? Take this solo. To me this is not poking fun at elderly women but, rather, a tremendous expression of sympathy with the inevitable heartbreak of the woman who realizes she is plain; recognizes what love is; and understands that she will never know it. Granted Katisha becomes a virago with the next line— didn't Shakespeare say something about Hell and a woman scorned?*

In silent sadness
I live alone!
The hope I cherished
All lifeless lies,
And all has perished
Save love, which never dies!
Oh, faithless one, this insult you shall rue!
In vain for mercy on your knees you'll sue.
I'll tear the mask from your disguising!

NANK. (aside).   Now comes the blow!
KAT. Prepare yourselves for news surprising!
NANK. (aside).   How foil my foe?
KAT. No minstrel he, despite bravado!
YUM. (aside, struck by an idea). Ha! ha! I know!
KAT.   He is the son of your——

[NANKI-POO, YUM-YUM, and CHORUS, interrupting, sing Japanese words, to drown her voice.

   O ni! bikkuri shakkuri to!
KAT. In vain you interrupt with this tornado!
  He is the only son of your——
ALL. O ni! bikkuri shakkuri to!
KAT. I'll spoil——
ALL. O ni! bikkuri shakkuri to!
KAT.   Your gay gambado!
  He is the son——
ALL. O ni! bikkuri shakkuri to!
KAT.   Of your——
ALL. O ni! bikkuri shakkuri to!
KAT. The son of your——
ALL. O ni! bikkuri shakkuri to! oya! oya! [55]

ENSEMBLE

KATISHA

Ye torrents roar!
Ye tempests howl!
Your wrath outpour
With angry growl!
Do ye your worst, my vengeance call
Shall rise triumphant over all!
Prepare for woe,
Ye haughty lords,
At once I go
Mikado-wards,
My wrongs with vengeance shall be crowned!
My wrongs with vengeance shall be crowned!

THE OTHERS

We'll hear no more,
Ill-omened owl,
To joy we soar,
Despite your scowl!
The echoes of our festival
Shall rise triumphant over all!
Away you go,
Collect your hordes;
Proclaim your woe
In dismal chords;
We do not heed their dismal sound,
For joy reigns everywhere around.

[KATISHA rushes furiously up stage, clearing the crowd away right and left, finishing on steps at the back of stage.

END OF ACT I

ACT II

SCENE.—KO-KO's Garden

YUM-YUM discovered seated at her bridal toilet, surrounded by maidens, who are dressing her hair and painting her face and lips, as she judges of the effect in a mirror. [56]

[55] O ni! bikkuri shakkuri to! . . . oya! oya!
 O ni = devil
 bikkuri = to be surprised or shocked
 shakkuri = hiccup
 to = a word that is used to close a quote
 oya = a common exclamation

Putting this all together, it would read something like this: "Oh! You she devil! We are so shocked by you it makes us hiccup! Bah!"

[56] The second-act opening to The Mikado ranks, in my opinion, as one of the most beautiful, musically and visually. And yet it always amazes me that any young girl—especially a young Japanese girl—should perform her bridal toilet in her erstwhile fiancé's garden!

THE MIKADO

Dye the coral lip—
(Shades of the future: the TV make-up man!)

[57] Words and music on page 474.

[58] *I've heard this very beautiful song interpreted many ways. To my way of thinking there is but one way to sing it. No one word should be emphasized more than another. The music itself will supply the necessary emphasis where required. The naïveté (conscious or unconscious) of Yum-Yum in her speech leading into the song should be maintained. This can best be done if one imagines a slowly turning wheel, never varying in its speed, and phrases the song to fit the turn of the wheel, allowing but one slight retard at the very end of each verse. As you look at the song you will see that it is actually phrased this way, and each phrase should be taken in one breath. Particular care should be taken with the following phrases: "I mean to rule the earth, As he the sky—(breath) We really know our worth, The sun and I! (breath) I mean to rule the earth, As he the sky— We really know our worth, (breath) The sun and I!" Originally this song was placed in the first act, coming just after the Quartet and Chorus "So please you, Sir" (see page 420). To lead into it Yum-Yum had additional dialogue: "How pitiable is the condition of a young and innocent child brought from the gloom of a ladies' academy into the full-blown blaze of her own marriage; and with a man for whom I care nothing! True, he loves me, but everybody does that." Within a very few days of the opening this dialogue had been cut, the present line taking its place, and the song transplanted to its present position in the second act.*

[59] Words and music on page 476.

[60] "Observe his flame." *Several times I have been questioned about whether this should not read "Observe her flame." Indeed, some number of years back, the late John Golden stopped me in the street to put the question. The answer is a definite No! The allusion is to His Majesty the Sun and his "flame," the Moon's Celestial Highness.*

SOLO—PITTI-SING *and* CHORUS OF GIRLS [57]

CHORUS.

Braid the raven hair—
   Weave the supple tress—
Deck the maiden fair,
   In her loveliness—
Paint the pretty face—
   Dye the coral lip—
Emphasize the grace
   Of her ladyship!
Art and nature, thus allied,
Go to make a pretty bride.

SOLO—PITTI-SING

Sit with downcast eye—
   Let it brim with dew—
Try if you can cry—
   We will do so, too.
When you're summoned, start
   Like a frightened roe—
Flutter, little heart,
   Colour, come and go!
Modesty at marriage-tide
Well becomes a pretty bride!

CHORUS

Braid the raven hair, etc.

[*Exeunt* PITTI-SING, PEEP-BO, *and* CHORUS.

YUM. Yes, I am indeed beautiful! Sometimes I sit and wonder, in my artless Japanese way, why it is that I am so much more attractive than anybody else in the whole world. Can this be vanity? No! Nature is lovely and rejoices in her loveliness. I am a child of Nature, and take after my mother.

[58] SONG—YUM-YUM [59]

The sun, whose rays
Are all ablaze
   With ever-living glory,
Does not deny
His majesty—
   He scorns to tell a story!
He don't exclaim,
"I blush for shame,
   So kindly be indulgent."
But, fierce and bold,
In fiery gold,
   He glories all effulgent!

   I mean to rule the earth,
      As he the sky—
   We really know our worth,
      The sun and I!

Observe his [60] flame,
That placid dame,
   The moon's Celestial Highness:
There's not a trace
Upon her face

Of diffidence or shyness:
She borrows light
That, through the night,
    Mankind may all acclaim her!
And, truth to tell,
She lights up well,
    So I, for one, don't blame her!

Ah, pray make no mistake,
    We are not shy;
We're very wide awake,
    The moon and I!

That placid dame

Enter PITTI-SING *and* PEEP-BO

YUM. Yes, everything seems to smile upon me. I am to be married to-day to the man I love best, and I believe I am the very happiest girl in Japan!

PEEP. The happiest girl indeed, for she is indeed to be envied who has attained happiness in all but perfection.

YUM. In "all but" perfection?

PEEP. Well, dear, it can't be denied that the fact that your husband is to be beheaded in a month is, in its way, a drawback. It does seem to take the top off it, you know.

PITTI. I don't know about that. It all depends!

PEEP. At all events, *he* will find it a drawback.

PITTI. Not necessarily. Bless you, it all depends!

YUM. (*in tears*). I think it very indelicate of you to refer to such a subject on such a day. If my married happiness *is* to be—to be——

PEEP. Cut short.

YUM. Well, cut short—in a month, can't you let me forget it? (*Weeping.*)

Enter NANKI-POO, *followed by* PISH-TUSH

NANK. Yum-Yum in tears—and on her wedding morn!

YUM. (*sobbing*). They've been reminding me that in a month you're to be beheaded! (*Bursts into tears.*)

PITTI. Yes, we've been reminding her that you're to be beheaded. (*Bursts into tears.*)

PEEP. It's quite true, you know, you *are* to be beheaded! (*Bursts into tears.*)

NANK. (*aside*). Humph! Now, [61] some bridegrooms would be depressed by this sort of thing! (*Aloud.*) A month? Well, what's a month? Bah! These divisions of time are purely arbitrary. Who says twenty-four hours make a day?

PITTI. There's a popular impression to that effect.

NANK. Then we'll efface it. We'll call each second a minute—each minute an hour—each hour a day—and each day a year. At that rate we've about thirty years of married happiness before us!

PEEP. And, at that rate, this interview has already lasted four hours and three-quarters!

[*Exit* PEEP-BO.

YUM. (*still sobbing*). Yes. How time flies when one is thoroughly enjoying oneself.

NANK. That's the way to look at it! Don't let's be downhearted! There's a silver lining to every cloud.

YUM. Certainly. Let's—let's be perfectly happy! (*Almost in tears.*)

PISH-TUSH. By all means. Let's—let's thoroughly enjoy ourselves.

[61] *For many years this line was read: "How some bridegrooms would be depressed . . ." It seems that one edition of the printed libretto contained this particular misprint, and it was not until many years had passed that the stage director, in looking over Gilbert's prompt book, discovered the error, one that gives quite a different reading and meaning to the line.*

THE MIKADO

[62] Quartettes of this description are very difficult to stage. Gilbert took the line of least resistance, yielding, I imagine, to Sullivan's probable insistence that this was a musical number which must in no way be disturbed. The result was that it became nothing more than a straight concert platform ensemble. Musically, it is fine and beautiful, but to me it was always uninteresting. The same was true of what is known as "The chippy-chopper trio" in the first act. That one I found more or less easy to restage and, while losing nothing of the music and words, imparting some action to it. But this quartette is more—much more—difficult, extremely so when it must be staged "in the round." I did eventually manage this, and in doing so, unwittingly prepared the ground for one of the most colossal "break-ups" it has been my lot to witness. I once began the number with the four people standing facing each other around a low Japanese table in the center of the stage. Unfortunately, in the preceding dialogue, Nanki-Poo had badly fluffed the words "married happiness." They came out as "harried mappiness." Not content to leave bad enough alone, he attempted to correct himself—"parried mappiness . . . er . . . married pappiness"—and by this time, he was lost, the other three were beginning to giggle, the audience was laughing, and the conductor picked up the introductory bars in an effort to save the situation. Everything would have been fine—if I had not staged them as I did. Coming face to face was too much. Yum-Yum's first line came out something like "Brightly dawns our giggling gig" and the rest followed suit. It was the most uproarious madrigal of all time, and the audience loved it! But . . . !

[63] The Pish-Tush, Frederick Bovill, who was at first intended to sing the bass line of the madrigal, could not, in spite of a fine baritone voice, plumb the necessary vocal depths to Sullivan's satisfaction. To ease this situation Gilbert created a new character, Go-To. He is usually the Noble Lord who demands of Nanki-Poo, just after his first entrance, who is he who asks this question.

[64] Words and music on page 478.

[65] It was the Martin Beck Theater. The year, 1939. The month, January. The performance, a mid-week matinee of The Mikado. I had made my final exit in Act I and had retired to my dressing room, had removed my black, heavy Ko-Ko tunic, and had donned a robe. I then stretched out on a settee, leaving instructions for my dresser to see to it that I was awake and properly dressed for my first entrance in Act II. With assurances from the dresser that this would be so, I relaxed. Suddenly there came a voice in my ear, the voice of the man who was singing the role of Go-To, saying, "Martyn, you're off!" My dresser had failed me! In a dazed state I grabbed my costume tunic, and foggily realized that Go-To had made his way from stage to dressing room to call me, and that a "stage-wait" of minutes was going on. I got onto the stage at last, still hooking up my costume, to find Nanki-Poo and Yum-Yum

PITTI. It's—it's absurd to cry. (*Trying to force a laugh.*)
YUM. Quite ridiculous! (*Trying to laugh.*)

[*All break into a forced and melancholy laugh.*

[62] MADRIGAL

[63] YUM-YUM, PITTI-SING, NANKI-POO, *and* PISH-TUSH [64]

Brightly dawns our wedding day;
  Joyous hour, we give thee greeting!
  Whither, whither art thou fleeting?
Fickle moment, prithee stay!
  What though mortal joys be hollow?
  Pleasures come, if sorrows follow:
Though the tocsin sound, ere long,
  Ding dong! Ding dong!
Yet until the shadows fall
Over one and over all,
Sing a merry madrigal—
      A madrigal!

Fal-la—fal-la! etc. (*Ending in tears.*)

Let us dry the ready tear,
  Though the hours are surely creeping
  Little need for woeful weeping,
Till the sad sundown is near.
  All must sip the cup of sorrow—
  I to-day and thou to-morrow;
This the close of every song—
  Ding dong! Ding dong!
What, though solemn shadows fall,
Sooner, later, over all?
Sing a merry madrigal—
      A madrigal!

Fal-la—fal-la! etc. (*Ending in tears.*)

[*Exeunt* PITTI-SING *and* PISH-TUSH.

[NANKI-POO *embraces* YUM-YUM. *Enter* KO-KO. [65]
NANKI-POO *releases* YUM-YUM.

KO. Go on—don't mind me.
NANK. I'm afraid we're distressing you.
KO. Never mind, I must get used to it. Only please do it by degrees. Begin by putting your arm round her waist. (NANKI-POO *does so.*) There; let me get used to that first.
YUM. Oh, wouldn't you like to retire? It must pain you to see us so affectionate together!
KO. No, I must learn to bear it! Now oblige me by allowing her head to rest on your shoulder.
NANK. Like that? (*He does so.* KO-KO *much affected.*)
KO. I am much obliged to you. Now—kiss her! (*He does so.* KO-KO *writhes with anguish.*) Thank you—it's simple torture!
YUM. Come, come, bear up. After all, it's only for a month.
KO. No. It's no use deluding oneself with false hopes.
NANK. } What do you mean?
YUM. }
KO. (*to* YUM-YUM). My child—my poor child! (*Aside.*) How shall I break it to her? (*Aloud.*) My little bride that was to have been?

YUM. (*delighted*). *Was* to have been?

KO. Yes, you never can be mine!

NANK.⎫ (*in ecstasy*). ⎧What!
YUM. ⎭   ⎩I'm so glad!

KO. I've just ascertained that, by the Mikado's law, when a married man is beheaded his wife is buried alive. [66]

YUM.⎫ Buried alive!
NANK.⎭

KO. Buried alive. It's a most unpleasant death.

NANK. But whom did you get that from?

KO. Oh, from Pooh-Bah. He's my Solicitor.

YUM. But he may be mistaken!

KO. So I thought; so I consulted the Attorney-General, the Lord Chief Justice, the Master of the Rolls, the Judge Ordinary, and the Lord Chancellor. They're all of the same opinion. Never knew such unanimity on a point of law in my life!

NANK. But stop a bit! This law has never been put in force.

KO. Not yet. You see, flirting is the only crime punishable with decapitation, and married men never flirt.

NANK. Of course, they don't. I quite forgot that! Well, I suppose I may take it that my dream of happiness is at an end!

YUM. Darling—I don't want to appear selfish, and I love you with all my heart—I don't suppose I shall ever love anybody else half as much—but when I agreed to marry you—my own—I had no idea—pet—that I should have to be buried alive in a month!

NANK. Nor I! It's the very first I've heard of it!

YUM. It—it makes a difference, doesn't it?

NANK. It *does* make a difference, of course.

YUM. You see—burial alive—it's such a stuffy death!

NANK. I call it a beast of a death.

YUM. You see my difficulty, don't you?

NANK. Yes, and I see my own. If I insist on your carrying out your promise, I doom you to a hideous death: if I release you, you marry Ko-Ko at once!

[67] TRIO.—YUM-YUM, NANKI-POO, *and* KO-KO [68]

YUM.   Here's a how-de-do!
              If I marry you,
          When your time has come to perish,
          Then the maiden whom you cherish
              Must be slaughtered, too!
              Here's a how-de-do!

NANK.   Here's a pretty mess!
              In a month, or less,
          I must die without a wedding!
          Let the bitter tears I'm shedding
              Witness my distress,
              Here's a pretty mess!

KO.   Here's a state of things!
              To her life she clings!
          Matrimonial devotion
          Doesn't seem to suit her notion—
              Burial it brings!
              Here's a state of things!

at their wits' end, wondering what to do or say next. The thought occurred to me that the best way to make some sort of profit out of a bad thing was just to speak the line Gilbert had allotted me—and it worked. The only trouble was that Derek Oldham, the Nanki-Poo, wittingly or unwittingly changed one word of his next line and said: "I'm afraid we're disturbing you."

[66] Gilbert's biographers have gone to great pains in many instances to point out the macabre ideas he had regarding fitting the punishment to the crime, and the punishment for beheading the heir apparent (see the Mikado's song "My object all sublime," pages 434-435 and Note 82) which included "boiling oil or melted lead." To me, the most macabre of all is the burying alive of the wife of any man who is beheaded. Personally, I don't think even Gilbert's Mikado could have dreamed that one up. This was Ko-Ko, who, knowing of his Emperor's propensity for "innocent merriment," just pulled it out of the hat for his own ends, bribing Pooh-Bah to support him in this! And this is the way I always tried to convey it.

[67] Of all the numbers in Gilbert and Sullivan operettas, this has probably turned out to be the one that draws the largest number of encores—including the famous Bells trio from H.M.S. Pinafore. My average with the Bells was five. With "Here's a how-de-do!" the record was eight, and the average six!

Through the years there have been many complaints regarding encores of any sort, and it became the policy at one time of the D'Oyly Carte to attempt to discourage them. Our musical director once told me that he was the person who decided when, and if, an encore should be taken. I'm afraid I took issue with him—over this very number—saying that it was the public which made the decision (probably aided and abetted by the performer on the stage). My first record of seven encores occurred that same evening!

In this matter of encores, and just as a matter of interest, I append a quotation from Sir Arthur Sullivan's diary dated 14th March 1885:—"New Opera, 'The Mikado' or 'The Town of Titipu,' produced at the Savoy Theatre with every sign of success. A most brilliant house. Tremendous reception. All went very well except Grossmith, whose nervousness nearly upset the piece. A treble encore for the 'Three Little Maids' and for 'The Flowers that Bloom in the Spring.' Seven encores taken—might have taken twelve! (The emphasis and the exclamation mark are mine.)"

[68] Words and music on page 481.

[69] *Nanki may have been serious in the first act regarding his suicide, but here I am sure that he is most certainly pulling a fast one. By this time he knows that Ko-Ko will never permit him to do such a thing. And I've always had a sneaking sort of feeling that he had some sneaking sort of idea that the Mikado and Katisha would shortly be on the scene, and that he was already planning ahead!*

[70] *I am not the only person who has at some time or other failed to make an entrance on cue (see Note 65). The D'Oyly Carte was in Boston in 1939 and playing The Mikado at the Colonial Theater. Derek Oldham was the Nanki-Poo and we had just reached the point where Ko-Ko has said: "Why, I shall have to be executed in your place!" to which Nanki replies: "It would certainly seem so!" At this point Ko-Ko turns upstage and sees Pooh-Bah, who has just entered—at least he should see him. On this occasion, however, Sydney Granville—of blessed memory—was not to be seen, either just in the wings, or even right off on the side of the stage. Many of the chorus were there and I tried to indicate to them that "Granny" was "off," but the idea didn't seem to penetrate! Derek was by this time getting somewhat frantic, and in a very hoarse stage whisper, said: "What's the matter?" From then on the dialogue went something like this (Derek and I taking and sharing Pooh-Bah's lines between us):*

ME.	*I think I see the Mikado approaching the city.*
DEREK.	*The Mikado!*
ME.	*Yes. He'll be here in ten minutes. He's probably coming to see . . . etc.*
DEREK.	*Very well, then—behead me.*
ME.	*What, now?*
DEREK.	*Certainly; at once.*
ME.	*Chop it off?*
DEREK.	*Chop it off, Ko-Ko!*
ME.	*My good sir, I don't go about . . . etc.* (POOH-BAH *rushes on*)
POOH-BAH.	*The Mikado and his suite . . .*
ME.	*We've said that.*
POOH-BAH.	*. . . and will be here in ten . . .*
ME.	*We've said that, too.*
POOH-BAH.	*As Lord High Execution . . .*
DEREK.	*I've said that . . .*
ME.	*Yes . . . and I've got to behead him in a month . . . etc.*

And we finally got back into the scene! PHEW! And all the time "Granny" had been in the wings, but out of sight, talking to the stage manager!

[71] *To all would-be do-it-themselves: Throw this line away; that is, as if unimportant. And add the word "Ko-Ko" in between the two, thus: "Chop it off, Ko-Ko, chop it off!" Gilbert never wrote it this way, but he never forbade it. And it is much funnier.*

[72] *A blue-bottle is one of those peculiarly large and dazzlingly blue—or green—flies, known in the United States as horseflies.*

ENSEMBLE

YUM-YUM *and* NANKI-POO	KO-KO
With a passion that's intense I worship and adore,	With a passion that's intense You worship and adore,
But the laws of common sense We oughtn't to ignore.	But the laws of common sense You oughtn't to ignore.
If what he says is true, 'Tis death to marry you!	If what I say is true, 'Tis death to marry you!
Here's a pretty state of things! Here's a pretty how-de-do!	Here's a pretty state of things! Here's a pretty how-de-do!

[*Exit* YUM-YUM.

KO. (*going up to* NANKI-POO). My poor boy, I'm really very sorry for you.

NANK. Thanks, old fellow. I'm sure you are.

KO. You see I'm quite helpless.

NANK. I quite see that.

KO. I can't conceive anything more distressing than to have one's marriage broken off at the last moment. But you shan't be disappointed of a wedding—you shall come to mine.

NANK. It's awfully kind of you, but that's impossible.

KO. Why so?

NANK. To-day I die. [69]

KO. What do you mean?

NANK. I can't live without Yum-Yum. This afternoon I perform the Happy Despatch.

KO. No, no—pardon me—I can't allow that.

NANK. Why not?

KO. Why, hang it all, you're under contract to die by the hand of the Public Executioner in a month's time! If you kill yourself, what's to become of me? Why, I shall have to be executed in your place!

NANK. It would certainly seem so!

Enter POOH-BAH [70]

KO. Now then, Lord Mayor, what is it?

POOH. The Mikado and his suite are approaching the city, and will be here in ten minutes.

KO. The Mikado! He's coming to see whether his orders have been carried out! (*To* NANKI-POO.) Now look here, you know—this is getting serious—a bargain's a bargain, and you really mustn't frustrate the ends of justice by committing suicide. As a man of honour and a gentleman, you are bound to die ignominiously by the hands of the Public Executioner.

NANK. Very well, then—behead me.

KO. What, now?

NANK. Certainly; at once.

POOH. Chop it off! Chop it off! [71]

KO. My good sir, I don't go about prepared to execute gentlemen at a moment's notice. Why, I never even killed a blue-bottle! [72]

POOH. Still, as Lord High Executioner——

KO. My good sir, as Lord High Executioner, I've got to behead him in a month. I'm not ready yet. I don't know how it's done. I'm going to take lessons. I mean to begin with a guinea pig, and work my way through the animal kingdom till I come to a Second Trombone. Why, you don't suppose that, as a humane man, I'd have accepted the post of Lord High Executioner if I hadn't thought the duties were purely nominal? I *can't* kill you—I can't kill anything! I can't kill anybody! (*Weeps.*)

NANK. Come, my poor fellow, we all have unpleasant duties to discharge at times; after all, what is it? If I don't mind, why should you? Remember, sooner or later it must be done.

KO. (*springing up suddenly*). *Must it?* I'm not so sure about that!

NANK. What do you mean?

KO. Why should I kill you when making an affidavit that you've been executed will do just as well? Here are plenty of witnesses—the Lord Chief Justice, Lord High Admiral, Commander-in-Chief, Secretary of State for the Home Department, First Lord of the Treasury, and Chief Commissioner of Police.

NANK. But where are they?

KO. There they are. They'll all swear to it—won't you? (*To* POOH-BAH.)

POOH. Am I to understand that all of us high Officers of State are required to perjure ourselves to ensure your safety?

KO. Why not? You'll be grossly insulted, as usual.

POOH. Will the insult be cash down, or at a date?

KO. It will be a ready-money transaction. [73]

POOH. (*Aside.*) Well, it will be a useful discipline. (*Aloud.*) Very good. Choose your fiction, and I'll endorse it! (*Aside.*) Ha! ha! Family Pride, how do you like *that*, my buck?

NANK. But I tell you that life without Yum-Yum——

KO. Oh, Yum-Yum, Yum-Yum! Bother Yum-Yum! Here, Commissionaire (*to* POOH-BAH), go and fetch Yum-Yum. (*Exit* POOH-BAH.) Take Yum-Yum and marry Yum-Yum, only go away and never come back again. (*Enter* POOH-BAH *with* YUM-YUM.) Here she is. Yum-Yum, are you particularly busy?

YUM. Not particularly.

KO. You've five minutes to spare?

YUM. Yes.

KO. Then go along with his Grace the Archbishop of Titipu; he'll marry you at once.

YUM. But if I'm to be buried alive?

KO. Now, don't ask any questions, but do as I tell you, and Nanki-Poo will explain all.

NANK. But one moment——

KO. Not for worlds. Here comes the Mikado, no doubt to ascertain whether I've obeyed his decree, and if he finds you alive I shall have the greatest difficulty in persuading him that I've beheaded you. (*Exeunt* NANKI-POO *and* YUM-YUM, *followed by* POOH-BAH.) Close thing that, for here he comes!

[*Exit* KO-KO

March.—Enter procession, heralding MIKADO, *with* KATISHA

Entrance of MIKADO *and* KATISHA [74]

("*March of the Mikado's troops.*")

CHORUS.	Miya sama, miya sama, [75]
	On n'm-ma no mayé ni
	Pira-Pira suru no wa
	Nan gia na
	Toko tonyaré tonyaré na?

DUET—MIKADO *and* KATISHA [76]

MIK.	From every kind of man
	Obedience I expect;
	I'm the Emperor of Japan—

| KAT. | And I'm his daughter-in-law elect! |
| | He'll marry his son |

[73] *Gilbert gives no directions regarding business here, but at this point Ko-Ko pulls out a bag, or a pile of money, which he clinks in front of Pooh-Bah. Pooh-Bah, having satisfied his crooked conscience, agrees, and Ko-Ko passes the bribe across. There have been times when an imp of mischief has seized me and I have done things that were not in the book. I once attached a longish piece of elastic to the money and, apparently inadvertently, missed Pooh-Bah's hand when passing the money over. He hurriedly—or as hurriedly as he could in all his padding— stooped to pick it up, only to see it flash back up into my hand. Well, it was a good gag—for one performance, after which the edict was "Out!" (I must confess that it has gone back in many times. And it is still a good gag!)*

[74] *The march is repeated twice. The Mikado and Katisha enter dancing the second time through.*

It has always seemed such a pity to me that present-day performances of The Mikado, as given by the D'Oyly Carte Company, should have the Emperor make his entrance on foot. Gilbert gives no instructions for how he should make it, so one must presume that he intended it that way. I always feel that following this Royal March something spectacular should happen (as, indeed, it should on Ko-Ko's entrance in the first act).

The film of The Mikado, made at Pinewood, England, in 1938, did give the Mikado a grand entrance. Here he was carried seated atop a magnificent litter. I'm afraid I have taken a frame from their celluloid whenever I've been called on to direct this show, stage or TV. Granted there was one occasion when one of the men carrying the litter stumbled, fell, and deposited the Mikado on the floor—but even that was spectacular if not effective.

[75] *Miya sama, etc. Contrary to popular belief—a belief that continued for some considerable time —this is not just jargon, nor is it, as it was once alleged a Japanese told Sullivan, who did not know the meaning of the words, "the foulest song ever sung in the lowest teahouse in Japan." Were this true my heart would bleed for the number of lovely young things who have, in amateur performances—not to mention professional ones—unwittingly given utterance to such soul-sullying syllables! But it is not true.*

Leslie Bailey's The Gilbert and Sullivan Book says that a well-known authority on things Japanese, Mr. Diosy, actually supplied Sullivan with some real Japanese music for these words; that the music was a famous Japanese war march, and the translation was:

> *Oh, my Prince, oh, my Prince,*
> *What is that fluttering in the wind*
> *Before your imperial charger?*
> *Know ye not it is the imperial banner*
> *Of silken brocade,*
> *The signal for chastisement of the rebels?*

[76] Words and music on page 485.

(He's only got one)
To his daughter-in-law elect.

MIK. My morals have been declared
Particularly correct;

KAT. But they're nothing at all, compared
With those of his daughter-in-law elect!
Bow—Bow—
To his daughter-in-law elect!

ALL. Bow—Bow—
To his daughter-in-law elect.

MIK. In a fatherly kind of way
I govern each tribe and sect,
All cheerfully own my sway—

KAT. Except his daughter-in-law elect!
As tough as a bone,
With a will of her own,
Is his daughter-in-law elect!

MIK. My nature is love and light—
My freedom from all defect—

KAT. Is insignificant quite,
Compared with his daughter-in-law elect!
Bow—Bow—
To his daughter-in-law elect!

ALL. Bow—Bow—
To his daughter-in-law elect!

[77] Words and music on page 487.

[78] An allusion to a number of German Lutheran
evangelists who were visiting England.

SONG—MIKADO *and* CHORUS

A more humane Mikado never
Did in Japan exist,
To nobody second,
I'm certainly reckoned
A true philanthropist.
It is my very humane endeavour
To make, to some extent,
Each evil liver
A running river
Of harmless merriment.

My object all sublime [77]
I shall achieve in time—
To let the punishment fit the crime—
The punishment fit the crime;
And make each prisoner pent
Unwillingly represent
A source of innocent merriment!
Of innocent merriment!

All prosy dull society sinners,
Who chatter and bleat and bore,
Are sent to hear sermons
From mystical Germans
Who preach from ten till four. [78]
The amateur tenor, whose vocal villainies
All desire to shirk,
Shall, during off-hours,

Extracted by terrified amateurs

Exhibit his powers
To Madame Tussaud's waxwork.

The lady who dyes a chemical yellow
Or stains her grey hair puce,
Or pinches her figger,
Is blacked like a nigger [79]
With permanent walnut juice.
The idiot who, in railway carriages,
Scribbles on window-panes,
We only suffer
To ride on a buffer
In Parliamentary trains. [80]

My object all sublime, etc.

CHORUS.   His object all sublime, etc.

The advertising quack who wearies
With tales of countless cures,
His teeth, I've enacted,
Shall all be extracted
By terrified amateurs.
The music-hall singer attends a series
Of masses and fugues and "ops"
By Bach, interwoven
With Spohr and Beethoven,
At classical Monday Pops. [81]

The billiard sharp whom any one catches,
His doom's extremely hard—
He's made to dwell—
In a dungeon cell
On a spot that's always barred.
And there he plays extravagant matches
In fitless finger-stalls
On a cloth untrue,
With a twisted cue
And elliptical billiard balls!

My object all sublime, etc. [82]

CHORUS.   His object all sublime, etc.

Enter POOH-BAH, KO-KO, and PITTI-SING. *All kneel*

(POOH-BAH *hands a paper to* KO-KO.)

KO. I am honoured in being permitted to welcome your Majesty. I guess the object of your Majesty's visit—your wishes have been attended to. The execution has taken place.

MIK. Oh, you've had an execution, have you?

KO. Yes. The Coroner has just handed me his certificate.

POOH. I am the Coroner. (KO-KO *hands certificate to* MIKADO.)

MIK. And this is the certificate of his death. (*Reads.*) "At Titipu, in the presence of the Lord Chancellor, Lord Chief Justice, Attorney-General, Secretary of State for the Home Department, Lord Mayor, and Groom of the Second Floor Front——"

POOH. They were all present, your Majesty. I counted them myself.

MIK. Very good house. I wish I'd been in time for the performance.

KO. A tough fellow he was, too—a man of gigantic strength. His struggles were terrific. It was really a remarkable scene.

MIK. Describe it.

[79] In modern English editions of the libretto and vocal score this line now reads:

"Or pinches her figure
Is painted with vigour . . ."

Sir Alan P. Herbert (see Princess Ida, page 374, Note 38) had provided Mr. Carte with several alternatives:

"Or stains her grey hair green,
Is taken to Dover
And painted all over
A horrible ultramarine."

"Or stains her grey hair puce,
Is made to wear feathers
In all the worst weathers,
And legibly labeled 'Goose.' "

"Or stains her grey hair blue
Is made to wear feathers
In all the worst weathers
And live in a draughty zoo."

Well—I must agree that Carte chose the best, but I am still somewhat fogged as to how it is possible to paint any one with "vigour and permanent walnut juice." What color is "vigour"? Or is it some sort of special pigment? Here again I have taken some liberty with the printed word and have had the Mikado sing either "painted, with vigour, with permanent walnut juice" or "painted with vigour, or stained with walnut juice."

[80] A nickname arising from the Railway Act of 1884 which laid down regulations and conditions for the railway such as the penny-a-mile fare.

[81] The Chappell and Company "Popular Concerts" held on Mondays at St. James's Hall in Piccadilly.

[82] For a gentleman whose sublime object it is to make each criminal a source of innocent merriment by fitting the punishment to the crime, donning a make-up that literally terrifies small children is in itself a crime for which a most fitting punishment should be evolved. I offer no prizes for suggestions. The more benign and bland the Mikado is the more humorous his lines make him become. An early photograph of Richard Temple, who created the role, depicts him in this manner. The only concession to the bizarre should be the complete blotting out of the actor's own eyebrows and the painting in of huge false ones, after the manner of the Japanese Emperor himself.

THE MIKADO

[83] Words and music on page 491.

[84] *Very shortly after the production I directed of the TV version of The Mikado, starring Groucho Marx as Ko-Ko and Helen Traubel as Katisha, I received a letter questioning Groucho's traditional ax. The letter said that an ax was not a snickersnee, and would I please explain. I looked the word up in the Oxford and in the Webster dictionaries and found that "snickersee" is a marrying of two words, "steken" (stick) and "snijen" (cut), and that it is, in effect, a knife used in cut-and-thrust fighting. I must confess I had always imagined Gilbert had invented the word. Ah, well—and lackaday! So the ax is technically wrong. But Ricketts designed it, and Carte approved it—in 1926.*

[85] *So now it becomes "sabre"! Was Ko-Ko also konnected with the Kavalry Korps?*

[86] *Very macabre humor, but rib-tickling humor for all that. And Madame Tussaud once said that the heads of many of the "aristos" actually smiled after the guillotine had fallen! Incidentally, Gilbert does mention Madame Tussaud in the Mikado's song. (Pronounced "Too-so.")*

TRIO AND CHORUS
KO-KO, PITTI-SING, POOH-BAH *and* CHORUS [83]

KO.
> The criminal cried, as he dropped him down,
> In a state of wild alarm—
> With a frightful, frantic, fearful frown,
> I bared my big right arm.
> I seized him by his little pig-tail,
> And on his knees fell he,
> As he squirmed and struggled,
> And gurgled and guggled,
> I drew my snickersnee! [84]
> Oh, never shall I
> Forget the cry,
> Or the shriek that shriekèd he,
> As I gnashed my teeth,
> When from its sheath
> I drew my snickersnee!

CHORUS

> We know him well,
> He cannot tell
> Untrue or groundless tales—
> He always tries
> To utter lies,
> And every time he fails.

PITTI.
> He shivered and shook as he gave the sign
> For the stroke he didn't deserve;
> When all of a sudden his eye met mine,
> And it seemed to brace his nerve;
> For he nodded his head and kissed his hand,
> And he whistled an air, did he,
> As the sabre true [85]
> Cut cleanly through
> His cervical vertebræ!

> When a man's afraid,
> A beautiful maid
> Is a cheering sight to see;
> And it's oh, I'm glad
> That moment sad
> Was soothed by sight of me!

CHORUS

> Her terrible tale
> You can't assail,
> With truth it quite agrees:
> Her taste exact
> For faultless fact
> Amounts to a disease.

POOH.
> Now though you'd have said that head was dead
> (For its owner dead was he),
> It stood on its neck, with a smile well-bred,
> And bowed three times to me! [86]
> It was none of your impudent off-hand nods,
> But as humble as could be;
> For it clearly knew

The deference due
To a man of pedigree!
And it's oh, I vow,
This deathly bow
Was a touching sight to see;
Though trunkless, yet
It couldn't forget
The deference due to me!

CHORUS

This haughty youth,
He speaks the truth
Whenever he finds it pays:
And in this case
It all took place
Exactly as he says!

[*Exeunt* CHORUS.

MIK. All this is very interesting, and I should like to have seen it. But we came about a totally different matter. A year ago my son, the heir to the throne of Japan, bolted from our Imperial Court.

KO. Indeed! Had he any reason to be dissatisfied with his position?

KAT. None whatever. On the contrary, I was going to marry him—yet he fled!

POOH. I am surprised that he should have fled from one so lovely!

KAT. That's not true.

POOH. No!

KAT. You hold that I am not beautiful because my face is plain. But you know nothing; you are still unenlightened. Learn, then, that it is not in the face alone that beauty is to be sought. My face is unattractive!

POOH. It is.

KAT. But I have a left shoulder-blade that is a miracle of loveliness. People come miles to see it. My right elbow has a fascination that few can resist.

POOH. Allow me!

KAT. It is on view Tuesdays and Fridays, on presentation of visiting card. As for my circulation, it is the largest in the world.

KO. And yet he fled!

MIK. And is now masquerading in this town, disguised as a Second Trombone.

KO. ⎫
POOH. ⎬ A Second Trombone!
PITTI. ⎭

MIK. Yes; would it be troubling you too much if I asked you to produce him? He goes by the name of——

KAT. Nanki-Poo.

MIK. Nanki-Poo.

KO. It's quite easy. That is, it's rather difficult. In point of fact, he's gone abroad!

MIK. Gone abroad! His address.

KO. Knightsbridge! [87]

KAT. (*who is reading certificate of death*). Ha!

MIK. What's the matter?

KAT. See here—his name—Nanki-Poo—beheaded this morning. Oh, where shall I find another? Where shall I find another?

[KO-KO, POOH-BAH, *and* PITTI-SING *fall on their knees.*

[87] Knightsbridge. *A thoroughfare in London running along the south side of Hyde Park. It was here that a Japanese Village had been built as a part of a Japanese exhibition. Naturally, the line brought a big laugh in those early days. When The Mikado was revived, however, Gilbert was the first to realize that, the exhibition having packed its pagodas and departed several years previously, Knightsbridge no longer had any particular power to produce a laugh. So he decreed that in all future performances Nanki-Poo's address should be localized to one of topical significance. That accounts for the fact that when playing in Boston I used the address "Wellesley"; in New York, "Jones' Beach"; and on one occasion I used "Broadhurst," the theater at which The Hot Mikado was running at the same time that we were at the Martin Beck. "Bojangles" Robinson was the Mikado in that production, which I regret to say I could not see because we were running concurrently. What does strike me most significantly about that particular season is that there were three Mikados running on Broadway simultaneously: the D'Oyly Carte Company's production, The Hot Mikado, and the Federal Theater's The Swing Mikado.*

[88] *As we played the scene, the Mikado did not address the line, "I forget the punishment, etc." to Katisha. What happened was this. As the Mikado laughed he dug Ko-Ko in the ribs—and by the way, Ko-Ko did not laugh at the end of his line. But he did laugh, and he did dig the Mikado in return, only to find himself the object of tremendous wrath. He promptly flung himself down on his knees again, instantly joined by Pooh-Bah and Pitti-Sing. The Mikado then directed the line at the three of them. It seems to me that this bit of action is an improvement on the directions in the text.*

[89] *This speech is broken by groans from the luckless three on the floor, thus:*

". . . boiling oil in it, I fancy." (Groan)
". . . but I'm not sure." (Groan)
". . . something humorous, but lingering . . ."
(Groans from Pooh and Pitti. Ko-Ko thinks he ought to laugh, tries, and fails miserably.)

One evening my laugh, quite inadvertently, happened to resemble a musical phrase from a popular tune that was a complete rage in England at the time, and the audience seemed to be inclined to pick it up. To make sure of this, I deliberately used the actual phrase at the next performance, and the result was that the audience went into hysterics. I was right—they did know the song. A house full of Gilbert and Sullivan fans, and they knew "The Woodpecker's Song"!

Unfortunately the Mikado made a protest to the stage director. Apparently he felt it caused him to lose face—er—dignity. All nontraditional laughs were decreed out from then on. Looking back on such instances of stuffed-shirtedness, I see more to induce "loss of face" in the business wherein Pooh-Bah, after complete collapse following ". . . or melted lead" is rocked back and forth by Ko-Ko and Pitti-Sing until he finally rolls over the top of both of them. The roll-over was Gilbert's idea, and I believe even that has often been cut in recent years. It's a great pity, for both Gilbert's occasional slapstick "business" and that of imaginative performers over the years has often been very funny.

[90] *A source of constant surprise to me is that Gilbert—and Sullivan—did not cut this number when they were cutting everything else. Polite applause is all it ever receives. Without it the show would move much faster, and when possible I have always had Katisha and the Mikado exit on his line, "Virtue is triumphant only in theatrical performances." It's such a good exit line, and the following dialogue between Ko-Ko and Pooh-Bah and Pitti-Sing carries on so much better than the song does.*

MIK. (*looking at paper*). Dear, dear, dear! this is very tiresome. (*To* KO-KO.) My poor fellow, in your anxiety to carry out my wishes you have beheaded the heir to the throne of Japan!

KO. I beg to offer an unqualified apology.

POOH. I desire to associate myself with that expression of regret.

PITTI. We really hadn't the least notion——

MIK. Of course you hadn't. How could you? Come, come, my good fellow, don't distress yourself—it was no fault of yours. If a man of exalted rank chooses to disguise himself as a Second Trombone, he must take the consequences. It really distresses me to see you take on so. I've no doubt he thoroughly deserved all he got. (*They rise.*)

KO. We are infinitely obliged to your Majesty——

PITTI. Much obliged, your Majesty.

POOH. Very much obliged, your Majesty.

MIK. Obliged? not a bit. Don't mention it. How *could* you tell?

POOH. No, of course we couldn't tell who the gentleman really was.

PITTI. It wasn't written on his forehead, you know.

KO. It might have been on his pocket-handkerchief, but Japanese don't use pocket-handkerchiefs! Ha! ha! ha!

MIK. Ha! ha! ha! [88] (*To* KATISHA.) I forget the punishment for compassing the death of the Heir Apparent.

KO. ⎫
POOH. ⎬ Punishment. (*They drop down on their knees again.*)
PITTI. ⎭

MIK. Yes. Something lingering, with boiling oil in it, I fancy. Something of that sort. I think boiling oil occurs in it, but I'm not sure. I know it's something humorous, but lingering, with either boiling oil or melted lead. [89] Come, come, don't fret—I'm not a bit angry.

KO. (*in abject terror*). If your Majesty will accept our assurance, we had no idea——

MIK. Of course——

PITTI. I knew nothing about it.

POOH. I wasn't there.

MIK. That's the pathetic part of it. Unfortunately, the fool of an Act says "compassing the death of the Heir Apparent." There's not a word about a mistake——

KO., PITTI., *and* POOH. No!

MIK. Or not knowing——

KO. No!

MIK. Or having no notion——

PITTI. No!

MIK. Or not being there——

POOH. No!

MIK. There should be, of course——

KO., PITTI., *and* POOH. Yes!

MIK. But there isn't.

KO., PITTI., *and* POOH. Oh!

MIK. That's the slovenly way in which these Acts are always drawn. However, cheer up, it'll be all right. I'll have it altered next session. Now, let's see about your execution—will after luncheon suit you? Can you wait till then?

KO., PITTI., *and* POOH. Oh, yes—we can wait till then!

MIK. Then we'll make it after luncheon.

POOH. I don't want any lunch.

MIK. I'm really very sorry for you all, but it's an unjust world, and virtue is triumphant only in theatrical performances.

GLEE [90]

438

PITTI-SING, KATISHA, KO-KO, POOH-BAH, *and* MIKADO

MIK. See how the Fates their gifts allot,
For A is happy—B is not.
Yet B is worthy, I dare say,
Of more prosperity than A!

KO., POOH., *and* PITTI. *Is* B more worthy?

KAT. I should say
He's worth a great deal more than A.

ENSEMBLE. {
Yet A is happy!
Oh, so happy!
Laughing, Ha! ha!
Chaffing, Ha! ha!
Nectar quaffing, Ha! ha! ha!
Ever joyous, ever gay,
Happy, undeserving A!
}

KO., POOH., *and* PITTI.
If I were Fortune—which I'm not—
B should enjoy A's happy lot,
And A should die in miserie—
That is, assuming I am B.

MIK. *and* KAT. But *should* A perish?

KO., POOH., *and* PITTI That should be
(Of course, assuming I am B).
B should be happy!
Oh, so happy!
Laughing, Ha! ha!
Chaffing, Ha! ha!
Nectar quaffing, Ha! ha! ha!
But condemned to die is he,
Wretched meritorious B!

[*Exeunt* MIKADO *and* KATISHA.

KO. Well, a nice mess you've got us into, with your nodding head and the deference due to a man of pedigree!

POOH. Merely corroborative [91] detail, intended to give artistic verisimilitude to an otherwise bald and unconvincing narrative.

PITTI. Corroborative detail indeed! Corroborative fiddlestick!

KO. And you're just as bad as he is with your cock-and-a-bull stories about catching his eye and his whistling an air. But that's so like you! You must put in your oar!

POOH. But how about your big right arm?

PITTI. Yes, and your snickersnee!

KO. Well, well, never mind that now. There's only one thing to be done. Nanki-Poo hasn't started yet—he must come to life again at once. (*Enter* NANKI-POO *and* YUM-YUM *prepared for journey.*) Here he comes. Here, Nanki-Poo, I've good news for you—you're reprieved.

NANK. Oh, but it's too late. I'm a dead man, and I'm off for my honeymoon.

KO. Nonsense! A terrible thing has just happened. It seems you're the son of the Mikado.

NANK. Yes, but that happened some time ago.

KO. Is this a time for airy persiflage? Your father is here, and with Katisha!

NANK. My father! And with Katisha!

KO. Yes, he wants you particularly.

POOH. So does she.

YUM. Oh, but he's married now.

[91] A number of years ago, in what was known as the D'Oyly Carte "Small Company," the principal comedian was ill. I was by this time the No. 1 understudy and going on for one of my early performances of Ko-Ko. Hilton Leyland was the Pooh-Bah, and Margaret Philo the Pitti-Sing. What happened to Hilton, who was a very solid performer with extremely good diction, I don't know. Perhaps he was delivering the line with more than his usual degree of unction and his tongue objected. Anyway, the line came out: "Merely cobbobobative detail . . ." That was all right, especially since he was wise enough not to attempt to correct it. But it infected Margaret. "Cobbobobative detail indeed!" says she. And then realized what she'd said and did try to correct it: "Corrolobate . . . corrolov . . . Oh! Stiddleficks!"

The audience began to laugh. I could not help it; my sense of humor got the better of me. Waiting until the uproar had completely died down, I delivered my next line with great deliberation: "And you're just as bad as he is . . ." and then I paused. I wasn't wrong. The audience picked up the inference, and poor "Maggie" broke up.

[92] *Traditionally, Pooh-Bah finds this a tremendous joke and breaks out into a very loud guffaw. Ko-Ko's reaction is promptly to faint. During one of our American tours I asked Derek Oldham if he thought he was strong enough to catch and hold me if I leaped into his arms at that point, the idea being that the sudden noise shocked me into it. Derek thought he was, and the resultant laugh from everybody, including Pitti-Sing and Pooh-Bah, whose stage laugh modulated into a real one, went on for what seemed like hours.*

[93] *Two encores are traditionally the limit for this duet—although the audience usually wants more—because Ko-Ko has to make a quick change on the side of the stage and doesn't want to become too breathless dancing and then have to re-enter in the same condition.*

[94] *Words and music on page 494.*

[95] *To make some sort of a change between the first time through and the first encore Nanki-Poo goes into a cadenza (Ko-Ko is seated on the floor):*

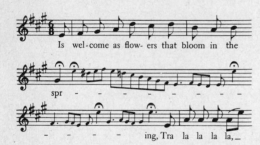

Ko-Ko then sings his verse, still seated, and for some inexplicable reason finds his big toe sticking up. He pushes it down with his fan, but it won't stay down. After several tries, he gets to his feet and tries once more to push it down, only to find that as it does so the other one comes up. That one is pushed down and up comes number one toe again. This is too much for him so he stamps on it, hurts himself badly, and hops off the stage nursing the damaged toe.

The second encore is mimed by Ko-Ko who brings on a big fan and draws a shocking caricature of Katisha on it, shows it to the audience, and ends up by making a sort of a bonnet out of it round Pooh-Bah's head.

The toe business, it is said, was invented by Henry Lytton. He trod on a tin-tack—a very short and sharp pointed nail used for tacking down stage cloths, and inadvertently lifted his big toe, a thing he didn't know he could do until that moment. The audience thought it was very funny, and the bit remained in. However, he only used one toe. I can never remember the time when I couldn't lift both toes up. Well—up to 1959!

[96] *Without any doubt whatsoever, I consider this the most beautiful contralto song, both for lyric and music, in the whole series.*

KO. But, bless my heart! what has that to do with it?

NANK. Katisha claims me in marriage, but I can't marry her because I'm married already—consequently she will insist on my execution, and if I'm executed, my wife will have to be buried alive.

YUM. You see our difficulty.

KO. Yes. I don't know what's to be done.

NANK. There's one chance for you. If you could persuade Katisha to marry you, [92] she would have no further claim on me, and in that case I could come to life without any fear of being put to death.

KO. I marry Katisha!

YUM. I really think it's the only course.

KO. But, my good girl, have you seen her? She's something appalling!

PITTI. Ah! that's only her face. She has a left elbow which people come miles to see!

POOH. I am told that her right heel is much admired by connoisseurs.

KO. My good sir, I decline to pin my heart upon any lady's right heel.

NANK. It comes to this: While Katisha is single, I prefer to be a disembodied spirit. When Katisha is married, existence will be as welcome as the flowers in spring.

[93] DUET—NANKI-POO *and* KO-KO
(*With* YUM-YUM, PITTI-SING, *and* POOH-BAH) [94]

NANK.   The flowers that bloom in the spring,
        Tra la,
    Breathe promise of merry sunshine—
    As we merrily dance and we sing,
        Tra la,
    We welcome the hope that they bring,
        Tra la,
      Of a summer of roses and wine.
        And that's what we mean when we say that a thing
        Is welcome as flowers that bloom in the spring.
          Tra la la la la la, etc.

ALL.   Tra la la la la, etc.

KO.   The flowers that bloom in the spring,
        Tra la,
    Have nothing to do with the case.
    I've got to take under my wing,
        Tra la,
    A most unattractive old thing,
        Tra la,
      With a caricature of a face
      And that's what I mean when I say, or I sing,
      "Oh, bother the flowers that bloom in the spring."
          Tra la la la la la, etc.

ALL.   Tra la la la la, Tra la la la, etc. [95]
      [*Dance and exeunt* NANKI-POO, YUM-YUM, POOH-BAH,
        PITTI-SING, *and* KO-KO.

Enter KATISHA

RECITATIVE *and* SONG—KATISHA [96]

Alone, and yet alive! Oh, sepulchre!
My soul is still my body's prisoner!
Remote the peace that Death alone can give—
My doom, to wait! my punishment, to live!

SONG

Hearts do not break!
They sting and ache
For old love's sake,
But do not die,
Though with each breath
They long for death
As witnesseth
The living I!
Oh, living I!
Come, tell me why,
When hope is gone,
Dost thou stay on?
Why linger here,
Where all is drear?
Oh, living I!
Come, tell me why,
When hope is gone,
Dost thou stay on?
May not a cheated maiden die?

KO. (*entering and approaching her timidly*). Katisha!

KAT. The miscreant who robbed me of my love! But vengeance pursues—they are heating the cauldron!

KO. Katisha—behold a suppliant at your feet! Katisha—mercy!

KAT. Mercy? Had you mercy on him? See here, you! You have slain my love. He did not love *me*, but he would have loved me in time. I am an acquired taste—only the educated palate can appreciate *me*. I was educating *his* palate when he left me. Well, he is dead, and where shall I find another? It takes years to train a man to love me. Am I to go through the weary round again, and, at the same time, implore mercy for you who robbed me of my prey—I mean my pupil—just as his education was on the point of completion? Oh, where shall I find another?

KO. (*suddenly, and with great vehemence*). Here!—Here!

KAT. What!!!

KO. (*with intense passion*). Katisha, for years I have loved you with a white-hot passion that is slowly but surely consuming my very vitals! [97] Ah, shrink not from me! If there is aught of woman's mercy in your heart, turn not away from a love-sick suppliant whose every fibre thrills at your tiniest touch! True it is that, under a poor mask of disgust, I have endeavoured to conceal a passion whose inner fires are broiling the soul within me! But the fire will not be smothered—it defies all attempts at extinction, and, breaking forth, all the more eagerly for its long restraint, it declares itself in words that will not be weighed—that cannot be schooled—that should not be too severely criticised. Katisha, I dare not hope for your love—but I will not live without it! Darling!

KAT. You, whose hands still reek with the blood of my betrothed, dare to address words of passion to the woman you have so foully wronged!

KO. I do—accept my love, or I perish on the spot!

KAT. Go to! Who knows so well as I that no one ever yet died of a broken heart!

KO. You know not what you say. Listen!

[98] SONG—KO-KO [99]

On a tree by a river a little tom-tit
Sang "Willow, titwillow, titwillow!"

[97] *As many have observed over the years, there is one particularly impish little devil who has attached itself to me, and at odd and unexpected intervals he makes his presence felt. He once got an idea into his head that it would be a good thing if I were to "break up" Katisha sometime during this scene. I, naturally, said, "No!" Then he suggested the way I could do it as I was making a quick change, and before I knew what I was doing I had approached a stagehand and had whispered some quick instructions to him. Then the imp and I went on. That imp was taking no chances; he was going to make sure that I carried out my—er—his idea.*

Normally, as Ko-Ko says: ". . . I have loved you with a white-hot passion that is slowly but surely consuming my very vitals!" he falls on her shoulder. Katisha roughly pushes him away, and he carries on with the lines. This night, however, when the line came, I knew exactly what that imp meant to do. The stagehand was ready. I leapt at one of the wings and shinnied up it as high as I could go, while the stagehand (the only other person in the theater who had any inkling of what I might be up to) did his best to hold the thing as steady as possible. As for Evelyn Gardiner (Katisha), her eyes popped out of her head. She rocked with laughter, and the more she broke up, the more the audience laughed. I didn't realize what I'd set up until what seemed like hours later, when the wave of laughter subsided and I spoke the next words: "Ah, shrink not from me!"

That did it. I regret to say that Eve couldn't speak another line that evening. I am happy to say, though, that such was the success of that imp's idea that Rupert D'Oyly Carte had a special framework built in at the back of the flat I used in order to ensure my safety and that of his scenery!

[98] *Words and music on page 496.*

[99] *This always used to be sung as a comedy song. It is said that the reason for this was that George Grossmith was unable to sing a straight number. Having been rehearsed in this manner, I too sang it as a comedy song—at first. We had been playing Washington, D. C., and during our visit—just following the last performance of The Mikado at the National Theater—I received a letter from a lady who said she thought it was a pity that so beautiful a number should be ruined by interpolating "vulgar" comedy business. Subconsciously, I believe I had always had a sneaking feeling that way myself, but this letter made me sit up and take notice. Our next stop was Chicago. The opening show was The Mikado. I asked our musical director if he could mute the strings for "Titwillow" as I intended to sing the song dead straight. After a little persuasion he agreed to do so. I have never been so grateful for a letter and a criticism. The effect on the audience was tremendous; the critics were unanimous in hailing a new song hit. The credit all belongs to the writer of that critical letter. She*

was so right. Any comedy should lie in the business that attends the dialogue that follows the song.

By the way, compare the poem of Nicholas Rowe, 17th-century poet, with Gilbert's 19th-century "Titwillow":

> To the brook and the willow that heard him
>   complain,
> Ah, Willow, Willow;
> Poor Colin sat weeping and told them his
>   pain,
> Ah, Willow, Willow; ah, Willow, Willow;
> Etc. . . .

On a tree by a river

And I said to him, "Dicky-bird, why do you sit
    Singing 'Willow, titwillow, titwillow'?"
"Is it weakness of intellect, birdie?" I cried,
"Or a rather tough worm in your little inside?"
With a shake of his poor little head, he replied,
    "Oh, willow, titwillow, titwillow!"

He slapped at his chest, as he sat on that bough,
    Singing "Willow, titwillow, titwillow!"
And a cold perspiration bespangled his brow,
    Oh, willow, titwillow, titwillow!
He sobbed and he sighed, and a gurgle he gave,
Then he plunged himself into the billowy wave,
And an echo arose from the suicide's grave—
    "Oh, willow, titwillow, titwillow!"

Now I feel just as sure as I'm sure that my name
    Isn't Willow, titwillow, titwillow,
That 'twas blighted affection that made him exclaim
    "Oh, willow, titwillow, titwillow!"
And if you remain callous and obdurate, I
Shall perish as he did, and you will know why,
Though I probably shall not exclaim as I die,
    "Oh, willow, titwillow, titwillow!"

[*During this song* KATISHA *has been greatly affected,
and at the end is almost in tears.*

KAT. (*whimpering*). Did he really die of love?
KO. He really did.
KAT. All on account of a cruel little hen?
KO. Yes.
KAT. Poor little chap!
KO. It's an affecting tale, and quite true. I knew the bird intimately.
KAT. Did you? He must have been very fond of her.
KO. His devotion was something extraordinary.
KAT. (*still whimpering*). Poor little chap! And—and if I refuse you, will you go and do the same?
KO. At once.
KAT. No, no—you mustn't! Anything but that! (*Falls on his breast.*) Oh, I'm a silly little goose!
KO. (*making a wry face*). You are!
KAT. And you won't hate me because I'm just a little teeny weeny wee bit bloodthirsty, will you?
KO. Hate you? Oh, Katisha! is there not beauty even in bloodthirstiness?
KAT. My idea exactly.

DUET—KATISHA *and* KO-KO

KAT.   There is beauty in the bellow of the blast,
        There is grandeur in the growling of the gale,
           There is eloquent outpouring
           When the lion is a-roaring,
        And the tiger is a-lashing of his tail!
KO.   Yes, I like to see a tiger
           From the Congo or the Niger,
        And especially when lashing of his tail!
KAT.   Volcanoes have a splendour that is grim,
        And earthquakes only terrify the dolts,
           But to him who's scientific

There's nothing that's terrific
In the falling of a flight of thunderbolts!

KO.   Yes, in spite of all my meekness,
If I have a little weakness,
It's a passion for a flight of thunderbolts!

BOTH.   If that is so,
Sing derry down derry!
It's evident, very,
Our tastes are one.
Away we'll go,
And merrily marry,
Nor tardily tarry
Till day is done!

KO.   There is beauty in extreme old age—
Do you fancy you are elderly enough?
Information I'm requesting
On a subject interesting:
Is a maiden all the better when she's tough?

KAT.   Throughout this wide dominion
It's the general opinion
That she'll last a good deal longer when she's tough.

KO.   Are you old enough to marry, do you think?
Won't you wait till you are eighty in the shade?
There's a fascination frantic
In a ruin that's romantic;
Do you think you are sufficiently decayed?

KAT.   To the matter that you mention
I have given some attention,
And I think I am sufficiently decayed.

BOTH.   If that is so,
Sing derry down derry!
It's evident, very,
Our tastes are one!
Away we'll go,
And merrily marry,
Nor tardily tarry
Till day is done!

[Exeunt together.

I shall perish as he did

Flourish. Enter the MIKADO, *attended by* PISH-TUSH *and Court*

MIK. Now then, we've had a capital lunch, and we're quite ready. Have all the painful preparations been made?

PISH. Your Majesty, all is prepared.

MIK. Then produce the unfortunate gentleman and his two well-meaning but misguided accomplices.

Enter KO-KO, KATISHA, POOH-BAH, *and* PITTI-SING.
They throw themselves at the MIKADO's *feet*

KAT. Mercy! Mercy for Ko-Ko! Mercy for Pitti-Sing! Mercy even for Pooh-Bah!

MIK. I beg your pardon, I don't think I quite caught that remark.

POOH. Mercy even for Pooh-Bah.

KAT. Mercy! My husband that was to have been is dead, and I have just married this miserable object. [100]

MIK. Oh! You've not been long about it!

KO. We were married before the Registrar.

POOH. I am the Registrar.

[100] *One of the fastest wedding ceremonies on record, I imagine!*

MIK. I see. But my difficulty is that, as you have slain the Heir Apparent——

Enter NANKI-POO *and* YUM-YUM. *They kneel*

NANKI. The Heir Apparent is *not* slain.

MIK. Bless my heart, my son!

YUM. And your daughter-in-law elected!

KAT. (*seizing* KO-KO). Traitor, you have deceived me! [101]

MIK. Yes, you are entitled to a little explanation, but I think he will give it better whole than in pieces.

KO. Your Majesty, it's like this: It is true that I stated that I had killed Nanki-Poo——

MIK. Yes, with most affecting particulars.

POOH. Merely corroborative detail intended to give artistic verisimilitude to a bald and——

KO. *Will* you refrain from putting in your oar? (*To* MIKADO.) It's like this: When your Majesty says, "Let a thing be done," it's as good as done—practically, it *is* done—because your Majesty's will is law. Your Majesty says, "Kill a gentleman," and a gentleman is told off to be killed. Consequently, that gentleman is as good as dead—practically, he *is* dead—and if he is dead, why not say so?

MIK. I see. Nothing could possibly be more satisfactory!

FINALE [102]

PITTI.	For he's gone and married Yum-Yum—
ALL.	Yum-Yum!
PITTI.	Your anger pray bury,
	For all will be merry,
	I think you had better succumb—
ALL.	Cumb—cumb!
PITTI.	And join our expressions of glee!
KO.	On this subject I pray you be dumb—
ALL.	Dumb—dumb!
KO.	Your notions, though many,
	Are not worth a penny,
	The word for your guidance is "Mum"—
ALL.	Mum—Mum!
KO.	You've a very good bargain in me.
ALL.	On this subject we pray you be dumb—
	Dumb—dumb!
	We think you had better succumb—
	Cumb—cumb!
	You'll find there are many
	Who'll wed for a penny,
	There are lots of good fish in the sea.
YUM. *and* NANK.	The threatened cloud has passed away,
	And brightly shines the dawning day;
	What though the night may come too soon,
	We've years and years of afternoon!
ALL.	Then let the throng
	Our joy advance,
	With laughing song
	And merry dance,
	With joyous shout and ringing cheer,
	Inaugurate our new career!
	Then let the throng, etc.

CURTAIN

[101] *As Katisha says this she seizes Ko-Ko around the throat and shakes him as a dog would shake a rat. One night the Katisha shook me so hard that my wig came off. (I was so hot it was only just floating on my head anyway.) Any slight accident of this kind is always good for a laugh for those onstage as well as out front. It was a bald-pated wig. Picking it up I hurriedly donned it again, only to realize it was on back to front, and that the bald part was at the back of my head. What could I do? Except just turn my back to the audience?*

Pooh-Bah's next line had an extra punch that night!

[102] *Originally the Finale began with Yum-Yum and Nanki-Poo going right into: "The threatened cloud has passed away." I imagine this was another thing Gilbert decided to fix the morning after the opening night. It's hard to conceive that, after seeing one performance, he could fail to realize that the ending was much too sudden as it stood. As it is now performed it's one of the most satisfying of Gilbert and Sullivan finales.*

If You Want to Know Who We Are

In spirited tempo

CHORUS

If you want to know who we are, _____

We are gen-tle-men of Ja - pan; _____ On ___

man - y a vase and jar, _____ On ___

man - y a screen and fan, _____

We fig-ure in live-ly paint: Our at-ti-tude's queer and

quaint, You're wrong if you think it ain't.___ Oh! _____ and

If you think we are work'd by

strings, _____ Like a Jap - a -nese mar-io - nette, _____

You ___ don't un - der - stand these things: _____

It is sim-ply Court et - i - quette. _____

Per - haps you sup-pose this throng_ Can't keep it up all day

A Wand'ring Minstrel

Lightly and gracefully

NANKI-POO

A wan-d'ring min - strel I, A thing of shreds ____ and

legato

patch - es, Of bal - lads, songs and snatch - es, And dream - y lull - a -

by! ___ My cat - a -logue is long, Thro' ev - 'ry pas - sion

rang-ing, And to your hu-mours chang-ing I tune_ my sup - ple

song! ___ I tune_ my sup - - - ple

Slowly, with expression *p*

song! Are you in sen - ti - men - tal mood? I'll sigh with you,

Oh; ___ sor - row! On maid - en's cold-ness do you brood? I'll

do so, too, Oh, _____ sor - row,_ sor - row! I'll charm your will-ing

ears With songs of lov-ers' fears, While sym-pa-thet-ic tears— My cheeks be-

dew,— Oh, _____ sor - row,_ sor - row!

March tempo

But if pa-tri-ot-ic sen-ti-ment is want-ed, I've

pa-tri-ot-ic bal-lads cut and dried; For wher-e'er our coun-try's ban-ner may be

planted, All oth-er lo-cal ban-ners are de-fied! Our war-ri-ors, in ser-ried ranks as-

sem - bled, Nev-er quail, or they con-ceal it if they do, And I

should-n't be sur-pris'd if na-tions trem - bled Be-fore the might-y troops, the troops of Ti - ti -

Cheerfully, but not too fast

pu!

And if you call for a

song of the sea, We'll heave the cap-stan round, With a yeo heave-ho, for the

wind is_ free, Her an-chor's a-trip and her helm's a-lee, Hur-rah for the home-ward

MEN

bound! Yeo-ho ___ heave-ho, ___ Hur-rah for the home-ward

NANKI-POO

bound! To lay a-loft in a howl-ing breeze May tick-le a lands-man's

taste, But the hap-piest hour a_ sail-or_ sees Is when he's down At an

rit.   *a tempo*

in-land town, With his Nan-cy on his knees, yeo-ho! And his arm_ a-round her

Behold the Lord High Executioner

Vigorous march tempo

ff

CHORUS of MEN

f

Be-hold the Lord High Ex - e - cu-tion-er!   A

per-son-age of no-ble rank and ti - tle,   A dig - ni-fied and po - tent

of - fi - cer,   Whose func - tions are par-tic - u - lar - ly vi - tal!   De-

mf

fer, _____ de - fer, _____ To the Lord High Ex - e -

cu - tion-er! De-fer, _____ de - fer, _____ To the no-ble Lord, to the

no - ble Lord, to the Lord High _____ Ex - e - - cu - tion - er!

KO-KO

Tak - en from the coun-ty jail By a set of cur - ious

chan - ces; Lib - er - a - ted then on bail, On my own re-cog - ni-

458

I've Got a Little List

Brightly and gracefully

mf

KO-KO

p   *leggiero*

1. As some day it may hap-pen that a
(2. There's the) nig-ger ser-e-nad-er and the
(3. And that) Ni-si Pri-us nui-sance, who just

vic-tim must be found, I've got a lit-tle list, I've got a lit-tle list Of so-
oth-ers of his race, And the pia-no or-gan-ist, I've got him on the list! And the
now is rath-er rife, The Ju-di-cial hu-mor-ist, I've got him on the list! All

ci-e-ty of-fend-ers who might well be un-der-ground, And who
peo-ple who eat pep-per-mint and puff it in your face, They
fun-ny fel-lows, com-ic men and clowns of pri-vate life, They'd

never would be miss'd, who nev - er would be miss'd! There's the pes - ti - len - tial nui - san - ces who
nev - er would be miss'd, they nev - er would be miss'd! Then the i - di - ot who prais - es, with en -
none of 'em be miss'd, they'd none of 'em be miss'd! And a - pol - o - get - ic states - men of a

write for au - to - graphs, All peo - ple who have flab - by hands and
thu - si - as - tic tone, All cen - tur - ies but this and ev - 'ry
com - pro - mis - ing kind, Such as What - d'ye - call - him, Thing - 'em - bob, and

ir - ri - tat - ing laughs, All chil - dren who are up in dates, and
coun - try but his own; And the la - dy from the prov - in - ces, who
like - wise Nev - er - mind, And 'St - 'st - 'st and What's - his - name, and

floor you with 'em flat, All per - sons who in shak - ing hands shake
dress - es like a guy, And "who does - n't think she waltz - es, but would
al - so You - know - who, The task of fill - ing up the blanks I'd

hands with you like that, And all third per-sons who on spoil-ing tête-à-têtes in-sist, They'd
rath-er like to try"; And that sin-gu-lar a-nom-a-ly, the la-dy nov-el-ist, I
rath-er leave to you. But it real-ly does-n't mat-ter whom you put up-on the list, For they'd

CHORUS of MEN

none of 'em be miss'd, they'd none of 'em be miss'd! He's got 'em on the list, he's
don't think she'd be miss'd, I'm sure she'd not be miss'd! He's got her on the list, he's
none of 'em be miss'd, they'd none of 'em be miss'd! You may put 'em on the list, you may

got 'em on the list, And they'll none of 'em be miss'd, they'll
got her on the list, And I don't think she'll be miss'd, I'm
put 'em on the list, And they'll none of 'em be miss'd, they'll

1.-2. KO-KO 3.

none of 'em be miss'd! 2. There's the
sure she'll not be miss'd! 3. And that
none of 'em be miss'd!

462

Three Little Maids from School

Gaily and gracefully

mf staccato

YUM-YUM, PEEP-BO and PITTI-SING

Three lit-tle maids from school are we, Pert as a school-girl well can be, Fill'd to the brim with girl-ish glee,—

YUM-YUM

Three lit-tle maids from school! Ev'-ry-thing is a source of— fun.

Were You Not to Ko-Ko Plighted

Slowly, with expression

NANKI-POO

Were you not to Ko-Ko plight-ed, I would say in ten-der tone, "Lov'd one, let us be u-nit-ed, Let us be each oth-er's own!" I would merge all rank and sta-tion, World-ly sneers are nought to

For He's Going to Marry Yum-Yum

Brightly

f leggiero

mp

rall.

Gracefully

PITTI-SING

a tempo

CHORUS   PITTI-SING

For __ he's go-ing to mar-ry Yum - Yum! Yum-Yum! Your

p   a tempo

an-ger pray bur-y, For all will be mer-ry, I think you had bet-ter suc-

find there— are man-y Who'll wed for a pen-ny, Who'll wed for a

pen-ny, There are lots of— good fish in the sea! There are

lots of good fish in the sea! There's lots of good fish, good fish in the

sea! There's lots of good fish, good fish in the sea, in the sea, in the

sea, in the sea, in the sea!

Braid the Raven Hair

Gracefully, but not fast

CHORUS of GIRLS

Braid the ra - ven hair,— Weave the sup - - ple tress,—

Deck the maid - en fair — In her love - - li - ness,

Paint the pret - ty face, Dye the cor - al lip, Em - pha - size the

The Moon and I

Slowly with expression

p YUM-YUM

1. The sun, whose rays Are all a-blaze With ev-er-liv-ing glo-ry,
2. Ob-serve his flame, That plac-id dame, The moon's Ce-les-tial High-ness;

Does not de-ny His maj-es-ty He scorns to tell a sto-ry!
There's not a trace Up-on her face Of dif-fi-dence or shy-ness:

He don't ex-claim, "I blush for shame, So kind-ly be in-dul-gent."
She bor-rows light That, thro' the night, Man-kind may all ac-claim her!

But, fierce and bold, In fie - ry gold, He glo - ries all ef - ful - gent!
And, truth to tell, She lights up well, So I, for one, don't blame her!

I mean to rule the earth, ___
Ah, pray make no mis - take, ___

___ As he the sky, We real - ly know our worth, ___ The sun and I!
___ We are not shy; We're ver - y wide a - wake, ___ The moon and I!

I mean to rule the earth, As he the sky, We real - ly know our worth, The sun and
Ah, pray make no mis - take, We are not shy; We're ver - y wide a - wake, The moon and

I!
I!

Brightly Dawns Our Wedding Day

In lively spirited tempo

f

YUM-YUM

f

f legato

1. Bright - ly dawns our wed - ding day; Joy - ous
(2. Let us) dry the read - y tear, Though the

hour, we give thee greet - ing! Whith - er,— whith - er art thou fleet - ing? Fick - le
hours are sure - ly creep - ing Lit - tle— need for woe - ful weep - ing, Till the

mo - ment, pri - thee stay! Fick - le— mo - ment, pri - thee stay!
sad sun - down is near, Till the— sad sun - down is near.

mf

Here's a How-De-Do

With exultant gaiety

YUM-YUM

Here's a how-de-do! If I mar-ry you, When your time has come to per-ish, Then the maid-en whom you cher-ish Must be slaugh-ter'd too! Here's a how-de-do! Here's a how-de-do!

482

From Every Kind of Man

My Object All Sublime

Very lively

ob-ject all sub-lime . . . fit the crime, The pun-ish-ment

fit the crime, The pun-ish-ment fit the crime, . . . make each pris-'ner pent Un-

will-ing-ly re-pre-sent A source of in-no-cent mer-ri-ment, Of in-no-cent mer-ri-ment!

hib - it his pow-ers To Ma - dame Tus-saud's wax-work. The
Spohr and Bee - tho - ven, At clas - si - cal Mon - day Pops. The

la - dy who dyes a chem - i - cal yel - low, Or stains her grey_ hair
bil - liard sharp whom an - y - one catch-es, His doom's ex - treme - ly

puce, Or pinch - es her fig - ger, Is black'd like a nig - ger With
hard, He's made to dwell in a dun - geon cell On a

per - ma - nent wal - nut juice. The i - diot who, in
spot that's al - ways barr'd. And there he plays ex -

rail - way car - riag - es, Scrib - bles on win - dow - panes, We
trav - a - gant match - es In fit - less fin - ger - stalls, On a

on - ly suf - fer To ride on a buf - fer In Par - lia - men - t'ry trains.}
cloth un - true, With a twist - ed cue, And el - lip - ti - cal bil - liard balls!}
My

a tempo

ob - ject all sub - lime I shall a - chieve in time, To

let the pun - ish - ment fit the crime, The pun - ish - ment fit the crime; And

make each pris - 'ner pent Un - will - ing - ly re - pre - sent A

source of in - no - cent mer - ri - ment, Of in - no - cent mer - ri - ment! -ment!

490

The Criminal Cried

With ease and not too fast

Ko-Ko 1. The

crim-i-nal cried, as he dropp'd him down, In a state_ of wild a-
shiv-er'd and shook as he gave the sign For the stroke he did-n't de-
tho' you'd have said that head was dead (For its own-er dead was

larm, With a fright-ful, fran-tic, fear-ful frown, I bar'd my big right
serve; When all of a sud-den his eye met mine, And it seem'd to brace his
he), It stood on its neck, with a smile well bred, And bow'd three times to

arm.__ I seiz'd him by his lit-tle pig-tail, And
nerve;__ For he nod-ded his head and kiss'd his hand, And he
me!__ It was none of your im-pu-dent off-hand nods, But as

on his knees fell he, As he squirm'd and strug-gled, And gur-gled and gug-gled, I
whis-tled an air,_ did he, As the sa-bre true Cut clean-ly through His
hum-ble as_ could be; For it clear-ly knew The def-er-ence due To a

drew my snick-er-snee, _____ my snick-er-snee!_ Oh,
cer-vi-cal ver-te-brae, _____ his ver-te-brae!_ When a
man of ped-i-gree, _____ of ped-i-gree!_ And it's

ne'er shall I For-get the cry, Or the shriek that shriek-ed he,_ As I
man's a-fraid, A beau-ti-ful maid Is a cheer-ing sight to see;_ And it's
oh, I vow, This death-ly bow Was a touch-ing sight to see;_ Though

gnash'd my teeth, When from_ its sheath I drew_ my snick-er-
oh,_ I'm glad That mo-ment sad I Was sooth'd by sight of
trunk-less, yet It could-n't for-get The def-er-ence due to

492

CHORUS

snee!___ We know him well, He can-not tell Un - true or ground-less
me!___ Her ter-ri-ble tale You can't as-sail, With truth it quite a-
me!___ This haugh-ty youth, He speaks the truth When - ev-er he finds it

tales;___ He al - ways tries To ut - ter lies, And
grees;___ Her taste ex - act For fault - less fact A -
pays;___ And in___ this case, It all___ took place Ex -

1.-2.
ev - 'ry time he fails.___ Pitti-Sing 2.He
mounts to a dis - ease.___ Pooh-Bah 3.Now
act - ly as he

3.
says! Ex-act - ly, ex-act - ly, ex-act - ly, ex-

act - ly as he says!___

493

The Flowers That Bloom in the Spring

In gay tempo

Nanki-Poo 1. The flow - ers that bloom in the spring, Tra - la, Breathe
Ko-Ko 2. The flow - ers that bloom in the spring, Tra - la, Have

molto leggiero

prom - ise of mer - ry sun - shine, As we mer - ri - ly dance and we
noth - ing to do with the case. I've got to take un - der my

sing, Tra - la, We wel - come the hope that they bring, Tra - la, Of a
wing, Tra - la, A most un - at - trac - tive old thing, Tra - la, With a

Tit-Willow

Slowly and with warmth

mp

p KO-KO

1. On a tree by a riv - er a lit - tle tom - tit Sang
(2. He) slapp'd at his chest, as he sat on that bough, Sing - ing
(3. Now I) feel just as sure as I'm sure that my name Is - n't

"Wil - low, tit - wil - low, tit - wil - low" And I said to him, "Dick - y - bird,
"Wil - low, tit - wil - low, tit - wil - low!" And a cold per - spi - ra - tion be -
Wil - low, tit - wil - low, tit - wil - low, That 'twas blight - ed af - fec - tion that

why do you sit Sing - ing 'Wil - low, tit - wil - low, tit -
span - gled his brow, Oh, wil - low, tit - wil - low, tit -
made him ex - claim, "Oh, wil - low, tit - wil - low, tit -

wil - low?"   "Is it weak-ness of in - tel - lect, bird - ie?" I cried, "Or a
wil - low!   He __ sobb'd and he sigh'd and a   gur - gle he gave, Then he
wil - low!"   And if you re - main cal - lous and   ob - du - rate, I Shall __

rath - er tough worm in your   lit - tle in - side?"   With a
plunged him - self in - to the   bil - low - y wave,   And an
per - ish as he did, and   you will know why,   Though I

shake of his poor lit - tle head, he re - plied, "Oh,   wil - low, tit - wil - low, tit -
ech - o a - rose from the   su - i - cide's grave, "Oh,   wil - low, tit - wil - low, tit -
prob - a - bly shall not ex - claim as I die, "Oh,   wil - low, tit - wil - low, tit -

wil - low!"
wil - low!"   2. He
          3. Now I   wil - low!"

497

Ruddigore
OR, THE WITCH'S CURSE

DRAMATIS PERSONÆ

MORTALS

SIR RUTHVEN MURGATROYD (*disguised as Robin Oakapple, a Young Farmer*)

RICHARD DAUNTLESS (*his Foster-Brother—a Man-o'-war's-man*)

SIR DESPARD MURGATROYD, OF RUDDIGORE (*a Wicked Baronet*)

OLD ADAM GOODHEART (*Robin's Faithful Servant*)

ROSE MAYBUD (*a Village Maiden*)

MAD MARGARET

DAME HANNAH (*Rose's Aunt*)

ZORAH }
RUTH } (*Professional Bridesmaids*)

GHOSTS

SIR RUPERT MURGATROYD (*the First Baronet*)

SIR JASPER MURGATROYD (*the Third Baronet*)

SIR LIONEL MURGATROYD (*the Sixth Baronet*)

SIR CONRAD MURGATROYD (*the Twelfth Baronet*)

SIR DESMOND MURGATROYD (*the Sixteenth Baronet*)

SIR GILBERT MURGATROYD (*the Eighteenth Baronet*)

SIR MERVYN MURGATROYD (*the Twentieth Baronet*)

AND

SIR RODERIC MURGATROYD (*the Twenty-first Baronet*)

Chorus of Officers, Ancestors, Professional Bridesmaids, and Villagers

ACT I

THE FISHING VILLAGE OF REDERRING, IN CORNWALL

ACT II

THE PICTURE GALLERY IN RUDDIGORE CASTLE

TIME

EARLY IN THE 19TH CENTURY

First produced at the Savoy Theatre on January 22, 1887

"What is the title of your new opera, Mr. Gilbert?"
"*Ruddygore*—or not so good as *The Mikado!*" replied W. S. G.

Shortly after the first night an acquaintance asked Gilbert:
"How is *Bloodygore* going on?"
"It is not *Bloodygore*, it is *Ruddygore!*"
"Oh! Well, that's the same thing!"
"Is it?" said Gilbert. "I suppose then, you will think that if I say I admire your ruddy countenance it's the same as if I said I like your bloody cheek! Well—it isn't—and I don't!"

THE MIKADO had been an immediate smash hit and was running well, so Sullivan turned his attention to writing a cantata, The Golden Legend. He had already promised this to the Leeds Festival for October 1886. The beginning of that year saw Gilbert still toying with his "magic lozenge" plot and approaching Sullivan about it. As before, the idea was rejected. Undeterred, Gilbert was soon back with an idea for a burlesque of the old-fashioned English "meller-drammer." In its way, it turned out to be but a thinly disguised, rehashed version of the "magic lozenge." Sullivan, however, knowing the type of show that Gilbert intended to burlesque, fell for the idea, and then found himself doing two things at once—writing a religious cantata, and an "Entirely Original Supernatural Opera"—Ruddygore (as it was originally spelled).

The main theme of the new piece was a whole picture gallery of ancestors, who step down from their frames and give one quarter-deck orders that it is life and death to disobey. This was an obvious modification of a play Gilbert had written some eighteen years previously, Ages Ago. It was at one of the rehearsals of this play that Gilbert and Sullivan had met.

There is a story told that Gilbert was at the opening performance of The Golden Legend in Leeds, and that he fell asleep and had to be awakened when the cantata came to an end. Asked by Sullivan, a little later, what he thought of the work, Gilbert replied: "Wonderful, my dear Sullivan, wonderful! I was transported to another world." I am afraid it is but a story.

The opening night of Ruddygore brought its crop of troubles, not the least of which was the picture frames that failed to open on cue. Further troubles came at the end of the performance. Gilbert and Sullivan had gone onstage to take their bows in response to the usual calls for "Author, Composer," when suddenly, through the applause there came a sound of hissing, and cries of "Boo! Give us back The Mikado! Take it away!" The critics took objection to the title, saying that it might, perhaps, pass in a smoking room, but "in the case of the ladies, on their lips such a title would scarcely sound pretty!" Mr. Carte and Arthur Sullivan were very concerned, and Gilbert was irritated beyond measure to think that his title, which to him just meant red blood, should have been interpreted as language more usually heard around the docksides. He promptly suggested that perhaps it should be called "Kensington Gore"* or "Robin and Richard Were Two Pretty Men." It was eventually decided to keep the title as it was but alter the spelling by one letter, and Ruddigore it became.

* Kensington Gore. A portion of the area surrounding the Albert Hall, Kensington.

In spite of all the negative reviews and the opprobrium hurled at Gilbert from the gallery on opening night, which might well have come from a claque hired for the purpose by some jealous competitor of Richard Carte's, the new piece ran for some twelve months or more. On page 269 of Leslie Bailey's Gilbert and Sullivan Book, he said: "Yet, when revived in 1937 the Manchester Guardian said: 'It is incomprehensible that Ruddigore should ever have been considered less attractive than the other comic operas in the Savoy series.'" I agree with the sentiment, but not with the date. Ruddigore was revived in 1922–3, and I remember appearing in the role of Robin as far back as 1929. Had he said 1947 I would be more inclined to accept the date, for during World War II the D'Oyly Carte Opera Company's wardrobe and stores were hit by a bomb. Much valuable property, scenery, costumes, etc. were lost, and the whole of Ruddigore literally went up in smoke. This occurred somewhere around 1941, and it was not until 1946 that Rupert D'Oyly Carte approached Peter Goffin to design the opera again. (Goffin had already redesigned The Yeomen of the Guard back in 1939—see Foreword, page 555.) This new production of Ruddigore made its first bow to the public at Newcastle-upon-Tyne in 1947. Manchester did not see it until some few weeks later. I will concede that this could be called a revival.

In the new production the biggest changes were in the second-act scenery, where once again a suggestion of pink plaster of Paris took the place of the good old, mullion-windowed, granite-walled baronial hall (see Foreword to The Yeomen of the Guard). The chorus of Bucks and Blades lost their colorful military uniforms and took on the appearance of escapees from a minstrel show on a day trip through Coney Island. And all this after Gilbert had spent many wearisome hours checking on the authenticity and accuracy of the twenty British regiments previously represented!

Another change was Robin's second-act costume. Gone were the bishop-like gaiters, the tight white pants, the gray cutaway coat, and the "black bag" wig streaked with gray and with two Napoleonic curls. In their place came long gray trousers, a vivid green frock coat, a startling ginger wig—dressed in Regency style—topped off with a silk hat of the same vivid green as the coat. As a bad Baronet Goffin's Robin reminded me more of an Irish gossoon at a barn dance than of a Cornish gentleman, villain or otherwise.

Mad Margaret underwent little enough change with respect to her costume, but a comparison of photographs of Jessie Bond in 1887 and Marjorie Eyre in 1932 always leaves me with the impression that Jessie's interpretation was rather on the lines of an extremely sad Iolanthe just before she went to live "at the bottom of that stream"—or just after! Marjorie's appearance was reminiscent of a cronelike creature in her younger days just about to take off on the broomstick she would appear, in the photograph, to be carrying. Cartoonists' impressions of Mad Margaret's second-act appearance reveal decided contrasts over the years. Jessie Bond seems to be a cross between Charley's Aunt, Sary Gamp and the Belle of New York, while Eileen Sharpe gives the impression of having crossed with the Pilgrim Fathers. In all fairness to Peter Goffin, and his predecessors, Mad Margaret was always intended to be something between a witch and a scarecrow.

Ruddigore

ACT I

SCENE.—*The fishing village of Rederring (in Cornwall).* ROSE MAYBUD'S *cottage is seen* L. [1]

Enter Chorus of Bridesmaids. They range themselves in front of ROSE'S *cottage*

CHORUS OF BRIDESMAIDS

Fair is Rose as bright May-day;
   Soft is Rose as warm west-wind;
   Sweet is Rose as new-mown hay—
   Rose is queen of maiden-kind!
   Rose, all glowing
      With virgin blushes, say—
   Is anybody going
      To marry you to-day?

SOLO—ZORAH

Every day, as the days roll on,
Bridesmaids' garb we gaily don,
Sure that a maid so fairly famed
Can't long remain unclaimed.
Hour by hour and day by day,
Several months have passed away,
Though she's the fairest flower that blows,
No one has married Rose!

CHORUS

Rose, all glowing
   With virgin blushes, say—
Is anybody going
   To marry you to-day?

Enter DAME HANNAH, *from cottage* [2]

HANNAH. Nay, gentle maidens, you sing well but vainly, for Rose is still heart-free, and looks but coldly upon her many suitors.

ZORAH. It's very disappointing. Every young man in the village is in love with her, but they are appalled by her beauty and modesty, and won't declare themselves; so, until she makes her own choice, there's no chance for anybody else.

RUTH. This is, perhaps, the only village in the world that possesses an endowed corps of professional bridesmaids who are bound to be on duty every day from ten to four—and it is at least six months since our services were required. The pious charity by which we exist is practically wasted!

ZOR. We shall be disendowed—that will be the end of it! Dame Hannah—you're a nice old person—*you* could marry if you liked.

[1] *In actual production the Bridesmaids are "discovered on," already facing Rose's cottage.*

[2] *Similarly, Dame Hannah is "discovered" as the curtain rises. She is seated upstage center, knitting. During one American tour, Evelyn Gardiner was the Dame Hannah, and she boasted of having knitted a scarf some ten feet long during those few moments she had at each performance.*

[3] Baronet. *A sort of civilian equivalent of a Warrant Officer in the Army. He is not a private nor an NCO; neither is he a commissioned officer; nor, in this case, is he a commoner, because of his title of "Sir," which is a hereditary one. But he is not Peer of the Realm, and, therefore, not a "Lord."*

    Bad Baronet. *This, to me, was always a funny line and is, of course, based on the fact that all "meller-drammers" of the day boasted a villain who was almost inevitably a Baronet.*

[4] *Baronets are always depicted as being very wealthy—which is not always true in real life. I once knew a very poor one.*

[5] Lord of Ruddigore. *Do not be misled. The use of the word "lord" is in no way an indication of his rank. It is on a par with the expression "monarch of all he surveys." Or, as one critic said of Gilbert and Sullivan shortly after the production of The Gondoliers, "They are 'Monarchs of all they Savoy'!"*

There's old Adam—Robin's faithful servant—he loves you with all the frenzy of a boy of fourteen.

HAN. Nay—that may never be, for I am pledged!

ALL. To whom?

HAN. To an eternal maidenhood! Many years ago I was betrothed to a god-like youth who woo'd me under an assumed name. But on the very day upon which our wedding was to have been celebrated, I discovered that he was no other than Sir Roderic Murgatroyd, one of the bad Baronets [3] of Ruddigore, and the uncle of the man who now bears that title. As a son of that accursed race he was no husband for an honest girl, so, madly as I loved him, I left him then and there. He died but ten years since, but I never saw him again.

ZOR. But why should you not marry a bad Baronet of Ruddigore?

RUTH. All baronets are bad; but was he worse than other baronets?

HAN. My child, he was accursed.

ZOR. But who cursed him? Not you, I trust!

HAN. The curse is on all his line and has been, ever since the time of Sir Rupert, the first Baronet. Listen, and you shall hear the legend:

LEGEND—HANNAH

Sir Rupert Murgatroyd
  His leisure and his riches [4]
He ruthlessly employed
  In persecuting witches.
With fear he'd make them quake—
He'd duck them in his lake—
    He'd break their bones
    With sticks and stones,
And burn them at the stake!

CHORUS.
      This sport he much enjoyed,
      Did Rupert Murgatroyd—
        No sense of shame
        Or pity came
      To Rupert Murgatroyd!

Once, on the village green,
  A palsied hag he roasted,
And what took place, I ween,
  Shook his composure boasted;
For, as the torture grim
Seized on each withered limb,
    The writhing dame
    'Mid fire and flame
Yelled forth this curse on him:

"Each lord [5] of Ruddigore,
  Despite his best endeavour,
Shall do one crime, or more,
  Once, every day, for ever!
This doom he can't defy,
However he may try,
    For should he stay
    His hand, that day
In torture he shall die!"

The prophecy came true:
  Each heir who held the title
Had, every day, to do
  Some crime of import vital;

> Until, with guilt o'erplied,
> "I'll sin no more!" he cried,
>   And on the day
>   He said that say,
> In agony he died!

CHORUS.   And thus, with sinning cloyed,
> Has died each Murgatroyd,
>   And so shall fall,
>   Both one and all,
> Each coming Murgatroyd!

[Exeunt Chorus of Bridesmaids.

Enter ROSE MAYBUD *from cottage, with small basket on her arm*

HAN. Whither away, dear Rose? On some errand of charity, as is thy wont?

ROSE. A few gifts, dear aunt, for deserving villagers. Lo, here is some peppermint rock for old gaffer Gadderby, a set of false teeth for pretty little Ruth Rowbottom, and a pound of snuff for the poor orphan girl on the hill.

HAN. Ah, Rose, pity that so much goodness should not help to make some gallant youth happy for life! Rose, why dost thou harden that little heart of thine? Is there none hereaway whom thou couldst love?

ROSE. And if there were such an one, verily it would ill become me to tell him so.

HAN. Nay, dear one, where true love is, there is little need of prim formality.

ROSE. Hush, dear aunt, for thy words pain me sorely. Hung in a plated dish-cover to the knocker of the workhouse door, with naught that I could call mine own, save a change of baby-linen and a book of etiquette, [6] little wonder if I have always regarded that work as a voice from a parent's tomb. This hallowed volume (*producing a book of etiquette*), composed, if I may believe the title-page, by no less an authority than the wife of a Lord Mayor, has been, through life, my guide and monitor. By its solemn precepts I have learnt to test the moral worth of all who approach me. The man who bites his bread, or eats peas with a knife, I look upon as a lost creature, and he who has not acquired the proper way of entering and leaving a room is the object of my pitying horror. There are those in this village who bite their nails, dear aunt, and nearly all are wont to use their pocket combs in public places. In truth I could pursue this painful theme much further, but behold, I have said enough.

HAN. But is there not one among them who is faultless, in thine eyes? For example—young Robin. He combines the manners of a Marquis with the morals of a Methodist. Couldst thou not love *him?*

ROSE. And even if I could, how should I confess it unto him? For lo, he is shy, and sayeth naught!

BALLAD—ROSE [7]

> If somebody there chanced to be
>   Who loved me in a manner true,
> My heart would point him out to me,
>   And I would point him out to you.

(*Referring
to book.*)
> But here it says of those who point—
>   Their manners must be out of joint—[8]
>   You *may* not point—
>   You *must* not point—
> It's manners out of joint, to point!

[6] *In The Yeomen of the Guard, the opera that was to follow, I make a reference to a "bundle" which Elsie Maynard carries on at her first entrance. (See page 563, Note 23.) I often wonder if, somehow or other, Mr. J. M. Gordon became mixed up in his operas. In Rose's case, it is her Bible, and it is visible.*

[7] *Words and music on page 537.*

[8] *A delicious example of the reasoning of a follower of Emily Post. Gilbert uses a similar theme later in the scene between Richard Dauntless and Sir Despard (see Note 43).*

Had I the love of such as he,
　　Some quiet spot he'd take me to,
Then he could whisper it to me,
　　And I could whisper it to you.

(*Referring*
to book.)

But whispering, I've somewhere met,
Is contrary to etiquette:
　　　Where can it be? (*Searching book.*)
　　　Now let me see—(*Finding reference.*)
　　　Yes, yes!
It's contrary to etiquette!

(*Showing it to* HANNAH)

If any well-bred youth I knew,
　　Polite and gentle, neat and trim,
Then I would hint as much to you,
　　And you could hint as much to him.

(*Referring*
to book.)

But here it says, in plainest print,
　　"It's most unladylike to hint"—
　　　You *may* not hint,
　　　You *must* not hint—
It says you mustn't hint, in print!
And if I loved him through and through—
　　(True love and not a passing whim),
Then I could speak of it to you,
　　And you could speak of it to him.

(*Referring*
to book.)

But here I find it doesn't do
To speak until you're spoken to.
　　　Where can it be? (*Searching book.*)
　　　Now let me see—(*Finding reference.*)
　　　Yes, yes!
"Don't speak until you're spoken to!"

[*Exit* HANNAH.

ROSE. Poor aunt! Little did the good soul think, when she breathed the hallowed name of Robin, that he would do even as well as another. But he resembleth all the youths in this village, in that he is unduly bashful in my presence, and lo, it is hard to bring him to the point. [9] But soft, he is here!

[ROSE *is about to go when* ROBIN [10] *enters and calls her.*

ROBIN. Mistress Rose!
ROSE. (*Surprised.*) Master Robin!
ROB. I wished to say that—it is fine.
ROSE. It is passing fine.
ROB. But we do want rain.
ROSE. Aye, sorely! Is that all?
ROB. (*Sighing.*) That is all.
ROSE. Good day, Master Robin!
ROB. Good day, Mistress Rose! (*Both going—both stop.*)
ROSE.) I crave pardon, I——
ROB. ∫ I beg pardon, I——
ROSE. You were about to say?——
ROB. I would fain consult you——
ROSE. Truly?
ROB. It is about a friend.
ROSE. In truth I have a friend myself.
ROB. Indeed? I mean, of course——
ROSE. And I would fain consult you——

[9] . . . *it is hard to bring him to the point. Rose is not quite so naïve as she, like several other of Gilbert's heroines, would appear to be.*

[10] *Robin's appearance and manner, from his first entrance and throughout this scene, must be the complete good-looking, gawky "hayseed." No hint of any sophistication. Unless this is so, this duet might just as well be thrown out the window.*

ROB. (*Anxiously.*) About him?

ROSE. (*Prudishly.*) About *her.*

ROB. (*Relieved.*) Let us consult one another.

DUET—ROBIN *and* ROSE [11]

[11] *Words and music on page 540.*

ROB.   I know a youth who loves a little maid—
    (Hey, but his face is a sight for to see!)
  Silent is he, for he's modest and afraid—
    (Hey, but he's timid as a youth can be!)

ROSE.   I know a maid who loves a gallant youth,
    (Hey, but she sickens as the days go by!)
  She cannot tell him all the sad, sad truth—
    (Hey, but I think that little maid will die!)

ROB.   Poor little man!

ROSE.   Poor little maid!

ROB.   Poor little man!

ROSE.   Poor little maid!

BOTH.   Now tell me pray, and tell me true,
  What in the world should the ${young\ man \brace maiden}$ do?

ROB.   He cannot eat and he cannot sleep—
    (Hey, but his face is a sight for to see!)
  Daily he goes for to wail—for to weep—
    (Hey, but he's wretched as a youth can be!)

ROSE.   She's very thin and she's very pale—
    (Hey, but she sickens as the days go by!)
  Daily she goes for to weep—for to wail—
    (Hey, but I think that little maid will die!)

ROB.   Poor little maid!

ROSE.   Poor little man!

ROB.   Poor little maid!

ROSE.   Poor little man!

BOTH.   Now tell me pray, and tell me true,
  What in the world should the ${young\ man \brace maiden}$ do?

ROSE.   If I were the youth I should offer her my name—
    (Hey, but her face is a sight for to see!)

ROB.   If I were the maid I should fan his honest flame—
    (Hey, but he's bashful as a youth can be!)

ROSE.   If I were the youth I should speak to her to-day—
    (Hey, but she sickens as the days go by!)

ROB.   If I were the maid I should meet the lad half way—
    (For I really do believe that timid youth will die!)

ROSE.   Poor little man!

ROB.   Poor little maid!

ROSE.   Poor little man!

ROB.   Poor little maid!

BOTH.   I thank you, ${miss, \brace sir,}$ for your counsel true;

Poor little man!
Poor little maid!

I'll tell that $\begin{Bmatrix} \text{youth} \\ \text{maid} \end{Bmatrix}$ what $\begin{Bmatrix} \text{he} \\ \text{she} \end{Bmatrix}$ ought to do!

[*Exit* ROSE.

[12] Ruthven. *Pronounced "Rivven." (See Act II, Note 55: "Without the elision . . .")*

[13] *Sir Ruthven is obviously a master of make-up and disguise. As Robin he appears to be little more than twenty-eight or so, and even then it means that he was only nine when he fled his home. His brother, who is younger, has every appearance of being the elder by some years. A similar situation is found in H.M.S. Pinafore with Ralph Rackstraw and Captain Corcoran. Corcoran, you will remember, had a daughter of twenty-one whom Ralph eventually married, and yet Ralph and Corcoran were babes in arms together. And didn't the Captain marry the baby farmer?*

[14] *. . . and see, he comes this way! I have never understood why Robin, on being told this, doesn't wait to greet his "beloved foster-brother." I once suggested to Mr. Carte that this line be cut, but, no, Gilbert had written it and it must stay. The only way I could ever make his exit appear at all sensible was to have him go off rapidly on his own line, "No, no—it cannot be!" and leave Adam to chase after him, as if to say, "Don't go—see—he comes this way!"*

[15] *The French people were, for a long time, deeply offended by this song. Indeed, quite an amount of official, top-level correspondence was exchanged on the subject. But how wrong they were! It was the British, as always, whom Gilbert was lampooning. What the boastful tar is saying is that a British sloop, on approaching a French frigate, and finding her not only fully armed but with some pretty accurate gunners aboard, actually turned tail and fled. Another case of "Blimey, wot I'd've done to 'im—if 'e 'adn't done it to me first!"*

ROB. Poor child! I sometimes think that if she wasn't quite so particular I might venture—but no—even then I should be unworthy of her!

He sits desponding. Enter OLD ADAM

ADAM. My kind master is sad! Dear Sir Ruthven [12] Murgatroyd——
ROB. Hush! As you love me, breathe not that hated name. [13] Twenty years ago, in horror at the prospect of inheriting that hideous title, and with it the ban that compels all who succeed to the baronetcy to commit at least one deadly crime per day, for life, I fled my home, and concealed myself in this innocent village under the name of Robin Oakapple. My younger brother, Despard, believing me to be dead, succeeded to the title and its attendant curse. For twenty years I have been dead and buried. Don't dig me up now.
ADAM. Dear master, it shall be as you wish, for have I not sworn to obey you for ever in all things? Yet, as we are here alone, and as I belong to that particular description of good old man to whom the truth is a refreshing novelty, let me call you by your own right title once more! (ROBIN *assents*.) Sir Ruthven Murgatroyd! Baronet! Of Ruddigore! Whew! It's like eight hours at the seaside!
ROB. My poor old friend! Would there were more like you!
ADAM. Would there were indeed! But I bring you good tidings. Your foster-brother, Richard, has returned from sea—his ship the *Tom-Tit* rides yonder at anchor, and he himself is even now in this very village!
ROB. My beloved foster-brother? No, no—it cannot be!
ADAM. It is even so—and see, he comes this way! [14]

[*Exeunt together.*

Enter Chorus of Bridesmaids

CHORUS

From the briny sea
  Comes young Richard, all victorious!
Valorous is he—
  His achievements all are glorious
Let the welkin ring
With the news we bring
  Sing it—shout it—
  Tell about it—
Safe and sound returneth he,
All victorious from the sea!

Enter RICHARD. *The girls welcome him as he greets old acquaintances*

BALLAD—RICHARD [15]

I shipped, d'ye see, in a Revenue sloop,
 And, off Cape Finistere,
  A merchantman we see,
  A Frenchman, going free,
So we made for the bold Mounseer,
  D'ye see?
We made for the bold Mounseer.

CHORUS. So we made for the bold Mounseer,
  D'ye see?
We made for the bold Mounseer.

But she proved to be a Frigate—and she up with her ports,
    And fires with a thirty-two!
        It come uncommon near,
        But we answered with a cheer,
    Which paralysed the Parley-voo,
        D'ye see?
    Which paralysed the Parley-voo!

CHORUS.   Which paralysed the Parley-voo,
        D'ye see?
    Which paralysed the Parley-voo!

Then our Captain he up and he says, says he,
    "That chap we need not fear,—
        We can take her, if we like,
        She is sartin for to strike,
    For she's only a darned Mounseer,
        D'ye see?
    She's only a darned Mounseer!

CHORUS.   For she's only a darned Mounseer,
        D'ye see?
    She's only a darned Mounseer!

But to fight a French fal-lal—it's like hittin' of a gal—
    It's a lubberly thing for to do;
        For we, with our faults,
        Why we're sturdy British salts,
    While she's only a poor Parley-voo,
        D'ye see?
    While she's only a poor Parley-voo!"

CHORUS.   While she's only a poor Parley-voo,
        D'ye see?
    While she's only a poor Parley-voo!

So we up with our helm, and we scuds before the breeze
    As we gives a compassionating cheer;
        Froggee answers with a shout
        As he sees us go about,
    Which was grateful of the poor Mounseer,
        D'ye see?
    Which was grateful of the poor Mounseer!

CHORUS.   Which was grateful of the poor Mounseer,
        D'ye see?
    Which was grateful of the poor Mounseer!

And I'll wager in their joy they kissed each other's cheek
    (Which is what them furriners do),
        And they blessed their lucky stars
        We were hardy British tars
    Who had pity on a poor Parley-voo,
        D'ye see?
    Who had pity on a poor Parley-voo!

CHORUS.   Who had pity on a poor Parley-voo,
        D'ye see?
    Who had pity on a poor Parley-voo!

(HORNPIPE) [16]

[*Exeunt* CHORUS.

For she's only a darned Mounseer,
D'ye see?

[16] Hornpipe. *Durward Lely, the creator of the role of Richard Dauntless, was responsible for the hornpipe which comes in here. When quite an old man, he came to see a performance of Ruddigore in Glasgow and then came backstage after the performance to visit me. "You know, Martyn," he said, as the actor playing Dick walked into my dressing room, "I said to W. S. G. at the first music rehearsal for Ruddigore that I thought Dick would quite naturally break into some sort of sailor's dance after such a salty sailor song. There was no music written for such a dance, and it seemed to me that Gilbert took no notice of me at the time, but the next day he asked me, as if he had thought of it, if I thought I could dance a hornpipe. I very rashly said I could, and the hornpipe was written. I learned twelve steps, and every tenor since has cursed me for speaking out of turn."*

Then, very glibly and with a whimsical smile, Mr. Lely added: "All tenors can sing—but I know only one who could dance as well!" What he really meant was, ". . . as well as I did," because I knew several tenors who both sang and danced the role. Not one of them liked the dance, and in any case it was the singing that was outstanding. In Durward Lely's case, it was both.

Enter ROB IN

ROB. Richard!

RICH. Robin!

ROB. My beloved foster-brother, and very dearest friend, welcome home again after ten long years at sea! It is such deeds as yours that cause our flag to be loved and dreaded throughout the civilised world!

RICH. Why, lord love ye, Rob, that's but a trifle to what we *have* done in the way of sparing life! I believe I may say, without exaggeration, that the marciful little *Tom-Tit* has spared more French frigates than any craft afloat! But 'tain't for a British seaman to brag, so I'll just stow my jawin' tackle and belay. (ROBIN *sighs.*) But 'vast heavin', messmate, what's brought *you* all a-cockbill?

ROB. Alas, Dick, I love Rose Maybud, and love in vain!

RICH. *You* love in vain? Come, that's too good! Why, you're a fine strapping muscular young fellow—tall and strong as a to'-gall'n'-m'st—taut as a forestay—aye, and a barrowknight to boot, if all had their rights!

ROB. Hush, Richard—not a word about my true rank, which none here suspect. Yes, I know well enough that few men are better calculated to win a woman's heart than I. I'm a fine fellow, Dick, and worthy any woman's love—happy the girl who gets me, say I. But I'm timid, Dick; shy—nervous—modest—retiring—diffident—and I cannot tell her, Dick, I cannot tell her! Ah, you've no idea what a poor opinion I have of myself, and how little I deserve it.

RICH. Robin, do you call to mind how, years ago, we swore that, come what might, we would always act upon our hearts' dictates?

ROB. Aye, Dick, and I've always kept that oath. [17] In doubt, difficulty, and danger I've always asked my heart what I should do, and it has never failed me.

RICH. Right! Let your heart be your compass, with a clear conscience for your binnacle light, and you'll sail ten knots on a bowline, clear of shoals, rocks, and quicksands! Well, now, what does my heart say in this here difficult situation? Why, it says, "Dick," it says—(it calls me Dick acos it's known me from a babby)—"Dick," it says, *"you* ain't shy—*you* ain't modest—speak you up for him as is!" Robin, my lad, just you lay me alongside, and when she's becalmed under my lee, I'll spin her a yarn that shall sarve to fish you two together for life!

ROB. Will you do this thing for me? Can you, do you think? Yes (*feeling his pulse*). [18] There's no false modesty about *you.* Your—what I would call bumptious self-assertiveness (I mean the expression in its complimentary sense) has already made you a bos'n's mate, and it will make an admiral of you in time, if you work it properly, you dear, incompetent old impostor! My dear fellow, I'd give my right arm for one tenth of your modest assurance!

SONG—ROBIN [19]

My boy, you may take it from me,
 That of all the afflictions accurst
  With which a man's saddled
  And hampered and addled,
 A diffident nature's the worst.
Though clever as clever can be—
 A Crichton of early romance—
  You must stir it and stump it,
  And blow your own trumpet,
 Or, trust me, you haven't a chance!

 If you wish in the world to advance,
 Your merits you're bound to enhance,

[17] *Robin must take a very dramatic pose at this point, remove his hat, holding it above his head, and place his free hand on his heart. If he wants to try to be very funny, at the end of the speech ". . . it has never failed me" he should replace his hat on his head, snapping it into place so hard that it comes down over his eyes.*

[18] *Robin pulls a watch from his fob pocket as he begins to feel Dick's pulse. When I had the part I went to great trouble to get an old vest-pocket chronometer from which I removed the works and then inserted some heavy lumps of metal. I used to hold it to my ear and shake it in an effort to get it started. The resulting clatter of loose lead could be heard all over the theater, and when I held it to my ear again and found to my satisfaction that it appeared to be going, I had to wait a second or two before I was able to proceed with my next line.*

[19] *Words and music on page 544.*

. . . stir it and stump it!

You must stir it and stump it,
And blow your own trumpet,
Or, trust me, you haven't a chance!

Now take, for example, *my* case:
I've a bright intellectual brain—
In all London city
There's no one so witty—
I've thought so again and again.
I've a highly intelligent face—
My features cannot be denied—
But, whatever I try, sir,
I fail in—and why, sir? [20]
I'm modesty personified!

If you wish in the world to advance, etc.

As a poet, I'm tender and quaint—
I've passion and fervour and grace—
From Ovid and Horace
To Swinburne and Morris,
They all of them take a back place.
Then I sing and I play and I paint:
Though none are accomplished as I,
To say so were treason:
You ask me the reason? [21]
I'm diffident, modest, and shy!

If you wish in the world to advance, etc.

[*Exit* ROBIN.

RICH. (*looking after him*). Ah, it's a thousand pities he's such a poor opinion of himself, for a finer fellow don't walk! Well, I'll do my best for him. "Plead for him as though it was for your own father"—that's what my heart's a-remarkin' to me just now. But here she comes! Steady! Steady it is! (*Enter* ROSE—*he is much struck by her.*) By the Port Admiral, but she's a tight little craft! Come, come, she's not for you, Dick, and yet—she's fit to marry Lord Nelson! [22] By the Flag of Old England, I can't look at her unmoved.

ROSE. Sir, you are agitated—

RICH. Aye, aye, my lass, well said! I am agitated, true enough!—took flat aback, my girl; but 'tis naught—'twill pass. (*Aside.*) This here heart of mine's a-dictatin' to me like anythink. Question is, Have I a right to disregard its promptings?

ROSE. Can I do aught to relieve thine anguish, for it seemeth to me that thou art in sore trouble? This apple—(*offering a damaged apple*).

RICH. (*looking at it and returning it*). No, my lass, 'tain't that: I'm—I'm took flat aback—I never see anything like you in all my born days. Parbuckle [23] me, if you ain't the loveliest gal I've ever set eyes on. There—I can't say fairer than that, can I?

ROSE. No. (*Aside.*) The question is, Is it meet that an utter stranger should thus express himself? (*Refers to book.*) Yes—"Always speak the truth."

RICH. I'd no thoughts of sayin' this here to you on my own account, for, truth to tell, I was chartered by another; but when I see you my heart it up and it says, says it, "This is the very lass for *you*, Dick"—"speak up to her, Dick," it says—(it calls me Dick acos we was at school together)—"tell her all, Dick," it says, "never sail under false colours—it's mean!" *That's* what my heart tells me to say, and in my rough, common-sailor fashion, I've said it, and I'm a-waiting for your reply.

[20] *The music should come to a full stop at this point so that Dick can interpolate: "I dunno!"*

[21] *The music again comes to a full stop and Dick this time interpolates: "No, I didn't." Before continuing with the song, Robin says: "Oh, sorry, I thought you did!"*

[22] *Later on in this scene Dick makes an allusion to the Admiral of the Fleet, who was at one time Lord Horatio Nelson. This would appear to set the date very early in the 19th century, in fact, before 1805.*

[23] *Parbuckle. A kind of sling formed by passing two ends of a rope around a heavy object and through a bight of the rope. The weight of the object keeps the knot tight. It was a form of sailor's knot used for raising guns, casks, etc. Dick obviously means, "Well, tie me up in a knot!"*

I'm a-tremblin', miss. Lookye here—(*holding out his hand*). That's narvousness!

ROSE (*aside*). Now, how should a maiden deal with such an one? (*Consults book.*) "Keep no one in unnecessary suspense." (*Aloud.*) Behold, I will not keep you in unnecessary suspense. (*Refers to book.*) "In accepting an offer of marriage, do so with apparent hesitation." (*Aloud.*) I take you, but with a certain show of reluctance. (*Refers to book.*) "Avoid any appearance of eagerness." (*Aloud.*) Though you will bear in mind that I am far from anxious to do so. (*Refers to book.*) "A little show of emotion will not be misplaced!" (*Aloud.*) Pardon this tear! (*Wipes her eye.*)

RICH. Rose, you've made me the happiest blue-jacket in England! I wouldn't change places with the Admiral of the Fleet, no matter who he's a-huggin' of at this present moment! [24] But, axin' your pardon, miss (*wiping his lips with his hand*), might I be permitted to salute the flag I'm goin' to sail under?

ROSE (*referring to book*). "An engaged young lady should not permit too many familiarities." (*Aloud.*) Once! (RICHARD *kisses her.*)

DUET—RICHARD *and* ROSE [25]

RICH.
    The battle's roar is over,
        O my love!
    Embrace thy tender lover,
        O my love!
      From tempests' welter,
        From war's alarms,
    O give me shelter
        Within those arms!
    Thy smile alluring,
    All heart-ache curing,
    Gives peace enduring,
        O my love!

ROSE.
    If heart both true and tender,
        O my love!
    A life-love can engender,
        O my love!
    A truce to sighing
        And tears of brine,
    For joy undying
        Shall aye be mine,
    And thou and I, love,
    Shall live and die, love,
    Without a sigh, love—
        My own, my love!

Enter ROBIN, *with* CHORUS OF BRIDESMAIDS

CHORUS

If well his suit has sped,
Oh, may they soon be wed!
Oh, tell us, tell us, pray,
What doth the maiden say?
In singing are we justified,
    Hail the Bridegroom—hail the Bride!
    Let the nuptial knot be tied:
        In fair phrases,
        Hymn their praises,
    Hail the Bridegroom—hail the Bride?

[24] A very obvious reference to Lady Hamilton.

[25] Though still retained in many editions of libretto and score, it has been many, many years since this duet was included in any of the D'Oyly Carte performances. I do not remember hearing it even as far back as 1923. As performed today, Robin's entrance with Chorus and Bridesmaids, "If well his suit has sped," is picked up on Rose's cue, "Once! (RICHARD kisses her.)"

ROB. Well—what news? Have you spoken to her?

RICH. Aye, my lad, I have—so to speak—spoke her.

ROB. And she refuses?

RICH. Why, no, I can't truly say she do.

ROB. Then she accepts! My darling! (*Embraces her.*) [26]

BRIDESMAIDS

Hail the Bridegroom—hail the Bride! etc.

ROSE (*aside, referring to her book*). Now, what should a maiden do when she is embraced by the wrong gentleman?

RICH. Belay, my lad, belay. You don't understand.

ROSE. Oh, sir, belay, I beseech you!

RICH. You see, it's like this: she accepts—but it's *me*.

ROB. You! (RICHARD *embraces* ROSE.)

BRIDESMAIDS [27]

Hail the Bridegroom—hail the Bride!
When the nuptial knot is tied——

ROB. (*interrupting angrily*). Hold your tongues, will you! Now then, what does this mean?

RICH. My poor lad, my heart grieves for thee, but it's like this: the moment I see her, and just as I was a-goin' to mention your name, my heart it up and it says, says it—"Dick, you've fell in love with her yourself," it says; "be honest and sailor-like—don't skulk under false colours—speak up," it says, "take her, you dog, and with her my blessin'!"

BRIDESMAIDS

Hail the Bridegroom—hail the Bride!——

ROB. Will you be quiet! Go away! (CHORUS *make faces at him and exeunt.*) Vulgar girls! [28]

RICH. What could I do? I'm bound to obey my heart's dictates.

ROB. Of course—no doubt. It's quite right—I don't mind—that is, not particularly—only it's—it *is* disappointing, you know.

ROSE (*to* ROBIN). Oh, but, sir, I knew not that thou didst seek me in wedlock, or in very truth I should not have hearkened unto this man, for behold, he is but a lowly mariner, and very poor withal, whereas thou art a tiller of the land, and thou hast fat oxen, and many sheep and swine, a considerable dairy farm and much corn and oil!

RICH. That's true, my lass, but it's done now, ain't it, Rob?

ROSE. Still it may be that I should not be happy in thy love. I am passing young and little able to judge. Moreover, as to thy character I know naught!

ROB. Nay, Rose, I'll answer for that. Dick has won thy love fairly. Broken-hearted as I am, I'll stand up for Dick through thick and thin! [29]

RICH. (*with emotion*). Thankye, messmate! that's well said. That's spoken honest. Thankye, Rob! (*Grasps his hand.*)

ROSE. Yet methinks I have heard that sailors are but worldly men, and little prone to lead serious and thoughtful lives!

ROB. And what then? Admit that Dick is *not* a steady character, and that when he's excited he uses language that would make your hair curl. Grant that—he does. It's the truth, and I'm not going to deny it. But look at his *good* qualities. He's as nimble as a pony, and his hornpipe is the talk of the Fleet! [30]

RICH. Thankye, Rob! That's well spoken. Thankye, Rob!

ROSE. But it may be that he drinketh strong waters which do bemuse

[26] *I regret to say that though Mr. Gilbert's directions say that Robin embraces Rose, he doesn't. Rose sees to this by repulsing him as soon as he makes the effort to embrace her and turns to her book of etiquette. At the same time Richard seizes Robin by the arm and forcibly drags him away.*

[27] *The Bridesmaids are a professional group and ready to hail any bridegroom—it doesn't matter which. To them a bridegroom is a bridegroom. It's a little like professional mourners at an Irish wake.*

[28] *Robin's irritation at the Bridesmaids is certainly understandable. Their reaction to him is also understandable—up to a point. There is every likelihood that they will be done out of a wedding!*
  One of the girls, just before she exits, turns and sticks her tongue out at Robin. It is this that really shocks him and causes him to say "Vulgar girls!" It was ever a joy to me to see that the girl entrusted with this piece of vulgarity had such a delightfully pink tongue, until I discovered that she always kept a supply of cochineal on hand.

[29] *As Ko-Ko says of Nanki-Poo in The Mikado, "Noble fellow!" But wait. Robin's attitude is only skin deep.*

[30] *Richard breaks into a step that purports to be part of the sailor's hornpipe—dum di di dum dum—dum dum! Robin watches him admiringly (?) and at the end turns to Rose and says: "There—and that's only a bit of it!" This line will not be found in any of the official editions of the libretto, but it is always spoken. Had Queen Victoria seen Ruddigore she would undoubtedly have remarked on this line, and probably on the interpolations used in Robin's song: "My boy, you may take it from me" (see Notes 20 and 21), as she did later regarding The Gondoliers (see page 667, Note 86).*

a man, and make him even as the wild beasts of the desert!

ROB. Well, suppose he does, and I don't say he don't, for rum's his bane, and ever has been. He *does* drink—I won't deny it. But what of that? Look at his arms—tattooed to the shoulder! (RICH. *rolls up his sleeves.*) No, no—I won't hear a word against Dick!

ROSE. But they say that mariners are but rarely true to those whom they profess to love!

ROB. Granted—granted—and I don't say that Dick isn't as bad as any of 'em. (RICH. *chuckles.*) You are, you know you are, you dog! a devil of a fellow—a regular out-and-out Lothario! But what then? You can't have everything, and a better hand at turning-in a dead-eye don't walk a deck! And what an accomplishment *that* is in a family man! No, no—not a word against Dick. I'll stick up for him through thick and thin!

RICH. Thankye, Rob, thankye. You're a true friend. I've acted accordin' to my heart's dictates, and such orders as them no man should disobey.

[31] *No doubt the heart should be their guide—if the heart of each had not been ruled by such a shrewd, cunning and calculating head!*

ENSEMBLE—RICHARD, ROBIN, ROSE

In sailing o'er life's ocean wide
Your heart should be your only guide; [31]
With summer sea and favouring wind,
Yourself in port you'll surely find.

SOLO—RICHARD

My heart says, "To this maiden strike—
    She's captured you.
She's just the sort of girl you like—
    You know you do.
If other man her heart should gain,
    I shall resign."
That's what it says to me quite plain,
    This heart of mine.

SOLO—ROBIN

My heart says, "You've a prosperous lot,
    With acres wide;
You mean to settle all you've got
    Upon your bride."
It don't pretend to shape my acts
    By word or sign;
It merely states these simple facts,
    This heart of mine!

SOLO—ROSE

Ten minutes since my heart said "white"—
    It now says "black."
It then said "left"—it now says "right"—
    Hearts often tack.
I must obey its latest strain—
    You tell me so. (*To* RICHARD.)
But should it change its mind again,
    I'll let you know.

(*Turning from* RICHARD *to* ROBIN, *who embraces her.*)

ENSEMBLE

In sailing o'er life's ocean wide
No doubt the heart should be your guide;
But it is awkward when you find
A heart that does not know its mind!

[*Exeunt* ROBIN *with* ROSE L., *and* RICHARD *weeping*, R.

Enter MAD MARGARET. *She is wildly dressed in picturesque tatters, and is an obvious caricature of theatrical madness.*

SCENA—MARGARET

Cheerily carols the lark
   Over the cot. [32]
Merrily whistles the clerk
   Scratching a blot.
     But the lark
     And the clerk,
     I remark,
   Comfort me not!

Over the ripening peach
   Buzzes the bee.
Splash on the billowy beach
   Tumbles the sea.
     But the peach
     And the beach
     They are each
   Nothing to me!
   And why?
   Who am I?
Daft Madge! Crazy Meg!
Mad Margaret! Poor Peg!
   He! he! he! he! he! (*chuckling*).

   Mad, I?
     Yes, very!
   But why?
     Mystery!
       Don't call!
         Whisht! whisht!
   No crime—
     'Tis only
   That I'm
     Love-lonely!
     That's all!

BALLAD—MARGARET [33]

To a garden full of posies
   Cometh one to gather flowers,
   And he wanders through its bowers
Toying with the wanton roses,
   Who, uprising from their beds,
   Hold on high their shameless heads
With their pretty lips a-pouting,
Never doubting—never doubting
   That for Cytherean posies
   He would gather aught but roses!

In a nest of weeds and nettles
   Lay a violet, half-hidden,
   Hoping that his glance unbidden
Yet might fall upon her petals.
   Though she lived alone, apart,
   Hope lay nestling at her heart,
But, alas, the cruel awaking

[32] Cot. *An accepted abbreviation of cottage, but in the manner in which Gilbert uses the word (quite correctly, by the way) it should be interpreted as* cote—*a place of shelter or a nest. And yet, if one gets down to basics, true interpretation doesn't matter, for these are but the ravings of a mentally deranged person, a person driven to madness by force of circumstances. One has only to look at Gilbert's directions for Margaret's character to see that she is but a thinly disguised version of Ophelia—"an obvious caricature . . ."*

   Read the lines assigned to each and you will find that, in spite of Mad Margaret's inanities, there is, as in the remarks of Ophelia, a deal of wisdom and meaning.

[33] *Although Phoebe was in no way mentally unstable, there is considerable similarity between her opening number in* The Yeomen of the Guard *and Mad Margaret's ballad here. Compare the sentiments, to say nothing of certain actual phrases; and Gilbert's directions, though phrased differently, come to the same thing (Bursts into tears).*

Set her little heart a-breaking,
For he gathered for his posies
Only roses—only roses!

(*Bursts into tears.*)

Enter ROSE

ROSE. A maiden, and in tears? Can I do aught to soften thy sorrow? This apple—(*offering apple*). [34]

MAR. (*Examines it and rejects it.*) No! (*Mysteriously.*) Tell me, are you mad?

ROSE. I? No! That is, I think not.

MAR. That's well! Then you don't love Sir Despard Murgatroyd? All mad girls love him. *I* love him. [35] I'm poor Mad Margaret—Crazy Meg!—Poor Peg! He! he! he! he! (*chuckling*).

ROSE. Thou lovest the bad Baronet of Ruddigore? Oh, horrible—too horrible!

MAR. You pity me? Then be my mother! The squirrel had a mother, but she drank and the squirrel fled! Hush! They sing a brave song in our parts—it runs somewhat thus: (*Sings.*)

"The cat and the dog and the little puppee [36]
Sat down in a—down in a—in a——"

I forget what they sat down in; but so the song goes! Listen—I've come to pinch her!

ROSE. Mercy, whom?

MAR. You mean "who".

ROSE. Nay! It is the accusative after the verb.

MAR. True. (*Whispers melodramatically.*) I have come to pinch Rose Maybud!

ROSE. (*Aside, alarmed.*) Rose Maybud!

MAR. Aye! I love him—he loved me once. But that's all gone, fisht! He gave me an Italian glance—thus (*business*)—and made me his. He will give *her* an Italian glance, and make *her* his. But it shall not be, for I'll stamp on her—stamp on her—stamp on her! Did you ever kill anybody? No? Why not? Listen—I killed a fly this morning! It buzzed, and I wouldn't have it. So it died—pop! So shall she!

ROSE. But, behold, *I* am Rose Maybud, and I would fain not die "pop."

MAR. You are Rose Maybud?

ROSE. Yes, sweet Rose Maybud!

MAR. Strange! They told me she was beautiful. [37] And *he* loves *you!* No, no! If I thought that, I would treat you as the auctioneer and land-agent treated the lady-bird—I would rend you asunder!

ROSE. Nay, be pacified, for behold I am pledged to another, and lo, we are to be wedded this very day!

MAR. Swear me that! Come to a Commissioner and let me have it on affidavit! I once made an affidavit—but it died—it died—it died! [38] But, see, they come—Sir Despard and his evil crew! Hide, hide—they are all mad—quite mad!

ROSE. What makes you think that?

MAR. Hush! They sing choruses in public. [39] That's mad enough, I think! Go—hide away, or they will seize you! Hush! Quite softly—quite, quite softly!

[*Exeunt together, on tiptoe.*

*Enter Chorus of Bucks and Blades, heralded
by Chorus of Bridesmaids* [40]

[34] (*Offering apple*). *Out of which one large bite has already been taken. Very obviously Margaret is not quite as mad as that.*

[35] *Mad Margaret is perhaps the sanest person on the stage. She knows she's mad and admits it.*

[36] *Sullivan must have written the tune for this unfinished couplet. If he didn't, then this is the second number Gilbert composed, because there is a tune and "it runs somewhat thus:"*

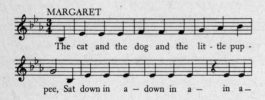

[37] *An almost identical joke will be found in Princess Ida:*

    KING GAMA: *Are you Hilarion? You were an exceedingly handsome child!*

[38] *. . . it died—it died—it died! My experience has been that the laugh comes on the first "it died." The repetition boosts the idea of madness, possibly, but it's really only gilding the lily.*

[39] *Gilbert is poking the most glorious fun at all "musical choruses," be they in grand opera, comic opera, Viennese opera, or just plain musicals. He's poking fun at Sullivan for having composed such things; at himself for having written them; at the public for listening to them seriously.*

[40] *The entrance of the male Chorus—the Bucks and the Blades—used to be a colorful sight. Twenty British regiments were represented, the*

CHORUS OF BRIDESMAIDS

Welcome, gentry,
For your entry
Sets our tender hearts a-beating.
Men of station,
Admiration
Prompts this unaffected greeting.
Hearty greeting offer we!

CHORUS OF BUCKS AND BLADES

When thoroughly tired
Of being admired
By ladies of gentle degree—degree,
With flattery sated,
High-flown and inflated,
Away from the city we flee—we flee!
From charms intramural
To prettiness rural
The sudden transition
Is simply Elysian,
So come, Amaryllis,
Come, Chloe and Phyllis,
Your slaves, for the moment, are we!

ALL. From charms intramural, etc.

CHORUS OF BRIDESMAIDS

The sons of the tillage
Who dwell in this village
Are people of lowly degree—degree.
Though honest and active,
They're most unattractive,
And awkward as awkward can be—can be.
They're clumsy clodhoppers
With axes and choppers,
And shepherds and ploughmen
And drovers and cowmen
And hedgers and reapers
And carters and keepers,
And never a lover for me!

BRIDESMAIDS

So, welcome, gentry, etc.

BUCKS AND BLADES

When thoroughly tired, etc.

Enter SIR DESPARD MURGATROYD

SONG AND CHORUS—SIR DESPARD

SIR D. Oh, why am I moody and sad?
CH. Can't guess!
SIR D. And why am I guiltily mad?
CH. Confess!
SIR D. Because I am thoroughly bad!
CH. Oh yes—
SIR D. You'll see it at once in my face.
Oh, why am I husky and hoarse?

uniform of each having been scrutinized most carefully by Gilbert to insure complete authenticity. It was an entrance that invariably evoked a big round of applause. The latest production, as designed by Peter Goffin, produced little or no applause, and yet in his way he was more logical in his approach. Why Gilbert decided to use a pageant of military dress uniforms in a Cornish fishing village passes my comprehension, since a buck is merely a dandy, a dashing fellow, and a blade is a gallant. But Gilbert was obviously looking for a male chorus entrance that would measure up to the entrance of the Dragoon Guards in Patience.

An extract from the first-night program carries this announcement:

In the First Act, Officers of the following Regiments are represented in the order in which they stand upon the stage:

7th Hussars	9th Lancers
1st Life Guards	Coldstream Guards
18th Hussars	19th Lancers
8th Light Dragoons	27th Regiment
Royal Engineers	17th Light Dragoons
Royal Horse Guards	Royal Artillery
Royal Horse Artillery	Scots Guards
52nd Light Infantry	10th Hussars
3rd Dragoon Guards	Grenadier Guards
12th Light Dragoons	15th Hussars

This chorus of Bridesmaids with the chorus of Bucks and Blades eventually turns into one of Sullivan's most delightful examples of counterpoint. Two separate and distinct melodies plus two distinct time signatures blend perfectly with each other.

CH.   Ah, why?
SIR D. It's the workings of conscience, of course.
CH.   Fie, fie!
SIR D. And huskiness stands for remorse,
CH.   Oh my!
SIR D.   At least it does so in my case!

SIR D. When in crime one is fully employed—
CH.   Like you—
SIR D. Your expression gets warped and destroyed:
CH.   It do.
SIR D. It's a penalty none can avoid;
CH.   How true!
SIR D.   I once was a nice-looking youth;
          But like stone from a strong catapult—
CH. (*explaining to each other*).   A trice—
SIR D. I rushed at my terrible cult—
CH. (*explaining to each other*).   That's vice—
SIR D. Observe the unpleasant result!
CH.   Not nice.
SIR D.   Indeed I am telling the truth!

SIR D. Oh, innocent, happy though poor!
CH.   That's we—
SIR D. If I had been virtuous, I'm sure—
CH.   Like me—
SIR D. I should be as nice-looking as you're!
CH.   May be.
SIR D.   You are very nice-looking indeed!
          Oh, innocents, listen in time—
CH.   We *doe*,
SIR D. Avoid an existence of crime—
CH.   Just so—
SIR D. Or you'll be as ugly as I'm—
CH. (*loudly*).   No! No!
SIR D.   And now, if you please, we'll proceed.

[*All the Girls express their horror of* SIR DESPARD. *As he approaches them they fly from him, terror-stricken, leaving him alone on the stage.*

SIR D. Poor children, how they loathe me—me whose hands are certainly steeped in infamy, but whose heart is as the heart of a little child. But what *is* a poor baronet to do, when a whole picture gallery [41] of ancestors step down from their frames and threaten him with an excruciating death if he hesitate to commit his daily crime? But ha! ha! I am even with them! (*Mysteriously.*) I get my crime over the first thing in the morning, and then, ha! ha! for the rest of the day I do good—I do good—I do good! (*Melodramatically.*) Two days since, I stole a child and built an orphan asylum. Yesterday I robbed a bank and endowed a bishopric. To-day I carry off Rose Maybud and atone with a cathedral! This is what it is to be the sport and toy of a Picture Gallery! But I will be bitterly revenged upon them! I will give them all to the Nation, and nobody shall ever look upon their faces again!

Enter RICHARD

RICH. Ax [42] your honour's pardon, but——
SIR D. Ha! observed! And by a mariner! What would you with me, fellow?

[41] Picture gallery. *This is the first indication that it is a ghostly gallery of pictures which keeps the holder of the (Bad) Baronetcy in line.*

[42] Ax. *Ask. Gilbert wrote it this way. And that is the way it has always been printed. But I never heard a Richard say anything other than "Axin'."*

RICH. Your honour, I'm a poor man-o'-war's-man, becalmed in the doldrums——

SIR D. I don't know them.

RICH. And I make bold to ax your honour's advice. Does your honour know what it is to have a heart?

SIR D. My honour knows what it is to have a complete apparatus for conducting the circulation of the blood through the veins and arteries of the human body.

RICH. Aye, but has your honour a heart that ups and looks you in the face, and gives you quarter-deck orders that it's life and death to disobey?

SIR D. I have not a heart of that description, but I have a Picture Gallery that presumes to take that liberty.

RICH. Well, your honour, it's like this—Your honour had an elder brother——

SIR D. It had.

RICH. Who should have inherited your title and, with it, its cuss.

SIR D. Aye, but he died. Oh, Ruthven!——

RICH. He didn't.

SIR D. He did *not?*

RICH. He didn't. On the contrary, he lives in this here very village, under the name of Robin Oakapple, and he's a-going to marry Rose Maybud this very day.

SIR D. Ruthven alive, and going to marry Rose Maybud! Can this be possible?

RICH. Now the question I was going to ask [43] your honour is— Ought I to tell your honour this?

SIR D. I don't know. It's a delicate point. I think you ought. Mind, I'm not sure, but I think so.

RICH. That's what my heart says. It says, "Dick," it says (it calls me Dick acos it's entitled to take that liberty), "that there young gal would recoil from him if she knowed what he really were. Ought you to stand off and on, and let this young gal take this false step and never fire a shot across her bows to bring her to? No," it says, "you did *not* ought." And I won't ought, accordin'.

SIR D. [44] Then you really feel yourself at liberty to tell me that my elder brother lives—that I may charge him with his cruel deceit, and transfer to his shoulders the hideous thraldom under which I have laboured for so many years! Free—free at last! Free to live a blameless life, and to die beloved and regretted by all who knew me!

DUET—SIR DESPARD *and* RICHARD [45]

RICH.	You understand?
SIR D.	I think I do;
	With vigour unshaken
	This step shall be taken.
	It's neatly planned.
RICH.	I think so too;
	I'll readily bet it
	You'll never regret it!
BOTH.	For duty, duty must be done;
	The rule applies to every one,
	And painful though that duty be,
	To shirk the task were fiddle-de-dee!
SIR D.	The bridegroom comes—
RICH.	Likewise the bride—
	The maidens are very

[43] *The word is still pronounced "ax." It is strange that Gilbert should have used this spelling in this one instance, but according to a recent printing of the original libretto this is axtually what he did.*

[44] *Gilbert wrote Sir Despard's speech as if he were making a statement of facts instead of asking a series of questions. I feel that question marks really should come as follows: ". . . my elder brother lives?"—"that I may charge him with his cruel deceit?"—"and transfer to his shoulders the hideous thraldom under which I have laboured for so many years?"—"Free?"*

With each question Richard should consider for just a moment and then nod his head. And on the last question, "Free?", nod his head vigorously. Then, and only then, does Sir Despard make his statement, "Free at last!" How could Richard be double-crossing Robin in the face of the enormous good deed he has just done?

[45] *I wonder if the nimble Durward Lely was responsible for the action carried out through the whole of this number? This question arises in my mind because the number is accompanied all the way by a wild skipping that is dignified by the term "dance." The tempo is fast, and it always tends to grow faster; there is a spate of words, and breathlessness is inevitable. Every Sir Despard and Dick Dauntless I ever knew would do their best to avoid any encore—but in vain. One tenor called it "a salt, mustard, vinegar, pepper" number. The first time through the number was all right, but the encore, or "pepper" part, was to be avoided like the plague, if possible. It seldom was possible.*

	Elated and merry; They are her chums.
SIR D.	To lash their pride Were almost a pity, The pretty committee!
BOTH.	But duty, duty must be done; The rule applies to every one, And painful though that duty be, To shirk the task were fiddle-de-dee!

[*Exeunt* RICHARD *and* SIR DESPARD.

Enter Chorus of Bridesmaids and Bucks

CHORUS OF BRIDESMAIDS

Hail the bride of seventeen summers:
    In fair phrases
    Hymn her praises;
Lift your song on high, all comers.
    She rejoices
    In your voices.
Smiling summer beams upon her,
Shedding every blessing on her:
    Maidens greet her—
    Kindly treat her—
You may all be brides some day!

CHORUS OF BUCKS

Hail the bridegroom who advances,
    Agitated,
    Yet elated.
He's in easy circumstances,
    Young and lusty,
    True and trusty.

Smiling welcome to the spring

Enter ROBIN, *attended by* RICHARD *and* OLD ADAM, *meeting* ROSE, *attended by* ZORAH *and* DAME HANNAH. ROSE *and* ROBIN *embrace.*

MADRIGAL

ROSE.	When the buds are blossoming, Smiling welcome to the spring, Lovers choose a wedding day— Life is love in merry May!
GIRLS.	Spring is green—Fal lal la! Summer's rose—Fal lal la!
ALL.	It is sad when summer goes, Fal la!
MEN.	Autumn's gold—Fal lal la! Winter's grey—Fal lal la!
ALL.	Winter still is far away— Fal la!
ALL.	Leaves in autumn fade and fall, Winter is the end of all. Spring and summer teem with glee: Spring and summer, then, for me! Fal la!
HANNAH.	In the spring-time seed is sown:

In the summer grass is mown:
In the autumn you may reap:
Winter is the time for sleep.

GIRLS.   Spring is hope—Fal lal la!
       Summer's joy—Fal lal la!
ALL.   Spring and summer never cloy.
       Fal la!
MEN.   Autumn, toil—Fal lal la!
       Winter, rest—Fal lal la!
ALL.   Winter, after all, is best—
       Fal la!

ALL.   Spring and summer pleasure you,
Autumn, aye, and winter too—
Every season has its cheer,
Life is lovely all the year!
       Fal la!

(*Gavotte*)

After Gavotte, enter SIR DESPARD

SIR D.   Hold, bride and bridegroom, ere you wed each other,
I claim young Robin as my elder brother!
His rightful title I have long enjoyed:
I claim him as Sir Ruthven Murgatroyd!

ALL.   O wonder!
ROSE (*wildly*). Deny the falsehood, Robin, as you should,
     It is a plot!
ROB.   I would, if conscientiously I could,
     But I cannot!
ALL.   Ah, base one!

SOLO—ROBIN

As pure and blameless peasant,
   I cannot, I regret,
Deny a truth unpleasant,
   I am that Baronet!

ALL.   He is that Baronet!

But when completely rated
   Bad Baronet am I,
That I am what he's stated
   I'll recklessly deny!

ALL.   He'll recklessly deny!

ROB. When I'm a bad Bart. I will tell taradiddles! [46]
ALL.   He'll tell taradiddles when he's a bad Bart.
ROB. I'll play a bad part on the falsest of fiddles. [47]
ALL.   On very false fiddles he'll play a bad part!
ROB. But until that takes place I must be conscientious—
ALL.   He'll be conscientious until that takes place.
ROB. Then adieu with good grace to my morals sententious!
ALL.   To morals sententious [48] adieu with good grace!

ZOR.   Who is the wretch who hath betrayed thee?
     Let him stand forth!
RICH. (*coming forward*). 'Twas I!
ALL.   Die, traitor!
RICH.   Hold! my conscience made me!
    Withhold your wrath!

[46] Taradiddles. *Trifling falsehoods; fibs.*

[47] Falsest of fiddles. *A sweet-sounding instrument that covers a multitude of villainies.*

[48] Morals sententious. *His Methodist morals, of course. But what about his marquisatorial manners?*

RUDDIGORE

[49] Richard's solo should be sung with all the inten-
    sity and passion with which Lohengrin sings
    about the swan.

SOLO—RICHARD [49]

Within this breast there beats a heart
 Whose voice can't be gainsaid.
It bade me thy true rank impart,
 And I at once obeyed.
I knew 'twould blight thy budding fate—
I knew 'twould cause thee anguish great—
But did I therefore hesitate?
 No! I at once obeyed!

ALL. Acclaim him who, when his true heart
Bade him young Robin's rank impart,
 Immediately obeyed!

SOLO—ROSE (*addressing* ROBIN)

Farewell!
Thou hadst my heart—
 'Twas quickly won!
But now we part—
 Thy face I shun!
Farewell!

Go bend the knee
 At Vice's shrine,
Of life with me
 All hope resign.
Farewell!

(*To* SIR DESPARD.) Take me—I am thy bride! [50]

BRIDESMAIDS

Hail the Bridegroom—hail the Bride!
When the nuptial knot is tied;
Every day will bring some joy
That can never, never cloy!

Enter MARGARET, *who listens*

SIR D. Excuse me, I'm a virtuous person now—
ROSE.. That's why I wed you!
SIR D. And I to Margaret must keep my vow!
MAR. Have I misread you?
Oh, joy! with newly kindled rapture warmed,
 I kneel before you! (*Kneels.*)
SIR D. I once disliked you; now that I've reformed,
 How I adore you! (*They embrace.*)

BRIDESMAIDS

Hail the Bridegroom—hail the Bride!
When the nuptial knot is tied;
Every day will bring some joy
That can never, never cloy!

ROSE. Richard, of him I love bereft,
  Through thy design,
Thou art the only one that's left,
  So I am thine! [51] (*They embrace.*)

[51] As Dame Carruthers says in The Yeomen of the
    Guard: "Marry? There be those who would
    marry but for a minute, rather than die old
    maids." With Meryll I would add: "Aye, I know
    one of them!" (See page 581, Note 67.)

BRIDESMAIDS

Hail the Bridegroom—hail the Bride!
Let the nuptial knot be tied!

DUET—ROSE *and* RICHARD

Oh, happy the lily
        When kissed by the bee;
And, sipping tranquilly,
        Quite happy is he;
And happy the filly
        That neighs in her pride;
But happier than any,
A pound to a penny,
A lover is, when he
        Embraces his bride!

DUET—SIR DESPARD *and* MARGARET

Oh, happy the flowers
        That blossom in June,
And happy the bowers
        That gain by the boon,
But happier by hours
        The man of descent,
Who, folly regretting,
Is bent on forgetting
His bad baronetting,
        And means to repent!

TRIO—HANNAH, ADAM, *and* ZORAH

Oh, happy the blossom
        That blooms on the lea,
Likewise the opossum
        That sits on a tree,
But when you come across 'em,
        They cannot compare
With those who are treading
The dance at a wedding,
While people are spreading
        The best of good fare!

SOLO—ROBIN

Oh, wretched the debtor
        Who's signing a deed!
And wretched the letter
        That no one can read!
But very much better
        Their lot it must be
Than that of the person
I'm making this verse on,
Whose head there's a curse on—
        Alluding to me! [52]

Repeat ensemble with Chorus
        (Dance)

[*At the end of the dance* ROBIN *falls senseless on the stage.* [53] *Picture.*

END OF ACT I

[52] As Robin comes to the end of his solo, which he has sung in the best "meller-dramatic" manner, Zorah steps forward and asks him to dance. He refuses the offer, because the transition from good to bad has already begun to take place. With a violent scowl on his face he storms off the stage and within the space of two minutes he changes his wig to that of the second act, applies make-up—heavy eyebrows, dark rings under his eyes, etc.—and changes his hat from a farmer's straw to a bad Baronet's silk topper. He flings a cape around his shoulders, seizes a hunting crop with a lash, and re-enters, cracking the whip, just as the Chorus reaches the end of the dance. All but Old Adam fly off, terrified and screaming. Old Adam pleads with Robin—now Sir Ruthven—but Robin cracks his whip again and the venerable Adam jumps like a jack-in-the-box and scuttles off the stage, followed by the bad Baronet who is still cracking his whip.

[53] No matter what the directions may say, in actual performance Robin never does fall down senseless. The final picture is that of a pleading Old Adam being lashed into evildoing by a fully conscious bad Baronet.

A thought that has often occurred to me is that perhaps Gilbert's directions fit in with the over-all picture of the second act. (See Notes 63 and 84.)

ACT II

SCENE.—*Picture Gallery in Ruddigore Castle. The walls are covered with full-length portraits of the Baronets of Ruddigore from the time of* JAMES I.—*the first being that of* SIR RUPERT, *alluded to in the legend; the last that of the last deceased Baronet,* SIR RODERIC.

Enter ROBIN *and* ADAM *melodramatically.* [54] *They are greatly altered in appearance,* ROBIN *wearing the haggard aspect of a guilty roué;* ADAM, *that of the wicked steward to such a man.*

DUET—ROBIN *and* ADAM

ROB.
I once was as meek as a new-born lamb,
 I'm now Sir Murgatroyd—ha! ha!
  With greater precision
  (Without the elision),
 Sir Ruthven [55] Murgatroyd—ha! ha!

ADAM.
And I, who was once his *valley-de-sham*,
 As steward I'm now employed—ha! ha!
  The dickens may take him—
  I'll never forsake him!
 As steward I'm now employed—ha! ha!

BOTH.
How dreadful when an innocent heart
Becomes, perforce, a bad young Bart.,
And still more hard on old Adam,
His former faithful *valley-de-sham!* [56]

ROB.
This is a painful state of things, old Adam!

ADAM. Painful, indeed! Ah, my poor master, when I swore that, come what would, I would serve you in all things for ever, I little thought to what a pass it would bring me! The confidential adviser to the greatest villain unhung! Now, sir, to business. What crime do you propose to commit to-day?

ROB. How should I know? As my confidential adviser, it's your duty to suggest something.

ADAM. Sir, I loathe the life you are leading, but a good old man's oath is paramount, and I obey. Richard Dauntless is here with pretty Rose Maybud, to ask your consent to their marriage. Poison their beer.

ROB. No—not that—I know I'm a bad Bart., but I'm not as bad a Bart. as all that. [57]

ADAM. Well, there you are, you see! It's no use my making suggestions if you don't adopt them.

ROB. (*melodramatically*). [58] How would it be, do you think, were I to lure him here with cunning wile—bind him with good stout rope to yonder post—and then, by making hideous faces at him, curdle the heart-blood in his arteries, and freeze the very marrow in his bones? How say you, Adam, is not the scheme well planned?

ADAM. It would be simply rude—nothing more. But soft—they come!

ADAM *and* ROBIN *retire up* [59] *as* RICHARD *and* ROSE *enter, preceded by Chorus of Bridesmaids*

DUET—RICHARD *and* ROSE

RICH.
Happily coupled are we,
 You see—
I am a jolly Jack Tar,
 My star,
And you are the fairest,

---

[54] An intermission is supposed to afford a moment or two of relaxation to the actors, as well as giving the audience the opportunity to stretch its legs and enjoy a smoke. Not so for Robin and Old Adam. In those few minutes—ten or fifteen at the most—they must make a complete change of costume and make-up, from wig through paint down to shoes. One must change from a simple innocent to a guilty roué, the other from a benign old faithful retainer to a wicked steward who is accessory before and after the fact to all the crimes committed by his villainous master. As a rule, we both made it, but it was always a case of walking from our respective dressing rooms and straight on to the stage without a pause. (Robin has a head start—see Note 52—but he needs every advantage he can get.)

[55] Sir Ruthven. "(Without the elision)." The only time the name is pronounced phonetically: Sir Ruth-ven.

[56] A punning play on valet de chambre. Later on in the text Robin addresses Old Adam as Gideon Crawle. There were originally six verses to this duet. Adam's verse, and the final verse for both, ran as follows:

ADAM. My name from Adam Goodheart, you'll find
 I've changed to Gideon Crawle—ha! ha!
 For a bad Bart's stew-ard
 Whose heart is much too-hard
 Is always Gideon Crawle—ha! ha!
BOTH. How providential when you find
 The face an index to the mind
 And evil men compelled to call
 Themselves by names like Gideon Crawle!

But Gilbert decided to keep the name of Old Adam Goodheart throughout the opera, so these two verses had to go. (See Note 67.)

[57] This line should be delivered in as exaggerated a manner as possible. Good old meller-drammer ham delivery: "No! NO! Not thart! I know I'm a bad Bart., but I'm not as bad a Bart. as all thart!"

[58] Gilbert's direction here should really read "exaggeratedly melodramatic." The last few lines should out-ham anything Robin has said previously: ". . . cu-u-r-r-dle the hear-r-r-rt-bur-lud in his arteries, and fer-r-r-re-e-e-eze the very ma-har-row in his bo-hones?"

[59] Robin and Adam actually exit left and keep their walk in time to the music, being very cloak-and-daggerish about it.

The richest and rarest
Of innocent lasses you are,
By far—
Of innocent lasses you are!
Fanned by a favouring gale,
You'll sail
Over life's treacherous sea
With me,
And as for bad weather,
We'll brave it together,
And you shall creep under my lee,
My wee!
And you shall creep under my lee!

For you are such a smart little craft—
Such a neat little, sweet little craft,
Such a bright little, tight little,
Slight little, light little,
Trim little, prim little craft!

CHORUS.   For she is such, etc.

ROSE.   [60] My hopes will be blighted, I fear,
My dear;
In a month you'll be going to sea,
Quite free,
And all of my wishes
You'll throw to the fishes
As though they were never to be;
Poor me!
As though they were never to be.
And I shall be left all alone
To moan,
And weep at your cruel deceit,
Complete;
While you'll be asserting
Your freedom by flirting
With every woman you meet,
You cheat—
With every woman you meet!

Though I am such a smart little craft—
Such a neat little, sweet little craft,
Such a bright little, tight little,
Slight little, light little,
Trim little, prim little craft!

CHORUS.   Though she is such, etc.

Enter ROBIN

ROB. Soho! pretty one—in my power at last, eh? Know ye not that I have those within my call who, at my lightest bidding, would immure ye in an uncomfortable dungeon? (*Calling.*) What ho! within there!

RICH. Hold—we are prepared for this (*producing a Union Jack*). [61] Here is a flag that none dare defy (*all kneel*), and while this glorious rag floats over Rose Maybud's head, the man does not live who would dare to lay unlicensed hand upon her!

ROB. Foiled—and by a Union Jack! But a time will come, and then——

ROSE. Nay, let me plead with him. (*To* ROBIN.) Sir Ruthven, have pity. In my book of etiquette the case of a maiden about to be wedded to one who unexpectedly turns out to be a baronet with a curse on

[60] *Rose's verse has not been sung by the D'Oyly Carte Company for many years. In a way, this is a pity, for it reveals that for all her apparent simplicity she is fully aware of a sailor's alleged legendary shortcomings.*

[61] *I always looked forward to appearing in Ruddigore at the Gaiety Theatre, Dublin, or in Cork, with mixed feelings. The Irish love Gilbert and Sullivan, but the producing of a Union Jack by Richard was the signal for prolonged bursts of cheers and hisses, boos and applause, according to the political leanings of those "in front." The noise would subside in time, and Richard was able to speak his next line, "Here is a flag that none dare defy." And that would be as far as he would get. More cheers, vociferous applause from the orchestra stalls, boxes and dress circle in an endeavor to drown out cries from the gallery of "Says you! Take it off the stage! Yah! Boo!" One Rose, appearing in Ireland, and so experiencing this reaction, for the first time, became really alarmed and in quite a loud stage whisper asked me: "Do you think we're safe?" Charles Goulding, playing Richard, heard her and said, "You are. I'm the one who's not. I'm holding the thing!" We always were safe—I think—because they always quieted down and I was able to carry on (although Dick never tried to finish his speech) with "Foiled—and by a Union Jack!" Then I'd strike a Napoleonic attitude, greatly enhanced by the spit-curls on my wig. The ensuing laugh relieved the tension and we were able to proceed.*

him is not considered. Time was when you loved me madly. Prove that this was no selfish love by according your consent to my marriage with one who, if he be not you yourself, is the next best thing—your dearest friend!

BALLAD—ROSE

In bygone days I had thy love—
    Thou hadst my heart.
But Fate, all human vows above,
    Our lives did part!
By the old love thou hadst for me—
By the fond heart that beat for thee—
By joys that never now can be,
    Grant thou my prayer!

ALL (*kneeling*).   Grant thou her prayer!

ROB. (*recit.*).   Take her—I yield!

ALL (*recit.*).   Oh, rapture!

CHORUS.   Away to the parson we go—
    Say we're solicitous very
That he will turn two into one—
    Singing hey, derry down derry!

RICH.   For she *is* such a smart little craft—
ROSE.   Such a neat little, sweet little craft—
RICH.   Such a bright little—
ROSE.   Tight little—
RICH.   Slight little—
ROSE.   Light little—
BOTH.   Trim little, slim little craft!

CHORUS.   For she *is* such a smart little craft, etc.

[*Exeunt all but* ROBIN.

ROB. For a week I have fulfilled my accursed doom! I have duly committed a crime a day! Not a great crime, I trust, but still, in the eyes of one as strictly regulated as I used to be, a crime. But will my ghostly ancestors be satisfied with what I have done, or will they regard it as an unworthy subterfuge? (*Addressing Pictures.*) Oh, my forefathers, wallowers in blood, there came at last a day when, sick of crime, you, each and every, vowed to sin no more, and so, in agony, called welcome Death to free you from your cloying guiltiness. Let the sweet psalm of that repentant hour soften your long-dead hearts, and tune your souls to mercy on your poor posterity! (*kneeling*). [62]

[*The stage darkens for a moment. It becomes light again, and the Pictures are seen to have become animated.*

CHORUS OF FAMILY PORTRAITS [63]

Painted emblems of a race,
    All accurst in days of yore,
Each from his accustomed place
    Steps into the world once more.

[*The Pictures step from their frames and march round the stage.*

Baronet of Ruddigore,
    Last of our accursèd line,
Down upon the oaken floor—
    Down upon those knees of thine.

[62] *Ignore the direction "kneeling." For as long as I remember Robin has always collapsed in a swoon on the steps at the foot of the picture of Sir Roderic. As soon as Robin has collapsed there is a complete blackout. The picture frames are opened "in the black," with a fortissimo passage on the timpani to drown out any rumbling noises made by the opening of the frames, and then the lights are faded in. The figures do not become animated immediately but are seen first in the poses of the painted portraits.*

[63] *During this chorus, I, as Robin, would be twisting and turning as if tormented by a frightful nightmare. Then I would suddenly spring to my feet, and, in great fear, try to leave the place, only to be stopped by the portraits as they stepped out of their frames. In my opinion this should be treated as if the whole of this scene, at least, is Robin's dream. (See Note 53.).*

Coward, poltroon, shaker, squeamer,
Blockhead, sluggard, dullard, dreamer,
Shirker, shuffler, crawler, creeper,
Sniffler, snuffler, wailer, weeper,
Earthworm, maggot, tadpole, weevil!
Set upon thy course of evil,
Lest the King of Spectre-Land
Set on thee his grisly hand!

[*The Spectre of* SIR RODERIC *descends from his frame.*]

SIR ROD.   Beware! beware! beware!
ROB.   Gaunt vision, who art thou
That thus, with icy glare
    And stern relentless brow,
    Appearest, who knows how?

SIR ROD.   I am the spectre of the late
    Sir Roderic Murgatroyd,
Who comes to warn thee that thy fate
Thou canst not now avoid.

ROB.   Alas, poor ghost!

SIR ROD.   The pity you
Express for nothing goes:
We spectres are a jollier crew
Than you, perhaps, suppose!

CHORUS.   We spectres are a jollier crew
Than you, perhaps, suppose!

. . . a jollier crew than you, perhaps, suppose!

[64] Words and music on page 546.

[65] *Reginald Burston, at one time the musical director of the "Small Co.," was the owner of a very handsome chow dog, and, like all chows, it was very much a one-man dog. It was Reggie's habit to take the dog into the musicians' room below the stage and leave it there during a performance, the door, of course, being closed. One Ruddigore night, however, someone went back into the musicians' room just after Reggie's return to the pit following the intermission, and forgot to close the door. The chow took full advantage of this and went roaming the theater in search of his master, eventually finding his way onto the stage just as Roderic's song came to an end. He walked straight to the footlights and stood, tail wagging, gazing down at Reginald Burston, who became paralyzed with shock at seeing his dog there. Suddenly regaining his voice, he called out in a loud voice, "Go home!" The chow never moved. One of the "Ghosts" stepped out of the chorus line and attempted to take the dog by the collar, only to be rewarded by a savage snap that could have been very bad had it made real contact. Reggie, by this time, had hurriedly made his way up from the pit, and the audience was treated to the spectacle of an immaculately clad figure in white tie and tails embarrassedly endeavoring to lead a wildly happy chow through a line of medieval ghosts who drew away to a respectful distance as the master and chow departed—through a picture frame!*

SONG—SIR RODERIC [64]

When the night wind howls in the chimney cowls, and the bat in the
    moonlight flies,
And inky clouds, like funeral shrouds, sail over the midnight skies—
When the footpads quail at the night-bird's wail, and black dogs bay
    at the moon,
Then is the spectres' holiday—then is the ghosts' high-noon!

CHORUS.   Ha! ha!
    Then is the ghosts' high-noon!

As the sob of the breeze sweeps over the trees, and the mists lie low
    on the fen,
From grey tomb-stones are gathered the bones that once were women
    and men,
And away they go, with a mop and a mow, to the revel that ends too
    soon,
For cockcrow limits our holiday—the dead of the night's high-noon!

CHORUS.   Ha! ha!
    The dead of the night's high-noon!

And then each ghost with his ladye-toast to their churchyard beds
    takes flight,
With a kiss, perhaps, on her lantern chaps, and a grisly grim "good-
    night";
Till the welcome knell of the midnight bell rings forth its jolliest tune,
And ushers in our next high holiday—the dead of the night's high-
    noon! [65]

CHORUS.   Ha! ha!
    The dead of the night's high-noon!

Their churchyard beds

ROB. I recognize you now—you are the picture that hangs at the end of the gallery.

SIR ROD. In a bad light. I am.

ROB. Are you considered a good likeness?

SIR ROD. Pretty well. Flattering.

ROB. Because as a work of art you are poor.

SIR ROD. I am crude in colour, but I have only been painted ten years. In a couple of centuries I shall be an Old Master, and then you will be sorry you spoke lightly of me.

ROB. And may I ask why you have left your frames?

SIR ROD. It is our duty to see that our successors commit their daily crimes in a conscientious and workmanlike fashion. It is our duty to remind you that you are evading the conditions under which you are permitted to exist.

ROB. Really, I don't know what you'd have. I've only been a bad baronet a week, and I've committed a crime punctually every day.

SIR ROD. Let us inquire into this. Monday?

ROB. Monday was a Bank Holiday.

SIR ROD. True. Tuesday?

ROB. On Tuesday I made a false income-tax return.

ALL. Ha! ha!

1ST GHOST. That's nothing.

2ND GHOST. Nothing at all.

3RD GHOST. Everybody does that.

4TH GHOST. It's expected of you.

SIR ROD. Wednesday?

ROB. (*melodramatically*). On Wednesday I forged a will.

SIR ROD. Whose will?

ROB. My own.

SIR ROD. My good sir, you can't forge your own will!

ROB. Can't I, though! I like that! I *did!* Besides, if a man can't forge his own will, whose will can he forge?

1ST GHOST. There's something in that.

2ND GHOST. Yes, it seems reasonable.

3RD GHOST. At first sight it does.

4TH GHOST. Fallacy somewhere, I fancy!

ROB. A man can do what he likes with his own?

SIR ROD. I suppose he can.

ROB. Well, then, he can forge his own will, stoopid! On Thursday I shot a fox. [66]

1ST GHOST. Hear, hear!

SIR ROD. That's better (*addressing Ghosts*). Pass the fox, I think? (*They assent.*) Yes, pass the fox. Friday?

ROB. On Friday I forged a cheque.

SIR ROD. Whose cheque?

ROB. Old Adam's.

SIR ROD. But Old Adam hasn't a banker.

ROB. I didn't say I forged his banker—I said I forged his cheque. On Saturday I disinherited my only son.

SIR ROD. But you haven't got a son.

ROB. No—not yet. I disinherited him in advance, to save time. You see—by this arrangement—he'll be born ready disinherited.

SIR ROD. I see. But I don't think you can do that.

ROB. My good sir, if I can't disinherit my own unborn son, whose unborn son can I disinherit?

SIR ROD. Humph! These arguments sound very well, but I can't help thinking that, if they were reduced to syllogistic form, they wouldn't hold water. Now quite understand us. We are foggy, but we don't

[66] *In England, particularly among hunting people, to shoot a fox is about the worst of crimes. It "simply isn't done."*

permit our fogginess to be presumed upon. Unless you undertake to—
well, suppose we say, carry off a lady? (*Addressing Ghosts.*) Those who
are in favour of his carrying off a lady? (*All hold up their hands except
a Bishop.*) Those of the contrary opinion? (*Bishop holds up his hands.*)
Oh, you're never satisfied! Yes, unless you undertake to carry off a lady
at once—I don't care what lady—any lady—choose your lady—you
perish in inconceivable agonies.

ROB. Carry off a lady? Certainly not, on any account. I've the greatest
respect for ladies, and I wouldn't do anything of the kind for worlds!
No, no. I'm not that kind of baronet, I assure you! If that's all you've
got to say, you'd better go back to your frames.

SIR ROD. Very good—then let the agonies commence.

[*Ghosts make passes.* ROBIN *begins to writhe in agony.*

ROB. Oh! Oh! Don't do that! I can't stand it!
SIR ROD. Painful, isn't it? It gets worse by degrees.
ROB. Oh—Oh! Stop a bit! Stop it, will you? I want to speak.

[SIR RODERIC *makes signs to Ghosts, who resume their attitudes.*

SIR ROD. Better?
ROB. Yes—better now! Whew!
SIR ROD. Well, do you consent?
ROB. But it's such an ungentlemanly thing to do!
SIR ROD. As you please. (*To Ghosts.*) Carry on!
ROB. Stop—I can't stand it! I agree! I promise! It shall be done!
SIR ROD. To-day?
ROB. To-day!
SIR ROD. At once?
ROB. At once! I retract! I apologize! I had no idea it was anything
like that!

CHORUS

He yields! He answers to our call!
    We do not ask for more.
A sturdy fellow, after all,
    This latest Ruddigore!
All perish in unheard-of woe
    Who dare our wills defy;
We want your pardon, ere we go.
For having agonized you so—
    So pardon us—
    So pardon us—
    So pardon us—
        Or die!

ROB.   I pardon you!
                 I pardon you!

ALL.   He pardons us—
                  Hurrah!

[*The Ghosts return to their frames.*

CHORUS.   Painted emblems of a race,
              All accurst in days of yore,
         Each to his accustomed place
              Steps unwillingly once more!

[*By this time the Ghosts have changed to pictures again.*
    ROBIN *is overcome by emotion.*

Enter ADAM

[67] Gideon Crawle, it won't do. (See Note 56.) Following Gilbert's decision to retain the name of Old Adam Goodheart, changes in the printing were not effected until the second edition. Someone, however, goofed. He overlooked one place when making corrections, and this was it. "Gideon Crawle" has been retained in every edition at this particular point until quite recently. The latest Chappell edition has been corrected and now reads "Old Adam." I feel, however, it is much more interesting to retain "Gideon Crawle." It makes it a sort of rarity in much the same way a postage stamp, imperfectly printed, becomes a collector's piece.

[68] This patter song is invariably cut, and has been since early in the life of Ruddigore. As performed today, Robin exits along with Adam.

[69] Postage-stamp prigging. Stealing of postage stamps, or the steaming of stamps off envelopes with the intention of using them again.

[70] Thimble-rigging. The shell game.

[71] Three-card delusion. A variation of the thimble trick, known in England as "Find the lady."

[72] And vote black or white as your leaders indite. Apropos of this, glance at the opening of the second act of Iolanthe. Private Willis sings a whole song on this one theme.

ADAM. My poor master, you are not well——

ROB. Gideon Crawle, [67] it won't do—I've seen 'em—all my ancestors —they're just gone. They say that I must do something desperate at once, or perish in horrible agonies. Go—go to yonder village—carry off a maiden—bring her here at once—any one—I don't care which—

ADAM. But——

ROB. Not a word, but obey! Fly!

[*Exit* ADAM.

RECIT. *and* SONG—ROBIN [68]

Away, Remorse!
   Compunction, hence!
Go, Moral Force!
   Go, Penitence!
To Virtue's plea
   A long farewell—
Propriety,
   I ring your knell!
Come, guiltiness of deadliest hue!
Come, desperate deeds of derring-do!

Henceforth all the crimes that I find in the *Times*,
  I've promised to perpetrate daily;
To-morrow I start, with a petrified heart,
  On a regular course of Old Bailey.
There's confidence tricking, bad coin, pocket-picking,
  And several other disgraces—
There's postage-stamp prigging, [69] and then, thimble-rigging, [70]
  The three-card delusion [71] at races!
Oh! a baronet's rank is exceedingly nice,
But the title's uncommonly dear at the price!

Ye well-to-do squires, who live in the shires,
  Where petty distinctions are vital,
Who found Athenæums and local museums,
  With views to a baronet's title—
Ye butchers and bakers and candlestick makers
  Who sneer at all things that are tradey—
Whose middle-class lives are embarrassed by wives
  Who long to parade as "My Lady,"
Oh! allow me to offer a word of advice,
The title's uncommonly dear at the price!

Ye supple M.P.'s, who go down on your knees,
  Your precious identity sinking,
And vote black or white as your leaders indite [72]
  (Which saves you the trouble of thinking),
For your country's good fame, her repute, or her shame,
  You don't care the snuff of a candle—
But you're paid for your game when you're told that your name
  Will be graced by a baronet's handle—
Oh! allow me to give *you* a word of advice—
The title's uncommonly dear at the price!

[*Exit* ROBIN.

Enter DESPARD *and* MARGARET. *They are both dressed in sober black of formal cut, and present a strong contrast to their appearance in Act I.*

DUET

DES.   I once was a very abandoned person—

MAR.   Making the most of evil chances.
DES.   Nobody could conceive a worse 'un—
MAR.   Even in all the old romances.
DES.   I blush for my wild extravagances,
                      But be so kind
                      To bear in mind,
MAR.   We were the victims of circumstances!

                                  (*Dance.*) [73]
       That is one of our blameless dances.

MAR.   I was once an exceedingly odd young lady—
DES.   Suffering much from spleen and vapours.
MAR.   Clergymen thought my conduct shady—
DES.   She didn't spend much upon linen-drapers.
MAR.   It certainly entertained the gapers.
                      My ways were strange
                      Beyond all range—
DES.   Paragraphs got into all the papers.

                             (*Dance.*)

DES.   We only cut respectable capers.

DES.   I've given up all my wild proceedings.
MAR.   My taste for a wandering life is waning.
DES.   Now I'm a dab at penny readings. [74]
MAR.   They are not remarkably entertaining.
DES.   A moderate livelihood we're gaining.
MAR.   In fact we rule
                      A National School. [75]
DES.   The duties are dull, but I'm not complaining.

                             (*Dance.*)
       This sort of thing takes a deal of training!

DES. We have been married a week.

MAR. One happy, happy week!

DES. Our new life—

MAR. Is delightful indeed!

DES. So calm!

MAR. So unimpassioned! (*wildly*). Master, all this I owe to you! See, I am no longer wild and untidy. My hair is combed. My face is washed. My boots fit!

DES. Margaret, don't. Pray restrain yourself. Remember, you are now a district visitor.

MAR. A gentle district visitor!

DES. You are orderly, methodical, neat; you have your emotions well under control.

MAR. I have! (*wildly*). Master, when I think of all you have done for me, I fall at your feet. I embrace your ankles. I hug your knees! (*Doing so.*)

DES. Hush. This is not well. This is calculated to provoke remark. Be composed, I beg!

MAR. Ah! you are angry with poor little Mad Margaret!

DES. No, not angry; but a district visitor should learn to eschew melodrama. Visit the poor, by all means, and give them tea and barley-water, but don't do it as if you were administering a bowl of deadly nightshade. It upsets them. Then when you nurse sick people, and find them not as well as could be expected, why go into hysterics?

MAR. Why not?

DES. Because it's too jumpy for a sick-room.

MAR. How strange! Oh, Master! Master!—how shall I express the all-absorbing gratitude that—(*about to throw herself at his feet*).

[73] *It is impossible to describe the sheer ludicrousness of the dances in this number, performed as they are in so staid a manner, with the emphasis on "modesty" and "respectability." They have to be seen to be believed.*

[74] Penny readings. *A form of mission-hall poetry readings of a particularly moral and religious character, the charge for admission being one penny.*

[75] National School. *One of a number of schools founded in 1811 to promote the education of the poor. In all probability they were forerunners of the council, or free schools, as opposed to the British high, grammar or public schools. (In the United States a public school and a high school are the equivalent of the English council schools. The American private school is the equivalent of the English public school.)*

[76] Basingstoke. A town some thirty or forty miles from London. But why did Gilbert select this place? Where is the hidden meaning? What is the hidden meaning? The whole thing's crazy. But so is Margaret.

[77] Not his young wife! A cat! On one occasion I made my entrance at this point and spoke my first words, "Despard! And his young wife!" At that exact moment the theater cat decided to explore the stage. The sight of a cat or a dog on the stage—especially when not part of the show —is calculated always to provoke laughter. This occasion was no exception. Pussy had come on from the opposite side of the stage, sniffed condescendingly at Despard and Margaret, seated but a few feet from her point of entrance, and then like The Cat That Walked By Itself, crossed the stage in a dignified manner, tail erect, making straight for me. The laughter grew, and when the animal arched its back and rubbed itself against my gaitered legs, with a purr that could be heard over and above the laughter, the house fell in. I waited until the cat had completed its antics around my ankles and had stalked off into the arms of a waiting stagehand. The laughter subsided. Then, and only then, did I speak my next line: "This visit is unexpected."

DES. Now! (*warningly*).

MAR. Yes, I know, dear—it shan't occur again. (*He is seated—she sits on the ground by him.*) Shall I tell you one of poor Mad Margaret's odd thoughts? Well, then, when I am lying awake at night, and the pale moonlight streams through the latticed casement, strange fancies crowd upon my poor mad brain, and I sometimes think that if we could hit upon some word for you to use whenever I am about to relapse—some word that teems with hidden meaning—like "Basingstoke" [76]—it might recall me to my saner self. For, after all, I am only Mad Margaret! Daft Meg! Poor Peg! He! he! he!

DES. Poor child, she wanders! But soft—some one comes—Margaret—pray recollect yourself—Basingstoke, I beg! Margaret, if you don't Basingstoke at once, I shall be seriously angry.

MAR. (*recovering herself*). Basingstoke it is!

DES. Then make it so.

Enter ROBIN. *He starts on seeing them*

ROB. Despard! And his young wife! This visit is unexpected. [77]

MAR. Shall I fly at him? Shall I tear him limb from limb? Shall I rend him asunder? Say but the word and——

DES. Basingstoke!

MAR. (*suddenly demure*). Basingstoke it is!

DES. (*aside*). Then make it so. (*Aloud.*) My brother—I call you brother still, despite your horrible profligacy—we have come to urge you to abandon the evil courses to which you have committed yourself, and at any cost to become a pure and blameless ratepayer.

ROB. But I've done no wrong yet.

MAR. (*wildly*). No wrong! He has done no wrong! Did you hear that!

DES. Basingstoke!

MAR. (*recovering herself*). Basingstoke it is!

DES. My brother—I still call you brother, you observe—you forget that you have been, in the eye of the law, a bad Baronet of Ruddigore for ten years—and you are therefore responsible—in the eye of the law—for all the misdeeds committed by the unhappy gentleman who occupied your place.

ROB. I see! Bless my heart, I never thought of that! Was I very bad?

DES. Awful. Wasn't he? (*to* MARGARET).

ROB. And I've been going on like this for how long?

DES. Ten years! Think of all the atrocities you have committed—by attorney as it were—during that period. Remember how you trifled with this poor child's affections—how you raised her hopes on high (don't cry, my love—Basingstoke, you know), only to trample them in the dust when they were at the very zenith of their fullness. Oh fie, sir, fie—she trusted you!

ROB. Did she? What a scoundrel I must have been! There, there—don't cry, my dear (*to* MARGARET, *who is sobbing on* ROBIN's *breast*), it's all right now. Birmingham, you know—Birmingham——

MAR. (*sobbing*). It's Ba—Ba—Basingstoke!

ROB. Basingstoke! Of course it is—Basingstoke.

MAR. Then make it so!

ROB. There, there—it's all right—he's married you now—that is, *I've* married you (*turning to* DESPARD)—I say, which of us has married her?

DES. Oh, *I've* married her.

ROB. (*aside*). Oh, I'm glad of that. (*To* MARGARET.) Yes, *he's* married you now (*passing her over to* DESPARD), and anything more disreputable than my conduct seems to have been I've never even heard of. But my mind is made up—I *will* defy my ancestors. I *will* refuse to obey their behests, thus, by courting death, atone in some degree for the infamy of my career!

MAR. I knew it—I knew it—God bless you—(*hysterically*).

DES. Basingstoke!

MAR. Basingstoke it is! (*Recovers herself.*)

PATTER-TRIO
ROBIN, DESPARD, *and* MARGARET [78]

ROB. My eyes are fully open to my awful situation—
I shall go at once to Roderic and make him an oration.
I shall tell him I've recovered my forgotten moral senses,
And I don't care twopence-halfpenny for any consequences.
Now I do not want to perish by the sword or by the dagger,
But a martyr may indulge a little pardonable swagger,
And a word or two of compliment my vanity would flatter,
But I've got to die to-morrow, so it really doesn't matter!

DES.   So it really doesn't matter—

MAR.   So it really doesn't matter—

ALL. So it really doesn't matter, matter, matter, matter, matter!

MAR. If I [79] were not a little mad and generally silly
I should give you my advice upon the subject, willy-nilly;
I should show you in a moment how to grapple with the question,
And you'd really be astonished at the force of my suggestion.
On the subject I shall write you a most valuable letter,
Full of excellent suggestions when I feel a little better,
But at present I'm afraid I am as mad as any hatter,
So I'll keep 'em to myself, for my opinion doesn't matter!

DES.   Her opinion doesn't matter—

ROB.   Her opinion doesn't matter—

ALL. Her opinion doesn't matter, matter, matter, matter, matter!

DES. If I had been so lucky as to have a steady brother
Who could talk to me as we are talking now to one another—
Who could give me good advice when he discovered I was erring
(Which is just the very favour which on you I am conferring),
My story would have made a rather interesting idyll,
And I might have lived and died a very decent indiwiddle.
This particularly rapid, unintelligible patter
Isn't generally heard, and if it is it doesn't matter!

ROB.   If it is it doesn't matter—

MAR.   If it ain't it doesn't matter—

ALL. If it is it doesn't matter, matter, matter, matter, matter!

[*Exeunt* DESPARD *and* MARGARET. [80]

Enter ADAM

ADAM (*guiltily*). Master—the deed is done!

ROB. What deed?

ADAM. She is here—alone, unprotected——

ROB. Who?

ADAM. The maiden. I've carried her off—I had a hard task, for she fought like a tiger-cat!

ROB. Great heaven, I had forgotten her! I had hoped to have died unspotted by crime, but I am foiled again—and by a tiger-cat! Produce her—and leave us!

[ADAM *introduces* DAME HANNAH, *very much excited, and exit.*

[78] *It was my great delight to watch as well as I could the faces of any of the audience I was able to see as I sang this verse. A degree of sadism on my part? Possibly. Conceit? Even more probably. Because I loved to see them turn purple as they struggled to take a breath for me, out of pure empathy. You see, I always took the whole of this verse in one breath!*

[79] *The original libretto, as presented by Reginald Allen in his book The First Night Gilbert and Sullivan, reveals a change of one word in the first line of this verse. Gilbert seems to have written: "If it were not a little mad and generally silly," but my recollections are that Mad Margaret always sang "I."*

Gilbert's "it" does seem to me more appropriate because Margaret is now apparently sane, and no mad person who is apparently sane will admit to insanity. And yet, as one proceeds with the verse, she does admit, "But at present I'm afraid I am as mad as any hatter." So perhaps, after all, it should be "I." Or perhaps not? Oh well, my opinion doesn't matter!

A second change involves Sullivan's alteration of the word "story" in Despard's verse to "existence" for the sake of musical scansion.

[80] *As a rule one encore at least was demanded for this trio. Very often there were two, and occasionally there would be a third encore. If a fourth should be called for, Old Adam would enter quickly and see to it that it was never taken. That would have meant singing the trio at a speed that even the strings couldn't have kept up with. One night, however, Despard and Margaret, convinced that Old Adam would be making his entrance as usual, proceeded on their way to their dressing rooms, following the third encore. For some reason, Old Adam didn't arrive, and there was nothing I could do. The applause kept up and there was one of those horrifying stage waits. Isidore Godfrey, our musical director, realizing that something was wrong, struck up a further encore, and I broke into my verse at a speed such that only the first and last words of each line could be heard. Despard and Margaret, hearing the music, dashed back onto the stage, both singing as best they could. Then Old Adam shot onto the stage (finally!) yelling, "Master—the deed is done!" as "guiltily" as it has ever been my pleasure (?) to hear. He should have felt guilty!*

ROB. Dame Hannah! This is—this is not what I expected.

HAN. Well, sir, and what would you with me? Oh, you have begun bravely—bravely indeed! Unappalled by the calm dignity of blameless womanhood, your minion has torn me from my spotless home, and dragged me, blindfold and shrieking, through hedges, over stiles, and across a very difficult country, and left me, helpless and trembling, at your mercy! Yet not helpless, coward sir, for approach one step—nay, but the twentieth part of one poor inch—and this poniard (*produces a very small dagger*) shall teach ye what it is to lay unholy hands on old Stephen Trusty's daughter!

ROB. Madam, I am extremely sorry for this. It is not at all what I intended—anything more correct—more deeply respectful than my intentions towards you, it would be impossible for any one—however particular—to desire.

HAN. Bah, I am not to be tricked by smooth words, hypocrite! But be warned in time, for there are, without, a hundred gallant hearts whose trusty blades would hack him limb from limb who dared to lay unholy hands on old Stephen Trusty's daughter!

ROB. And this is what it is to embark upon a career of unlicensed pleasure!

[HANNAH, *who has taken a formidable dagger from one of the armed figures, throws her small dagger to* ROBIN.

HAN. Harkye, miscreant, you have secured me, and I am your poor prisoner; but if you think I cannot take care of myself you are very much mistaken. Now then, it's one to one, and let the best man win!

[*Making for him.* [81]

ROB. (*in an agony of terror*). Don't! don't look at me like that! I can't bear it! Roderic! Uncle! Save me!

RODERIC *enters, from his picture. He comes down the stage*

ROD. What is the matter? Have you carried her off?

ROB. I have—she is there—look at her—she terrifies me!

ROD. (*looking at* HANNAH). Little Nannikin!

HAN. (*amazed*). Roddy-doddy!

ROD. My own old love! Why, how came *you* here?

HAN. This brute—he carried me off! Bodily! But I'll show him! (*about to rush at* ROBIN).

ROD. Stop! (*To* ROB.) What do you mean by carrying off this lady? Are you aware that once upon a time she was engaged to be married to me? I'm very angry—very angry indeed.

ROB. Now I hope this will be a lesson to you in future not to——

ROD. Hold your tongue, sir.

ROB. Yes, uncle. [82]

ROD. Have you given him any encouragement?

HAN. (*to* ROB.). Have I given you any encouragement? Frankly now, have I?

ROB. No. Frankly, you have not. Anything more scrupulously correct than your conduct, it would be impossible to desire.

ROD. You go away.

ROB. Yes, uncle.   [*Exit* ROBIN.

ROD. This is a strange meeting after so many years!

HAN. Very. I thought you were dead.

ROD. I am. I died ten years ago.

HAN. And are you pretty comfortable?

ROD. Pretty well—that is—yes, pretty well.

HAN. You don't deserve to be, for I loved you all the while, dear;

[81] *A splendid mock fight takes place between Robin and Dame Hannah, who chases him around the stage. At one point she pauses to strop her large, swordlike weapon on a stone step. Robin, after one look, attempts to strop his little dagger on the sole of his shoe. But it is not the sword that really demoralizes him; it is the fearsome look on the face of this dear old lady.*

[82] *Yes, uncle. Robin speaks these words both on this occasion and on the one on which he exits, a few lines below, in the shrill falsetto tones of a small boy who is decidedly frightened of his uncle. When he finally exits, he does so sucking his thumb.*

and it made me dreadfully unhappy to hear of all your goings-on, you bad, bad boy!

BALLAD—HANNAH [83]

There grew a little flower
'Neath a great oak tree:
When the tempest 'gan to lower
Little heeded she:
No need had she to cower,
For she dreaded not its power—
She was happy in the bower
Of her great oak tree!
Sing hey,
Lackaday!
Let the tears fall free
For the pretty little flower
And the great oak tree!

[83] *Words and music on page 548*

BOTH.

Sing hey,
Lackaday! etc.

When she found that he was fickle,
Was that great oak tree,
She was in a pretty pickle,
As she well might be—
But his gallantries were mickle,
For Death followed with his sickle,
And her tears began to trickle
For her great oak tree!

BOTH.

Sing hey,
Lackaday! etc.

Said she, "He loved me never,
Did that great oak tree,
But I'm neither rich nor clever,
And so why should he?
But though fate our fortunes sever,
To be constant I'll endeavour,
Aye, for ever and for ever,
To my great oak tree!"

BOTH.

Sing hey,
Lackaday! etc.

[Falls weeping on RODERIC's *bosom.*

Enter ROBIN, *excitedly, followed by all the characters and Chorus of Bridesmaids*

ROB. Stop a bit—both of you.

ROD. This intrusion is unmannerly.

HAN. I'm surprised at you.

ROB. I can't stop to apologize—an idea has just occurred to me. A Baronet of Ruddigore can only die through refusing to commit his daily crime.

ROD. No doubt.

ROB. Therefore, to refuse to commit a daily crime is tantamount to suicide!

ROD. It would seem so.

ROB. But suicide is, itself, a crime—and so, by your own showing, you ought never to have died at all!

RUDDIGORE

[84] *See Note 53. The whole of the second act would, I believe, become much more logical and believable if, as soon as Robin says, "Undoubtedly!" time could be taken to effect a transformation and the whole scene whisked back to the finale of Act I—provided one used Gilbert's printed directions at that point. In that event, Sir Roderic would be given the opportunity to return to his frame and become a portrait again. But to leave him on the stage "practically alive" is in a way more ghoulish than the gallery of ghosts.*

[85] *During the final chorus Old Adam is beckoned off by Robin. He shortly returns with a tray bearing a decanter of sherry and several glasses already filled. There is one exception: a half-filled glass. Robin, taking two glasses at a time, hands one to Roderic and one to Hannah, who accept; one to Despard, who would accept, and one to Margaret, who refuses for both. The half-glass of sherry he offers to Richard and a full one to Zorah, with whom Richard is paired off. Richard takes both, compares them, and hands the half-glass to Zorah. Finally, Robin and Rose take a glass apiece and all is fun and games as the curtain falls.*

  P.S. It actually was fun and games after the curtain fell as well because real sherry was always served in that final chorus.

ROD. I see—I understand! Then I'm practically alive!

ROB. Undoubtedly! [84] (SIR RODERIC *embraces* HANNAH.) Rose, when you believed that I was a simple farmer, I believe you loved me?

ROSE. Madly, passionately!

ROB. But when I became a bad baronet, you very properly loved Richard instead?

ROSE. Passionately, madly!

ROB. But if I should turn out *not* to be a bad baronet after all, how would you love me then?

ROSE. Madly, passionately!

ROB. As before?

ROSE. Why, of course!

ROB. My darling! (*They embrace.*)

RICH. Here, I say, belay!

ROSE. Oh sir, belay, if it's absolutely necessary!

ROB. Belay? Certainly not!

FINALE [85]

ROB.
Having been a wicked baronet a week,
Once again a modest livelihood I seek.
    Agricultural employment
    Is to me a keen enjoyment,
For I'm naturally diffident and meek!

ROSE.
When a man has been a naughty baronet,
And expresses his repentance and regret,
    You should help him, if you're able,
    Like the mousie in the fable,
That's the teaching of my Book of Etiquette.

RICH.
If you ask me why I do not pipe my eye,
Like an honest British sailor, I reply,
    That with Zorah for my missis,
    There'll be bread and cheese and kisses,
Which is just the sort of ration I enjye!

DES. *and* MAR.
Prompted by a keen desire to evoke,
All the blessed calm of matrimony's yoke,
    We shall toddle off to-morrow,
    From this scene of sin and sorrow,
For to settle in the town of Basingstoke!

ALL.
For happy the lily
    That's kissed by the bee;
And, sipping tranquilly,
    Quite happy is he;
And happy the filly
    That neighs in her pride;
But happier than any,
A pound to a penny,
A lover is, when he
    Embraces his bride!

CURTAIN

If Somebody There Chanced to Be

Moderate Waltz tempo

ROSE

1. If some-bod-y there chanced to be   Who loved me in a man - ner true,   My heart would point him out to me,   And I would point him out to you.   But here__ it__

2. If an - y well-bred youth I knew,   Po - lite and gen - tle, neat and trim,   Then I would hint as much to you,   And you could hint as much to him.   But here__ it__

(Referring to book of Etiquette)

537

says of those— who— point, Their man - ners must be out of
says in plain - est— print, "It's most un - la - dy - like to

joint. You may not point, you must not point, It's
hint." You may not hint, you must not hint, It

man - ners out of joint, to point! Ah!————— Had
says you must - n't hint, in print! Ah!————— And

I the love of such— as he, Some qui - et spot he'd
if I loved him through and through (True love and not a

take— me to, Then he could whis - per it to me,——
pass - ing whim), Then I could speak of it to you,——

I Know a Youth

Gracefully

ROBIN

1. I know a youth who loves a lit-tle maid (Hey, but his face is a sight for to see!).
2. He can-not eat, and he can-not sleep (Hey, but his face is a sight for to see!).

Si-lent is he, for he's mod-est and a-fraid (Hey, but he's tim-id as a youth can be!).
Dai-ly he goes for to wail for to weep (Hey, but he's wretch-ed as a youth can be!).

ROSE

I know a maid who loves a gal-lant youth
She's ver-y thin, and she's ver-y pale

(Hey, but she sick-ens as the days go by!). She can-not tell him all the
(Hey, but she sick-ens as the days go by!). Dai - ly she goes for to

sad,— sad— truth (Hey, but I think that lit-tle maid will die!).
weep— for to wail (Hey, but I think that lit-tle maid will die!).

rall.

ROBIN
mp a tempo
ROSE
ROBIN

Poor lit-tle man! Poor lit-tle maid! Poor lit-tle man!
Poor lit-tle maid! Poor lit-tle man! Poor lit-tle maid!

ROSE
mf BOTH

Poor lit-tle maid!}
Poor lit-tle man! } Now tell me pray, and tell me true,

What in the world___ should the {maid-en
{young man do?

1.

My Boy, You May Take It from Me

Fast and vivaciously

ROBIN

1. My boy, you may take it from me, That of all the af-flic-tions ac-
2. Now take, for ex-am-ple, my case: I've a bright in-tel-lec-tu-al
3. As a po-et, I'm ten-der and quaint, I've pas-sion and fer-vour and

curst With which a man's sad-dled And ham-pered and ad-dled, A
brain, In all Lon-don cit-y There's no one so wit-ty, I've
grace, From Ov-id and Hor-ace To Swin-burne and Mor-ris, They

dif-fi-dent na-ture's the worst. Though clev-er as clev-er can be, A
thought so a-gain and a-gain. I've a high-ly in-tel-li-gent face, My
all of them take a back place. Then I sing and I play and I paint: Though

Crich-ton of ear - ly ro - mance, . . . You must stir it and stump it, And
fea-tures can-not be de - nied, But, what - ev - er I try, sir, I
none are ac-com-plished as I, To say so were trea - son: You

mf

blow your own trum-pet, Or, trust me, you have-n't a chance!
fail in and why, sir? I'm mod-es-ty per-son-i - fied!
ask me the reas-on? I'm dif-fi-dent, mod-est, and shy!

If you

p   *mf*

cresc.

wish in the world to ad-vance, Your mer-its you're bound to en-hance, You must stir it and stump it, And

cresc.

1.-2.   **3.**

blow your own trum-pet, Or, trust me, you have-n't a chance!   chance!

mf   *sf*

When the Night Wind Howls

Fast and with energy

SIR RODERIC

1. When the
(2. As the)
(3. And)

marcato

sempre staccato

night wind howls in the chim-ney cowls, and the bat in the moon-light flies, And
sob of the breeze sweeps o-ver the trees and the mists lie low on the fen, From
then each ghost with his la-dye-toast to their church-yard beds take flight, With a

ink-y clouds, like fu-ner-al shrouds, sail o-ver the mid-night
grey tomb-stones are gath-ered the bones that once were wom-en and
kiss, per-haps, on her lan-tern chaps, and a gris-ly grim "good-

skies, When the foot-pads quail at the night bird's wail, and
men, And a-way they go, with a mop and a mow, to the
night!" Till the wel-come knell of the mid-night bell rings

There Grew a Little Flower

Slowly, with sentiment

HANNAH

1. There
(2. When she)
(3. Said)

grew a lit - tle flow - er 'Neath a great oak tree: When the
found that he was fick - le, Was that great oak tree, She was
she, "He loved me nev - er, Did that great oak tree, But I'm

tem - pest 'gan to low - er Lit - tle heed - ed she: No
in a pret - ty pick - le, As she well might be, But his
neith - er rich nor clev - er, And so why should he? But though

need had she to cow - er, For she dread - ed not its pow - er, She was
gal - lan - tries were mick - le, For death fol - lowed with his sick - le, And her
fate our for - tunes sev - er, To be con - stant I'll en - deav - our, Aye, for -

The Yeomen of the Guard

OR, THE MERRYMAN AND HIS MAID

DRAMATIS PERSONÆ

SIR RICHARD CHOLMONDELEY (*Lieutenant of the Tower*)

COLONEL FAIRFAX (*under sentence of death*)

SERGEANT MERYLL (*of the Yeomen of the Guard*)

LEONARD MERYLL (*his Son*)

JACK POINT (*a Strolling Jester*)

WILFRED SHADBOLT (*Head Jailer and Assistant Tormentor*)

THE HEADSMAN

FIRST YEOMAN

SECOND YEOMAN

FIRST CITIZEN

SECOND CITIZEN

ELSIE MAYNARD (*a Strolling Singer*)

PHŒBE MERYLL (*Sergeant Meryll's Daughter*)

DAME CARRUTHERS (*Housekeeper to the Tower*)

KATE (*her Niece*)

Chorus of Yeomen of the Guard, Gentlemen, Citizens, etc.

SCENE.—*Tower Green.*

Date, 16th Century.

First produced at the Savoy Theatre on October 3, 1888

OVER the years many reviewers have compared the role of Jack Point with that of Punchinello. This has given rise in the minds of many people to the suspicion that Gilbert was, perhaps, guilty of plagiarism. I do not recall ever having read of Punchinello's being compared with Jack Point, but surely that is the way it should be: The Yeomen of the Guard was written, composed and produced in 1888; I Pagliacci in 1892!

Gilbert was accused of plagiarism, however—if not of outright theft. The weekly magazine Punch attacked Gilbert lustily, sarcastically alluding to Yeomen as "the new and original opera, by the unknown team of Gillivan and Sulbert, The Beefeater's Bride, or, The Merryman and His Maritana." It then proceeded to point out all the similarities in the plot to the Fitzball–Wallace opera Maritana. Practically every other critic made some reference to this similarity, but none was so overwhelmingly and devastatingly belligerent as Punch. The Times did not consider the plot particularly strong, and said the resemblance to Maritana was so obvious that it could have been taken as a parody, "did not the serious tone of Mr. Gilbert's work preclude such a thought." It went on to say that even at his worst (evidently a reflection of their opinion regarding this latest work of Gilbert's) he was head and shoulders above the usual run of playwrights.

There is no doubt that there are similarities in practically every twist of The Yeomen to Maritana, but even Maritana was not original, it having been based upon a French play by d'Ennery, Don César de Bazan. I think, if we go back far enough, we will find that Hamlet was far from being an original plot—but is it any the less a masterpiece?

The Yeomen of the Guard owes its existence to an advertisement in a suburban London railway station. Ruddigore was beginning to show signs of a permanent drop in box-office receipts, and a new piece was being demanded. Gilbert was ready with a plot. The same old plot, modified slightly, but still the same old plot—a magic lozenge! Sullivan was just as ready with a refusal. The same old refusal, and with no modification. His diary reveals such phrases as "a puppet show," "not human," "not possible to feel any sympathy," "don't see my way to setting it."

History does not record why Gilbert should have been waiting for a train at Uxbridge one fateful night, nor why the train was late in arriving at that suburban station some twelve miles from London. But that he was so waiting, and that the train was late, turned out to be a most fortunate thing for Carte, Sullivan, himself—and ourselves and posterity.

As Gilbert paced up and down the platform, probably fuming at the tardiness of the train, his eye was caught by an advertisement for the Tower Furnishing Company which depicted a view of the Tower of London, a gray-bearded "Beefeater" in the foreground clad in his resplendent mutton-sleeved, ruff-collared, scarlet uniform, black velvet hat, and bearing a halberd.

The Tower of London! What a setting for an opera! What a title for an opera! As he got into the train his agile mind began to picture images—stage settings, costumes, Beefeaters, headsmen's blocks. Give it a modern treatment, he thought, a sort of up-to-date Sorcerer. Yes, his magic lozenge—a philter. Yes, indeed! What a setting for such a plot! But he changed his mind.

He saw an item in the theatrical column of The Sporting Times that read: "A real comic opera dealing with neither topsy-turvydom nor fairies [a very obvious dig at Iolanthe], but a genuine dramatic story, would be a greater novelty and a more splendid success than anything we are likely to see during the present dramatic season." Leslie Bailey advances the theory that this paragraph had much to do with Gilbert's change of heart, and I am inclined to agree. Popular opinion to the contrary, Gilbert was not the adamant curmudgeon who was not "open to conviction."

But why did he call it a comic opera? It is tragedy. Neither Gilbert nor anyone else connected with the piece ever called it a "comic" opera. It is billed, and always has been billed, as "an entirely new and original opera"! The word "comic" does not appear.

At first the piece was titled The Tower of London, and Sullivan was much relieved when he heard Gilbert's new idea. On receiving an outline of the plot, he confided his great pleasure to his diary: "no topsy-turvydom . . . very human . . . and funny also." (A comic opera after all?) Later on Gilbert discarded the title The Tower of London, feeling unsure of it. He also eschewed another, The Tower Warders, on the grounds that none but the very few knew that Beefeaters were called Tower Warders. He did suspect that The Beefeaters was right. Sullivan, however, was just as unsure in his mind of that title as Gilbert had been of the first two. It was Sir Arthur's suggestion that the title be changed to The Yeomen of the Guard. He had felt that "Beefeater" was an ugly word. According to the Oxford Dictionary, it is a derivative of hlaf-æta, a menial servant. It was originally used contemptuously in reference to "a well-fed menial."

Did Sullivan and Gilbert make a technical mistake when they decided on their final title? In a way. Both the Yeomen of the Guard and the Tower Warders are popularly known as Beefeaters, but the Yeomen are a distinct body and are stationed at St. James's Palace, performing their duties only on state occasions. With the exception of a red-and-gold cross-belt worn from the left shoulder to the right hip, which in former days supported an arquebus, the uniforms of both bodies are similar. The Captain of the Yeomen is appointed by the Lord Chamberlain's office, and the rank and file are selected from NCOs and Warrant Officers of the Regular Army who have distinguished themselves during their service. The Tower Warders are officially known as the Yeomen Warders of the Tower and, to complicate matters, are extraordinary members of the Yeomen of the Sovereign's Bodyguard!

Gilbert said that he was going to set the piece in the Elizabethan period. The programs indicate that the date is the 16th century—very definitely Elizabethan. A sketch from W. S. G.'s notebook depicts one of the Tower Warders with the initials E. R. embroidered on the breast of the uniform—Elizabeth Regina. However, a sketch of Courtice Pounds as Fairfax, at the time of the original opening, reveals the initials H. R. on his uniform—Henry Rex. This places the date no later than 1547. (Henry VIII was King of England 1509–47; then came Edward VI and Mary I; Elizabeth did not come to the throne until 1558.) There is nothing wrong with the period given in the program. What then made Gilbert change his mind about the actual date? He did, as will be seen later in the actual text of the libretto and my comments thereon.

That The Yeomen of the Guard ever reached fruition is a source of amazement. Gilbert was not only in constant pain from gout, but in a growing state of anxiety over the rapidly approaching opening night—not so much because of his departure from his usual format, but out of concern and a conviction that "further alterations" would have to be made if the piece were to achieve any sort of success. Sullivan was, by now, practically a chronic invalid and working under tremendous pressure. Petty quarrels were constantly flaring up. The morning of the opening night Sullivan heard from Gilbert that Sergeant Meryll's song in the first act was wholly irrelevant, that the act began with a solo, serious in character; went on with a chorus, serious and martial; then a song, grim; and after that, a trio, sentimental! Sergeant Meryll's song was cut little more than half an hour before the curtain went up. On that same opening night, Jessie Bond, sitting onstage beside her spinning wheel, already in a state of nerves, was fretted by Gilbert to such an extent that she reached a point of positive sickness and became the first, and probably only, person to put Gilbert in his place without suffering any consequences. "For heaven's sake," she screamed at him, "go away, or I'll never be able to sing a note!" Gilbert went—nor was he seen, front or backstage, until it was time for him to go "on" with Sullivan and acknowledge the plaudits and cries of the audience for "Author!" "Composer!"

The Yeomen of the Guard and The Mikado are the two operas which have undergone the most radical changes of scenery design and decor. Less radical changes were made in Ruddigore, The Gondoliers and Princess Ida. The Mikado changes, though radical, were logical; but The Yeomen of the Guard. . . .

The London Daily Telegraph said in its review of the first night in 1888, ". . . the one set, designed by Hawes Craven, elicited the first round of applause. It shows the Tower, as solidly built, to all appearance, as the original edifice a little lower down the river." In 1939, Peter Goffin's design took its place, and I regret to say that not only did the solidity vanish, but all resemblance to the Tower of London vanished with it. In the place of a grim, gray-stone fortalice, there arose a massive structure that bore every appearance of having been built of pink plaster of Paris, and which completely dwarfed the players on the stage. One must be grateful for the fact that at least the Beefeaters' uniforms were left untouched; but Jack Point's second-act costume is one with which I will never agree. I wore it, yes, but I did not like it. I didn't agree with it, so I couldn't like it. What, never? No, never. What, never? No, never! It offended me to such an extent that I spent some hours in the British Museum searching for any sort of clue that would, even if only vaguely, reconcile the new design with that of any court jester the world has known, and eventually came to the conclusion that it had been based entirely on some early prints of the Italian clown Grimaldi.

This new production was due to make its bow to the public in Southsea, near Portsmouth, in the second or third week of September 1939. Hitler, however, put a spoke in that wheel by marching into Poland that month. The theaters were closed as soon as war was declared on the Sunday following, and Mr. Carte was as quick to invoke the war clause in all contracts and declare them null and void. I was as quickly signed up by the late C. B. Cochran to star in a revue to open in Manchester as soon as theaters were allowed to reopen. This happened much earlier than was expected and the revue opened that November. The D'Oyly Carte did not get going again until late in December, when at last the new Yeomen was revealed to the public. It was not until 1946 that I eventually wore and performed in that confounded costume.

Just before I went on for my first entrance, Rupert D'Oyly Carte came to me in my dressing room and with an enigmatic smile gently reminded me of my statement back in '39—that I could not wear that second-act "clown get-up." I'm afraid that I replied with an equally enigmatic smile, saying (and thinking to myself as I said it: You've got to earn a living, me lad!): "Mr. Carte, like Pooh-Bah, 'I do it. It revolts me—but I do it.' And also like Grosvenor, though perhaps not as cheerfully, 'I do it on compulsion.'"

Carte smiled again, thought a moment, and then added: "And as you yourself will say in a very short while: 'Use is everything, and you will come in time to like it.'"

He had the last word. I did get used to it—but I did not come to like it.

The Yeomen of the Guard

ACT I

SCENE.—*Tower Green*

PHŒBE *discovered spinning* [1]

SONG—PHŒBE [2]

When maiden loves, she sits and sighs,
    She wanders to and fro;
Unbidden tear-drops fill her eyes,
And to all questions she replies
    With a sad "heigho!"
   'Tis but a little word—"heigho!"
   So soft, 'tis scarcely heard—"heigho!"
    An idle breath—
    Yet life and death
May hang upon a maid's "heigho!"

When maiden loves, she mopes apart,
    As owl mopes on a tree;
Although she keenly feels the smart,
She cannot tell what ails her heart,
    With its sad "Ah me!"
   'Tis but a foolish sigh—"Ah me!"
   Born but to droop and die—"Ah me!"
    Yet all the sense
    Of eloquence
Lies hidden in a maid's "Ah me!" (*Weeps.*)

Enter WILFRED

WIL. Mistress Meryll!

PHŒ. (*looking up*). Eh! Oh! it's you, is it? You may go away, if you like. Because I don't want you, you know.

WIL. Haven't you anything to say to me?

PHŒ. Oh yes! Are the birds all caged? The wild beasts all littered down? All the locks, chains, bolts, and bars in good order? Is the Little Ease [3] sufficiently uncomfortable? The racks, pincers, and thumbscrews all ready for work? Ugh! you brute!

WIL. These allusions to my professional duties are in doubtful taste. I didn't become a head jailer because I like head-jailing. I didn't become an assistant tormentor because I like assistant-tormenting. We can't *all* be sorcerers, you know. (PHŒBE, *annoyed.*) Ah! you brought that upon yourself.

PHŒ. Colonel Fairfax is *not* a sorcerer. He's a man of science and an alchemist.

WIL. Well, whatever he is, he won't be one long, for he's to be beheaded to-day for dealings with the devil. His master nearly had him last night, when the fire broke out in the Beauchamp [4] Tower.

PHŒ. Oh! how I wish he had escaped in the confusion! But take care; there's still time for a reply to his petition for mercy.

[1] *The most nervous person in the whole company on the opening night was undoubtedly Jessie Bond who had the role of Phoebe. Gilbert was making a radical departure from the usual chorus opening, and the curtain goes up on a solo. Even Gilbert was a little awed by what he had done. Would the public, used as it was to finding comic twists in all of Gilbert's apparently serious speeches, accept unabashed the tearful sentiment? They did, and they have ever since. Thomas Dunhill described this song as "an exquisite piece of lyrical music . . . halting here and there so that the singer may breathe the most musical of sighs."*

   In my opinion this is one of the two most beautiful openings of the series. The other? Iolanthe, of course.

[2] Words and music on page 593.

[3] *Little Ease. The allusion here is to a particularly uncomfortable dungeon in the Tower wherein one could not stand, sit or lie with any degree of comfort. The term is also given to the pillory, the stocks and—possibly—the rack.*

[4] *Pronounced in the English fashion: Beecham.*

WIL. Ah! I'm content to chance that. This evening at half-past seven—ah!

PHŒ. You're a cruel monster to speak so unfeelingly of the death of a young and handsome soldier.

WIL. Young and handsome! How do *you* know he's young and handsome?

PHŒ. Because I've seen him every day for weeks past taking his exercise on the Beauchamp Tower.

WIL. Curse him!

PHŒ. There, I believe you're jealous of *him*, now. Jealous of a man I've never spoken to! Jealous of a poor soul who's to die in an hour!

WIL. I am! I'm jealous of everybody and everything. I'm jealous of the very words I speak to you—because they reach your ears—and I mustn't go near 'em!

PHŒ. How unjust you are! Jealous of the words you speak to me! Why, you know as well as I do that I don't even like them.

WIL. You used to like 'em.

PHŒ. I used to *pretend* I liked them. It was mere politeness to comparative strangers.

[*Exit* PHŒBE, *with spinning wheel.*

WIL. I don't believe you know what jealousy is! I don't believe you know how it eats into a man's heart—and disorders his digestion—and turns his interior into boiling lead. Oh, you are a heartless jade to trifle with the delicate organization of the human interior!

[*Exit* WILFRED.

Enter Crowd of Men and Women, followed by Yeomen of the Guard. [5]

CHORUS (*as Yeomen march on*)

Tower Warders,
Under orders,
Gallant pikemen, valiant sworders!
Brave in bearing,
Foemen scaring,
In their bygone days of daring!
Ne'er a stranger
There to danger—
Each was o'er the world a ranger;
To the story
Of our glory
Each a bold contributory!

CHORUS OF YEOMEN

In the autumn of our life,
Here at rest in ample clover,
We rejoice in telling over
Our impetuous May and June.
In the evening of our day,
With the sun of life declining,
We recall without repining
All the heat of bygone noon.

SOLO—2ND YEOMAN [6]

This the autumn of our life,
This the evening of our day;
Weary we of battle strife,
Weary we of mortal fray.

[5] *The Peter Goffin production (see Foreword, page 555) introduced a radical change here. The opera opened to an inset—a room, Phoebe's room in Sergeant Meryll's quarters. Shadbolt was seen only through an open window. Phoebe made her usual exit, Shadbolt disappeared from the window, and the stage was blacked out. The inset was then rapidly removed, revealing a full stage and Tower Green. All this is good thinking, but it has always caused a very bad delay. From the first I was conscious of this and have often wondered why the change was not so arranged that it became a transformation scene in full view of the audience. I've always been a believer in doing things openly that cannot be done perfectly under cover, and perhaps making profit out of doing so.*

(I've recently heard that the D'Oyly Carte Company has done away completely with the inset idea and has returned to Gilbert's original directions. That is a pity, for surely it is incongruous for a young lady to be discovered spinning on Tower Green, instead of in her own room.)

[6] *This song was originally given to Sergeant Meryll who led the Yeomen of the Guard on. I do not know when this was changed, but I am convinced that the portrayer of the role must have been very relieved. The dialogue following the chorus, currently given to the 2nd Yeoman, was also Sergeant Meryll's. But after his second speech, he just had to remain standing while Dame Carruthers sang her solo. I have no hesitation in assuming that Gilbert made the switch the morning after the opening for the simple reason that Phoebe would have asked her question about Fairfax's reprieve (see page 560) almost immediately upon her father's appearance.*

But our year is not so spent,
    And our days are not so faded,
But that we with one consent,
    Were our lovèd land invaded,
      Still would face a foreign foe,
      As in days of long ago.

CHORUS.   Still would face a foreign foe,
              As in days of long ago.

PEOPLE.	YEOMEN.
Tower Warders, under orders, etc.	This the autumn of our life, etc.

[Exeunt Crowd. Manent Yeomen.

Enter DAME CARRUTHERS

DAME. A good day to you!

2ND YEOMAN. Good day, Dame Carruthers. Busy to-day?

DAME. Busy, aye! the fire in the Beauchamp last night has given me work enough. A dozen poor prisoners—Richard Colfax, Sir Martin Byfleet, Colonel Fairfax, Warren [7] the preacher-poet, and half-a-score others—all packed into one small cell, not six feet square. Poor Colonel Fairfax, who's to die to-day, is to be removed to No. 14 in the Cold Harbour that he may have his last hour alone with his confessor; and I've to see to that.

2ND YEO. Poor gentleman! He'll die bravely. I fought under him two years since, and he valued his life as it were a feather!

PHŒ. He's the bravest, the handsomest, and the best young gentleman in England! He twice saved my father's life; and it's a cruel thing, a wicked thing, and a barbarous thing that so gallant a hero should lose his head—for it's the handsomest head in England!

DAME. For dealings with the devil. Aye! if all were beheaded who dealt with *him*, there'd be busy doings on Tower Green.

PHŒ. You know very well that Colonel Fairfax is a student of alchemy—nothing more, and nothing less; but this wicked Tower, like a cruel giant in a fairy-tale, must be fed with blood, and that blood must be the best and bravest in England, or it's not good enough for the old Blunderbore. [8] Ugh!

DAME. Silence, you silly girl; you know not what you say. I was born in the old keep, and I've grown grey in it, and, please God, I shall die and be buried in it; and there's not a stone in its walls that is not as dear to me as my own right hand.

SONG WITH CHORUS—DAME CARRUTHERS *and* YEOMEN [9]

When our gallant Norman foes
    Made our merry land their own,
      And the Saxons from the Conqueror were flying,
At his bidding it arose,
    In its panoply of stone,
      A sentinel unliving and undying.

Insensible, I trow,
    As a sentinel should be,
      Though a queen to save her head should come a-suing,
There's a legend on its brow
    That is eloquent to me,
      And it tells of duty done and duty doing.

    "The screw may twist and the rack may turn,
    And men may bleed and men may burn,

[7] *Contrary to the belief of a number of people, Richard Colfax, Sir Martin Byfleet and Warren, the preacher-poet, are not the names of actual people. Each is a name invented by Gilbert. Byfleet is, however, the name of a town in Surrey, and Colfax is reminiscent of Carfax, a junction of four roads in Oxford. It also happens to be the name of the Vice-President of the United States, 1869–73! I'll bet you didn't know that.*

[8] Blunderbore. *The name of the giant in "Jack the Giant Killer." The word most likely came from "blunderbuss" which, apart from being a musket with a flaring muzzle, also means a blustering, noisy fellow (1654). It later became blunderhead and still later, dunderhead.*

[9] *Words and music on page 595.*

O'er London town and its golden hoard
I keep my silent watch and ward!"

CHORUS.   The screw may twist, etc.

Within its wall of rock
  The flower of the brave
    Have perished with a constancy unshaken. [10]
From the dungeon to the block,
  From the scaffold to the grave,
    Is a journey many gallant hearts have taken.

And the wicked flames may hiss
  Round the heroes who have fought
    For conscience and for home in all its beauty,
But the grim old fortalice [11]
  Takes little heed of aught
    That comes not in the measure of its duty.

  "The screw may twist and the rack may turn,
  And men may bleed and men may burn,
  O'er London town and its golden hoard
  I keep my silent watch and ward!"

CHORUS.   The screw may twist, etc.

[*Exeunt all but* PHŒBE. *Enter* SERGEANT MERYLL.

PHŒ. Father! Has no reprieve arrived for the poor gentleman?

MER. No, my lass; but there's one hope yet. Thy brother Leonard, who, as a reward for his valour in saving his standard and cutting his way through fifty foes who would have hanged him, has been appointed a Yeoman of the Guard, will arrive to-day; and as he comes straight from Windsor, where the Court is, it may be—it *may* be—that he will bring the expected reprieve with him.

PHŒ. Oh, that he may!

MER. Amen to that! For the Colonel twice saved my life, and I'd give the rest of my life to save his! And wilt thou not be glad to welcome thy brave brother, with the fame of whose exploits all England is a-ringing?

PHŒ. Aye, truly, if he brings the reprieve.

MER. And not otherwise?

PHŒ. Well, he's a brave fellow indeed, and I love brave men.

MER. *All* brave men?

PHŒ. Most of them, I verily believe! But I hope Leonard will not be too strict with me—they say he is a very dragon of virtue and circumspection! Now, my dear old father is kindness itself, and——

MER. And leaves thee pretty well to thine own ways, eh? Well, I've no fears for thee; thou hast a feather-brain, but thou'rt a good lass.

PHŒ. Yes, that's all very well, but if Leonard is going to tell me that I may not do this and I may not do that, and I must not talk to this one, or walk with that one, but go through the world with my lips pursed up and my eyes cast down, like a poor nun who has renounced mankind—why, as I have *not* renounced mankind, and don't mean to renounce mankind, I won't have it—there!

MER. Nay, he'll not check thee more than is good for thee, Phœbe! He's a brave fellow, and bravest among brave fellows, and yet it seems but yesterday that he robbed the Lieutenant's orchard.

Enter LEONARD MERYLL [12]

LEON. Father!

[10] *Although Gilbert writes the words: ". . . a constancy unshaken" the line should be sung with the thought, "their constancy . . ." in mind. The allusion is to those who went to the block rather than prove inconstant, and not to the constant executions which were taking place in the Tower.*

[11] *Fortalice. The medieval name for a fortress. Stems from the same root as the musical expression forte—fortis—strong, loud.*

[12] *Sergeant Meryll's "wholly irrelevant song" (see Foreword, page 555) came at this point. I quote the second verse:*

When at my Leonard's deeds sublime
A soldier's pulse beats double time,
  And brave hearts thrill,
  As brave hearts will
At tales of martial glory;
I burn with flush of pride and joy,
A pride unbittered by alloy,
To find my boy—my darling boy—
  The theme of song and story!

(The exclamation mark was Gilbert's.)

MER. Leonard! my brave boy! I'm right glad to see thee, and so is Phœbe!

PHŒ. Aye—hast thou brought Colonel Fairfax's reprieve?

LEON. Nay, I have here a despatch for the Lieutenant, but no reprieve for the Colonel!

PHŒ. Poor gentleman! poor gentleman!

LEON. Aye, I would I had brought better news. I'd give my right hand —nay, my body—my life, to save his!

MER. Dost thou speak in earnest, my lad? [13]

LEON. Aye, father—I'm no braggart. Did he not save thy life? and am I not his foster-brother?

MER. Then hearken to me. Thou hast come to join the Yeomen of the Guard!

LEON. Well?

MER. None has seen thee but ourselves?

LEON. And a sentry, who took but scant notice of me.

MER. Now to prove thy words. Give me the despatch, and get thee hence at once! Here is money, and I'll send thee more. Lie hidden for a space, and let no one know. I'll convey a suit of Yeoman's uniform to the Colonel's cell—he shall shave off his beard, so that none shall know him, and I'll own him as my son, the brave Leonard Meryll, who saved his flag and cut his way through fifty foes who thirsted for his life. He will be welcomed without question by my brother-Yeomen, I'll warrant that. Now, how to get access to the Colonel's cell? (*To* PHŒBE.) The key is with thy sour-faced admirer, Wilfred Shadbolt.

PHŒ. (*demurely*). I think—I say, I *think*—I can get anything I want from Wilfred. I think—mind I say, I *think*—you may leave that to me.

MER. Then get thee hence at once, lad—and bless thee for this sacrifice.

PHŒ. And take my blessing, too, dear, dear Leonard!

LEON. And thine, eh? Humph! Thy love is newborn; wrap it up carefully, lest it take cold and die.

TRIO—PHŒBE, LEONARD, MERYLL

PHŒ.   Alas! I waver to and fro!
      Dark danger hangs upon the deed!

ALL.   Dark danger hangs upon the deed!

LEON.   The scheme is rash and well may fail,
      But ours are not the hearts that quail,
      The hands that shrink, the cheeks that pale
        In hours of need!

ALL.   No, ours are not the hearts that quail,
      The hands that shrink, the cheeks that pale
        In hours of need!

MER.   The air I breathe to him I owe:
      My life is his—I count it naught!

PHŒ. *and* LEON. That life is his—so count it naught!

MER.   And shall I reckon risks I run
      When services are to be done
      To save the life of such an one?
        Unworthy thought!

PHŒ. *and* LEON. And shall we reckon risks we run
      To save the life of such an one?

[13] . . . my lad. *I do not remember ever having heard a Sergeant Meryll use the word "my." Gilbert wrote the line that way, yes, and how it came to be dropped I do not know, unless it was the same reason that I have: the line has a much more fatherly reading without it.*

[14] The Lieutenant. *Being a thoroughly English story, this is pronounced "Leftenant." This pronunciation goes back to 1450 and is based on the old French "luef" for "lieu," and the Scandinavian forms "luf" and "lufftenand."*

[15] *As opposed to Richard Colfax, etc. (see Note 7), Sir Richard Cholmondeley was an actual person and a Lieutenant of the Tower. If there were any reason for his name to be spoken during the course of the opera it would be pronounced "Chumley," and if anybody asks why, I can only say that it is probably for the same reason that Connecticut is pronounced Co-nett-i-c't.*

[16] Colonel. *In the 16th century the word was "Coronel"—an adaptation of the French "coronel," which came from the Italian "Colonnello." It was a three-syllable word and not reduced in pronunciation until the turn of the century. So it could be argued that Fairfax should be alluded to as "Cor-o-nel." It's not done, however.*

[17] and [18] and [19] *It is impossible not to picture Fairfax as a great, gallant and philosophical gentleman when one hears these three speeches. Later developments cause one to wonder whether this is not the philosophy of bravado. Whether or not this is true, these speeches do eventually seem to prove how easily the philosophy of man, facing an apparently inevitable doom, can change, once the inevitability is removed; that man is only as philosophically gallant as the circumstances demand.*

[20] Words and music on page 598. (See also Patience, page 219, Note 6.)

ALL.   Unworthy thought!
We may succeed—who can foretell?
May heaven help our hope—farewell!

LEONARD *embraces* MERYLL *and* PHŒBE, *and then exit.* PHŒBE *weeping.*

MER. Nay, lass, be of good cheer, we may save him yet.

PHŒ. Oh! see, father—they bring the poor gentleman from the Beauchamp! Oh, father! his hour is not yet come?

MER. No, no—they lead him to the Cold Harbour Tower to await his end in solitude. But softly—the Lieutenant [14] approaches! He should not see thee weep.

Enter FAIRFAX, *guarded. The* LIEUTENANT [15] *enters, meeting him.*

LIEUT. Halt! Colonel [16] Fairfax, my old friend, we meet but sadly.

FAIR. Sir, I greet you with all good-will; and I thank you for the zealous care with which you have guarded me from the pestilent dangers which threaten human life outside. In this happy little community, Death, when he comes, doth so in punctual and business-like fashion; and, like a courtly gentleman, giveth due notice of his advent, that one may not be taken unawares. [17]

LIEUT. Sir, you bear this bravely, as a brave man should.

FAIR. Why, sir, it is no light boon to die swiftly and surely at a given hour and in a given fashion! Truth to tell, I would gladly have my life; but if that may not be, I have the next best thing to it, which is death. Believe me, sir, my lot is not so much amiss! [18]

PHŒ. (*aside to* MERYLL). Oh, father, father, I cannot bear it!

MER. My poor lass!

FAIR. Nay, pretty one, why weepest thou? Come, be comforted. Such a life as mine is not worth weeping for. (*Sees* MERYLL.) Sergeant Meryll, is it not? (*To* LIEUT.) May I greet my old friend? (*Shakes* MERYLL'S *hand.*) Why, man, what's all this? Thou and I have faced the grim old king a dozen times, and never has his majesty come to me in such goodly fashion. Keep a stout heart, good fellow—we are soldiers, and we know how to die, thou and I. Take my word for it, it is easier to die well than to live well—for, in sooth, I have tried both. [19]

BALLAD—FAIRFAX [20]

Is life a boon?
   If so, it must befall,
   That Death, whene'er he call,
Must call too soon.
   Though fourscore years he give,
   Yet one would pray to live
Another moon!
   What kind of plaint have I,
   Who perish in July?
   I might have had to die,
Perchance, in June!

Is life a thorn?
   Then count it not a whit!
   Man is well done with it;
Soon as he's born
   He should all means essay
   To put the plague away;
And I, war-worn,
   Poor captured fugitive,
   My life most gladly give—

I might have had to live
Another morn!

[*At the end*, PHŒBE *is led off, weeping, by* MERYLL.

FAIR. And now, Sir Richard, I have a boon to beg. I am in this strait for no better reason than because my kinsman, Sir Clarence Poltwhistle, one of the Secretaries of State, has charged me with sorcery, in order that he may succeed to my estate, which devolves to him provided I die unmarried.

LIEUT. As thou wilt most surely do.

FAIR. Nay, as I will most surely *not* do, by your worship's grace! I have a mind to thwart this good cousin of mine.

LIEUT. How?

FAIR. By marrying forthwith, to be sure!

LIEUT. But heaven ha' mercy, whom wouldst thou marry?

FAIR. Nay, I am indifferent on that score. Coming Death hath made of me a true and chivalrous knight, who holds all womankind in such esteem that the oldest, and the meanest, and the worst-favoured of them is good enough for him. So, my good Lieutenant, if thou wouldst serve a poor soldier who has but an hour to live, find me the first that comes—my confessor shall marry us, and her dower shall be my dishonoured name and a hundred crowns [21] to boot. No such poor dower for an hour of matrimony!

LIEUT. A strange request. I doubt that I should be warranted in granting it.

FAIR. There never was a marriage fraught with so little of evil to the contracting parties. In an hour she'll be a widow, and I—a bachelor again for aught I know!

LIEUT. Well, I will see what can be done, for I hold thy kinsman in abhorrence for the scurvy trick he has played thee.

FAIR. A thousand thanks, good sir; we meet again on this spot in an hour or so. I shall be a bridegroom then, and your worship will wish me joy. Till then, farewell. (*To Guard.*) I am ready, good fellows.

[*Exit with Guard into Cold Harbour Tower.*

LIEUT. He is a brave fellow, and it is a pity that he should die. Now, how to find him a bride at such short notice? Well, the task should be easy! [22]

[*Exit.*

Enter JACK POINT *and* ELSIE MAYNARD, *pursued by a crowd of men and women.* POINT *and* ELSIE *are much terrified*; POINT, *however, assuming an appearance of self-possession.* [23]

CHORUS

Here's a man of jollity,
    Jibe, joke, jollify!
Give us of your quality,
    Come, fool, follify!

If you vapour vapidly,
River runneth rapidly,
    Into it we fling
    Bird who doesn't sing!

Give us an experiment
In the art of merriment;
    Into it we throw
    Cock who doesn't crow!

[21] Crown. *An English coin, similar in size to a silver dollar and approximately of the same value (in those days): five shillings. No such poor dower indeed.*

It is grossly unfair to analyze any plot of Gilbert's because not one of them will bear analysis; and to probe too deeply can ruin the pleasure of illogicality. Nevertheless, as Gilbert held up the mirror to the foibles of human nature for us to laugh at, I feel that he would have been equally ready for the mirror to be held up to the foibles of Gilbert for him to chuckle over.

Colonel Fairfax makes an extraordinary offer, with the aid of the Lieutenant—to "the first that comes" his dishonored name, and "a hundred crowns to boot" for one hour of matrimony. All this in order to diddle his cousin out of an estate which would devolve to him, provided Fairfax died unmarried. Surely, by virtue of marriage, his wife becomes his heir, and unless he intends to make another will immediately after the ceremony, leaving the estate elsewhere, it will automatically go to her. So why the bait of "a hundred crowns"?

One must presume that the estate is so involved that he could not make such a will, or he would have done so earlier as the simplest means of doing Poltwhistle in the eye, without having to resort to marriage. And it cannot be argued that as a convicted and condemned criminal his estate would automatically be confiscated by the Crown. If that were the case, Poltwhistle could never have benefited, so why frame Fairfax in the first place? One might argue that as one of the Secretaries of State, that is exactly what Poltwhistle was doing, but I don't believe Gilbert meant it that way. It was a purely personal thing.

However, things being what they are, it is quite evident that Fairfax had no thought of escape or he would not contemplate a chance and hurried marriage with "the first that comes."

I suppose we should be grateful that Gilbert did not go very deeply into the logic of this situation. If he had—well—possibly there would have been no Yeomen of the Guard. And that would be a pity!

[22] *What makes the Lieutenant so sure that his "task should be easy"? It seems to suggest that he holds the distaff side of the City of London's citizenry to be extremely mercenary. I would prefer to see this line cut. To borrow a phrase that Gilbert, as a barrister at law, must have used in court at some time or another: Objection—on the grounds that it suggests a foregone conclusion on the part of the witness!*

[23] *Elsie and Point used to make their entrance according to Gilbert's directions. That is, they entered together, pursued by the crowd. The Goffin production ended that. Then, each entered separately, brought on by two groups of citizens. However, Goffin did concede one prop which Elsie had always carried—a bundle tied up in an old green cotton kerchief. This she would throw into the wings, offstage. No one ever knew why she brought it on in the first place, until one day the whole thing was ex-*

563

plained by Mr. Gordon, the stage director. In his view she was a little too vigorous in throwing it and he called her attention to it.

"But," says she, "I have to throw it hard to get it over the heads of the citizens and out of sight offstage."

"I know," replies Mr. Gordon, "but it must not look as if you throw it so hard. Remember, it contains all your personal belongings."

Our Elsie couldn't help it. "But surely, Mr. Gordon, there's no china in it, is there?"

"Of course not," he answers, "but you carry your Bible in it!"

Elsie was silent for a moment. Then quite seriously she said, "Yes, I see. I didn't know that. But do you think the audience does?"

[24] Words and music on page 600.

[25] This may well be put down as the one number which Gilbert composed. Sullivan was completely stumped when he received the lyric. The rhythm was strange and unlike anything Gilbert had done before. Sullivan took the only course open to him and called W. S., saying that it seemed apparent that he had had a tune in his mind when he wrote the lyric, and would he come over and hum whatever it was? Gilbert explained that he had heard some sailors (members of the crew of his own yacht) singing a chantey, the tune and form of which had haunted him, and that was what he had had in mind. The chantey was:

Come and I will sing to you.
What will you sing to me?
I will sing you one, O!
What is your one, O?
One of them is all alone,
And ever will remain so . . .

The style of the lyric is curious, and as Leslie Bailey says: ". . . one that is believed to be a corruption of an old Cornish carol." ("Green Grow the Rushes" is still another variant.) He then goes on to say that Sullivan promptly wrote a new tune to Gilbert's words. Yes, new—and yet so old that the first time I heard it I was struck by its familiarity. So who did write it? It's hard to say, but without Gilbert, Sullivan would never have put this particular melody down on paper.

The Yeomen of the Guard was the second of the operas I saw. (The first? The Gondoliers.) I was a student at the Royal College of Music at the time and went with a couple of others to the Prince's Theatre and splurged three shillings and sixpence on standing room at the back of the dress circle. As I walked out of the theater that night I said to my companions, "There's a part I would love to play, and one day I think I will." A derisive laugh was all I received. But almost three years to the day, and of all things, in the town of my father's and mother's birth, I gave my first performance of Jack Point, and—as Alice said, curiouser and curiouser, one of my derisive friends happened to be out front. He did not know I was scheduled to appear, nor did I know that he was out front. I think I received my greatest tribute from him after the show that night. He called around to see me for the express purpose of apologizing for having laughed!

Banish your timidity,
And with all rapidity
Give us quip and quiddity—
Willy-nilly, O!

River none can mollify;—
Into it we throw
Fool who doesn't follify,
Cock who doesn't crow!

POINT (*alarmed*). My masters, I pray you bear with us, and we will satisfy you, for we are merry folk who would make all merry as ourselves. For, look you, there is humour in all things, and the truest philosophy is that which teaches us to find it and to make the most of it.

ELSIE (*struggling with one of the crowd*). Hands off, I say, unmannerly fellow!

POINT (*to 1st Citizen*). Ha! Didst thou hear her say, "Hands off"?

IST CIT. Aye, I heard her say it, and I felt her do it! What then?

POINT. Thou dost not see the humour of that?

IST CIT. Nay, if I do, hang me!

POINT. Thou dost not? Now observe. She said, "Hands off!" Whose hands? Thine. Off whom? Off *her*. Why? Because she is a woman. Now, had she *not* been a woman, thine hands had not been set upon her at all. So the reason for the laying on of hands is the reason for the taking off of hands, and herein is contradiction contradicted! It is the very marriage of *pro* with *con*; and no such lopsided union either, as times go, for *pro* is not more unlike *con* than man is unlike woman—yet men and women marry every day with none to say, "Oh, the pity of it!" but I and fools like me! Now wherewithal shall we please you? We can rhyme you couplet, triolet, quatrain, sonnet, rondolet, ballade, what you will. Or we can dance you saraband, gondolet, carole, pimpernel, or Jumping Joan.

ELSIE. Let us give them the singing farce of the Merryman and his Maid—therein is song and dance too.

ALL. Aye, the Merryman and his Maid!

[24] DUET—ELSIE *and* POINT [25]

POINT.   I have a song to sing, O!

ELSIE.   Sing me your song, O!

POINT.   It is sung to the moon
By a love-lorn loon,
Who fled from the mocking throng, O!
It's the song of a merryman, moping mum,
Whose soul was sad, and whose glance was glum,
Who sipped no sup, and who craved no crumb,
As he sighed for the love of a ladye.
Heighdy! heighdy!
Misery me, lackadaydee!
He sipped no sup, and he craved no crumb,
As he sighed for the love of a ladye.

ELSIE.   I have a song to sing, O!

POINT.   What is your song, O?

ELSIE.   It is sung with the ring
Of the songs maids sing
Who love with a love life-long, O!

It's the song of a merrymaid, peerly proud,
Who loved a lord and who laughed aloud
At the moan of the merryman, moping mum,
Whose soul was sad, and whose glance was glum,
Who sipped no sup, and who craved no crumb,
   As he sighed for the love of a ladye.
     Heighdy! heighdy!
     Misery me, lackadaydee!
     He sipped no sup, etc.

POINT.   I have a song to sing, O!

ELSIE.   Sing me your song, O!

POINT.   It is sung to the knell
     Of a churchyard bell,
And a doleful dirge, ding dong, O!
It's a song of a popinjay, bravely born,
Who turned up his noble nose with scorn
At the humble merrymaid, peerly proud,
Who loved a lord, and who laughed aloud
At the moan of a merryman, moping mum,
Whose soul was sad, and whose glance was glum,
Who sipped no sup, and who craved no crumb,
   As he sighed for the love of a ladye.

BOTH.   Heighdy! heighdy!
     Misery me, lackadaydee!
     He sipped no sup, etc.

ELSIE.   I have a song to sing, O!

POINT.   Sing me your song, O!

ELSIE.   It is sung with a sigh
     And a tear in the eye,
For it tells of a righted wrong, O!
It's a song of the merrymaid, once so gay,
Who turned on her heel and tripped away
From the peacock popinjay, bravely born,
Who turned up his noble nose with scorn
At the humble heart that he did not prize:
So she begged on her knees, with downcast eyes,
For the love of the merryman, moping mum,
Whose soul was sad, and whose glance was glum,
Who sipped no sup, and who craved no crumb,
   As he sighed for the love of a ladye.

BOTH.   Heighdy! heighdy!
     Misery me, lackadaydee!
His pains were o'er, and he sighed no more,
For he lived in the love of a ladye.

1ST CIT. Well sung and well danced!
2ND CIT. A kiss for that, pretty maid!
ALL. Aye, a kiss all round.
ELSIE (*drawing dagger*). Best beware! I am armed!
POINT. Back, sirs—back! This is going too far.
2ND CIT. Thou dost not see the humour of it, eh? Yet there is humour in all things—even in this. (*Trying to kiss her.*)
ELSIE. Help! help!

The Yeomen of the Guard *does not rank among the top three operas in popularity, but this duet ranks among the most popular numbers in the series. It also ranks among the most difficult, especially for Jack Point. A running entrance, followed by a spate of dialogue that must be kept up to pitch in order to gain and keep the attention of the crowd—thus saving himself and Elsie from a ducking—leaves Point in a breathless condition. The number begins with a moderate dance step and goes into a legato vocal passage, with a well articulated and steady rhythm. To obtain the full beauty of the melody and lyric the whole thing must flow easily and smoothly. This is no easy task for an already breathless performer. Also, action is called for throughout the number, including dance steps and an inevitable encore, by the end of which Point is in a state of utter exhaustion. I eventually turned this exhaustion to some good account, even emphasizing it in order to convey the impression that Point was not the fittest of men. After some discussion with a specialist I began to use make-up that would indicate that Point was, even then, suffering from a heart condition. By doing this I set up a situation that would justify Point's eventual fate (see Note 92).*

It's a song of a popinjay, bravely born . . .

[26] . . . there is a limit to my folly. *The true jester, never missing an opportunity. But Jack Point is in love with Elsie and there should be no doubt of this from the outset.*

[27] *Electuary. A medicine consisting of a powder or other ingredient. I imagine it must be of a particularly vile flavor because it is always mixed with honey, jam or syrup.*

[28] *There is no thought, nor should there be, in the Lieutenant's mind of a solution to his and Fairfax's problem until this moment, when his task assumes for the first time an appearance of easy accomplishment.*

[29] *Gilbert was at this time doing all he could to help Sullivan. He apparently permitted him to cut two lines from each verse of his original lyric for this trio and, furthermore, presented alternative lyrics, varying in rhythm, for Sullivan to choose from. From the Lieutenant's verse:*

. . . about to lose his head?

he cut: { No harm to you can thence arise, / In half an hour, poor soul, he dies.

From Elsie's verse:

. . . I sorely need.

he cut: { Unfortunately, life and death / Have hung, till lately, on a breath.

From Point's verse:

. . . any one but me,

he cut: { The circumstances of this case / May set such fancies out of place;

and the word "so" of the next line was changed to "yet."

The alternative rhythm for the last lines of the first verse was:

LIEUT. What matter though his head should fall,
This trifling blow need not appal.
Most men who wed, so poets tell,
Have lost both head and heart as well!

Enter LIEUTENANT *with Guard. Crowd falls back*

LIEUT. What is this pother?

ELSIE. Sir, we sang to these folk, and they would have repaid us with gross courtesy, but for your honour's coming.

LIEUT. (*to Mob*). Away with ye! Clear the rabble. (*Guards push Crowd off, and go off with them.*) Now, my girl, who are you, and what do you here?

ELSIE. May it please you, sir, we are two strolling players, Jack Point and I, Elsie Maynard, at your worship's service. We go from fair to fair, singing, and dancing, and playing brief interludes; and so we make a poor living.

LIEUT. You two, eh? Are ye man and wife?

POINT. No, sir; for though I'm a fool, there is a limit to my folly. [26] Her mother, old Bridget Maynard, travels with us (for Elsie is a good girl), but the old woman is a-bed with fever, and we have come here to pick up some silver to buy an electuary [27] for her.

LIEUT. Hark ye, my girl! Your mother is ill? [28]

ELSIE. Sorely ill, sir.

LIEUT. And needs good food, and many things that thou canst not buy?

ELSIE. Alas! sir, it is too true.

LIEUT. Wouldst thou earn an hundred crowns?

ELSIE. An hundred crowns! They might save her life!

LIEUT. Then listen! A worthy but unhappy gentleman is to be beheaded in an hour on this very spot. For sufficient reasons, he desires to marry before he dies, and he hath asked me to find him a wife. Wilt thou be that wife?

ELSIE. The wife of a man I have never seen!

POINT. Why, sir, look you, I am concerned in this; for though I am not yet wedded to Elsie Maynard, time works wonders, and there's no knowing what may be in store for us. Have we your worship's word for it that this gentleman will die to-day?

LIEUT. Nothing is more certain, I grieve to say.

POINT. And that the maiden will be allowed to depart the very instant the ceremony is at an end?

LIEUT. The very instant. I pledge my honour that it shall be so.

POINT. An hundred crowns?

LIEUT. An hundred crowns!

POINT. For my part, I consent. It is for Elsie to speak.

TRIO—ELSIE, POINT, *and* LIEUTENANT [29]

LIEUT. How say you, maiden, will you wed
A man about to lose his head?
For half an hour
You'll be a wife,
And then the dower
Is yours for life.
A headless bridegroom why refuse?
If truth the poets tell,
Most bridegrooms, ere they marry, lose
Both head and heart as well!

ELSIE. A strange proposal you reveal,
It almost makes my senses reel.
Alas! I'm very poor indeed,
And such a sum I sorely need.
My mother, sir, is like to die,
This money life may bring.

Bear this in mind, I pray, if I
Consent to do this thing!

POINT.   Though as a general rule of life
I don't allow my promised wife,
My lovely bride that is to be,
To marry any one but me,
    Yet if the fee is promptly paid,
    And he, in well-earned grave,
Within the hour is duly laid,
    Objection I will waive!
    Yes, objection I will waive!

ALL.   Temptation, oh, temptation,
    Were we, I pray, intended
To shun, whate'er our station,
    Your fascinations splendid;
Or fall, whene'er we view you,
Head over heels into you?
    Temptation, oh, temptation, etc.

[*During this, the* LIEUTENANT *has whispered to* WILFRED (*who has entered*). WILFRED *binds* ELSIE'S *eyes with a kerchief, and leads her into the Cold Harbour Tower.* [30]

LIEUT. And so, good fellow, you are a jester?

POINT. Aye, sir, and like some of my jests, out of place.

LIEUT. I have a vacancy for such an one. Tell me, what are your qualifications for such a post?

POINT. Marry, sir, I have a pretty wit. I can rhyme you extempore; I can convulse you with quip and conundrum; I have the lighter philosophies at my tongue's tip; I can be merry, wise, quaint, grim, and sardonic, one by one, or all at once; I have a pretty turn for anecdote; I know all the jests—ancient and modern—past, present, and to come; I can riddle you from dawn of day to set of sun, and, if that content you not, well on to midnight and the small hours. Oh, sir, a pretty wit, I warrant you—a pretty, pretty wit!

RECITATIVE AND SONG—POINT [31]

I've jibe and joke
    And quip and crank
For lowly folk
    And men of rank.
I ply my craft
    And know no fear,
But aim my shaft
    At prince or peer.
At peer or prince—at prince or peer,
I aim my shaft and know no fear!

I've wisdom from the East and from the West,
    That's subject to no academic rule;
You may find it in the jeering of a jest,
    Or distil it from the folly of a fool.
I can teach you with a quip, if I've a mind;
    I can trick you into learning with a laugh;
Oh, winnow all my folly, and you'll find
    A grain or two of truth among the chaff!

I can set a braggart quailing with a quip,
    The upstart I can wither with a whim;

[30] There is some similarity at this point between The Mikado and The Yeomen of the Guard. Ko-Ko gives up his fiancée on the condition that Nanki-Poo forfeit his head in a month; Jack Point gives up the girl he loves on the assurance that Fairfax will die that day. Both Fairfax and Nanki-Poo escape their fate, and both Ko-Ko and Point lose their loved ones. However, Ko-Ko's sacrifice was to save his own head; Point's is to help save the life of Bridget Maynard. Ko-Ko was utterly selfish; Point is completely unselfish, and utterly gallant (in spite of his making a jest of it). His final line before the trio is not just passing the buck; he is really encouraging Elsie for her mother's sake.

As Elsie is led off by Shadbolt there is a moment when Point would reverse the decision and races after her, but he is stopped by the Lieutenant. The chance of a permanent job once again brings out the true jester—a man of wit and wisdom.

[31] Gilbert was a modern jester and in this song is really describing his own philosophy. But it isn't in the same jocular way in which he describes himself in Princess Ida where it was Gilbert the cynic, living, as he put it, "up to my reputation."

He may wear a merry laugh upon his lip,
　But his laughter has an echo that is grim!
When they're offered to the world in merry guise,
　Unpleasant truths are swallowed with a will—
For he who'd make his fellow-creatures wise
　Should always gild the philosophic pill!

LIEUT. And how came you to leave your last employ?

POINT. Why, sir, it was in this wise. My Lord was the Archbishop of Canterbury, and it was considered that one of my jokes was unsuited to His Grace's family circle. In truth, I ventured to ask a poor riddle, sir—Wherein lay the difference between His Grace and poor Jack Point? His Grace was pleased to give it up, sir. And thereupon I told him that whereas His Grace was paid £10,000 a year [32] for being good, poor Jack Point was good—for nothing. 'Twas but a harmless jest, but it offended His Grace, who whipped me and set me in the stocks for a scurril rogue, and so we parted. I had as lief not take post again with the dignified clergy.

LIEUT. But I trust you are very careful not to give offence. I have daughters.

POINT. Sir, my jests are most carefully selected, and anything objectionable is expunged. If your honour pleases, I will try them first on your honour's chaplain.

LIEUT. Can you give me an example? Say that I had sat me down hurriedly on something sharp?

POINT. Sir, I should say that you had sat down on the spur of the moment. [33]

LIEUT. Humph! I don't think much of that. Is that the best you can do?

POINT. It has always been much admired, sir, but we will try again.

LIEUT. Well, then, I am at dinner, and the joint of meat is but half cooked.

POINT. Why then, sir, I should say that what is *underdone* cannot be helped. [34]

LIEUT. I see. I think that manner of thing would be somewhat irritating.

POINT. At first, sir, perhaps; but use is everything, and you would come in time to like it.

LIEUT. We will suppose that I caught you kissing the kitchen wench under my very nose.

POINT. Under *her* very nose, good sir—not under yours! *That* is where I would kiss her. Do you take me? Oh, sir, a pretty wit—a pretty, pretty wit!

LIEUT. The maiden comes. Follow me, friend, and we will discuss this matter at length in my library.

POINT. I am your worship's servant. That is to say, I trust I soon shall be. But, before proceeding to a more serious topic, can you tell me, sir, why a cook's brain-pan is like an overwound clock?

LIEUT. A truce to this fooling—follow me.

POINT. Just my luck; my best conundrum wasted! [35]

[*Exeunt.*

Enter ELSIE *from Tower, led by* WILFRED, *who removes the bandage from her eyes, and exit*

RECITATIVE AND SONG—ELSIE [36]

'Tis done! I am a bride! Oh, little ring,
　That bearest in thy circlet all the gladness

. . . he who'd make his fellow-creatures wise

Should always gild the philosophic pill!

[32] £10,000 *a year. Ten thousand pounds, but the line is delivered ". . . ten thousand a year." I found, however, that in the United States it was necessary to say it in full because I received so many inquiries about what I meant. "Ten thousand what?" I would be asked.*

[33] *As the Lieutenant says, I don't think much of that—but as Jack Point says, it has always been much admired, and what is more, still is!*

[34] *. . . cannot be helped. Synonymous with "cannot be served." Gilbert also intended it to be synonymous with "inevitable"!*

[35] *There have been many suggested answers to this conundrum but, like the "official utterances" of Sir Joseph Porter, it is "unanswerable." In any case, one could not overwind clocks in the 16th century; they hadn't been invented yet. And that would seem to be as good an answer as any. (See The Mikado, page 421, Note 36.)*

[36] *The whole of this song is an indictment of those who would marry in haste (for money) and repent at leisure.*

That lovers hope for, and that poets sing,
    What bringest thou to me but gold and sadness?
A bridegroom all unknown, save in this wise,
To-day he dies! To-day, alas, he dies!

Though tear and long-drawn sigh
    Ill fit a bride,
No sadder wife than I
    The whole world wide!
      Ah me! Ah me!
      Yet maids there be
Who would consent to lose
    The very rose of youth,
      The flower of life,
    To be, in honest truth,
      A wedded wife,
        No matter whose!

Ah me! what profit we,
    O maids that sigh,
Though gold, though gold should live
If wedded love must die?

Ere half an hour has rung,
    A widow I!
Ah, heaven, he is too young,
    Too brave to die!
      Ah me! Ah me!
      Yet wives there be
So weary worn, I trow,
    That they would scarce complain,
      So that they could
In half an hour attain
    To widowhood,
      No matter how!

O weary wives
    Who widowhood would win,
Rejoice that ye have time
    To weary in.

                [*Exit* ELSIE *as* WILFRED *re-enters.*

WIL. (*looking after* ELSIE). 'Tis an odd freak, for a dying man and his confessor to be closeted alone with a strange singing girl. I would fain have espied them, but they stopped up the keyhole. *My* keyhole!

Enter PHŒBE *with* MERYLL. MERYLL *remains in the background,
unobserved by* WILFRED

PHŒ. (*aside*). Wilfred—and alone! [37]

WIL. Now what could he have wanted with her? That's what puzzles me!

PHŒ. (*aside*). Now to get the keys from him. (*Aloud.*) Wilfred—has no reprieve arrived?

WIL. None. Thine adored Fairfax is to die.

PHŒ. Nay, thou knowest that I have naught but pity for the poor condemned gentleman.

WIL. I know that he who is about to die is more to thee than I, who am alive and well.

PHŒ. Why, that were out of reason, dear Wilfred. Do they not say that a live ass is better than a dead lion? No, I don't mean that!

[37] *Wilfred carries on his belt an actual thumbscrew and a bunch of huge keys. The thumbscrew in my day was a practical model. I well remember on one occasion Hilton Leyland as Shadbolt was demonstrating the "nice regulation of a thumbscrew," and failed to regulate it to the essential "hundredth part of a single revolution." His involuntary "ouch!" was a revelation in histrionic sincerity. Yes, he had really trapped his thumb, and a blackened nail bore witness to this for many days.*

In spite of the directions that Gilbert gives just before Wilfred's thumbscrew speech, Phoebe does not remove the keys until the moment when Wilfred catches his thumb in his own little instrument of torture.

A lot that Gilbert wrote for The Yeomen of the Guard never got even so far as being set to music. One song written for Wilfred will perhaps indicate why this was so:

    *The kerchief on your neck of snow
    I look on as a deadly foe,
    It goeth where I may not go,
    And stops there all day long . . .*

is the way the song begins. It ends:

    *The cat you fondled, soft and sly,
    He lieth where I may not lie!
    We're not on terms, that cat and I!
    I do not like that cat!*

Upon thy breast
My loving head would rest

[38] *Words and music on page 608.*

[39] *Jessie Bond, the creator of the role of Phoebe, remarks very scathingly in her memoirs on some of the business carried out in this duet. That is, after she left the Company. "I think it is wicked," she writes, "that there should be this vulgarity in one of the loveliest songs in the operas. . . . Sir William Gilbert . . . intended that his words should be heard . . . and they never are today. Sir Arthur would not have stood it. The air was too sweet to be drowned by silly laughter." Jessie herself, or so she says, would not allow W. H. Denny (the father of Reginald Denny) to do so much as give her a slightly humorous look. "I won't have any movement while I'm singing my song!"*

In all fairness to later Phoebes I must say that I fear Jessie was getting on in years when she wrote about Shadbolt swaying and ogling, and Phoebe scratching his chin and pulling his hair. Oh yes—it all takes place, but only in the encore. Something I think Jessie forgot. Something else she forgot, too, is that Gilbert gives specific directions at one point for the return of the keys right in the middle of the song, which entails the entrance of Meryll. There's movement for you, Jessie! And Phoebe must somehow distract Wilfred's attention. I would not say that she has to ogle him, but she certainly has to become very coy while she replaces the keys, and Wilfred must react to her advances. More movement! There has to be. I have a deep conviction that directions to cover all this would be found in Gilbert's own prompt copy. His Bab sketch seems to indicate something of his thoughts in this direction.

WIL. Oh, they say that, do they?

PHŒ. It's unpardonably rude of them, but I believe they put it in that way. Not that it applies to thee, who art clever beyond all telling!

WIL. Oh yes, as an assistant-tormentor.

PHŒ. Nay, as a wit, as a humorist, as a most philosophic commentator on the vanity of human resolution.

[PHŒBE *slyly takes bunch of keys from* WILFRED'S *waistband and hands them to* MERYLL, *who enters the Tower, unnoticed by* WILFRED.

WIL. Truly, I have seen great resolution give way under my persuasive methods (*working a small thumbscrew*). In the nice regulation of a thumbscrew—in the hundredth part of a single revolution lieth all the difference between stony reticence and a torrent of impulsive unbosoming that the pen can scarcely follow. Ha! ha! I am a mad wag.

PHŒ. (*with a grimace*). Thou art a most light-hearted and delightful companion, Master Wilfred. Thine anecdotes of the torture-chamber are the prettiest hearing.

WIL. I'm a pleasant fellow an I choose. I believe I am the merriest dog that barks. Ah, we might be passing happy together——

PHŒ. Perhaps. I do not know.

WIL. For thou wouldst make a most tender and loving wife.

PHŒ. Aye, to one whom I really loved. For there is a wealth of love within this little heart—saving up for—I wonder whom? Now, of all the world of men, I wonder whom? To think that he whom I am to wed is now alive and somewhere! Perhaps far away, perhaps close at hand! And I know him not! It seemeth that I am wasting time in not knowing him.

WIL. Now say that it is I—nay! suppose it for the nonce. Say that we are wed—suppose it only—say that thou art my very bride, and I thy cheery, joyous, bright, frolicsome husband—and that, the day's work being done, and the prisoners stored away for the night, thou and I are alone together—with a long, long evening before us!

PHŒ. (*with a grimace*). It is a pretty picture—but I scarcely know. It cometh so unexpectedly—and yet—and yet—*were* I thy bride——

WIL. Aye!—wert thou my bride——?

PHŒ. Oh, how I would love thee!

SONG—PHŒBE [38]

Were I thy bride,
Then all the world beside
Were not too wide
    To hold my wealth of love—
Were I thy bride!

Upon thy breast [39]
My loving head would rest,
    As on her nest
        The tender turtle dove—
Were I thy bride!

This heart of mine
Would be one heart with thine,
    And in that shrine
        Our happiness would dwell—
Were I thy bride!

And all day long
Our lives should be a song:
    No grief, no wrong

Should make my heart rebel—
Were I thy bride!

The silvery flute,
The melancholy lute,
Were night-owl's hoot
To my low-whispered coo—
Were I thy bride!

The skylark's trill
Were but discordance shrill
To the soft thrill
Of wooing as I'd woo—
Were I thy bride!

MERYLL *re-enters; gives keys to* PHŒBE, *who replaces them at* WILFRED'S *girdle, unnoticed by him. Exit* MERYLL.

The rose's sigh
Were as a carrion's cry
To lullaby
Such as I'd sing to thee,
Were I thy bride!

A feather's press
Were leaden heaviness
To my caress.
But then, of course, you see,
I'm not thy bride!

[*Exit* PHŒBE.

WIL. No, thou'rt not—not yet! But, Lord, how she woo'd! I should be no mean judge of wooing, seeing that I have been more hotly woo'd than most men. I have been woo'd by maid, widow, and wife. I have been woo'd boldly, timidly, tearfully, shyly—by direct assault, by suggestion, by implication, by inference, and by innuendo. But this wooing is not of the common order: it is the wooing of one who must needs woo me, if she die for it!

[*Exit* WILFRED.

Enter MERYLL, *cautiously, from Tower*

MER. (*looking after them*). The deed is, so far, safely accomplished. The slyboots, how she wheedled him! What a helpless ninny is a love-sick man! He is but as a lute in a woman's hands—she plays upon him whatever tune she will. But the Colonel comes. I' faith, he's just in time, for the Yeomen parade here for his execution in two minutes!

Enter FAIRFAX, *without beard and moustache,*
and dressed in Yeoman's uniform

FAIR. My good and kind friend, thou runnest a grave risk for me!
MER. Tut, sir, no risk. [40] I'll warrant none here will recognise you. You make a brave Yeoman, sir! So—this ruff is too high; so—and the sword should hang thus. Here is your halberd, sir; carry it thus. The Yeomen come. Now remember, you are my brave son, Leonard Meryll.
FAIR. If I may not bear mine own name, there is none other I would bear so readily.
MER. Now, sir, put a bold face on it, for they come.

FINALE—ACT I

Enter Yeomen of the Guard

[40] *No risk? I cannot say if the wearing of beards and mustaches was compulsory for the Tower warders in the 16th century, but it was certainly usual and inclines one to wonder how it is that the sight of a clean-shaven young man did not give rise to at least a question.*

CHORUS

Oh, Sergeant Meryll, is it true—
    The welcome news we read in orders?
Thy son, whose deeds of derring-do
Are echoed all the country through,
    Has come to join the Tower Warders?
If so, we come to meet him,
That we may fitly greet him,
And welcome his arrival here
With shout on shout and cheer on cheer.
    Hurrah! Hurrah! Hurrah!

RECITATIVE—SERGEANT MERYLL

Ye Tower Warders, nursed in war's alarms,
    Suckled on gunpowder, and weaned on glory,
Behold my son, whose all-subduing arms
    Have formed the theme of many a song and story!
    Forgive his aged father's pride; nor jeer
    His aged father's sympathetic tear!

(Pretending to weep.)

CHORUS

Leonard Meryll!
Leonard Meryll!
Dauntless he in time of peril!
Man of power,
Knighthood's flower,
Welcome to the grim old Tower,
To the Tower, welcome thou!

RECITATIVE—FAIRFAX

Forbear, my friends, and spare me this ovation,
I have small claim to such consideration;
The tales that of my prowess are narrated
Have been prodigiously exaggerated!

CHORUS

'Tis ever thus!
Wherever valour true is found,
True modesty will there abound.

COUPLETS

1ST YEOMAN. Didst thou not, oh, Leonard Meryll!
    Standard lost in last campaign,
    Rescue it at deadly peril—
    Bear it safely back again?

CHORUS.   Leonard Meryll, at his peril,
    Bore it safely back again!

2ND YEOMAN. Didst thou not, when prisoner taken,
    And debarred from all escape,
    Face, with gallant heart unshaken,
    Death in most appalling shape?

CHORUS.   Leonard Meryll, faced his peril,
    Death in most appalling shape!

FAIR. *(aside)*. Truly I was to be pitied, [41]
    Having but an hour to live,

[41] *Fairfax's aside is an aside to Meryll, who should show concern for fear of his being overheard.*

I reluctantly submitted,
I had no alternative!

(*Aloud.*)   Oh! the tales that are narrated
Of my deeds of derring-do
Have been much exaggerated,
Very much exaggerated,
Scarce a word of them is true!

CHORUS.   They are not exaggerated, etc.

Enter PHŒBE. [42] *She rushes to* FAIRFAX. *Enter* WILFRED

RECITATIVE

PHŒ.   Leonard!
FAIR. (*puzzled*). I beg your pardon? [43]
PHŒ.   Don't you know me?
I'm little Phœbe!

FAIR. (*still puzzled*). Phœbe? Is this Phœbe?
What! little Phœbe? (*Aside.*) Who the deuce may *she* be?
It can't be Phœbe, surely?
WIL.   Yes, 'tis Phœbe——
Your sister Phœbe! Your own little sister!
ALL.   Aye, he speaks the truth;
'Tis Phœbe!
FAIR. (*pretending to recognise her*). Sister Phœbe!
PHŒ.   Oh, my brother!
FAIR.   Why, how you've grown! I did not recognise you!
PHŒ.   So many years! Oh, brother! [44]
FAIR.   Oh, my sister!
WIL.   Aye, hug him, girl! There are three thou mayst hug——
Thy father and thy brother and—myself!
FAIR.   Thyself, forsooth? And who art thou thyself?
WIL.   Good sir, we are betrothed. (FAIRFAX *turns inquiringly to*
      PHŒBE.)
PHŒ.   Or more or less——
But rather less than more!
WIL.   To thy fond care
I do commend thy sister. Be to her
An ever-watchful guardian—eagle-eyed!
And when she feels (as sometimes she does feel)
Disposed to indiscriminate caress,
Be thou at hand to take those favours from her!
ALL.   Be thou at hand to take those favours from her!
PHŒ.   Yes, yes.
Be thou at hand to take those favours from me!

TRIO—WILFRED, FAIRFAX, AND PHŒBE

WIL.   To thy fraternal care
Thy sister I commend;
From every lurking snare
Thy lovely charge defend:
And to achieve this end,
Oh! grant, I pray, this boon—
She shall not quit thy sight:
From morn to afternoon—
From afternoon to night
From seven o'clock to two—
From two to eventide—

[42] *Phoebe's sudden appearance on the scene should come as a shock to Meryll, and cause him further concern. Phoebe knows who "Leonard Meryll" really is, but Fairfax does not know that she is, ostensibly, his sister, and might, therefore, let the cat out of the bag—and the fat would really be in the fire. (Who did Fairfax think the girl with Meryll was when he met them as he was being removed from the Beauchamp Tower? I imagine we must assume he was too occupied with his then impending doom to give the question much thought.)*

[43] *Fairfax, though puzzled, realizes he ought to know who the girl is. He directs the aside to Meryll and so finds out. Meryll interjects a stage-whispered aside in reply: "Your sister!" This aside is not to be found in any libretto but is always spoken. My reading of this is that there should be no reply from Meryll. Fairfax's aside should be to himself and it should be the lumbering Wilfred who supplies the answer when Fairfax, covering up well, sings: "It can't be Phoebe, surely?"*

    Once recognized, Phoebe takes full advantage of her opportunities, nor is Fairfax slow to reciprocate, both of them embracing and hugging, to the consternation of Meryll and the lugubrious approval of Shadbolt.

[44] *Sullivan's help in building the humor of this point is delightful, writing, as he does, several repetitions of "Oh, my brother!" and "Oh, my sister!" with enthusiastic embraces between each.*

From dim twilight to 'leven at night
She shall not quit thy side!

ALL. From morn to afternoon, etc.

PHŒ. So amiable I've grown,
    So innocent as well,
That if I'm left alone
    The consequences fell
    No mortal can foretell.
So grant, I pray, this boon—
    I shall not quit thy sight:
From morn to afternoon—
    From afternoon to night—
From seven o'clock to two—
    From two to eventide—
From dim twilight to 'leven at night
    I shall not quit thy side.

ALL. From morn to afternoon, etc.

FAIR. With brotherly readiness, [45]
    For my fair sister's sake,
At once I answer "Yes"—
    That task I undertake—
    My word I never break.
I freely grant that boon,
    And I'll repeat my plight.
From morn to afternoon—   (*kiss*)
    From afternoon to night—   (*kiss*)
From seven o'clock to two—   (*kiss*)
    From two to evening meal—   (*kiss*)
From dim twilight to 'leven at night
    That compact I will seal.   (*kiss*)

ALL. From morn to afternoon, etc.

[*The bell of St. Peter's* [46] *begins to toll. The Crowd enters; the block is brought onto the stage, and the Headsman takes his place.* [47] *The Yeomen of the Guard form up. The* LIEUTENANT *enters and takes his place, and tells off* FAIRFAX *and two others to bring the prisoner to execution.* WILFRED, FAIRFAX, *and two Yeomen exeunt to Tower.*

CHORUS (*to tolling accompaniment*)

The prisoner comes to meet his doom;
The block, the headsman, and the tomb.
The funeral bell begins to toll—
May Heaven have mercy on nis soul!

SOLO—ELSIE, *with* CHORUS

Oh, Mercy, thou whose smile has shone
    So many a captive heart upon;
Of all immured within these walls,
        To-day the very worthiest falls!

Enter FAIRFAX *and two other Yeomen from Tower in great excitement*

FAIR. My lord! I know not how to tell
    The news I bear!
I and my comrades sought the prisoner's cell—
    He is not there!

[45] *Fairfax has begun to enjoy himself, and in doing so reveals (at least, to my mind) that he is not the gallant gentleman he appeared to be when we first met him. He is very much the Don Juan and leading Phoebe on at this point, to the visible distress of Meryll. And he also would appear to have forgotten that he is now a married man!*

[46] *St. Peter's. The Tower's own church, situated within the walls.*

[47] *This is one of the biggest dramatic moments of the entire series. The block is brought onto the stage and placed in position by two assistants to the Headsman. They are clad in black from head to foot and wear masks which completely conceal their faces. They are followed by the Headsman himself, who is similarly clad, and bearing an ax. A real ax. He takes his position behind the block and, at the appropriate time, just before the chorus begins to sing "The Prisoner Comes to Meet His Doom," drops it, one point of the blade downward, into the wooden block with a very ominous thud. This has never failed to bring an audible gasp from the audience.*

The best-laid plans of mice and men, however, "gang aft agley"—and, I might add, of Gilbertian Headsmen! The man normally playing the part of the Headsman was taken ill at the last moment on one occasion and the Company's property man was hurriedly pressed into the job. Everything seemed to be going splendidly. The assistants—a couple of "experts" obtained locally and rehearsed just before the curtain went up— placed the block in its precise position. The newly recruited Headsman, without any rehearsal, made a slow, stately and dignified entrance and took his position behind the block, raising and dropping the ax right on cue. At this point, I suppose, the mask must have dropped in the way of his vision, for the ax missed the block by an inch or two—and his toes by a mere fraction of an inch. He went on for the role many times afterward and never again missed the block, but he always made sure that his feet were wide apart.

ALL.
          He is not there!
     They sought the prisoner's cell—he is not there!

          TRIO—FAIRFAX *and two* Yeomen

          As escort for the prisoner
               We sought his cell, in duty bound;
          The double gratings open were,
               No prisoner at all we found!

          We hunted high, we hunted low,
               We hunted here, we hunted there—
          The man we sought with anxious care
               Had vanished into empty air!

                              [*Exit* LIEUTENANT.

GIRLS.
          Now, by my troth, the news is fair,
          The man has vanished into air!

ALL.
          As escort for the prisoner
               They sought his cell in duty bound, etc.

          Enter WILFRED, *followed by* LIEUTENANT

LIEUT.
          Astounding news! The prisoner fled!
     (*To* WILFRED.) Thy life shall forfeit be instead! [48]

                         (WILFRED *is arrested.*)

WIL.
          My lord, I did not set him free,
          I hate the man—my rival he!

                         (WILFRED *is taken away.*)

MER.
          The prisoner gone—I'm all agape!
          Who could have helped him to escape?

PHŒ.
          Indeed I can't imagine who!
          I've no idea at all—have you?

          Enter JACK POINT

DAME.
          Of his escape no traces lurk,
          Enchantment must have been at work!

ELSIE (*aside to* POINT).
          What have I done! Oh, woe is me!
          I am his wife, and he is free!

POINT.
          Oh, woe is *you*? Your anguish sink!
          Oh, woe is *me*, I rather think!
          Oh, woe is *me*, I rather think!
          Yes, woe is *me*, I rather think!
               Whate'er betide
               You are his bride,
               And I am left
               Alone—bereft!
          Yes, woe is *me*, I rather think!
          Yes, woe is *me*, I rather think!

          ENSEMBLE—LIEUTENANT *and* CHORUS

          All frenzied with despair I rave,
               The grave is cheated of its due.
          Who is the misbegotten knave
               Who hath contrived this deed to do?
          Let search be made throughout the land,

[48] *Gilbert's directions are very explicit:* (WILFRED *is arrested*). *The Lieutenant is also very definite: "Thy life shall forfeit be . . ." In spite of his protestations, Wilfred is taken away by the two assistant headsmen. But—just wait and see!*

[49] A thousand marks. *Now obsolete in England. The mark was in use in the 15th and 16th centuries. A money of account representing a mark weight of silver—13s 4d. The Lieutenant was offering a not inconsiderable sum of money, especially for those days.*

Or $\left\{\begin{matrix} \text{his} \\ \text{my} \end{matrix}\right\}$ vindictive anger dread—

A thousand marks [49] to him $\left\{\begin{matrix} \text{he'll} \\ \text{I'll} \end{matrix}\right\}$ hand

Who brings him here, alive or dead.

[*At the end,* ELSIE *faints in* FAIRFAX'S *arms; all the Yeomen and populace rush off the stage in different directions, to hunt for the fugitive, leaving only the Headsman on the stage, and* ELSIE *insensible in* FAIRFAX'S *arms.*

END OF ACT I

ACT II

SCENE.—*The same.—Moonlight*

Two days have elapsed

Women and Yeomen of the Guard discovered

CHORUS

Night has spread her pall once more,
    And the prisoner still is free:
Open is his dungeon door,
    Useless now his dungeon key!
He has shaken off his yoke—
    How, no mortal man can tell!
Shame on loutish jailer-folk—
    Shame on sleepy sentinel!

Enter DAME CARRUTHERS *and* KATE

SOLO—DAME CARRUTHERS

Warders are ye?
    Whom do ye ward?
Bolt, bar, and key,
    Shackle and cord,
Fetter and chain,
    Dungeon of stone,
All are in vain—
    Prisoner's flown!
Spite of ye all, he is free—he is free!
Whom do ye ward? Pretty warders are ye!

CHORUS OF WOMEN. Pretty warders are ye, etc.

CHORUS

YEOMEN.   Up and down, and in and out,
Here and there, and round about;
Every chamber, every house,
Every chink that holds a mouse,
Every crevice in the keep,
Where a beetle black could creep,
Every outlet, every drain,
Have we searched, but all in vain.

WOMEN.   Warders are ye?
    Whom do ye ward? etc.

[*Exeunt all.*

Enter JACK POINT, *in low spirits, reading from a huge volume*

POINT (*reads*). "The Merrie Jestes of Hugh Ambrose. [50] No. 7863. The Poor Wit and the Rich Councillor. A certayne poor wit, being anhungered, did meet a well-fed councillor. 'Marry, fool,' quoth the councillor, 'whither away?' 'In truth,' said the poor wag, 'in that I have eaten naught these two dayes, I do wither away, and that right rapidly!' The councillor laughed hugely, and gave him a sausage." Humph! the councillor was easier to please than my new master the Lieutenant. I would like to take post under that councillor. Ah! 'tis but melancholy mumming when poor heart-broken, jilted Jack Point must needs turn to Hugh Ambrose for original light humour!

Enter WILFRED, *also in low spirits* [51]

WIL. (*sighing*). Ah, Master Point!

POINT (*changing his manner*). [52] Ha! friend jailer! Jailer that wast—jailer that never shalt be more! Jailer that jailed not, or that jailed, if jail he did, so unjailerly that 'twas but jerry-jailing, or jailing in joke—though no joke to him who, by unjailerlike jailing, did so jeopardise his jailership. Come, take heart, smile, laugh, wink, twinkle, thou tormentor that tormentest none—thou racker that rackest not—thou pincher out of place—come, take heart, and be merry, as I am!—(*aside, dolefully*)—as I am!

WIL. Aye, it's well for thee to laugh. Thou hast a good post, and hast cause to be merry.

POINT (*bitterly*). Cause? Have we not all cause? Is not the world a big butt of humour, into which all who will may drive a gimlet? See, I am a salaried wit; and is there aught in nature more ridiculous? A poor, dull, heart-broken man, who must needs be merry, or he will be whipped; who must rejoice, lest he starve; who must jest you, jibe you, quip you, crank you, wrack you, riddle you, from hour to hour, from day to day, from year to year, lest he dwindle, perish, starve, pine, and die! Why, when there's naught else to laugh at, I laugh at myself till I ache for it! [53]

WIL. Yet I have often thought that a jester's calling would suit me to a hair.

POINT. Thee? Would suit *thee*, thou death's head and cross-bones?

WIL. Aye, I have a pretty wit—a light, airy, joysome wit, spiced with anecdotes of prison cells and the torture chamber. Oh, a very delicate wit! I have tried it on many a prisoner, and there have been some who smiled. [54] Now it is not easy to make a prisoner smile. And it should not be difficult to be a good jester, seeing that thou art one.

POINT. Difficult? Nothing easier. Nothing easier. Attend, and I will prove it to thee!

SONG—POINT [55]

Oh! a private buffoon is a light-hearted loon, [56]
    If you listen to popular rumour;
From the morn to the night he's so joyous and bright,
    And he bubbles with wit and good humour!
He's so quaint and so terse, both in prose and in verse,
    Yet though people forgive his transgression,
There are one or two rules that all family fools
    Must observe, if they love their profession.
        There are one or two rules,
        Half a dozen, may be,
        That all family fools,
        Of whatever degree,
    Must observe, if they love their profession.

[50] Hugh Ambrose. *I rather imagine that Joe Miller and his Joke Book would be a modern counterpart.*

[51] *How is it that Wilfred, arrested two days previously and threatened with execution (see Note 48), is now roaming the Tower grounds quite free? As Head Jailer, would he have been acquitted quite so soon? Of complicity, possibly, but of negligence of his duty, I doubt. But he is free and, quite obviously, has lost his job.*

[52] *As Point speaks, he puts the volume of Hugh Ambrose's "merrie jestes" down on the steps at the back of the stage, or at whatever position he is seated.*

[53] *. . . till I ache for it! A very important line that must not be thrown away. It is, in effect, a prophecy. (See Note 92 on the death of Jack Point.)*

[54] *Gilbert's joke here is the enlargement of the fact that most comedy is based on the misfortunes of others. The man who slips on a banana skin and falls heavily, with the woman with a small boy saying: "Oh please, do that again; my little son didn't see it."*

How right Jack Point is with his reply! It is the easiest thing in the world to be a good jester —always providing!

[55] *Words and music on page 612.*

[56] *Gilbert gives some of the soundest advice in this song. All would-be jesters should read, mark, learn and inwardly digest it—if they wish to succeed!*

It is usual to sing only the first three verses, keeping the last two for the encore. If a further encore is required, then it is the last verse only that is repeated.

"I have known that old joke from my cradle!"

[57] Half-a-crown. A monetary piece, the equivalent of two shillings and sixpence (2s 6d). (See Note 21.)

[58] Possibly a bitter allusion to Point's similar predicament.

If you wish to succeed as a jester, you'll need
To consider each person's auricular:
What is all right for B would quite scandalise C
(For C is so very particular);
And D may be dull, and E's very thick skull
Is as empty of brains as a ladle;
While F is F sharp, and will cry with a carp
That he's known your best joke from his cradle!
When your humour they flout,
You can't let yourself go;
And it *does* put you out
When a person says, "Oh,
I have known that old joke from my cradle!"

If your master is surly, from getting up early
(And tempers are short in the morning),
An inopportune joke is enough to provoke
Him to give you, at once, a month's warning.
Then if you refrain, he is at you again,
For he likes to get value for money;
He'll ask then and there, with an insolent stare,
"If you know that you're paid to be funny?"
It adds to the tasks
Of a merryman's place,
When your principal asks,
With a scowl on his face,
If you know that you're paid to be funny?

Comes a Bishop, maybe, or a solemn D.D.—
Oh, beware of his anger provoking!
Better not pull his hair—don't stick pins in his chair;
He don't understand practical joking.
If the jests that you crack have an orthodox smack,
You may get a bland smile from these sages;
But should they, by chance, be imported from France,
Half a crown [57] is stopped out of your wages!
It's a general rule,
Though your zeal it may quench,
If the family fool
Tells a joke that's too French,
Half-a-crown is stopped out of his wages!

Though your head it may rack with a bilious attack,
And your senses with toothache you're losing,
Don't be mopy and flat—they don't fine you for that,
If you're properly quaint and amusing!
Though your wife ran away with a soldier that day, [58]
And took with her your trifle of money;
Bless your heart, they don't mind—they're exceedingly kind—
They don't blame you—as long as you're funny!
It's a comfort to feel,
If your partner should flit,
Though *you* suffer a deal,
They don't mind it a bit—
They don't blame you—so long as you're funny!

POINT. And so thou wouldst be a jester, eh?
WIL. Aye!
POINT. Now, listen! My sweetheart, Elsie Maynard, was secretly wed to this Fairfax half an hour ere he escaped.

WIL. She did well.

POINT. She did nothing of the kind, so hold thy peace and perpend. Now, while he liveth she is dead to me and I to her, and so, my jibes and jokes notwithstanding, I am the saddest and the sorriest dog in England!

WIL. Thou art a very dull dog indeed.

POINT. Now, if thou wilt swear that thou didst shoot this Fairfax while he was trying to swim across the river [59]—it needs but the discharge of an arquebus on a dark night—and that he sank and was seen no more, I'll make thee the very Archbishop of jesters, and that in two days' time! Now, what sayest thou?

WIL. I am to lie?

POINT. Heartily. But thy lie must be a lie of circumstance, which I will support with the testimony of eyes, ears, and tongue.

WIL. And thou wilt qualify me as a jester?

POINT. As a jester among jesters. I will teach thee all my original songs, my self-constructed riddles, my own ingenious paradoxes; nay, more, I will reveal to thee the source whence I get them. Now, what sayest thou? [60]

WIL. Why, if it be but a lie thou wantest of me, I hold it cheap enough, and I say yes, it is a bargain!

DUET—POINT *and* WILFRED

BOTH.
    Hereupon we're both agreed,
        All that we two
        Do agree to
    We'll secure by solemn deed,
        To prevent all
        Error mental.

POINT.
    You on Elsie are to call
        With a story
        Grim and gory;

WIL.
    How this Fairfax died, and all
        I declare to
        You're to swear to.

BOTH.
        Tell a tale of cock and bull,
        Of convincing detail full
          Tale tremendous
          Heaven defend us!
        What a tale of cock and bull! [61]

BOTH.
    In return for $\left\{\begin{array}{l}\text{your}\\\text{my}\end{array}\right\}$ own part
    You are$\left.\begin{array}{l}\\\end{array}\right\}$
    I am$\left.\begin{array}{l}\\\end{array}\right\}$ making
    Undertaking
    To instruct $\left\{\begin{array}{l}\text{me}\\\text{you}\end{array}\right\}$ in the art
    (Art amazing,
    Wonder raising)

POINT.
    Of a jester, jesting free. [62]
        Proud position—
        High ambition!

WIL.
    And a lively one I'll be,
        Wag-a-wagging,
        Never flagging!

[59] The river. *The Thames—pronounced Temms.*

[60] *Point has picked up the book of "merrie jestes" which he shows to Wilfred, who makes a grab at it. But Jack withholds it from Wilfred as he inquires, "What sayest thou?" When Wilfred agrees to the terms, Point puts the book down again and they shake hands, and Jack breaks into a joyous dance step which Wilfred awkwardly tries to copy.*

[61] *At the end of each phrase, Point performs a pirouette, closely watched by Wilfred who endeavors to do the same thing.*

[62] *Point takes a position here similar to one in preparation for rond de jamb. Wilfred, who also attempts to copy this, loses his balance and staggers across the stage.*

[63] *During the closing music, Point and Wilfred link arms, dance over to the book, pick it up between them, and dance off, book held in front as if reading it. For the encore, Point re-enters, carrying the book, and places it in its old position. Wilfred follows and watches with a rather crafty look on his face. The last verse is sung in the same way as before, and again they dance over to the book, pick it up, and begin to dance off. Wilfred, however, suddenly stops and distracts Jack's attention by pointing to the other side of the stage, as if someone were approaching. When Jack turns to see who it is, Wilfred seizes the book from him and rushes off in great glee, hotly chased by Point who realizes that he has been tricked.*

[64] *It becomes increasingly obvious, to me anyway, that Fairfax is not the great and gallant gentleman.*

BOTH.   Tell a tale of cock and bull, etc.

[*Exeunt together.* [63]

Enter FAIRFAX

FAIR. Two days gone, and no news of poor Fairfax. The dolts! They seek him everywhere save within a dozen yards of his dungeon. So I am free! Free, but for the cursed haste [64] with which I hurried headlong into the bonds of matrimony with—Heaven knows whom! As far as I remember, she should have been young; but even had not her face been concealed by her kerchief, I doubt whether, in my then plight, I should have taken much note of her. Free? Bah! The Tower bonds were but a thread of silk compared with these conjugal fetters which I, fool that I was, placed upon mine own hands. From the one I broke readily enough —how to break the other!

BALLAD—FAIRFAX

Free from his fetters grim—
    Free to depart;
Free both in life and limb—
    In all but heart!
Bound to an unknown bride
    For good and ill;
Ah, is not one so tied
    A prisoner still?

Free, yet in fetters held
    Till his last hour,
Gyves that no smith can weld,
    No rust devour!
Although a monarch's hand
    Had set him free,
Of all the captive band
    The saddest he!

Enter MERYLL

FAIR. Well, Sergeant Meryll, and how fares thy pretty charge, Elsie Maynard?
MER. Well enough, sir. She is quite strong again, and leaves us to-night.
FAIR. Thanks to Dame Carruthers' kind nursing, eh?
MER. Aye, deuce take the old witch! Ah, 'twas but a sorry trick you played me, sir, to bring the fainting girl to me. It gave the old lady an excuse for taking up her quarters in my house, and for the last two years I've shunned her like the plague. Another day of it and she would have married me! (*Enter* DAME CARRUTHERS *and* KATE.) Good Lord, here she is again! I'll e'en go. (*Going.*)
DAME. Nay, Sergeant Meryll, don't go. I have something of grave import to say to thee.
MER. (*aside*). It's coming.
FAIR. (*laughing*). I' faith, I think I'm not wanted here. (*Going.*)
DAME. Nay, Master Leonard, I've naught to say to thy father that his son may not hear.
FAIR. (*aside*). True, I'm one of the family; I had forgotten!
DAME. 'Tis about this Elsie Maynard. A pretty girl, Master Leonard.
FAIR. Aye, fair as a peach blossom—what then? [65]
DAME. She hath a liking for thee, or I mistake not.
FAIR. With all my heart. She's as dainty a little maid as you'll find in a midsummer day's march.

[65] *There is no question in my mind that Fairfax took Elsie to Sergeant Meryll's house so that he might have the opportunity of seeing more of her. After all, it was "his father's house," and he is "one of the family." I rather imagine that both his soliloquy and song ("Two days gone" and "Free from his fetters grim") were inspired by thoughts of Elsie.*

DAME. Then be warned in time, and give not thy heart to her. Oh, *I* know what it is to give my heart to one who will have none of it!

MER. (*aside*). Aye, *she* knows all about that. (*Aloud.*) And why is my boy to take heed of her? She's a good girl, Dame Carruthers.

DAME. Good enough, for aught I know. But she's no girl. She's a married woman.

MER. A married woman! Tush, old lady—she's promised to Jack Point, the Lieutenant's new jester.

DAME. Tush in thy teeth, old man! As my niece Kate sat by her bed-side to-day, this Elsie slept, and as she slept she moaned and groaned, and turned this way and that way—and, "How shall I marry one I have never seen?" quoth she—then, "An hundred crowns!" quoth she—then, "Is it certain he will die in an hour?" quoth she—then, "I love him not, and yet I am his wife," quoth she! Is it not so, Kate?

KATE. Aye, aunt, 'tis even so.

FAIR. Art thou sure of all this?

KATE. Aye, sir, for I wrote it all down on my tablets.

DAME. Now, mark my words: it was of this Fairfax she spake, and he is her husband, or I'll swallow my kirtle! [66]

MER. (*aside*). Is it true, sir?

FAIR. (*aside to* MERYLL). True? Why, the girl was raving! (*Aloud.*) Why should she marry a man who had but an hour to live?

DAME. Marry? There be those who would marry but for a minute, rather than die old maids. [67]

MER. (*aside*). Aye, I know one of them!

QUARTET—FAIRFAX, SERGEANT MERYLL, DAME CARRUTHERS,
and KATE [68]

Strange adventure! Maiden wedded
    To a groom she's never seen—
        Never, never, never seen!
Groom about to be beheaded,
    In an hour on Tower Green!
        Tower, Tower, Tower Green!
Groom in dreary dungeon lying,
Groom as good as dead, or dying,
For a pretty maiden sighing—
    Pretty maid of seventeen! [69]
        Seven—seven—seventeen!

Strange adventure that we're trolling:
    Modest maid and gallant groom—
        Gallant, gallant, gallant groom!—
While the funeral bell is tolling,
    Tolling, tolling, Bim-a-boom!
        Bim-a, Bim-a, Bim-a-boom!
Modest maiden will not tarry;
Though but sixteen [69a] years she carry,
She must marry, she must marry,
    Though the altar be a tomb—
        Tower—Tower—Tower tomb!

[*Exeunt* DAME CARRUTHERS, MERYLL, *and* KATE.

FAIR. So my mysterious bride is no other than this winsome Elsie! By my hand, 'tis no such ill plunge in Fortune's lucky bag! I might have fared worse with my eyes open! But she comes. Now to test her princi-ples. 'Tis not every husband who has a chance of wooing his own wife! [70]

[66] Kirtle. A woman's gown, skirt or outer petticoat. I rather imagine that Gilbert's allusion is to defi-nition two.
    Dame Carruthers' entire statement should come as a complete surprise to both Meryll and Fairfax—though in Fairfax's case the surprise and the shock are of a quite pleasant nature, even though he does dissemble. "True? Why, the girl was raving."

[67] See Ruddigore, page 522, Note 51. ROSE: "Thou art the only one that's left . . ."

[68] Words and music on page 615.

[69] and [69a] Seventeen? Sixteen? How old was Elsie?

[70] Care should be taken in speaking this line, viz.: " 'Tis not every husband who has a chance of wooing his own wife!" It should not be spoken, as one Fairfax insisted: ". . . of wooing his own wife!" The implication is quite different.

Enter ELSIE

FAIR. Mistress Elsie!

ELSIE. Master Leonard!

FAIR. So thou leavest us to-night?

ELSIE. Yes, Master Leonard. I have been kindly tended, and I almost fear I am loth to go.

FAIR. And this Fairfax. Wast thou glad when he escaped?

ELSIE. Why, truly, Master Leonard, it is a sad thing that a young and gallant gentleman should die in the very fullness of his life.

FAIR. Then when thou didst faint in my arms, it was for joy at his safety?

ELSIE. It may be so. I was highly wrought, Master Leonard, and I am but a girl, and so, when I am highly wrought, I faint.

FAIR. Now, dost thou know, I am consumed with a parlous jealousy?

ELSIE. Thou? And of whom?

FAIR. Why, of this Fairfax, surely!

ELSIE. Of Colonel Fairfax?

FAIR. Aye. Shall I be frank with thee? Elsie—I love thee, ardently, passionately! (ELSIE *alarmed and surprised*.) Elsie, I have loved thee these two days—which is a long time—and I would fain join my life to thine!

ELSIE. Master Leonard! Thou art jesting!

FAIR. Jesting? May I shrivel into raisins if I jest! I love thee with a love that is a fever—with a love that is a frenzy—with a love that eateth up my heart! What sayest thou? Thou wilt not let my heart be eaten up?

ELSIE (*aside*). Oh, mercy! What am I to say?

FAIR. Dost thou love me, or hast thou been insensible these two days?

ELSIE. I love all brave men.

FAIR. Nay, there is love in excess. I thank heaven there are many brave men in England; but if thou lovest them all, I withdraw my thanks.

ELSIE. I love the bravest best. But, sir, I may not listen—I am not free —I—I am a wife!

FAIR. Thou a wife? Whose? His name? His hours are numbered—nay, his grave is dug and his epitaph set up! Come, his name?

ELSIE. Oh, sir! keep my secret—it is the only barrier that Fate could set up between us. My husband is none other than Colonel Fairfax!

FAIR. The greatest villain unhung! The most ill-favoured, ill-mannered, ill-natured, ill-omened, ill-tempered dog in Christendom!

ELSIE. It is very like. He is naught to me—for I never saw him. I was blindfolded, and he was to have died within the hour; and he did not die—and I am wedded to him, and my heart is broken!

FAIR. He was to have died, and he did *not* die? The scoundrel! The perjured, traitorous villain! Thou shouldst have insisted on his dying first, to make sure. 'Tis the only way with these Fairfaxes.

ELSIE. I now wish I had!

FAIR. (*aside*). Bloodthirsty little maiden! (*Aloud*.) A fig for this Fairfax! Be mine—he will never know—he dares not show himself; and if he dare, what art thou to him? Fly with me, Elsie—we will be married to-morrow, and thou shalt be the happiest wife in England!

ELSIE. Master Leonard! I am amazed! Is it thus that brave soldiers speak to poor girls? Oh! for shame, for shame! I am wed—not the less because I love not my husband. I am a wife, sir, and I have a duty, and—oh, sir!—thy words terrify me—they are not honest—they are wicked words, and unworthy thy great and brave heart! Oh, shame upon thee! shame upon thee!

FAIR. Nay, Elsie, I did but jest. I spake but to try thee—— (*Shot heard.*) [71]

Enter MERYLL *hastily*

MER. (*recit.*). Hark! What was that, sir?
FAIR.   Why, an arquebus—
    Fired from the wharf, unless I much mistake.
MER. Strange—and at such an hour! What can it mean?

Enter CHORUS

CHORUS

Now what can that have been—
    A shot so late at night,
    Enough to cause a fright!
What can the portent mean?

Are foemen in the land?
    Is London to be wrecked?
    What are we to expect?
What danger is at hand?
    Let us understand
    What danger is at hand!

LIEUTENANT *enters, also* POINT *and* WILFRED

RECITATIVE

LIEUT. Who fired that shot? At once the truth declare!
WIL.   My lord, 'twas I—to rashly judge forbear!
POINT. My lord, 'twas he—to rashly judge forbear!

DUET *and* CHORUS—WILFRED *and* POINT

WIL.   Like a ghost his vigil keeping—
POINT.   Or a spectre all-appalling—
WIL.   I beheld a figure creeping—
POINT.   I should rather call it crawling—
WIL.   He was creeping—
POINT.   He was crawling—
WIL.   He was creeping, creeping—
POINT.   Crawling!
WIL.   He was creeping—
POINT.   He was crawling—
WIL.   He was creeping, creeping—
POINT.   Crawling!

WIL.   Not a moment's hesitation—
            I myself upon him flung,
    With a hurried exclamation
            To his draperies I hung;
    Then we closed with one another
    In a rough-and-tumble smother;
    Colonel Fairfax and no other
            Was the man to whom I clung!

ALL.   Colonel Fairfax and no other
            Was the man to whom he clung!

WIL.   After mighty tug and tussle—
POINT.   It resembled more a struggle—
WIL.   He, by dint of stronger muscle—
POINT.   Or by some infernal juggle—

[71] A revolver or a rifle loaded with a blank cartridge was generally used here. On one occasion, however, someone blundered and forgot to load the weapon. Result: one faint click! After a moment of deathly silence, Meryll proceeded and the musical director picked up the cue, Meryll singing, "Hark! What was that, sir?"

From then on we devised a standby for the gun, in the shape of a five-foot plank, a screw-eye and a piece of rope. Properly used, this can be a perfect substitute for the sound of a gun shot. It turned out to be a most fortunate standby, for on one occasion a gun license could not be obtained in time.

WIL. From my clutches quickly sliding—

POINT. I should rather call it slipping—

WIL. With a view, no doubt, of hiding—

POINT. Or escaping to the shipping—

WIL. With a gasp, and with a quiver—

POINT. I'd describe it as a shiver—

WIL. Down he dived into the river,
And, alas, I cannot swim.

ALL. It's enough to make one shiver—
With a gasp and with a quiver,
Down he dived into the river;
It was very brave of him!

WIL. Ingenuity is catching;
With the view my king [72] of pleasing,
Arquebus from sentry snatching—

POINT. I should rather call it seizing—

WIL. With an ounce or two of lead
I despatched him through the head!

ALL. With an ounce or two of lead
He despatched him through the head!

WIL. I discharged it without winking,
Little time I lost in thinking,
Like a stone I saw him sinking—

POINT. I should say a lump of lead.

ALL. He discharged it without winking,
Little time he lost in thinking.

WIL. Like a stone I saw him sinking—

POINT. I should say a lump of lead.

WIL. Like a stone, my boy, I said—

POINT. Like a heavy lump of lead.

WIL. Like a stone, my boy, I said—

POINT. Like a heavy lump of lead!

WIL. Anyhow, the man is dead,
Whether stone or lump of lead! [73]

ALL. Anyhow, the man is dead,
Whether stone or lump of lead!
Arquebus from sentry seizing,
With the view his king of pleasing,
Wilfred shot him through the head,
And he's very, very dead.
And it matters very little whether stone or lump of lead;
It is very, very certain that he's very, very dead!

RECITATIVE—LIEUTENANT

The river must be dragged—no time be lost;
The body must be found, at any cost.
To this attend without undue delay;
So set to work with what despatch ye may!

[*Exit.*

ALL. Yes, yes,
We'll set to work with what despatch we may!

---

[72] *There can be no doubt at this point that the action of the play is set in the reign of Henry VIII.*

[73] *Wilfred, in pantomime, begins to enlarge on his statement to the Lieutenant while Point feels in his pouch for a coin, which he produces. He then taps Wilfred on the shoulder and suggests they should settle the matter of how Fairfax sank by the toss of a coin. Wilfred agrees and Point tosses the coin. As the chorus finishes ". . . very, very dead" Wilfred cries "Stone!" Point uncovers the coin and in great triumph cries, "Lead!" Wilfred grabs the coin and examines it, probably with the idea that it is a double-headed trick coin. Point manages to retrieve the coin and return it to his pouch just before Wilfred is picked up and carried off.*

[Four men raise WILFRED, *and carry him off on their shoulders.*

CHORUS

Hail the valiant fellow who
Did this deed of derring-do!
Honours wait on such an one;
By my head, 'twas bravely done!
Now, by my head, 'twas bravely done!

[Exeunt all but ELSIE, POINT, FAIRFAX, *and* PHŒBE. [74]

POINT (*to* ELSIE, *who is weeping*). Nay, sweetheart, be comforted. This Fairfax was but a pestilent fellow, and, as he had to die, he might as well die thus as any other way. 'Twas a good death.

ELSIE. Still, he was my husband, and had he not been, he was nevertheless a living man, and now he is dead; and so, by your leave, my tears may flow unchidden, Master Point.

FAIR. And thou didst see all this?

POINT. Aye, with both eyes at once—this and that. The testimony of one eye is naught—he may lie. But when it is corroborated by the other, it is good evidence that none may gainsay. Here are both present in court, ready to swear to him! [75]

PHŒ. But art thou sure it was Colonel Fairfax? Saw you his face?

POINT. Aye, and a plaguey ill-favoured face too. A very hang-dog face —a felon face—a face to fright the headsman himself, and make him strike awry. Oh, a plaguey, bad face, take my word for 't. (PHŒBE *and* FAIRFAX *laugh.*) How they laugh! 'Tis ever thus with simple folk— an accepted wit has but to say "Pass the mustard," and they roar their ribs out!

FAIR. (*aside*). If ever I come to life again, thou shalt pay for this, Master Point!

POINT. Now, Elsie, thou art free to choose again, so behold me: I am young and well-favoured. I have a pretty wit. I can jest you, jibe you, quip you, crank you, wrack you, riddle you——

FAIR. Tush, man, thou knowest not how to woo. 'Tis not to be done with time-worn jests and thread-bare sophistries; with quips, conundrums, rhymes, and paradoxes. 'Tis an art in itself, and must be studied gravely and conscientiously. [76]

TRIO—ELSIE, PHŒBE, *and* FAIRFAX [77]

FAIR.

A man who would woo a fair maid
Should 'prentice himself to the trade,
        And study all day,
        In methodical way,
How to flatter, cajole, and persuade;
He should 'prentice himself at fourteen,
And practise from morning to e'en;
        And when he's of age,
        If he will, I'll engage,
He may capture the heart of a queen!

ALL.

        It is purely a matter of skill,
        Which all may attain if they will:
            But every Jack,
            He must study the knack
        If he wants to make sure of his Jill!

ELSIE.

If he's made the best use of his time,
His twig he'll so carefully lime
        That every bird

[74] *A most extraordinary lighting change takes place here. Can it be that the sun is so elated that it needs must burst out of a midnight sky? I can think of no other reason, because in spite of the shot occurring "so late at night," the stage is suddenly flooded with light and the shadows of night disappear.*

[75] *Point is lying, we know. He, himself, knows. Phoebe knows. Fairfax knows. It is only Elsie who doesn't know. And the only thing that Point doesn't know is that Phoebe and Fairfax do.*

**Study all day,
In methodical way**

[76] *Jack, by gesture, asks Fairfax to teach him the art of wooing, and with each verse Jack grows happier.*

[77] *Words and music on page 617.*

[78] *Elsie reaches out her hand and lightly touches Point's face. He takes her hand in his and reverently kisses the finger tips.*

[79] *Phoebe—the minx—takes Point by one of the ears of his jester's cap and draws him to one side. She then proceeds to egg him on, only to deliver a resounding slap over his ear (his real ear) when she reaches the appropriate line. Business is varied in the encores (there are usually two). In the first one, Point, now aware of her intention, eggs her on, practically offering his face to be slapped, but at the last moment he substitutes his folly-stick. In the second encore, he tries the same trick, but Phoebe fools him by slapping the other side of his face.*

[80] *Point listens to all that Fairfax has to say with his back turned to Fairfax and Elsie. Fairfax begins at last to reveal himself in his true colors, indulging in the most caddish piece of chicanery. Every word he speaks can be taken to mean that it is Point to whom he is alluding.*

[81] *Phoebe also begins to realize that perhaps Fairfax is not all that he appears to be.*

[82] *Fairfax, that great, gallant, most parfit knyght, plays the dirtiest of tricks on Point, and doesn't even pay Phoebe the courtesy of acknowledging her presence. Elsie seems to have some of the tar rubbed off onto her.*

Will come down at his word,
Whatever its plumage or clime.
He must learn that the thrill of a touch [78]
May mean little, or nothing, or much:
 It's an instrument rare,
 To be handled with care,
And ought to be treated as such.

ALL.   It is purely a matter of skill, etc.

PHŒ.   Then a glance may be timid or free, [79]
It will vary in mighty degree,
 From an impudent stare
 To a look of despair
That no maid without pity can see!
And a glance of despair is no guide—
It may have its ridiculous side;
 It may draw you a tear
 Or a box on the ear;
You can never be sure till you've tried!

ALL.   It is purely a matter of skill, etc.

FAIR. (*aside to* POINT). [80] Now, listen to me—'tis done thus—(*aloud*)—Mistress Elsie, there is one here who, as thou knowest, loves thee right well!

POINT (*aside*). That he does—right well!

FAIR. He is but a man of poor estate, but he hath a loving, honest heart. He will be a true and trusty husband to thee, and if thou wilt be his wife, thou shalt lie curled up in his heart, like a little squirrel in its nest!

POINT (*aside*). 'Tis a pretty figure. A maggot in a nut lies closer, but a squirrel will do.

FAIR. He knoweth that thou wast a wife—an unloved and unloving wife, and his poor heart was near to breaking. But now that thine unloving husband is dead, and thou art free, he would fain pray that thou wouldst hearken unto him, and give him hope that thou wouldst one day be his!

PHŒ. (*alarmed*). [81] He presses her hands—and he whispers in her ear! Ods bodikins, what does it mean?

FAIR. Now, sweetheart, tell me—wilt thou be this poor good fellow's wife?

ELSIE. If the good, brave man—*is* he a brave man?

FAIR. So men say.

POINT (*aside*). That's not true, but let it pass.

ELSIE. If the brave man will be content with a poor, penniless, untaught maid——

POINT (*aside*). Widow—but let *that* pass.

ELSIE. I will be his true and loving wife, and that with my heart of hearts!

FAIR. My own dear love! (*Embracing her.*)

PHŒ. (*in great agitation*). Why, what's all this? Brother—brother—it is not seemly!

POINT (*also alarmed, aside*). Oh, I can't let *that* pass! (*Aloud.*) Hold, enough, Master Leonard! An advocate should have his fee, but methinks thou art over-paying thyself!

FAIR. Nay, that is for Elsie to say. I promised thee I would show thee how to woo, and herein lies the proof of the virtue of my teaching. [82] Go thou, and apply it elsewhere! (PHŒBE *bursts into tears.*)

QUARTET—ELSIE, PHŒBE, FAIRFAX, *and* POINT [83]

ELSIE *and* FAIR.
    When a wooer
      Goes a-wooing,
    Naught is truer
      Than his joy.
    Maiden hushing
      All his suing—
    Boldly blushing—
      Bravely coy!

ALL.
    Oh, the happy days of doing!
    Oh, the sighing and the suing!
    When a wooer goes a-wooing,
      Oh, the sweets that never cloy!

PHŒ. (*weeping*)
    When a brother
      Leaves his sister
    For another,
      Sister weeps.
    Tears that trickle,
      Tears that blister—
    'Tis but mickle
      Sister reaps!

ALL.
    Oh, the doing and undoing,
    Oh, the sighing and the suing,
    When a brother goes a-wooing,
    And a sobbing sister weeps!

POINT.
    When a jester
      Is outwitted,
    Feelings fester,
      Heart is lead!
    Food for fishes
      Only fitted,
    Jester wishes
      He was dead!

ALL.
    Oh, the doing and undoing,
    Oh, the sighing and the suing,
    When a jester goes a-wooing,
    And he wishes he was dead!

[*Exeunt all but* PHŒBE, *who remains weeping*. [84]

PHŒ. And I helped that man to escape, and I've kept his secret, and pretended that I was his dearly loving sister, and done everything I could think of to make folk believe I *was* his loving sister, and this is his gratitude! Before I pretend to be sister to anybody again, I'll turn nun, and be sister to everybody—one as much as another!

Enter WILFRED

WIL. In tears, eh? What a plague art thou grizzling for now?

PHŒ. Why am I grizzling? Thou hast often wept for jealousy—well, 'tis for jealousy I weep now. Aye, yellow, bilious, jaundiced jealousy. So make the most of that, Master Wilfred.

WIL. But I have never given thee cause for jealousy. The Lieutenant's cook-maid and I are but the merest gossips!

PHŒ. Jealous of thee! Bah! I'm jealous of no craven cock-on-a-hill, who crows about what he'd do an he dared! I am jealous of another and a better man than thou—set that down, Master Wilfred. And he

[83] Words and music on page 622.

[84] *Fairfax and Elsie go off together. Point follows, heartbroken and pleading. Just before he disappears from sight, Fairfax administers the coup de grâce, stopping him with an imperious gesture which says, It's no use. Elsie doesn't even throw Point a glance. This is a very touching moment. As the three go off, Jack still pleading, Phoebe is left, watching and weeping. At one time there would be the beginnings of applause that could grow and break the mood. It is possible, however, for Phoebe to hold the audience absolutely quiet by a little trick of stage technique. She can, by a gesture, quite deliberately maintain complete quiet. The impact of her next line becomes much the greater, and it also helps to introduce the comedy of her speech far more subtly.*

[85] *Margaret Philo, the Phoebe of the Small Company, on one occasion had allowed her thoughts to drift, jumped up from the stump on which she had seated herself, and delivered the line: "Whom thou hast just shot through the bottom, and who lies at the head of the river!"*

[86] *Cockatrice. A serpent in fable, hatched from a cock's egg, supposedly able to kill with a glance. Figuratively applied to persons, male and female, in the 16th century. By the time of the 18th century, it also meant whore.*

is to marry Elsie Maynard, the little pale fool—set that down, Master Wilfred—and my heart is wellnigh broken! There, thou hast it all! Make the most of it!

WIL. The man thou lovest is to marry Elsie Maynard? Why, that is no other than thy brother, Leonard Meryll!

PHŒ. (*aside*). Oh, mercy! what have I said?

WIL. Why, what manner of brother is this, thou lying little jade? Speak! Who is this man whom thou hast called brother, and fondled, and coddled, and kissed!—with my connivance, too! Oh Lord! with my connivance! Ha! should it be this Fairfax! (PHŒBE *starts*.) It is! It is this accursed Fairfax! It's Fairfax! Fairfax, who——

PHŒ. Whom thou hast just shot through the head, and who lies at the bottom of the river! [85]

WIL. A—I—I may have been mistaken. We are but fallible mortals, the best of us. But I'll make sure—I'll make sure. (*Going.*)

PHŒ. Stay—one word. I think it cannot be Fairfax—mind, I say I *think*—because thou hast just slain Fairfax. But whether he be Fairfax or no Fairfax, he is to marry Elsie—and—and—as thou hast shot him through the head, and he is dead, be content with that, and I will be thy wife!

WIL. Is that sure?

PHŒ. Aye, sure enough, for there's no help for it! Thou art a very brute—but even brutes must marry, I suppose.

WIL. My beloved! (*Embraces her.*)

PHŒ. (*aside*). Ugh!

Enter LEONARD, *hastily*

LEON. Phœbe, rejoice, for I bring glad tidings. Colonel Fairfax's reprieve was signed two days since, but it was foully and maliciously kept back by Secretary Poltwhistle, who designed that it should arrive after the Colonel's death. It hath just come to hand, and it is now in the Lieutenant's possession!

PHŒ. Then the Colonel is free? Oh, kiss me, kiss me, my dear! Kiss me, again, and again!

WIL. (*dancing with fury*). Ods bobs, death o' my life! Art thou mad? Am I mad? Are we *all* mad?

PHŒ. Oh, my dear—my dear, I'm wellnigh crazed with joy. (*Kissing* LEONARD.)

WIL. Come away from him, thou hussy—thou jade—thou kissing, clinging cockatrice! [86] And as for thee, sir, devil take thee, I'll rip thee like a herring for this! I'll skin thee for it! I'll cleave thee to the chine! I'll—oh! Phœbe! Phœbe! Who is this man?

PHŒ. Peace, fool. He is my brother!

WIL. Another brother! Are there any more of them? Produce them all at once, and let me know the worst!

PHŒ. This is the real Leonard, dolt; the other was but his substitute. The *real* Leonard, I say—my father's own son.

WIL. How do I know this? Has he "brother" writ large on his brow? I mistrust thy brothers! Thou art but a false jade!

[*Exit* LEONARD

PHŒ. Now, Wilfred, be just. Truly I did deceive thee before—but it was to save a precious life—and to save it, not for me, but for another. They are to be wed this very day. Is not this enough for thee? Come— I am thy Phœbe—thy very own—and we will be wed in a year—or two— or three, at the most. Is not that enough for thee?

Enter MERYLL, *excitedly, followed by* DAME CARRUTHERS
(*who listens, unobserved*)

MER. Phœbe, hast thou heard the brave news?

PHŒ. (*still in* WILFRED'S *arms*). Aye, father.

MER. I'm nigh mad with joy! (*Seeing* WILFRED.) Why, what's all this?

PHŒ. Oh, father, he discovered our secret through my folly, and the price of his silence is——

WIL. Phœbe's heart.

PHŒ. Oh dear, no—Phœbe's hand.

WIL. It's the same thing!

PHŒ. *Is* it? [87]

[*Exeunt* WILFRED *and* PHŒBE.

MER. (*looking after them*). 'Tis pity, but the Colonel had to be saved at any cost, and as thy folly revealed our secret, thy folly must e'en suffer for it! (DAME CARRUTHERS *comes down.*) Dame Carruthers!

DAME. So this is a plot to shield this arch-fiend, and I have detected it. A word from me, and three heads besides his would roll from their shoulders!

MER. Nay, Colonel Fairfax is reprieved. (*Aside.*) Yet, if my complicity in his escape were known! Plague on the old meddler! There's nothing for it—(*aloud*)—Hush, pretty one! Such bloodthirsty words ill become those cherry lips! (*Aside.*) Ugh!

DAME (*bashfully*). Sergeant Meryll!

MER. Why, look ye, chuck—for many a month I've—I've thought to myself—"There's snug love saving up in that middle-aged bosom for some one, and why not for thee—that's me—so take heart and tell her—that's thee—that thou—that's me—lovest her—thee—and—and—well, I'm a miserable old man, and I've done it—and that's me!" But not a word about Fairfax! The price of thy silence is——

DAME. Meryll's heart?

MER. No, Meryll's *hand*.

DAME. It's the same thing!

MER. *Is* it! [88]

DUET—DAME CARRUTHERS *and* SERGEANT MERYLL [89]

DAME.

Rapture, rapture
    When love's votary,
Flushed with capture,
    Seeks the notary,
        Joy and jollity
        Then is polity;
        Reigns frivolity!
Rapture, rapture!

MER.

Doleful, doleful!
    When humanity
With its soul full
    Of satanity,
        Courting privity,
        Down declivity
        Seeks captivity!
Doleful, doleful!

DAME.

Joyful, joyful!
    When virginity
Seeks, all coyful,

[87] *As Phoebe says this, she boxes Wilfred's ear.*

[88] *Meryll takes a leaf out of his daughter's book, but one must assume that, in Meryll's case, it is more pretense than reality.*

[89] *The D'Oyly Carte Company has cut this duet for many years, with Meryll and Carruthers making their exit on the ear-boxing.*

Man's affinity;
　　Fate all flowery,
　　Bright and bowery,
　　Is her dowery!
Joyful, joyful!

MER.　　　Ghastly, ghastly!
　　　When man, sorrowful,
Firstly, lastly,
　　Of to-morrow full,
　　　After tarrying,
　　　Yields to harrying—
　　　Goes a-marrying.
Ghastly, ghastly!

BOTH.　　　Rapture, etc.

[*Exeunt* DAME *and* MERYLL.

FINALE

Enter Yeomen and Women

CHORUS OF WOMEN

(ELEGIACS)

Comes the pretty young bride, a-blushing, timidly shrinking—
Set all thy fears aside—cheerily, pretty young bride!
Brave is the youth to whom thy lot thou art willingly linking!
Flower of valour is he—loving as loving can be!
Brightly thy summer is shining,
Fair as the dawn of the day;
　　Take him, be true to him—
　　Tender his due to him—
Honour him, love and obey!

Enter DAME, PHŒBE, *and* ELSIE *as Bride*

TRIO—PHŒBE, ELSIE, *and* DAME CARRUTHERS

'Tis said that joy in full perfection
　　Comes only once to womankind—
That, other times, on close inspection,
　　Some lurking bitter we shall find.
If this be so, and men say truly,
My day of joy has broken duly.

With happiness $\begin{Bmatrix} \text{my} \\ \text{her} \end{Bmatrix}$ soul is cloyed—

This is $\begin{Bmatrix} \text{my} \\ \text{her} \end{Bmatrix}$ joy-day unalloyed!

ALL.　　Yes, yes, with happiness her soul is cloyed!
This is her joy-day unalloyed!

Flourish. Enter LIEUTENANT

[90] *The Lieutenant must have been put up to this by Fairfax.*

LIEUT.　　Hold, pretty one! [90] I bring to thee
　　News—good or ill, it is for thee to say.
Thy husband lives—and he is free,
　　And comes to claim his bride this very day!

ELSIE.　　No! no! recall those words—it cannot be!

ENSEMBLE

KATE *and* CHORUS
Oh, day of terror! Day of tears!
Who is the man who, in his pride,
Claims thee as his bride?

DAME CARRUTHERS *and* PHŒBE
Oh, day of terror! Day of tears!
The man to whom thou art allied
Appears to claim thee as his bride.

LIEUT., MERYLL, *and* WILFRED
Come, dry these unbecoming tears,
Most joyful tidings greet thine ears,
The man to whom thou art allied
Appears to claim thee as his bride.

ELSIE
Oh, Leonard, come thou to my side,
And claim me as thy loving bride!
Oh, day of terror! Day of tears!

Flourish. Enter COLONEL FAIRFAX, *handsomely dressed, and attended by other Gentlemen*

FAIR. (*sternly*).   All thought of Leonard Meryll set aside.
Thou art mine own! I claim thee as my bride. [91]

ALL.   Thou art his own! Alas! he claims thee as his bride.

ELSIE.   A suppliant at thy feet I fall;
Thine heart will yield to pity's call!

FAIR.   Mine is a heart of massive rock,
Unmoved by sentimental shock!

ALL.   Thy husband he!

ELSIE (*aside*).   Leonard, my loved one—come to me.
They bear me hence away!
But though they take me far from thee,
My heart is thine for aye!
My bruised heart,
My broken heart,
Is thine, my own, for aye!
(*To* FAIRFAX.)   Sir, I obey!
I am thy bride;
But ere the fatal hour
I said the say
That placed me in thy power
Would I had died!
Sir, I obey!
I am thy bride!

(*Looks up and recognises* FAIRFAX.) Leonard!

FAIR.   My own!

ELSIE.   Ah! (*Embrace.*)

ELSIE *and*   ⎰With happiness my soul is cloyed,
FAIR.   ⎱This is our joy-day unalloyed!

ALL.   Yes, yes!
With happiness their souls are cloyed,
This is their joy-day unalloyed!

Enter JACK POINT

POINT.   Oh, thoughtless crew!
Ye know not what ye do!
Attend to me, and shed a tear or two—
For I have a song to sing, O!

ALL.   Sing me your song, O!

[91] One very charming lady whom I met at a party after a performance of The Yeomen of the Guard said to me: "You know, Mr. Green, if I had been in Elsie's shoes, I would have asked him for a divorce at once for the cruel joke he had played on me."

591

[92] *Gilbert's directions are "Point falls insensible . . ."
It is on record, however, that after hearing from
Mr. Carte that Henry Lytton (later Sir Henry
Lytton) was playing it on tour as a death scene,
Gilbert replied: "It's just what I want. Point
should die, and the end of the opera should be
tragedy." His direction "falls insensible" was for
the sake of Grossmith, who was really incapable
of serious acting. He was a "funnyman" and
thought people would not accept anything else.
According to the late J. M. Gordon, Grossmith
didn't even fall insensible, he only pretended to.
And as the curtain was coming down, he would
waggle his toes and wink at the audience.*

*Jack Point's "death" has been a tradition now
for many years, and I naturally followed that
tradition. But I never really believed it possible
for anyone to die simply of a broken heart. Apparently, neither did Gilbert. Does he not say,
through the mouth of Katisha: "Go to—no one
ever yet died of a broken heart"?*

*However, a severe shock such as Jack Point
experiences could prove too much for someone
already suffering from undernourishment and a
serious cardiac condition! After discussion with
a heart specialist, I began to play the role from
its opening as a man suffering from such a condition. My make-up suggested it in the first act,
and, thanks to a quick change of make-up, my
appearance later on became more and more that
of a man whose death was imminent. Point, the
jester, sees the final joke of which he is a butt.
And "there's naught else to laugh at." So he
"laughs at himself until he dies for it."*

POINT.
It is sung to the moon
By a love-lorn loon,
Who fled from the mocking throng, O!
It's the song of a merryman, moping mum,
Whose soul was sad, and whose glance was glum,
Who sipped no sup, and who craved no crumb,
As he sighed for the love of a ladye!

ALL.
Heighdy! heighdy!
Misery me, lackadaydee!
He sipped no sup, and he craved no crumb,
As he sighed for the love of a ladye!

ELSIE.
I have a song to sing, O!

ALL.
What is your song, O?

ELSIE.
It is sung with the ring
Of the songs maids sing
Who love with a love life-long, O!
It's the song of a merrymaid, nestling near,
Who loved her lord—but who dropped a tear
At the moan of the merryman, moping mum,
Whose soul was sad, and whose glance was glum,
Who sipped no sup, and who craved no crumb,
As he sighed for the love of a ladye!

ALL.
Heighdy! heighdy!
Misery me, lackadaydee!
He sipped no sup, and he craved no crumb,
As he sighed for the love of a ladye!

[FAIRFAX *embraces* ELSIE *as* POINT *falls insensible at their feet.* [92]

CURTAIN

When Maiden Loves

Moderately fast

PHOEBE

1. When maid - en loves, she sits and sighs, She wan-ders to and fro; Un - bid - den tear-drops fill her eyes, And to all ques-tions she re-plies With a sad "heigh - ho!"

2. When maid - en loves, she mopes a - part, As owl mopes on a tree; Al - though she keen - ly feels the smart, She can-not tell what ails her heart, With its sad "Ah me!"

'Tis but a lit - tle word, "heigh-ho!" So soft, 'tis scarce - ly heard, "heigh-ho!"

'Tis but a fool - ish sigh, "Ah me!" Born but to droop and die, "Ah me!"

594

When Our Gallant Norman Foes

Majestically, but not too slow

DAME CARRUTHERS

1. When our
2. With -

gal-lant Nor-man foes Made our mer-ry land their own, And the Sax-ons from the Con-quer-or were
in its wall of rock The flow-er of the brave Have

fly-ing, At his bid-ding it a-rose, In its pan-o-ply of stone, A
shak-en. From the dun-geon to the block, From the scaf-fold to the grave, Is a

sen-ti-nel un-liv-ing and un-dy-ing. In - sen-si - ble, I trow, As a
jour-ney man-y gal-lant hearts have tak - en. And the wick-ed flames may hiss Round the

sen-ti-nel should be, Tho' a queen to save her head should come a - su - ing; There's a
he-roes who have fought For con-science and for home in all its beau-ty; But the

le-gend on its brow That is el - o-quent to me, And it tells of du - ty
grim old for-ta-lice Takes lit-tle heed of aught That comes not in - the

rall.   a tempo   p
done_ and du-ty do - ing.}
meas-ure of its du - ty.}   "The screw may twist and the

rall.   p a tempo

cresc.
rack_ may turn, And men may bleed and men_ may burn, O'er Lon-don town and its

cresc.   f

596

gold - en hoard I keep my silent watch and ward! The screw may twist and the

rack may turn, And men may bleed and men may burn, O'er Lon-don town and its

gold - en hoard I keep my si - lent watch and ward!"

watch and ward!"

Is Life a Boon?

Slowly with expression

FAIRFAX

1. Is life a boon? If so, it must be-fall That Death, when-e'er he call, Must call too soon. Though four-score years he give, Yet one would pray to live An-oth-er

2. Is life a thorn? Then count it not a whit! Nay, count it not a whit! Man is well done with it; Soon as he's born He should all means es-say To put the plague a-

moon! What kind of plaint have I,
way; And I, war - worn,

Who per - ish in Ju -
Poor cap - tured fu - gi -

rit   *p a tempo*

ly, Who per - ish in Ju - ly?
tive, My life most glad - ly ___ give,

I might have had to
I might have had to

cresc.

die, ___ Per - chance, in June! }
live ___ An - oth - er morn! }

I might have had to

1. *p rit*   *a tempo*

die, ___ Per - chance, in June!

p rit   *f a tempo*

2.

live, ___ to live An - oth - er morn!

follow the voice   *f a tempo*

I Have a Song to Sing, O!

In well-articulated, steady tempo

mf

POINT

mp

1. I have a song to sing, O!

mp

mf ELSIE

Sing me your song, O!

POINT

p

It is

mf

p

sung to the moon By a love-lorn loon, Who fled from the mock-ing throng, O! It's the

song of a mer-ry-man, mop-ing mum, Whose soul was sad, and whose glance was glum, Who

sipped no sup, and who craved no crumb, As he sighed for the love of a la-dye.

Heigh-dy! heigh-dy! Mis-er-y me, lack-a-day-dee! He

sipped no sup, and he craved no crumb, As he sighed for the love of a la-dye!

sipped no sup, and who craved no crumb, As he sighed for the love of a la - dye!

mp
Heigh - dy! heigh - dy! Mis - er - y me, lack - a - day - dee! He

sipped no sup, and he craved no crumb, As he sighed for the love of a la - dye!

mp POINT
3. I have a song to sing, O!

mf ELSIE
POINT
p
Sing me your song, O! _____ It is

603

sung to the knell Of a church-yard bell, And a dole-ful dirge, ding dong, O! It's a

song of a pop-in-jay, brave-ly born, Who turned up his no-ble nose with scorn At the

hum-ble mer-ry-maid, peer-ly proud, Who lov'd a lord, and who laugh'd a-loud At the

moan of the mer-ry-man, mop-ing mum, Whose soul was sad, and whose glance was glum, Who

sipped no sup, and who craved no crumb, As he sighed for the love of a la-dye!

Heigh - dy! heigh - dy! Mis - er - y me, lack - a - day - dee! He

sipped no sup, and he craved no crumb, As he sighed for the love of a la - dye!

mp ELSIE

4. I have a song to sing, O!

mf POINT   ELSIE

Sing me your song, O! _____ It is

sung with a sigh And a tear in the eye, For it tells of a right - ed wrong, O! It's a

song of the mer-ry-maid, once so gay, Who turned on her heel and tripped a-way From the

pea-cock pop-in-jay, brave-ly born, Who turned up his no-ble nose with scorn At the

hum-ble heart that he did not prize; So she begged on her knees, with down-cast eyes, For the

love of the mer-ry-man, mop-ing mum, Whose soul was sad and whose glance was glum, Who

sipped no sup, and who craved no crumb, As he sighed for the love of a la-dye!

Heigh - dy! heigh - dy! Mis - er - y me, lack - a - day - dee! His

pains were o'er, and he sighed no more, For he lived in the love of a la - dye!

Heigh - dy! heigh - dy! Mis - er - y me, lack - a - day - dee! His pains were o'er, and he

sighed no more, For he lived in the love of a la - dye! __

Were I Thy Bride

Gracefully

PHOEBE

Were I thy bride, Then all the world be - side Were not too wide To hold my wealth of love, Were I thy bride!

Up-on thy breast My lov - ing head would rest, As on her

nest The ten-der tur-tle dove, Were I thy bride!

This heart of mine Would be one heart with thine, And in that shrine Our hap-pi-ness would dwell, Were I thy bride!

And all day long Our lives should be a song: No grief, no wrong Should make my heart re-bel, Were

Were I thy bride! The ro - se's

sigh Were as a car-rion's cry To lull-a - by Such as I'd sing to thee,

Were I thy bride! A feath - er's

press Were lead - en heav-i - ness To my ca - ress. But then, of course, you see,

I'm not thy bride!

Oh, a Private Buffoon

Quick but not hurriedly

POINT

1. Oh, a
2. If you
3. If your
4. Comes a
5. Tho' your

pri-vate buf-foon is a light-heart-ed loon, If you lis-ten to pop-u-lar
wish to suc-ceed as a jest-er, you'll need To con-sid-er each per-son's au-
mas-ter is sur-ly, from get-ting up ear-ly (And tem-pers are short in the
Bish-op, may-be, or a sol-emn D. D. Oh, be-ware of his an-ger pro-
head it may rack with a bil-ious at-tack, And your sen-ses with tooth-ache you're

ru - mour;   From the morn to the night he's so
ric - 'lar: What is all right for B would quite
morn - ing),   An in - op - por - tune joke is e -
vok - ing!   Bet - ter not pull his hair, don't stick
los - ing,   Don't be mo - py and flat, they don't

joy - ous and bright, And he bub - bles with wit and good
scan - dal - ize C   (For C is so ver - y par -
nough to pro - voke Him to give you, at once, a month's
pins in his chair; He don't - un - der - stand prac - ti - cal
fine you for that, If you're prop - er - ly quaint and a -

612

hu - mour! He's so quaint and so terse, both in
tic - 'lar!); And D may be dull, and E's
warn - ing. Then if you re - frain, he is
jok - ing. If the jests that you crack have an
mus - ing! Tho' your wife ran a - way with a

prose and in verse; Yet though peo - ple for - give his trans -
ver - y thick skull Is as emp - ty of brains as a
at you a - gain, For he likes to get val - ue for
or - tho - dox smack, You may get a bland smile from these
sol - dier that day, And took with her your tri - fle of

gres - sion, There are one or two rules that all
la - dle; While F is F sharp, and will
mon - ey; He'll ask then and there, with an
sag - es; But should they, by chance, be im -
mon - ey; Bless your heart, they don't mind, they're ex -

fam - i - ly fools Must ob - serve, if they love their pro -
cry with a carp That he's known your best joke from his
in - so - lent stare, "If you know that you're paid to be
port - ed from France, Half - a - crown is stopp'd out of your
ceed - ing - ly kind, They don't blame you, as long as you're

fes - sion!   There   are   one   or   two   rules,   Half - a -
cra - dle!   When   your   hu - mour   they   flout,   You   can't
fun - ny?"   It   adds   to   the   task   Of   a
wag - es!   It's   a   gen - er - al   rule,   Tho'   your
fun - ny!   It's   a   com - fort   to   feel,   If   your

doz - en,   may   be,   That   all   fam - i - ly   fools,   Of   what -
let   your - self   go;   And   it   does   put   you   out   When   a
mer - ry - man's   place,   When   your   prin - ci - pal   asks,   With   a
zeal   it   may   quench,   If   the   fam - i - ly   fool   Tells   a
part - ner   should   flit,   Tho'   you   suf - fer   a   deal,   They   don't

ev - er   de - gree,   Must   ob - serve,   if   they   love   their   pro -
per - son   says: "Oh,   I   have   known   that   old   joke   from   my
scowl   on   his   face,   If   you   know   that   you're   paid   to   be
joke   that's   too   French,   Half - a - crown   is   stopp'd   out   of   his
mind   it   a   bit;   They   don't   blame   you,   so   long   as   you're

1. - 2. - 3. - 4.   **5.**

fes - sion!
cra - dle!"
fun - ny?
wag - es!   fun - ny!

Strange Adventure

Lightly as a Gavotte

p

f KATE

1. Strange ad - ven - ture! Maid - en wed - ded To a
2. Strange ad - ven - ture that we're troll - ing: Mod - est

f

p ENSEMBLE   *f* KATE

groom she'd_nev - er_ seen! Nev - er, nev - er, nev - er seen! Groom a -
maid and_gal - lant_ groom! Gal - lant, gal - lant, gal - lant groom! While the

p   *f*

ENSEMBLE

bout_ to be be - head - ed, In an_ hour on Tow - er Green! Tow - er,
fun - 'ral bell is toll - ing, Toll - ing,_ toll - ing, Bim - a - boom! Bim - a,

mp

A Man Who Would Woo a Fair Maid

Lively and gracefully

Fairfax 1. A
(Elsie 2. If he's)

man who would woo a fair maid _____ Should 'pren-tice him-self to the
made the best use of his time, _____ His twig he'll so care-ful-ly

trade, _____ And stud-y all day, In me-thod-i-cal way, How to
lime, _____ That ev-er-y bird Will come down at his word, _____ What-

flat - ter, ca - jole and per - suade. He should 'pren - tice him - self at four -
ev - er its plum - age or clime. He must learn that the thrill of a

teen, And prac - tice from morn - ing to e'en; And
touch May mean lit - tle, or noth - ing, or much; It's an

when he's of age, If he will, I'll en - gage, He may cap - ture the heart of a
in - stru - ment rare, To be hand - led with care, And ought to be treat - ed as

queen, the heart of a queen!
such, ought to be treat - ed as such.

It is pure - ly a mat - ter of skill, Which

all may at - tain if they will:___ But ev - er - y Jack, He must

stud - y the knack If he wants to make sure of his Jill! If he

wants to make sure___ of his Jill!

Elsie 2. If he's

PHOEBE

Then a

glance may be tim - id or free,___ It will var - y in might - y de - gree,___ From an

im - pu-dent stare To a   look of des-pair That no maid with-out pi - ty can see;   And a

glance of des-pair is no guide,   It may have its ri-dic-u-lous side;   It may

draw you a tear Or a   box on the ear; You can   nev- er be sure till you've

rall.   ALL THREE

tried! Nev - er be sure till you've tried!   It is

rit.   *follow the voice*   *a tempo*
                                            mf

pure - ly a mat - ter of   skill,—   Which   all   may at-tain   if they will:—   But

p

ev - er - y Jack He must stud - y the knack If he wants to make sure of his

Jill! If he wants to make sure, ____ to make sure ____

of ____ his Jill! Sure ____ of ____ his Jill! If he

wants to make sure of his Jill! Yes, ev - er - y Jack Must

stud - y the knack If he wants ____ to make sure of ____ his Jill! ____

follow the voice

When a Wooer Goes A-Wooing

In an easy flowing movement

ELSIE

When a woo-er Goes a - woo-ing, Naught is

FAIRFAX

tru-er Than his joy. Maid - en hush-ing All his su - ing, Bold - ly blush-ing, Brave - ly

ELSIE

coy! Bold - ly blush-ing, Brave - ly coy!

Oh, the hap - py days of do - ing! Oh, the sigh - ing and the su - ing! When a

su - ing, When a broth - er goes a - woo-ing, And a sob-bing sis - ter

weeps! When a jest - er Is out - wit - ted, Feel - ings fes - ter, Heart is

lead! Food for fish - es On - ly fit - ted, Jest - er wish - es He was

dead! Food for fish - es On - ly fit - ted, Jest - er wish - es He was

dead! Oh, the do - ing and un - do - ing, Oh, the sigh - ing and the

su - ing, When a jest - er goes a - woo - ing, And he wish - es he ____ was

dead! Oh, the do - ing and un - do - ing, Oh, the sigh - ing and the

su - ing, When a jest - er goes a - woo - ing, And he wish - es he ____ was dead, He

wish - es he was dead! ____

The Gondoliers

OR, THE KING OF BARATARIA

DRAMATIS PERSONÆ

THE DUKE OF PLAZA-TORO (*a Grandee of Spain*)

LUIZ (*his Attendant*)

DON ALHÁMBRA DEL BOLERO (*the Grand Inquisitor*)

MARCO PALMIERI
GIUSEPPE PALMIERI
ANTONIO
FRANCESCO
GIORGIO
ANNIBALE
} (*Venetian Gondoliers*)

THE DUCHESS OF PLAZA-TORO

CASILDA (*her Daughter*)

GIANETTA
TESSA
FIAMETTA
VITTORIA
GIULIA
} (*Contadine*)

INEZ (*the King's Foster-mother*)

Chorus of Gondoliers and Contadine, Men-at-Arms, Heralds, and Pages

Act I: THE PIAZZETTA, VENICE

Act II: PAVILION IN THE PALACE OF BARATARIA

(*An interval of three months is supposed to elapse
between Acts I and II*)

Date 1750

First produced at the Savoy Theatre on December 7, 1889

"A VERDICT of emphatic and unanimous approval was passed last night by a brilliant house upon Mr. W. S. Gilbert and Sir Arthur Sullivan's new comic opera. . . ." So said the Sunday Times on December 8, 1889, in its review of The Gondoliers. It also added that Gilbert and Sullivan had "scored their greatest triumph since The Mikado."

In The Gondoliers, unlike any of the other operas in the series, a full twenty minutes elapse before one hears a word of spoken dialogue. This does not imply that Gilbert, for once, considered the words of less importance than the music, or that he had in any way suggested such a thing to Sullivan. It is just that he went to extreme pains to satisfy, as far as he possibly could, Sullivan's desires regarding the music.

At about this time Richard D'Oyly Carte was in the process of building a new theater to be known as the Royal English Opera House, and he had approached Sullivan to compose a grand opera with which to open it. This was Sullivan's opportunity to do something he had long desired. But to compose a grand opera one needs a book, just as for a comic opera, and quite naturally—especially after The Yeomen of the Guard—he turned to Gilbert. However, Gilbert did not think he could do his best work in a truly serious opera. Besides, he did not believe that Carte's new theater, situated in the wrong place, at the top of Shaftesbury Avenue, would achieve any popularity. He, therefore, turned Sullivan down, but it was all very friendly. In fact, he suggested that Sullivan should approach a more serious writer—Julian Sturgis, for instance. On the other hand, he suggested that he and Sullivan should work together on a new comic opera at the same time.

Sullivan took the advice regarding Sturgis but once again said that "I have lost all taste for comic opera. In fact, it is not too much to say that it has become distasteful to me." He was adamant in his insistence that if he and Gilbert were to work together again, the piece should be of a much more dramatic nature and the music should have greater importance than in their previous pieces. Gilbert retorted that their one step toward grand opera (or, as Sullivan had put it, more serious work)—The Yeomen of the Guard—had not had such an outstanding success that they could assume the public wanted that sort of stuff. (This lack of success on the part of Yeomen was a great disappointment to Sullivan. Lack of success! It ran nearly a year.) Despite Gilbert's very common-sense approach to the matter, Sullivan repeated his assertion that he could not and would not consider a return to their former style.

With that he went off to the Riviera, leaving Gilbert in London to cope with the problems that the Savoy Theatre and the production of The Yeomen of the Guard were now suffering. George Grossmith was on the point of leaving the company in order to resume his career as an Entertainer at the Piano; Rutland Barrington had already left; two other principals wanted to leave; and Jessie Bond was asking for more money. All this reached Sullivan's ears while he was still abroad, and he wrote to Gilbert saying that "this inclination on the part of the company to disintegrate might give us a chance to renew our collaboration on different lines." This was simply a broad hint to Gilbert that he should think again about more serious works, with the music occupying first place. Gilbert answered with a polite but firm No, adding that the librettist of a grand opera was always drowned by the composer. Sullivan came back with a snorter. If any sacrifices had been made, it was he who had made them and not Gilbert; and it was he who would have to continue making them if he were to carry on with comic opera. From now on he wanted to do work where the music was of paramount importance; where the words would merely suggest, and not govern. Then, quite innocently, he asked if there was any way that this could be accomplished.

Gilbert promptly "blew his top."

"Are you under the astounding impression that you have been effacing yourself in all our pieces?" he wrote. "If you mean that I am to supply a libretto subordinate to the music, consequently making the librettist subordinate to the composer, then there is no way to be found that would be satisfactory to both! You," he continued, "are as adept in your profession as I am in mine. If we meet, it must be as Master and Master, not as Master and Servant."

That final line! Sullivan heartily agreed, and said as much in a letter to Carte, adding that if this could be carried out it would remove a great deal of unnecessary friction . . . for . . . excepting vocal rehearsals and two orchestral rehearsals, he was but a cipher in the theater.

Carte showed this letter to Gilbert, and the "cat was among the pigeons" again. The ensuing quarrel became known as the "cipher quarrel," and it had not been resolved, one way or the other, by the time the first rough draft of The Gondoliers was down on paper. Another contributing cause of Gilbert's rising irascibility was his difference with Jessie Bond over her salary. He was tired to death, he said, of artists who thought they were responsible for the success of the operas, and he intended to put a stop to that sort of thing. "I'll write an opera in which there will be no principal parts!" Unfortunately for him, that is impossible. Someone in the cast is bound to stand out. And no matter how the author tries, one character, and it may well turn out to be one of the small parts, will be better drawn, better written, or better what-have-you. It is inevitable. However, Gilbert wrote The Gondoliers with this determination in mind.

The Gondoliers was the first of the Gilbert and Sullivan operas to be honored by a command performance at the order of Queen Victoria. The whole company was transferred, lock, stock and barrel, to Windsor Castle for the occasion, the performance taking place before her Majesty; her son Edward, Prince of Wales; her grandson Prince George (later to become King George V); and other princes and princesses of the Blood Royal. There is one nice little story that was told in The Era, a theatrical weekly:

Her Majesty had observed that certain additions had been made to the text by some of the principals, and after the performance she asked Mr. Carte the reason for that.

"Those, Your Majesty," said Mr. Carte, "are what we call gags."

"Gags?" replied the Queen. "I thought gags were things that were put by authority into people's mouths."

"These gags, Your Majesty," said Mr. Carte, "are things these people put into their own mouths without authority."

Legend has had it that the program for the Royal Command Performance did not bear the name of W. S. Gilbert and that this was the cause of deep resentment to him and gave rise to another terrific quarrel. He virtually accused Sullivan of toadying to royalty, and of being, if not responsible for, at least cognizant of, this omission. A scrutiny of the special program for the Royal Command Performance reveals the words "Written by W. S. Gilbert. Composed by Sir Arthur Sullivan." In September of the same year, The Mikado was accorded a similar honor at Balmoral Castle, where again the special program for that performance reveals the same credits, and in both cases in that order.

One very interesting fact about The Gondoliers is that during its run at the Savoy Theatre, Ivanhoe was produced at the Royal English Opera House. In spite of the fact that Queen Victoria had once said to Sullivan, "You are capable of better things, Sir Arthur. You should write a grand opera," she never went to see Ivanhoe. But she did see The Gondoliers—and at a command performance! Gilbert was not present at either of the command performances, but, strangely enough, neither was Sullivan. The conductor for The Gondoliers was Mr. Frank Cellier, and for The Mikado, Mr. F. W. Halton.

The famous so-called "carpet quarrel" took place shortly afterward and, for all practical considerations, brought a brilliantly successful collaboration to an end. Gilbert returned from the Continent to find that he had been billed by Mr. Carte for what he thought was an excessive amount—£500— for restoring carpets at the Savoy. One thing led to another, Sullivan seemed to side with Carte, and the relationship broke up. Many years later the quarrel was made up and two new pieces, Utopia, Limited and The Grand Duke, were ultimately produced. But neither was a success. Utopia ran for only 245 performances, while The Grand Duke achieved the shortest run of all— except Thespis—with just 123. Sullivan did write more, and so did Gilbert, but not in collaboration. The famous partnership was finally and irrevocably at an end. Sullivan died in 1901, leaving behind two completed, rough drafts of fifteen numbers of The Emerald Isle, book by Basil Hood. The score was eventually completed by Edward German. Before the run of Ivanhoe came to an end Sullivan must have realized his mistake. Standing with him one day in the theater watching a performance of Ivanhoe, a companion said to Sullivan, "I like it."

"That's more than I do," said Sullivan. "A cobbler should stick to his last."

To all intents and purposes the partnership really ceased with The Gondoliers, and it is with that opera that we bring this volume to an end.

The Gondoliers

ACT I

SCENE.—*The Piazzetta, Venice. The Ducal Palace on the right*

FIAMETTA, GIULIA, VITTORIA, *and other Contadine discovered,*
each tying a bouquet of roses [1]

CHORUS OF CONTADINE [2]

List and learn, ye dainty roses,
 Roses white and roses red,
Why we bind you into posies
 Ere your morning bloom has fled
By a law of maiden's making,
Accents of a heart that's aching,
Even though that heart be breaking,
 Should by maiden be unsaid:
Though they love with love exceeding,
They must seem to be unheeding—
Go ye then and do their pleading,
 Roses white and roses red!

FIAMETTA

Two there are for whom in duty,
 Every maid in Venice sighs—
Two so peerless in their beauty
 That they shame the summer skies.
We have hearts for them, in plenty,
 They have hearts, but all too few,
We, alas, are four-and-twenty!
 They, alas, are only two!
We, alas!

CHORUS.   Alas!

FIA.   Are four-and-twenty,
They, alas!

CHORUS.   Alas!

FIA.   Are only two.

CHORUS.   They, alas, are only two, alas!
Now ye know, ye dainty roses,
Why we bind you into posies,
 Ere your morning bloom has fled,
 Roses white and roses red!

[*During this chorus* ANTONIO, FRANCESCO, GIORGIO, *and other Gondoliers*
have entered unobserved by the Girls—at first two, then two more,
then four, then half a dozen, then the remainder of the Chorus.

[1] Though not his best, this ranks high as a Sullivan choral opening; for color, it has no peer. The romantic Piazzetta, with the Grand Canal in the background; the Contadine in their multicolored national costumes; the roses white and roses red! It's a feast for the eyes.

[2] Words and music on page 671.

SOLI

FRANC.	Good morrow, pretty maids; for whom prepare ye These floral tributes extraordinary?
FIA.	For Marco and Giuseppe Palmieri, The pink and flower of all the Gondolieri.
GIU.	They're coming here, as we have heard but lately, To choose two brides from us who sit sedately.
ANT.	[3] Do all you maidens love them?
ALL.	Passionately!
ANT.	These gondoliers are to be envied greatly!
GIOR.	But what of us, who one and all adore you? Have pity on our passion, we implore you!
FIA.	These gentlemen must make their choice before you;
VIT.	In the meantime we tacitly ignore you.
GIU.	When they have chosen two that leaves you plenty— Two dozen we, and ye are four-and-twenty.

FIA. *and* VIT. Till then, enjoy your *dolce far niente.* [4]

ANT.   With pleasure, nobody *contradicente!*

[5] SONG—ANTONIO *and* CHORUS

For the merriest fellows are we, tra la,
That ply on the emerald sea, tra la;
With loving and laughing,
And quipping and quaffing,
We're happy as happy can be, tra la—
As happy as happy can be!

With sorrow we've nothing to do, tra la,
And care is a thing to pooh-pooh, tra la;
And Jealousy yellow,
Unfortunate fellow,
We drown in the shimmering blue, tra la—
We drown in the shimmering blue!

FIA. (*looking off*). See, see, at last they come to make their choice—
Let us acclaim them with united voice.

[MARCO *and* GIUSEPPE *appear in gondola at back.*

CHORUS (*Girls*). Hail, hail! gallant gondolieri, ben venuti!
Accept our love, our homage, and our duty.

[MARCO *and* GIUSEPPE *jump ashore—the Girls salute them.*

[6] DUET—MARCO *and* GIUSEPPE, *with* CHORUS OF GIRLS

MAR. *and* GIU.	Buon' giorno, signorine!
GIRLS.	Gondolieri carissimi! Siamo contadine!
MAR. *and* GIU. (*bowing*)	Servitori umilissimi! Per chi questi fiori— Questi fiori bellissimi?
GIRLS.	Per voi, bei signori O eccellentissimi!

[3] Antonio was the second role I played in The Gondoliers. The first was Luiz. See Note 15.

[4] Dolce far niente. *Pleasant inactivity. (Toward the girls? Or themselves?)*

[5] *When I was offered this role, I didn't know if I could do it. It entails a dance, and I was still feeling the effects of a war wound in my left knee. But I accepted the offer and promptly rented a studio where every day I practiced dancing in front of a mirror until I thought I could get away with it on one leg. (I did!)*

During the 1926 London season (at the Princess Theatre), Sir Malcolm Sargent (or Dr., as he was then) was in the chair and took the number much too slowly for me to be able to dance. When I complained he told me that if he continued at the speed at which I wanted, my words would be heard, yes, but the words of the chorus would be lost. I asked him if he knew what the chorus words were.

"I can't remember just now," he said, "but whatever they are they will be lost."

"Well," I replied, "I remember them. They are 'Tra la la la'!"

The number was taken at my tempo.

[6] Translation:

MAR. and GIU.	Good day, ladies!
GIRLS.	Dear gondoliers! We are peasant girls!
MAR. and GIU.	Your most humble servants! For whom are these flowers— These most beautiful flowers?
GIRLS.	For you, O most good and Excellent sirs!
MAR. and GIU.	O Heaven!
GIRLS.	Good day, noble sirs!
MAR. and GIU.	We are only gondoliers. Ladies, we love you!
GIRLS.	We are but peasant girls.
MAR. and GIU.	Ladies!
GIRLS.	Peasant girls! Noble sirs!
MAR. and GIU.	Gondoliers! Poor gondoliers!

[*The Girls present their bouquets to* MARCO *and* GIUSEPPE, *who are overwhelmed with them, and carry them with difficulty.*

MAR. *and* GIU. (*their arms full of flowers*). O ciel'!

GIRLS.	Buon' giorno, cavalieri!
MAR. *and* GIU. (*deprecatingly*).	Siamo gondolieri.
(*To* FIA. *and* VIT.)	Signorina, io t' amo!
GIRLS (*deprecatingly*).	Contadine siamo.
MAR. *and* GIU.	Signorine!
GIRLS (*deprecatingly*).	Contadine!
(*Curtseying to* MAR. *and* GIU.)	Cavalieri.
MAR. *and* GIU. (*deprecatingly*).	Gondolieri!
	Poveri gondolieri!
CHORUS.	Buon' giorno, signorine, etc.

[7] DUET—MARCO *and* GIUSEPPE [8]

We're called *gondolieri*,
But that's a vagary,
It's quite honorary
    The trade that we ply.
For gallantry noted
Since we were short-coated,
To beauty devoted,
    Giuseppe }
    Are Marco } and I;

When morning is breaking,
Our couches forsaking,
To greet their awaking
    With carols we come.
At summer day's nooning,
When weary lagooning,
Our mandolins tuning,
    We lazily thrum.

When vespers are ringing,
To hope ever clinging,
With songs of our singing
    A vigil we keep,
When daylight is fading,
Enwrapt in night's shading,
With soft serenading
    We sing them to sleep.

We're called *gondolieri*, etc.

RECIT.—MARCO *and* GIUSEPPE [9]

MAR.	And now to choose our brides!
GIU.	As all are young and fair,
	And amiable besides,
BOTH.	We really do not care
	A preference to declare.
MAR.	A bias to disclose
	Would be indelicate— .

[7] Marco and Giuseppe, always ready to serenade the ladies, carry mandolins slung across their backs.

[8] Words and music on page 674.

[9] Giuseppe was my fourth role in The Gondoliers. (I had already appeared as the Duke.) The D'Oyly Carte Company was due to make its first tour of Canada in the winter season of 1926–27, immediately following the 1926 London season at the Princess Theatre. During this season I was rehearsed in the role and then dispatched to whatever city or town in which the D'Oyly Carte Small Company was appearing, to give a trial performance. Apparently I passed the test and then went on to perform the role throughout that coast-to-coast Canadian tour. But I didn't keep it for long after our return to England. In June of 1927 the Small Company was disbanded and some of the principals were transferred to the Repertory Company. Among them was Leslie Rands, the Small Company's Giuseppe. I was, at this time, also understudying Henry Lytton. It was, quite rightly, considered foolish to have two understudies on stage simultaneously, if it could be avoided, so I had to relinquish the role. The only roles I retained until taking over the principal comedy roles in 1934 were comparatively small ones that could not conflict with my understudying Henry Lytton.

GIU.   And therefore we propose
                  To let impartial Fate
                  Select for us a mate!

ALL.   Viva!

GIRLS.   A bias to disclose
                  Would be indelicate—

MEN.   But how do they propose
                  To let impartial Fate
                  Select for them a mate?

GIU.   These handkerchiefs upon our eyes be good enough to bind,

MAR.   And take good care that both of us are absolutely blind;

BOTH.   Then turn us round—and we, with all convenient despatch,
          Will undertake to marry any two of you we catch!

ALL.   Viva!
They undertake to marry any two of { us they catch!
                             { them they catch!

[The Girls prepare to bind their eyes as directed.

FIA. (*to* MARCO).   Are you peeping?
                  Can you see me?

MAR.   Dark I'm keeping,
                  Dark and dreamy!

                                 (MARCO *slyly lifts bandage*).

VIT. (*to* GIUSEPPE).   If you're blinded
                  Truly, say so.

GIU.   All right-minded
                  Players play so!   (*slyly lifts bandage*).

FIA. (*detecting* MARCO).   Conduct shady!
                  They are cheating!
               Surely they de-
                  Serve a beating!   (*replaces bandage*).

VIT. (*detecting* GIUSEPPE). This too much is;
                  Maidens mocking—
               Conduct such is
                  Truly shocking!   (*replaces bandage*).

ALL.   You can spy, sir!
                    Shut your eye, sir!
               You may use it by and by, sir!
                    You can see, sir!
                    Don't tell me, sir!
              That will do—now let it be, sir!

CHORUS OF GIRLS.   My papa he keeps three horses,
                 Black, and white, and dapple grey, sir;
              Turn three times, then take your courses,
              Catch whichever girl you may, sir!

CHORUS OF MEN.   My papa, etc.

*[MARCO and GIUSEPPE turn round, as directed, and try to catch the girls.
Business of blind-man's buff. Eventually MARCO catches GIANETTA,
and GIUSEPPE catches TESSA. The two girls try to escape, but in*

vain. The two men pass their hands over the girls' faces to discover their identity.

GIU.   I've at length achieved a capture!
(*guessing.*)   This is Tessa! (*removes bandage*). [10] Rapture, rapture!

MAR. (*guessing*).   To me Gianetta fate has granted!
(*removes bandage*).
Just the very girl I wanted!

GIU. (*politely to* MAR.). If you'd rather change——

TESS.   My goodness!
This indeed is simple rudeness.

MAR. (*politely to* GIU.). I've no preference whatever—

GIA.   Listen to him! Well, I never!
(*Each man kisses each girl.*)

GIA.   Thank you, gallant *gondolieri!*
In a set and formal measure
It is scarcely necessary
To express our pleasure.
Each of us to prove a treasure,
Conjugal and monetary,
Gladly will devote our leisure,
Gay and gallant *gondolieri.*
Tra, la, la, la, la, la, etc.

TESS.   Gay and gallant *gondolieri,*
Take us both and hold us tightly,
You have luck extraordinary;
We might both have been unsightly!
If we judge your conduct rightly,
'Twas a choice involuntary;
Still we thank you most politely,
Gay and gallant *gondolieri!*
Tra, la, la, la, la, la, etc.

CHORUS OF GIRLS. [11]   Thank you, gallant *gondolieri;*
In a set and formal measure,
It is scarcely necessary
To express our pleasure.
Each of us to prove a treasure
Gladly will devote our leisure,
Gay and gallant *gondolieri!*
Tra, la, la, la, la, la, etc.

Fate in this has put his finger—
Let us bow to Fate's decree,
Then no longer let us linger,
To the altar hurry we!

[*They all dance off two and two*—GIANETTA *with* MARCO, TESSA *with* GIUSEPPE.

Flourish. A gondola arrives [12] *at the Piazzetta steps, from which enter the* DUKE OF PLAZA-TORO, *the* DUCHESS, *their daughter* CASILDA, *and their attendant* LUIZ, *who carries a drum.* [13] *All are dressed in pompous but old and faded clothes.*

Entrance of DUKE, DUCHESS, CASILDA, *and* LUIZ

[10] In the D'Oyly Carte production, Tessa and Gianetta did not appear on the stage until the last moment, slipping unobserved (they hoped) into the ring of girls circling around Marco and Giuseppe. Of course, they were invariably observed and the illusion of being caught at random was spoiled. I am sure that Gilbert had them on the stage from the very beginning as part of the chorus, and when I have directed the opera I have done it this way. The effect is excellent and natural. And my two principal ladies never seemed to mind.

[11] A glance at the vocal score reveals one of Sullivan's most enchanting examples of countertempo—2/4 time against 3/4:

[12] A gondola must have a gondolier, so quite obviously one Gondolier must have missed all the previous fun, unless he made an unobtrusive exit in order to pick up the ducal party. To overcome this glaring faux pas, I decided, when directing The Gondoliers, to divide the piece into five scenes: three were in Act I and two in Act II. Scene 1, Act I came to an end and the stage blacked out as the Gondoliers and Contadine danced off for their weddings. This allowed for a time lapse and permitted a Gondolier to take his place among the ducal party without evoking comment. Nor was the audience left staring for several seconds at a brightly lighted—and blank—stage.

[13] *Luiz gives a roll on his drum at the end of each line. It is a very slack drum, and the roll in consequence is very dull:*

THE GONDOLIERS

[14] Plaza-Toro. *The plaza de toros is the bull ring.*

[15] *The very first Gilbert and Sullivan role I appeared in was that of Luiz. I auditioned one week; was called for a second audition the next week; signed a contract the third week; joined the Small Company the fourth week; and appeared as Luiz the sixth week!*

[16] *I was never happy with this line, nor with the later line where the Duke hopes the Grand Inquisitor is deaf. They are not funny lines, they never were funny lines, and they never will be funny lines. Maybe I feel even more strongly today about making fun of a handicap in this manner than I once did, but I always wanted to cut them, and when I became responsible for the direction of a production of this opera, cut them I did. In any case, the laugh really belongs to Luiz, and the Duke's hope in each case is an unnecessary gilding of the lily.*

DUKE. From the sunny Spanish shore,
The Duke of Plaza-Tor!—[14]

DUCH. And His Grace's Duchess true—

CAS. And His Grace's daughter, too—

LUIZ. And His Grace's private drum
To Venetia's shores have come:

ALL. If ever, ever, ever
They get back to Spain,
They will never, never, never
Cross the sea again—

DUKE. Neither that Grandee from the Spanish shore,
The noble Duke of Plaza-Tor'—

DUCH. Nor His Grace's Duchess, staunch and true—

CAS. You may add, His Grace's daughter, too—

LUIZ. Nor His Grace's own particular drum
To Venetia's shores will come:

ALL. If ever, ever, ever
They get back to Spain,
They will never, never, never
Cross the sea again!

DUKE. At last we have arrived at our destination. This is the Ducal Palace, and it is here that the Grand Inquisitor resides. As a Castilian hidalgo of ninety-five quarterings, I regret that I am unable to pay my state visit on a horse. As a Castilian hidalgo of that description, I should have preferred to ride through the streets of Venice; but owing, I presume, to an unusually wet season, the streets are in such a condition that equestrian exercise is impracticable. No matter. Where is our suite?

LUIZ (*coming forward*). Your Grace, I am here. [15]

DUCH. Why do you not do yourself the honour to kneel when you address His Grace?

DUKE. My love, it is so small a matter! (*To* LUIZ.) Still, you may as well do it. (LUIZ *kneels.*)

CAS. The young man seems to entertain but an imperfect appreciation of the respect due from a menial to a Castilian hidalgo.

DUKE. My child, you are hard upon our suite.

CAS. Papa, I've no patience with the presumption of persons in his plebeian position. If he does not appreciate that position, let him be whipped until he does.

DUKE. Let us hope the omission was not intended as a slight. I should be much hurt if I thought it was. So would he. (*To* LUIZ.) Where are the halberdiers who were to have had the honour of meeting us here, that our visit to the Grand Inquisitor might be made in becoming state?

LUIZ. Your Grace, the halberdiers are mercenary people who stipulated for a trifle on account.

DUKE. How tiresome! Well, let us hope the Grand Inquisitor is a blind gentleman. [16] And the band who were to have had the honour of escorting us? I see no band!

LUIZ. Your Grace, the band are sordid persons who required to be paid in advance.

DUCH. That's so like a band!

DUKE (*annoyed*). Insuperable difficulties meet me at every turn!

DUCH. But surely they know His Grace?

LUIZ. Exactly—they know His Grace.

DUKE. Well let us hope that the Grand Inquisitor is a deaf gentleman. A cornet-à-piston would be something. You do not happen to possess the accomplishment of tootling like a cornet-à-piston?

LUIZ. Alas, no, Your Grace! But I can imitate a farmyard.

DUKE (doubtfully). I don't see how that would help us. I don't see how we could bring it in.

CAS. It would not help us in the least. We are not a parcel of graziers come to market, dolt!

DUKE. My love, our suite's feelings! (To LUIZ.) Be so good as to ring the bell and inform the Grand Inquisitor that his Grace the Duke of Plaza-Toro, Count Matadoro, Baron Picadoro——[17]

DUCH. And suite—

DUKE. And suite—have arrived at Venice, and seek——

CAS. Desire—

DUCH. Demand!

DUKE. And demand an audience.

LUIZ. Your Grace has but to command. (Rising.)

DUKE (much moved). I felt sure of it—I felt sure of it! (Exit LUIZ into Ducal Palace.) And now my love—(aside to DUCHESS) Shall we tell her? I think so—(aloud to CASILDA) And now, my love, prepare for a magnificent surprise. It is my agreeable duty to reveal to you a secret which should make you the happiest young lady in Venice!

CAS. A secret?

DUCH. A secret which, for State reasons, it has been necessary to preserve for twenty years.

DUKE. When you were a prattling babe of six months old you were married by proxy to no less a personage than the infant son and heir of His Majesty the immeasurably wealthy King of Barataria!

CAS. Married to the infant son of the King of Barataria? Was I consulted? (DUKE shakes his head.) It was a most unpardonable liberty!

DUKE. Consider his extreme youth and forgive him. [18] Shortly after the ceremony that misguided monarch abandoned the creed of his forefathers, [19] and became a Wesleyan Methodist of the most bigoted and persecuting type. The Grand Inquisitor, determined that the innovation should not be perpetuated in Barataria, caused your smiling and unconscious husband to be stolen and conveyed to Venice. A fortnight since the Methodist Monarch and all his Wesleyan Court were killed in an insurrection, and we are here to ascertain the whereabouts of your husband, and to hail you, our daughter, as Her Majesty, the reigning Queen of Barataria! (Kneels.)

During this speech LUIZ *re-enters* [20]

DUCH. Your Majesty! (Kneels.)

DUKE. It is at such moments as these that one feels how necessary it is to travel with a full band.

CAS. I, the Queen of Barataria! But I've nothing to wear! We are practically penniless!

DUKE. That point has not escaped me. Although I am unhappily in straitened circumstances at present, my social influence is something enormous; and a Company, to be called the Duke of Plaza-Toro, Limited, is in course of formation to work me. An influential directorate has been secured, and I shall myself join the Board after allotment.

CAS. Am I to understand that the Queen of Barataria may be called upon at any time to witness her honoured sire in process of liquidation?

[17] *The reading of the Duke's titles is another gilding of the lily, but here it's delicious gilding. The Duke of Bull Square! Count Bull Killer! Baron Bull Provoker! Note how the succession of titles indicates their degree of importance. By the way, he reads all of this from an enormous visiting card.*

[18] *The Duke carries out some nice business here with his cape. Taking it from behind he brings it across his chest in a bunch, as if rocking a baby in swaddling clothes. And, of course, he allows a sufficiently long pause for the line and the action to achieve their full impact.*

[19] *The "creed of his forefathers" is, of course, an obvious one, and his renunciation of it to become a Wesleyan Methodist would come as a tremendous shock, especially of the type which Gilbert defines. But why no one ever takes objections to these lines I can't imagine, unless it is the business that goes with it. The Duke's wig is "full bottomed." By taking the two long "ears" between his teeth he gives the impression of being a very old, long-gray-bearded gentleman. Perhaps it is the ensuing laugh that removes any thought of insult.*

[20] *Luiz should make his entrance at a point where he does not hear the reference to Casilda's husband or to her being a queen. All he should hear is the Duchess of Plaza-Toro saying, "Your Majesty!" At the same time he must be onstage with sufficient time left at his disposal to re-affix his drum (which he had removed immediately after the quartette "From the Sunny Spanish Shore"). Then, as the Duke and Duchess kneel, he gives a long, dull roll on the drum. Without this the Duke's next line means nothing.*

DUCH. The speculation is not exempt from that drawback. If your father should stop, it will, of course, be necessary to wind him up.

CAS. But it's so undignified—it's so degrading! A Grandee of Spain turned into a public company? Such a thing was never heard of!

DUKE. My child, the Duke of Plaza-Toro does not follow fashions—he leads them. He always leads everybody. When he was in the army he led his regiment. He occasionally led them into action. He invariably led them out of it.

[21] Words and music on page 679.

SONG—DUKE OF PLAZA-TORO [21]

In enterprise of martial kind,
    When there was any fighting,
He led his regiment from behind—
    He found it less exciting.
But when away his regiment ran,
    His place was at the fore, O—
        That celebrated,
        Cultivated,
        Underrated
            Nobleman,
    The Duke of Plaza-Toro!

ALL.   In the first and foremost flight, ha, ha!
You always found that knight, ha, ha!
        That celebrated,
        Cultivated,
        Underrated
            Nobleman,
    The Duke of Plaza-Toro!

He led his regiment from behind—

When, to evade Destruction's hand,
    To hide they all proceeded,
No soldier in that gallant band
    Hid half as well as he did.
He lay concealed throughout the war,
    And so preserved his gore, O!
        That unaffected,
        Undetected,
        Well-connected
            Warrior,
    The Duke of Plaza-Toro!

In the first and foremost flight . . .

ALL.   In every doughty deed, ha, ha!
He always took the lead, ha, ha!
        That unaffected,
        Undetected,
        Well-connected
            Warrior,
    The Duke of Plaza-Toro!

When told that they would all be shot
    Unless they left the service,
That hero hesitated not,
    So marvellous his nerve is.
He sent his resignation in,
    The first of all his corps, O!
        That very knowing,
        Overflowing,
        Easy-going

Paladin,
The Duke of Plaza-Toro!

ALL.
To men of grosser clay, ha, ha!
He always showed the way, ha, ha!
That very knowing,
Overflowing,
Easy-going
Paladin,
The Duke of Plaza-Toro!

[*Exeunt* DUKE *and* DUCHESS *into Grand Ducal Palace. As soon as they have disappeared,* LUIZ *and* CASILDA *rush to each other's arms.*

RECIT. AND DUET—CASILDA *and* LUIZ

O rapture, when alone together
    Two loving hearts and those that bear them
May join in temporary tether,
    Though Fate apart should rudely tear them.

CAS.
Necessity, Invention's mother,
    Compelled me to a course of feigning—
But, left alone with one another,
    I will atone for my disdaining!

AIR [22]

CAS.
Ah, well-beloved,
Mine angry frown
Is but a gown
That serves to dress
My gentleness!

LUIZ.
Ah, well-beloved,
Thy cold disdain,
It gives no pain—
'Tis mercy, played
In masquerade!

BOTH.
Ah, well-beloved, etc.

CAS. O Luiz, Luiz—what have you said? What have I done? What have I allowed you to do?

LUIZ. Nothing, I trust, that you will ever have reason to repent. (*Offering to embrace her.*)

CAS. (*withdrawing from him*). Nay, Luiz, it may not be. I have embraced you for the last time.

LUIZ (*amazed*). Casilda!

CAS. I have just learnt, to my surprise and indignation, [23] that I was wed in babyhood to the infant son of the King of Barataria!

LUIZ. The son of the King of Barataria? The child who was stolen in infancy by the Inquisition?

CAS. The same. But of course, you know his story.

LUIZ. Know his story? Why, I have often told you that my mother was the nurse to whose charge he was entrusted!

CAS. True. I had forgotten. Well, he has been discovered, and my father has brought me here to claim his hand.

LUIZ. But you will not recognize this marriage? It took place when you were too young to understand its import.

[22] *Originally this duet, following Casilda's recitative, was a ballad for Luiz, the first verse of which was as follows:*

Thy wintry scorn I dearly prize,
    Thy mocking pride I bless;
Thy scorn is love in deep disguise,
    Thy pride is lowliness.
Thy cold disdain
It gives no pain.
'Tis mercy played
In masquerade.
Thine angry frown
Is but a gown
That serves to dress
Thy gentleness!

The ballad ends with the couplet:

Oh, happy he who is content to gain
    Thy scorn, thy angry frown, thy disdain!

The current and now accepted duet is, of course, a précis of the original ballad which reached print only in the first edition.

[23] *My first Casilda was a Miss Mabel Sykes, known to all and sundry as "Bill" Sykes! She was an excellent Casilda, if only she could have overcome her "surpwise and indrigation"! Poor darling—she never did. Later on, she invariably said either "married il infalcy" or "married in ilfancy." See page 668, Note 88.*

641

CAS. Nay, Luiz, respect my principles and cease to torture me with vain entreaties. Henceforth my life is another's.

LUIZ. But stay—the present and the future—they are another's; but the past—that at least is ours, and none can take it from us. As we may revel in naught else, let us revel in that!

CAS. I don't think I grasp your meaning.

LUIZ. Yet it is logical enough. You say you cease to love me?

CAS. (demurely). I say I may not love you.

LUIZ. Ah, but you do not say you did not love me?

CAS. I loved you with a frenzy that words are powerless to express—and that but ten brief minutes since!

LUIZ. Exactly. My own—that is, until ten minutes since, my own—my lately loved, my recently adored—tell me that until, say a quarter of an hour ago, I was all in all to thee! (Embracing her.)

CAS. I see your idea. It's ingenious, but don't do that. (Releasing herself.)

LUIZ. There can be no harm in revelling in the past.

CAS. None whatever, but an embrace cannot be taken to act retrospectively.

LUIZ. Perhaps not!

CAS. We may recollect an embrace—I recollect many—but we must not repeat them.

LUIZ. Then let us recollect a few! (A moment's pause, as they recollect, then both heave a deep sigh.)

LUIZ. Ah, Casilda, you were to me as the sun is to the earth!

CAS. A quarter of an hour ago?

LUIZ. About that.

CAS. And to think that, but for this miserable discovery, you would have been my own for life!

LUIZ. Through life to death—a quarter of an hour ago!

CAS. How greedily my thirsty ears would have drunk the golden melody of those sweet words a quarter—well, it's now about twenty minutes since. (Looking at her watch.)

LUIZ. About that. In such a matter one cannot be too precise.

CAS. And now our love, so full of life, is but a silent, solemn memory!

LUIZ. Must it be so, Casilda?

CAS. Luiz, it must be so! [24]

DUET—CASILDA and LUIZ [25]

LUIZ.
There was a time—
　　A time for ever gone—ah, woe is me!
It was no crime
　　To love but thee alone—ah, woe is me!
One heart, one life, one soul,
　　One aim, one goal—
Each in the other's thrall,
　　Each all in all, ah, woe is me!

BOTH.
Oh, bury, bury—let the grave close o'er
The days that were—that never will be more!
Oh, bury, bury love that all condemn,
And let the whirlwind mourn its requiem!

CAS.
Dead as the last year's leaves—
　　As gathered flowers—ah, woe is me!
Dead as the garnered sheaves,
　　That love of ours—ah, woe is me!
Born but to fade and die

[24] In my opinion, if Gilbert had a fault it was that he could and would and did work a gag to death. Witness the scene that takes place in the above dialogue, starting with Luiz' "But stay—the present and the future . . ." Current official editions have made a number of cuts and today the scene reads more easily and faster.

　　When a long gag very similar to this is put to music, as in Nanki-Poo's wooing of Yum-Yum in The Mikado (see page 421), it stands up better.

[25] Words and music on page 681.

When hope was high,
Dead and as far away
As yesterday!—ah, woe is me!

BOTH.   Oh, bury, bury—let the grave close o'er, etc.

Re-enter from the Ducal Palace the DUKE *and* DUCHESS, *followed by*
DON ALHAMBRA BOLERO, *the Grand Inquisitor.*

DUKE. My child, allow me to present to you His Distinction Don
Alhambra Bolero, the Grand Inquisitor of Spain. It was His Distinction who so thoughtfully abstracted your infant husband and
brought him to Venice.

DON AL. So this is the little lady who is so unexpectedly called upon
to assume the functions of Royalty! And a very nice little lady, too!

DUKE. Jimp, [26] isn't she?

DON AL. Distinctly jimp. Allow me! (*Offers his hand. She turns away
scornfully.*) Naughty temper!

DUKE. You must make some allowance. Her Majesty's head is a little
turned by her access of dignity.

DON AL. I could have wished that Her Majesty's access of dignity had
turned it in this direction.

DUCH. Unfortunately, if I am not mistaken, there appears to be some
little doubt as to His Majesty's whereabouts.

CAS. (*aside*). A doubt as to his whereabouts? Then we may yet be
saved!

DON AL. [27] A doubt? Oh dear, no—no doubt at all! He is here, in
Venice, plying the modest but picturesque calling of a gondolier. I can
give you his address—I see him every day! In the entire annals of our
history there is absolutely no circumstance so entirely free from all
manner of doubt of any kind whatever! Listen, and I'll tell you all
about it.

SONG—DON ALHAMBRA
(*with* DUKE, DUCHESS, CASILDA, *and* LUIZ) [28]

I stole the Prince, and brought him here,
    And left him gaily prattling
With a highly respectable gondolier,
Who promised the Royal babe to rear,
And teach him the trade of a timoneer
    With his own beloved bratling.

        Both of the babes were strong and stout,
            And, considering all things, clever.
        Of that there is no manner of doubt—
        No probable, possible shadow of doubt—
            No possible doubt whatever.

But owing, I'm much disposed to fear,
    To his terrible taste for tippling,
That highly respectable gondolier
Could never declare with a mind sincere
Which of the two was his offspring dear,
    And which the Royal stripling!

        Which was which he could never make out
            Despite his best endeavour.
        Of *that* there is no manner of doubt—
        No probable, possible shadow of doubt—
            No possible doubt whatever.

[26] Jimp. *A word of Scandinavian origin, 1508:
slender, slim, graceful, delicate, neat. According
to the Oxford Dictionary, it was introduced into
English literature in the 19th century. Might one
hazard a guess that Gilbert was perhaps responsible?*

*As the Duke makes this remark, "Jimp, isn't
she?" he pokes the Don in the ribs, and the
Don, in returning the compliment, bruises his
finger tips on the Duke's breastplate. A few lines
later, as the Don says, ". . . had turned it in
this . . ." he starts to poke the Duke, remembers the breastplate just in time and instead of
using his fingers, does the digging with his long
stick.*

[27] *Sidney Granville, as he himself admitted, had a
one-track mind. Every performance was identical. Each gesture and movement came on the
same syllable or word. It was his habit, during
this speech, to take a pinch of snuff from a box
which he kept in his right-hand pocket, thus:
"Oh dear, no—no doubt at all! [Hand in pocket]
He is here, in Venice, [Brings snuffbox out] plying the modest but picturesque calling of a gondolier. [Flips open lid of box] I can give you his
address—[Takes a pinch of snuff from box] I see
him every day! [A sniff up each nostril] In the
entire annals of our history there is absolutely no
circumstance so entirely free from all manner of
doubt of any kind whatever! [Two more sniffs]
Listen, [Closes lid] and I'll tell you all about it."
[Places snuffbox back in pocket, takes lace handkerchief from left cuff and gracefully wipes his
nose]*

*One day the snuffbox wasn't there. The result
was chaos and confusion. Not one word of the
dialogue could he remember because there wasn't
a gesture to go with it, and his song, "I Stole
the Prince," became more of a concerted number
than even Gilbert and Sullivan ever intended,
all the others taking any line they could remember and trying to adapt it to their own characters.*

[28] *Words and music on page 684.*

I stole the Prince, and brought him here

Time sped, and when at the end of a year
   I sought that infant cherished,
That highly respectable gondolier
Was lying a corpse on his humble bier—
I dropped a Grand Inquisitor's tear—
   That gondolier had perished.

   A taste for drink combined with gout,
      Had doubled him up for ever.
   Of *that* there is no manner of doubt—
   No probable, possible shadow of doubt—
      No possible doubt whatever.

The children followed his old career—
   (This statement can't be parried)
Of a highly respectable gondolier:
Well, one of the two (who will soon be here)—
But *which* of the two is not quite clear—
   Is the Royal Prince you married!

   Search in and out and round about,
      And you'll discover never
   A tale so free from every doubt—
   All probable, possible shadow of doubt—
      All possible doubt whatever!

CAS. Then do you mean to say that I am married to one of two gondoliers, but it is impossible to say which?

DON AL. Without any doubt of any kind whatever. But be reassured: the nurse to whom your husband was entrusted is the mother of the musical young man who is such a past-master of that delicately modulated instrument (*indicating the drum*). She can, no doubt, establish the King's identity beyond all question.

LUIZ. Heavens, how did he know that?

DON AL. My young friend, a Grand Inquisitor is always up to date. (*To* CAS.) His mother is at present the wife of a highly respectable and old-established brigand, who carries on an extensive practice in the mountains around Cordova. Accompanied by two of my emissaries, he will set off at once for his mother's address. She will return with them, and if she finds any difficulty in making up her mind, the persuasive influence of the torture chamber will jog her memory.

RECIT.—CASILDA *and* DON ALHAMBRA

CAS.   But, bless my heart, consider my position!
                I am the wife of one, that's very clear;
            But who can tell, except by intuition,
                Which is the Prince, and which the Gondolier?

DON AL.   Submit to Fate without unseemly wrangle:
                Such complications frequently occur—
            Life is one closely complicated tangle:
                Death is the only true unraveller!

QUINTET—DUKE, DUCHESS, CASILDA, LUIZ, *and* GRAND INQUISITOR [29]

ALL.   Try we life-long, we can never
                Straighten out life's tangled skein,
            Why should we, in vain endeavor,
                Guess and guess and guess again?

LUIZ.   Life's a pudding full of plums,

[29] *This quintet is staged in the D'Oyly Carte Company just as the madrigal in* The Mikado *and the "Tower Tomb" quartet in* The Yeomen of the Guard *are staged—as a straight concert item. To my mind any lengthy and static musical number, no matter how good from a musical point of view, can become just a little boring. Some sort of action, no matter how slight, should be introduced. That is easy enough to say but difficult to carry out. Of the three, the one in* The Mikado *is the easiest. This one, "Try We Life-Long," is the hardest. I was able to introduce some animation by using Gilbert's own Bab sketch—reproduced on the next page—as a model.*

DUCH.   Care's a canker that benumbs.

ALL.   Life's a pudding full of plums,
              Care's a canker that benumbs.
         Wherefore waste our elocution
         On impossible solution?
         Life's a pleasant institution,
              Let us take it as it comes!

         Set aside the dull enigma,
            We shall guess it all too soon;
         Failure brings no kind of stigma—
            Dance we to another tune!
              String the lyre and fill the cup,
              Lest on sorrow we should sup.
         Hop and skip to Fancy's fiddle,
         Hands across and down the middle—
         Life's perhaps the only riddle
              That we shrink from giving up!

[*Exeunt all into Ducal Palace except* LUIZ, *who goes off in gondola.* [30]

Hop and skip to Fancy's fiddle

[30] *If the act is presented in three scenes, Scene 2 ends here.*

Enter Gondoliers and Contadine, followed by MARCO, GIANETTA, GIUSEPPE, *and* TESSA

CHORUS

         Bridegroom and bride!
            Knot that's insoluble,
            Voices all voluble
         Hail it with pride.
         Bridegroom and bride!
            We in sincerity
            Wish you prosperity,
         Bridegroom and bride!

[31] SONG—TESSA [32]

TESS.   When a merry maiden marries,
         Sorrow goes and pleasure tarries;
            Every sound becomes a song,
            All is right, and nothing's wrong!
         From to-day and ever after
         Let our tears be tears of laughter.
            Every sigh that finds a vent
            Be a sigh of sweet content!
         When you marry, merry maiden,
         Then the air with love is laden;
            Every flower is a rose,
               Every goose becomes a swan,
            Every kind of trouble goes
               Where the last year's snows have gone!

CHORUS.   Sunlight takes the place of shade
               When you marry, merry maid!

TESS.   When a merry maiden marries,
         Sorrow goes and pleasure tarries;
            Every sound becomes a song,
            All is right, and nothing's wrong.
         Gnawing Care and aching Sorrow,

[31] *Tessa's song must be numbered among the best as far as soubrette songs go. It is probably the truest soubrette number in the whole series—full of joy and happiness with the underlying suggestion of the ever constant blindness of love.*

[32] *Words and music on page 687.*

Gnawing Care and aching Sorrow,
Get ye gone until to-morrow

[33] *This scene is one of the longest dialogue scenes in the entire series. It is the longest in The Gondoliers. For this reason, it must bubble along from beginning to end. Giuseppe doesn't really mean that "it's a bad omen" if the Don is an undertaker. And it is not really an aside; he should say it to the other three. If the Don hears, it doesn't really matter. They are young, they have just been married, and they are ribbing the beejay out of him.*

The Don is a bass, he is portly, and he is dressed in black. But that does not mean that he is slow or ponderous. He, in his way, must bubble along as well.

Get ye gone until to-morrow;
    Jealousies in grim array,
    Ye are things of yesterday!
When you marry, merry maiden,
Then the air with joy is laden;
    All the corners of the earth
        Ring with music sweetly played,
    Worry is melodious mirth,
        Grief is joy in masquerade;

CHORUS.   Sullen night is laughing day—
                  All the year is merry May!

At the end of the song, DON ALHAMBRA *enters at back. The Gondoliers and Contadine shrink from him, and gradually go off, much alarmed.*

GIU. And now our lives are going to begin in real earnest! What's a bachelor? A mere nothing—he's a chrysalis. He can't be said to live—he exists.

MAR. What a delightful institution marriage is! Why have we wasted all this time? Why didn't we marry ten years ago?

TESS. Because you couldn't find anybody nice enough.

GIA. Because you were waiting for *us*.

MAR. I suppose that *was* the reason. We were waiting for you without knowing it. (DON ALHAMBRA *comes forward.*) Hallo!

DON AL. Good morning. [33]

GIU. If this gentleman is an undertaker it's a bad omen.

DON AL. Ceremony of some sort going on?

GIU. (*aside*). He *is* an undertaker! (*Aloud.*) No—a little unimportant family gathering. Nothing in *your* line.

DON AL. Somebody's birthday I suppose?

GIA. Yes, mine!

TESS. And mine!

MAR. And mine!

GIU. And mine!

DON AL. Curious coincidence! And how old may you all be?

TESS. It's a rude question—but about ten minutes.

DON AL. Remarkably fine children! But surely you are jesting?

TESS. In other words, we were married about ten minutes since.

DON AL. Married! You don't mean to say you are married?

MAR. Oh yes, we are married.

DON AL. What, both of you?

ALL. All four of us.

DON AL. (*aside*). Bless my heart, how extremely awkward!

GIA. You don't mind, I suppose?

TESS. You were not thinking of either of us for yourself, I presume? Oh, Giuseppe, look at him—he was. He's heart-broken!

DON AL. No, no, I wasn't! I wasn't!

GIU. Now, my man (*slapping him on the back*), we don't want anything in your line to-day, and if your curiosity's satisfied—you can go!

DON AL. You mustn't call me your man. It's a liberty. I don't think you know who I am.

GIU. Not we, indeed! We are jolly gondoliers, the sons of Baptisto Palmieri, who led the last revolution. Republicans, heart and soul, we hold all men to be equal. As we abhor oppression, we abhor kings: as we detest vain-glory, we detest rank: as we despise effeminacy, we despise wealth. We are Venetian gondoliers—your equals in everything except our calling, and in that at once your masters and your servants.

DON AL. Bless my heart, how unfortunate! One of you may be Baptisto's son, for anything I know to the contrary; but the other is no less a personage than the only son of the late King of Barataria.

ALL. What!

DON AL. And I trust—I *trust* it was that one who slapped me on the shoulder and called me his man!

GIU. One of us a king!

MAR. Not brothers!

TESS. The King of Barataria!

GIA. Well, who'd have thought it!

} *Together*.

MAR. But which is it?

DON AL. What does it matter? As you are both Republicans, and hold kings in detestation, of course you'll abdicate at once. Good morning! (*Going*.)

GIA. *and* TESS. Oh, don't do that! (MARCO *and* GIUSEPPE *stop him*.)

GIU. Well, as to that, of course there are kings and kings. When I say that I detest kings, I mean I detest *bad* kings.

DON AL. I see. It's a delicate distinction.

GIU. Quite so. Now I can conceive a kind of king—an ideal king—the creature of my fancy, you know—who would be absolutely unobjectionable. A king, for instance, who would abolish taxes and make everything cheap, except gondolas——

MAR. And give a great many free entertainments to the gondoliers——

GIU. And let off fireworks on the Grand Canal, and engage all the gondolas for the occasion——

MAR. And scramble money on the Rialto among the gondoliers.

GIU. Such a king would be a blessing to his people, and if I were a king, that is the sort of king I would be.

MAR. And so would I!

DON AL. Come, I'm glad to find your objections are not insuperable.

MAR. *and* GIU. Oh, they're not insuperable.

GIA. *and* TESS. No, they're not insuperable.

GIU. Besides, we are open to conviction.

GIA. Yes; they are open to conviction.

TESS. Oh! they've often been convicted.

GIU. Our views may have been hastily formed on insufficient grounds. They may be crude, ill-digested, erroneous. I've a very poor opinion of the politician who is not open to conviction.

TESS. (*to* GIA.). Oh, he's a fine fellow!

GIA. Yes, that's the sort of politician for *my* money!

DON AL. Then we'll consider it settled. Now, as the country is in a state of insurrection, it is absolutely necessary that you should assume the reins of Government at once; and, until it is ascertained which of you is to be king, I have arranged that you will reign jointly, so that no question can arise hereafter as to the validity of any of your acts.

MAR. As one individual?

DON AL. As one individual.

GIU. (*linking himself with* MARCO). Like this? [34]

DON AL. Something like that.

MAR. And we may take our friends with us, and give them places about the Court?

DON AL. Undoubtedly. That's always done!

MAR. I'm convinced!

GIU. So am I!

TESS. Then the sooner we're off the better.

GIA. We'll just run home and pack up a few things (*going*)——

[34] Here Marco and Giuseppe strike a pose. One can hardly call it "linking" with each other. One places his outstretched left arm on the other's shoulders and vice versa. At the same time they do a little jump and take a coup de pied position. This position is the one they strike from now on whenever they are alluded to as "Your Majesty."

[35] As Tessa speaks her final line, she and Giuseppe move upstage and seat themselves on the steps just below the gondola landing stage. They should remain absorbed in themselves, but not in any way obtrude themselves during Gianetta's song. Marco should stand in some easy position and listen, while the Don stands dead center.

There always seems to be a great temptation on Giuseppe's part to do a little more love-making than he should (he's supposed to be completely absorbed in his new wife, of course) while seated on the steps. The degree of excess always seems to grow with the degree of Tessa's prettiness. I must admit that I, when playing the part, had no difficulty at all in being absorbed in my "new wife." She was extremely pretty.

[36] As Gianetta sings in the first verse, "Ah me, you men will never understand . . ." she lays a hand on the Don's arm, and he is not unaware of this. As she sings it again in the second verse she makes a move as if to do the same thing. This time the Don is ready—and waiting—to cover her hand with his own. But she fools him. Instead of laying her hand on his arm she lays it on her own heart.

Between the two verses she should turn to Marco who takes her in his arms for a moment. Similarly, as she sings, "But Marco's quite another thing," she turns back to the Don for the hand business at the appropriate line.

DON AL. Stop, stop—that won't do at all—ladies are not admitted.
ALL. What!
DON AL. Not admitted. Not at present. Afterwards, perhaps. We'll see.
GIU. Why, you don't mean to say you are going to separate us from our wives!
DON AL. (aside). This is very awkward! (Aloud.) Only for a time—a few months. After all, what is a few months?
TESS. But we've only been married half an hour! (Weeps.) [35]

FINALE—ACT I

SONG—GIANETTA [36]

Kind sir, you cannot have the heart
Our lives to part
From those to whom an hour ago
We were united!
Before our flowing hopes you stem,
Ah, look at them,
And pause before you deal this blow,
All uninvited!
You men can never understand
That heart and hand
Cannot be separated when
We go a-yearning;
You see, you've only women's eyes
To idolize
And only women's hearts, poor men,
To set *you* burning!
Ah me, you men will never understand
That woman's heart is one with woman's hand!

Some kind of charm you seem to find
In womankind—
Some source of unexplained delight
(Unless you're jesting),
But what attracts you, I confess,
I cannot guess,
To me a woman's face is quite
Uninteresting!
If from my sister I were torn
It could be borne—
I should, no doubt, be horrified,
But I could bear it;—
But Marco's quite another thing—
He is my King,
He has my heart and none beside
Shall ever share it!
Ah me, you men will never understand
That woman's heart is one with woman's hand!

RECIT.—DON ALHAMBRA

Do not give way to this uncalled-for grief,
Your separation will be very brief.
To ascertain which is the King
And which the other,
To Barataria's Court I'll bring
His foster-mother;
Her former nurseling to declare
She'll be delighted.

That settled, let each happy pair
Be reunited.

MAR., GIU., GIA.,   Viva! His argument is strong!
   TESS.   Viva! We'll not be parted long!
                Viva! It will be settled soon!
                Viva! Then comes our honeymoon!

[*Exit* DON ALHAMBRA.

QUARTET—MARCO, GIUSEPPE, GIANETTA, TESSA [37]

GIA.   Then one of us will be a Queen,
             And sit on a golden throne,
                With a crown instead,
                Of a hat on her head,
             And diamonds all her own!
      With a beautiful robe of gold and green,
             I've always understood;
                I wonder whether
                She'd wear a feather?
             I rather think she should!
ALL.   Oh, 'tis a glorious thing, I ween,
             To be a regular Royal Queen!
             No half-and-half affair, I mean,
             But a right-down regular Royal Queen!

MAR.   She'll drive about in a carriage and pair,
             With the King on her left-hand side,
                And a milk-white horse,
                As a matter of course,
             Whenever she wants to ride!
      With beautiful silver shoes to wear
             Upon her dainty feet;
                With endless stocks
                Of beautiful frocks
             And as much as she wants to eat!
ALL.   Oh, 'tis a glorious thing, I ween, etc.

TESS.   Whenever she condescends to walk,
             Be sure she'll shine at that,
                With her haughty stare
                And her nose in the air,
             Like a well-born aristocrat!
      At elegant high society talk
             She'll bear away the bell,
                With her "How de do?"
                And her "How are you?"
             And "I trust I see you well!"
ALL.   Oh, 'tis a glorious thing, I ween, etc.

GIU.   And noble lords will scrape and bow,
             And double themselves in two,
                And open their eyes
                In blank surprise
             At whatever she likes to do.
      And everybody will roundly vow
             She's fair as flowers in May,
                And say, "How clever!"
                At whatsoever
             She condescends to say!

[37] *It is on record that Queen Victoria, at the command performance, particularly enjoyed this quartet. One of the cast described the Queen as "a little squat figure in black," and went on to say that she was seen to be beating time with them as they sang ". . . a regular Royal Queen . . ."*

ALL. Oh, 'tis a glorious thing, I ween,
To be a regular Royal Queen!
No half-and-half affair, I mean,
But a right-down regular Royal Queen!

Enter Chorus of Gondoliers and Contadine

CHORUS

Now, pray, what is the cause of this remarkable hilarity?
This sudden ebullition of unmitigated jollity?
Has anybody blessed you with a sample of his charity—
Or have you been adopted by a gentleman of quality?

MAR. *and* GIU. [38] Replying, we sing
As one individual,
As I find I'm a king,
To my kingdom I bid you all.
I'm aware you object
To pavilions and palaces,
But you'll find I respect
Your Republican fallacies.

CHORUS. As they know we object
To pavilions and palaces,
How can they respect
Our Republican fallacies?

MARCO *and* GIUSEPPE

MAR. For every one who feels inclined,
Some post we undertake to find
Congenial with his frame of mind—
And all shall equal be.

GIU. The Chancellor in his peruke—
The Earl, the Marquis, and the Dook,
The Groom, the Butler, and the Cook—
They all shall equal be.

MAR. The Aristocrat who banks with Coutts—
The Aristocrat who hunts and shoots—
The Aristocrat who cleans our boots—
They all shall equal be!

GIU. The Noble Lord who rules the State—
The Noble Lord who cleans the plate—

MAR. The Noble Lord who scrubs the grate—
They all shall equal be!

GIU. The Lord High Bishop orthodox—
The Lord High Coachman on the box—

MAR. The Lord High Vagabond in the stocks—
They all shall equal be!

BOTH. For every one, etc.

Sing high, sing low, [39]
Wherever they go,
They all shall equal be! [40]

CHORUS. Sing high, sing low,
Wherever they go,
They all shall equal be!

[38] *This duet, if properly done, is very amusing. Marco and Giuseppe strike their pose as "one individual" and proceed to sing as if they were, each taking a part of each line and turning his head to the other as they sing, thus:*

GIU. *Replying, we*
MAR. *sing*
As one indi-
GIU. *vidual,*
As I find I'm a
MAR. *king,*
To my kingdom I
GIU. *bid you all.*
I'm aware you ob-
MAR. *ject*
To pavilions and
GIU. *palaces,*
But you'll find I re-
MAR. *spect*
Your Republican
GIU. *fallacies.*
You'll find I re
MAR. *spect*
Your Republican
GIU. *fallacies.*

(The repeat of "you'll find I respect . . ." is not shown in the libretto. Nevertheless, this is how it is sung.)

[39] *A traditional conundrum is asked of all new-comers to the D'Oyly Carte Company. Question: Who are the two Chinese characters in The Gondoliers? Answer: Sing Hi and Sing Lo.*

[40] *The suggestion that it was Gilbert's intention to write an opera in which no one principal would stand out above another is perhaps emphasized in these lines.*

The Earl, the Marquis, and the Dook,
The Groom, the Butler, and the Cook,
The Aristocrat who banks with Coutts,
The Aristocrat who cleans the boots,
The Noble Lord who rules the State,
The Noble Lord who scrubs the grate,
The Lord High Bishop orthodox,
The Lord High Vagabond in the stocks—

For every one, etc.

> Sing high, sing low,
> Wherever they go,
>   They all shall equal be!
>
> Then hail! O King,
>   Whichever you may be,
> To you we sing,
>   But do not bend the knee.
> Then hail! O King.

MARCO *and* GIUSEPPE (*together*)

Come, let's away—our island crown awaits me—
Conflicting feelings rend my soul apart!
The thought of Royal dignity elates me,
But leaving thee behind me breaks my heart!

(*Addressing* GIANETTA *and* TESSA.)

GIANETTA *and* TESSA (*together*)

Farewell, my love; on board you must be getting;
But while upon the sea you gaily roam,
Remember that a heart for thee is fretting—
The tender little heart you've left at home!

GIA.

> [41] Now, Marco dear, [42]
> My wishes hear:
>   While you're away
> It's understood
> You will be good,
>   And not too gay.
> To every trace
> Of maiden grace
>   You will be blind,
> And will not glance
> By any chance
>   On womankind! [43]
> If you are wise,
> You'll shut your eyes
>   Till we arrive,
> And not address
> A lady less
>   Than forty-five.
> You'll please to frown
> On every gown
>   That you may see;
> And, O my pet,
> You won't forget
>   You've married me!

[41] *This solo and the one following should be very touching, and should be staged with full attention centered on the two separate couples, in order—first, Gianetta and Marco, then Tessa and Giuseppe.*

[42] *Words and music on page 690.*

To every trace
Of maiden grace
You will be blind

[43] *The Bab sketch might seem to suggest that some comedy should be introduced during this number. For instance, Giuseppe would begin to flirt with one of the other girls and be caught by Tessa who would promptly slap his hand. I disagree strongly with this interpretation. There is a great similarity between this number and "Tit-willow" (The Mikado, Note 99). If there is any comedy it must arise from the situation, not by interpolated visual gags.*

Lighting is of extreme importance, too, in my opinion. The D'Oyly Carte Company always kept the stage practically "full-up." I have felt that a fully lighted stage detracts from the beauty of the song's sentiment. Not only that, it keeps a whole chorus in full view, and try as one may, one cannot keep a chorus so still and quiet that it does not intrude into the scene.

But take the stage to "black," and just spot each soloist and her partner as they sing, and the eye cannot wander. And if the eye doesn't wander, the ear won't either. Finally, spot the four as they come together for the last quartette, fading out on the last note. Then a "sudden death full-up." The effect is tremendous.

And O my darling, O my pet,
Whatever else you may forget
In yonder isle beyond the sea,
Do not forget you've married me!

**You'll sit and mope
All day, I hope**

TESS.
You'll lay your head
Upon your bed
At set of sun.
You will not sing
Of anything
To any one.
You'll sit and mope
All day, I hope,
And shed a tear
Upon the life
Your little wife
Is passing here.
And if so be
You think of me,
Please tell the moon!
I'll read it all
In rays that fall
On the lagoon:
You'll be so kind
As tell the wind
How you may be,
And send me words
By little birds
To comfort me!

And O my darling, O my pet,
Whatever else you may forget,
In yonder isle beyond the sea,
Do not forget you've married me!

QUARTET.   O, my darling, O my pet, etc.

CHORUS (*during which a "Xebeque" [44] is hauled alongside the quay*)

Then away we go to an island fair
That lies in a Southern sea:
We know not where, and we don't much care,
Wherever that isle may be.

THE MEN (*hauling on boat*).
One, two, three,
Haul!
One, two, three,
Haul!
One, two, three,
Haul!
With a will!

ALL.
When the breezes are a-blowing [45]
The ship will be going,
When they don't we shall all stand still!
Then away we go to an island fair,
We know not where, and we don't much care,
Wherever that isle may be.

[44] Xebeque (Xebec). Originally a Spanish two-masted vessel plying in the Mediterranean, lateen-rigged, but with some square sail. Formerly a warship. (The figurehead of the D'Oyly Carte Company's "Xebeque" was a recumbent nude figure of a warriorlike man carrying a spear or trident.)

[45] These lines invariably remind me of "Rock-a-bye Baby."

SOLO—MARCO

Away we go
  To a balmy isle,
Where the roses blow
  All the winter while.

ALL (*hoisting sail*). [46]

Then away we go to an island fair
  That lies in a Southern sea:
Then away we go to an island fair,
  Then away, then away, then away!

[*The men embark on the "Xebeque,"* MARCO *and* GIUSEPPE *embracing* GIANETTA *and* TESSA. *The girls wave a farewell to the men as the curtain falls.*

END OF ACT I

ACT II

SCENE.—*Pavilion in the Court of Barataria.* MARCO *and* GIUSEPPE, *magnificently dressed, are seated on two thrones, occupied in cleaning the crown and the sceptre. The Gondoliers are discovered, dressed, some as courtiers, officers of rank, etc., and others as private soldiers and servants of various degrees. All are enjoying themselves without reference to social distinctions—some playing cards, others throwing dice, some reading, others playing cup and ball, "morra," [47] etc.*

CHORUS OF MEN *with* MARCO *and* GIUSEPPE

Of happiness the very pith
      In Barataria you may see:
A monarchy that's tempered with
      Republican Equality.
This form of government we find
The beau ideal of its kind—
A despotism strict combined
      With absolute equality!

MARCO *and* GIUSEPPE [48]

Two kings, of undue pride bereft,
      Who act in perfect unity,
Whom you can order right and left
      With absolute impunity.
Who put their subjects at their ease
By doing all they can to please!
And thus, to earn their bread-and-cheese,
      Seize every opportunity.

CHORUS.   Of happiness the very pith, etc.

MAR. Gentlemen, we are much obliged to you for your expressions of satisfaction and good feeling—[49] I say, we are much obliged to you for your expressions of satisfaction and good feeling.

ALL. We heard you.

MAR. We are delighted, at any time, to fall in with sentiments so charmingly expressed.

ALL. That's all right.

[46] *Much business and making of farewells goes on at this point. It should be hammed up as much as possible. It is by way of being a burlesque of a Verdi opera and the same extravagant moves and gestures are required as were requested of Grossmith by Sullivan in The Sorcerer.*

[47] Morra. *A variation of mora, a popular early 18th-century game in Italy. One player guesses the number of fingers concealed by another player.*

[48] *Marco and Giuseppe, resplendent in their kingly dress, still carrying crown and sceptre as well as polishing brush and cloth, march down to front center of the stage. At one point the duet is held up for a second as they audibly breathe on each object to be polished and then vigorously commence to rub as they start singing again, thus:*

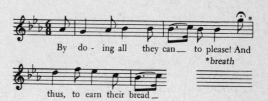

[49] *The surrounding gondoliers, now gentlemen of the Court, take no notice of Marco, so in repeating his line he raises his voice.*

GIU. At the same time there is just one little grievance that we should like to ventilate.

ALL (*angrily*). What?

GIU. Don't be alarmed—it's not serious. It is arranged that, until it is decided which of us two is the actual King, we are to act as one person.

GIORGIO. Exactly.

GIU. Now, although we act as *one* person, we are, in point of fact, *two* persons. [50]

ANNIBALE. Ah, I don't think we can go into that. It is a legal fiction, and legal fictions are solemn things. Situated as we are, we can't recognize two independent responsibilities.

GIU. No; but you can recognize two independent appetites. It's all very well to say we act as one person, but when you supply us with only one ration between us, I should describe it as a legal fiction carried a little too far.

ANNI. It's rather a nice point. I don't like to express an opinion off-hand. Suppose we reserve it for argument before the full Court? [51]

MAR. Yes, but what are we to do in the meantime?

MAR. *and* GIU. We want our tea.

ANNI. I think we may make an interim order for double rations on their Majesties entering into the usual undertaking to indemnify in the event of an adverse decision?

GIOR. That, I think, will meet the case. But you must work hard—stick to it—nothing like work.

GIU. Oh, certainly. We quite understand that a man who holds the magnificent position of King should do something to justify it. We are called "Your Majesty"; we are allowed to buy ourselves magnificent clothes; our subjects frequently nod to us in the streets; the sentries always return our salutes; and we enjoy the inestimable privilege of heading the subscription lists to all the principal charities. In return for these advantages the least we can do is to make ourselves useful about the Palace.

SONG—GIUSEPPE *with* CHORUS [52]

Rising early in the morning,
    We proceed to light the fire,
Then our Majesty adorning
    In its workaday attire,
        We embark without delay
        On the duties of the day. [53]

First, we polish off some batches
Of political despatches,
    And foreign politicians circumvent:
Then, if business isn't heavy,
We may hold a Royal *levée*,
    Or ratify some Acts of Parliament.
Then we probably review the household troops—
With the usual "Shalloo humps!" and "Shalloo hoops!" [54]
Or receive with ceremonial and state
An interesting Eastern potentate.
    After that we generally
    Go and dress our private *valet*—
(It's a rather nervous duty—he's a touchy little man)—
    Write some letters literary
    For our private secretary—
He is shaky in his spelling, so we help him if we can.
    Then, in view of cravings inner,

[50] *In spite of Gilbert's italics the emphasis in Giuseppe's speech should be as follows:* "Now, although we act as one person, we are, in point of fact, two persons." *The emphasis on the word* "one," *if any, should be in Giuseppe's previous lines:* ". . . until it is decided which of us two is the actual King, we are to act as one person."

[51] *Compare Annibale's lines with those of Pooh-Bah and Pish-Tush in The Mikado:* "We might reserve that point." "True, it could be argued six months hence, before the full Court."

[52] *Words and music on page 694.*

The duties of the day

[53] *According to one member of the cast at the command performance,* "Queen Victoria was very amused when Barrington sang of the duties of a Republican monarch."

[54] *Shalloo humps! Shalloo hoops! The Sergeant-Major's way of giving the old-fashioned military order* "Shoulder arms." *The modern order is* "Slope arms," *and is given as* "Slo-o-pe Hipe!"

We go down and order dinner;
Then we polish the Regalia and the Coronation Plate—
        Spend an hour in titivating
        All our Gentlemen-in-Waiting;
Or we run on little errands for the Ministers of State.
        Oh, philosophers may sing
        Of the troubles of a King;
Yet the duties are delightful, and the privileges great;
        But the privilege and pleasure
        That we treasure beyond measure
Is to run on little errands for the Ministers of State.

CHORUS. Oh, philosophers may sing, etc.

After luncheon (making merry
On a bun and glass of sherry),
        If we've nothing in particular to do,
We may make a Proclamation,
Or receive a Deputation—
        Then we possibly create a Peer or two.
Then we help a fellow-creature on his path
With the Garter or the Thistle or the Bath [55]
Or we dress and toddle off in semi-state
To a festival, a function, or a *fête*.
        Then we go and stand as sentry
        At the Palace (private entry),
Marching hither, marching thither, up and down and to and fro,
        While the warrior on duty
        Goes in search of beer and beauty
(And it generally happens that he hasn't far to go).
        He relieves us, if he's able,
        Just in time to lay the table,
Then we dine and serve the coffee, and at half-past twelve or one,
        With a pleasure that's emphatic,
        We retire to our attic
With the gratifying feeling that our duty has been done!
        Oh, philosophers may sing
        Of the troubles of a King,
But of pleasures there are many and of worries there are none;
        And the culminating pleasure
        That we treasure beyond measure
Is the gratifying feeling that our duty has been done!

CHORUS. Oh, philosophers may sing, etc.

[*Exeunt all but* MARCO *and* GIUSEPPE.

GIU. [56] Yes, it really is a very pleasant existence. They're all so singularly kind and considerate. You don't find them wanting to do this, or wanting to do that, or saying "It's my turn now." No, they let us have all the fun to ourselves, and never seem to grudge it.

MAR. It makes one feel quite selfish. It almost seems like taking advantage of their good nature.

GIU. How nice they were about the double rations.

MAR. Most considerate. Ah! there's only one thing wanting to make us thoroughly comfortable.

GIU. And that is?

MAR. The dear little wives we left behind us three months ago.

GIU. Yes, it *is* dull without female society. We can do without everything else, but we can't do without that.

[55] Garter, Thistle, Bath. *Orders of knighthood.*

We retire to our attic

[56] *During this dialogue Giuseppe picks up a mandolin similar to that used in Act I. (It's probably the same one.) With this he quietly accompanies Marco as the latter sings the next solo. The orchestration is scored in such a way as to suggest the plucking of the strings of such an instrument.*

MAR. And if we have that in perfection, we have everything. There is only one recipe for perfect happiness.

[57] *With the possible exception of "A Wandering Minstrel" in The Mikado, this song of Marco's is probably the most popular and widely sung tenor aria of the whole series. This, no doubt, is because it is more readily acceptable out of context as a solo. An interesting comparison is found between this aria and a ballad that Sullivan wrote, "A Life That Lives for You." Throughout both numbers there is a definite similarity, and the coda, if transposed, is identical for several bars:*

"Take a Pair of Sparkling Eyes"

"A Life That Lives for You"

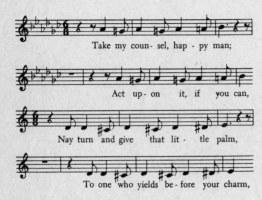

Take my coun-sel, hap-py man;

Act up-on it, if you can,

Nay turn and give that lit-tle palm,

To one who yields be-fore your charm,

But, as Sullivan said when it was once suggested that a tune of his was very like that of another composer: "Quite likely—for after all, we only have eight notes between us."

[58] *Words and music on page 698.*

[57] SONG—MARCO [58]

Take a pair of sparkling eyes,
 Hidden, ever and anon,
  In a merciful eclipse—
Do not heed their mild surprise—
 Having passed the Rubicon,
  Take a pair of rosy lips;
Take a figure trimly planned—
 Such as admiration whets
  (Be particular in this);
Take a tender little hand,
 Fringed with dainty fingerettes,
  Press it—in parenthesis;—
Ah! Take all these, you lucky man—
Take and keep them, if you can!

Take a pretty little cot—
 Quite a miniature affair—
  Hung about with trellised vine,
Furnish it upon the spot
 With the treasures rich and rare
  I've endeavoured to define.
Live to love and love to live—
 You will ripen at your ease,
  Growing on the sunny side—
Fate has nothing more to give.
 You're a dainty man to please
  If you are not satisfied.
Ah! Take my counsel, happy man;
Act upon it, if you can!

Enter Chorus of Contadine, running in, led by FIAMETTA *and* VITTORIA. *They are met by all the Ex-Gondoliers, who welcome them heartily.*

SCENA—CHORUS OF GIRLS, QUARTET, DUET *and* CHORUS

Here we are, at the risk of our lives,
From ever so far, and we've brought your wives—
And to that end we've crossed the main,
And don't intend to return again!

FIA. Though obedience is strong,
   Curiosity's stronger—
 We waited for long,
   Till we couldn't wait longer.

VIT. It's imprudent, we know,
   But without your society
 Existence was slow,
   And we wanted variety—

ALL. So here we are, at the risk of our lives,
 From ever so far, and we've brought your wives—
 And to that end we've crossed the main,
 And don't intend to return again!

Enter GIANETTA *and* TESSA. *They rush to the arms of* MARCO *and* GIUSEPPE

GIU.	Tessa!
TESS.	Giuseppe!
GIA.	Marco!
MAR.	Gianetta!

Embrace.

TESSA *and* GIANETTA

TESS.	After sailing to this island—
GIA.	Tossing in a manner frightful,
TESS.	We are all once more on dry land—
GIA.	And we find the change delightful,
TESS.	As at home we've been remaining—
	We've not seen you both for ages,
GIA.	Tell me, are you fond of reigning?—
	How's the food, and what's the wages?
TESS.	Does your new employment please ye?—
GIA.	How does Royalizing strike you?
TESS.	Is it difficult or easy?—
GIA.	Do you think your subjects like you?
TESS.	I am anxious to elicit,
	Is it plain and easy steering?
GIA.	Take it altogether, is it
	Better fun than gondoliering?
BOTH.	We shall both go on requesting
	Till you tell us, never doubt it;
	Everything is interesting,
	Tell us, tell us all about it!
CHORUS.	They will both go on requesting, etc.
TESS.	Is the populace exacting?
GIA.	Do they keep you at a distance?
TESS.	All unaided are you acting,
GIA.	Or do they provide assistance?
TESS.	When you're busy, have you got to
	Get up early in the morning?
GIA.	If you do what you ought not to,
	Do they give the usual warning?
TESS.	With a horse do they equip you?
GIA.	Lots of trumpeting and drumming?
TESS.	Do the Royal tradesmen tip you?
GIA.	Ain't the livery becoming!
TESS.	Does your human being inner
	Feed on everything that nice is?
GIA.	Do they give you wine for dinner;
	Peaches, sugar-plums, and ices?
BOTH.	We shall both go on requesting
	Till you tell us, never doubt it;
	Everything is interesting,
	Tell us, tell us all about it!
CHORUS.	They will both go on requesting, etc.

MAR. This is indeed a most delightful surprise!

TESS. Yes, we thought you'd like it. You see, it was like this. After you left we felt very dull and mopey, and the days crawled by, and you never wrote; so at last I said to Gianetta, "I can't stand this any longer; those two poor Monarchs haven't got any one to mend their stockings

[59] *On December 18, 1926, the D'Oyly Carte Company made its first transatlantic trip (from Liverpool) in many years for a coast-to-coast-and-back tour of Canada, opening in Montreal on January 4, 1927, with The Gondoliers. Tessa's line ". . . and, thank goodness, that's done" was spoken with a wealth of meaning that did not go unappreciated by a very appreciative audience. Tessa was such a bad sailor.*

[60] *. . . until Nurse turns up. This should be a straight allusion to Luiz' mother. The manner in which the line is spoken, if too "cute," can easily give the impression that Giuseppe was saying "Nursie," which is a very cheap laugh and certainly not Gilbert.*

[61] *Words and music on page 702.*

[62] *Xeres, Manzanilla, Montero. The first two are unquestionably sherries and so I'm reasonably certain that Montero was also a sherry. But upon reference to the Webster and Oxford dictionaries I find that the only existing reference to Montero is as "a huntsman's cap with a flap"!*

With respect to this musical number as a whole, it is the only one that would today resemble what is called a production number. The Sunday (London) Times said of it in 1899: "The theme is inspiriting; the dance, a treat to witness, executed with a precision and élan that professional dancers might envy. Nothing to equal them has been done before at the Savoy." The same paper also took note of the comparatively short skirts worn by the ladies for the first time, and how very gratifying it was to have it "revealed to a curious world that the Savoy chorus (ladies, of course) are a very well-legged lot." It is significant that although Gilbert directed and produced the operas himself and in at least one case designed the ladies' dresses (Patience: The Rapturous Maidens), a choreographer, Mr. John d'Auban, was brought in to arrange the incidental dances, with the one exception of The Gondoliers, when a special choreographer was engaged for this number.

or sew on their buttons or patch their clothes—at least, I hope they haven't—let us all pack up a change and go and see how they're getting on." And she said, "Done," and they all said, "Done"; and we asked old Giacopo to lend us his boat, and *he* said, "Done"; and we've crossed the sea, and, thank goodness, *that's* done; [59] and here we are, and—and—*I've* done!

GIA. And now—which of you is King?

TESS. And which of us is Queen?

GIU. That we shan't know until Nurse turns up. [60] But never mind that—the question is, how shall we celebrate the commencement of our honeymoon? Gentlemen, will you allow us to offer you a magnificent banquet?

ALL. We will!

GIU. Thanks very much; and, ladies, what do you say to a dance?

TESS. A banquet *and* a dance! O, it's too much happiness!

CHORUS *and* DANCE [61]

Dance a cachucha, fandango, bolero,
Xeres we'll drink—Manzanilla, Montero—[62]
Wine, when it runs in abundance, enhances
The reckless delight of that wildest of dances!
    To the pretty pitter-pitter-patter,
    And the clitter-clitter-clitter-clatter—
        Clitter—clitter—clatter,
        Pitter—pitter—patter,
    Patter, patter, patter, patter, we'll dance.
Old Xeres we'll drink—Manzanilla, Montero;
For wine, when it runs in abundance, enhances
The reckless delight of that wildest of dances!

(*Cachucha*)

The dance is interrupted by the unexpected appearance of DON ALHAMBRA, *who looks on with astonishment.* MARCO *and* GIUSEPPE *appear embarrassed. The others run off, except Drummer Boy, who is driven off by* DON ALHAMBRA.

DON AL. Good evening. Fancy ball?

GIU. No, not exactly. A little friendly dance. That's all. Sorry you're late.

DON AL. But I saw a groom dancing, and a footman!

MAR. Yes. That's the Lord High Footman.

DON AL. And, dear me, a common little drummer boy!

GIU. Oh no! That's the Lord High Drummer Boy.

DON AL. But surely, surely the servants'-hall is the place for these gentry?

GIU. Oh dear no! *We* have appropriated the servant's-hall. It's the Royal Apartment, and accessible only by tickets obtainable at the Lord Chamberlain's office.

MAR. We really must have some place that we can call our own.

DON AL. (*puzzled*). I'm afraid I'm not quite equal to the intellectual pressure of the conversation.

GIU. You see, the Monarchy has been re-modelled on Republican principles.

DON AL. What!

GIU. All departments rank equally, and everybody is at the head of his department.

DON AL. I see.

MAR. I'm afraid you're annoyed.

DON AL. No. I won't say that. It's not quite what I expected.

GIU. I'm awfully sorry.

MAR. So am I.

GIU. By the by, can I offer you anything after your voyage? A plate of macaroni and a rusk?

DON AL. (*preoccupied*). No, no—nothing—nothing.

GIU. Obliged to be careful?

DON AL. Yes—gout. [63] You see, in every Court there are distinctions that must be observed.

GIU. (*puzzled*). There are, are there?

DON AL. Why, of course. For instance, you wouldn't have a Lord High Chancellor play leapfrog with his own cook.

MAR. Why not?

DON AL. Why not! Because a Lord High Chancellor is a personage of great dignity, who should never, under any circumstances, place himself in the position of being told to tuck in his tuppenny, except by noblemen of his own rank. A Lord High Archbishop, for instance, might tell a Lord High Chancellor to tuck in his tuppenny, but certainly not a cook, gentlemen, certainly not a cook.

GIU. Not even a Lord High Cook?

DON AL. My good friend, that is a rank that is not recognized at the Lord Chamberlain's office. No, no, it won't do. I'll give you an instance in which the experiment was tried.

SONG—DON ALHAMBRA, *with* MARCO *and* GIUSEPPE [64]

DON AL.
There lived a King, as I've been told,
In the wonder-working days of old,
When hearts were twice as good as gold,
 And twenty times as mellow.
Good-temper triumphed in his face,
And in his heart he found a place
For all the erring human race
 And every wretched fellow.
When he had Rhenish wine to drink
It made him very sad to think
That some, at junket or at jink, [65]
 Must be content with toddy. [66]

MAR. *and* GIU.
With toddy, must be content with toddy.

DON AL.
He wished all men as rich as he
(And he was rich as rich could be),
So to the top of every tree
 Promoted everybody.

MAR. *and* GIU.
Now, that's the kind of King for me—
He wished all men as rich as he,
So to the top of every tree
 Promoted everybody!

DON AL.
Lord Chancellors were cheap as sprats,
And Bishops in their shovel hats [67]
Were plentiful as tabby cats—
 In point of fact, too many.
Ambassadors cropped up like hay,
Prime Ministers and such as they
Grew like asparagus in May,
 And Dukes were three a penny.
On every side Field-Marshals gleamed,

[63] *Gilbert suffered from gout himself. So it was on his mind.*

[64] *Words and music on page 706.*

[65] Junket . . . jink. *Junket means to make merry with good cheer; to go on a pleasure excursion. Jink means to elude by a quick turn; the winning of a card game, "Spoil five, twenty-five, or forty-five." High jinks: a name for various frolics at drinking parties.*

[66] Toddy. *Scotch whisky, or rum, with sugar and hot water. (As opposed to this good-tempered king's preference for Rhenish wines. There's no disputing tastes!)*

[67] Shovel hat. *A stiff, broad-brimmed hat, turned up at the sides and with a shovellike curve in front and at back; a typical cleric's hat.*

THE GONDOLIERS

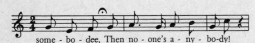

some - bo - dee, Then no - one's a - ny - bo-dy!

Small beer [68] were Lords-Lieutenant deemed,
With Admirals the ocean teemed
All round his wide dominions.

MAR. *and* GIU. With Admirals all round his wide dominions.

DON AL. And Party Leaders you might meet
In twos and threes in every street
Maintaining, with no little heat,
Their various opinions.

MAR. *and* GIU. Now that's a sight you couldn't beat—
Two Party Leaders in each street
Maintaining, with no little heat,
Their various opinions.

DON AL. That King, although no one denies
His heart was of abnormal size,
Yet he'd have acted otherwise
If he had been acuter.
The end is easily foretold,
When every blessed thing you hold
Is made of silver, or of gold,
You long for simple pewter.
When you have nothing else to wear
But cloth of gold and satins rare,
For cloth of gold you cease to care—
Up goes the price of shoddy.

MAR. *and* GIU. Of shoddy, up goes the price of shoddy.

DON AL. In short, whoever you may be,
To this conclusion you'll agree,
When every one is somebodee, [69]
Then no one's anybody!

MAR. *and* GIU. Now that's as plain as plain can be,
To this conclusion we agree—

ALL. When every one is somebodee,
Then no one's anybody!

GIANETTA *and* TESSA *enter unobserved. The two girls, impelled by curiosity, remain listening at the back of the stage.*

DON AL. And now I have some important news to communicate. His Grace the Duke of Plaza-Toro, Her Grace the Duchess, and their beautiful daughter Casilda—I say their beautiful daughter Casilda——
GIU. We heard you.
DON AL. Have arrived at Barataria, and may be here at any moment.
MAR. The Duke and Duchess are nothing to us.
DON AL. But the daughter—the beautiful daughter! Aha! Oh, you're a lucky dog, one of you!
GIU. I think you're a very incomprehensible old gentleman.
DON AL. Not a bit—I'll explain. Many years ago when you (whichever you are) were a baby, you (whichever you are) were married to a little girl who has grown up to be the most beautiful young lady in Spain. That beautiful young lady will be here to claim you (whichever you are) in half an hour, and I congratulate that one (whichever it is) with all my heart.
MAR. Married when a baby!
GIU. But we were married three months ago!

DON AL. One of you—only one. The other (whichever it is) is an unintentional bigamist.

GIA. *and* TESS. (*coming forward*). Well, upon my word!

DON AL. Eh? Who are these young people?

TESS. Who are we? Why their wives, of course. We've just arrived.

DON AL. Their wives! Oh dear, this is very unfortunate! Oh dear, this complicates matters! Dear, dear, what will Her Majesty say?

GIA. And do you mean to say that one of these Monarchs was already married?

TESS. And that neither of us will be a Queen?

DON AL. That is the idea I intended to convey. (TESSA *and* GIANETTA *begin to cry.*)

GIU. (*to* TESSA). Tessa, my dear, dear child——

TESS. Get away! perhaps it's you!

MAR. (*to* GIA.). My poor, poor little woman!

GIA. Don't! Who knows whose husband you are?

TESS. And pray, why didn't you tell us all about it before they left Venice?

DON AL. Because, if I had, no earthly temptation would have induced these gentlemen to leave two such extremely fascinating and utterly irresistible little ladies!

TESS. There's something in that.

DON AL. I may mention that you will not be kept long in suspense, as the old lady who nursed the Royal child is at present in the torture chamber, waiting for me to interview her.

GIU. Poor old girl. Hadn't you better go and put her out of her suspense?

DON AL. Oh no—there's no hurry—she's all right. She has all the illustrated papers. However, I'll go and interrogate her, and, in the meantime, may I suggest the absolute propriety of your regarding yourselves as single young ladies. Good evening!

[*Exit* DON ALHAMBRA.

GIA. Well, here's a pleasant state of things!

MAR. Delightful. One of us is married to two young ladies, and nobody knows which; and the other is married to one young lady whom nobody can identify!

GIA. And one of us is married to one of you, and the other is married to nobody.

TESS. But which of you is married to which of us, and what's to become of the other? (*About to cry.*)

GIU. It's quite simple. Observe. Two husbands have managed to acquire three wives. Three wives—two husbands. (*Reckoning up.*) That's two-thirds of a husband to each wife.

TESS. O Mount Vesuvius, here we are in arithmetic! My good sir, one can't marry a vulgar fraction! [70]

GIU. You've no right to call me a vulgar fraction.

MAR. We are getting rather mixed. The situation is entangled. Let's try and comb it out.

QUARTET—MARCO, GIUSEPPE, GIANETTA, TESSA

> In a contemplative fashion,
> 　　And a tranquil frame of mind,
> Free from every kind of passion,
> 　　Some solution let us find. [71]
> Let us grasp the situation,
> 　　Solve the complicated plot—
> Quiet, calm deliberation
> 　　Disentangles every knot.

[70] Vulgar fraction. *A mathematical term that is synonymous with a common fraction using a numerator and denominator (as opposed to a decimal fraction).*

[71] *It's paradoxical that Gilbert should have been writing these words at the same time that he, Sullivan and Carte were all seething with animosity; and that Sullivan should then have set the words to what is one of the outstanding examples of countermelody extant; and that having written them and set them, both should then forget them and indulge in a quarrel so violent that it ended the collaboration and culminated in litigation.*

THE GONDOLIERS

TESS.   I, no doubt, Giuseppe wedded—
      That's, of course, a slice of luck.
  He is rather dunder-headed,
      Still distinctly, he's a duck.

THE OTHERS. In a contemplative fashion, etc.

GIA.   I, a victim, too, of Cupid,
      Marco married—that is clear.
  He's particularly stupid,
      Still distinctly, he's a dear.

THE OTHERS. Let us grasp the situation, etc.

MAR.   To Gianetta I was mated;
      I can prove it in a trice:
  Though her charms are overrated,
      Still I own she's rather nice.

THE OTHERS. In a contemplative fashion, etc.

GIU.   I to Tessa, willy-nilly,
      All at once a victim fell.
  She is what is called a silly,
      Still she answers pretty well.

THE OTHERS. Let us grasp the situation, etc.

MAR.   Now when we were pretty babies
           Some one married us, that's clear—

GIA.   And if I can catch her
            I'll pinch her and scratch her,
        And send her away with a flea in her ear.

GIU.   He whom that young lady married,
           To receive her can't refuse.

TESS.   If I overtake her
            I'll warrant I'll make her
        To shake in her aristocratical shoes!

GIA. (*to* TESS.).   If she married your Giuseppe
           You and he will have to part—

TESS. (*to* GIA.).   If I have to do it
            I'll warrant she'll rue it—
       I'll teach her to marry the man of my heart!

TESS. (*to* GIA.).   If she married Messer Marco
           You're a spinster, that is plain—

GIA. (*to* TESS.).   No matter—no matter
           If I can get at her
       I doubt if her mother will know her again!

ALL.   Quiet, calm deliberation
           Disentangles every knot!

                        [*Exeunt, pondering.* [72]

MARCH. *Enter procession of Retainers, heralding approach of* DUKE, DUCHESS, *and* CASILDA. *All three are now dressed with the utmost magnificence.* [73]

CHORUS OF MEN, *with* DUKE *and* DUCHESS

With ducal pomp and ducal pride
  (Announce these comers,
    O ye kettle-drummers!)
Comes Barataria's high-born bride.
  (Ye sounding cymbals clang!)
She comes to claim the Royal hand—
  (Proclaim their Graces,
    O ye double basses!)
Of the King who rules this goodly land.
  (Ye brazen brasses bang!)

[72] With the added direction, should it be decided to present the second act in two scenes: "Blackout on Scene 1."

[73] The entrance of the ducal party gains added impetus and drive if the act is presented in two scenes. From "Black" the lights "Fade in" to the accompaniment of highly ceremonial music, and immediately the Procession of Retainers begins to make its dignified and martial entrance, followed by the swaggering appearance of the Duke, Duchess and Casilda. The impact is far greater if carried out in this way than by letting the previous scene run down and attempting to bring it back into gear without the aid of some lighting gimmick. I am convinced that Gilbert, had he been in possession of the necessary lighting equipment, would have directed it in this manner.

DUKE *and* DUCH.   This polite attention touches
                  Heart of Duke and heart of Duchess.
                      Who resign their pet
                      With profound regret.
                  She of beauty was a model
                  When a tiny tiddle-toddle,
                      And at twenty-one
                      She's excelled by none!

CHORUS.   With ducal pomp and ducal pride, etc.

DUKE [74] (*to his attendants*). Be good enough to inform His Majesty that His Grace the Duke of Plaza-Toro, Limited, [75] has arrived, and begs——

CAS. Desires——

DUCH. Demands——

DUKE. And demands an audience. (*Exeunt attendants.*) And now, my child, prepare to receive the husband to whom you were united under such interesting and romantic circumstances.

CAS. But which is it? There are two of them!

DUKE. It is true that at present His Majesty is a double gentleman; but as soon as the circumstances of his marriage are ascertained, he will, *ipso facto*, boil down to a single gentleman—thus presenting a unique example of an individual who becomes a single man and a married man by the same operation.

DUCH. (*severely*). I have known instances in which the characteristics of both conditions existed concurrently in the same individual.

DUKE. Ah, he couldn't have been a Plaza-Toro.

DUCH. Oh! couldn't he, though!

CAS. Well, whatever happens, I shall, of course, be a dutiful wife, but I can never love my husband.

DUKE. I don't know. It's extraordinary what unprepossessing people one can love if one gives one's mind to it.

DUCH. I loved your father.

DUKE. My love—that remark is a little hard, I think? Rather cruel, perhaps? Somewhat uncalled-for, I venture to believe?

DUCH. It was very difficult, my dear; but I said to myself, "That man is a Duke, and I *will* love him." Several of my relations bet me I couldn't, but I did—desperately!

SONG—DUCHESS [76]

    On the day when I was wedded
      To your admirable sire,
    I acknowledge that I dreaded
      An explosion of his ire.
    I was overcome with panic—
    For his temper was volcanic,
      And I didn't dare revolt,
      For I feared a thunderbolt!
    I was always very wary,
      For his fury was ecstatic—
    His refined vocabulary
      Most unpleasantly emphatic.
        To the thunder
          Of this Tartar
        I knocked under
          Like a martyr;
        When intently
          He was fuming,

[74] *The role of the Duke of Plaza-Toro marked my first appearance on Broadway (the Martin Beck Theater, 1934).*

[75] *Limited. A limited company in England is the equivalent of a corporation in the United States. I was a little worried when I did not receive the laugh that usually accompanied this line. When it was explained to me I very naturally wanted to change the word to incorporated. For some time I resisted the temptation, but one night I succumbed—not only in the second act but in the first as well: "A Company to be known as the Duke of Plaza-Toro, Incorporated . . ." and, of course, ". . . the Duke of Plaza-Toro, Incorporated, has arrived." I knew as well as everybody else that I was committing sacrilege, and at the next performance I went back to the official lines. But the laugh was never again half so big.*

[76] *For many years this gem of a comic song was smothered to quite a large extent by comedy business interpolated by the Duke. I can't emphasize too often the fact that great Gilbert comedy should not be embroidered by too much business. Heaven knows, I've indulged in plenty in my day, but never to a point where I was competing with the basic comedy of the words.*

THE GONDOLIERS

[77] During this verse there is some business given to the Duchess but it is only to emphasize the words of the song, and whatever laughs there are belong to her. The Duke has no right to butt in at any time; he only responds.

[78] On the same occasion that I used the "Incorporated" I naturally had to alter this expression. It became "as an Incorporated Company."

I was gently
Unassuming—
When reviling
Me completely,
I was smiling
Very sweetly:
Giving him the very best, and getting back the very worst—
That is how I tried to tame your great progenitor—at first!
But I found that a reliance [77]
On my threatening appearance,
And a resolute defiance
Of marital interference,
And a gentle intimation
Of my firm determination
To see what I could do
To be wife and husband too
Was the only thing required
For to make his temper supple,
And you couldn't have desired
A more reciprocating couple.
Ever willing
To be wooing,
We were billing—
We were cooing;
When I merely
From him parted,
We were nearly
Broken-hearted—
When in sequel
Reunited,
We were equal-
Ly delighted.
So with double-shotted guns and colors nailed unto the mast,
I tamed your insignificant progenitor—at last!

CAS. My only hope is that when my husband sees what a shady family he has married into he will repudiate the contract altogether.

DUKE. Shady? A nobleman shady, who is blazing in the lustre of unaccustomed pocket-money? A nobleman shady, who can look back upon ninety-five quarterings? It is not every nobleman who is ninety-five quarters in arrear—I mean, who can look back upon ninety-five of them! And this, just as I have been floated at a premium! Oh fie!

DUCH. Your Majesty is surely unaware that directly your Majesty's father came before the public he was applied for over and over again.

DUKE. My dear, Her Majesty's father was in the habit of being applied for over and over again—and very urgently applied for, too—long before he was registered under the Limited Liability Act. [78]

RECIT.—DUKE

To help unhappy commoners, and add to their enjoyment,
Affords a man of noble rank congenial employment;
Of our attempts we offer you examples illustrative:
The work is light, and, I may add, it's most remunerative.

DUET—DUKE *and* DUCHESS

DUKE.   Small titles and orders
               For Mayors and Recorders
                  I get—and they're highly delighted—

DUCH.	They're highly delighted!
DUKE.	M.P.'s baronetted, [79] Sham Colonels gazetted, [80] And second-rate Aldermen knighted—
DUCH.	Yes, Aldermen knighted.
DUKE.	Foundation-stone laying I find very paying: It adds a large sum to my makings—
DUCH.	Large sums to his makings.
DUKE.	At charity dinners The best of speech-spinners, I get ten per cent on the takings—
DUCH.	One-tenth of the takings.
DUCH.	I present any lady Whose conduct is shady Or smacking of doubtful propriety—
DUKE.	Doubtful propriety.
DUCH.	When Virtue would quash her, [81] I take and whitewash her, And launch her in first-rate society—
DUKE.	First-rate society!
DUCH.	I recommend acres Of clumsy dressmakers— Their fit and their finishing touches—
DUKE.	Their finishing touches.
DUCH.	A sum in addition They pay for permission To say that they make for the Duchess—
DUKE.	They make for the Duchess!
DUKE.	Those pressing prevailers, The ready-made tailors, Quote me as their great double-barrel— [82]
DUCH.	Their great double-barrel.
DUKE.	I allow them to do so, Though Robinson Crusoe Would jib at their wearing apparel—
DUCH.	Such wearing apparel!
DUKE.	I sit, by selection, Upon the direction Of several Companies bubble—[83]
DUCH.	All Companies bubble!
DUKE.	As soon as they're floated, I'm freely bank-noted— I'm pretty well paid for my trouble—
DUCH.	He's paid for his trouble!
DUCH.	At middle-class party

[79] M.P.'s baronetted. *Members of Parliament elevated to a Baronetcy. This carries the title "Sir," but unlike a knighthood's title, it is hereditary. A knighthood is for the lifetime of the holder only.*

[80] Colonels gazetted. *When an officer of His or Her Majesty's armed forces receives a commission his name appears in the Royal Gazette belonging to whichever service he is commissioned into, giving name, rank, and all—if any—promotions.*

The best of speech-spinners

[81] When Virtue would quash her. *It was not unknown for some peeresses to be seen with a woman whom the breath of scandal had touched—for a fee, of course! To be seen in the company of a duchess would mean that the breath of scandal was merely idle, malicious gossip.*

[82] Double-barrel. *A sporting gun with two barrels. In this case the expression is used as a colloquialism to indicate their pièce-de-résistance.*

[83] Companies bubble. *The allusion is to the stock jobbing companies and especially to the "South Sea Bubble." The South Sea scheme was inaugurated by the South Sea Company in 1720 for the purpose of taking up the whole of the national debt, but it collapsed in the same year; i.e., the bubble burst!*

Lure simpletons into your clutches—

[84] Few people, it seems, know the real definition of the word "hoodwink." Literally, it is to blindfold the eyes with a hood, bandage, or the like. Gilbert's use of the word is figurative—to throw dust in someone's eyes.

[85] Enter Marco and Giuseppe. I once experienced the most harrowing of "stage waits" at this point. Marco and Giuseppe failed to appear; they had trusted to the summons of a call boy to warn them of their impending entrance. They did not normally make their entrance until I had said, as if seeing them in the distance, "Ah! Their Majesties!" Then, as they entered, I would bow, saying, "Your Majesty!" I realized that they were not there, and my line became, "Ah-h-h-h! Their Majesties are late!"

I blathered away in this wing and that wing, calling for "Page?" "Boy?" "Herald?" "John?" —any name that I could think of. There was neither stage manager, assistant stage manager, nor even a chorus boy or girl to be seen. Asking the Duchess and Casilda to excuse me as "I had to see a gondolier about the King," I went offstage. There was one lone stagehand in a corner. I addressed him in a loud voice, saying, "Inform Their Majesties that the Duke of Plaza-Toro is waiting." Then, in a stage whisper, I added to the startled stagehand, "For heaven's sake, get the Gondoliers down," and returned to the stage, where I tried to get our musical director to take up an encore for the duet. But no one seemed to know where to start, and anyway the audience was beginning to enjoy our embarrassment, so I let it ride.

Fortunately, at that moment, a clatter, clatter, gasp, gasp was heard offstage and the Kings arrived, breathing heavily. It was too good an opportunity to miss. With an elaborate bow, I said, "Ah! At last, Their Breathless Majesties!" The rest of the scene was a mixture of gasps from the Gondoliers, cackles from Casilda, and guffaws from the gallery.

               I play at *écarté*—
               And I'm by no means a beginner—

DUKE (*significantly*). She's not a beginner.

DUCH.   To one of my station
           The remuneration—
               Five guineas a night and my dinner—

DUKE.   And wine with her dinner.

DUCH.   I write letters blatant
           On medicines patent—
               And use any other you mustn't—

DUKE.   Believe me you mustn't—

DUCH.   And vow my complexion
           Derives its perfection
               From somebody's soap—which it doesn't—

DUKE (*significantly*). It certainly doesn't!

DUKE.   We're ready as witness
           To any one's fitness
               To fill any place or preferment—

DUCH.   A place or preferment.

DUCH.   We're often in waiting
           At junket or *fêting*,
               And sometimes attend an interment—

DUKE.   We enjoy an interment.

BOTH.   In short, if you'd kindle
           The spark of a swindle,
               Lure simpletons into your clutches—
                  Yes; into your clutches.
       Or hoodwink [84] a debtor,
       You cannot do better

DUCH.   Than trot out a Duke or a Duchess—

DUKE.   A Duke or a Duchess!

Enter MARCO *and* GIUSEPPE [85]

DUKE. Ah! Their Majesties. Your Majesty! (*Bows with great ceremony.*)

MAR. The Duke of Plaza-Toro, I believe?

DUKE. The same. (MARCO *and* GIUSEPPE *offer to shake hands with him. The* DUKE *bows ceremoniously. They endeavour to imitate him.*) Allow me to present——

GIU. The young lady one of us married?

(MARCO *and* GIUSEPPE *offer to shake hands with her.* CASILDA *curtsies formally. They endeavour to imitate her.*)

CAS. Gentlemen, I am the most obedient servant of one of you. (*Aside.*) Oh, Luiz!

DUKE. I am now about to address myself to the gentleman whom my daughter married; the other may allow his attention to wander if he likes, for what I am about to say does not concern him. Sir, you will find in this young lady a combination of excellences which you would search for in vain in any young lady who had not the good fortune to be my daughter. There is some little doubt as to which of you is the gentleman I am addressing, and which is the gentleman who is allowing his attention to wander; but when that doubt is solved, I shall say (still addressing the attentive gentleman), "Take her, and may she make you happier than her mother has made me."

DUCH. Sir!

DUKE. If possible. And now there is a little matter to which I think I am entitled to take exception. I come here in state with Her Grace the Duchess and Her Majesty my daughter, and what do I find? Do I find, for instance, a guard of honour to receive me? No!

MAR. *and* GIU. No.

DUKE. The town illuminated? No!

MAR. *and* GIU. No.

DUKE. Refreshment provided? No!

MAR. *and* GIU. No.

DUKE. A Royal salute fired? No!

MAR. *and* GIU. No.

DUKE. Triumphal arches erected? No!

MAR. *and* GIU. No.

DUKE. The bells set ringing?

MAR. *and* GIU. No.

DUKE. Yes—one—the Visitors', and I rang it myself. It is not enough! It is not enough!

GIU. Upon my honour, I'm very sorry; but you see, I was brought up in a gondola, and my ideas of politeness are confined to taking off my cap to my passengers when they tip me.

DUCH. That's all very well in its way, but it is not enough.

GIU. I'll take off anything else in reason.

DUKE. But a Royal Salute to my daughter—it costs so little.

CAS. Papa, I don't want a salute.

GIU. My dear sir, as soon as we know which of us is entitled to take that liberty she shall have as many salutes as she likes.

MAR. As for guards of honour and triumphal arches, you don't know our people—they wouldn't stand it.

GIU. They are very off-hand with us—very off-hand indeed.

DUKE. Oh, but you mustn't allow that—you must keep them in proper discipline, you must impress your Court with your importance. You want deportment—carriage——

GIU. We've got a carriage.

DUKE. [86] Manner—dignity. There must be a good deal of this sort of thing—(*business*)—and a little of this sort of thing—(*business*)—and possibly just a *Soupçon* of this sort of thing!—(*business*)—and so on. Oh, it's very useful, and most effective. Just attend to me. You are a King—I am a subject. Very good——

(*Gavotte*)

DUKE, DUCHESS, CASILDA, MARCO, GIUSEPPE [87]

DUKE.
I am a courtier grave and serious
　Who is about to kiss your hand:
Try to combine a pose imperious
　With a demeanour nobly bland.

MAR. *and* GIU.
Let us combine a pose imperious
　With a demeanour nobly bland.

(MARCO *and* GIUSEPPE *endeavour to carry out his instructions.*)

DUKE.
That's, if anything, *too* unbending—
　Too aggressively stiff and grand;

(*They suddenly modify their attitudes.*)

[86] *It was probably this speech which accounted for Queen Victoria's question to Richard D'Oyly Carte and his reference to "quote gags" (see Foreword, page 630).*

　Each time Gilbert gives a direction—business in the libretto—the Duke demonstrates the sort of thing he means, at the same time ad-libbing a few words to emphasize his gestures, viz.: (As he bows extravagantly): "Ah! Your Majesty— honored." (As he peers at the Kings through his spyglass): "Ah ha. Saw you·in the park. Any time you're passing—pass!" (After crossing the stage and calling Marco and Giuseppe to him): ". . . and possibly just a Soupçon . . ."

　(Giuseppe cuts in): "A soup song?"

　(The Duke corrects him): "Soupçon. A French word. A touch of—something of this sort." (If possible, peering at and pointing to a lady in the audience): "Ah—I see you, you little heart killer!" (And with that he blows several kisses)

[87] *Words and music on page 711.*

	Now to the other extreme you're tending— Don't be so deucedly condescending!
DUCH. *and* CAS.	Now to the other extreme you're tending— Don't be so dreadfully condescending!
MAR. *and* GIU.	Oh, hard to please some noblemen seem! At first, if anything, *too* unbending; Off we go to the other extreme— Too confoundedly condescending!
DUKE.	Now a gavotte perform sedately— Offer your hand with conscious pride; Take an attitude not too stately, Still sufficiently dignified.
MAR. *and* GIU.	Now for an attitude not too stately, Still sufficiently dignified.

(*They endeavour to carry out his instructions.*)

DUKE (*beating time*). Oncely, twicely—oncely, twicely—
Bow impressively ere you glide.

(*They do so.*)

	Capital both—you've caught it nicely! That is the style of thing precisely!
DUCH. *and* CAS.	Capital both—they've caught it nicely! That is the style of thing precisely!
MAR. *and* GIU.	Oh, sweet to earn a nobleman's praise! Capital both—we've caught it nicely! Supposing he's right in what he says, This is the style of thing precisely!

[GAVOTTE. *At the end exeunt* DUKE *and* DUCHESS, *leaving* CASILDA *with* MARCO *and* GIUSEPPE.

GIU. (*to* MARCO). The old birds have gone away and left the young chickens together. That's called tact.

MAR. It's very awkward. We really ought to tell her how we are situated. It's not fair to the girl.

GIU. Then why don't you do it?

MAR. I'd rather not—you.

GIU. I don't know how to begin. (*To* CASILDA.) Er—Madam—I [88]— we, that is, several of us——

CAS. Gentlemen, I am bound to listen to you; but it is right to tell you that, not knowing I was married in infancy, I am over head and ears in love with somebody else.

GIU. Our case exactly! W*e* are over head and ears in love with somebody else! (*Enter* GIANETTA *and* TESSA.) In point of fact, with our wives!

CAS. Your wives! Then you are married?

TESS. It's not our fault.

GIA. We knew nothing about it.

BOTH. We are sisters in misfortune.

CAS. My good girls, I don't blame you. Only before we go any further we must really arrive at some satisfactory arrangement, or we shall get hopelessly complicated.

QUINTET AND FINALE
MARCO, GIUSEPPE, CASILDA, GIANETTA, TESSA

[88] Madam—I— *Marco should interrupt Giuseppe with a whispered "We!" before Giuseppe continues with his speech. See also page 641, Note 23.*

ALL.   Here is a case unprecedented! [89]
    Here are a King and Queen ill-starred!
    Ever since marriage was first invented
    Never was known a case so hard!

MAR. *and* GIU. I may be said to have been bisected, [90]
    By a profound catastrophe!

CAS., GIA., TESS. Through a calamity unexpected
    I am divisible into three!

ALL.   O moralists all,
    How can you call
   Marriage a state of unitee,
  When excellent husbands are bisected,
   And wives divisible into three?
    O moralists all,
    How can you call
   Marriage a state of union true?

CAS., GIA., TESS. One-third of myself is married to half of ye or you,

MAR. *and* GIU. When half of myself has married one-third of ye or you?

Enter DON ALHAMBRA, *followed by* DUKE, DUCHESS, *and all the* CHORUS

FINALE

RECIT.—DON ALHAMBRA

Now let the loyal lieges gather round—
The Prince's foster-mother has been found!
She will declare, to silver clarion's sound,
The rightful King—let him forthwith be crowned!

CHORUS.   She will declare, etc.

[DON ALHAMBRA *brings forward* INEZ, *the Prince's foster-mother*.

TESS.   Speak, woman, speak—
DUKE.   We're all attention!
GIA.   The news we seek—
DUCH.   This moment mention.
CAS.   To us they bring—
DON AL.   His foster-mother.
MAR.   Is he the King?
GIU.   Or this my brother?

ALL.   Speak, woman, speak, etc.

RECIT.—INEZ

The Royal Prince was by the King entrusted
To my fond care, ere I grew old and crusted;
When traitors came to steal his son reputed,
My own small boy I deftly substituted!
The villains fell into the trap completely—
I hid the Prince away—still sleeping sweetly:
I called him "son" with pardonable slyness—
His name, Luiz! Behold his Royal Highness!

[*Sensation.* LUIZ *ascends the throne, crowned and robed as King.*

CAS. (*rushing to his arms*). Luiz!
LUIZ. Casilda! (*Embrace.*)

[89] *Here is a case unprecedented! While discussing Gilbert and Sullivan in general and The Gondoliers in particular, I happened to remark on the fact that it was Sullivan's habit to compose his operas, and indeed all of his works, while seated at his desk, sipping weak gin and water. To my surprise my companion was not at all concerned about the gin and water, but was vastly intrigued by the fact that, unlike many composers of musical shows today, he not only didn't use a piano but arranged and scored the whole of the orchestration himself!*

[90] *I may be said to have been bisected. Gilbert becomes inconsistent about his mathematics. Giuseppe has stated earlier, "Three wives—two husbands. That's two-thirds of a husband to each wife." Correct, if we're talking about three women and two men.*
 However, here the "vulgar fractions" make sense only if you regard Casilda, Gianetta and Tessa as being embodied in one queenly woman, and Marco and Giuseppe as combined in one kingly man.
 Now try this on your friends!

ALL.
> Is this indeed the King?
> Oh, wondrous revelation!
> Oh, unexpected thing!
> Unlooked-for situation!

MAR., GIA.,
GIU., TESS.
> This statement we receive
> With sentiments conflicting;
> Our hearts rejoice and grieve,
> Each other contradicting;
> To those whom we adore
> We can be reunited—
> On one point rather sore,
> But, on the whole, delighted! [91]

LUIZ.
> When others claimed thy dainty hand,
> I waited—waited—waited,

DUKE.
> As prudence (so I understand)
> Dictated—tated—tated.

CAS.
> By virtue of our early vow
> Recorded—corded—corded.

DUCH.
> Your pure and patient love is now
> Rewarded—warded—warded.

ALL.
> Then hail, O King of a Golden Land,
> And the high-born bride who claims his hand!
> The past is dead, and you gain your own,
> A royal crown and a golden throne!

[*All kneel:* LUIZ *crowns* CASILDA.

ALL.
> Once more *gondolieri*,
> Both skilful and wary,
> Free from this quandary
> Contented are we.
> From Royalty flying,
> Our gondolas plying,
> And merrily crying
> Our "*premé*," "*stalì!*" [92]

So good-bye, cachucha, fandango, bolero—
We'll dance a farewell to that measure—
Old Xeres, adieu—Manzanilla—Montero—
We leave you with feelings of pleasure! [93]

CURTAIN

[91] Was Gilbert at all conscious of the applicability of these words to his relationship with Sullivan when he wrote them? And was Sullivan, when he set them to music? Probably not; but they certainly might have been penned as a description of everyone's feelings about smoothing the path for the writing of The Gondoliers.

[92] These are gondoliers' cries. Premé—push in or press down; Stalì—stop or stand there!

[93] What comment can I make here other than to say that the last line, like so many others before, speaks for me better than I could for myself?

Roses White and Roses Red

Moderately bright CHORUS of GIRLS

List and learn, list and learn, List and learn, ye dain-ty ros-es, Ros-es white and ros-es red, Why we bind you in-to po-sies Ere_ your morn-ing bloom has fled. By a law of maid-en's mak-ing, Ac-cents of— a heart that's ach-ing, E-ven

though that heart be break-ing, Should by maid-en be un-said:

Though they love with love ex-ceed-ing, They must seem to be un-heed-ing, Go ye

then and do their plead-ing,

Ros - es white and ros - es

red!

List and learn,

list and learn, ye dain-ty ros-es, Ros-es white and ros-es

red, Why we bind you in - to po - sies Ere_ your morn - ing bloom_ has

fled. List and learn, list and learn, Ros - es white and ros - es

red, Ros - - - es, oh list, list _ and

learn, List _ and learn, _____ Oh, ros - es white_ and

red! _____

We're Called Gondolieri

In lively, very spirited tempo

MARCO and GIUSEPPE

We're called _____ gon-do-lier-i, But that's a va-ga-ry,_ It's_ quite hon-or-a-ry_ The_ trade that_ we_ ply._

For gal - - lant-ry not-ed Since we were short coat-ed,_ To_ beau-ty_ de-

vot - ed, — Giu - sep - pe — and _ I! _

When morn-ing is break-ing, Our

couch-es for - sak-ing, To greet their a - wak-ing With car-ols we come. At

sum-mer day's noon-ing, When wea - ry la - goon-ing, Our man - - do-lins tun -

dim. ____ *p*

- ing, We la - - - zi - ly _____ thrum. Tra-la-la-la-

la, Our— man-do - lins— tun-ing, We— la - - si-ly thrum. Tra-la-la-la - la-la - la, Tra-la-la-la - la-la - la, Tra-la-la-la - la, Tra-la-la-la - la!_____ When ves - pers are ring-ing, To hope ev-er cling-ing,—With— songs of— our— sing-ing— A— vig-il— we— keep._____

When day-light is fad - ing, En-wrapt in night's

In Enterprise of Martial Kind

Bright martial tempo

DUKE

1. In _ en - ter - prise of mar - tial kind, When there was an - y _
2. When, to e - vade De - struc-tion's hand, To hide they all _ pro -
3. When told that they would all be shot Un - less they left _ the _

fight - ing, He _ led his reg'- ment from be - hind, He found it less _ ex -
ceed - ed, No _ sol - dier in that gal - lant band Hid half as well _ as _
ser - vice, That he - ro hes - i - tat - ed not, So mar - vel - lous _ his _

cit - ing. But _ when a - way his reg'-ment ran, His place was at the fore, O! That
he did. He _ lay con-ceal'd through-out the war, And so pre-serv'd his gore, O! That
nerve is. He _ sent his re - sig - na-tion in, The first of _ all his corps, O! That

cel - e - brat - ed, Cul - ti - vat - ed, Un - der - rat - ed No - ble - man, The Duke of Pla - za_
un - af - fect - ed, Un - de - tect - ed, Well - con - nect - ed War - ri - or, The Duke of Pla - za_
ver - y know - ing, O - ver - flow - ing, Eas - y - go - ing Pal - a - din, The Duke of Pla - za_

To - ro! In the first and fore - most flight, ha, ha! You al - ways found that knight, ha, ha! That
To - ro! In ev - 'ry dough - ty deed, ha, ha! He al - ways took the lead, ha, ha! That
To - ro! To men of gross - er clay, ha, ha! He al - ways showed the way, ha, ha! That

cel - e - brat - ed, Cul - ti - vat - ed, Un - der - rat - ed No - ble - man, The Duke of_ Pla - za_
un - af - fect - ed, Un - de - tect - ed, Well - con - nect - ed War - ri - or, The Duke of_ Pla - za_
ver - y know - ing, O - ver - flow - ing, Eas - y - go - ing Pal - a - din, The Duke of_ Pla - za_

1. - 2.
To - ro!
To - ro!

3.
To - ro!

680

There Was a Time

Slowly with expression

LUIZ

There was a time, A time for-ev-er gone, ah, woe is me! It was no crime To love but thee a-lone, ah, woe is me! One heart, one life, one soul, One aim, one goal, Each in the oth-er's thrall, Each all in all, ah, woe is

me, ah, woe is me!

Casilda (upper)
Luiz (lower) Oh, bur-y, bur-y, let the grave close o'er The

days that were, that nev-er will be more! Oh, bur-y, bur-y love that all con -

demn, And let the whirl-wind mourn its re - qui - em!

CASILDA

Dead as the last year's leaves, As gath-er'd flow'rs, ah, woe is me!

Dead as the gar-ner'd sheaves, That love of ours, ah, woe is me! Born but to fade and

I Stole the Prince

Brightly, but not too fast

DON ALHAMBRA

1. I stole the Prince, and I brought him here, And left him gai - ly prat - tling With a high - ly re - spect - a - ble gon - do - lier, Who

2. But ow - ing, I'm much dis - posed to fear, To his ter - ri - ble taste for tip - pling, That high - ly re - spect - a - ble gon - do - lier Could

3. Time sped, and when at the end of a year, I sought that in - fant cher - ished, That high - ly re - spect - a - ble gon - do - lier Was

4. The chil - dren fol - lowed his old ca - reer (This state - ment can't be par - ried) Of a high - ly re - spect - a - ble gon - do - lier: Well,

prom-ised the Roy - al babe to rear, And teach him the trade of a
nev - er de-clare with a mind sin-cere Which of the two was his
ly - ing a corpse on his hum - ble bier, I dropp'd a Grand In-
one of the two (who will soon be here), But which of the two it is

ti - mon - eer With his own be - lov - ed brat - ling.
off - spring dear,— And which the Roy - al strip - ling!
quis - i - tor's tear,— That gon - do - lier had per - ished! A
not quite clear, Is the Roy - al Prince you mar - ried! Search

Both of the babes were strong and stout, And, con - sid - er - ing all things,
Which was which he could nev-er make out De - spite his best en -
taste for drink, com - bined with gout, Had dou - bled him up for -
in and out and round a - bout And you'll dis - cov - er

clev - er. Of that there is no man - ner of doubt, No
deav - our. Of that there is no man - ner of doubt, No
ev - er. Of that there is no man - ner of doubt, No
nev - er A tale so free from ev - er - y doubt, All

mf

prob - a - ble, pos - si - ble sha - dow of doubt, No pos - si - ble doubt what-
prob - a - ble, pos - si - ble sha - dow of doubt, No pos - si - ble doubt what-
prob - a - ble, pos - si - ble sha - dow of doubt, No pos - si - ble doubt what-
prob - a - ble, pos - si - ble sha - dow of doubt, All pos - si - ble doubt what-

1.-2.-3.

DUCHESS and CASILDA

ev - er. No pos - si - ble doubt what - ev - er!
ev - er. No pos - si - ble doubt what - ev - er!
ev - er. No pos - si - ble doubt what - ev - er!

4.

ev - er. A tale so free from ev - 'ry doubt, All prob - a - ble, pos - si - ble

sha - dow of doubt, All pos - si - ble doubt what - ev - er!

When a Merry Maiden Marries

In light and graceful tempo

TESSA

1. When a mer-ry maid-en
2. When a mer-ry maid-en

mar - ries, Sor - row goes and pleas-ure tar - ries; Ev - 'ry sound be - comes a
mar - ries, Sor - row goes and pleas-ure tar - ries; Ev - 'ry sound be - comes a

song, All is right and noth-ing's wrong! From to-day and ev - er
song, All is right and noth-ing's wrong! Gnaw-ing Care and ach - ing

af - ter Let our tears be tears of laugh - ter, Ev - 'ry sigh that finds a
Sor - row, Get ye gone un - til to - mor - row; Jeal - ous - ies in grim ar -

veut   Be a   sigh   of   sweet con - tent!   When you mar-ry, mer-ry
ray,   Ye are   things   of   yes - ter-day!   When you mar-ry, mer-ry

maid - en,   Then the   air with love is   lad - en; Ev-'ry flow'r is   a
maid - en,   Then the   air with joy is   lad - en; All the cor-ners of   the

rose, Ev - 'ry   goose   be-comes a   swan,   Ev-'ry kind of trou - ble
earth Ring with mu - sic sweet-ly   played,   Wor-ry is mel - o - dious

goes Where   the last   year's snows have gone!   Sun-light takes the place of
mirth, Grief   is   joy   in mas - quer-ade;   Sul - len night is laugh-ing

O My Darling, O My Pet

Slowly, but not dragging

GIANETTA

Now, Mar-co dear, My wish-es hear: While you're a-way It's un-der-stood You will be good, And not too gay.

To ev-'ry trace Of maid-en grace You will be blind, And will not glance by an-y chance On wo-man-kind!

If you are wise, You'll shut your eyes Till we ar-rive, And not ad-dress A la-dy less Than for-ty-five.

You'll please to frown On ev-'ry gown That you may see; And, O my pet, You won't for-get You've mar-ried me!

cresc.

_p_

_mf_

And, O my dar - ling, O my pet, What - ev - er else you may for-

mf espressivo

TESSA

get, In yon-der isle be-yond the sea, Do not for- get, Do not for-get You've mar-ried me! You'll

_p_

_p_

lay your head Up-on your bed At set of sun. You will not sing Of an- y-thing To an-y-one. You'll

sit and mope All day, I hope, And shed a tear Up-on the life Your lit-tle wife Is pass-ing here.   And

if   so   be You think of me, Please tell the moon: I'll read it   all   In rays that fall On the la-goon: You'll

be   so   kind   As tell the   wind How you may be, And send me words By lit-tle birds To com-fort me! And, O   my

dar - ling, O   my pet, What-ev - er   else   you   may   for-get, In yon-der isle be-yond the

Rising Early in the Morning

Quickly but not too fast

GIUSEPPE

Ris-ing ear-ly in the morn-ing, We pro-ceed to light the fire, Then our Maj-es-ty a-dorn-ing In its work-a-day at-tire, — We em-bark with-out de-lay On the du-ties of the day. First, we pol-ish off some batch-es Of po-lit-i-cal des-patch-es, And for-eign pol-i-ti-cians cir-cum-lunch-eon (mak-ing mer-ry On a bun and glass of sher-ry), If we've noth-ing in par-tic-u-lar to

vent;   Then, if bus'-ness is-n't heav-y, We may hold a Roy-al le-vée, Or
do,   We may make a Proc-la-ma-tion, Or re-ceive a dep-u-ta-tion,Then we

rat-i-fy some Acts of Par-lia-ment.   Then we prob-a-bly re-view the house-hold
pos-si-bly cre-ate a Peer or two.   Then we help a fel-low crea-ture on his

troops   With the u-sual"Shal-loo humps" and "Shal-loo hoops!"   Or re-
path,   With the Gar-ter, or the This-tle, or the Bath.   Or we

ceive with cer-e-mo-ni-al and state An in-ter-est-ing East-ern po-ten-
dress and tod-dle off in sem-i-state, To a fes-ti-val, a func-tion or a

tate. Af-ter that we gen-er-al-ly Go and dress our pri-vate val-et (It's a rath-er ner-vous
fête. Then we go and stand as sen-try At the Pal-ace (pri-vate en-try),March-ing hith-er, march-ing

duty, he's a touch-y lit-tle man), Write some let-ters lit-er - a-ry For our pri-vate sec-re-
tith-er, up and down and to and fro, While the war-ri-or on du-ty Goes in search of beer and

ta-ry: He is shak-y in his spell-ing, so we help him if we can. Then, in
beau-ty (And it gen-er-al-ly hap-pens that he has-n't far to go). He re-

view of crav-ings in-ner, We go down and or-der din-ner; Then we pol-ish the Re-ga-lia and the
lieves us, if he's a-ble, Just in time to lay the ta-ble, Then we dine and serve the cof-fee, and at

mp

Cor-o-na-tion plate, Spend an hour in tit-i-vat-ing All our Gen-tle-men-in-Wait-ing; Or we
half-past twelve or one, With a pleas-ure that's em-phat-ic, We re-ti-re to our at-tic With the

mf *p*

run on lit-tle er-rands for the Min-is-ters of State. Oh, — phi-los-o-phers may sing Of the
grat-i-fy-ing feel-ing that our du-ty has been done! Oh, — phi-los-o-phers may sing Of the

mf *p*

trou - bles of a King; Yet the du - ties are de - light - ful, and the
trou - bles of a King; But of pleas - ures there are man - y and of

priv - i - leg - es great; But the priv - i - lege and pleas - ure That we
wor - ries there are none; And the cul - mi - nat - ing pleas - ure That we

treas - ure be - yond meas - ure Is to run on lit - tle er - rands for the
treas - ure be - yond meas - ure Is the grat - i - fy - ing feel - ing that our

1. Min - is - ters of State. Af - ter du - ty has been

2. *rit*

rit.

fo done!

f *a tempo*

Take a Pair of Sparkling Eyes

Moderately and with warmth

MARCO

1. Take a pair of spark - ling eyes,___ Hid - den, ev - er and a-
2. Take a pret - ty lit - tle cot,___ Quite a min - ia - ture af-

non,___ In a mer - ci - ful e - clipse.___ Do not
fair,___ Hung a - bout with trel - liss'd vine,___ Fur - nish

heed their mild sur - prise,___ Hav - ing pass'd the Ru - bi - con.___ Take a
it up - on the spot___ With the trea - sures rich and rare___ I've en-

pair of ros - y lips; _____ Take a fig - ure trim - ly
deav - our'd to _ de - fine. _____ Live to love and love to

plann'd, Such as ad - mi - ra - tion whets _ (Be par - tic - u - lar in
live, _ You will rip - en at your ease, _ Grow - ing on the sun - ny

this); Take a ten - der lit - tle hand, _ Fring'd with dain - ty fin - ger -
side. Fate has noth - ing more to give. _ You're a dain - ty man to

ettes, _ Press _____ it, press it in pa - ren - the -
please, If _____ you're not sat - is - fied, not _ sat - is -

Take my coun-sel, hap-py man;

Act up-on it, if you can, if you

can, if you can, Act up-on it, if you can,⎯ hap-py

man, if⎯ you can!⎯

Dance a Cachucha

Brilliantly and gaily

CHORUS

Dance a ca - chu - cha, fan - dan - go, bo - le - ro, Xe - res_ we'll_ drink, Man - za - nil - la, Mon - te - ro, Wine, when_ it_ runs in a -

702

dance, Old Xe-res we'll drink, Man-za-nil-la, Mon-te-ro, For wine, when it

runs in a-bun-dance, en-hanc-es The reck-less de-light of that

wild-est of danc-es, that wild-est of danc-es, The reck-less de-light!

Dance a ca-chu-cha, fan-dan-go, bo-le-ro, Xe-res we'll

drink, Man-za-nil-la, Mon-te-ro, Wine, when it runs in a-bun-dance, en-

There Lived a King

Brightly, but not too fast

DON ALHAMBRA

There lived a King, as I've been told, In the won-der-work-ing days of old, When hearts were twice as good as gold, And twen-ty times as mel-low. Good tem-per tri-umphed in his face, And in his heart he found a place For

So to the top of ev'ry tree Promoted ev'rybody. Now

and GIUSEPPE

that's the kind of King for me, He wished all men as rich as he,

So to the top of ev'ry tree Promoted ev'rybody! Lord

ALHAMBRA

Chan-cel-lors were cheap as sprats, And Bish-ops in their shov-el hats Were
King, al-though no one de-nies His heart was of ab-nor-mal size, Yet

plen-ti-ful as tab-by cats, In point of fact, too man-y. Am-
he'd have act-ed oth-er-wise If he had been a cut-er. The

bas-sa-dors cropped up like hay, Prime Min-is-ters and such as they Grew
end is eas-i-ly fore-told, When ev-'ry bless-ed thing you hold Is

like as-par-a-gus in May, And Dukes were three a pen-ny. On
made of sil-ver, or of gold, You long for sim-ple pew-ter. When

ev-'ry side Field Mar-shals gleam'd, Small beer were Lords Lieu-ten-ant deem'd, With
you have noth-ing else to wear But cloth of gold and sat-ins rare, For

Ad-mi-rals the o-cean teem'd, All round his wide do-min-ions. With
cloth of gold you cease to care, Up goes the price of shod-dy. Of

MARCO

and GIUSEPPE

Ad-mi-rals a-round his wide do-min-ions. And
shod-dy, up goes the price of shod-dy. In

DON
ALHAMBRA

Par - ty Lead - ers you might meet In twos and threes in ev - 'ry street, Main-
short, who - ev - er you may be, To this con - clu - sion you'll a - gree, When

MARCO

tain - ing, — with no — lit - tle heat, Their var - i - ous o - pin - ions. Now
ev - 'ry - one is — some - bod - ee, Then no one's an - y - bod - y! Now

f

and GIUSEPPE

that's a sight you could - n't beat, Two Par - ty Lead - ers in each street Main-
that's as plain as plain can be, To this con - clu - sion we a - gree, When

1.   *p* DON

tain - ing, — with no — lit - tle heat, Their var - i - ous o - pin - ions! That
ev - 'ry - one is — some - bod - ee, Then no one's an - y -

p

2.

bod - y!

f

710

I Am a Courtier Grave and Serious

Slowly like a Gavotte

mf cresc.   *f*   *p*

p DUKE

dim.   *p*

1. I— am a cour-tier grave and ser-ious Who— is a-bout to kiss your hand: Try— to com-bine a pose im-per-ious With— a de-mean-our no-bly bland.

MARCO and GIUSEPPE

Let us com-bine a pose im-per-ious With a de-

DUKE

mean - our no - bly bland! That's, if an - y - thing, too un - bend - ing, Too ag -

gres - sive - ly _ stiff and grand; Now to the oth - er ex - treme you're tend - ing, Don't be so

CASILDA and DUCHESS

deu - ced - ly con - de - scend - ing! Now to the oth - er ex - treme you're_

MARCO and GIUSEPPE

tend - ing, Don't be so dread - ful - ly con - de - scend - ing! Oh, hard to

please some no - ble - men seem! At first, if an - y - thing, too un -

praise! Cap-i-tal, both, cap-i-tal, both, we've caught it nice-ly! Sup-pos-ing he's

right in what he says, This is the style of thing pre-

CASILDA and DUCHESS

cise-ly! Cap-i-tal, both, cap-i-tal, both, you've caught it nice-ly! That is the

style of thing pre-cise-ly! That is the style of thing, the style

of thing pre-cise-ly!

A NOTE ABOUT THE PIANO ARRANGEMENTS

I DERIVED the piano arrangements contained in this volume exclusively from the original piano scores, published in London during the composer's lifetime. I also found great help in listening to the recordings of the D'Oyly Carte Opera Company, considered the most dependable custodian of the Gilbert and Sullivan tradition.

In making these arrangements, my guiding principle was the strict and faithful observance of Sullivan's style and spirit. Not once have I touched or altered a single harmony of the composer. It would have been, in my opinion, an anachronistic and unstylish sacrilege to "modernize" the crystal-clear purity of Sullivan's conception.

My only aim was to make all these songs playable and enjoyable to the great mass of Sullivan admirers who possess average pianistic technique. In Sullivan's piano scores, the melody appeared only in the voice line and was (with rare exceptions) almost completely banished from the piano part. Dynamic marks and phrasing were fragmentary or entirely missing.

I made it my task to integrate the melody with the piano parts. All ensemble parts were condensed into one vocal line. The only deviation from this rule occurs in a number of *Ruddigore* ("There Grew a Little Flower"), where a charming countermelody, which could not be entirely omitted, needed an additional voice line. I found it advisable to substitute English terminology for the monotonously simple and mostly nondescriptive Italian indications for mood and tempo as used in Sullivan's published scores. Within reasonable limits I also added dynamic marks and did not neglect the phrasing of the melodies.

In order to bring the songs within the range of the average voice, I had to transpose more than a third of them into a practical key. All the introductions and postludes are from the original score. In a very few cases the extreme length of choral numbers necessitated the careful and respectful omission of a number of bars, but I have religiously abstained from violating Sullivan's music even by adding one single note which is not his own.

In spite of all my endeavor to simplify the songs pianistically, a few of them remain not quite easy to play—for instance, the opening chorus of *The Mikado* ("If You Want to Know Who We Are"). Sullivan was not a "piano composer" in the sense that, for instance, Puccini and George Gershwin were. These two worked at the piano and consequently wrote excellently for the piano. Sullivan visualized everything orchestrally. His spirited string or woodwind figures often become very hard when transcribed for the piano keyboard.

May I be allowed to close with a personal note in the nature of a candid confession: The months of work spent on this volume converted me from a complacent listener into a fervent admirer of Sullivan's genius.

ALBERT SIRMAY

MARTYN GREEN *is uniquely qualified to be the authority on Gilbert and Sullivan. A star of the famous D'Oyly Carte Opera Company for more than twenty years, he became the unsurpassed master of the classic comedy roles and the tongue-tripping patter songs of Gilbert and Sullivan.*

Mr. Green's talents are based on sound musicianship. He received early training from his father, William Green, a noted tenor of the English stage, and he later studied at the Royal College of Music.

Martyn Green served over four years in World War I with the Royal Fusiliers, and for the same length of time, during World War II, he was the very model of a modern Air Force Squadron Leader, seeing service in California and Southeast Asia.

Since 1952 he has made his home in New York, where his versatility, both as actor and producer, has led to assignments on the stage, TV, records, and in films. Savoyards have seen him in the motion-picture version of The Mikado and in The Gilbert and Sullivan Story; for TV he staged and adapted the hilarious Groucho Marx Mikado, and he directed himself in Trial by Jury for "Omnibus." His recordings of the lilting Gilbert and Sullivan operettas are undoubtedly being enjoyed at this very moment from Penzance to Tokyo.

LUCILLE CORCOS *supplied not only the basic conception of this book, but also its entire galaxy of illustrations. She was born in New York City in 1908 and has been a Gilbert and Sullivan fan since high-school days, when she designed sets for H.M.S. Pinafore and was a sister and a cousin and an aunt. She has exhibited in the Metropolitan Museum of Art, the Whitney Museum, the Art Institute of Chicago and the Carnegie Institute, as well as in major European and South American museums. Her drawings have been appearing for years in Vanity Fair, Vogue, Harper's Bazaar, Fortune, Life and Holiday. Most recently, Miss Corcos has been applying her charming talent to illustrating children's books—notably a four-volume edition of Grimm's Fairy Tales—for the Limited Editions Club.*

ALBERT SIRMAY, *creator of the piano arrangements, studied piano at the Royal Academy of Music in Budapest. He wrote twelve operettas which were produced in Budapest, Vienna, Berlin, and London. In 1923, in Vienna, he met Max Dreyfus, the dean of American music publishers, who offered Sirmay a position in his publishing house. Sirmay has subsequently become a musical adviser and editor to almost a whole generation of young American composers. Sirmay was one of George Gershwin's intimate friends. He edited all of Gershwin's compositions starting with the Rhapsody in Blue up to and including the score of Porgy and Bess.*